Rob Ventura's thoroughly Reformed exposition of Paul's greatest epistle is packed full of insights for preachers and teachers of God's Word. His approach strikes an excellent balance. He discusses the details of each verse without getting overly technical. He quotes great theologians of the Augustinian/Reformed tradition while letting the Scriptures speak for themselves. His commentary is exegetical, doctrinal, and warmly practical, containing helpful applications for both believers and unbelievers at the end of every section. This is a reliable and highly recommended exposition for people who want to be like Ezra in studying, obeying, and teaching God's Word (Ezra 7:10).

JOEL R. BEEKE
President, Puritan Reformed Theological Seminary,
Grand Rapids, Michigan

As readers, as ministers, as pastors, we can never get to the bottom of Romans. Rob Ventura in his study of the letter particularly assists those who preach and teach the epistle. This commentary is carefully outlined with helpful exegetical comments along with theological reflection. It especially stands out for its focus on application and for quotes from luminaries from the past.

TOM SCHREINER
James Buchanan Harrison Professor of New Testament
Interpretation, The Southern Baptist Seminary,
Louisville, Kentucky

If preachers around the world were to expound on Romans, as Steven J. Lawson in his foreword to this commentary wishes they would, they might think it too daunting a task. The sheer number of commentaries on Romans is overwhelming, and they are often aimed at the academy of scholars rather than the pastor of a local church. Rob Ventura has mined these resources, includes a list of his favorite evangelical commentaries for preaching through Romans, and provides his own solid and theologically grounded insights in a way that is most helpful for those who have the weekly charge to proclaim God's Word. For each section, he lays out the general theme, provides a homiletical outline, a summary, key exegetical and practical insights (the latter are often alliterative). What is unique is his inclusion of suggested applications from the text for the non-Christian. His diligent research covering the long history of the interpretation of Romans and his own discerning reading of the text will be a most welcome resource for pastors. I highly recommend it.

DAVID E. GARLAND
Professor of Christian Scriptures,
George W. Truett Theological Seminary, Baylor University, Waco

With flair but no fluff, this well-organized study models how to think through Romans from the ground up. It will aid preachers and teachers in grasping both the stately trees (verses) and magnificent forest (the whole epistle) of the sublime gospel presentation called Romans. Notable features include (1) effective citation of dozens of commentators from previous centuries, (2) careful attention to the Greek text, and (3) the author's zeal to see people saved through Jesus the Messiah whom Romans presents. We all need Him. This book skillfully unpacks, and packages for the reader, the power of God for salvation contained and explained in Romans.

ROBERT W. YARBROUGH
Professor of New Testament, Covenant Theological Seminary,
St. Louis, MO

There are few books of Scripture more important to understand and expound than Paul's great epistle to the Romans. Its doctrinal exposition of the gospel is unique in Scripture. But it is crucially important to communicate its profound teachings practically, popularly, and passionately. This is the value of Rob Ventura's exposition of the book. He provides the student and the preacher with a clear and straightforward exposition and also potent and timely application of the letter. May God give Rob's work wonderful usefulness in spreading Romans life-changing gospel truths.

SAM WALDRON
President, Covenant Baptist Theological Seminary
and One of the Pastors of Grace Reformed Baptist Church,
Owensboro, Kentucky

Rob Ventura is an author, scholar, and pastor-preacher with the gift of expressing New Testament theology in clear, elegant prose. Reading him in full flow in his new commentary on Romans affords the simple pleasure of watching an expert do what they do best. He has plundered the finest commentators on this letter, giving the book a delightful fragrance, and so has put every succeeding expositor and preacher of Romans in his debt. In this fine achievement, he clothes conservative evangelical proclamation with a refreshing intellectual rigor. For everyone whose task and delight it is to explain the meaning and relevance of the Word of God, this book is an indispensable resource. Not only does it help us understand the meaning of this mighty letter but, from the manifested principles of interpretation and application, it illumines all of Scripture's relevance to us. Tolle Lege! Take up and read!

GEOFF THOMAS
Former Pastor Alfred Place Baptist Church Aberystwyth, Wales

This is a splendidly rich and extremely useful volume, written in a style reminiscent of Spurgeon's *Treasury of David*. It abounds with pithy outlines of the biblical text, insightful exegetical analysis, select quotations from classic commentaries, and suggested points of application. From now on, this will be the first resource I'll turn to when studying any passage from Romans.

PHIL JOHNSON
Executive Director, Grace to You

In Rob Ventura's commentary on the book of Romans, he states that Paul's purpose in writing this letter to this church was fivefold: biographical, theological, practical, pastoral, and missional. The same can be said about this new work. Furthermore, its deep insights and simplicity make it useful to all believers – the seasoned expositor, the Sunday school teacher, the parent leading family devotions, and the recent convert.

PAUL WASHER
Founder and Director of HeartCry Missionary Society

EXPOSITORY OUTLINES & OBSERVATIONS *on* ROMANS

Hints and Helps for Preachers and Teachers

Rob Ventura

MENTOR
Encouraging Christians to Think

About the cover: Along with the Colosseum representing Rome, this striking depiction should remind us that many faithful Christians boldly gave their lives for the sake of Christ and the gospel, even as the apostle Paul did. May we be as faithful should we be called to this end. Likewise, the clouds surrounding the Colosseum are a powerful reminder of that great cloud of witnesses who have gone before us. May this encourage us to be like them as we run the race towards heaven, looking unto Jesus, the author and finisher of our faith.

Copyright © Rob Ventura 2023

Hardback ISBN 978-1-5271-1012-0
Ebook ISBN 978-1-5271-1070-0

10 9 8 7 6 5 4 3 2 1

Published in 2023
in the
Mentor Imprint
by
Christian Focus Publications Ltd.,
Geanies House, Fearn, Ross-shire,
IV20 1TW, Scotland, Great Britain

www.christianfocus.com

Cover design by Daniel Van Straaten
Printed by Bell & Bain, Glasgow

FSC
www.fsc.org

MIX
Paper | Supporting
responsible forestry
FSC® C007785

CONTENTS

FOREWORD

If I had my way, every preacher in the world would expound the book of Romans from his pulpit. If I could exert the influence, I would orchestrate every church around the globe to be under the direct influence of the preaching of Romans. If I had the power, I would ensure that every Christian was well-versed in this monumental book.

Think about the incredible effect this epistle by the apostle Paul would have upon countless lives. Pause to recognize the powerful ripple effect a rich study in Romans would bring to any church. Unquestionably, our doctrine would be stronger, and our beliefs would be deeper. Our worship would be higher, and our lives would be holier. Our fellowship would be closer, and our outreach would be stronger. All this—and far more—would be the result of the steady preaching of the book of Romans.

This is why I am grateful for this book, *Expository Outlines and Observations on Romans*, by Rob Ventura. Contained in this helpful commentary are insightful observations from the text of Romans, combined with homiletical outlines and personal applications. Further, there are quotations and footnotes from noted theologians and trusted expositors that will assist any preacher or teacher in better understanding what this epistle sets forth. Moreover, this book shows the practical relevance of how Romans can be better lived on a daily basis.

Throughout the centuries, the preaching of the book of Romans has inevitably led to history-altering reformations and revivals. I truly believe that as you expound the inexhaustible riches of this epistle, God will visit your pulpit ministry with extraordinary power and abundant blessings. Quite simply, God will honor the man who honors His word.

May you be one of these faithful men who digs into the rich veins of the profound truths contained in Romans. May you explore and excavate the priceless treasures contained in these deep mines. And may you bring to your congregation the vast spiritual wealth found in this matchless epistle.

Steven J. Lawson
President, OnePassion Ministries
Dallas, Texas

PREFACE

The book of Romans, which supremely showcases the central doctrines of the Christian faith, has given rise to many outstanding commentaries over the centuries. So many resources on this masterful book give a wealth of spiritual riches for the preacher as he works his way through this letter which Luther called, "the chief part of the New Testament."[1] Calvin said of it, "When one gains the knowledge of this epistle, he has an entrance opened to him to all the most hidden treasures of Scripture."[2]

While Romans is a well-served letter, surprisingly, I did not find many resources which gave me quick, accessible, expository nuggets to help me prepare Greek-informed,[3] hermeneutically-sound, and homiletically-clean sermons in time for preaching each week.

Further, I noticed that few of the commentaries I used had any real practical and pointed applications to help bring home the truths of the

---

1   Luther also said in his preface to his commentary on Romans that this epistle is "the very purest Gospel, and is worthy not only that every Christian should know it word for word, by heart, but occupy himself with it every day, as the daily bread of the soul. It can never be read or pondered too much, and the more it is dealt with the more precious it becomes, and the better it tastes."

2   It has also been called among other things "the Constitution of Christianity," "the Christian Manifesto," and "the Cathedral of the Christian faith" as cited in the *King James Bible Commentary*, p. 1390.

3   The exegetical and explanatory remarks in this commentary are based on the Greek text. When parsing is done, I am parsing in shorthand so that for example, instead of writing aorist tense, active voice, verb, I shorten it to (Grk. aorist, active, verb), etc. Further, while I did all of my own Greek exegesis on every verse, I acknowledge that in addition to the resources mentioned in this book, at points I found helpful insights on the Greek text from the website: www.preceptaustin.org and from Earnest R. Campbell, *A Commentary of Romans* (Silverton, OR: Canyonview Press, 1987). Additionally, while my commentary is very different from the old commentary written by H. P. Liddon called *Explanatory Analysis of St. Paul's Epistle to the Romans* (1893), the reader should note that the idea for "observations" on the text was initially sparked in my mind by Liddon's work. Since his book is rare and out of print, I did not mention it in my top thirty commentaries on Romans. Finally, please note that I wrote this commentary Coram Deo, that is, with the constant conviction that I was writing in God's presence. Therefore, whenever I quoted or borrowed the thoughts of others either from a book or a sermon, I earnestly endeavored to footnote it as a matter of conscience. I hope that the abundant footnoting enhances further study and does not unduly detract from the flow of the content.

text to the hearts and minds of my hearers. To address these matters, I wrote the book that you are now reading.[4]

This material comes from my personal study and verse-by-verse preaching through this excellent epistle.[5] I hope that this work will prove profitable to all who read it, but especially to preachers and teachers as they labor to instruct their hearers out of the precious Word of God, line upon line, and precept upon precept (Isa. 28:10).[6]

To God alone be the glory,

Rob Ventura 2023

Author's Acknowledgments

I am grateful to D. Scott Meadows, who for a long time has been involved in editing various works I have written. Scott is a pastor and theologian, and also a dear friend who has been a great help to me over the years. Brother, thank you for all your diligent labors in editing this entire volume.

I want to thank my fellow pastor, Jack Buckley, who is always an encouragement to me. Jack, laboring with you for over a decade and a half now in the church has been a tremendous joy to my soul. You are a true servant of the Savior and my dearest friend in the Lord.

I would thank the congregation I am privileged to pastor in Rhode Island, Grace Community Baptist Church, for their faithful love and encouragement regularly expressed to me.

I thank my dear friend and former systematic theology professor, Pastor Greg Nichols, for his outstanding instruction on Romans, whether privately on the phone or publicly in preaching. "Grandpa," the time you have spent meticulously going through this entire manuscript and making useful suggestions throughout has been a tremendous help to me.[7]

I thank my longtime friend Dr. William Downing for being an extra set of eyes on this manuscript and making helpful exegetical suggestions throughout.

Furthermore, I thank my "Romans readers" for making valuable comments on this commentary: Jack Buckley, Michael Ives, Rob Hill, Dan Crichton, Dr. Robert J. Burrelli Jr., Bob Tetrault, Robert Gemma, Paul Smalley and Tim Weiner. Brothers, I am greatly indebted to all of you for

---

4 I have outlined every section of this epistle in order to aid those who prepare weekly sermons.

5 For a helpful plan on how to preach through Romans, I encourage the reader to see Robert W. Yarbrough's comments in the *ESV Expository Commentary*, Vol. 10 (Romans-Galatians), pp. 30-32.

6 Unless otherwise indicated, Scripture references are taken from the New King James Version.

7 I am honored to be the general editor for Greg's multivolume systematic theology. These volumes can be purchased on amazon.com.

your kindness to me.[8] I am thankful as well to The Five Solas Foundation for its financial contribution to this project.[9]

I appreciate my students who took my course on Romans over the years. You all were a delight to teach and made beneficial remarks on this work.

Lastly, I thank my beloved family. You all are a special treasure. I am grateful for your selflessly allowing me to serve the Lord and His church.

I dedicate this book to every true preacher and teacher of the gospel. May this volume be a help to you in effectively proclaiming, explaining and applying that glorious good news of Jesus Christ, which is indeed the power of God to salvation for everyone who believes (Rom. 1:16).[10]

---

8   There are a few others that I want to acknowledge and thank who have been a continual help and encouragement to me along the way in writing this book: Jim Domm, Jeffery Smith, John Reuther, Dave Chanski, David Charles, Jerry Doman, John Sgambato, Robin Dziuba, Mark Raines, Allyn Meyers, Tabitha Harris, Paul Farese and Libby Koziarski.

9   www.thefivesolasfoundation.org.

10   I also dedicate this book to my dear unsaved family members and friends. I have written this volume with a deliberate evangelistic emphasis so that you might see your need of Jesus, believe on Him, and be saved.

MY TOP 30 EVANGELICAL COMMENTARIES FOR PREACHING THROUGH ROMANS[11]

1 John Murray, *The New International Commentary on the New Testament, Romans*
2 Douglas Moo, *The New International Commentary on the New Testament, Encountering the Book of Romans*
3 Thomas Schreiner, *Baker Exegetical Commentary on the New Testament*
4 Leon Morris, *The Pillar New Testament Commentary*
5 John Harvey, *Exegetical Guide to the Greek New Testament, A Commentary on Romans*
6 Colin Kruse, *The Pillar New Testament Commentary*
7 David E. Garland, *Tyndale New Testament Commentaries*
8 Frank Thielman, *Zondervan Exegetical Commentary on the New Testament*
9 Charles Hodge, *Geneva Series Commentary*
10 John MacArthur, *The MacArthur New Testament Commentary*
11 R. C. Sproul, *The Gospel of God*
12 Richard Longnecker, *The New International Greek Testament Commentary*
13 Robert Mounce, *The New American Commentary*
14 Grant Osborne, *The IVP New Testament Commentary Series, & Osborne, Verse by Verse*
15 David Peterson, *Biblical Theology for Christian Proclamation*
16 Michael F. Bird, *The Story of God Bible Commentary*
17 Geoffrey B. Wilson, *A Digest of Reformed Comment*
18 Robert W. Yarbrough, *ESV Expository Commentary*
19 Robert Rogland, *Romans A Study Manual*
20 R. Kent Hughes, *Romans Righteousness from Heaven*
21 Robert Haldane, *Exposition of the Epistle to the Romans*
22 Stuart Olyott, *The Gospel As It Really Is*
23 James Montgomery Boice, *Romans*
24 Tony Merida, *Christ-Centered Exposition*
25 Daniel M. Doriani, *Reformed Expository Commentary*
26 Anthony Thiselton, *Discovering Romans*
27 Alva J. McClain, *The Gospel of God's Grace*

28   E. H. Gifford, *Romans*

29   J. G. Vos, *Romans*

30   William S. Plumer, *Commentary on Romans.*

---

11 I would also recommend the standard commentaries written by Matthew Henry, William Burkitt, Matthew Poole and John Calvin along with sermonic multi-volume sets of Martyn Lloyd-Jones and Donald Grey Barnhouse as there is much useful material there for the expositor. Also, when my top commentaries are quoted in this book, I just list the author and page number.

THE BOOK OF ROMANS (A BRIEF OVERVIEW)[12]

Format: 16 chapters, 433 verses.

Author: The apostle Paul (Rom. 1:1). No evangelical scholar has ever seriously challenged the matter of Pauline authorship. Paul used Tertius, his amanuensis (his scribe or secretary), to help produce this letter (Rom. 16:22). Paul was a native of the city of Tarsus (an ancient city in south-central modern-day Turkey); was from the tribe of Benjamin; was brought up as a strict Pharisee; was converted to and by Christ on the road to Damascus and later wrote thirteen New Testament epistles (cf. Acts 9:1-25; 22:3; 26:13; Phil. 3:5).

Date and background: Around A.D. 57, while Paul was nearing the end of his third missionary journey (Acts 18:22ff). Most likely he wrote this letter while he was in Corinth preparing to bring relief funds to the needy believers in Jerusalem (Rom. 15:25, 26). This idea is based on the fact that in Romans 16:23, Paul mentions that Gaius was hosting him at the time he was writing this letter. Scholars suggest that this Gaius most likely was the one who lived in the city of Corinth (cf. 1 Cor. 1:14).[13]

Main theme: The glorious gospel of Jesus Christ (Rom. 1:1, 9, 15-17; 3:21-26; 15:16, 19, 20, 29; 16:25).[14]

Recipients: Believers living in Rome, the capital city of Italy (Rom. 1:7), some of whom were Paul's friends and missionary co-workers, such as Priscilla and Aquila (Rom. 16:1-16).[15] Mostly, the recipients were individuals who were saved on the day of Pentecost under Peter's powerful preaching and then went back to Rome as Christians (cf. Acts 2:10). The congregation at Rome was a combination of Jewish and Gentile converts (Rom. 1:5, 6, 13; 2:17; 3:9; 4:1; 11:13).

---

12 For more detailed information on this book, see the introduction section to Romans in the commentaries by Murray, Morris, Moo and Schreiner.

13 *Archaeology Study Bible* p. 1667.

14 This includes the great doctrines of justification by faith alone, sanctification and glorification, which Paul will expound throughout this letter.

15 Some scholars say that it was most likely Priscilla and Aquila who gave Paul updates regarding the church at Rome (cf. 1 Cor. 1:11).

Purpose: For Paul to introduce himself to this church, which he had neither founded nor visited, in preparation for a personal visit to them (Rom. 1:10, 11; 15:23).[16] As the inspired apostle, he wrote to the congregation at Rome to give and reinforce apostolic instructions for their church life together (Rom. 15:15). He addresses such matters, among others, as the universal need of the gospel for all people, justification and sanctification, the Holy Spirit and the believer, election and God's plan for Israel, the Christian life and spiritual gifts, the believer's relationship to government, and unity and divisions in the congregation. Another purpose in writing to them while he was a missionary was to give them a summary sketch of what he believed about the gospel. Then, having seen the gospel of grace which he taught and preached on the mission field, he desired that they would help contribute to his gospel-spreading endeavors further to the west, in a way comparable to what the Antioch church had done for him w (cf. Acts 13:1-3; 14:21; 15:22; 18:22 with Rom. 15:20-24).[17] In summary, we can say that Paul's purpose in writing this letter to this church was fivefold: *biographical, theological, practical, pastoral, and missional.*

Outline: I have found two to be the most helpful.[18] The first is a broad outline:

Salutation: 1:1 to 1:17
Sin: 1:18 to 3:20
Salvation: 3:21 to 5:21
Sanctification: 6:1 to 8:39
Sovereignty: 9:1 to 11:36
Service: 12:1 to 16:27

The second stems from a central theme in this book concerning "the righteousness of God"[19] which could be called the "thesis statement" of this entire epistle as stated in 1:17:

---

16 It is interesting to see the warm reception that Paul received from the brethren in Rome and various parts of Italy when he arrived there (Acts 28:11-15). This is a good indication that they gladly received this epistle which he wrote to them about three years earlier.

17 This overview should help us to understand that the book of Romans is much more than a systematic theology, as some tend to read it.

18 The first outline comes mainly from Bruce Wilkinson and Kenneth Boa, *Talk Thru the Bible* (Thomas Nelson Publishers, 1983), 371. The second comes mainly from the unpublished notes of Pastor W. R. Downing. Downing has been a gospel minister for more than 45 years and currently is a pastor of Sovereign Grace Baptist Church of Silicon Valley, California. He also leads Pacific Institute for Religious Studies in Morgan Hill, California (www.sgbcsv.org). There are two other outlines which are broader than the two above that I also like: Chapters 1-8, the *doctrinal* portion of this epistle; Chapters 9-11, the *historical* portion of this epistle; Chapters 12-16, the *practical* portion of this epistle. Or, Chapters 1-8, the *presentation* of the gospel; Chapters 9-11, the *plan* of the gospel; Chapters 12-16, the *practice* of the gospel.

19 Paul discusses this central subject in this letter in 1:17; 3:21-22; 10:3.

Righteousness of God *required* from humanity: 1:18 to 3:20
Righteousness of God *revealed* in Christ alone: 3:21 to 3:26
Righteousness of God *received* by faith alone: 3:27 to 5:21
Righteousness of God *realized* in sanctification: 6:1 to 8:11
Righteousness of God *retained* in glorification: 8:12 to 8:39
Righteousness of God *rejected* by non-elect Israel: 9:1 to 11:36
Righteousness of God *reproduced* in a converted life: 12:1 to 16:27

ROMANS
CHAPTER ONE

Text: Romans 1:1

General theme: Paul's Credentials

Homiletical outline of the verse:
 A. **His second name:** Paul
 B. **His servanthood:** a bondservant of Jesus Christ
 C. **His status:** called *to be* an apostle
 D. **His separation:** separated to the gospel of God.

Summary of section: The opening words of Romans 1:1-17 break nicely into three parts: verses 1 to 7; verses 8 to 15; and verses 16 and 17. Interestingly, the first seven verses (which form the introduction to this epistle, and are a summary of the entire book), constitute a single sentence in the Greek text. Perhaps Paul wrote this way from sheer excitement. He was so thrilled about the gospel that his words gushed forth abundantly! Additionally, this is his longest and most formal introduction in any of his letters, which might be due to the fact that he is writing to a church which he neither founded nor visited.

Exegetical & Practical Insights:
In this verse, Paul sets forth his credentials as a minister of Christ:

Obs. 1- That the name **Paul** (his official Roman name) is derived from a Latin word which means "the little one."[1] Note his humility in putting forth this name. Even though his Jewish name was Saul (after Israel's famous first king), now he is willing to be known as the little or small one, who preached Christ, the truly great One. Additionally, it is interesting to consider how King Saul in the Old Testament started out well (popular and well-liked by the people etc., see 1 Sam. 9-11), but ended badly (committed suicide by falling on his own sword to avoid being captured in battle, see 1 Sam. 31). However, Saul in the New Testament started out badly (breathing murderous threats against the disciples of

---

1 Leon Morris makes this same point. Morris, p. 36.

the Lord, see Acts 9), but ended well (becoming a servant of Christ and His church).[2] All of this happened because of Jesus' distinguishing grace toward him.

Obs. 2- That Paul was willing to use his Roman name "Paul" as he started his gospel ministry to the Gentiles. He did this most likely so that his Jewish name would not be a stumbling block to them. Clearly, he was willing to "become all things to all men that he might indeed win some" (1 Cor. 9:19-23).

Obs. 3- That he identifies himself here as the **bondservant of**[3] **Jesus Christ.**[4] Literally, he is the "slave"[5] of Jesus Christ.[6] Paul chose a very strong Greek word to describe his relationship with the Lord. While the word has a wide range of meanings, in summary, it denotes total servitude.[7] It describes the sole commitment of one person to another, being absolutely ready to do their bidding (Acts 9:6a).[8] Paul was the slave who entirely *belonged* to Jesus Christ in all aspects of his life. Of course, when he speaks of being a slave of Jesus Christ we should never think of this relationship as one of cruelty or compulsion, but rather one of complete commitment, devotion, and a willing allegiance wrought in his heart by the free grace and love of Jesus.

Obs. 4- That Paul was **called** "an apostle," (or we could take the words to mean "a called apostle,"[9] the words *to be* are not in the Greek text), highlights the divine manner of his apostleship, showing us that he was directly commissioned by God to this apostolic office. Paul did not seek this position on his own nor force his way into it. Rather, his apostleship was a heavenly, sovereign calling which was "not from men, nor through a man, but through Jesus Christ and God the Father who raised Him from the dead" (see Gal. 1:1). The word *called* is used in verses 6 and 7 of this chapter as well, but there the references are not of a call to a unique apostolic office, but first of a sovereign call to Christ for salvation through the gospel (v. 6) and then, second, of a call to be holy, a saint (v.7).

Obs. 5- That the word **apostle** comprises two Greek words, and in this context, denotes being "commissioned," "sent out," or "dispatched" by another. The word carries the idea of being an authorized delegate and appointed messenger of Christ sent to do a specific task.[10] Paul was

---

2 I am not the first commentator to make this observation.

3 Grk. genitive of possession.

4 I will dwell more on the meaning of the name *Jesus Christ* in verse 3.

5 For a helpful treatment of *slavery* in the ancient world and this entire subject in connection to Paul's use of the word, I recommend reading John MacArthur's book called *Slave: The Hidden Truth about Your Identity in Christ*.

6 Note that at one time, Paul, just like the rest of us, prior to salvation, was a slave to sin (Rom. 6:16-17).

7 No doubt Paul also had other servants of God in mind who were called a similar thing such as Abraham and Joshua (cf. Gen. 26:24; Josh. 24:29).

8 Mounce, 633.

9 Morris, 38.

10 What an amazing thing it is to see the glorious, transforming grace of God in Paul's life. It changed him from Paul the antagonist to Paul the apostle! It changed him from Paul

an "apostle" in the official sense of the word, although he was one "born out of due time" (1 Cor. 15.8). Unlike the other apostles, he did not sit directly under Jesus' earthly ministry, but was made an apostle after His ascension. He qualified for this unique honor because he saw the risen Lord Jesus Christ and then was directly called by Him (cf. Acts 1:22b; 9:1-16; 1 Cor. 9:1). Incidentally, since no one can meet these qualifications in our day, there can be no present day apostles in this sense.[11]

Obs. 6- That the word **separated** also comprises two Greek words, and it means to "mark off from others," or to "set apart for some purpose." The word in Greek is in the perfect tense, stressing Paul's present state of separation to his vocational preaching of the gospel from the time he was called to it. Generally speaking, we can say that there were three separations in his life:

1- When he was separated from his mother's womb for God's calling in his life (Gal.1:15), much like the calling of Jeremiah in Jeremiah chapter one.

2- When he was separated at conversion to Jesus to preach the gospel to the Gentiles (Acts 9:15), and then

3- When the Holy Spirit said "separate" him to Me for the *official* work of missions (Acts 13:2).[12] Commentator James R. Edwards insightfully comments that,

> The Greek word for set apart [separated] is the normal Greek rendering of the Hebrew word for "Pharisee," which probably means "to separate."[13] If Paul is indulging in a word play, he seems to indicate that he now is a different kind of Pharisee from what he had been. Previously he had been a Pharisee separated *from* Gentiles; now he is separated *for* them![14]

Obs. 7- That Paul was separated **to**[15] or for the sake of; **the gospel of God** signifies the specific purpose for his separation as an apostle. Paul was separated "for the service of"[16] proclaiming God's gospel or "good news." Further, the words "gospel of God"[17] tell us that God the Father is the author of this history-altering, life-transforming message. He is its architect and divine designer. What an amazing thought! The God from whom we deserve nothing but His wrath (as Paul will soon discuss) has good news for us. He is the God who "so loved the world that He gave

---

the persecutor to Paul the preacher!

11 Ephesians 2:20 also makes it clear that the apostles were foundational in God's plan for the church. They understood that their apostolic office would not continue. Thus Paul, for example, throughout his missionary journeys appointed "elders in every church" (Acts 14:23), so that elders would oversee local congregations after the apostles left the scene (cf. Titus 1:5-9).

12 Many commentators have made these three observations.

13 The word also has its roots in the Aramaic language which Paul spoke.

14 Edwards, 28.

15 The preposition with the accusative case can denote purpose.

16 Phillips translation.

17 Grk. genitive of source. These words could also be understood as a possessive genitive, i.e., the gospel which belongs to God. Cf. Rom. 15:16.

His only begotten Son, that whoever believes in Him should not perish but have everlasting life" (John 3:16).

Note also that this is the first occurrence of the word *gospel* in this epistle. Interestingly, not only does this book begin on a "gospel note," but as something of a bookend to it, it closes on this same note as well. This shows us clearly that the gospel is the major theme of this letter (cf. Rom. 16:25).[18]

Consider three things about the gospel:

First, *its connotation*. The word *gospel*, as stated above means, "good news" or "glad tidings." The Greek word is *euaggelion* which is comprised of two Greek words that mean "good" and "message."

Second, *its concepts*. Its biblical-historical use is found in the Septuagint and it refers to the Old Testament footmen who announced the "good news" of freedom from Babylonian captivity in the sixth century B.C. (cf. Isa. 52:7-10; Rom. 10:15). As these Jewish exiles traveled over the mountains back to Jerusalem, these heralds zealously went before the people, announcing this joyful and exciting news. Additionally, scholars tell us that the term "gospel" was not invented by Paul, but was already used in his day by the Romans regarding Roman imperial propaganda.[19] In the first century, there was what was called the "good news" or "the gospel" of the Caesars. Such "good news" referred to "an announcement of 'glad tidings' regarding a birthday, rise to power, or decree of the emperor that was to herald the fulfillment of hopes for peace and well-being in all the world."[20]

Having said these two things about the gospel, of course, the gospel that we preach is much grander and more glorious than the aforementioned examples. For one thing, the gospel we preach is God's Emancipation Proclamation; it is a decree of freedom, not merely from physical enemies and oppression as the case was with the Hebrew exiles, but from spiritual enemies and spiritual oppression. And for another thing, the good news we proclaim is not about a mere man (such as Caesar), but rather about the all-powerful God-man, Jesus Christ, who alone is to be worshiped.

Third, *its components*. Essentially, there are four.

i) the gospel is a message about God (v. 1, God, as holy, righteous, and just, who must punish sin, Rom. 6:23a. God who is a God of love, who sent His Son into the world to save sinners, cf. 1 Tim. 1:15).

ii) the gospel is a message about man as a lost, ruined, and rebellious sinner against God, who has fallen short of His glory and thus is under His wrath and just judgment (Rom. 1:18; 3.23).

---

18 Paul will repeat several of the major themes found here in verses 1 to 5, in Romans chapter 16 verses 25 to 27.

19 I first heard of this from Dr. Douglas Moo in his very helpful online course on Romans which could be found here for free: https://www.biblicaltraining.org/romans/douglas_moo.

20 Mounce, 303.

iii) the gospel is a message about Jesus Christ, the Son of God, the sinners' substitute. It is about the Lord who willingly paid the penalty for our sins by taking them upon Himself and being punished for them at the cross. Jesus then was buried and rose again on the third day as the Father's validation of His completed and accepted work on our behalf (cf. Matt. 26:28; Acts 2:32, 33; Rom. 3:21-26; 5:8; Gal. 1:1; 3:10-14; 1 Cor. 15:1-4).[21]

iv) the gospel is about the two demands for all who would receive its benefits namely, expressing repentance toward God for our sins against Him, and faith toward our Lord Jesus Christ who died as a sacrifice for our sins (Mark 1:15; Rom. 1:16; 5:1; Acts 20:20, 21).[22]

Suggested applications from the text for the church:

1- Remember that like Paul, all believers are called to serve Christ with the same bondservant disposition.[23] Do you?

2- Regard your pastors/elders highly for their work's sake because they, like Paul, also derive their authority from Christ. Although they are not apostles, they are called of God to lead Jesus' church.[24]

3- Resolve to discover if Christ is giving new pastors in your church who exemplify Christ-like, apostolic characteristics. Look for men[25] who, like Jesus and Paul, are servants first and foremost; men who preach the gospel, not psychology, philosophy, politics, or their own preferences.

Suggested application from the text for the non-Christian:[26]

1- Recall that God is not only the author of the gospel, but He is the revealer of it. Therefore, you are accountable to Him to respond to it immediately in true repentance and faith.

Text: Romans 1:2-7

General theme: The Glorious Gospel

Homiletical outline of the verses:

A. The continuity of the gospel: [2] which He promised before through His prophets in the Holy Scriptures,

---

21 Note that the apostle Paul will expound in detail the heart of the gospel in this regard in 3:21-26, a text of Scripture that Martin Luther called, "The chief point, and the very central place of the epistle, and of the whole Bible."

22 For some helpful material on the gospel, I strongly recommend reading the following books: *Evangelism and the Sovereignty of God* by J. I. Packer, *Today's Evangelism: Its message and methods* by Ernest C. Reisinger, *The Gospel Call & True Conversion* by Paul Washer, and *What is the Gospel* by Greg Gilbert.

23 Cf. Rom. 6:22; 1 Cor. 7:22; Col. 4:12.

24 Cf. 1 Thess. 5:12, 13.

25 Cf. 1 Tim. 3:1, 2.

26 The reader should note that in this section of the commentary I apply the saving truths of the texts to the non-Christian. I do this because I believe that in all of our preaching, we are to address the lost, obeying Paul's admonition to "do the work of an evangelist," fulfilling our ministries (2 Tim. 4:5).

B. The content of the gospel: [3] concerning His Son Jesus Christ our Lord, who was born of the seed of David according to the flesh, [4] *and* declared *to be* the Son of God with power according to the Spirit of holiness, by the resurrection from the dead.

C. The commission of the gospel: [5] Through Him we have received grace and apostleship for obedience to the faith among all nations for His name, [6] among whom you also are the called of Jesus Christ; [7] To all who are in Rome, beloved of God, called *to be* saints: Grace to you and peace from God our Father and the Lord Jesus Christ.

Exegetical & Practical Insights:
Having mentioned the gospel in the previous verse:

Obs. 1- (v. 2) That although the gospel is good news, it is not new news! The gospel of Christ is not a theological novelty or some "Johnny-come-lately story."[27] It is not an afterthought in the mind of God, as though it were some Plan B. Rather, it was that **which God promised before**[28] or previously, or in advance, having pre-announced it; **through** or by means of; **His prophets** that is, His Old Testament spokesmen; **in** or by; **the Holy** or set apart from that which is common or distinct from other books; **Scriptures** or writings.[29] In other words, the gospel has always been a part of the true religion of God and has always been known and believed by the true people of God (see Gal. 3:8). The gospel is not a break with the past, rather it is the continuation and consummation of it. From the book of Genesis with its first gospel promise (the *protoevangelium*; see Gen. 3:15) and all the way through Scripture, (Gen. 3:15; Deut. 18:15; Ps. 16:12; Ps. 22:1, 16; Isa. 6:14; 53, Jer. 23:6; Dan. 9:26 etc.), we see that the Bible speaks about the *doing, dying, and rising* of Jesus Christ our Lord on our behalf (cf. Luke. 24:25, 26; 44; John 5:46; Acts 10:43; 1 Cor. 15:1-4). Thus, John Calvin was right when he said, "Christ came not on the earth unexpectedly, nor did he introduce a doctrine of a new kind and not heard of before, inasmuch as he, and his gospel too, had been promised and expected from the beginning of the world."[30] Further, note that Paul's words here in verse two could be somewhat polemical. It could be that he was defending himself against the Judaizers who often thought that he preached against Moses and the law of God.[31] These men taught that Paul proclaimed some innovative message when he preached the gospel, some new fad that was unheard of in the Jewish Scriptures. Clearly, this was not the case, for the gospel of Christ is neither new nor anti-Jewish, and it is absolutely found in the Old Testament Bible.

Obs. 2- (v. 3) That the central subject of the gospel is Christ. He is the featured Person of the gospel in the Godhead. Even though it is God the Father who planned our salvation from eternity past (Eph. 1:4), and in

---

27 Merida, p. 10.

28 Grk. aorist, middle, verb.

29 Cf. Rom. 15:4.

30 Calvin, p. 43.

31 MacArthur mentions this point on page 12 of his commentary on Romans.

time, God the Holy Spirit regenerates His elect people according to the divine plan of salvation (Titus 3:5), the gospel, the good news message of the Bible, is centered in or **concerning** the preposition meaning "about" or "with reference to" Jesus Christ. In this sense then, we could say that the gospel is not a *what*, but a *who*. The gospel at its core is the good news concerning Jesus' person and work (cf. 1 Cor. 15:1-4). Jesus is the chief point and critical center of the message. As Calvin says, "This is a principal passage in which we are taught that the whole gospel is bound up in Christ, so that if anybody moves a single foot away from Christ they withdraw themselves from the gospel."[32]

Obs. 3- That Christ is God's **Son**. He is His unique Son, the eternal Son (not a created, redeemed and adopted son as believers are, cf. Rom. 8:14, 15), His Son in the sense of equality with the Father (cf. John 10:30). Christ is the second person of the Blessed Trinity. He is the Son of God. He is God the Son. He is the Supreme Being (John 1:1; Rev. 1:8).

Obs. 4- That His *distinctive name* **Jesus** means "God saves" (the word *Jesus* being the Greek equivalent to the Hebrew term, *Yeshua* or in English, Joshua) which means "the Lord is salvation" (cf. Matt. 1:21). This name is used most often in Scripture with reference to the personal, human, Hebrew name of our Lord. *His distinguished title*, **Christ**, is the equivalent Greek term for the Hebrew word *Messiah* found in the Old Testament. It affirms that Jesus is God's promised anointed and appointed One sent from Him to be His great Messianic King, Mediator, Ruler and mighty Deliverer who would shepherd His people (cf. Matt. 2:4; 16:16).[33] *His divine designation*, **Lord**, means that He is the sovereign master over all things who rules and reigns supreme.[34] It means that all authority in heaven and on earth are in His hands. Thus, "all things are subject to him, and we are bound to serve him"[35] (cf. Matt. 28:18). This designation also signifies Jesus' divine nature and it translates the Old Testament word for Lord *Jehovah* multiple times in the Septuagint (the Greek translation of the Hebrew Scriptures).

Obs. 5- That Christ became a man. He was **born of the seed of David** as foretold in 2 Sam. 7:11-14. He is from King David's posterity, or his

---

32 *Reformation Commentary on Scripture, Romans*, p. 21.

33 The Old Testament has much to say about Jesus the Messiah. There are many predictions concerning Him. It tells us for example that He would be the promised Seed of the woman who would crush the head of the serpent (Gen. 3:15). It tells us that He would be born of a virgin and be the incarnate Son of God (Isa. 7:14). It tells us that He would be born in Bethlehem (Mic. 5:2). It tells us that He would be despised by the Jews (Isa. 53:2-3). It tells us He would die a sacrificial death in the place of the guilty, being pierced through on account of their sins (Ps. 22: 1, 16; Isa. 53:5; Dan. 9:26). It tells us that He would not be left in the grave, that is, He would be raised from the dead (Ps. 16:10). It tells us that He would ascend to heaven (Ps. 68:18), to name a few things.

34 While in Rome, the popular saying was "Caesar is Lord!" Christians would reply back by saying "Christ is Lord!" The point is, they realized that in the ultimate sense, Jesus Christ was the supreme Lord over all things.

35 *The Commentary of Dr. Zacharias Ursinus on the Heidelberg Catechism* (Grand Rapids, MI: Wm. B. Eerdmans, 1956), 202.

family line. He is from his lineage as the promised Messiah had to be (cf. Acts 13:23). This was so both *legally* through Joseph, his appointed father (see Matt. 1), and *biologically* through Mary as his human mother (see Luke 3).[36]

Obs. 6- Jesus Christ, the Son of God, actually became man—a real man, 100% man. He came **according to the flesh**[37] (not sinful flesh, for He had no sin).[38] He came into the world with a true human soul and body. Jesus, who was truly and fully God, through the incarnation, became truly and fully man, being born of a woman (Gal. 4:4). Remaining what He had always been (namely, God), He became something that he had never been (namely, man). He is the God-man; one person, with two natures. He is God "manifested in the flesh" (1 Tim. 3:16), real flesh. He did not only "appear" or "seem" to be human as the heretical group known as the Docetists falsely taught. But again, real man, with flesh, blood, and bones (cf. Luke 24:39). All of this was so that through His sacrificial work on the cross in our place, we might be delivered from the penalty of our sins (1 Cor. 15:3). This is what Jesus did at Calvary for sinners. This is the work He willingly undertook and accomplished in our stead as our sinless representative and surety.

Obs. 7- (v. 4) That in a unique way, Jesus' resurrection from the dead (v. 4b) **declared** or "distinguished," and "demonstrated" Him; **to be the Son of God with power** or with sovereign strength. The resurrection was the pivotal point which marked the end of His humiliation on the earth and initiated the beginning of His exaltation into glory; **according to the Spirit of holiness,** there has been much scholarly discussion concerning the language of "the Spirit of holiness" and what it means (whether Jesus' own inner spirit or disposition of holiness, versus the Holy Spirit etc.); however, the words in this context seem to refer to the Holy Spirit.[39]

This is made clear especially when we compare this verse, which goes on to speak about Jesus' resurrection from the dead, with Rom. 8:11 and other places where there are obvious links between the Holy Spirit and Jesus' resurrection. Luther's comment on this phrase is noteworthy. He says that: The apostle uses the expression "Spirit of holiness" in place of the "Holy Spirit," but that is of no significance, for He is the same Spirit who, according to His divine work, is called either "Holy Spirit" or "Spirit of holiness;" **by** or out of; **the resurrection from the dead.**[40] This language does not, of course, imply that at His resurrection, Jesus became the Son of God, for He was already God's Son (1:3). Rather, it means that uniquely, His resurrection from the grave was the clear

---

36 Do not miss the point here in connection to the last phrase of Jesus as God's Son, that Paul is stressing both the *deity* and the *humanity* of Christ.

37 Cf. 9:5.

38 John 8:46; 2 Cor. 5:21; Heb. 4:15; 1 Pet. 2:22; 1 John 3:5.

39 Harvey says, "Since 'spirit of holiness' is a literal translation of the Hebrew *ruach qodesh* (Ps. 51:16; Isa. 63:10-11), that phrase is best understood as a reference to the Holy Spirit." Harvey, 67.

40 Paul also mentions Jesus' resurrection in 4:25 and 10:9.

line of demarcation which separated Him from the rest of humanity, proving beyond any doubt His exclusive Sonship, and then afterwards, His entrance into His mediatorial reign as the exalted Lord of glory and David's great king (v.3, cf. Ps. 2:6-8; 110:1; Acts 2:29, 30; 1 Cor. 15:20-25).

Obs. 8- (v. 5) That the opening words **through Him** refer to Jesus as "the agent in bestowing grace and appointing unto apostleship;"[41] **we have received**;[42] or laid hold of, once for all time; **grace,** "received" not *earned* grace.[43] Grace is never meritorious. It is not what God gives us for keeping the Ten Commandments, or for being baptized, or for joining a particular church. Instead, grace is that which is freely given to sinners out of God's kind, benevolent heart.

This is the first time of many times that the word "grace" appears in this epistle.[44] But what exactly is grace? Grace, or as Paul speaks about it in this context, saving grace,[45] is a virtue or trait in God that speaks about His unmerited, unearned, and uncaused favor and goodwill toward us in Christ, which continues all of our days. For Paul, "the word grace at times seems to function as shorthand for all that God has done for His people in Christ."[46] Grace is getting what we do not deserve from God, namely, His pardon, peace, joy, and deliverance from His wrath for our sins against Him. It is about we who warranted nothing from our Maker but His judgment, instead getting everything that is good from Him for nothing. All of this is ours "through the redemption that is in Christ Jesus" (Rom. 3:24).

Obs. 9- That Paul's **apostleship** which he and the other apostles received through "Him" (again, through the agency of Jesus) is described here regarding three definitive things.

First, he tells us the *purpose* of his apostleship when he speaks of it being **for** or with a view to; **obedience** literally, a hearing under or being submissive; **to the faith**, that is, the objective faith of the gospel.[47] This speaks primarily about compliance to that message upon initially hearing it, and responding to its demands of repentance and faith (cf. Acts 20:21). Further, the language of "obedience to the faith" connotes saved people, by the power and the enablement of the Holy

---

41 McBeth, 29.

42 Grk. aorist, active, verb.

43 Cf. Rom. 15:15, 16, where Paul says that "grace" was also given to him in order that he might be a "minister of Jesus Christ to the Gentiles, ministering the gospel of God." See also Rom. 12:3.

44 Cf. See 1:7; 3:24; 4:4, 16; 5:2, 15, 17, 20, 21; 6:1, 14, 15; 11:5, 6; 12:3, 6; 15:15; 16:20, 24.

45 I agree with John Murray when he says, "Grace and apostleship could mean the grace of apostleship. It is more likely, however, that 'grace' is here the more general unmerited favor of God. The apostle was never forgetful of the grace and mercy by which he had been saved and called into the fellowship of Christ (*cf.* 1 Cor. 15:10; Gal. 1:15; 1 Tim. 1:13-16; 2 Tim. 1:9; Tit. 3:5-7)." Murray, p. 13. This view seems to go better with the general flow of the passage.

46 Matthew Harmon, Philippians, *A Mentor Commentary*, p. 75.

47 Paul ends this glorious epistle on the same note of obedience to the faith as something of a bookend to this entire letter (cf. 16:26).

Spirit, expressing evangelical compliance to the objective faith of the Christian religion as expressed in God's Word.[48]

Second, Paul speaks here of the *scope* of his apostleship when he says that it is **among**, the preposition denoting the sphere of his apostolic labors; **all the nations**, that is, the Gentile nations, not just the Jews (cf. Matt. 28:19). Third, he speaks about the *goal* of his apostleship when he says that it is **for** or on behalf of; **His name**, that is Jesus' name, not his own.[49]

Obs. 10- (v. 6) That Paul writes that these believers at Rome were **among whom you also are,** that is, among all the Gentile nations spoken of in the previous verse. Simply stated, although they were not "called" to be apostles as Paul was (see v. 1), they were, nonetheless, **the called of Jesus Christ**[50] i.e., those who personally belonged to Him.

Obs. 11- (v. 7) That in Paul addressing these Christians broadly as **all who are in Rome** may mean that there was not a single church in Rome, but multiple local churches in that city (cf. Rom. 16:5, 14, 15). McDonald suggests, "There were several gatherings of believers in the city and this salutation embraces them all."[51] What an amazing thought it is to consider that in the midst of this extremely pagan city, God had a people! Yes, God has chosen ones in the darkest and distant parts of the earth. He has them all throughout the world, in all kinds of obscure and spiritually dim places, since He shows no partiality among humanity (cf. Acts 10:34, 35; 18:9, 10, Rev. 5:9). **Beloved of God** emphasizes that believers are dearly loved, valued and treasured by God. Note that every single believer, regardless of who they are or where they are from, is an object of God's divine love. The church, composed of believing Jews and Gentiles, is individually and collectively cherished by the Lord, being His "own special people."[52] The church is the apple of God's eye. It is precious to Him, being in the "bosom of His affection," as the theologian John Murray says.[53]

Obs. 12- That these Christians, just like all true believers in all ages, were **called** *to be* **saints** (or saints by Divine calling; the words *to be* as with verse one, are not in the Greek text). Their salvation, just like everyone's salvation — Paul's included — began not with themselves, but with God, for it is God who always starts the call to salvation (1 Cor. 1:9, 30). He issues the divine summons to those whom He chooses for salvation, for they are "called according to His purpose" (Rom. 8:28).

---

48   In the apostle's mind there is a true connection between faith and obedience to the things of God. Simply stated, Paul was no antinomian and he definitely held to the Lordship of Christ. He preached that a life of faith which alone justifies us before God, is never alone without a life of corresponding obedience to the things of God (cf. John 14:15; James 2:14-26; 1 John 2:4).

49   Note that all ministry, whatever it is, is to have this main view in focus in view.

50   Grk. genitive of possession. See the following verse for an exposition of the word "called."

51   McDonald, 1676.

52   Cf. Deut. 33:3, with 1 Pet. 2:9-10.

53   Murray, p. 15.

Their calling to Christ is rooted in their predestination by the decree of God, which calling always brings about their justification, which always brings about their sanctification, and which always ends in their glorification. This calling takes place in time, as they are *effectually* and *savingly* called *to* God through the gospel (cf. Rom. 8:30; 11:29; 1 Thess. 1:4, 5; 2 Tim. 1:9).[54]

Further, that they were called "saints" meant that because of their relationship with God through Christ, they were now a consecrated people, sanctified in Christ Jesus (cf. 1 Cor. 1:2). By virtue of the new birth, they were "separate ones," whose lives were now to be "set apart" unto God from the world and sin. They were those who, because they were radically changed *within*, were now to live distinctly Christian lives *without* in the midst of a crooked and perverse generation (cf. Phil. 2:15). They were those who, by the help and grace of God, by the enablement of the Holy Spirit, were to live morally pure and different from others around them. They were called to be holy, even as God Himself is holy (cf. Lev. 11:44; 1 Pet. 1:16).

Additionally, the fact that Paul says that they were "called saints" shows that this is not something that would happen to them in the *future* when they died, but was, in fact, a *present* reality for them. According to Scripture, a saint is not some individual who at last enters some "special honorary status" after death. No, a saint is a saved, living, breathing believer who is in this world, but is not of the world. He is a Christian! She is a Christian! This is what these Romans were. This is what you are, believer.

However, remember that this was not what the Romans were before conversion.[55] Paul says they were *called* saints, *not born* saints. The point is, they were once just as ungodly as others living in Rome at that time (Rom. 6:17, 18). They also were once "dead in trespasses and sins," being "alienated from the life of God," just as we all were "because of the ignorance that [was] in them, because of the blindness of their heart" (Eph. 2:1; 4:18). Now, however, by the great transforming power of the gospel, they were made new people in Jesus. They had become the salt of the earth. The light of the world (Matt. 5:13, 14).

Obs. 13- That the benediction, **grace to you and peace from God our Father and the Lord Jesus Christ,** is one which appears in all of Paul's epistles. True spiritual "grace" or goodwill and unmerited favor, is that which refers to all the spiritual blessings which God in Christ confers upon His people (as mentioned above in the comments on v. 5); and "peace" which is not the absence of turmoil, but inner serenity in the midst of it, is that which comes exclusively "from" or out of as its source; "God our Father and the Lord Jesus Christ." Augustine warmly writes:

---

54 This divine summons from God is not merely the general external call that all people hear when the gospel is preached, but rather that which is internal, and effectual and always produces salvation (cf. Matt. 10:27).

55 See the second half of Romans 1, and Romans 2.

> Grace then is from God the Father and the Lord Jesus Christ, by which
> our sins, which had turned us from God, are forgiven; and from them
> also is this peace, whereby we are reconciled to God. Since through grace
> hostilities dissolve once sins are remitted, now we may cling in peace to
> him from whom our sins alone had torn us…. But when these sins have
> been forgiven through faith in our Lord Jesus Christ, we shall have peace
> with no separation between us and God.[56]

Moreover, note that based on these words, that grace and peace come
"from God our Father and the Lord Jesus Christ," it is clear that Jesus
must, in fact, be God.[57] As the Bible commentator Robert Haldane rightly
said, "Here again we see an incontrovertible proof of the deity of Jesus
Christ; for, if He were not God, He could not without impiety be thus
joined with, or invoked along with, the Father to impart blessings, of
which God alone is the author."[58]

Suggested applications from the text for the church:
1- Love the gospel; think about all that God has done for you
through it.
2- Live in the gospel; regularly preach it to yourself, remembering
how it tells you about your election, justification, sanctification, and
glorification, etc.
3- Live out the gospel; adorn it as a child of God. Commend it to the
world through how you live. Do not discredit it.
4- Let loose the gospel; share it as far and wide as you possibly can
to the lost.

Suggested application from the text for the non-Christian:
1- Believe the gospel. This is God's message for you.

Text: Romans 1:8-15

General theme: Paul's Pastoral Heart

Homiletical outline of the verses:
A. His praise: [8]First, I thank my God through Jesus Christ for you all,
that your faith is spoken of throughout the whole world.
B. His prayers: [9]For God is my witness, whom I serve with my spirit
in the gospel of His Son, that without ceasing I make mention of you
always in my prayers, [10]making request if, by some means, now at last I
may find a way in the will of God to come to you.
C. His plans: [11]For I long to see you, that I may impart to you some
spiritual gift, so that you may be established— [12]that is, that I may be
encouraged together with you by the mutual faith both of you and me.
[13]Now I do not want you to be unaware, brethren, that I often planned to

---

56 *Ancient Christian Commentary on Scripture, Romans* p. 14.

57 Paul already hinted at this matter in 1:3a.

58 Haldane, p. 36.

come to you (but was hindered until now), that I might have some fruit among you also, just as among the other Gentiles.

D. His passion: [14] I am a debtor both to Greeks and to barbarians, both to wise and to unwise. [15] So, as much as is in me, *I am* ready to preach the gospel to you who are in Rome also.

Summary of section: Verses 8-15 are considered the second part of Paul's introduction to this epistle, which sets the stage for his presentation of the gospel (v. 16ff). In this section we have the apostle opening the window of his heart to the Romans. Here he builds a bridge to his readers before he launches into his main treatise in this book, for, as John MacArthur writes, Paul is saying to the Romans, in effect, "Before I show you my theology, I am going to show you myself."[59]

Exegetical & Practical Insights:
Obs. 1- That having established his apostolic credentials with the Romans in verse one of this chapter, Paul now writes to these believers on a very personal note. Notice the multiple number of first-person singular references to Paul. "I" is used in each verse from 8 to 15. Here, Paul is letting the Romans know how he felt about them, how he loved them. It is striking to see this about him. Whereas we might think that the apostle was a distant individual, aloof from people, nothing could be further from the truth. Paul loved people, just as all pastors should. He loved the brethren, just as we all should. Moreover, it is striking to note that he returns once again to using the first-person singular regarding himself in 15:22, showing us that all of his high-level theology that he shares with the Romans in this letter from the beginning to the end is rooted in a pastoral relationship with them. All of it is couched in special Christian love and concern for them.

Obs. 2- (v. 8) That the opening word **first** is not being used chronologically so that Paul will say in the following words, *second, third, or fourth.* Nor is the word being used in terms of what is most important. Rather, the word *first* here is used by the apostle in order to grab his readers' attention with what he is going to say to them right at the beginning of this letter. He is using the word as a preface to this epistle and could be understood as saying "at the outset."[60]

Obs. 3- That when Paul says **I thank**[61] the present tense verb "thank" shows that this is what he did continually.[62] Paul is always ready to give thanks to God for the churches. He does this in most of his epistles. The only exception is the epistle to the Galatians, and this was due to the fact that many of them were "turning away so soon from Him who called

---

59 MacArthur, p. 32

60 Harvey notes that the postpositive particle in the Greek text *men* without *de* following adds emphasis. Harvey, p. 18.

61 Grk. present, active, verb.

62 Thiselton notes that the Greek word-group *eucharisteo* occurs 46 times in the Pauline corpus, showing us that indeed the apostle was a thankful man. Thiselton, p. 72.

you in the grace of Christ to a different gospel" (Gal. 1·6). Thankfulness, as Paul expressed it, is to be a distinguishing mark for all ministers regarding their people. Really, it should be a distinguishing mark of all of God's people in their lives, in contrast to unbelievers who are typically *un*thankful (cf. Rom. 1:21).

Obs. 4- That Paul's use of **my God** highlights his personal piety and what the essence of true saving faith is all about. In other words, his words emphasize his real, spiritual, personal relationship with God. For Paul, God was not some vague idea or concept; he was not some mere "man upstairs." Rather, He was his Redeemer. He was his God by virtue of salvation in Christ (cf. Phil. 1:3; 1 Cor. 1:4; 2 Tim. 1:12). John MacArthur makes a good point when he says, that "no pagan would have made such a statement, nor would have most Jews referred to God with a personal pronoun. For Paul, God was not a theological abstraction but a beloved Savior and close friend."[63]

Obs. 5- That Paul thanks his God for the Romans, **through** or by the agency of; **Jesus Christ.** Why did he do this? Well, besides the fact that God became "his God" *through* Christ (that is, through Christ's person and work in his place), he did this also, because, as Christians we do all things with reference to our God through Jesus our Advocate. Paul did this because, according to the Bible, even though we are saved, we are not fit in and of ourselves to approach the holy God of Scripture. Rather, we need a high priest. We need a go-between, and (blessed be God) we have one in our Lord! It is through Him that we have "access by one Spirit to the Father" (Eph. 2:18). It is through Jesus' mediation and merits that we can make our approaches to the Almighty and His great grace (Rom. 5:2). For as Paul says in 1 Tim. 2:5, "There is one God and one Mediator between God and men, the Man Christ Jesus" (cf. John 14:14).

Obs. 6- That concerning the Romans, Paul says that he thanks God, not merely for *some* of them, but **for** or on account of **you all.** No one was excluded from his gratitude to God in this regard. In the church, our hearts are to be grateful for each of the brethren without exception, even despite their deficiencies, dispositions, and any trivial differences we might have with them. Additionally, we are to pray for all the saints, whomever they are, as Paul instructs us in Eph. 6:18.[64]

Obs. 7- That Paul gives the specific reason of his thanksgiving for the Romans when he says that it was **that** or because; their **faith,** that is, their trust and confidence in Christ and ultimately their Christianity lived out before others; was **being spoken**[65] **of** or declared, and this continually; **throughout** the preposition denoting sphere; **the whole world** (the words

---

63 MacArthur, p. 34.

64 For a detailed exposition of this verse, and the verses surrounding it, I point the reader to *Spiritual Warfare, A Biblical and Balanced Perspective* by Brian Borgman and Rob Ventura, (Reformation Heritage Books).

65 Grk. present tense verb. The Greek word is intensive in form with the added *kata* and so it is an emphatic expression of their testimony. Simply stated, their lives were announcing the truth of the gospel everywhere they went.

"whole world" being used as an obvious hyperbole from the apostle cf. John 12:19).[66] Here the apostle is not speaking literally, saying that every single person, in every single corner on the face of the planet, had heard about the faith of the Romans. Rather, he is simply saying that the faith of the Romans was being spoken of in many places; it was known throughout the "then world," that is, throughout the Roman Empire (cf. 1 Thess. 1:8-10).[67]

Obs. 8- (v. 9) That as Paul confirms that he regularly thanked God for each and every one of the Romans (v. 8a), he begins this verse by saying: **For** a verification of this fact; **God is my witness**. We should note that Paul's language here is not meant to suggest that the Romans doubted this about him. Rather, so as to plainly set forth the fact of this matter, he calls God as his defense. The apostle, as it were, puts himself under oath saying even further in the second part of the verse that he prays for the Romans **without ceasing** or constantly; **making mention** of them **always** or at all times; in his prayers. This language of how earnestly and consistently the apostle prayed for the believers in Rome should be a challenge for all of us as Christians. Think about it: if Paul could pray this way for people whom he barely knew, how much more should we pray for those whom we know quite well![68]

Obs. 9- That when Paul speaks here of **serving**[69] God **with** or in; **my spirit in the gospel of His Son,** his language of "my spirit" speaks most likely of his own human spirit, as fueled by the Holy Spirit of God. This word "serving" is used in the Septuagint to refer exclusively to service rendered to a deity, such as a priest would offer in a temple. In the New Testament, it always refers to service that is religious in nature (see Luke 2:37; Acts 7:7, 42). Here, then, the apostle unveils his *inner life* to us as a believer (cf. Acts 24:14), and says that with his whole heart, "my spirit," he worshiped the true and living God "in" or with reference to the gospel or the good news of His Son which had so radically affected his life.[70] The gospel (which is all about Christ) was the center of Paul's

---

66 The word "world" in Scripture can have various meanings. Sometimes it may mean the "physical world" (cf. John 1:9). Sometimes it could mean "the people of the world" (cf. John 1:10). Sometimes it could mean the "then world of the first century," etc. (cf. Luke 2:1).

67 We should not miss the significance of this important statement from Paul, written in the context of Christianity as an illegal religion and Christians being severely persecuted under Nero's reign. Despite this humanly insurmountable opposition, the Roman church was making a significant impact for Christ and the gospel. Their godliness and obedience to their Lord had them "shining as lights" in a dark place and fulfilling their identity as the "salt of the earth." No wonder their faith was being spoken of "throughout the whole world."

68 MacArthur expresses this thought in a popular way when he says that the saints in Rome were never taken off Paul's "prayer list." MacArthur, p. 38.

69 Grk. present, active, verb.

70 Alva McClain says on page 48 of his commentary on Romans, "The place of Paul's priestly service was 'in the gospel of His Son.' Paul was no priest ministering at a mundane altar, ministering a sacrifice which could never take away sins. But he had an altar nevertheless: 'We have an altar, whereof they have no right to eat who serve the tabernacle' (Heb. 13:10). Paul has an altar in the gospel of the Son of God. That is our place of service,

life. It was that which shaped him and then motivated him as a Christian
in all of his labors for the Lord.

Further, maybe this language stands in contrast to his former days as
a Pharisee. Generally speaking, the Pharisees were very much concerned
with outward religious deeds and observances while not being inwardly
right with God (cf. Matt. 23:26, 27). Now, however, since Paul had been
born again, and given a new spiritual heart (Ezek. 36:26), he says that he
served God with his spirit (cf. Rom. 2:28-29). This was now what the core
of his religion was like, as a true child of God, because of the salvation
he experienced in Jesus. It was from this new inward spring that the
outward aspects of Christianity (such as praying, fasting and going to
church) came forth from his life.

Obs. 10- That this is the second time in the opening chapter that
Paul mentions the word *gospel* (cf. v. 1). All of this is preparatory for
what he will say about the gospel in verses 16 and 17 of this chapter and
throughout the rest of this book.

Obs. 11- (v. 10) That as Paul speaks further about his prayer and
his affection for the Romans, he says that he was continually **making
request**[71] to God, that **if by some means now, at last he may find a way**
or, more literally from the Greek, might have a good, prosperous, and
successful journey; **in the will of God to come to them.**

In the first part of this verse, we see something of the *constancy* of
Paul's prayer life to the Lord. In the second part, we see something of
the *compliance* of it, as he very delicately balances his desire to visit the
Romans, which at this point he had not yet done, in the sovereign will
of God. The apostle clearly understood, as we all should, the words of
Solomon in Proverbs 16:9 that "a man's heart plans his way but the LORD
directs his steps." Paul grasped that all of his plans to visit the church in
Rome had to be submitted to God who disposes of all things as He wills
(cf. Rom. 15:32, also Acts 21:14; James 4:13-15). Lastly, it is interesting to
note here that when Paul finally arrived at Rome, he did not arrive as
a free missionary of the Lord, but as an arrested prisoner of the Lord,
showing us again the truthfulness of Proverbs 16:9 as quoted above
(cf. Acts. 28:16).[72]

Obs. 12- (v. 11) That the word **for** in the verse is explanatory,
amplifying to us why it is Paul wants to find a way in the will of God to
come to the Romans as expressed in the previous verse. The word **long**
or earnestly desire, expresses the ongoing aim that Paul had. The word

---

at the altar of the cross of Christ. We are to stand and persuade sinners to come there and
be cleansed. Our priestly service today is not a wafer, not a cup of wine. Our service today
involves that for which those things stand: the cross, His broken body."

71 Grk. present, middle, participle.

72 Paul's journeys might not seem too prosperous (cf. Acts 14:19; 21:27 etc.).
Nevertheless, we know that they were because God was with him, sustaining and guiding
him in all that he did (cf. Acts 18:10). Further, God so worked things out for Paul (Rom. 8:28),
that in the Lord's will He granted the apostle to be able to stay in Rome for "two whole
years... preaching the kingdom of God and teaching the things which concern the Lord
Jesus Christ with all confidence no one forbidding him" (cf. Acts 28:30-31).

that expresses the purpose for the visit and is further explained in the next verse. And so why did the apostle long to see the Romans? He tells us: so that **I may impart** or I[73] may share or give and distribute; **to you some** (or some kind of);[74] **spiritual gift** or gracious bestowal; **so that** or to the end that or for the purpose that; **you may be established**[75] that is, made thoroughly strong and stable in the faith (cf. Rom. 16:25).[76]

Obs. 13- That what Paul speaks of imparting to the Romans here was not, most likely, "a miraculous gift of the Spirit," of the kind spoken of in Romans 12:6 or in 1 Corinthians chapters 12 to 14, such as gifts of healings, speaking with tongues, and prophecies, etc.[77] Rather, he seems to speak of an overall spiritual benefit, most likely an instruction or insight connected to the Christian gospel. This interpretation seems to fit best in this specific setting. Really then, in one sense, it could be said that the teaching of this entire letter to the Romans was a "spiritual gift" to them which would establish them as Christians. Concerning this gift, Leon Morris rightly says, "The term is used here in the more general sense of anything that builds up the spiritual life." He writes, "There is no reason to think that Paul has the special gifts in mind here, and the indefinite form of the expression (some spiritual gift) favors the more general concept."[78]

Obs. 14- (v. 12) That as Paul more fully explains and expands his thought here from the previous verse, and perhaps qualifies it,[79] he says that through the imparting of a spiritual gift or benefit to the Romans, he may also **be encouraged together** with them **by** or through the means of; **the mutual faith** or belief in the truth (belief in the Lord); **of you and me.** What is the point? It is that as they fellowship together in the things of Christ, they impart the spiritual benefit of joy and encouragement to each other.

The two words "encouraged together" in our English Bibles are one compound word in the original language. The word carries the idea of being strengthened or comforted by others. This is a benefit of our fellowship as believers. Our fellowship is to be about building one another up in our most holy faith (Jude 20). We are to encourage one another through our prayers and insights from the Word of God.

---

73 The use of the first person singular here "I" makes it clear that Paul is not speaking of imparting some supernatural gift of the Holy Spirit to the Romans. He knew very well that only the Spirit Himself could do this, for as he says in 1 Corinthians 12:11 "but one and the same Spirit works all these things, distributing to each one individually as He wills."

74 Since Paul does not exactly spell out what the spiritual gift is, we should not be dogmatic at this point.

75 Grk. aorist, passive, verb.

76 The Greek passive form of the verb underscoring to us that this spiritual establishing of the Romans was not ultimately done by themselves, but rather, by God, who Himself establishes His people.

77 For a useful treatment of these topics, see *Signs of the Apostles* by Walter Chantry and *Charismatic Chaos* by John MacArthur.

78 Morris, p. 60.

79 Thiselton, p. 74.

R. C. Sproul rightly says that, "This is the way the church is supposed to function, each member of the body being comforted and ministered to by the others."[80] Spurgeon concurs:

> Paul wanted his faith to establish theirs, and their faith to establish his. Christians grow rich by the exchange of spiritual commodities; and I am afraid some Christians are very poor because they do not engage in the spiritual bartering with one another. You know how it was in the old-time, "They that feared the Lord spake often one to another." Shall I tell you how it is now? They that fear not the Lord speak often one against another. That is a very sad difference. Oh, for more Christian communion; for when we blend our "mutual faith", we are "comforted together"; each believer grows stronger as he cheers his brother in the Lord.[81]

Further, we see that although Paul had a vital relationship with Christ, nonetheless, he treasured mutual fellowship in the Lord. The point is, he was not beyond needing this as a believer. Christian fellowship is for all of God's people, from the least of them to the greatest, and it is never to be one-sided. It is never to be for just receiving and not giving. But about giving and receiving, "iron sharpening iron."[82] In commenting on this matter, John Calvin said of Paul,

> See to what degree of modesty his pious heart submitted itself, so that he disdained not to seek confirmation from unexperienced beginners: nor did he speak dissemblingly, for there is no one so void of gifts in the Church of Christ, who is not able to contribute something to our benefit: but we are hindered by our envy and by our pride from gathering such fruit from one another.[83]

Obs. 15- (v. 13) That as he typically does in his letters, Paul uses the language of, **I do not want you to be unaware** literally, without knowledge, or ignorant, when he is highlighting something that his readers did not know or that he deemed especially important for them to know.[84] Paul uses this expression several times throughout his letters (cf. 11:25; 1 Cor. 10:1; 12:1; 1 Thess. 4:13). What was it that the apostle wanted the Roman brethren to be aware of?[85] He tells us when he says **that** expressing the content of his thought; **I often planned**[86] or purposed

---

80 Sproul, p. 30.

81 Spurgeon, p. 12.

82 Prov. 27:17.

83 Calvin, p. 58.

84 Thiselton notes that Paul's use here of a double negative ("do not"/"unaware") was used for the sake of emphasis. Thiselton, p. 74. Perhaps Paul speaks so forcefully because he does not want the Romans to have any question about his sincerity of heart toward them.

85 This is the first time in this epistle that the apostle addresses the Romans as "brethren." This word was used "of those who belong to the same religious group and here makes the appeal more personal and effective" (Rogers and Rogers, p. 316). The term speaks about those who are part of Jesus' family, highlighting their close spiritual relationship with one another.

86 Grk. aorist, middle, verb.

beforehand;[87] **to come to you but was hindered** or prevented; until now. When Paul speaks here about planning to come to the Romans but being *hindered*, why was this? Was it because Satan hindered him as some scholars suggest (cf. 1 Thess. 2:18)? Maybe. Paul does not say. But it could be that this was so because of all of his pressing ministerial duties that were upon him while on the mission field. Also, notice that it is not until 15:22, 23 that he picks up again his reason for being *hindered* in coming to the Romans. Talk about a long digression! What then was one of the main purposes for Paul's planning to come to the Romans? He says it was that he might have **some fruit**, that is "spiritual fruit,"[88] among them also just as among the other Gentiles.[89]

Obs. 16- (v. 14) That the verb **I am** in the verse is in the present tense, showing Paul's continual compulsion.[90] Here we see his eagerness and great desire for evangelizing the lost. Simply stated, he felt a debt to everyone because knowing what he had been saved *from* (hell and eternal destruction), he knew what he had been saved *for* (namely, to see others delivered from such a plight). Also, note that this is the first of Paul's three "I am" statements in this section of Scripture (cf. vv. 15-16, where he says, "*I am ready* to preach," and "*I am not ashamed* of the gospel of Christ").

The noun **debtor**[91] literally means to owe a debt to someone or something. In this setting, it carries two meanings: first, it refers to Paul's divine obligation *to Christ* (who paid Paul's sin debt to God at the cross) to carry out the commission of preaching the good news of salvation in Him, a commission which Jesus entrusted to his care. Then second, it refers to his obligation *to all people* to share this wonderful Savior with them (cf. Acts 9:15).[92] Note also the universality of the gospel for all people everywhere. Paul says that he had a binding moral commitment to preach to all men. For him, there was no class or race distinction among people, whether they were **Greeks** that is, those from Greece, who spoke Greek; or **barbarians,** i.e., Gentiles, non-Greeks, whether they were **wise** or **unwise**, that is to say, whether they were educated or not. Here the

---

87 This was Paul's serious desire that he wanted to accomplish as the Lord willed. It was that for which he had planned, and not merely a sudden impulse.

88 MacArthur says that Paul's intent in coming to the Romans was "not to make a social call" but to obtain some fruit among the believers in Rome, even as among the rest of the Gentiles to whom he ministered. He says, "Paul's ministry was an unending quest for spiritual fruit. His preaching, teaching, and writing were not ends in themselves. The purpose of all true ministry for God is to bear fruit in His name and with His power and for His glory." MacArthur, p. 45.

89 The imagery is of gathering a spiritual harvest of souls through the preaching of the gospel as Paul went to the capital city of the Gentile world (cf. Phil. 1:22).

90 Cf. 1 Cor. 9:16.

91 Paul uses this word two other times in Romans (cf. 8:12; 15:27), and one other time in Galatians 5:3.

92 Also consider that as Christians we have an obligation to Christ to fulfill the great commission (cf. Acts 8:1-4). We are to preach to all people for as Spurgeon rightly said, "He who knows what he's been saved from, knows what he's been saved for." Further, note what Paul was not a debtor to in Rom. 8:12).

apostle's desire is very much in line with our Lord's Great Commission in Matthew 28:18-20; Mark 16:15; Luke 24:46-49. From Paul, we learn that the gospel knows no bounds. The gospel he preached, and the gospel we are to preach, crosses all cultural, ethnic and economic lines. It must be preached to all people, in all places, regardless of who they are, or where they are, either socially, spiritually, mentally, or materially or based on their color or creed.[93]

Obs. 17- (v. 15) That when Paul uses the language, **So as much as is in me,** these words can be understood as him saying, "that in view of what I just said in the previous verse 'as far as my ability will carry me,'[94] I am absolutely prepared to discharge my debt as I have been appointed." Paul says that he was **ready**[95] to do this, which emphasizes his eagerness in this regard. He says, "I am zealous **to preach the gospel to you who are in Rome.**" The Greek aorist tense of the verb **preach** stresses Paul's resoluteness to do this. The question has often been asked why Paul was so zealous to preach the gospel to these believers in Rome when they were already saved. Perhaps the most obvious answer to the question was to further their understanding of the gospel after they had first believed. Additionally, in saying what he said, his words demonstrate his great courage. I mention this because the city of Rome was the hub of the Roman Empire, a place which was staunchly polytheistic and did not tolerate at this time the monotheistic beliefs of Christianity. The point is, Paul was very willing to go into an extremely hostile situation in order to preach Jesus. May we be willing to do the same!

Suggested applications from the text for the church:

1- Never forget that the gospel you believe is being spoken of by others *concerning you*—so adorn it well.

2- Never forget that if you believe the true gospel, it will establish you in the faith.[96] Is what you believe establishing you in the Christian faith?

Suggested application from the text for the non-Christian:

1- Never forget that while you are not saved, you are spiritually lost before God; you are liable to His judgment because of your sins against Him. Therefore, you desperately need "the gospel of His Son." This gospel tells you that God Himself has provided a substitute for sinners like you, even Jesus. At Calvary, Jesus paid the penalty due to sinners by facing God's wrath on their behalf, dying on the cross with their sins upon Him. He did this for all who trust in Him alone to be saved.

---

93 Cf. Col. 3:11.

94 Phillips translation.

95 In his commentary on Romans, McBeth mentions that this Greek word comes from a word which means to be out of breath, as from running. The point is, in Paul's use of this word, he is setting forth his 'overwhelming passion to preach the unsearchable riches of [Jesus'] grace.' McBeth, p. 41.

96 Cf. Rom. 16:25.

Text: Romans 1:16-17

General theme: God's Way of Salvation

Homiletical outline of the verses:
    A. Paul's praise for the gospel: [16] For I am not ashamed of the gospel of Christ, for it is the power of God to salvation for everyone who believes, for the Jew first and also for the Greek.
    B. Paul's proclamation of the gospel: [17] For in it the righteousness of God is revealed from faith to faith; as it is written, "The just shall live by faith."

Summary of section: Verses 16, 17 of this chapter are a transitional point in this letter. In some respects, these verses bring a close to the opening portion of this epistle, while at the same time, they prepare the reader for Paul's explanation of why people need the gospel. Really these magnificent verses are Paul's thesis statement and key focus concerning this entire book.

Exegetical & Practical Insights:
    Obs. 1- (v. 16) That in verses 16 to 18 of this chapter, there are four uses of the explanatory conjunction, **for** which are linked to and explain to us why each previous statement of the apostle Paul was so. The reason Paul was ready to preach the gospel to those who were in Rome (v. 15) was because, as he says in 16a, with the first use of the word "for" or because, **I am not ashamed of the gospel of Christ.**
    But we may ask, "Why was Paul not ashamed of the gospel of Christ?" He tells us with the second use of the word *for*, in 16b, **for it is the power of God to salvation for everyone who believes for the Jew first and also for the Greek.** Next, we might ask, "Why is this so?" Paul tells us with his third use of the word *for* when he writes in 17a, **for in it the righteousness of God is revealed from faith to faith; as it is written,** *The just shall live by faith.*
    Finally, then, in answering the question comprehensively of why we desperately need the gospel, of which Paul is not ashamed (v. 16a), which is the power of God for all who believe, for the Jew first and also the Greek (v. 16b), because in it the righteousness of God is revealed (v. 17), he tells us the reason in verse 18, when he says, with his fourth use of the word *for*, **the wrath of God is revealed from heaven against all ungodliness and unrighteousness of men, who suppress the truth in unrighteousness.**[97] This is why Paul is so zealous to preach the gospel at Rome (v. 15). He has given us reason after reason for each preceding statement. This is what this sequence of explanatory conjunctions shows us, and they are vitally important for us to grasp as we seek to understand Paul's line of reasoning and argumentation, which he employs throughout this epistle.

---

97 With this last *"for"* clause (v. 18), the apostle begins to open the next major section of this book which goes from 1:18 to 3:20, demonstrating clearly why all people need the good news of Jesus.

Obs. 2- That the word **ashamed** is a Greek present tense verb indicating a habitual disposition. It carries the idea of being embarrassed by something that has been done. The point is, Paul was not at all ashamed of the truths of the gospel, which were all about what Christ has done in His life, death, burial and resurrection.[98] The question has been asked, "Why does Paul tell the Romans that he was not ashamed of the gospel?" In other words, why begin this sentence with this statement of negation? Scholars list several reasons. Some say that Paul may have been thinking of the words of the Lord Jesus Christ, when He said, "For whoever is ashamed of Me and My words in this adulterous and sinful generation, of him the Son of Man also will be ashamed when He comes in the glory of His Father with the holy angels" (Mark 8:38). Others say that Paul was using a figure of speech known as *litotes*. This type of speech speaks positively by means of a negation, as when someone says that "so-and-so is not a bad vocalist," meaning actually that they are rather skilled. And so it could be that when Paul says that he was not ashamed of the gospel, he was simply saying that he was very enthusiastic about it.

Furthermore, Paul might be thinking specifically in contrast to the Jews of his day. They were very much ashamed of the message he preached, when he told them that in order to be delivered from God's judgment because of their sins against Him, they needed to put their faith in Jesus who hung on a cursed tree in order that they might be saved. This message was absolutely scandalous for them. It was a stumbling block and an affront (1 Cor. 1:23a). However, it was true nonetheless (cf. Isa. 53; 1 Cor. 1:24).

The last proposal is that Paul was speaking in strong contrast to the pagan Gentiles of his day. They could not possibly imagine that God could or would come to this earth as a man. MacArthur says, "The idea of the incarnation, not to mention the crucifixion, was utter folly to Greek thinking. To those rationalists nothing could be more absurd than the idea of an incarnate God giving Himself to be crucified in order to secure salvation, holiness, and eternal life for a fallen world."[99]

While each interpretation is reasonable and may be exactly what Paul is saying, I believe that in general it is best to understand his words as a bold way of saying that despite the various adversities that came his way either from the unbelieving Jews or pagan Gentiles in his preaching of the gospel, and despite what they thought about it, he was completely confident in the gospel since it is "the power of God to salvation for everyone who believes, for the Jew first and also for the Greek. For in it the righteousness of God is revealed."

The sense is he was setting forth a defiant response to all the negative reactions to the gospel which were expressed by many throughout

---

98 Paul did not say, "I am not afraid" to preach the gospel, for according to his own testimony, at times he experienced this (cf. 1 Cor. 2:1-5). We all can relate to that. Nonetheless, we must still preach the gospel anyway, God helping us.

99 John MacArthur, 1 Corinthians, p. 46.

the Roman Empire, both from Jews and Gentiles (cf. 1 Cor. 1:23 with Gal. 6:14). Or, as Calvin says,

> This is an anticipation of an objection; for he declares beforehand, that he cared not for the taunts of the ungodly; and he thus provides a way for himself, by which he proceeds to pronounce an eulogy on the value of the gospel, that it might not appear contemptible to the Romans. He indeed intimates that it *was* contemptible in the eyes of the world; and he does this by saying, that he was not ashamed of it. And thus he prepares them for bearing the reproach of the cross of Christ, lest they should esteem the gospel of less value by finding it exposed to the scoffs and reproaches of the ungodly; and, on the other hand, he shows how valuable it was to the faithful.[100]

Obs. 3- That once again, in telling us why he was not ashamed **of the gospel of Christ** (cf. 1:1 for its meaning), he says in 16b that the ultimate reason for this was because the gospel **is the power** or divine strength; **of God**[101] or the might which belongs to Him, **to salvation.** Now while it is true that the Greek word for power (*dunamis*) is the basis of our English word dynamite, it should be noted that this does not mean that Paul is saying here that the gospel is the "explosive dynamite power of God," since at this time dynamite had not yet been invented. Rather, what he means is that the gospel of Christ is the mighty instrument through which the great *saving* power of God dynamically operates in order to rescue men and women from their sins (cf. 1 Cor. 1:18). Simply stated, the plain preaching of the message of Jesus' death and His resurrection from the dead on our behalf is the sovereign, supernatural means through which God's great omnipotence works in order to bring spiritually dead sinners to new life in His Son. This good news of Christ is, as the Puritan William Gurnall said, "The chariot wherein the Spirit rides victoriously when he makes his entrance into the hearts of men."

What an amazing thing the gospel is then! And no wonder Paul was not ashamed of it. This is why we should not be ashamed of it either. We should proclaim it faithfully and fearlessly as far and wide as we can, for when we do, the power of God is momentously at work. Moreover, the verb, "it is," is in the present tense telling us what is continually true of the gospel and its power. As it is proclaimed, it will continue to be the power of God to salvation for sinners.

Finally, we should note that the word "power" would have certainly resonated with the believers at Rome since Rome was considered to be the great "power" or "strong arm" of the world, having conquered the entire known world at that time. Thus, Romans naturally appreciated the matters of power or strength.[102] However, Paul here is speaking to these believers and to us about a much *grander, glorious* power! He is not

---

100 Calvin, pp. 61, 62.

101 Grk. genitive of possession.

102 A few commentators highlight this point. One is James R. Edwards, *New International Biblical Commentary on Romans* (1992), 39.

speaking about the power of men or military, which could only command people but never truly change them. Rather, he is speaking about the power of the gospel, which has the strength to turn dead sinners into living saints, to turn rebels into righteous people, and to turn those who were lost and on their way to hell into saved individuals who are on their way to heaven. Truly then, the gospel is the power of God!

Obs. 4- That Paul tells us that the gospel is the power of God **to** or perhaps better translated, resulting in or unto; **salvation.** This is the first time that the word salvation is mentioned in this letter. To be sure, this is what the gospel is all about. The word "salvation" means to deliver, or to rescue. So, the all-important question is: "From what does the gospel deliver and rescue?" Verse 18 answers: "The wrath of God." Along with delivering us from *sin, self, and Satan,* it chiefly delivers us from the dreadful *penalty* and *punishment* for our sins against God—an eternity in hell under His judgment (cf. Matt. 25:46a; 2 Thess. 1:9). All of this is because our loving, merciful, sinless, sin-bearing substitute Jesus Christ bore that penalty and punishment for us in our place at the cross (Rom. 5:6-9). However, there is more to it than this. The gospel also delivers us presently from the *power* of sin (Rom. 6), and the ongoing *pollution* of sin (2 Cor. 5:17; Gal. 1:4), and one day (praise be to God) it will deliver us from the very *presence* of sin altogether (2 Pet. 3:13; Rev. 21:27). What a day that is going to be!

Obs. 5- That from the human standpoint, the power of the gospel to salvation is only for those who **believe**[103] or are believing. Here, Paul teaches us that not only is salvation received by faith and not by our works, but he also places a limit on the participants of the gospel. He says, it is only **for everyone** or all without distinction, who individually trusts (this is what the word "believe" means) in the finished work of Christ alone for their salvation. On the cross, Jesus made a once-for-all, perfect atonement for our sins (cf. Rom. 5:11). Each one who believes in Him and His accomplishment on our behalf will be saved in this life and be received into glory in the life to come.

Concerning the matter of *belief* at this early point in this letter, William Tyndale correctly notes, "The sum and whole cause of the writing of this letter is to prove that we are justified by faith alone. If you deny this proposition, not only will this letter and all that Paul writes, but the whole of Scripture, be so locked up that you should never understand it to your soul's health."[104]

Obs. 6- That true biblical faith, belief, is much more than mere "mental assent" to the gospel. It is not just knowing and agreeing that Jesus lived, died, was buried and rose again on the third day (cf. James 2:19).[105] Rather, true biblical faith (which is a gift of God, cf. Eph. 2:8), is, as I mentioned

---

103 Grk. present, active, participle. Paul's doctrine of salvation through faith alone, in Christ alone, will be expounded throughout this commentary.

104 *Reformation Commentary on Scripture, Romans* p. 9.

105 Historically, theologians say that biblical faith is made up of three aspects: *knowledge, assent, and trust.*

above, a total, unreserved, and unshakable trust in the finished work of Christ alone for salvation, who died on the cross as a sacrifice for our sins. It is forsaking all other confidences in ourselves, our works, our religious upbringing, our baptism, our church membership, our own so-called "goodness" and everything else, to rely solely and entirely on what Jesus did 2000 years ago in our place. It is depending completely on the One who lived a perfect life for us, and on the cross died a substitutionary death for us. As the Westminster Shorter Catechism wonderfully says concerning the question, What is faith? "Faith in Jesus Christ is a saving grace, whereby we receive and rest upon him alone for salvation, as he is offered to us in the gospel."

Obs. 7- That when Paul says that the gospel is **for the Jew first and also for the Greek,** he is telling us two things. First, the gospel is for all people everywhere indiscriminately. No one is to be excluded from hearing its message. It is to be preached to all without distinction (cf. Matt. 28:19). Second, when Paul speaks about the gospel going to the Jew "first" he is not speaking here of the Jews as better than or above the Greeks. Rather, he is speaking *historically.* He is speaking *chronologically,* for throughout redemptive history from the Old Testament to the New, the Jews, that is to say, the Israelites, received God's special revelation before others (cf. Rom. 9:4). They received it first in order of time. This is why Paul and Barnabas could say to the Jews in their own day that "it was necessary that the word of God should be spoken to you first" (Acts 13:46).

Obs. 8- (v. 17) That the opening word **For** explains why the gospel is the power of God to salvation for everyone who believes, for the Jew first and also for the Greek (v.16). This is because **in it,** i.e., the gospel, or we might say "by means of the gospel" the righteousness of God is revealed as Paul says here.

Obs. 9- That before he was converted, the Protestant Reformer Martin Luther seriously stumbled over this verse. Luther said that he hated the phrase, **"the righteousness of God."** This is because he understood it to mean the righteous character which God *is* in His own nature, or the attribute of His justice in Himself, the strictness whereby a just and holy God must punish our sins. Now that God is just and holy and must punish the sins of sinners is without question (cf. Ex. 34:7b; Ezek. 18:20; Rom. 6:23a). The problem, however, with Luther's original interpretation of this passage was that Paul had something else in mind. I say this primarily for three reasons.

First, because whatever this righteousness of God is that Paul is writing of here, it has to be connected with the good news of God in this context (v.16), and surely the fact that God must punish our sins is not good news! As a matter of fact, this is terrible news for the sinner. And thus, such a misunderstanding of the phrase drove the spiritually lost Luther to misery.

Second, this righteousness of God must be a righteousness which is perfectly accepted in His eyes. And third, this righteousness is received by faith alone (as Paul speaks of in the next verse) and can cover all of our *un*righteousness, so that we can be delivered from God's wrath, as Paul speaks of in verse 18. And so then, what righteousness of God (or righteousness *from* God, that is to say, a God-provided, God-approved righteousness)[106] is there which (1) is connected to the gospel, (2) makes unbelievers totally acceptable in God's sight, and (3) is received by faith alone and enables them to escape His wrath due them, for their unrighteousness before Him?

What righteousness is this that covers all their sins and faulty self-righteousness, which is like filthy rags in God's sight (Isa. 64:6)? According to the Bible, there is only one such righteousness: it is the spotless righteousness of Christ, which God Himself freely gives or imputes i.e., credits to sinners the moment they believe in Jesus.[107] This is the *commending* righteousness of Christ, which He, the God-man, worked out for us as our federal head and legal representative. He did this through His perfect sinless life of *active obedience* in keeping all the commandments of God for us which we broke (cf. Isa. 42:21; Matt. 5:17). This obedience is the only righteousness that makes us acceptable to God and enables us to stand before His infinite righteousness. This along with Jesus' atoning death for us in His *passive obedience* on the cross, which cancels out our guilt, are the only grounds of our acceptance before God.[108] It is this which delivers us from the wrath to come, for as the hymn writer wonderfully said:

Jesus, Thy blood and righteousness,
my beauty are, my glorious dress;
midst flaming worlds, in these arrayed,
with joy shall I lift up my head.

Bold shall I stand in thy great day,
for who aught to my charge lay?
Fully absolved through these I am,
From sin and fear, from guilt and shame.[109]

---

106 Grk. genitive of source or origin.

107 I was helped in my understanding of this verse by the exposition of Pastor Greg Nichols. This message can be found on sermonaudio.com. Also, Nichols deals with this topic in his book *Doctrine of Christ*.

108 We can say then in sum that the righteousness of God in view is not the righteousness which God is in Himself (in His own character), for if this were the case, it would seem strange that Paul says in 10:3 that the Jews were ignorant of it, for surely they knew that God was righteous in His person. They knew that righteousness was an attribute which belonged to Him. Rather, it is the righteousness (or the flawless virtue and merit) of Christ Himself (which the Jews would not accept nor submit to; cf. John 9:16, 19:15; Rom. 10:3) which God freely gives to those who believe on Jesus alone for life and salvation. It is also worth noting that the view, that the righteousness of God is that righteousness which is from Him in Christ, was the view that was taken by the Synod of Dordrecht (1618-1619) and the Westminster Assembly (1645). This point is cited in *The Dordrecht Bible Commentary*, Volume VI. p. 6.

109 What a beautiful thought to consider that according to Holy Scripture God not only sees Christ *in* us, and *with* us, and *for* us, but *on* us as well! Simply stated, when God

The Old Testament predicted that Christ would be our righteousness in such passages as Isaiah 56:1 and Jeremiah 23:5-6.[110] Additionally, Paul makes it plain in Romans 5:15-19 that although Adam's sin was imputed to us, nonetheless, "so also by the one Man's obedience (Jesus), many will be made righteous" (cf. Rom.10:3-4; 1 Cor. 1.30; 2 Cor. 5:21; Eph. 1:6b; Phil. 3:9, which all set forth this same truth).[111]

Obs. 10- That the verb **revealed** is a Greek present tense verb. It means that whenever the gospel is proclaimed, the righteousness of God that sinners desperately need in order to be made right with Him is continually and compassionately manifested to them, for "by that saving message God unveils his saving work."[112] The preaching of the gospel is the revelation of God's righteousness so that when the Gospel is proclaimed in truth, the way of salvation is unleashed to the lost like a flood; it goes forth into the world accomplishing God's eternal purpose of drawing specific sinners to Himself. Strikingly, Paul uses this exact word "revealed" in the next verse in this chapter. However, there he says that *the wrath of God* "is revealed" rather than His righteousness.

Obs. 11- That when Paul speaks here of the righteousness of God being **from faith to faith**, literally, "out of faith into faith," the idea is that the righteousness of God which is set forth in the gospel message is received by faith from "start to finish" or from "first to last."[113] The point is, it becomes our full possession by means of faith alone from the beginning of our Christian lives all the way to the end.[114] Perfect righteousness before God is never that which we can ever earn or obtain by our own strivings since all that we do is tainted with sin (Isa. 64: 6; Rom. 3:23; 4:4-5; Eph. 2:8-9).[115] Rather, it is a free gift given to sinners and

---

says of His Son, "This is my beloved Son in whom I am well pleased" (Matt. 3:17), He says the same of us!

110 Cf. Psalm 98:1-2; Daniel 9:24 and Malachi 4:2.

111 I find it surprising that many commentators do not connect this "righteousness of God" with the "righteousness of Christ," who is God (cf. Rom. 9:5). To me, this is an oversight. The righteousness of Christ is that which Paul speaks of in several places in this epistle and it most certainly exalts our Lord's person and work, which is what the heart of the gospel is all about. The real question to ask then when we are dealing with the matter of "the righteousness of God" is not first, *what* is it, but *who* is it? It should also be noted that after this verse, Paul will leave off this topic of the righteousness of God until he has brought forth his full indictment against human sin. He will take it up again in Romans 3:21 as something of a bookend to this section of Scripture dealing with the reason why all people need it.

112 Yarbrough, p. 41.

113 Most commentators understand these words in this way.

114 Cf. Phil. 3:9.

115 It is shocking to think that with such a clear presentation to the Christians living in *Rome* of how the gospel is received (namely, by faith alone as presented in this verse and in the previous one) that any works-based system of salvation could ever come from such a city. Yet, this is exactly what happened a few hundred years later in *Roman* Catholicism. Therefore, we have a serious warning to take careful heed to these words and to teach them to others after us, so that they will continue to "contend earnestly for the faith once for all delivered to the saints" (Jude 3).

received by means of believing.[116] This righteousness is "to all and on all who believe" (cf. Rom. 3:21-22). As the great fifth century preacher John Chrysostom rightly said: "You do not receive God's righteousness by toils and labors, but you receive it by a gift from above contributing one thing only from yourself, namely, believing."[117]

Obs. 12- That in Paul's free use of the Habakkuk quote, *"The just,* i.e., believers; *shall live by faith"* (Hab. 2:4, the first of his many [approximately sixty] times in this book that he will quote from the Old Testament), he is saying that just as believers in Habakkuk's day escaped the wrath of God (inflicted upon the inhabitants of Jerusalem through the Babylonians) by means of faith, so also, this is the way that sinners in all ages will escape His wrath. This shows us again that "faith-righteousness is not a new doctrine."[118] Paul is telling us that we are rescued from God's judgment through believing God's Word, that is to say, the word of the gospel which tells us to trust in Christ's person and accomplished work at Calvary alone for our deliverance. This has always been and will always be God's exclusive way of justifying the guilty (cf. Rom. 4; Gal. 3:11).[119]

Suggested applications from the text for the church:

1- Know the gospel as it is set forth in Romans 1:16-17 because many do not. Many think that in the gospel the way to health, wealth, and prosperity is revealed. Others think that in it the way to live a "successful Christian life" is revealed. Neither of these is what the Bible tells us. Rather, it teaches that in the gospel the righteousness of God is revealed. The gospel has the great remedy for man's great malady. The gospel tells us how God accepts us in His sight, according to His own standard, and that acceptance and standard is found in His Son.

2- Rejoice in the gospel because it is good news, particularly for you as a believer.

Suggested application from the text for the non-Christian:

1- Understand that the gospel is the very thing that you need. This is because you lack the perfect righteousness of God which you must have to enter into heaven which the gospel alone provides through Christ (cf. Rom. 3:10; Gal. 3:10).

---

116 Note also that faith is not the ground of our acceptance with God; rather faith is the open hand that receives the righteousness of Christ that God offers to us.

117 Chrysostom, *Hom. Rom.*2. as quoted in Michael F. Bird p. 40.

118 J. P. McBeth, p. 44. This point would have also been significant for Paul's Jewish readers.

119 Many commentators plausibly suggest that Paul's citation from Habakkuk here also makes the point that the Christian life not only begins but continues to the end by faith in Christ. This interpretation is consistent with the verse's previous phrase. Paul describes what this "life of faith" entails, practically speaking, especially from Romans 12 onward.

Text: Romans 1:18-32

General theme: God's wrath and the foolish exchange.

Homiletical outline of the verses:

 A. The reality of God's wrath: [18] For the wrath of God is revealed from heaven against all ungodliness and unrighteousness of men, who suppress the truth in unrighteousness.

 B. The reason for God's wrath: [19] because what may be known of God is manifest in them, for God has shown *it* to them. [20] For since the creation of the world His invisible *attributes* are clearly seen, being understood by the things that are made, *even* His eternal power and Godhead, so that they are without excuse, [21] because, although they knew God, they did not glorify *Him* as God, nor were thankful, but became futile in their thoughts, and their foolish hearts were darkened. [22] Professing to be wise, they became fools, [23] and changed the glory of the incorruptible God into an image made like corruptible man—and birds and four-footed animals and creeping things.

 C. The result of God's wrath: [24] Therefore God also gave them up to uncleanness, in the lusts of their hearts, to dishonor their bodies among themselves, [25] who exchanged the truth of God for the lie, and worshiped and served the creature rather than the Creator, who is blessed forever. Amen. [26] For this reason God gave them up to vile passions. For even their women exchanged the natural use for what is against nature. [27] Likewise also the men, leaving the natural use of the woman, burned in their lust for one another, men with men committing what is shameful, and receiving in themselves the penalty of their error which was due. [28] And even as they did not like to retain God in *their* knowledge, God gave them over to a debased mind, to do those things which are not fitting; [29] being filled with all unrighteousness, sexual immorality, wickedness, covetousness, maliciousness; full of envy, murder, strife, deceit, evil-mindedness; *they are* whisperers, [30] backbiters, haters of God, violent, proud, boasters, inventors of evil things, disobedient to parents, [31] undiscerning, untrustworthy, unloving, unforgiving, unmerciful; [32] who, knowing the righteous judgment of God, that those who practice such things are deserving of death, not only do the same but also approve of those who practice them.

Summary of section: In verses 18 to 32 of this chapter, and actually all the way through 3:20, the apostle paints a picture of lost humanity's plight before a holy God because of their sins against Him as he launches into his universal indictment against the human race. In these verses he shows the worldwide condemnation of all people, and explains why it is that all people, in all places and in all generations, absolutely need to receive the gospel of Christ, which is the power of God unto salvation for everyone who believes (vv. 16-17).

Exegetical & Practical Insights:

Obs. 1- (v. 18) That the word **for** in Greek is an explanatory conjunction, showing why all people need Christ and His righteousness credited to their account. The apostle is giving the reason for what he just said in verses 16 and 17 of this chapter, and at the same time explaining why he was so desirous to preach Jesus everywhere.

Obs. 2- That the word **wrath**[120] is not to be understood as an out-of-control burst of anger from the Almighty God. Sometimes when we hear the word "wrath," we think of it as one "flying off the handle," becoming belligerent, like that of human wrath. This is not the idea in this word. Rather, it signifies "both the attitude and the action of God toward sin and toward those who practice it."[121] To state the matter another way, God's wrath is, as John Murray has rightly said: "The holy revulsion of God's being against that which is the contradiction of his Holiness."[122]

Obs. 3- That according to this verse, the God of the Bible has wrath against sinful humanity. Paul describes it as the wrath *of* **God**[123] that is to say, it is wrath which belongs to or comes from Him. If we were to search our Bibles thoroughly, we would see that there are hundreds of references to God's anger and wrath against human sin. God's wrath against human sin is that which is called forth by the wickedness of His creatures. It is a manifestation of His holiness and justice; His righteous response toward our *un*righteousness, as the rest of the verse tells us.

Obs. 4- That far from declaring that God's wrath against sinners is merely a future event, such as Paul speaks of in Romans 2:5, he says that it is a present-day reality. The wrath of God *is* **revealed** or is being revealed or disclosed, present tense verb, showing us that this is what is happening continually. God's wrath *is already* here (cf. John 3:36). It is already being manifested, and while it is manifested in many ways against unrepentant sinners, the specific way Paul mentions is set forth three times in this chapter. In verses 24, 26, 28, he speaks about God "giving up" the ungodly *to* their sins as a judgment upon them *for* their sins. Note further that this phraseology of something being "revealed" is, as I mentioned above, the same terminology that is used in 1:17. However, in that verse we read about the righteousness of God being "revealed" through the gospel, while in Romans 1:18 Paul teaches that simultaneously God's wrath is being "revealed," and this **from heaven** or the place from where God rules and reigns. There is a positive and a negative here. On the positive note, the gospel presents the magnificent message of Christ, who Himself became the wrath-absorber for all who believe in Him (cf. 3:25). On the negative note, God is judging all day long the ungodly who reject Him (cf. Ps. 7:11).

---

120 The topic of God's wrath is mentioned throughout this book: 2:8, 3:5, 4:15, 5:9, 9:22, and 12:19.

121 Robert Rogland, p. 15.

122 Murray, p. 35.

123 Grk. genitive of source.

Obs. 5- That God's wrath is aimed **against** not merely toward, but more literally from the Greek text, upon; **all** not just some, but all; **ungodliness and unrighteousness of men** that is to say, lost humanity, unsaved people, Jews and Gentiles alike. The word *ungodliness* here speaks about our *attitude toward God*. It has to do with "our relation to a sovereign God,"[124] and since it is the first sin mentioned, clearly it is vile in God's sight. The term has to do with impiety or a lack of reverence and respect for the Lord our Creator. It is a disdaining of Him. It is a snubbing our noses at the Savior, not having Him in our highest thoughts or in our minds. The word literally means "to be *un*like God" or "god-*less*." *Un*righteousness (being repeated at the end of the verse for the sake of emphasis), speaks mainly about our *actions toward others*. In this setting, it has to do with morality and man's injustices and wrongdoings in the world. The word speaks about not conforming to what is "right." It denotes mostly anything that is inconsistent with love for our fellow human beings. Putting these two words together, we see that they collectively speak of the failure of humanity to uphold the requirements set forth in the two tables of God's law, which are found in the Ten Commandments.[125] The first table tells us that we are to love the Lord our God with all our heart, souls, mind and strength. The second table says that we are to love our neighbors as ourselves. Clearly, then, fallen humanity has not done these things as God requires. Thus, His wrath is just.

Obs. 6- That in describing the ungodly and unrighteous, Paul says after this, that they are not those who seek the truth. Rather, he says that they **suppress the truth**. The word "suppress" is a verb which is derived from two words in the Greek language. It carries the idea of strongly holding down or hindering something. Note also that the word is a present, active, participle, highlighting to us the continual nature of such suppression from the unsaved. How then do they suppress it? Paul tells us when he says that they suppress the truth **in** that is, in the realm or through the practice of **unrighteousness**, which is to say, through their sinful living, they seek to dull their senses to it.

But what truth *specifically*? The use of the definite article "the" in the text, and in this context, seems to point in the direction of the truth about God, as the Creator and Maker of all things (including the ungodly themselves), since the following verses speak of Him in this way, specifically verses 19 to 21. This is truth about God which they clearly know and clearly perceive but do not respond to accordingly.[126]

Obs. 7- (v. 19) That the word **because** in the beginning of the sentence (the strong inferential Greek particle), gives further reason

---

124 The *King James Bible Commentary*, p. 1398.

125 I am not the first commentator to observe this.

126 McBeth in his commentary on Romans says, "Those who 'hold down the truth' are just as much liars as those who pervert the truth. To pervert, cover, change, conceal, or withhold the truth is to lie. To hold down the greatest truth is the biggest lie. God is the biggest truth, and to live as if there were no God is to live the biggest lie." McBeth, p. 50.

and rationale for God's wrath being revealed on the ungodly and for its being completely just. As a matter of fact, from verses 19 to 23, Paul gives several arguments to prove this point again and again. Here he gives two lines of evidence concerning God's revelation of Himself to all people as the Creator of all things, evidence which sinners resist and reject.

He writes: **What may be known of God** or knowable about Him; **is manifested** or evident; **in them**[127] **for God** (literally, God Himself, the word God being emphatic in the Greek text); **has shown it**[128] or has made clear once for all time; **to them.** In what specific way has God made Himself known to His creatures in this regard? The answer seems to be through two voices namely, *the voice of conscience* and *the voice of creation*, as the rest of the verse suggests.[129]

The word conscience appears over twenty-five times in the New Testament, and it literally means a "co-knowledge," that is, a knowledge together with oneself — a moral awareness. The word comprises two Latin words: *con* which means "with," and *science*, which means "knowledge." Thus, when Paul speaks of a knowledge of God manifesting within the sinner, he is referring to the knowledge that conscience supplies. This is a sensible understanding of this phrase, since Paul goes on later in chapter two to employ the word "conscience" directly, and to explain its operation in condemning the unrighteous (cf. Rom. 2:14-16).

Therefore, according to the apostle, within each of us, there is a knowledge that God exists. Conscience, as the Puritan Thomas Brooks said, is "God's preacher in the bosom" and acts as a "domestic chaplain" in our hearts telling us that there is a God.[130] Such knowledge is written into our DNA. Thus, Calvin was right when he said, in his famous *Institutes of the Christian Religion,*

> ...from this we conclude that it is not a doctrine that must first be learned in school, but one of which each of us is master from his mother's womb and which nature itself permits no one to forget, although many strive with every nerve to this end.[131]

And:

> ....there is within the human mind, and indeed by natural instinct, an awareness of divinity. This we take to be beyond controversy. To prevent anyone from taking refuge in the pretense of ignorance, God himself has implanted in all men a certain understanding of his divine majesty. Ever renewing its memory, he repeatedly sheds fresh drops. Since, therefore,

---

127 Although some commentators prefer the idea of the preposition *en* be translated as "among" so as to say that the knowledge of God was that which had been communicated to people collectively, I think, contextually speaking, that "in" is the better choice.

128 Grk. aorist, active, verb.

129 Note the double force of the present tense and aorist tense in this verse.

130 Note that it is not merely that there are gods plural in the world, but one God truly, as the definite article in the Greek text emphasizes. A literal rendering of the words is: that which is known of *the* God is plainly evident in them, for God made it clear to them.

131 P. 46 of the Ford Lewis Battles edition of Calvin's Institutes.

men one and all perceive that there is a God and that he is their Maker, they are condemned by their own testimony because they have failed to honor him and to consecrate their lives to his will.[132]

Not only is there the *subjective* witness in ourselves that there is a God, but Paul says in 19b that there is an *objective* witness to this fact. It is the external witness that God has given to us in creation. Paul writes that what may be known of God is manifested in them, for God has shown it "to them." The apostle is not speaking of what may be known of God savingly, for this only comes through what is commonly called *special revelation* (or that revelation which comes only through the Word of God), but *general revelation* which is that revelation of God through what He has made as Paul speaks of here. His language is reminiscent of Psalm 19:1-4. It may be that he had this passage in mind:

> The heavens declare the glory of God
> And the firmament shows His handiwork.
> Day unto day utters speech,
> And night unto night reveals knowledge.
> There is no speech nor language
> Where their voice is not heard.
> Their line has gone out through all the earth,
> And their words to the end of the world.
> In them He has set a tabernacle for the sun.[133]

The questions should be asked, "How good is God's general revelation at proving that He exists to mankind, even to people without the Bible? Is such revelation effective? Do things made really prove that there is a Maker?" According to the inspired apostle, the answer is yes, without a doubt. Verse 20 explains:

> For since the creation of the world [right from the days of Adam onward throughout the centuries], His invisible *attributes* are clearly seen, being understood by the things that are made, *even* His eternal power and Godhead, so that they are without excuse, i.e., they are guilty.[134]

Obs. 8- (v. 20) That the opening word **for** explains how God shows Himself to all people (v.19). For **since by the creation of the world His invisible attributes are clearly seen.**[135] The point? His attributes are not

---

132 Ibid., pp. 43, 44.

133 Paul will also quote from this passage in Romans 10:18. In doing this I believe that in that context he is showing that, through God's created order, all people have heard of God and thus all are without excuse for not responding to the fact that there is a God, and they need His gospel to be saved.

134 It is clear in this verse that Paul has answered the age-old question of "What about the heathen who have never heard about the one true living God?" Paul says they have heard, because they have received revelation concerning God both internally and externally and yet they suppress the light God has given them and thus are justly under His divine judgment.

135 Note Paul's play on words: The *invisible* God has made himself *visible*.

hidden in a corner somewhere, but are plainly visible.[136] Literally they are, "looked down upon," that is to say, thoroughly considered and this continually (as the present tense verb highlights); **being understood**[137] or constantly perceived and grasped; **by the things that are made** or created (cf. Heb. 11:3).

The sum of the matter is that the natural world is loud and clear concerning the fact that there is a Creator God. Specifically, as Paul says in this verse, there are two things about the unseen God that are visible for all to see. First, there is His **eternal:** or infinite; **power** or His great might and strength in how He created all things, governs all things, sustains all things, and preserves all things in His universe. And second, there is **His Godhead** or deity; that is to say, that He is One who is like no other, who is the sole unoriginated source of such tremendous power.[138] What then is the consequence of all of this visible knowledge from the invisible God that He gives to individuals? Since what may be known of Him is manifested *in* them and *to* them (v. 19), what results from this *for* them?[139] Paul gives the answer when he writes at the end of verse 20, saying **so that they are**[140] "continually"; **without excuse.**[141] These words in English are one word in Greek and it literally means *not a word from,* or more simply, *having nothing to say.* These words are being used here in the judicial sense.[142] In this language Paul is acting as a prosecuting attorney, saying that such people are without legal defense.[143] He is saying that they are without a valid reason for their rejection of God since general revelation about Him is so effective. Clearly, then, he is teaching us that the problem with humanity is not that they lack the knowledge that there is one true and living God. Rather, he says that they just will not respond correctly to it.

Obs. 9- (v. 21) That Paul gives another reason why God's wrath against sinners is just and right and that they are inexcusable before Him. He begins the sentence with the same word in verse 19 of this chapter,

---

136 Grk. present, passive, verb.

137 Grk. present, passive, participle.

138 The word "eternal" here should be understood as modifying both nouns, *power and Godhead.*

139 Gifford takes these words as expressing "not a mere result, but a purpose," Gifford, p. 63.

140 Grk. (present, active, verb).

141 Tom Schreiner helpfully says that, "God has stitched into the fabric of the human mind his existence and power, so that they are instinctively recognized when one views the created world." Schreiner, p. 86.

142 This is the Greek word that Paul uses in Romans 2:1.

143 Chrysostom says, "Will the heathen say at the judgment that they were ignorant of God? Did they not hear the heaven sending forth a voice while the well-ordered harmony of all things spoke out more clearly than a trumpet? Did you not see the hours of night and day remaining constantly unmoved, the good order of winter, spring and the other seasons remaining both fixed and unmoved?... Yet God did not set so great a system of teaching before the heathen in order to deprive them of any excuse but so that they might come to know him. It was by their failure to recognize him that they deprive themselves of every excuse" (as quoted in Kruse, p. 91).

reinforcing what he has written, when he says: **Because although they knew God, they did not glorify him as God nor were thankful, but became futile in their thoughts, and their foolish hearts were darkened.**

When the apostle speaks about the unconverted in some sense knowing God,[144] that is to say, they knew Him definitively,[145] the context tells us that he is speaking about them knowing or recognizing Him as the Creator. They knew Him in the sense that He was their Maker and they were His creatures (and so in this sense, of course, biblically speaking there are no such things as atheists or agnostics).[146] They knew Him with reference to His "eternal power and deity" (v. 20). Nevertheless, Paul says that **they did not glorify** or honor, regard, respect, or reverence Him, nor were they thankful.[147] What an indictment this is! Although humanity knew that God existed, they did not truly give praise to Him *as* God or in a manner which is befitting such a glorious Being. They did not extol Him as the great Potentate that He is by acknowledging Him in all their ways. Further, they were not sincerely grateful to Him (just as many in our day are ungrateful to Him as well). So what did they do? With sharp contrast, Paul says concerning them **but** they **became futile**[148] **in** that is, in the realm of or in the sphere of; **their thoughts** or speculations; **and their foolish hearts**, a term which speaks symbolically of their inner beings, who they really were within, "the center of man's moral and spiritual nature;"[149] **were darkened.**[150]

What a horrible commentary this is on fallen humanity. When people will not have the true and living God in their hearts and lives, they become "futile" or devoid of truth and "vain" in their thoughts or inward reasoning and thinking. Their "foolish" or senseless and unintelligent hearts were "darkened," which is to say, since they ignored the truth of God, their hearts became spiritually dim, so that they could not comprehend the truth of God (cf. Eph. 4:17-18).

Obs. 10- (v. 22) That as Paul describes and gives proof of the futile way in which people refuse to honor and glorify God, he says:[151] **professing**[152] or more literally, constantly asserting and affirming; **to be wise** or

---

144 It is striking that in the Greek text Paul literally writes, "because they knew the God" which is to say, they knew *the* "only true and living God." The point is, they know that this very God exists and thus they are further "without excuse."

145 Grk. aorist, active, participle.

146 This is why I am a proponent of presuppositional apologetics.

147 Clearly then such individuals fall short of what the most famous question in the *Westminster Shorter Catechism* answers asks in Question #1: "What is the chief end of man? Man's chief end is to glorify God, and to enjoy him forever."

148 Grk. aorist, passive, verb.

149 McBeth, p. 54.

150 Grk. aorist, passive, verb. Note the two passive forms of the verbs suggesting something of God's divine judgment upon such individuals.

151 Paul might have in his mind some of the philosophers in his day at this point (cf. 1 Cor. 2:1-16).

152 Grk. present, active, participle.

sophisticated; **they became fools**[153] or utter fools,[154] a Greek word which is related to our English word "moron."[155] There is something particularly ridiculing in this remark. In a true sense, from God's perspective, those who are outside of Christ are foolish (cf. 1 Cor. 1:20). As a matter of fact, since in Christ and in Christ alone are hidden "all the treasures of wisdom and knowledge," unsaved men and women are not to be lauded and thought of by us as wise, especially when it comes to spiritual matters (cf. Jer. 10:14; Ps. 14:1; Col. 2:3). Rather, according to Paul the exact opposite is true! While we can recognize their God-given intellectual gifts in some matters, they are nonetheless horrible theologians and unsafe spiritual guides altogether.

Obs. 11- (v. 23) That Paul here shows how the foolishness of men who reject God is displayed. Connecting his thought to the previous verse with the word **and**, he says that unbelievers; **changed**[156] or exchanged, modified and altered definitively; **the glory** or splendor and majesty; **of the incorruptible** or imperishable and immortal; **God into an image** or likeness; **made like corruptible** or perishable; **man and birds and four-footed animals and creeping things.**

The word "changed" here means to "make otherwise." It carries the idea of replacing one thing for something else. Thus, along with the ungodly not glorifying God, nor being thankful to Him, and having foolish hearts, they also became idolaters who violate the First and Second Commandments of God. They changed the glory or perfections of God for their idolatry, and it is striking to see that the very first thing that man substitutes for God is himself! Self is the true object of worship for the unbeliever. His own glory, his own honor, his own praise, instead of the glory, honor, and praise of God. People who reject the one, true, living God, even go further and make "gods" with their own hands: birds, and four-footed animals, and creeping things; idols which were common among pagans in the ancient world; gods which are no gods at all (cf. Ps. 115:4-8; Isa. 44:9-20; Jer. 16:19-21; Acts 17: 22-34).

It is vital for us to note from this verse the downward spiritual spiral that begins to happen in the lives of people who reject general revelation about God. The point is, a *denial* of God always leads to *defilement* of life, whether morally, spiritually, or physically. Paul speaks about this in the following verses. In essence, what he says here and in the rest of the chapter is that man's *aversion to* God led to his *diversion from* God which ultimately led to his *perversion before* God. This further explains why,

---

153 Grk. aorist, passive, verb.

154 The aorist tense of the verb highlights a definitive transaction. They, having rejected God, became fools, once for all time, without God's sovereign intervention to save them. Also, the aorist passive verb parallels the two verbs in verse 21b. Harvey, p. 38.

155 E. H. Gifford notes that "self-conceit and folly go hand in hand." Gifford, p. 64.

156 Grk. aorist, active, verb. Note also that this word occurs in verses 25 and 26. It appears three times in these verses corresponding with God's threefold response of "giving them up."

according to verse 18, the wrath of God is being revealed from heaven against all ungodliness and unrighteousness of men.[157]

Obs. 12- (v. 24) That in this verse, along with verses 26 and 28, Paul tells us how God responds to the wickedness of men who reject what may be clearly known of Him. Here the apostle sets forth the result of the reaction to what comes forth from God's holy being toward such individuals, showing us again why it is that each and every one of us desperately needs to receive deliverance from His wrath through the saving message of His Son. Additionally, in verses 24 to 31 of this chapter, the apostle explains how the present-day manifestation of the wrath of God (1:18) is being displayed against sinners who reject Him. Such wrath has been understood by theologians to be God's "divine or judicial abandonment" of such individuals.[158] Simply stated, because people will not have God to be their God, His current judgment against them is that He ceases restraining them in their lives, letting them go headlong into their sins with all of its catastrophic consequences. This judgment is tragic and terrifying! When God lets go of an individual who refuses to have Him as his God, that person will eventually sink deeper and deeper into a wicked and wayward lifestyle, one which will not only bring great harm to himself, but also to others.

Such an act by God toward a person leaves him completely helpless against the darkness of his own heart. When this happens, great spiritual and moral problems will be compounded, just as we are seeing throughout the world in our day. And so instead of thinking that living life without God-regulated, ethical boundaries is a mark of "a progressive society," as some tell us, the truth is, it is an evidence of God's abandonment, as Paul insists in these verses. These are marks of His displeasure toward a depraved people and He judges such wickedness by "giving them up to such things" (cf. 24, 26, 28).[159] In essence, God says to sinners who reject

---

157 R. C. Sproul says, "As the theory goes, religion begins in a primitive stage of what we call 'animism.' Animism is a superstitious belief concerning spirits inhabiting inanimate things like rocks, trees and animals. Simplistic, primitive religion began when men worshipped the spirits that dwell in the trees. But then as men progressed intellectually and historically, they moved into more sophisticated and complex forms of polytheism. Then, it developed into henotheism, which is the belief that each nation or each group has one god that is sovereign over the geographical boundaries of that particular group: a god for the Philistines, a god for the Amorites, a god for the Jewish people and so on. Finally, in the evolutionary scale of development, a sophisticated and complex variety of monotheism is reached. This theory, assumed by many scholars around the world, is on a collision course with what Paul writes in Romans 1. Paul is not teaching an evolution of religion, but a devolution of religion; not a progress, but a regress. He is saying that monotheism is not something that appears late as a result of human striving, growing in achievement. Rather man begins with monotheism, with a clear understanding of the God of heaven and earth. It is because of man's sinful reaction to this one God, that religion deteriorates into idolatry." Sproul, pp. 46, 47.

158 C. S. Lewis is noted as saying that there are two kinds of people in the world. There are those who say to God, "Thy will be done," and there are those to whom God says, "thy will be done."

159 Importantly, although we are told in these verses that God "gave up" such individuals to their sinful lifestyles, we are not told that He totally "gave up on" them. This is always a crucial matter to remember. This should encourage us to preach the

the light of His general revelation, "Since you would not have Me, I will let you go down the path of your own choosing, the path of destruction." He says: "You want your sins? Your sins you can have with all of their dreadful ramifications in your life!" In summary: God gives up such individuals to the sins that they sought for themselves. He allows them to reap what they sow.[160] And although at times the ungodly mock God saying, "He doesn't judge sin, because look: we go on living as freely and sinfully as we like without any judgment coming to us," they fail to realize that this is His very judgment toward them.

Consequently, Paul says in verse 24: **therefore** or for this reason, the word indicating that "the retribution to follow finds its grounds in the antecedent sins and is therefore justifiable;"[161] **God gave them up**[162] or quite literally, He abandoned them or handed them over,[163] the word itself carrying a judicial aspect,[164] **to uncleanness in** denoting the sphere or realm of their uncleanness;[165] **the lust**[166] **of their hearts to dishonor**[167] or to continually shame; **their bodies among themselves.**

This verse summarizes all that Paul is going to say in the following verses. This text acts as a catch-all for what is to come. The word "uncleanness" is made up of two Greek words which quite literally mean "without being pure or clean." Broadly speaking, it refers to anything that is filthy or dirty. Here, it is being used in the sense of a sexually *im*pure and *im*moral life. This impurity is, "in the lust," or in the sinful desires and sensual cravings, of their hearts (that is, their fallen hearts, or the core of who we are by nature in Adam).[168]

Paul is saying that the consequence of this current-day judgment of God is to "dishonor their bodies among themselves." The verb "dishonor" means "to treat with indignity or to insult; it means to treat disgracefully or to degrade." And so, instead of honoring and preserving their bodies, they dishonor them by means of sexual immorality. Unsaved people treat their bodies beneath their original design, thus robbing themselves and others of true dignity. Since they do not *honor* God, as Paul speaks of in

---

gospel to others so that they might be saved and brought out of their sinful, immoral state (cf. 1 Cor. 6:9-11).

160 Cf. Gal. 6:7.

161 The *King James Bible Commentary,* p. 1400.

162 Grk. aorist, active, verb.

163 Douglas Moo insightfully says that "Paul's use of the verb 'hand over' to describe this retribution has its roots in the OT, where it is regularly used in the stereotyped formula according to which God 'hands over' Israel's enemies so that they may be defeated in battle. And, in an ironic role reversal, the same formula is used when God hands his own people over to another nation as punishment for their sins. Somewhat similarly, Paul here alleges that God has 'handed over' people to 'uncleanness'" (Moo, NICNT, p. 110).

164 Rogers and Rogers, p. 317.

165 Or perhaps better translated "through or by the lust of their hearts."

166 McBeth notes that the plural word in the Greek text, "Denotes the many avenues they practiced in the expression of their affection." McBeth, p. 57.

167 Grk. present, middle, verb.

168 Cf. Jer. 17:9; Mark 7:20-23

verse 21 of this chapter, he says here that God judges them by allowing them to *dishonor* themselves among or with themselves according to their own depraved dispositions. The punishment *for* their sins is that God has surrendered them *to* their sins! God allows them to run with their sins which were in them by nature as sinners, and this to their great hurt morally, mentally, spiritually, and emotionally speaking.

Obs. 13- (v. 25) That as God's judgment continues with Him handing the ungodly over to this terrible cycle of ever-increasing sin in their lives, the apostle says that such individuals, **exchanged the truth of God for the lie, and worshiped and served the creature rather than the Creator, who is blessed forever. Amen.**[169] It is striking to note here that Paul tells us that although people will not worship the true and living God, they are still worshipers nonetheless. As an image-bearer of God, man is instinctively and intrinsically religious. Paul speaks about such individuals having "exchanged"[170] or of their own choice definitively swapped out,[171] "the[172] truth of God"[173] that is to say, the truth that He has revealed to men about Himself as Creator, as spoken of in the previous verses, for "the lie" or falsehood (the lie here, in this context seems to be the lie of false worship or religion). Specifically, Paul seems to have in mind the lie of idolatry or the giving of one's affections and devotions to something other than God.

Further, notice the connection between this verse and the previous one with respect to sexual uncleanness. When a society does not worship the God of the Bible, who, as Paul says at the end of this verse, is "blessed" or praised; "forever" or eternally; that society devolves to sexual immorality and deviant behavior, much as is happening all over the world. To state the matter another way, we will always become what we worship. Whatever captures our hearts will always be reflected in our lives.

And so when such idolatry has gripped people, how do they live? Paul says that they "worshiped"[174] or reverenced, "and served"[175] or devoted

---

169 It is interesting to see Paul giving the "Amen," a word which denotes a strong affirmation and can be understood as him saying, "truly" or "so be it," having just mentioned God who is blessed forever. Paul's piety flows from his heart as he thinks about the God who redeemed him in Christ, who is blessed forever, especially in light of all of the sin he has been describing. John MacArthur rightly says, "Perhaps unable to continue discussing such vile things without coming up for air, as it were, Paul inserted a Jewish common doxology about the true God, the Creator who is blessed forever. Amen. Paul could not resist adding that refreshing thought in the sea of filth he was describing. That word of praise of the Lord served, by utter contrast, to magnify the wickedness of idolatry and all other ungodliness." Macarthur, p. 104.

170 Grk. aorist, active, verb.

171 The word suggests a volitional choice, Rogers and Rogers, p. 317.

172 The definite article is used here in the Greek text.

173 Grk. genitive of possession.

174 Grk. aorist, passive, verb.

175 Grk. aorist, active, verb. Note that both verbs "worshiped" and "served" are religious terms and are both in the aorist tense, which refers to a definitive act of *entire* exchange.

themselves wholly to, "the creature rather than" or instead of, "the Creator." Paul's play on words here of "creature/Creator" underscores the *godless exchange* (or we could say *extremely foolish exchange*) that happens when God judges people by leaving them in the cesspool of their own sins. When He leaves people in such a state, there is no level too low for them to sink to, as the following verses show.

Obs. 14- (vv. 26-27) That the two obvious sins spoken against here are the sins of lesbianism and homosexuality.[176] First, Paul speaks in verse 26, not of God giving up such depraved individuals to a "good, healthy, normal lifestyle" which He approves of and we all should accept. No, rather he writes: **for this reason** giving the justification for the ensuing judgment;[177] **God gave them up** or delivered them over **to** or unto **vile**, literally disgraceful and degrading sinful; **passions** or cravings especially of a sexual nature. Paul says God gave them up to great wickedness. Then, in explaining how this was so, he says: **For** an explanatory conjunction, for **even their women exchanged**[178] **the natural use** or the common function of the body according to God's creation of it; **for what is against** or contrary to **nature** that is to say, that for which our bodies were designed.

(v. 27) Likewise[179] or in a similar way; **also the men leaving** or forsaking and abandoning; **the natural use of the woman, burned** or were passionately inflamed **in their lust** or sexual cravings and longings;[180] **for** or toward; **one another,**[181] **men with men**, literally from the Greek text,

---

176 Five things concerning this topic which are worth considering. First, we must understand that both of these sins are an abomination to the Lord. Despite what some tell us in our day—even calling them "alternative lifestyles" the God of the Bible strictly forbids such practices, even if such individuals are in a so-called "loving, committed relationship" (cf. Lev. 18:22; Lev. 20:13; 1 Cor. 6:9). Second, that although there are many today who laud such practices as homosexuality and lesbianism and the like, the Bible calls them in the passage shameful. Third, the sins of homosexuality and lesbianism are, as these verses teach, the result of a person denying and disobeying God. To state the matter another way, when people continue in sin and unbelief as a pattern of life, God gives them over to even more depravity which is in their hearts and these are some such sins. Fourth, (and now to add some more perspective), homosexuality and lesbianism are not to be viewed as the most wicked sins in all the world, for while surely they are among the gross, debased sins that people practice, we see that Romans chapter one lists them among the many sins that people commit (cf. vv. 28-31). They stand at the top of the list, but they are not the only sins. Fifth, we should note that although many people in the world are given over to such sins, it does not mean that there is no hope for such people. For we have a 2000-year-old record in the Bible which tells us that even some of the members at the church in Corinth had lived this way and yet, through the power of the gospel, they had been washed, sanctified, and justified (cf. 1 Cor. 6:11). And so although God gave up such people *to* their sins, He did not give up on them *in* their sins.

177 Rogers and Rogers, p. 317.

178 It is interesting to note that Paul does not say that such individuals were "born this way," but rather, that they "exchanged" the natural use for what is against nature.

179 The adverb expressing the manner of their rebellion.

180 The Greek noun means to reach out for something.

181 John MacArthur notes that in the United States and many other Western countries it is not uncommon for homosexual males to have over 300 partners (not in a lifetime) but in a year. MacArthur, pp. 105, 106.

men in men; **committing**[182] or continually working among themselves; **what is shameful** or disgraceful and unbecoming; **and receiving**[183] or constantly getting; **in themselves the penalty** or recompense; **of their error** or wanderings from the truth sexually and morally speaking; **which was due** or was warranted for such a lifestyle.[184]

Obs. 14- (v. 28) That as mentioned earlier, this is the third and final place in this chapter where we are told that as a penalty for their perversion, God "gave them up" to their sinful ways. Strikingly, we are told that because people **did not like** or see it right; **to retain**[185] or habitually keep and have; **God in their knowledge** or thinking as has been seen concerning them in verses 19 to 23 of this chapter; that **in similar fashion** or as it is in this passage "even as" in judgment; **God gave them over to a debased** or an undiscerning; **mind.** And so in summary, we see that God's judgment against sinners continues to progress: *first*, it affects their worship; *second*, it affects their bodies; and *third*, it affects their minds.

The point is, because people suppressed the truth of God revealed to them thinking that a knowledge of God was useless, their minds, "the whole reasoning faculty, intellectual and moral, all that conspires in doing a good action,"[186] became useless. Thus, as a consequence of men's sins, God gave them a reprobate mind, or more literally, a mind that "fails the test" of what God approves. It is a mind that lacks sound judgment morally and spiritually speaking (cf. Eph. 4:18). It is a mind which produces futile thinking, a mind which is not set on the things of God, but is set on the things of the flesh (cf. Rom. 8:5-9). And this, in order **to do**[187] or to continually practice as a pattern of life; those things which are continually; **not fitting**[188] or proper in His sight.

Obs. 15- (vv. 29-31) That this is Paul's longest list of sins found in all of his letters, highlighting the clear signs of a depraved, God-abandoned mind. Here is a dark list of over twenty additional sins that characterize those who are under God's judgment. While this list is not exhaustive, it certainly conveys the sins that enslave much of the godless world around us. As Paul begins to describe such things, he says not merely that such people are occasionally doing them, but rather are, **being filled**[189] not merely tainted with a bit, but saturated and overflowing with; **all** or

---

182 Grk. present, middle, participle.

183 Grk. present, active, participle.

184 This may be a reference to some type of sexually-transmitted disease, whether that be syphilis, STDs or Aids. Note also that Paul says contrary to what some think, sin does have a penalty. Paul says elsewhere: "Do not be deceived. God is not mocked; for whatever a man sows, that he will also reap, for he who sows to his flesh will of the flesh reap corruption" (Gal. 6:7-8).

185 Grk. present, active, verb.

186 E. H. Gifford, p. 66.

187 Grk. present, active, verb.

188 Grk. present, active, participle.

189 Grk. perfect, passive, participle.

every kind of; **unrighteousness** or injustice or that which is contrary or opposed to what is right and just; **sexual immorality** or fornication and all other sexually immoral acts, whether adultery, prostitution, or bestiality, etc. This word is the origin of our English word pornography; **wickedness** or mischief or evil, the desire to harm others; **covetousness** or an insatiable lust for more and more, greed; **maliciousness** or ill will and spite; **full** "the adjective which describes the state of being thoroughly characterized by something;"[190] of **envy** or resentment that goes beyond jealousy to begrudge the fact that a person has what he has; **murder** or homicide, to intentionally take the life of another; **strife** or discord and contention, constant wrangling and quarreling; **deceit** or trickery or craftiness; **evil mindedness** or one who plans to ruin others; **whisperers** or gossips, talebearers,

(**v. 30**) **backbiters** or slanderers, literally those who speak down against others, those who badmouth people; **haters of God** or those who have nothing to do with and are hostile toward His way, will, and Word; **violent** or brutal; **proud** or conceited and arrogant, literally, appearing above others; **boasters** or loudmouths and braggarts; **inventors of evil things,** that is, creators of new forms of wickedness, seeking out new ways to be sinful; **disobedient to parents**, that is, breakers of the Fifth Commandment and rebellious to their God-given authority; refusing to do what they say, being unpersuaded by their wisdom,

(**v. 31**) **undiscerning** or without moral and spiritual sensitivity, being senseless and foolish; **untrustworthy** or breaking promises and agreements; **unloving** literally, without love toward one's own family members; **unforgiving** or better translated heartless or without affection, "the term describes someone who lacks positive feelings for others;"[191] and **unmerciful** or without pity, cruel, callous and unwilling to show compassion to those in need.

Obs. 15- (v. 32) That if all of the aforementioned sins were not enough to mention, Paul has more to say. He gives one final indictment concerning the lost, saying of them: **who knowing**[192] not being ignorant of God's displeasure with these sinful activities, but who being thoroughly aware with certainty[193] (as the aorist tense of the verb suggests with the intensive form of the Greek verb); **the righteous** or just **judgment** (or verdict); **of God** (that is, the judgment that belongs to Him, which judgment they

---

190 Harvey, p. 97.

191 Ibid.

192 Grk. aorist, active, participle.

193 "Paul's conclusion is that the heathen are never without a witness to the presence and personality of God. They have the witness of nature and the witness of their own conscience. However, the heathen have deliberately suppressed these witnesses to the truth and have consistently opted for a lie in place of the truth. They have chosen the course of idolatry, which is always accompanied by debauchery. Thus, God has revealed His wrath from heaven against all ungodliness and unrighteousness of men who suppress the truth of God. In addition, God gave them up to idolatry, to passions of infamy, and to an undiscerning and unapproving mind." The *King James Bible Commentary*, p. 1400.

sense in their own consciences);[194] **that** the conjunction providing the content of what humans know; **those who practice**[195] or habitually carry out and commit; **such things,** i.e., these sorts of sin; **are deserving** or worthy of **death** which is the consequence of such a life, being either punishment from God, or perhaps even capital punishment;[196] **not only do**[197] or are doing; **the same but** in contrast to this and in addition to it; **approve**[198] or agree with, and enthusiastically support; **those who practice them.**

Plainly, Paul's list of the sins of the lost has reached its peak! In some sense, we see its fullest manifestation of people going from bad to worse, for now, Paul tells us that they are not only going headlong into sin for themselves, but are also regularly consenting to and taking pleasure in those who practice them. These people are affirming the evil of others and taking delight in them—just as we see happening all around us.[199] John Murray helpfully comments:

> However severe has been the apostle's delineation of the depravity of men, he has reserved for the end the characterization which is the most damning of all. It is that of the consensus of men in the pursuit of iniquity. The most damning condition is not the practice of iniquity, however much that may evidence our abandonment of God and abandonment to sin; it is that together with the practice there is also the support and encouragement of others in the practice of the same. To put it bluntly, we are not only bent on damning ourselves but we congratulate others in the doing of those things that we know have their issue in damnation. We hate others as we hate ourselves and render therefore to them the approval of what we know merits damnation. Iniquity is most aggravated when it meets with no inhibition from the disapproval of others and when there is collective, undissenting approbation.[200]

Suggested applications from the text for the church:

1- This passage teaches us that we are to be extremely thankful to God for delivering us from His wrath through the wrath-absorbing work of His Son on the cross.

2- This passage should produce in us a prayerfulness so that we regularly call on the Lord to save those who are currently under His wrath.

---

194 Cf. Rom. 2:14-15.

195 Grk. present, active, participle.

196 Note that this is the first time that death appears in this epistle, but it will show up later in the following chapters. Thiselton, p. 91.

197 Grk. present, active, participle.

198 Grk. present, active, verb.

199 John MacArthur says, "To justify one's own sin is wicked enough, but to approve and encourage others to sin is immeasurably worse. Even the best of societies have had those within them who were blatantly wicked and perverse. But a society that openly condones and defends such evils as sexual promiscuity, homosexuality, and the rest has reached the deepest level of corruption." MacArthur, p. 109.

200 Murray, p. 53.

3- This passage challenges us regularly to mortify our own sins by the power of the Spirit (Rom. 8:12-14), knowing that all sin, even sin in the saints, displeases God.

4- This passage instructs us regarding the crucial fact that although many claim to be "atheist," or "agnostic," according to our text no such individuals exist. No, Paul says that all people everywhere know from "the things that are made" that God exists. Therefore all are without excuse.

5- This passage calls us not to live as "practical atheists." Not that we are truly atheist of course, but rather that when it comes to hard times in our lives, even we as Christians can act as if there is no God.

6- This passage should motivate us to put away our own idols, idols of the mind, and idols of the heart (1 Jn. 5:21).

Suggested application from the text for the non-Christian:

1- This passage should cause you to flee at once from the wrath of God which is both present and coming, to Christ the only Savior of sinners.

ROMANS
CHAPTER TWO

Text: Romans 2:1-16

General theme: God's indictment against the deceived moralist

Homiletical outline of the verses:

A. The inconsistency of the judgmental moralist: [1] Therefore you are inexcusable, O man, whoever you are who judge, for in whatever you judge another you condemn yourself; for you who judge practice the same things.

B. The integrity of the judgment of God: [2] But we know that the judgment of God is according to truth against those who practice such things. [3] And do you think this, O man, you who judge those practicing such things, and doing the same, that you will escape the judgment of God? [4] Or do you despise the riches of His goodness, forbearance, and longsuffering, not knowing that the goodness of God leads you to repentance? [5] But in accordance with your hardness and your impenitent heart you are treasuring up for yourself wrath in the day of wrath and revelation of the righteous judgment of God, [6] who "will render to each one according to his deeds": [7] eternal life to those who by patient continuance in doing good seek for glory, honor, and immortality; [8] but to those who are self-seeking and do not obey the truth, but obey unrighteousness— indignation and wrath, [9] tribulation and anguish, on every soul of man who does evil, of the Jew first and also of the Greek; [10] but glory, honor, and peace to everyone who works what is good, to the Jew first and also to the Greek. [11] For there is no partiality with God.

C. The inescapability of the judgment of God on the last day: [12] For as many as have sinned without law will also perish without law, and as many as have sinned in the law will be judged by the law [13] (for not the hearers of the law *are* just in the sight of God, but the doers of the law will be justified; [14] for when Gentiles, who do not have the law, by nature do the things in the law, these, although not having the law, are a law to themselves, [15] who show the work of the law written in their hearts, their conscience also bearing witness, and between themselves *their* thoughts accusing or else excusing *them*) [16] on the day when God will judge the secrets of men by Jesus Christ, according to my gospel.

Summary of section: In verses 1 to 16 of this chapter, the apostle continues his discussion of the universal condemnation of all men, showing why all people everywhere are guilty before God, under His wrath, and need to receive the good news message of Christ for the saving of their souls. Paul sets forth this argument so that "every mouth may be stopped and all the world may become guilty before God" (Rom. 3:19), and so that they may go to Jesus, the only Savior of sinners for mercy and forgiveness. In these verses specifically, the apostle addresses the *deceived moralist.*[1] Having already addressed *depraved humanity* in general in the previous chapter and then addressing the *deluded Jews* of his day in verses 17 to 29 of this chapter, he now has in view either Gentile or Jewish individuals who have set up for themselves their own code of conduct by which they have assured themselves that they are right with God. These people believe, for example, that since they have treated others nicely and have not murdered any one, God is pleased with them. They believe that based on their moralities God accepts them because of who they are and what they have done. They consider themselves to be "good people," and may in fact be better than most. But they are ignorant of the fact that from God's perspective, according to Ecclesiastes 7:20, "there is not a just man on the earth who does good and does not sin."

Paul is going to challenge such people. He is going to show them that even on their best days, apart from being in saving union with Christ[2] by faith in Him alone and being covered by His righteousness, they are completely undone before the Almighty who is absolutely holy.[3]

---

1 I realize that many commentators take the words in this section of Scripture to be speaking specifically about the Jews only. However, I am not convinced this is the case, especially since verse one has the universal language of "whoever you are who judge." Furthermore, although Paul begins this section of Scripture with the word "therefore" which normally would connect it to the previous words, I think that he is extending his argument further to include a second category of people, namely, the deceived moralist. The apostle seems to be speaking of any person from any background, whether Jew or Gentile, who looks down his nose at others; any person who considers himself to be holier when, in fact, according to the Word of God, they are not. I also understand verses 17 to 29 of this chapter to speak specifically about a third category of people, because in verse 17 there seems to be a very clear shift in Paul's thinking to this third group when he says: "Indeed you are called a Jew." In summary, I believe that broadly speaking in 1:18-32 Paul is dealing with *depraved humanity* in general. In 2:1-16 he is dealing with the *deceived moralist*, and then in 2:17-29, he is dealing with a *deluded Jew.*

2 Union with Christ is a topic that Paul deals with more in Romans chapters five, six and seven.

3 If anyone could be accepted by God based on how well he lived, surely, it would have been the Apostle Paul himself. Paul was one who advanced in Judaism beyond many of his own contemporaries in his own nation (Gal. 1:14). He was one who could say of himself that concerning the righteousness that is in the law, he was "blameless" (Phil. 3:6).

Exegetical & Practical Insights:

Obs. 1- (v. 1) That the word **therefore** in the beginning of this verse is an inferential conjunction which could be understood as Paul saying "for this reason." Here he is saying that lost humanity (of whom he spoke in the previous chapter), are guilty before God for their own sins and also because they consent to and commend the sins of others (1:32). Additionally, he speaks now to the deceived moralists, declaring that they likewise deserve God's wrath because they not only tolerate wickedness in others, but they practice the very things that they condemn in them.[4] He says that they are just as bad, thus justifying again God's judgment upon them. The word **inexcusable** is the same Greek word that he uses in 1:20, when he speaks about the unsaved who know that there is one true and living God and yet reject Him. Therefore, he says they are "without excuse." In using the same Greek word here, the apostle tells them that although they condemn others for their gross immoralities, they are just as guilty.

When Paul addresses the moralist in this verse as **O man,**[5] it seems that he was not actually zeroing in on one particular person in the church at Rome. This would not make much sense since he did not know most people there. Further, it would seem a bit out of place for him to go after just one person in the congregation. In view of this, I agree with most commentators when they say that Paul is simply using a style of writing called diatribe.[6] This is a particular teaching device whereby he addresses a single imaginary person who represents an entire group of people in a conversation or debate in order to teach others a crucial point. The instruction is this: for us to justify ourselves as being okay with God and to believe that we do not need the salvation that Christ offers on the grounds that others are apparently worse than we are is hypocrisy in the highest degree. To gloss over our own sins and condemn the sins of others is great duplicity before the Almighty. Strikingly, Paul uses the word judge *three times* in this verse, showing his actual point at hand. The sense of the word **judge**[7] means to judge self-righteously or to be one who continually passes judgment on others. Interestingly, the word is the same word that our Lord used in Matthew 7:1 when he said, "judge not, that you be not judged."[8]

---

4 This seems to be the best way to understand the conjunction "therefore" in verse one, although it is hard to be dogmatic at this point and many commentators struggle with its exact meaning. To me, the conjunction looks both backward and forward linking the central content of thoughts together.

5 Note that the noun for man is in the vocative case, the case of direct address. Here Paul is being very forthright in his words.

6 This literary style of writing which typically involves using questions and answers to make various points was quite common in Paul's day.

7 The present tense verb is used all three times.

8 Of course, this in no way means that as believers we are not to use judgment or discernment in life. As Paul says in 2 Corinthians 2:15, "But he who is spiritual judges all things." Furthermore, Jesus said in Matthew 7:24, "Do not judge according to appearance, but judge with righteous judgment." Paul (and Jesus in other places) is speaking against having moral standards to which one's own behavior does not conform, and then goes and

Paul goes on in the second part of the verse to give the reason why the moralist is without excuse before God when he judges: **for** an explanatory conjunction; **in whatever you judge another you condemn yourself** or more literally, you call judgment down on or against yourself; **for** explaining the reason why they are condemned; **you who judge practice**[9] or are practicing; **the same things.** Now, while it may not be that the self-righteous, self-inflated moralist actually practiced each and every sin which he condemned others for practicing, if he were seriously to look at the sin of his own heart then he would find many offenses of which he is guilty as well. This is especially true in view of the fact that in the final day God will judge "the secrets of men by Jesus Christ" (v. 16a).

Obs. 2- (v. 2) That having spoken of the twisted judgment of the deceived moralist, Paul now speaks about the truth of the judgment of God, to straighten out such a one. In speaking about the general, innate knowledge which all people should have as image bearers of God, he says: **But we know that** the conjunction giving the content of what we know; **the judgment of God**[10] or the judgment that belongs to God; **is according to** or is in line with the truth, *not* appearance, but the **truth** that is the objective truth of God Himself and His infallible law which Paul mentions in verses 12 to 15 of this chapter. This truth stands in opposition to the inconsistent, subjective standard found in man; **against** or upon; **those who practice such things.** Thus, the smug moralist who in his own self-assessment thinks he is better than others and right with God apart from Christ is not so, for God will judge all people "according to the truth." Or as John Murray aptly says, "in accordance with the facts of the case."[11] Simply stated, when God judges men on the final Day of Judgment,[12] which is in view in this context (cf. v. 16), His assessment of the matter will be entirely correct. This is because His judgment is based upon the truth, the whole truth, and nothing but the truth.

Obs. 3- (v. 3) That in this verse, Paul brings home the application of what he has been saying in the two previous verses to such self-deceived individuals. His question is rhetorical; the answer to it is that those who judge others and yet are sinning themselves will absolutely not escape the judgment of God in the last day. This is why he is writing this section of Scripture: apparently, according to this verse, the self-righteous man or woman thinks that they will actually escape God's eternal condemnation. On the one hand, they think this because they are completely ignorant of the righteous character and just judgment of God, who judges "according to truth." On the other hand, they think this because they judge themselves by the wrong standard, misunderstanding the depths of their own depravity. They judge themselves either by themselves or

---

condemns others for their sins. This is hypocrisy in the highest degree.

9   Grk. present, active, verb.

10 Grk. genitive of possession.

11 Murray, p. 57.

12 Which judgment takes place at the last day when Christ returns to close out this age and usher in the age to come (cf. Matt. 25:31-46; 13:36-43; 2 Tim. 4:1).

by others, forgetting that in the final day this will not be the standard of God's judgment (cf. 2 Cor. 10:12). The standard will be God's perfect law as summarized in the Ten Commandments, and those commandments will not only judge our external actions, but also our internal thoughts and the intents of our hearts and minds as well (cf. Matt. 5:21-30; Rom. 7:7-14). When it does, all except those who are true Christians will be found guilty and thus be condemned by God. As Paul says in Romans 3:19, "Now we know that whatever the law says, it says to those who are under the law, that every mouth may be stopped, and all the world may be guilty before God."

Here, once again, the apostle is, as it were, getting in the hypocrite's face. He is getting into the mind of this man when he says: **And do you think** (the word think in Greek is a word which is related to our English word logic); **this, O man, you who judge those practicing such things, and doing the same that** the word giving the content of his false hope; **you** literally, you yourself **will escape**[13] or be delivered from, **the judgment of God?** The apostle is saying: "Are you really reckoning in this way? *Really?*" He is showing the utter foolishness of such reasoning, completely shutting it down. Thus, Paul obliterates all such false thinking.

Obs. 4- (v. 4) That having just spoken of the future judgment of God in verse 3 of this chapter, now Paul engagingly writes to the moralist who refuses to go to Christ in order that he might be saved from God's coming wrath, saying: **Or do you despise** or scorn and value so little; **the riches** or wealth; **of His goodness** or kindness; **forbearance** or bearing with us in our sins and rebellion against Him; **and longsuffering** or God's great patience in postponing His punishment; **not knowing**[14] or more literally, being continually ignorant and unaware of the fact; **that the goodness of God leads you to repentance**[15] or a change of mind, produced in a person by the grace of God,[16] which is to issue forth in a change of life.[17]

What exactly is Paul addressing here? Just this: every single day of their lives, unsaved people despise the riches of God's goodness, forbearance, and longsuffering which He displays toward them as He gives them ample opportunity to turn and trust in Christ. They despise these blessings by not making proper use of them. Whereas in the previous verse, Paul dealt with people's erroneous thoughts concerning the final Day of Judgment and their having to meet God, now he is dealing with their apparent ignorance as to the purpose of God's goodness toward them in this life. Such people have completely misread His forbearance.

---

13 Grk. future, middle, verb.

14 Grk. present active participle.

15 This is the first time that the word *repentance* appears in Romans.

16 Cf. Acts 5:31; 11:18; 2 Tim. 2:25.

17 Perhaps my all-time favorite definition of repentance comes from the Westminster Shorter Catechism question 87: "Repentance unto life is a saving grace, whereby a sinner, out of a true sense of his sin, and apprehension of the mercy of God in Christ, doth, with grief and hatred of his sin, turn from it unto God, with full purpose of, and endeavour after, new obedience."

They think God does not care about their sins. They have misread His character, not knowing that such general kindness to them was not intended to give them cause to continue in their sins. But rather it is an inducement to flee from the coming wrath to Christ for life and salvation through repentance toward God and faith in our Lord Jesus Christ (cf. Acts 20:21).[18] Such people have wrongly exegeted God and His benevolence; thus, Solomon was correct when he said in Ecclesiastes 8:11, "Because the sentence against an evil work is not executed speedily, therefore the heart of the sons of men is fully set in them to do evil."[19] The English Puritan, Stephen Charnock, stated the matter well:

> Because God is slow to anger, men are more fierce in sin, and not only continue in their old rebellions, but heap new upon them. If he spared them for three transgressions, they will commit four.... They invert God's order, and bind themselves stronger to iniquity by that which should bind them faster to their duty. A happy escape at sea makes men go more confidently into the deeps afterward.[20]

Consequently, Chrysostom warns, "God shows us his kindness in order to lead us to repentance, not in order that we might sin even more. If we do not take advantage of this opportunity, the punishment we shall receive will be all the greater."[21]

Obs. 5- (v. 5) That Paul here tells us what the result is for those who presume upon God's goodness to them. He writes: **But in accordance with**, or in proportion to, or because of,[22] (thus showing again that the judgment is not random, but just); **your hardness** or callousness;[23] **and your impenitent** or unrepentant or non-changing **heart** figuratively describing one's inward self, one's person; **you are treasuring up**[24] **for yourself wrath in the day of wrath and revelation** or the uncovering or the exposing; **of the righteous judgment of God** that is, the righteous judgment that belongs to and comes from Him.

The sense in these words is that such people are gradually, moment after moment, day after day, week after week, month after month, year after year, gathering up for themselves judgment that will break forth on them; something akin to a surge swelling behind a dam ready to burst. Or as McDonald says, they are "treasuring up judgment for themselves, as if they were building up a fortune of gold and silver. But what a

---

18 A parallel passage in this regard can be found in 2 Peter 3:9, 10.

19 John MacArthur succinctly says here, "The purpose of the kindness of God is not to excuse men of their sin but to convict them of it and lead them to repentance." MacArthur, p. 120.

20 Stephen Charnock, *The Existence and Attributes of God*, vol. 2, p. 509.

21 *Ancient Christian Commentary on Scripture, Romans* p. 53.

22 McBeth, p. 68.

23 MacArthur notes that, "This is the word from which we get the medical term *sclerosis* [which is a hardening of body tissues]. Such physical hardening is an ideal picture of the spiritual condition of hearts that have become unresponsive and insensitive to God." MacArthur, p. 120.

24 Grk. present, active, verb.

fortune that will be in the day when God's wrath is finally revealed at the judgment."[25]

This is a sobering Scripture to be sure. It teaches us that non-Christians have a spiritual savings account with God, whereby every day that they sin, they make a deposit for themselves and accumulate more and more wrath for the day of wrath at the return of Christ (cf. 1 Thess. 1:10; Rev. 6:12-17; 20:11, 12) and the revelation (or the revealing) of the righteous judgment of God. Paul is saying that the self-righteous moralist who thinks he or she will escape the judgment of God and receive nothing from Him will actually receive a huge payout on the Day of Judgment. That payout is God's punishment for their sins against Him. It is His eternal wrath in hell which He will release upon the ungodly, for surely He has a record of every single day of their lives and how they have lived before Him in impenitence and a refusal to go to Jesus for forgiveness (cf. Rom. 6:23a).

Obs. 6- (vv. 6-7) That in these verses all the way to verse 16 of this chapter, Paul sets forth *the principle* that God will use on the Day of Judgment to declare who was truly saved in this life and who was not. As he continues to speak about the Day of Judgment to the deceived moralist (as he has done in verses 2, 3, and 5 and will do in verse 16), he reiterates what the Bible teaches in many places: that in the final analysis there will be only two types of people in the world, and the evidence of which group a person belongs to spiritually will be revealed in how they lived (cf. Matt. 7:21-23; 12:33-37; Matt. 16:27; 25:31-46; John 5:28-29).[26] These two sorts; believers or unbelievers, sheep or goats, gave evidence of their spiritual state by how they conducted their lives on the earth, either as true born-again Christians who had been given new hearts to walk in the ways of God (cf. Ezek. 36:26-27), or as worldlings, or false professors of faith, showing no fruit of true salvation (cf. Gal. 5:19-26). Simply stated, on the final day, our lives will be the validation of either our salvation or damnation, and if we were truly converted, we would have lived a life of gospel obedience to the things of Jesus (v. 7). The judgment will be a judgment *according to evidence*. As MacArthur remarks, "God does not judge on the basis of religious profession, religious relationships, or religious heritage. But among other standards, He judges on the basis of the products of a person's life."[27]

Of course, none of this denies the fact that as Christians we are 100% accepted before God both in this life and in the life to come on the sole basis of the blood and righteousness of Christ and not by our lives of obedience to the things of God. On Judgment Day, it is Jesus'

---

25 McDonald, p. 1681.

26 Do not lose sight of the fact which many commenters have noted: that the subject matter in these verses is *judgment* (vv. 2, 3, 5, 6, & 16) not *justification*. For if one misses this point, one can be confused and misconstrue Paul here to be teaching salvation by works, which of course he is not, as the whole book of Romans and the entire Bible shows. Scripture teaches that good works are the *fruit* of salvation, never the *root* of salvation (Eph. 2:8-10).

27 MacArthur, p. 128.

life and death for us which alone commends us to God (Rom. 5:9-11). And of course, none of this denies the fact that salvation is not based on our works at all, but only on the finished work of Christ alone (cf. Rom. 4:5-8; Eph. 2:8-9). Thus, our present-day justification through faith alone, in Christ alone, will be the same as our future justification. However, the point of this passage is to teach us that those who have been truly saved through faith alone, on the ground of Christ alone, will show that fact by living a transformed life in the here and now.[28] By God's grace and the help of the Holy Spirit, true believers do live differently from others in the world because they are different now that they are saved. Thus, Paul could say in 2 Corinthians 5:21, "Therefore, if anyone is in Christ he is a new creation; old things have passed away; behold, all things have become new."

In summary, on the Day of Judgment, God **will render**[29] or give back in recompense; **to each one** i.e., no one will be excluded, regardless if he is a Jew or Greek; **according to his deeds** not according to what he said about himself but again, according to what was true of him as demonstrated by how he lived, as Paul says in verse 6.[30] Then, in describing the deeds of the true Christian, who has been saved by grace alone, through faith alone, he says in verse 7 that they will receive: **eternal life,** (the state of an unending, joyful communion with God through Jesus), **by patient continuance in doing good** (as all Christians are called to do, cf. Gal. 6:10); **seek for glory,** that is, God's glory on this earth and glory in the life to come with God (cf. 5:2); **honor,** that is, honor from God when He will say to all of His true people, "Well done, good and faithful servant" (Matt. 25:21a); **and immortality** when they will put off their perishable bodies and put on that which is imperishable in the eternal state (cf. 1 Cor. 15:50-55).

Obs. 7- (vv. 8-11) That in contrast to the godly in verse 7, here Paul begins by saying that the lifestyle of the unbeliever will also be manifested on the Day of Judgment. In describing their way of life, he says that they are those who are: **self-seeking** or extremely selfish, caring nothing for others; **and do not obey**[31] or continually refuse to submit to or be persuaded by; **the truth,** that is, the truth about God, the truth about His Word, the truth about the gospel; **but obey**[32] or habitually follow; **unrighteousness** or wrongdoing, that which is not right in the eyes of God or men; and thus the results for them in the final day will be; **indignation** or fervent burning anger; **and wrath, tribulation** or great affliction; **and anguish** or extreme trouble and distress; **on** or better understood upon; **every soul of man** or all people without distinction;

---

28 James deals with this in James 2:14-26.

29 Grk. future, active, verb.

30 Cf. Rev. 2:23; 20:12.

31 Grk. present, active, verb.

32 Grk. present, passive, participle.

who does;[33] or continues to work out to its full end; **evil, of the Jew first and also of the Greek,** that is, non-Jews, the rest of the human race.

However, in now describing the outcome of the believing-righteous, he says in verse 10: **but glory, honor, and peace to everyone who works what is good, to the Jew first and also to the Greek.** Paul then tells us why all these things will be so in verse 11: **For there is no** none whatsoever; **partiality** or showing favoritism; **with God.** McDonald remarks, "In human courts of law, preference is shown to the good-looking, wealthy, and influential; but God is strictly impartial. No considerations of race, place, or face will ever influence Him."[34]

Obs. 8- (v. 12) That having established the fact that God's judgment is according to truth, as Paul says in verse two of this chapter, now he tells us that God will also judge a person in the final day according to the light they had received. He highlights this in connection with the inescapability of God's judgment.[35] In simple terms, this means that God will not unjustly hold anyone responsible for what they never possessed. Paul has already told us in 1:19 of this epistle that what may be known of God is plain to all people, because God has shown it to them through what He has made. Therefore, all people everywhere are without excuse concerning the fact that there is a God and that they are accountable to Him. Through the external voice of creation and the internal voice of conscience, God has made Himself known in some sense to everyone. In these verses, Paul continues to speak about the Jews and Gentiles and the principles that God will use in judging each of them, saying first in verse 12a of the Gentiles: **for**[36] **as many as have sinned**[37] or missed the mark of righteousness before God; **without law**[38] that is to say, without

---

33 Grk. present, middle, participle.

34 McDonald, p. 1683.

35 The light that the Gentiles have received is really threefold: the light of nature, the voice of conscience, and the law of God written on their hearts.

36 The explanatory conjunction is being used in this verse, and in verse 13 and verse 14 to support the claim of verse 11 that God is no respecter of persons. On the final Day of Judgment when Christ returns, all who have not been converted will stand guilty before Him and will not be able to claim innocence, since both Jews and Gentiles have sinned whether they had the law or not. Thus, the dreadful consequences for both are the same.

37 It is interesting to note the aorist tense of the verb being used here summing up the entire conduct of the lives of such individuals in one word. Furthermore, we should note that one does not actually need to hear the gospel to sin and perish. They sin because they are sinners, and perish because they sin, whether they ever hear the gospel or not. Dr. Waldron is right when he says that it is "sometimes said that man's only sin is unbelief or failure to believe the gospel. It is said, 'It is not the sin question, but the Son question.'" Waldron says, "The saying is false. Men do not go to hell only for rejecting Christ." They go to hell because they are sinners.

38 Observe that this is the first time, out of over seventy times, that Paul will use the word "law" in this book. This term is especially important to the apostle, having three primary meanings. Sometimes it refers to the Ten Commandments or the Decalogue, the moral law (3:19-20). Sometimes it refers to the Old Testament Scriptures (3:21b). Sometimes it refers to a standard of behavior or a general rule or principle etc. (3:27; 4:15; 7:21, 23). I agree with Leon Morris when he says that "Paul uses the term *law* in a bewildering variety of ways. Typically it is the law of Moses, the law of the Old Testament. Thus, even though neither Moses nor the Bible is mentioned, plainly this is meant when it speaks of

the law in codified form, the Ten Commandments; **will also perish** or be eternally damned, destroyed and ruined; **without law** (or without reference to the law, again, dealing with them according to the light that they received; they would not perish because they did not have the Mosaic law, but rather, because they have sinned). Furthermore, **as many have sinned in the law** (that is the Jews, who had God's law revealed to them at Sinai); **will be judged by** (or according to); **the law** (the law they received and were well trained in). Thus, we see again, that God's judgment of people is always with fairness. It is according to the light received, for God's impartiality does not exclude His taking this into account. In truth, whether people had great light or not, all are still under condemnation and need to be saved. As Leon Morris rightly states,

> The Gentile, it is true, cannot be accused of breaking the law, for he does not have the law. But when he does the right, as he sometimes does, this shows that he in fact knows what right is. He may not have the law, but his conduct shows that what the law requires is written in his heart. He is guilty when he does wrong. The Jew cannot claim that he will automatically be saved because God has given him the law: he has not kept it! Nor can the Gentile automatically be saved because he never had the law and so did not break it: he sinned against the light he had. People are judged according to the light they have, not according to the light they do not have. So all are caught up in final condemnation.[39]

Obs. 9- (v. 13) That Paul here addresses the folly of those who think that merely listening to the law (in whatever context that might be) will grant them safety on the day of wrath. To the contrary, he says that it is not enough to merely be **hearers of the law,** such as was the case, for example, with the Jew who heard the law expounded to them week after week in the synagogue. The point he makes as he continues to speak about the final Day of Judgment (v. 16) is this: it will not be those who simply sat under the teaching of God's Word that will be **just** or upright; **in the sight of God.** [40] But rather, it will be only those who having heard such teaching and gone to Christ for salvation who become; **the doers of the law** because they, in fact, were true Christians. In the last day, only such people will be declared; **justified**[41] or not guilty.[42] John MacArthur

---

the Jews as having 'in the law the embodiment of truth and knowledge' (2:20). It is difficult to be certain of all the occasions when he means the law of Moses, for the context does not always put the matter beyond doubt, and we must bear in mind that in this epistle he never speaks of 'the law of Moses' in set terms. Nor can we say that 'the law' as opposed to 'law' means the Mosaic law, since both usages can apply either to the Mosaic law or to law in general." Morris, p. 143.

39 Morris, p. 121.

40 Note the force of the contrast in the Greek text through the use of the word "not" *ou* and "but" *alla*.

41 Grk. future, passive, verb.

42 Note that this is the first time that the verb *justified* is used in this book. It will play a prominent role throughout Romans. Since Paul says in chapter 3:20 that "by the deeds of the law no flesh will be justified in his sight," it is clear that he is not contradicting himself in this passage.

correctly notes, "The idea here is not that obeying the law will produce justification, because Scripture makes clear that justification comes only through faith (Rom. 3:24-28). But they will be demonstrated to be the just by the evidence of their doing God's holy law."[43]

In other words, the pattern of a person's life will be the evidence either of their justification or of their damnation in the final day. Their lives will be proof positive of whether or not they were the real deal. The true Christian should not be troubled at all about this, since by the transforming power of the gospel they have in fact become evangelical "doers of the law," and this not in order *to be* saved, but *because* they are saved. Since God has written His law on their hearts at conversion (Jer. 31:33), they do walk in His ways by the enablement of the Holy Spirit as a pattern of life, having been saved by free grace (Rom. 8:4).[44]

Obs. 10- (vv. 14-15) That Paul is returning to his original thought in verse 12a with reference to Gentiles, who were not given the Ten Commandments as a people and yet; **by nature do the things in the law, these although not having the law are a law to themselves.**[45] Indirectly, Paul is explaining the age-old question of how God can be just in sending people to hell who never had received the law of God. He answers the question of how is it fair for Gentiles to perish if they did not have the "special revelation" of God's commandments telling them what was right and what was wrong. Paul's answer to this question is simple: it is because the **Gentiles** or non-Jews are "a law to themselves."[46] He says that this law is theirs **by nature** (v. 14a), which law is the law of God. As image bearers of God, the essence of God's moral law is in them.[47] He says in verse 15 that they **show**[48] or continually manifest and display;

---

43 MacArthur, pp. 139, 140.

44 They walk in the ways of God as a pattern of life, not *perfectly,* but *purposely.*

45 I agree with one of my former seminary professors, Dr. Sam Waldron, whose unpublished notes on the section of Scripture have influenced my thinking. He says in summary, that although some suggest that Romans 2:12a, 14, 15 is speaking of regenerate, Christian Gentiles, this is not the case. Waldron says that when these verses speak of those who "do by nature the things of the law" and have "the work of the law written in their hearts," they speak of those who have only the light of nature and who, therefore, cannot be saved. Paul does not say in these words that "the law" is written *on* their hearts, which is what would happen in regeneration (Jer. 31:33). No, rather, he merely says that they show "the work of the law" *in* their hearts. This is what all people have in them by virtue of being made in the image of God. Furthermore, in the Greek, the word, *written,* agrees in case with work, not law. Nowhere in the Bible are Christians ever called "a law to themselves."

46 John Murray is right when he says, "This expression should not be understood in the sense of popular current use when we say that a man is a law to himself. It means almost the opposite, that they themselves, by reason of what is implanted in their nature, confront themselves with the law of God. They themselves reveal the law of God to themselves— their persons is the medium of revelation." Murray, p. 73.

47 Murray is also correct when he says, "The law referred to is definite and can be none other than the law of God specified in the preceding verses as the law which the Gentiles in view did not have, the law the Jews did have and under which they were, the law by which men will be condemned in the day of judgment. It is not therefore a different law that confronts the Gentiles who are without the law but the same law brought to bear upon them by a different method of revelation." Murray, p. 74.

48 Grk. present, middle, verb.

the work of the law (or the work that the law requires, namely, to point
out what is right and wrong, thus making non-Christians inexcusable
before the Almighty);[49] **written** the word alluding to the law of God as
written upon tables of stone as seen in the Old Testament, cf. Exo. 31:18;
in not on, but in; **their hearts, their conscience** or inner co-knowledge
with oneself; **also bearing witness** or testifying in support of something;
and between or among; themselves as a joint witness; **their thoughts
accusing**[50] which is a legal term that means to bring charges against, or
to call out, evidencing further proof of the work of the law in the heart,
and this continually as the present tense verb highlights; **or excusing** *or*
defending; them.[51]

    Obs. 11- (v. 16) That the apostle here announces when those who have
sinned, whether with or without the law will be judged (cf. v. 3, 5, 12).
Paul says that this will happen; **in the day when God will judge the
secrets** or hidden things, not just the public sins, but concealed sins (the
word from where we derive our English word cryptic); **of men** that is, all
people, Jews or Gentiles; **by** or through the agency of; **Jesus Christ** (God's
great, final, eschatological, judge, cf. John 5:22; Acts 17:31); **according
to** or in line with; **my gospel,** that is to say, the gospel Paul preached,
which was given to him "through the revelation of Jesus Christ"
(cf. Gal. 1:11-12).[52]

---

49   A classic example of this is seen in the case of Abimelech in Genesis 20:1-18. We
also see something of the law of God working in the heart of an individual before it was
actually given on Sinai in Joseph (cf. Gen. 39:9).

50   Grk. present, middle, participle.

51   Dr. Sam Waldron has a helpful threefold summary of this section of Scripture in his
unpublished class notes (Prolegomena to Systematic Theology including introduction to
systematic theology and apologetics, page 144) when he writes, "1- This passage confirms
the teaching of Romans 1 as to the reality of the knowledge of the living God and those
without special revelation. 'The work of the law is written in their hearts' and, thus, they
confront themselves with both the precepts and the penalty of the law of God. Thus, they
know the one, true, and living God because they know Him specifically in His position
as lawgiver. Further, they know this God by nature and by means of their own hearts
and, thus, this knowledge must be absolutely universal among those who possess human
nature. 2- This passage brings to completion the teaching of Romans one concerning the
source of their knowledge of God. In Romans 1:19, 20 the source of this knowledge is
external creation. In Romans 2:15 the thought is added that man's own nature and heart
revealed the knowledge of God. Thus, Kuiper is right when he says that man has a twofold
office in revelation. He is both a source of and the recipient of revelation. Kuiper says, 'If the
cosmos is the theater of revelation, in this theater man is both actor and spectator.' 3- This
passage expands the teaching of Romans 1 as to the extent of their knowledge of God by
nature and creation. Not only do men know God, but they have an extensive knowledge of
the moral requirements of His law. This might be deduced from the fact that men according
to Romans 1:18-20 know the character of the living God. Since the moral law of God is
simply the transcript or account of His character as it comes to bear upon or controls the
regulation of human conduct, to know God truly is to know something of His law. All of
this is confirmed by Romans 2:12a, 14, and 15."

52   It is interesting to see Paul using the language of "my gospel" here and at the end
of this epistle in 16:25. Why does he do this especially when he knows according to his
own words, that the gospel belongs to God (1:1)? I am sure many reasons could be given,
but perhaps this language is meant to stress to the Romans exactly what he believed as a
missionary-evangelist. Paul knew that many charged him with false things (cf. 3:8; 6:1 such
as antinomianism, etc.). And so this language of "my gospel" gives clear testimony to what
he taught and believed contrary to what others said about him.

Suggested applications from the text for the church:

1- If you are a true Christian, cease from judging others self-righteously at once as Jesus commands (cf. Matt. 7:1-7).

2- If you are a true Christian, be thankful that the goodness of God has led you to repentance. Be thankful for the goodness, forbearance, and long-suffering that God in grace displays toward you every day of your life.

3- If you are a true Christian, always remember that in the last day in the fullest sense God will grant you eternal life, glory, honor, and immortality.

Suggested application from the text for the non-Christian:

1- If you would become a true Christian, and be ready for the Day of Judgment, then you must prepare now to meet your God through Jesus. You do this by turning from your sins and trusting in His work on the cross alone as your only hope of acceptance with the Almighty.

Text: Romans 2:17-29

General theme: Practice what you preach (the sin of religious hypocrisy)

Homiletical outline of the verses:

A. Profession without practice: [17] Indeed you are called a Jew, and rest on the law, and make your boast in God, [18] and know *His* will, and approve the things that are excellent, being instructed out of the law, [19] and are confident that you yourself are a guide to the blind, a light to those who are in darkness, [20] an instructor of the foolish, a teacher of babes, having the form of knowledge and truth in the law. [21] You, therefore, who teach another, do you not teach yourself? You who preach that a man should not steal, do you steal? [22] You who say, "Do not commit adultery," do you commit adultery? You who abhor idols, do you rob temples? [23] You who make your boast in the law, do you dishonor God through breaking the law? [24] For "the name of God is blasphemed among the Gentiles because of you," as it is written.

B. Ritual without regeneration: [25] For circumcision is indeed profitable if you keep the law; but if you are a breaker of the law, your circumcision has become uncircumcision. [26] Therefore, if an uncircumcised man keeps the righteous requirements of the law, will not his uncircumcision be counted as circumcision? [27] And will not the physically uncircumcised, if he fulfills the law, judge you who, *even* with *your* written *code* and circumcision, *are* a transgressor of the law? [28] For he is not a Jew who *is one* outwardly, nor *is* circumcision that which *is* outward in the flesh; [29] but *he is* a Jew who *is one* inwardly; and circumcision *is that* of the heart, in the Spirit, not in the letter; whose praise *is* not from men but from God.

Summary of section: In verses 17 to 29 of this chapter, Paul deals directly with the deluded Jew. Here as he continues his diatribe style of writing, he makes this quite plain in 17a.[53]

Exegetical & Practical Insights:

Obs. 1- (v. 17) That as the apostle continues his case study on humanity, this is the first time he speaks directly about the Jews. Just in case such individuals thought that they would escape the wrath of God because they were religious, even God's "chosen people," Paul says no. As a matter of fact, all of their religious privileges only increased their accountability before the Lord, therefore, because of his great love for them,[54] his countrymen after the flesh,[55] the apostle would not neglect to speak to them (cf. Rom. 10:1). In essence, he takes away "religion" as the root of their acceptance with God. He says:

Indeed you are called or have had the name placed upon you; **a Jew** a name of privilege which originally designated a member of the tribe of *Judah* and then over the centuries was applied generally to all of the Israelites; **and rest on**[56] or continually rely on; **the law, and make your boast**[57] or constant brag; **in God.**[58]

When the apostle speaks of the Jews "resting on" the law, it means that they were placing all of their hopes upon it to make them right with God. This word carries the sense of leaning on something for support. It is, as A. T. Robertson rightly notes, the "picture of blind and mechanical reliance on the Mosaic law."[59] The Jews were hoping that by keeping the commandments to the best of their abilities they would in fact one day be made right with the Lord. The issue with this is that God never intended that His law would make anyone right with Him.[60] The problem with this type of man-made salvation (taught by every religion in the world except for true, biblical Christianity) is that Paul tells us plainly in Romans 3:20 that "by the deeds of the law no flesh will be justified in His sight, for by the law is the knowledge of sin."[61]

---

53 Robert Mounce is correct when he notes that verse 17 begins with a series of conditional clauses, each which assumes its premise to be true. Mounce, p. 98.

54 I believe that Paul's love for the Jews should be reflected by all believers, having our great desire for them, like that of all people, that they would come to know God in truth through Christ.

55 Cf. Rom. 9:1-3.

56 Grk. present, middle, verb.

57 Grk. present, middle, verb.

58 Note that most verbs in this section of Scripture carry the force of the present tense verb.

59 Robertson, Vol. 4. p. 338.

60 I hold to the historic, Reformed threefold use of the law of God so that first, it acts *evangelically* as a mirror to show us our sinfulness before the Lord in order to drive us to trust in Christ alone for salvation. Second, it acts *civilly* to prevent and restrain evil in society. Third, it acts *morally* for the Christian to know how to walk pleasingly before his God. For further discussion on this matter, I point the reader to *A Puritan Theology* by Beeke and Jones, pp. 555-71.

61 Matthew Henry has famously said that if anyone would be justified in God's sight

When the apostle speaks about the Jew making his "boast in God," the sense seems to be that he is proudly bragging that God had made Himself known to the Jewish people specifically and not to others. Because God had favored the Jews, they took this as partiality. Thus, they went around looking down their noses at the Gentiles. However, the Jews failed to consider that God's favoring of them was not because they were so mighty, but rather because He was so merciful and remembered the oath that He swore to their fathers (cf. Deut. 7:7, 8). This arrogant disposition amounted to an ugly kind of boasting in God. It was really a self-centered, religious swagger, which ultimately showed that they trusted in who they were ethnically in connection to Jehovah for salvation, instead of a true relationship with Him through God's Son Jesus, in whom alone is eternal life (cf. John 3:16).[62]

Obs. 2- (vv. 18-20) That in these verses Paul continues to address the matters that he knew the Jews of his time most certainly believed about themselves. As a matter of fact, they would have heartily consented to all that he says in these words. Thus, the apostle is setting them up for his challenge in verses 21 to 24 of this chapter. As he continues to speak of their self-confidence, he says: **and know *His* will**[63] **and approve**[64] or continually affirm and accept as genuine; **the things that are excellent** or matter; **being instructed**[65] or more literally, continually catechized; **out of the law, and are confident**[66] or more literally, have been proudly confident and continue to be so; **that you yourself are a guide** or spiritual and qualified leader (although Jesus said they were not, cf. Matt. 15:14; 23:24, 26); **to the blind,** that is, the spiritually blind; **a light** (who unfortunately were not willing to come to Christ, who is the light of the world cf. John 8:12);[67] **to those who are in darkness,** that is, spiritual darkness; **an instructor** or corrector, a schoolmaster; **of the foolish,** i.e., those who are unthinking and mindless, ignorant; **a teacher of babes** that is, the spiritually immature; **having the form** or shape, or essence; **of knowledge and truth,** that is, objective truth; **in the law.**

Obs. 3- (vv. 21-23) That Paul here now turns the tables on his imaginary opponent and goes into "attack mode." Following the example of the Lord Jesus (cf. Matt. 23), he reveals the religious hypocrisy of the Jews by means of five rhetorical questions, showing them their absolute lack of any inherent righteousness and thus their desperate need to be saved

---

by keeping His law, they would have to keep it *perfectly, perpetually, and personally* all of their days, which of course, none of us has since everyone is a sinner. This is bad news, and it puts us under the curse of God's law (Gal. 3:10). But blessed be God, that Christ "has redeemed us from the curse of the law, having become a curse for us" (Gal. 3:13).

62 Paul here may have been thinking of the words found in Jeremiah 9:24.

63 Or more literally *the* will.

64 Grk. present, active, participle.

65 Grk. present, passive, participle.

66 Grk. perfect, active, verb.

67 Note that according to Isaiah 49:6 the Jews were called to be a light to the nations, but sadly they did not fulfill that calling. The church now is to fulfill that role (Matt. 28: 18-20).

by Messiah Jesus. The apostle seeks to blast away the false securities of his fellow Jews and says to them:

You, therefore or consequently, an inferential conjunction drawing a conclusion from the preceding words; **who teach**[68] or are teaching; **another, do you not teach yourself? You who preach**[69] or are proclaiming; **that a man should not steal** (the Greek word steal, from where we get our English word kleptomania; a violation of the eighth commandment); **do you steal? You who say**[70] or are continually saying; **"Do not commit adultery"** (a violation of the seventh commandment, which is not only committed by the actual act itself, but through one's lusting in his heart after another person as Jesus said in Matthew 5:28); **do you commit adultery? You who abhor** or more literally consider them a foul and repugnant thing;[71] **idols** or images, false gods, that which is made with men's hands; **do you rob temples** that is, commit sacrilege,[72] a violation of the first commandment, the second commandment, and the eighth commandment?[73] **You who make your boast**[74] constantly;[75] **in the law, do you dishonor**[76] or continually disgrace and degrade; **God through** or by means of; **breaking** or transgressing and violating; **the law?**[77]

What then is the sum of the matter? It is that the lives of unsaved Jews (whom Paul was addressing) were full of falsehood, having a *profession* of faith without being in true *possession* of it—not unlike the lives of many "religious people" in our day. They "talked the talk," but they did not "walk the walk." They were catechized, *but* they were not converted. Simply stated, they were religious, *but* they were not the real deal. They had their ceremonies, *but* they were not saved by Christ. In other words, they had a "form of godliness" but denied its power, of whom Paul says, "turn away!" (1 Tim. 3:5). They were, as John MacArthur rightly says: " ... much like corrupt police officials or judges, whose lives are in direct contradiction of the laws they have sworn to uphold and enforce.

---

68 Grk. present, active, participle.

69 Grk. present, active, participle.

70 Grk. present, active, participle.

71 Leon Morris notes that this word is connected with the Greek word that means "break wind" and words denoting a smell. He said the word means to "turn from something on account of the stench, and thus to abhor, detest." Morris, p. 136.

72 Scholars debate whether this is a reference to pagan temples or perhaps to Jews who robbed the Jerusalem Temple by not paying the money required of every Jew for its upkeep etc. In commenting on this verse Chrysostom says, "It was strictly forbidden for the Jews to touch any of the treasures deposited in heathen temples, because they would be defiled. But Paul claims here that the tyranny of greed has persuaded them to disregard the law at this point." *Ancient Christian Commentary on Scripture, Romans* p. 71.

73 Note how many things in this list break the law of God, the very thing in which the Jews made their boast (cf. v. 23).

74 Grk. present, middle, verb.

75 Cf. 4:1-3.

76 Grk. present, active, verb.

77 Obviously, not every single Jew in Paul's day committed all of these sins.

And because of their greater responsibility, they bring upon themselves greater punishment when they break those laws."[78]

Obs. 4- (v. 24) That this verse gives the consequence of such a high-talk, low-walk lifestyle of the deluded Jew. Here Paul tells what the specific result was among the nations when he writes: **For the name of God** that is, all that God stands for in His essence and character, all that He is in His person;[79] **is blasphemed**[80] or habitually spoken ill of or disapprovingly among the Gentiles; **because of you** or on account of you, that is, on account of your God*less*, two-faced conduct; **as** or just as; **it is written** that is to say, written in Isa. 52:5; Ezek. 36:20.

Obs. 5- (vv. 25-29) That having dismantled many of the false confidences in which the Jews prided themselves, Paul now goes after one last main thing that they trusted in, the performance of which they thought would absolutely make them right with God. This final matter was the rite of circumcision;[81] a ceremony which God Himself had commanded His Old Covenant people to do as a mark of His covenant with Abraham and His descendants (cf. Gen. 17).[82] This matter of circumcision was not a bad thing. In fact, in and of itself, it was a good thing in what it represented. The problem, however, was that the Jews thought that circumcision exempted them from God's judgment for their sins against Him. They thought that the ceremony of circumcision protected them from God's wrath. There was even a general teaching among the Rabbis that one who was circumcised was guaranteed entrance into the kingdom of God on the final day. But, was physical circumcision categorically a passport into glory? Does partaking of this rite, or any rite for that matter, without experiencing the reality to which the sign points, really help someone? Paul says no, surely not![83]

He writes: **For circumcision is indeed** or certainly; **profitable** not that which justifies, but that which is of use as an identification marker; **if you keep**[84] or continue to keep; **the law; but if you are a breaker** or transgressor; **of the law, your circumcision has become uncircumcision. Therefore** Paul is drawing a conclusion from what he just said in verse 25; **if an uncircumcised man keeps the righteous requirements of the law, will not his uncircumcision be counted** or reckoned and regarded; **as circumcision? And will not the physically uncircumcised, if he**

---

78 MacArthur, p. 155.

79 For further study on the topic of the names of God, I refer the reader to *Lectures in Systematic Theology,* Volume 1, Doctrine of God, by Greg Nichols. There Nichols defines the names of God as His "self-designations, by which he makes himself known in respect to his personal characteristics, his interpersonal relations, and his economic and official functions" (p. 582).

80 Grk. present, passive, verb.

81 Or the cutting away and removal of the foreskin of the male member.

82 Cf. Ex. 12:44-49.

83 Recall also that the early church in Acts 15:1-12, had already answered this matter in the negative.

84 Grk. present, active, verb.

fulfills[85] or is achieving; **the law, judge** or deem; **you who,** *even* **with** *your* **written** *code* (or what is stated in the Ten Commandments); **and circumcision,** *are* **a transgressor of the law?** And then in stating why this is so, Paul writes lastly:

For a summary confirmation of the foregoing words; **he is not a Jew** that is a true Jew; **who** *is one* **outwardly,** that is, by just being a mere physical descendant of Abraham;[86] **nor** a negative conjunction; *is* **circumcision that which** *is* **outward in the flesh; but**[87] or in strong contrast to this; *he is* **a Jew** (a true Jew, Abraham's spiritual seed, a child of God, a believer in Messiah Jesus); **who** *is one* **inwardly,** or in the hidden places; **and circumcision** *is that* **of the heart**[88] or the inner man, "not just a literal cutting of the body but the spiritual reality of surgery on the old, unregenerate nature;"[89] **in** referring to the instrumentality of; **the Spirit,** i.e., the Holy Spirit; **not in the letter;** or just with outward, mechanical observance to the law; **whose praise** or approval;[90] *is* **not from men but** emphasizing the antithesis; **from** or out of as its source;[91] **God** (whose praise alone matters most).

Paul in these verses, (specifically in verses 25 to 27), has firstly set forth the fact that any outward sign, even one ordained by God, is worthless if it is not connected with an inward work of grace in the heart.[92] In theoretical language, he argues that a circumcised Jew who transgresses the law is fundamentally no different than an uncircumcised Gentile. Essentially, he says, he might just as well *be* as an uncircumcised Gentile! Consequently, the upstanding behavior of an uncircumcised Gentile actually condemns the hypocritical Jew who is not living in accord with the light he has received.

And secondly, in these verses (28, 29), Paul lets us know that God is not a ritualist. He does not prescribe "salvation by surgery" (that

---

85 Grk. present, active, participle.

86 Cf. Rom. 9:6.

87 The strong Greek adversative.

88 Without this kind of circumcision no one will go to heaven (cf. Deut. 10:16; Deut. 30:6; Jer. 4:4; John 3:3-8; Col. 2:11).

89 McDonald, p. 1685.

90 Several commentators note how Paul here might be engaging in a play on words and this is because the word "Jew" is derived from the patriarch "Judah" whose name means praise (cf. Gen. 29:35; Gen. 49:8). Additionally, the apostle is highlighting for us that the real Jew was one who is truly concerned with God's praise above all things, not the praise of men (cf. 1 Sam. 16:7).

91 Here Paul seems to be referring to that supernatural, sovereign work of God in regenerating sinners and making them believers. This act involves the cutting away of our old human natures, and the implanting of a new spiritual disposition within us through the agency of the Holy Spirit.

92 I think that Charles Hodge's comment is spot on: "Whenever true religion declines, the disposition to lay undue stress on external rites is increased. The Jews, when they lost their spirituality, supposed that circumcision had the power to save them. 'Great is the virtue of circumcision,' they cried; 'no circumcised person enters hell.' The Christian Church, when it lost its spirituality, taught that water in baptism washed away sin. How large a part of nominal Christians rest all their hopes on the idea of the inherent efficacy of external rights!" (Hodge, p. 68).

is to say, salvation by circumcision), and this is because the only way to be delivered from His just judgment is by putting our trust in the finished work of Christ His Son, who died as a sacrifice for our sins (cf. Rom. 3:21-26). The one who does this is the true Jew. This is the one who truly is Abraham's seed (cf. John 8:56; Gal. 3:29).

Suggested applications from the text for the church:

1- Examine yourself to see if you are in the faith, with the evidence of a transformed, gospel-centered life, realizing that a mere profession of faith, without biblical fruit, will not save (cf. Matt. 7:21-23; Gal. 5:22-25). Look to your life and see if you are the real deal.

2- Steer yourself away from having double standards in your life whereby you say one thing and yet you violate it by doing something else, for in doing this you live hypocritically.

3- Comfort yourself with the fact that it is by God's grace that you are in "the faith" and have a "true faith."

4- Guard yourself from trusting in anything but Christ alone for salvation. Not your baptism, nor your church membership, nor your church attendance, etc.

Suggested application from the text for the non-Christian:

1- Rest by faith on nothing other than Jesus' shed blood and righteousness as the only grounds of your acceptance with God. Not your good works, not your religious upbringing, not your family relations, etc., but Christ and Christ alone. Confess with the hymn writer of old saying:

> My hope is built on nothing less,
> Than Jesus' blood and righteousness;
> I dare not trust the sweetest frame,
> But wholly lean on Jesus' name.
> On Christ, the solid Rock, I stand;
> All other ground is sinking sand,
> All other ground is sinking sand.

ROMANS
CHAPTER THREE

Text: Romans 3:1-8

General theme: The Jewish Advantage Answered

Homiletical outline of the verses:

   A. Jewish question: [1] What advantage then has the Jew, or what *is* the profit of circumcision?

   Paul's answer: [2] Much in every way! Chiefly because to them were committed the oracles of God.

   B. Jewish question: [3] For what if some did not believe? Will their unbelief make the faithfulness of God without effect?

   Paul's answer: [4] Certainly not! Indeed, let God be true but every man a liar. As it is written:

   "That You may be justified in Your words,
   And may overcome when You are judged."

   C. Jewish question: [5] But if our unrighteousness demonstrates the righteousness of God, what shall we say? *Is* God unjust who inflicts wrath? (I speak as a man.)

   Paul's answer: [6] Certainly not! For then how will God judge the world?

   D. Jewish question: [7] For if the truth of God has increased through my lie to His glory, why am I also still judged as a sinner? [8] And *why* not *say,* "Let us do evil that good may come"?—as we are slanderously reported and as some affirm that we say.

   Paul's answer: Their condemnation is just.

Summary of section: This chapter breaks nicely into three distinct sections (1-8; 9-20; 21-31)[1] and is particularly important to Paul's entire presentation of the gospel. As he continues to answer the question of why all people need to be saved by means of the gospel (vv. 1-20), and what the heart of the gospel is all about (vv. 21-31), he begins firstly in verses 1 to 8 by setting forth an imaginary dialogue between himself

---

1   A general outline can be: The *why* of Jewish selection (vv. 1-8), the *wickedness* of sinners (vv. 9-20), and the *way* of Jesus' salvation (vv. 21-31).

and a Jewish objector to the gospel.[2] Since Paul had a Jewish background, he was quite familiar with the thinking of such people in his day. Here, then, he anticipates responses from his unsaved kinsmen and answers them so that they will see their need for the Messiah Jesus.[3]

Further, in the first eight verses, Paul responds to the obvious objection that would come from any Jewish person having just read the opening two chapters of this epistle. Having just placed Gentiles and Jews on equal footing before God as guilty, the apostle now answers the question of whether or not being Jewish meant anything at all. The question would go something like this, "If we Jews are condemned and lost and under the wrath of God just like everyone else, was all that God did for us for nothing?" Some of Paul's Gentile readers at Rome might have said: "Absolutely." Paul says instead: "This is not the case."

In fact, in this section of Scripture, Paul seeks to balance all that he said in the previous chapters. John MacArthur rightly says,

> The apostle did not teach that Jewish heritage and the Mosaic law ceremonies were not important. Because they were God-given, they had tremendous importance. But they were not in Paul's day, and had never been, the means of satisfying the divine standard of righteousness. They offer Jews great spiritual advantages, but they did not provide spiritual security.[4]

Exegetical & Practical Insights:

Obs. 1- (v. 1)[5] That as Paul begins his theoretical diatribe so as to address potential pushback from the Jews, he begins by saying: **What advantage** or what preeminence;[6] **then**[7] **has the Jew, or what *is* the profit** or value; **of circumcision**[8] (that is to say, being part of the Abrahamic covenant)?[9] Paul will answer this question more definitively in the next verse. But again, note that in view of what he has been writing in the

---

2 Some commentators say that Paul here is raising arguments that he himself would have raised as an unbelieving Jew regarding the gospel.

3 A couple of commentators point out some thematic links in the opening words of this chapter with the following words that Paul will speak of later in this book. The question of Jewish privileges 3:1=9:1-5. Has God failed? 3:3=9:6; 11:1-2. Some Jews failed/Some Jews faithful 3:3=9:27; 11:5. Is God unjust? 3:5=9:4. Righteousness of God 3:5=10:3. Why does God condemn? 3:7=9:19. Equality between Jews and Gentiles 3:9=10:12. Israel's failure in the Torah 3:9=9:30-10:21 (taken from Bird, p. 95).

4 MacArthur, p. 166.

5 Verses 1-8 in this chapter are notorious among commentators for containing some of the most difficult portions of Scripture in this epistle. While I agree with this assessment to some extent, I found that after I understood what Paul was doing here, preaching through this material was quite useful and encouraging.

6 This Greek word carries the meaning "over and above" or "exceedingly abundantly."

7 Moo notes that Paul frequently uses the words "what, then" in Romans to raise questions about what he has taught and to so further his argument (cf. 3:9; 6:15; 7:7; 11:7, Moo, NICNT, p. 180).

8 Grk. genitive of source, "profit derived from circumcision."

9 Paul began touching on this topic back in 2:25ff.

previous chapters, he wants his audience to know that God's selection
of the Jews was a tremendous privilege, for to them were given "the
adoption, the glory, the covenants, the giving of the law, the service
of God, and the promises; of whom are the fathers and from whom,
according to the flesh, Christ came, who is over all, the eternally blessed
God. Amen" (Rom. 9:4, 5). Yes, being Jewish had great advantage[10]—
however, it did not have an absolute advantage. It had abundant benefit,
but not an ultimate, salvific benefit before God.

Obs. 2- (v. 2) That as Paul answers the question of his Jewish
opponent (as found in verse 1) he swiftly sets forth their chief
advantage when he writes: **Much** or great; **in** or according to;
every way or manner![11] **Chiefly** or mainly as the principal advantage;
because a conjunction of content;[12] **to them were committed** or entrusted;
the oracles or the sayings and utterances; **of God**[13] or that which
belong to Him. Here Paul highlights the primary benefit that the Jews
had when he said that to them were committed "the oracles of God."
Simply stated, in God's goodness to them, the Jews received the sacred
Old Testament Scriptures.[14] They had been made the "depositories of
God's special revelation."[15]

Obs. 3- (vv. 3-4) That as Paul continues his dialogue with his
imaginary Jewish opponent, he asks his second question and then
immediately answers it in verse four. He writes: **For what if some** (not all,
but some);[16] **did not believe? Will their unbelief make the faithfulness** or
the covenantal loyalty; **of God without effect** or powerless? **Certainly not**[17]

---

10 Cf. Deut. 4:8; 7:1-11; Ps. 147:19, 20; Amos 3:2.

11 William Cowper wrote of Israel saying:

They and they only amongst all mankind,
Received the transcript of the eternal mind,
Were trusted with his own engraven laws,
And constituted guardians of his cause;
Theirs were the prophets, theirs the priestly call,
And theirs by birth the Saviour of us all.

See also Rom. 9:3-5.

12 Harvey, p. 76.

13 Grk. genitive of possession.

14 Two side matters here. First, think of what a tremendous privilege it is for us as
Christians to have the full revelation of God's mind given to us in the New Testament.
Indeed, as believers, we are of all people most blessed! Second, think how sad it is that the
Jews who had the Old Testament Scriptures, which clearly point to Christ (Luke 24:25-27;
44-45; John 1:45; 5:45), and did not profit many of them, since they rejected Him (John 1:11).

15 Murray, p. 92.

16 Note that God will always have a believing remnant amongst the Jewish people
(cf. Rom. 11:1-7). There was and will always be an "Israel" within "Israel" (cf. Rom. 9:6-13).

17 The phrase *me genoito* expresses utter shock and denotes the most extreme negation
or "the abhorrence of an inference which may be falsely drawn from the argument,"
Rogers and Rogers, p. 321. MacArthur says that this phrase was the "strongest negative
Greek expression and usually carried the connotation of impossibility." MacArthur, p. 172.
Cf. Rom. 6:1-2. For a similar Old Testament expression, see Gen. 44:17; Josh. 22:29; 1 Kings
21:3.

or let not this be!¹⁸ **Indeed** or but; **let**¹⁹ **God be true** or faithful;²⁰ **but every man** each and every person; **a liar.**²¹ **As** or just as; **it is written**²² or stands written:²³ "**That** the conjunction indicating purpose; **You** (God); **may be justified** or proven right; **in Your words, And may overcome**²⁴ or be victorious, and conquer; **when You** (God); **are judged**" that is, judged negatively by sinful man.

Paul's question in verse three would have been very relevant in the minds of most Jews, because historically the nation had been very unfaithful to the Lord their God. Much of the Old Testament contains examples of this. Ultimately, it was because of their spiritual infidelity to Jehovah through their idolatry that He sent them into exile. The question that Paul is asking here is, "Will the treachery of the Jews against God make the trustworthiness of His character and conduct toward them to be of no use?" He answers and says: "By no means, no, not at all." In no way will the fickleness of God's people change His faithfulness in accomplishing His holy will concerning them.

One clear practical way in which this matter is seen is in Jehovah sending the Redeemer *to* Israel for saving many *within* Israel. Even though God promised in many places in the Old Testament that He would send the Savior, even the Messiah Jesus, who would save His people from their sins (Isa. 53; 59:20; Matt. 1:21), yet many Jews did not—and still do not believe on Him (Isa. 53:1a; John 1:11). Nonetheless, God has saved and will continue to save a remnant of Jewish people through Jesus "according to the election of grace" until the Lord returns,²⁵ even though the greater portion of the nation of Israel has rejected Him (cf. Rom. 10:6-11; 11:1-6). Thus, the *faith-lessness* of men will never cancel out the *faith-fulness* of God. Paul says that this is unthinkable, for even if all people on the face of the planet were to agree that this was so, it would only prove one thing: that all people on the face of the planet are liars and that God is

---

18 Paul uses this phrase nine other times in Romans to express strong denial, always after the question (3:6, 31; 6:2, 15; 7:7, 13; 9:14; 11:1, 11), Harvey, p. 77. McBeth says that the term "expresses horror." It is "the strongest denial." McBeth, p. 97.

19 The imperative strengthens the force of what Paul is saying.

20 God's truthfulness standing, in stark opposition to man's falsehood.

21 Calvin said that these words, "Let God be true and every man a liar," contain "the primary axiom of all Christian philosophy." Calvin, p. 116.
Haldane says, "Whenever, then, the Divine testimony is contradicted by human testimony, let man be accounted a liar." Haldane, p. 112.

22 Grk. perfect, passive, verb.

23 Psalm 51:4.

24 A second verb of purpose. Harvey, p. 78.

25 This is seen throughout the Old Testament in God saving many of the patriarchs, the prophets, Abraham, and David as is mentioned in chapter 4 of this book. This is also seen in New Testament times in God saving thousands of Jews on the Day of Pentecost (Acts 2:41; see also 4:4) and "myriads of Jews" (Acts 21:20) after that, including the apostle Paul himself (Acts 9:1-19).

true. Again, in supporting his claim, Paul quotes from Psalm 51:4, saying of God:[26]

"That You may be justified in Your words,
And may overcome when You are judged."[27]

Chrysostom remarks,

> Paul is saying something like this: "Even if every one of the Jews was an unbeliever ... God would only be the more justified." What does the word justify mean? It means that if there were a trial and an examination of the things which God had done for the Jews and also of what they had done to him, the victory would be with God, and all the right would be on his side.[28]

Obs. 4- (vv. 5-6) That in these verses Paul asks and answers the third set of hypothetical questions that he anticipates coming from his Jewish opponents. In this next argument, he is clear in verse five that he speaks "as a man" or in human terms. He is using an argument that would have been familiar to the people in his day. He writes:

But if our, that is, the Jews; **unrighteousness** or injustice; **demonstrates** or brings out and establishes; **the righteousness of God** that is, His justice and recompense against human sin;[29] **what shall we say?** *Is* God **unjust** or unfair; **who inflicts**[30] or more literally, brings upon; **wrath?**[31] **(I speak**[32] **as a man.) Certainly not**[33] or by no means, may it never come to pass. **For then** or if that were so;[34] **how** or in what way; **will God judge**[35] **the world?**

What is Paul saying here? Speaking as his own imaginary challenger, he says: "If my sin makes God look good because it gives Him an occasion to demonstrate His justice against me, have not I given Him a grand

---

26 In the original setting of this Psalm, David was repenting of his unfaithfulness to the Lord through his committing adultery with Bathsheba. In view of this, as Paul thinks about his question at hand, he takes a portion of the Psalm to prove that God is always faithful in all that He does concerning His people, whether it be in keeping promises to bless His people or to chasten them for their sins (as the case was with David at this time). Despite what sinful people say or do, His purposes and plans will prevail on the earth.

27 Other similar texts of Scripture in this regard can be found in Ps. 89:30-37; Rom. 9:6-13; 2 Tim. 2:13; Heb. 10:23.

28 *Ancient Christian Commentary on Scripture, Romans*, p. 81.

29 Here the reference is to the divine attribute or strict justice of God, as opposed to His justifying righteousness that He gives to sinners who believe in His Son, which is revealed in the gospel, cf.1:17.

30 Grk. present, active, participle.

31 Note that Paul brings up the issue of wrath once again here, cf. 1:18, 2:8, 4:15, 5:9, 9:22, 12:19.

32 Or "I am speaking," present tense active verb.

33 Grk. negative particle with aorist, middle, verb.

34 Rogers and Rogers, p. 321.

35 Grk. future, active, verb.

opportunity to reveal Himself as just? And if so, how then can it be right for Him to condemn me?" In other words, if we give God a platform to set forth Himself as righteous through our sin, then in fact we should sin even more and make Him look even better, and He should not hold us accountable for it. Thus, the argument here is given to make it seem unjust for God to punish sinners. Now if ever there was twisted human logic, surely this was it!

This is as bizarre as someone saying, "If robbing homes gives opportunity to show the skills of a police officer in apprehending such individuals, *why not rob homes?*" The answer is: we do not do such things because they are wrong and violate the Eighth Commandment. We do not do such things because they cause great harm to others! So again, the apostle uses a very strong Greek term to indicate that this is "certainly not" the case. The sense in his language is "banish such base reasoning." Ultimately God does not need anything from us, especially our sin, in order to demonstrate that He is righteous. He is righteous with or without our sin. And if He ever needed our sin in order to show something about Himself, how then would He be able to judge the world in the final day in truth? He could not, at least not righteously. Thus, Paul shows us that this whole argument is skewed.

Obs. 5- (vv. 7-8) That as Paul takes up a fourth and final objection from an imaginary opponent, he speaks as the objector to the gospel one last time.

For if the truth of God has increased or abounded; **through** or by **my lie** or falsehood; **to His glory** or praise so that others admire the character of God; **why am I also still judged as a sinner? And** *why* **not**[36] *say,* **"Let us do** or practice; **evil** that is, do as much wickedness as we can since it promotes God's glory; **that** or for the purpose that; **good may come"?—as we are slanderously reported** as teaching; **and as some affirm**[37] or are continually asserting; **that we say. Their** or all who draw such a conclusion; **condemnation** or damnation by God; **is just** or well deserved.

This argument is like the previous one, in that the hypothetical opponent argues different words that are similar in meaning, saying: "If my falsehood enhances God's truthfulness and so increases His glory or praise, then why am I still condemned as a sinner?" This question is just as inappropriate and absurd as the last question in the previous verses. It is just as flawed, and yet this fourth matter is more personal than the aforementioned matters. Here, a particular attack is made on Paul's own ministry in verse eight. As he no doubt thinks of some of his Jewish detractors, he says on their behalf: "And *why* not say, 'Let us do evil that good may come'?—as we are slanderously reported and as some affirm

---

36 The negative particle being used in a rhetorical question expecting the answer "no," Rogers and Rogers, p. 321.

37 Grk. present, active, verb.

that we say."[38] To which Paul ends this section of Scripture by saying: Their condemnation is just.

Unlike the three questions that were set forth in the previous verses, all Paul can say now is that any who says that he taught they should do evil that good may come are absolutely deserving of the judgment of God. He says that what such people get from the Lord on the final day is well deserved.

Suggested applications from the text for the church:
1- Never forget the great spiritual advantages that have been given to us in the gospel as Christians and rejoice in them. Further, never forget the great blessings that we have in the gospel ordinances of the Lord's Supper and baptism (v. 1).

2- Never forget that no amount of human unbelief or unfaithfulness will ever overthrow the work of God on the earth, especially regarding the advancement of His truth and the good of His church (v. 2).

3- Never forget to know and engage in the popular ideas of the day, as Paul did. However, always do this with a view to bringing people to faith in Christ, not merely to win arguments (vv. 3-8).

Suggested application from the text for the non-Christian:
1- Never forget that according to verse six of this chapter, God will, in fact, judge the world. Thus today is the day to seek the Lord while He may be found, and to call upon Him while He is near (cf. Isa. 53: 6, 7).

Text: Romans 3:9-20

General theme: Biblical Anthropology

Homiletical outline of the verses:
A. The conclusion concerning human sin: [9] What then? Are we better *than they?* Not at all. For we have previously charged both Jews and Greeks that they are all under sin.
B. The catalog of human sin: [10] As it is written:
"There is none righteous, no, not one; [11] There is none who understands; There is none who seeks after God. [12] They have all turned aside; They have together become unprofitable; There is none who does good, no, not one." [13] "Their throat *is* an open tomb; With their tongues they have practiced deceit"; "The poison of asps *is* under their lips"; [14] "Whose mouth *is* full of cursing and bitterness." [15] "Their feet *are* swift to shed blood; [16] Destruction and misery *are* in their ways; [17] And the way of peace they have not known." [18] "There is no fear of God before their eyes."

---

38 Could it be that Paul's detractors were accusing him of antinomianism, that is, being someone who taught that since Christ paid our sin debt in full, now we can live our lives in any way that we want, sin included? It seems they were. However, for the apostle, nothing could be further from the truth, for he regularly taught that instead of the gospel making people law*less* when they received it in truth, it actually makes them law-*abiding*, Cf. Rom. 3:31; Titus 1:1.

C. The conviction for human sin: [19] Now we know that whatever the law says, it says to those who are under the law, that every mouth may be stopped, and all the world may become guilty before God. [20] Therefore by the deeds of the law no flesh will be justified in His sight, for by the law *is* the knowledge of sin.

Summary of section: In these verses, the apostle reaches the height of his argument concerning why all people everywhere need to be saved. He does this as he sums up God's case against all humanity. Having shown in the previous chapters the universal need for the gospel of Christ, Paul now as it were, puts the final nail in the coffin as he drives home his point with significant power and scriptural authority.

Exegetical & Practical Insights:
Obs. 1- (v. 9) That as he for the first time in this letter aligns himself with his fellow Jews ethnically speaking, he writes:
What then[39] or what inference should be drawn from all that I have been saying; **Are we**[40] we who are Abraham's natural descendants; **better** or more preferred above others because of all of our religious privileges; *than they?* (That is, they who are non-Jews, Gentiles). **Not at all** or by no means.[41]

The point is, the Jews have no superior, salvific advantage over Gentiles in regard to their standing before God. **For** an explanatory conjunction; **we have previously charged** a forensic word carrying a tone of legal accusation; **both Jews and Greeks that they are all under sin** not only *in* sin but *under* it,[42] that is, under the dominion of sin as a controlling, ruling, and reigning spiritual principle (cf. Gal. 3:22).[43] What is Paul doing in this verse? He is speaking as a prosecuting attorney for the Lord. He is putting all humanity on a level playing field before

---

39 In the Greek text this verse begins in the same way that verse one of this chapter begins.

40 I realize that some commentators take the plural "we" to refer to Paul and his fellow believers at Rome asking them rhetorically: "Are we, that is, we Christians, better than they, that is to say, better than they who are Jews and Greeks," and while this is certainly possible, personally I think that Paul is speaking here in the *national* sense, not in the *spiritual* sense.

41 That Paul here does not use the stronger expression, *me genoito* (or certainly not), as he did previously in verses 4 and 6 of this chapter should not surprise us. To me, it would seem a bit redundant and out of place for the general tone of what he is discussing here in this verse.

42 They are under Adam's *representative* sin since he is their federal head (5:12). They are born with *Original* Sin (Gen. 6:5). And they commit *actual* sin (3:23), much of the various types of sin that Paul has been speaking of in the previous chapters.

43 This is the first time that the word *sin* appears in Romans. Sin is failure to live up to God's moral law as found in the Ten Commandments (1 John 3:4). It is rebellion against God and His ways. It is saying in one's heart and by one's life: I will not live as He says, I will live how I want to live. Sin is cosmic treason as R. C. Sproul has famously said. It is spiritual treason. It is as another has said, "That which *defiles* a man and *defies* God." It is moral leprosy. It is to wander from the path of uprightness as defined by our maker. It is that which the holy, flawless God of the Bible hates and promises to punish (cf. Ps. 11:7; Ezek. 18:20).

the Almighty. He is saying that in the eyes of God, no one—regardless of who they are (religious or not), or regardless of who they think they are—stands taller in God's sight. The reason for this is, as he says in verse 9b, *all* are under sin.

Obs. 2- (vv. 10-18) That as he validates his accusation concerning all being under sin, and thus all are sinners, he quotes several[44] Old Testament texts from the Psalms, Ecclesiastes, and Isaiah, providing us with fourteen indictments so as to prove his point.[45] He demonstrates the truthfulness of what he just wrote from the Bible. And interestingly enough, the various texts that he quotes which speak about man's sinfulness were all spoken to *both Jews and Gentiles alike*, showing us that from God's perspective, this is how He views *all people* who are without Christ.

He writes:

As or just as or even as; **it is written**[46] that is written in the Old Testament and stands written forever:

"There is[47] and will never be; **none** that is, not a single exception;[48] **righteous,**[49] that is, a person who is completely upright and morally innocent in and of himself before God and His law;[50] **no, not one;**

There is and never will be; **none who understands**[51] or continually and comprehensively grasps the things of God spiritually speaking while not saved;[52] **There is none who seeks**[53] or is continually seeking out in truth;[54] **after God.**[55] **They have all** that is, all without exception;

---

44 Leon Morris highlights that by stacking all of these texts together, Paul follows a common rabbinical practice of stringing texts together like beads in order to prove their point. This was called "pearl stringing." Or more formally *testimonia*, Morris, p. 166.

45 Note that this is the longest series of quotes in the New Testament, coming from seven different texts of Scripture. Also, note that Paul is quoting from the Septuagint rather than the Hebrew Old Testament Bible.

46 Grk. perfect, passive, verb.

47 Grk. present, active, verb.

48 Notice the repetition of the words "none" and "no, not one" for the sake of emphasis. Consider also that Paul is continuing the courtroom setting in these words as the language carries a legal tone.

49 A keynote in this epistle and the critically important reason why people need the gospel, cf. 1:16-17.

50 Of course the only exception to this is Jesus Christ our Lord; He is the Lord our righteousness, cf. Jer. 23:6; 2 Cor. 5:21.

51 Grk. present, active, participle.

52 Cf. 1 Cor. 2:14.

53 Grk. present, active, participle.

54 Of course this does not mean that there are no "religious people" in the world who are not seeking after God or an experience with God, because many are. Some do this for intellectual reasons and others for mystical reasons. However, Paul is telling us that they are not seeking God in truth with a heart to be saved by Him through His Son, Jesus. They are not seeking Him as hell-deserving sinners who desperately need a Savior to forgive them of their sins. Furthermore, Paul could be saying here that there is none who seeks God, apart from God initiating this whole matter, cf. John 6:65.

55 Thanks be to God that although this is true, He sought us out nonetheless! See also John 6:37.

turned aside[56] that is, they have definitively departed and deviated from the path of truth according to God Himself;[57] **They have together** that is, all of fallen humanity as one; **become unprofitable** or spiritually useless and depraved;[58]

There is none who does[59] or is doing; **good** that is morally good, or spiritually good apart from Christ;[60] **no, not: one."**

And then, in speaking as a spiritual physician, Paul gives a portrait of the lost human condition as he metaphorically describes man and says:

"Their throat from where we derive our English word larynx or voice box; *is* **an open tomb** or a grave;

With their tongues or in their speech; **they have practiced deceit**[61] or were deceiving, or habitually practicing deception;

"The poison of asps (the words being used figuratively of a venomous Egyptian snake, depicting unbelievers as having deadly fangs); *is* **under their lips"**;

"Whose mouth *is* **full**[62] or continuously packed and brimming over; **of cursing** or profanity; **and bitterness** or resentment."

"Their feet *are* **swift** or fast to; **shed blood**;

Destruction or utter ruin; **and misery** or affliction and distress; *are* **in their ways** or on the path they travel;

And the way of peace or harmony, tranquility and shalom; **they have not known** that is, known experientially." **"There is** and remains to be; **no fear** or dread or holy reverence; **of God before** or in front of; **their eyes."**

What a horrible picture of fallen humanity this is, and yet, how true it is! "This, then, is God's X-ray of the human race."[63] Here Paul highlights three aspects of all nonbelievers and says that before the perfect, holy God of the Bible they are:

1- depraved in *character* (vv. 10-12)
2- depraved in *conversation* (vv. 13,14)
3- depraved in *conduct* (vv. 15-18).[64]

Obs. 3- (vv. 19-20) Having taught the depravity of man from Scripture, Paul goes on in verses 19 to 20 to expose the sinfulness of man even

---

56 Grk. aorist, active, verb.

57 Here Paul highlights for us that it is not only that people have not understood the things of God or sought Him as they should, but they have perverted the way of righteousness through sinful living. cf. Isa. 53:6.

58 MacArthur notes that the Hebrew equivalent of the Greek term translated unprofitable here was often used to describe milk that had turned sour and rancid, thereby becoming unfit to drink or to be used to make butter, cheese, or anything else edible. He says that in ancient Greek literature the word was even used of the senseless laughter of a moron. MacArthur, p. 186.

59 Grk. present, active, participle.

60 Cf. Rom. 8:8.

61 Grk. imperfect, active, verb.

62 Grk. present, active, verb.

63 McDonald, p. 1686.

64 McClain notes something similar to this in his commentary on Romans, p. 96.

further by using the law of God. In setting forth the use of the law (which is to shut the mouth of unbelievers who often justify themselves and their actions) and declare them guilty before Him, he says in these verses:

Now a conjunction introducing the conclusion of his argument; **we** (we believers, we who are the people of God, we who make up the apostolate); **know**[65] or continue to understand and are acknowledging;[66] **that** the conjunction expressing the content of the knowledge; **whatever** or as many things as; **the law** that is, the moral law of God as summarized in the Ten Commandments;[67] **says**[68] or continues to say, for it is always speaking God's will and is always abiding; **it says**[69] **to those who are under** or in the realm of the legal jurisdiction of; **the law, that** or for the purpose that; **every mouth,** not just the Jews, but every mouth, that is, every single person's mouth; **may be stopped**[70] or silenced once for all time with no objections to render to the charges brought against them;[71] **and all** each and every person, be they Jew or Gentile as Paul has been speaking of in the previous words; **the world may become guilty**[72] or liable to judgment and wrath[73] for their sins; **before God.**[74]

Therefore or because of what was just stated in the former verse, explaining why every mouth will be stopped and all brought under judgment, a causal conjunction; **by** or out of, or on the basis of; **the deeds of the law** or actions that the law requires;[75] **no flesh,** that is, no human being, no person, Jew or Gentile even with their best obedience

---

65 The verb here carries a present tense meaning. Rogers and Rogers, p. 322.

66 Cf. 2:2.

67 Some take the word *law* here as a general reference to the entire Old Testament and say that the pronoun *whatever* points back to those text references in the previous verses. This could be so; however I am not thoroughly convinced it is.

68 Grk. present, active, verb.

69 Grk. present, active, verb.

70 Grk. aorist, passive, verb.

71 No one will ever become a true Christian until his or her mouth is closed before the Almighty God as a guilty individual. As Lloyd-Jones famously said, "You do not begin to be a Christian, until your mouth is shut, is stopped, and you are speechless and have nothing to say. You put up your arguments, and produce all your righteousness; then the Law speaks and it all withers to nothing—becomes 'filthy rags' and 'dung,' and you have nothing to say."

72 In most human courts when charges have been laid against a person, afterward the accused is allowed to speak for himself. Here Paul says that in the final Day of Judgment, people of their own accord will have nothing to say to defend themselves. Their own consciences will accuse them, saying in the language of Job, "If I justify myself, mine own mouth shall condemn me: *if I say,* I am perfect, it shall also prove me perverse" (Job 9:20, KJV).

73 Cf. 1:18.

74 The courtroom scene of one standing before God as condemned continues to be in view. This word *guilty* is a legal, judicial term which pictures "God both as the one offended and as the judge who weighs the evidence and pronounces the verdict. The image, then, is of all humanity standing before God, accountable to him for willful and inexcusable violations of his will, awaiting the sentence of condemnation that their actions deserve." Moo, NICNT, p. 205.

75 For a helpful discussion of the matter of "the deeds of the law" or the "works of the law" in connection with New Perspective theology, I refer the reader to Moo, NICNT, pp. 206ff.

to God's commandments whatsoever (for even our best obedience to the things of God is imperfect, and tainted with sin); **will be justified**[76] or rendered righteous and acquitted on the final Day of Judgment apart from Christ;[77] **in His sight** or before Him; **for** an explanatory conjunction; **by** or through the means of **the law** (again, the Ten Commandments); *is* **the knowledge** that is, the ethical and moral knowledge, and awareness; **of sin**[78] (not the knowledge of salvation, but of our transgressions before God, showing us why it is that we desperately need to be saved because of our violations of it).[79]

In these words, Paul is anticipating someone pushing back to what he just wrote in the previous verses with reference to his catalog of sin. Perhaps he expects a person saying: "Paul, in your string of texts, I am not guilty of all of those things, so things cannot really be too bad with me." To which Paul replies essentially with the words of James when he writes in James 2:10, "for whoever shall keep the whole law, and yet stumble in one point, he is guilty of all."

Again, the apostle shows a major function of the law of God toward the unconverted, which is to stop them from justifying themselves.[80] As J. P. McBeth aptly remarks, "The office of the law is not justification from sin, but conviction of sin and condemnation for sin."[81] Luther said it is not "to justify but to terrify." Spurgeon concurs and says,

> All the law can do is to show us our sin. The law is a mirror, and looking in it you can see your spots; but you cannot wash in a looking-glass. If you want to be cleansed from your stains, you must go somewhere else. The object of the law of God is not to cleanse us, but to show us how much cleansing we need; to reveal our disease, not to find a remedy for it.[82]

The law of God is meant to show unbelievers their lost estate before Him and their desperate need to be saved by Jesus. Thus, ironically, the law helps them by leaving them helpless before the Almighty.[83] Of course, all that Paul is saying here is preparatory for what he is going to say in the following verses of this chapter. Here he has set us up to receive the good news of Christ who suffered and died under the curse of God's

---

76 Grk. future, passive, verb. Cf. Rom. 9:31, 32.

77 This is because no one has kept the commandments of God perfectly, as God requires.

78 Clearly then the law was not given to us so that we can boast in our so-called attempts to keep it, for if we do this, we forget that the law is spiritual and examines our motives and thoughts and finds us wanting (cf. 2:23; 7:14).

79 Cf. Gal. 3:24.

80 See Romans 7:7 to see how the law of God was used in Paul's own life to bring conviction of sin.

81 McBeth, 114.

82 Spurgeon, p. 21.

83 Perhaps the best teaching on how to use the law of God in evangelizing the lost comes from the well-known evangelist, Ray Comfort. His material can be found at: livingwaters.com.

law in the place of sinners who put their faith in Him alone for life and salvation (Gal. 3:10-14).

Suggested applications from the text for the church:

1- In these verses there is a call to humility because the catalog of sin in view in our verses once marked us out as well, to one degree or another.

2- In these verses there is a call to eagerness to use the Ten Commandments to bring conviction of sin to the lost since the Commandments help reveal sin and then to preach Christ to them.

3- In these verses there is a call to gratitude toward Christ who has liberated us from the penalty, power, and pollution of sin and has made us free to serve Him.[84]

Suggested application from the text for the non-Christian:

1- In these verses there is a call to eagerly seek Christ, the only Savior of sinners who can deliver you because according to God, you are totally guilty before Him (cf. Isa. 55:6, 7).

Text: Romans 3:21-26

General theme: God's method of justifying sinners through Christ[85]

Homiletical outline of the verses:

A. Manifestation: [21] But now the righteousness of God apart from the law is revealed, being witnessed by the Law and the Prophets, [22] even the righteousness of God.

B. Appropriation: through faith in Jesus Christ, to all and on all who believe. For there is no difference; [23] for all have sinned and fall short of the glory of God.

C. Justification: [24] being justified freely by His grace.

D. Redemption: through the redemption that is in Christ Jesus.

E. Propitiation: [25] whom God set forth *as* a propitiation by His blood, through faith, to demonstrate His righteousness, because in His forbearance God had passed over the sins that were previously committed, [26] to demonstrate at the present time His righteousness, that He might be just and the justifier of the one who has faith in Jesus.

Summary of section: In these verses, the apostle sets forth the gospel most magnificently.[86] He condenses so much theological truth concerning the splendor of Christ's work on our behalf into a small scope. These verses are so significant that most scholars consider them the very heart

---

84 Blessed be God, that in glory He will liberate us from the presence of sin!

85 These are glorious verses which very plainly teach us what the Reformers regularly proclaimed namely, that salvation is by grace alone (v. 24) through faith alone (v. 22) because of Christ alone (vv. 21-25) and not by one's works (v. 21b).

86 Note that this paragraph is one long sentence in the original text.

and center of this entire epistle.[87] Leon Morris even says that they are "possibly the most important single paragraph ever written."[88] These words are the buildup and explanation of all that Paul has been presenting back from chapter 1:17, where he spoke about the gospel containing the righteousness of God.

Here he shows specifically, beginning in verse 21, first, that God's righteousness was historically manifested in the apostolic generation, "But now the righteousness of God... is revealed."

Second, he shows that God's righteousness is not accomplished by people keeping the Ten Commandments for he tells us it is "apart from the law." And third, he says that God's righteousness is in accord with the testimony of the Old Testament, for he writes that it is "witnessed by the law and the prophets." Having shown us very vividly in the previous words that all are under sin and thus God's wrath abides upon them, Paul now turns from "diagnosis to cure"[89] as he turns his attention to humanity's only hope for escaping God's judgment due to them.

Exegetical & Practical Insights:

Obs. 1- (vv. 21-24) That the opening word **But** is a conjunction highlighting a transition from the previous bad news to the good news of Christ; **now**[90] which is an emphatic adverb strengthening the force of what is being said;[91] **the righteousness of God**,[92] or the righteousness which is from God in Christ, i.e., Christ's perfect righteousness,[93] "not that by which God is righteous but that with which he clothes man when he justifies the ungodly;"[94] **apart from the law** or wholly without "the aid

---

87 Luther, in a marginal note attached to his German translation, arrests the attention of the reader, saying, "Take heed to what is here. It is the central and most important passage of the epistle, and indeed the entire Scripture." Calvin coincided with Luther in opinion: "There is probably no passage in the whole Bible of greater significance as regards the justifying righteousness of God." (As quoted in the *Preacher's Complete Homiletical Commentary* on the Epistle of St. Paul the Apostle to the Romans, p. 89).

88 Morris, p. 173.

89 Doriani, p. 9.

90 Spurgeon says, in commenting on these words, "Now there comes in a new principle—the principle of grace, which accomplishes what the law never could accomplish; that is, the free justification of all the guilty ones who believe in Jesus. And this justification is a righteous one, seeing that it is based upon 'the redemption that is in Christ Jesus.'" Spurgeon, p. 28.

91 Note again, that these two little words here represent a dramatic turning point in this epistle in a bright, positive direction. Moreover, in using these words here, "But now," Paul is certainly thinking *logically*; that is to say, he is advancing his current argument. He is also thinking *temporally*; referring to that which took place in history right there and then in the first century in the apostolic generation, "at the present time," cf. v. 26, when God was pleased, in the fullness of time, to send forth His Son, who was born of a woman, born under the law, to redeem those who were under the law, that we might receive the adoption as sons (cf. Gal. 4:4-5).

92 The major theme of this whole letter, cf. 1:16-17.

93 See my comments on 1:17. Not the faulty righteousness of man which other religions extol, but will absolutely come short of meeting God's standard of perfection in the final day (cf. Eccles. 7:20; Gal. 3:10).

94 Augustine, as quoted in the *Ancient Christian Commentary on Scripture, Romans*, p. 95.

of the law"[95] (being completely separate from our own personal obedience and faulty self-righteous strivings to keep the Mosaic law which are always defective); **is revealed**[96] or more literally "stands manifested,"[97] being set forth finally and forevermore through Christ's accomplished work at Calvary; **being witnessed**[98] or spoken of and continually testified; **by** a preposition denoting agency; **the Law** or the Old Testament as a whole; **and the Prophets**[99] that is, the Old Testament prophets who spoke prophetically about this matter in Scripture (showing that this God-ordained method of justification before God was not something new with Paul); **even the righteousness of God, through faith,**[100] signifying the manner through which the righteousness of God is personally received for ourselves (faith being the sole means of our salvation);[101] **in Jesus Christ;**[102] and Jesus Christ alone; **to all and on all who believe**[103] or are trusting and exercising faith in Him.[104] **For** an explanatory conjunction telling us why the righteousness of God is received through faith in Jesus Christ to all and on all who believe; **there is**[105] and there will always be; **no difference** or distinction when it comes to people's need for the gospel,[106] "the Jew has no special privilege and the Gentile is at no disadvantage,"[107] **for** another explanatory conjunction explaining the previous verse; **all,** i.e., each and every person Jew or Gentile; **have sinned**[108] that is, sinned in their lives through personal acts of sin, through "evil moral acts often committed with the body, which are directed against God, which violate His revealed will either by commission or omission;"[109]

---

95 Calvin, as quoted in *Reformation Commentary on Scripture,* Romans, p. 158.

96 Grk. perfect, passive, verb.

97 Note also, how it is that as the wrath of God continues to be revealed against sinners (1:18), so also when we preach the completed work of Christ, we are continually proclaiming that which was once for all manifested.

98 Grk. present, passive, participle.

99 The combination of the terms "law and the prophets" is typically a reference to the entire Old Testament. Isaiah 46:13; 51:8; Jeremiah 23:5-6; Daniel 9:24; (cf. Romans 1:2).

100 Note not *because* of faith, for faith is never the ground for our justification. No, faith is the instrumental means of our justification, but never the basis of it. Cf. Philippians 3:9.

101 McDonald defines faith as, "utter reliance on the living Lord Jesus Christ as one's only Savior from sin and one's only hope for heaven." McDonald, p. 1687.

102 Martin Bucer, the German Protestant in the Reformed tradition and contemporary of Luther and Calvin (1491-1551), said, "Our cause is ever supported by these verses from the chief apostle and Christ's chosen instrument. No other apostle ever inculcated in us the doctrine that righteousness comes to all people solely by faith in Jesus Christ, who died for us. Let us fix our minds on this very thing with greater depth and carefully weigh the matter with a worthy examination." *Reformation Commentary on Scripture,* Romans, p. 164.

103 Grk. present, active, participle.

104 I believe that Paul repeats here what he said in the first part of verse 22 for the sake of emphasis.

105 Grk. present, active, verb.

106 Cf. Rom. 10:12.

107 McDonald, p. 1687.

108 Grk. aorist, active, verb. The aorist tense verb perhaps referring to our original fall in Adam.

109 *Lectures in Systematic Theology,* Volume 2, Doctrine of Man, by Greg Nichols.

and fall short[110] or habitually come short of; **the glory** (not just the Law of God), but, the moral glory and excellence; **of God** in His essential character and nature;[111] **being justified**[112] or declared or reckoned not guilty, i.e., forgiven[113] (hence accounted positively righteous,[114] never to be condemned);[115] **freely** or without any cost or charge to us (without any works, or merit or any performance on our part, but simply as a gift); **by His grace** or God's unmerited favor and kindness to those who do not deserve such things (the phrase "by His grace" stating the divine cause by which we are "justified freely"); **through** the word pointing to the judicial ground of our justification; **the redemption,**[116] that is, the payment price which was made to God[117] in order to satisfy His divine justice for our sins against Him and to free us from our guilt and penalty for sin;[118] **that is in** the preposition identifying the unique agent of our redemption, "that is in," or connected to, and paid for exclusively by; **Christ Jesus.**[119]

Obs. 2- (v. 25) That in this verse Paul explains *how* the redemptive work of Christ actually functions (cf. v. 24). He expounds *why* it is that Jesus' death in our place completely satisfies all the claims of divine justice against us. Notice what he writes:

---

110 Grk. present, active, verb. The present tense verb referring to our own actual sin.

111 John Piper has called the glory of God, "The infinite beauty and greatness of His manifold perfections."

112 Grk. present, passive, participle. The present tense form of the verb should not concern us who understand justification as a single, one time act that it is. Here Paul is simply using this tense to speak about what God does in time, once for all time, the moment people believe.

113 Note, not "made righteous." This is what happens in *sanctification.*

114 This is the positive side of justification so that it is not only "just as if we have never sinned," but also "just as if we are perfect in God's sight."

115 "Justified" is a legal term straight from the law courts in Paul's day. The picture is that of God the great Judge of humanity on His royal throne in His courtroom pronouncing a criminal acquitted [just or righteous], dismissing judgment against him. Justification is a declarative word from God to the believing sinner. It is His permanent verdict, which will never be revoked by Him, or lost by the one who has received it. One of my favorite definitions for justification is found in the *Westminster Shorter Catechism* where the writers say in Q. 33 that justification is: "an act of God's free grace, wherein he pardoneth all our sins, and accepteth us as righteous in his sight, only for the righteousness of Christ imputed to us, and received by faith alone."

116 MacArthur says that "The imagery behind this Greek word comes from the ancient slave market. It meant paying the necessary ransom to obtain the prisoner or slave's release." John MacArthur, *One Faithful Life* (2019), p. 277.

117 Not the devil as some have erroneously thought throughout the centuries.

118 The great Puritan John Owen said that redemption is "The freeing of a man from misery by the intervention of a ransom" (Taken from Spurgeon sermon on Isaiah 53:10).

119 Note that this is Paul's first use of the title "Christ Jesus" in this epistle, as other commentators have noted. Maybe Paul did this in order to emphasize that the redemption that was made on our behalf as foretold by the "law and the prophets" came about through Messiah Jesus as had been predicted. Note also that since we are told here that our redemption comes to us in Christ Jesus, it is clear that our salvation is a purchased and precious gift. It was a gift of infinite value and worth, which cost the Son of God His all so that we might be saved.

whom God[120] that is to say, God the Father, the One who is the chief architect and source of our redemption;[121] **set forth**[122] not hid in a corner but publicly displayed for all to see (or perhaps better understood, eternally purposed);[123] *as* **a propitiation**[124] that is, a wrath-absorber (or an appeasement who stopped divine anger by a sacrificial offering), which offering Jesus was; **by His blood**[125] that is, the blood of Christ,[126] which speaks of His sacrifice and death,[127] which was the exclusive basis of the propitiation;[128] **through faith** not good deeds, not baptism, not law keeping, but "through faith" explaining the instrumental means in

---

120 Note the amazing love of God being set forth here! Having described in the opening chapters of this book, man's great rebellion against God and thus the appropriateness of God's wrath, Paul tells us that God in Christ appeases His own wrath against us. Although the God of the Bible is a God of strict justice who must punish our sins (for this is what His Holiness demands), nonetheless He is also a God of great abounding love, willing to rescue us from such a horrible plight through the wrath-absorbing work of His Son in our place. This is the God who so loved the world that He gave his only begotten Son that whoever believes in Him should not perish but have everlasting life (John 3:16). Along these lines, Tony Merida makes this helpful comment, "To be clear, the picture is not of the Father as an angry old man and Jesus as a nice and mild man who offers to satisfy the rage of his crazy dad. There is unity in the action and purpose in this work. The Father puts the Son forward, and the Son willingly obeys the Father. Love and justice motivated the cross event. We should remember both of these attributes when considering the cross. What motivated the atonement? Both love and justice." Merida, p. 55.

121 This plan of redemption, being devised by God the Father in complete cooperation with Christ and the Holy Spirit, is what is known as the Covenant of Redemption.

122 Grk. aorist, middle, verb.

123 Commentators discuss the meaning of this verb taking one of two options. *Contextually,* "set forth" is probably better because as Robert Mounce correctly says, "The text is explaining how God went about establishing his redemptive program." Mounce, p. 117, ft. 20. However, *theologically* speaking (and even *grammatically* speaking), based on the makeup of the verb with the preposition attached to it, the second option of "eternally purposed" is true as well.

124 Commentators often connect this word with the Old Testament mercy seat. This is because this Greek word is the same as used for the mercy seat in the Septuagint. For this reason, I have no problem understanding propitiation in this way *in part* along with my other definition given above. I say this because just as the Old Testament mercy seat was the place where sacrificial blood was sprinkled so as to reconcile God with His old covenant people, in like manner Jesus is now our mercy seat where we, through his blood, are reconciled to Him. Furthermore, commentators often discuss the difference between propitiation (to avert or appease God's wrath by a sacrifice) and expiation (to take away or remove guilt, to make amends) through the atonement of Christ. Which is the better word? Personally, I would opt for propitiation. However, expiation does highlight for us another aspect of Christ's work in our place. For a helpful treatment of this topic, I point the reader to Anthony Thiselton, *Discovering Romans,* pp. 108-10; Leon Morris, *The Apostolic Preaching of the Cross,* pp. 179ff. Additionally, it should be noted that for believing Jews reading this verse in Paul's day they would have also understood the language of propitiation in connection to God providing a sacrifice for them such as He did on the Day of Atonement or *Yom-Kippur.* As they thought about Jesus' death, they would have understood that He was the ultimate fulfillment of this event.

125 Cf. Rom. 5:9; Eph. 1:7; Col. 1:20; Rev. 1:5.

126 Cf. Lev. 17:11.

127 Jesus' blood also has connections to all the Old Testament sacrifices and the entire sacrificial system, fulfilling completely all that they foreshowed once for all time (John 1:29; 19:30; Heb. 10:4-14).

128 Hence, Jesus cried out on the cross, saying, "it is finished" (John 19:30).

which God applies Jesus' propitiatory sacrifice to us;[129] **to demonstrate**
or to give proof of (so as to uphold God's integrity in view of what some
might consider His leniency); **His righteousness,** i.e., His justice and
holiness, the uprightness of His method of justifying sinners; **because**
or on account of; **in His forbearance** or patience and long-suffering;
God had passed over[130] not ignored, but "passed over;" **the sins** that is,
the forgiven sins of the redeemed under the Old Covenant which were
"not historically punished till in the death of Christ on the cross;"[131]
that were previously committed. In explaining these words, McDonald
well observes:

> This refers to the sins committed before the death of Christ. From Adam
> to Christ, God saved those who put their faith in Him on the basis of
> whatever revelation He gave them. Abraham, for example, believed God,
> and it was reckoned to him for righteousness (Gen. 15:6). But how could
> God do this righteously? A sinless substitute had not been slain. The
> blood of a perfect Sacrifice had not been shed. In a word, Christ had not
> died. The debt had not been paid. God's righteous claims had not been
> met. How then could God save believing sinners in the OT period? The
> answer is that although Christ had not yet died, God knew that He *would*
> die, and He saved men on the basis of the still-future work of Christ. Even
> if OT saints didn't know about Calvary, *God* knew about it, and He put
> all the value of Christ's work to their account when they believed God.
> In a very real sense, OT believers were saved on credit. They were saved
> on the basis of a price still to be paid. They looked forward to Calvary;
> we look back to it.[132]

The writers of the historic London Baptist Confession of Faith of 1689 say
something similar:

> The price of redemption was not actually paid by Christ till after His
> incarnation. Yet the virtue, efficacy, and benefit of it was imparted to
> the elect in every age since the beginning of the world, in and by those
> promises, types, and sacrifices that revealed Him as the seed that would
> bruise the serpent's head and the Lamb slain from the foundation of the
> world. He is the same yesterday, and today, and forever.[133]

---

129 Note also that faith is not the *ground* of our acceptance with God; only the death
of Christ is. We are not justified "on account of faith," but "through faith," and faith alone.

130 The sense to me seems to be that God "passed over" the *sins* of His Old Testaments
saints in that He delayed an "official punishment" for them, not, as some commentators
suggest, in that He *just* overlooked them or *did not regard them*, not dealing with them
because they were symbolically atoned for through the sacrificial system. This calls into
question the righteous character of God. I take the words as suggesting that God forgave
the sins of His people and covered them completely based on what Christ would come and
do for them. Thus, this illustrates the necessity and certainty of the atonement.

131 McBeth, 123, 124.

132 McDonald, 1690.

133 The London Baptist Confession of Faith of 1689, Chapter 8, paragraph 6 (updated
version for the 21st century by Founders Press).

Obs. 3- (v. 26) That as Paul speaks further about the timeframe of Jesus' propitiation concerning its purpose in history, he writes: **to demonstrate** or to publicly give proof; **at the present time;**[134] that is, at the cross 2000 years ago, where Jesus willingly and openly made propitiation to God the Father for us, by becoming our propitiatory offering in our place; **His** (God the Father's) **righteousness; that** the word denoting purpose; **He might be**[135] and always remain; **just** or upright in His character; **and the justifier** or the vindicator; **of the one who has faith** that is, a true belief and confidence; **in Jesus** (alone).[136]

What is Paul saying? Having told us in verse 25 that God publicly set forth His Son on the cross of Calvary as the One who drank up all of His bitter wrath against us as our wrath-bearing substitute, now in verse 26, he gives us two important reasons why this was done. The first was to demonstrate "at the present time" that although God was long-suffering in passing over the sins of Old Testament saints, He forgave their sins and imputed righteousness to them on credit through what Christ would eventually come and do (as Paul says that God did in the next chapter with reference to Abraham and David). Nonetheless, so that God could not be charged with any injustice in doing this and so uphold His righteous character, Christ came, and made an "official atonement" when He died on the cross for our sins.

Second, Paul amplifies why it is that Christ would be the propitiation for our sins at this time in history by saying that it was to demonstrate that God might be "just and the justifier" of the one who has faith in Jesus. Simply stated, in the death of Christ, God did two things. On the one hand, He upheld His own law and justice, because it was satisfied in His Son. On the other hand, He could be the justifier (or the one who declares sinners who put their trust in Jesus not guilty), since Jesus paid their sin debt for them when He bore their sins "in His own body on the tree" (cf. 1 Pet. 2:24). In summary, through Jesus' cross, God's mercy can be granted without His justice being compromised. At the cross, justice and mercy kissed! And at the cross justice and love intersected! This answers the vital question of how it is that God could satisfy His own demands against sinful people and yet demonstrate His amazing grace toward them. What a glorious God He is!

Suggested applications from the text for the church:

1- In these verses there is an encouragement to carefully ponder the truths contained in them because they are theologically rich and for our spiritual good.

2- In these verses there is an exhortation to praise God for such wonderful good news given to us in His wonderful Son.

---

134 In contrast to that which was previous (cf. v. 25).

135 Grk. present, active, verb.

136 I believe that our Lord's human name here is significant, putting a personal touch and precious reminder of the One who loved us and gave Himself for us.

Suggested application from the text for the non-Christian:
1- In these verses there is an entreaty to remember that while you are not justified by God, you are condemned by Him and so you must seek Christ for salvation.

Text: Romans 3:27-31

General theme: Salvation Transformation

Homiletical outline of the verses:
A. Humiliation: [27] Where *is* boasting then? It is excluded. By what law? Of works? No, but by the law of faith. [28] Therefore we conclude that a man is justified by faith apart from the deeds of the law.

B. Integration: [29] Or *is He* the God of the Jews only? *Is He* not also the God of the Gentiles? Yes, of the Gentiles also, [30] since *there is* one God who will justify the circumcised by faith and the uncircumcised through faith.

C. Affirmation: [31] Do we then make void the law through faith? Certainly not! On the contrary, we establish the law.

Summary of section: The apostle here describes three powerful and profound implications which are to be produced in us who have received the aforementioned gospel in truth. Having just spoken in the previous words about Christ's crowning work in our place, he now sets forth some crucial results that are to be implemented from it.

Exegetical & Practical Insights:
Obs. 1- (v. 27) That it might seem a bit odd here that Paul begins this verse how he does by speaking against self-glorying, especially since he has just spoken in great detail about all that God in Christ has done for sinners apart from their works. However, since the apostle understood that the human heart (Christian or otherwise), has much pride in it, the Holy Spirit led him to deal with this issue and so, as he concludes his discussion from verse twenty one, he writes: "**Where *is* boasting** or the act of glorying and pride; **then** or therefore?"[137]

Paul responds by saying: **It is excluded,**[138] literally he says, it is shut out and completely eliminated once for all time. Next, he asks how it is that all boasting is excluded: **By** or through; **what law** or, as almost all commentators suggest, what *principle or rule*? **Of works** that is to say, our own efforts, which of course cannot be the case since our own efforts would produce the exact opposite result. **No** an emphatic negation being used for the sake of emphasis; **but**[139] or on the contrary; **by** or through; **the law of faith** that is to say, believing, for as John Murray rightly says,

---

137 Paul is saying rhetorically that really there is no ground or basis for this at all, since in the final analysis, before God we have done all the *sinning* and He has done all the *saving*.

138 Grk. aorist, passive, verb.

139 The strong adversative.

faith is "*self*-renouncing whereas works are *self*-congratulatory."[140] Faith looks away from oneself, works looks to oneself. Or, as Matthew Henry wonderfully put it,

> Now, if justification were by the works of the law, boasting would not be excluded. How should it? If we were saved by our own works, we might put the crown upon our own heads. But *the law of faith*, that is, the way of justification by faith, doth for ever [sic] exclude boasting; for faith is a depending, self-emptying, self-denying grace, and casts every crown before the throne; therefore it is most for God's glory that thus we should be justified.[141]

Obs. 2- (v. 28) That just in case Paul was not clear in all that he has been saying up to this point in this epistle (or more immediately in verses 20-26 of this chapter), regarding faith being the sole means of one being saved and not their works, he writes so that none should miss it:

Therefore or as a result of what he just said in the previous verse; **we** (we who are believers, we who hold to the apostolic gospel as set forth in Scripture); **conclude**[142] or are always holding and maintaining; **that a man** a word signifying the human race in general, a person, whoever the person is, and wherever the person is from, be that a Jew or Gentile; **is justified** or rendered righteous and vindicated in God's sight; **by faith**[143] that is, solely by means of faith (or trust in the completed work of Christ alone); **apart** or completely separate; **from the deeds of the law** or anything that we attempt to do in order to bridge the gap between our sins and God's moral perfection, since "by the deeds of the law no flesh will be justified in His sight," v. 19.[144]

---

140 Murray, p. 123.

141 Henry, p. 312.

142 Grk. present, middle verb.

143 *Believing* instead of *achieving*, Phillips translation.

144 Cf. Rom. 9:30-33. It is worth noting that this verse was one of the key verses in the New Testament which sparked the Protestant Reformation and brought great light to the glorious doctrine of *sola fide*, which teaches us that God pardons sinners not through what they do for themselves, but through faith in what Christ has done for them. As a matter of fact, R. C. Sproul said this verse more than any other single verse in Scripture most clearly articulates the doctrine of justification by faith alone. Sproul, p. 96.

John Trapp, the great Puritan, rightly said concerning it, "Here we have Paul showing himself to be a pure Lutheran." John Trapp, *A Commentary on the New Testament*, p. 495. Furthermore, it is this passage which is so clear about this matter of justification by faith alone that Luther in his German translation of the Bible inserted the word alone into the text. Of course, Luther was severely criticized by the Catholic Church for doing this; however, this is the plain sense of the passage, and thus Luther felt right in doing it. In fact, historians tell us that there were others before Luther in the Catholic Church who interpreted this verse in this way. So Luther was not being novel, but just typically bold. In answering his Roman Catholic objectors, the story goes that Luther (in adopting some of Paul's language from 2 Corinthians chapter 11) said: "If your papists make much useless fuss about the word sola, tell him that Dr. Martin Luther will have it so, for I ask: are the papists doctors? So am I. Are they learned? So am I. Are they preachers? So am I. Are they theologians? So am I. Therefore the word alone shall remain in my New Testament and although all papal donkeys get furious about it they shall not take it out."

Obs. 3- (vv. 29-30) That Paul here makes both a practical and theological point. *Practically speaking* he is indirectly dealing with the issue of racial segregation. In the first century, this was happening between unsaved Jews and Gentiles regularly. This was because many Jews considered the Gentiles dogs, being the type of people whose minds were "always intent upon idolatry," as one famous Rabbinic sage wrote. And many Gentiles despised the Jews. Sadly, however, when these individuals were converted, the sin of racial segregation did not die speedily. Paul deals with this in several places in his epistles[145] but perhaps most notably in Galatians 3:28 when he writes: "There is neither Jew nor Greek, there is neither slave nor free, there is neither male nor female; for you are all one in Christ Jesus."

Secondly, *theologically speaking*, he says that since there is one God who saves through one way (viz., faith in His Son v. 28; 30), He is thus the God of all who believe on Christ regardless of who they are or where they are from. In other words, as Paul says in Romans 10:12: there is no distinction between Jew and Greek, for the same Lord over all is rich to all who call upon him, for whoever calls on the name of the Lord shall be saved. Paul asks here:

Or *is He* **the God of the Jews only** or exclusively? *Is He* **not** an emphatic adverb stressing the certainty of the matter which anticipates a positive response; **also the God of the Gentiles? Yes** or most certainly; **of the Gentiles also,**[146] **since** or more literally, since *indeed*, a composite particle adding force to Paul's statement[147] and explaining why God is the God of both Jews and Gentiles; *there is* **one God**[148] **who will justify the circumcised by faith** (that is the Jews), **and the uncircumcised through faith** (that is the Gentiles).[149]

Obs. 4- (v. 31) That having once again earnestly defended in this section of Romans the doctrine of justification before God by faith alone, on the ground of Christ's work alone, because of grace alone, apart from anything that we do (vv. 27, 28), Paul anticipates and answers a very logical question with reference to Christians and the moral law of God. The question relates to antinomianism (a teaching which says that since we are saved completely by God's grace in Christ, wholly apart from what we do, the Ten Commandments are no longer relevant as a moral rule and

---

145 Cf. Eph. 2:14-15; Col. 3:11.

146 Sproul, in quoting Hodge, says: "We Gentiles may now look up to heaven, and confidently say, 'Thou art our Father, though Abraham be ignorant of us, and though Israel acknowledge us not.'" Sproul, p. 97.

147 Longenecker, p. 449. See also, 8:9, 17.

148 As the apostle sets forth the monotheistic belief of the Bible, namely, that there is only one God which the Jews regularly confess in their own Shema, he is stressing the point that therefore He must equally be the same God to all who know Him in truth. Furthermore, Paul again is showing us that his doctrine of justification by faith alone for all who believe is rooted in his belief that there is one God. Thus, He saves all in one way.

149 I do not believe we should quibble over the two different uses of the prepositions in this verse *ek, dia*. Both of them highlight to us the means through which God justifies sinners, although the former may be stressing the source of the matter, and the latter, the instrument or agency of it.

guide for our lives as Christians). The question is this: since we do not get right with God by our attempts to keep the law, does this mean that the law of God counts for nothing?[150] Paul's answer is decisive. He writes:[151]

Do we then or therefore; **make void**[152] or go on living and nullifying; **the law**[153] **through faith? Certainly not** or perish the thought![154] **On the contrary** or quite the opposite;[155] **we** (we who are Christians, we who have been justified by God's grace alone in Christ alone); we **establish**[156] that is, we continually confirm, uphold, and validate it by how we live;[157] **the law.**[158]

What is Paul saying? He is saying that although we are not saved by *law-keeping*, when we become saved, we do not become *lawbreakers*. Since the law of God is written on our hearts in regeneration,[159] and Christ told us that if we love Him we will keep His commandments,[160] as believers (in contrast to how non-believers live who go around breaking the commandments of God all the time by lying and stealing and blaspheming God's name, etc.), we, by the power of the Spirit, seek to uphold His statutes, not in order to be made right with God, but because we have already been made right with Him through Christ. Out of love and gratitude for all that God has freely done for us in Jesus, we seek to keep the commandments of God (cf. 8:1-4).

Suggested applications from the text for the church:

1- There is to be no boasting in self, but only in the Savior.

2- There is to be no discrimination, but an assimilation of God's people.

3- There is to be no antinomianism, but an evangelical keeping of the commandments of God for His glory and our good.

Suggested application from the text for the non-Christian:

1- Do not let your self-importance, or self-righteousness keep you out of the kingdom of God. Rather, see yourself in truth as God sees you, namely, as a lost, hell-deserving sinner, and then go to Christ by faith alone quickly to be saved by Him.

---

150 Paul takes up this matter again in 6:1.

151 The Phillips translation of the Bible on this verse is memorable. It says, "Are we then undermining the Law by this insistence on faith? Not a bit of it! We put the law in its proper place."

152 Grk. present, active, verb.

153 In the Greek text, the word *law* is emphatic.

154 The most emphatic negative in the Greek language.

155 The strong Greek adversative.

156 Grk. present, active, verb.

157 Spurgeon was right when he said, "There is no one who so much loves the law of God, and delights in it after the inward man, as the one who has been justified by faith" (cf. Rom. 7:12; 22).

158 Alva McClain in his commentary on Romans, "There is only one religion in all the world that can save men and still establish, exalt, and honor the law: Christianity. All of the systems that are based on legality, on salvation by works, dishonor the law, because nobody ever kept it." McClain, p. 111.

159 Cf. Jer. 31:33.

160 Cf. John 14:15.

ROMANS
CHAPTER FOUR

.

Text: Romans 4:1-8

General theme: The Case of Abraham (I). The exemplification of justification by faith alone apart from works.

Homiletical outline of the verses:

    A. What Abraham received: [1] What then shall we say that Abraham our father has found according to the flesh? [2] For if Abraham was justified by works, he has *something* to boast about, but not before God. [3] For what does the Scripture say? "Abraham believed God, and it was accounted to him for righteousness."

    B. How Abraham received it: [4] Now to him who works, the wages are not counted as grace but as debt. [5] But to him who does not work but believes on Him who justifies the ungodly, his faith is accounted for righteousness, [6] just as David also describes the blessedness of the man to whom God imputes righteousness apart from works: [7] "Blessed *are those* whose lawless deeds are forgiven, And whose sins are covered; [8] Blessed *is the* man to whom the Lord shall not impute sin."

Summary of section: In verses 1 to 25 of this chapter (which breaks neatly into three sections, 1-8; 9-12; 13-25), Paul appeals to the example of Abraham (and then later David), in order to prove and illustrate the argument that he has been establishing up to this point in this letter (and has just reiterated in 3:28). Specifically, he has been teaching that justification before a holy God is a free gift, received by faith alone to all who believe (vv. 4:1-3; 23-25), not by our works (vv. 4-8), nor by circumcision (vv. 9-12), nor by keeping the Ten Commandments (vv. 13-25). His case study of the patriarch was not only powerful and persuasive for his Jewish readers at Rome, but is also of great use to all Christians in every generation for its timeless gospel principles.[1]

---

1 MacArthur helpfully notes that, "by using Abraham as the supreme scriptural example of justification, or salvation, by faith *alone*, Paul was storming the very citadel of traditional Judaism. By demonstrating that Abraham was not justified by works, the

Exegetical & Practical Insights:

Obs. 1- (vv. 1-3) That as Paul illustrates the truth of justification by faith alone and not by one's works through the life of Abraham, he begins by saying:

What then or better translated "therefore," a word of summary in view of all that he has just been saying in the previous chapter; **shall we say that Abraham** (who was perhaps the most notable individual in Judaism, the one whom the Jews extolled);[2] **our father**[3] or forefather; **has found**[4] that is to say, discovered when he was first saved and discovered to be true all of his days; **according to** or with reference to; **the flesh,** which is to say, with reference to his own experience?

Paul is asking here: "Did Abraham learn that a person, even he himself, gets right with God by what he does, or by faith alone?" Clearly, he learned it was by faith alone, as Paul says in verse three of this chapter. Yet, in speaking against what some Jews thought at that time concerning Abraham, Paul uses a hypothetical in the first part of verse two:

For the conjunction explaining the relevance of verse one to his overall argument;[5] **if** or assuming that; **Abraham was justified** or made right with God; **by works** that is, by the labors of his own hands, something he did by his own performance, etc., **he has**[6] and continues to have *something* **to boast about** or brag about; **but not**[7] **before** or in the presence of; **God,** who saw Abraham in truth, as a sinner in need of the Savior and His righteousness. **For** a conjunction explaining the last half of the preceding verse, specifically why Abraham had no grounds for boasting in himself; **what does the Scripture** that is, the inspired writing of the Old Testament as found in Genesis 15:6; **say**[8] or continue to tell us?[9]

---

apostle demolished the foundation of rabbinical teaching—that a man is made right with God by keeping the law, that is, on the basis of his own religious efforts and works. If Abraham was not and could not have been justified by keeping the law, then no one could be. Conversely, if Abraham was justified solely on the basis of his faith in God, then everyone else must be justified in the same way, since Abraham is the biblical standard of a righteous man." MacArthur, p. 233.

2 Abraham was so revered in Judaism that in rabbinic writing the rabbis affectionately called him, "a bag of myrrh," saying, "just as myrrh is the most excellent of spices, so Abraham was the chief of all righteous men." Longenecker, p. 477.

3 I believe that Paul here in referring to Abraham as "our father" along with speaking *ethnically* is also speaking *spiritually*. Abraham is the spiritual father of all true believers in Christ whether they are Jews or Gentiles, as explained later in this chapter.

4 Grk. perfect, active, verb.

5 Harvey, p. 106.

6 Grk. present, active, verb.

7 The combination of the two words in the Greek text are very strong, showing the folly of the opening thoughts of this verse.

8 Grk. present, active, verb.

9 Here Paul gives a key question which must be the foundation for all that we believe and the basis upon which we always argue all of our points theologically speaking, namely, "what does the Scripture say?" Not, "what is my preference?" Not, "what is my opinion?" Not, "what does a church denomination teach?" No, but, "what does the Word of God say?"

"**Abraham believed**[10] or put his complete trust in; **God** and His Word,[11] **and it was** (in return); **accounted**[12] or reckoned[13] once for all time; **to him** that is to Abraham himself, a sinner like the rest of us (cf. Rom. 3:10, 23); **for righteousness** that is to say, a perfect standing with the Almighty."[14]

What is Paul's point in appealing to this Genesis passage? It is to demonstrate what he has been showing throughout this entire epistle: that faith is the singular means through which a person receives righteousness and is made right with God. In the original context of Genesis 15, we see that God promised Abraham that one would come from his own body and be his heir (Isaac). Although Abraham had been childless for over eighty years and his wife Sarah had never conceived and was well past childbearing, nevertheless, he still believed that God would perform what He promised. He believed that the Lord could and would do what He said, which means that he took God at His Word, and, as a result, God gave him a right standing with Himself.

To state the matter another way, in Genesis 15:6, where we are told that "Abraham believed God and it was credited to him for righteousness," nothing at all is mentioned there about him working in order to be made right with the Lord. There is nothing about his law-keeping or circumcision as the grounds of this. No, Abraham was justified by faith *alone*. Faith was the singular channel through which he was counted righteous.[15] Moreover, it is important to stress again that this entire matter of Abraham being justified by faith in God and in His Messiah who was to come (for Abraham rejoiced to see Jesus' day, *and he saw it and was glad*, cf. John 8:56) is crucial to Paul's whole argument in this chapter, because Abraham's status was so significant to the minds of the Jewish people.[16]

Obs. 2- (vv. 4-5) That as Paul continues to contrast the way of works-righteousness with the way of faith-righteousness, he draws out two theological implications from what he just said about Abraham's justification in Genesis 15. Here in using an illustration from the business world, he writes first in verse 4:

---

10 Grk. aorist, active, verb.

11 The sense of this word in the Hebrew text is that Abraham said *amen* to God!

12 Grk. aorist, active, verb.

13 This word is a bookkeeping term that can be applied metaphorically to human beings, Kruse, p. 206. Abraham believed God and so God, as it were, took out his ledger and put it down to Abraham's account as righteousness.

14 It is important to note that Paul ends this chapter by quoting this text once again in verse 22. He does this as something of a bookend to his whole argument at hand, highlighting its importance to us.

15 Sadly, scholars tell us that some rabbis used Genesis 15:6 to say that Abraham was justified by works, his faith being a work. However, such individuals forget that faith before God is never considered in the Bible to be meritorious. No, faith is a gift from God, not that which is inherent in the believer (Eph. 2:8).

16 It is striking to consider that in the Genesis 15:6 passage we have appearing together for the very first time in the Bible the three words of *belief, accounted,* and *righteousness,* and when they do, they are all connected with Abraham.

Now to him who works[17] (i.e., the moralist, the self-righteous man, the religionist, the externalist) or is working and laboring so as to gain acceptance with God on his own merit which is not possible because of human sin; **the wages** or payments; **are not counted** or credited; **as** or in accord with; **grace** or free mercy and kindness (for if this were the case, grace would no longer be grace, Rom. 11:6!); **but** or instead; **as** or in accord with; **debt** that is, one's due, something owed to them.

Now in taking this metaphor and applying it to the gospel, Paul says secondly in verse 5:

But to him who does not work, that is, does not rely on his own supposed goodness and effort before God; does not try to earn his salvation through self-effort; **but believes**[18] or is believing and completely trusting, in contrast to the one who works in verse 4; **on Him who justifies** or declares not guilty; **the ungodly**[19] that is, those who are lost, and wretched, as we all are by nature and practice; **his faith** that is, his trust in Christ who died for the ungodly (5:6), which is the reason why God can justify them; **is accounted** or reckoned to his account; **for righteousness** again, a right standing with God.

What is Paul's argument? He is making the case that salvation is not a reward of one's works, but rather a free gift of God in Christ by faith alone.[20] He is showing that when a man works for a living and gets his paycheck at the end of the week, he is entitled to what he has earned from his employer. He does not get paid as a gift of grace. No, he gets paid what he is justly owed. He gets paid out of what is due him for his services rendered. This earning of salvation is not God's gospel way of justifying sinners. It never was and never will be. Thank God for this, for if in the final analysis we are rewarded according to our deeds, which are always full of sin, we would be damned forever.

In contrast to verse 4, again, Paul says in verse 5 (as shocking as it would seem to the Jews who were works-oriented people, cf. Luke 18:9-14), that to the one who does not work, but believes on Him, that is, God and His promises in Christ to save us, his faith is accounted to him for righteousness. He says to the one who does not try to work for his salvation, but instead abandons all hope in himself ever to be made right with God by what he does or what he is, to this one who believes, his faith is the means through which God accepts and justifies him.[21] This is what Abraham found, for as Paul will go on to show in

---

17 Grk. present, active, participle.

18 Grk. present, active, participle.

19 What a joy it is to know that God saves the ungodly. He takes wretched and ruined people and regards them as righteous because of His Son. He takes slaves of sin and makes them servants of Christ when they come to God broken and in need of the forgiveness that Jesus offers in the cross. Yet those who see themselves as commendable before God in and of themselves, will never be justified in God's sight. These are the self-deceived and self-righteous, of whom Jesus said in Luke 5:32: I have not come to call the righteous, but sinners, to repentance.

20 Paul speaks about this topic plainly again in Rom. 6:23.

21 Faith is always the means whereby we receive the righteousness of God in Christ,

the following verses, he was accepted by God through faith alone, long before he ever obeyed the Lord by being circumcised or by keeping any of His commandments.

Obs. 3- (vv. 6-8) That having established the fact that the patriarch Abraham was reckoned as righteous before God by means of faith alone and not works, Paul, knowing that according to the Old Testament Scripture, "by the mouth of two or three witnesses everything should be established," now brings forth another witness in this regard: King David.[22] In doing this, he puts the final nail in the coffin of a works salvation scheme to demonstrate the truth of justification by faith alone. Having spoken of Abraham, and now David, he sets forth as his examples the two most illustrious people in the Old Testament. Thus, I agree with Bible commentator Robert Haldane when he wrote:

> Nothing could be so well calculated to convince both Jewish and Gentile believers, especially the former, how vain is the expectation of those who look for justification by their own works. Abraham was a patriarch eminently holy, the head of the nation of Israel, the friend of God, the father of all who believe, in whose seed all the nations of the world were to be blessed. David was a man according to God's own heart, the progenitor (ancestor), of the Messiah, his great personal type, and a chosen and anointed king of Israel. If, then, Abraham had not been justified by his works, but by the righteousness of God imputed to him through faith, and David, speaking by the Spirit of God, had declared that the only way in which a man can receive justification is by his sin being covered by the imputation of that righteousness, who could suppose that it was to be obtained by any other means?[23]

Paul quotes Psalm 32:1-2, a psalm in which David wrote:

just as or even as, a subordinate conjunction backing up and adding to what Paul just wrote concerning Abraham; **David also** or in the same way; **describes** or speaks about; **the blessedness** that is, the happiness; **of the man** that is, human kind in general, whoever they are, man, woman, boy or girl; **to whom God imputes** or credits and puts to his account; **righteousness** or approval with Himself, and divine favor; **apart** or completely separate; **from works:**

"**Blessed** or, more literally, extremely happy and joyful;[24] *are those whose lawless deeds* or violations and transgressions; **are forgiven** literally canceled out and sent away (being removed from us legally and judiciously as far as the east is from the west, never to be remembered anymore). **And whose sins are covered** that is, thoroughly concealed

---

but again, it is never meritorious. The only thing that is meritorious in connection to faith is the object that it lays hold of, namely, God in Christ in the gospel.

22 It is worth noting how very different these two men were and yet God's method of justifying them was the same.

23 Haldane, pp. 159-60.

24 Without negating the fact that as Christians we will experience various heartaches, sadness, and trouble in the world (cf. Acts 14:22), we should nonetheless be a joyful people in Christ, because all of our sins have been forgiven through Him.

from God's divine justice and buried away once for all time, never to be brought into judgment in the final day; **Blessed** *is the* **man to whom the** LORD **shall not** or by no means, under no circumstances, a double negation in the Greek text; **impute** or credit to his account; **sin** or offense."

What is so striking in the words of this psalm is that David wrote them *after* he had grievously sinned by committing adultery with Bathsheba and by setting up the murder of her husband Uriah. The point is, as he is writing about the blessedness of those whose lawless deeds and sins are forgiven and the happiness of the man to whom the Lord shall not impute sin—he is the man! He is writing *personally* not *theoretically*. He is writing *practically* about what he experienced in his own life.[25] David found that God graciously credits righteousness and forgiveness to individuals through faith and not on account of works. This is the heart of the gospel! This is the core of the good news that the God of heaven grants to believing sinners.

Suggested applications from the text for the church:

1- Since according to the Bible, there has always been only one way of salvation which is through faith alone, on the ground of Christ alone, because of God's grace alone, and every believer before or after Abraham and David has known this, we must totally reject any system of belief that teaches otherwise.

2- Since according to the Bible, the gospel that we believe has been saving people throughout history, including Abraham and David, then we ought to have great confidence in proclaiming it.

3- Since according to the Bible, all of a Christian's lawless deeds have been completely forgiven in the courtroom of heaven, having been wiped away once for all time because of Jesus, we are to rejoice greatly. And so, do we? Do you?

Suggested application from the text for the non-Christian:

1- Would you be blessed? Would you have all of your lawless deeds forgiven? Then learn what Abraham and David learned, namely, that our works cannot save us, but the substitutionary work of Christ can. Believe on this Christ and His accomplished work alone and be saved.

Text: Romans 4:9-12

General theme: The Case of Abraham (II). The explanation of justification by faith alone apart from works.

Homiletical outline of the verses:

A. The questions asked: [9]*Does* this blessedness then *come* upon the circumcised *only*, or upon the uncircumcised also? For we say that faith was accounted to Abraham for righteousness. [10a]How then was it accounted? While he was circumcised, or uncircumcised?

---

25 Cf. Ps. 51.

B. The answers given: [10b]Not while circumcised, but while uncircumcised. [11]And he received the sign of circumcision, a seal of the righteousness of the faith which *he had while still* uncircumcised, that he might be the father of all those who believe, though they are uncircumcised, that righteousness might be imputed to them also, [12] and the father of circumcision to those who not only *are* of the circumcision, but who also walk in the steps of the faith which our father Abraham *had while still* uncircumcised.

Summary of section: In these opening verses, we have the apostle moving from the "how" of justification to the "when" of justification.[26] Here, as Moo says, "Paul notes another significant aspect of the reckoning of Abraham's faith for righteousness—it took place before he was circumcised."[27] In dealing with circumcision once again (see Rom. 2:25-29), the apostle shows us how much the Jews needed teaching regarding this matter. For them, circumcision was essential for one to be made right with God, for as we are told in Acts 15:1: "And certain men came down from Judea and taught the brethren, 'Unless you are circumcised according to the custom of Moses, you cannot be saved.'"[28] Paul once again deals with this issue plainly, setting the record straight in the first part of these verses. He shows that Abraham was justified *before* he was ever circumcised (cf. Gen. 15; Gen. 17), which means he was justified while still uncircumcised and thus he could be the father of *all* believers, both Jews and Gentiles. The result? Again, Moo answers wisely when he says,

---

26 As a side note here, we could also say that Paul is dealing with the error of *salvation by ceremony*, whether it be the ceremony or rite of circumcision or anything else we might think we can partake of that makes us right with God apart from faith alone in Christ alone. MacArthur wisely notes on page 250 of his commentary on Romans that "the relevance of this basic truth for our own day is great. Although few people, even Jews, now believe that circumcision brings salvation, countless millions firmly trust in some other form of religious ceremony or activity to make them right with God. Among those claiming the name of Christ, the Roman Catholic Church is by far the greatest offender. Throughout its history, it has taught salvation by human works, made effective through the mediation of the Catholic priest." I would also mention the so-called "Churches of Christ" and any other heretical group that teaches salvation by water baptism or baptismal regeneration. Such teaching is a complete denial of the gospel as found in Romans, and everywhere else in the Bible. It denies what Paul has said several times in this chapter alone (v. 3, 5, 6, 9, 10, 11), namely, that God credits righteousness to the believing sinner by faith alone and not anything he does with his own hands.

27 Moo, NIGNT, p. 267.

28 Concerning this matter, MacArthur notes in his commentary, pp. 247, 248: "Most Jews in New Testament times were thoroughly convinced that circumcision was not only the unique mark that set them apart from all other men as God's chosen people but was also the means by which they became acceptable to God. Many Jews believe that salvation was based on their obedience to God and being circumcised, and that, therefore their eternal security rested in that rite. In his commentary on *The book of Moses*, Rabbi Menachem wrote, 'Our Rabbins [rabbis] have said that no circumcised man will ever see hell' (fol. 43, col. 3). The *Jalkut Rubem* taught that 'Circumcision saves from hell' (num. 1) and the *Midrash Millim* that 'God swore to Abraham that no one who was circumcised should be sent to hell'" (fol. 7, col. 2).

Paul thereby makes clear that it is not necessary to be Jewish to become a member of the people of God. Faith *alone*—apart from works (4:3-8), apart from circumcision (4:9-12)—is sufficient to gain entrance into Abraham's spiritual 'family.' It becomes evident here that Abraham is much more than an 'example' of faith. As the recipient and mediator of the promise, his experience becomes paradigmatic for his spiritual progeny.[29]

Exegetical & Practical Insights:

Obs. 1- (vv. 9-12) That having just spoken in verses 7-8 of this chapter about our receiving justification before God through faith alone, with the positive result of God imputing perfect righteousness to us in Christ, covering all of our sins, now Paul asks:

Does **this blessedness then** that is, the blessedness of salvation, this spiritual richness and happiness that Paul just spoke of; *come* **upon** or pertain to; **the circumcised** (the Jews); *only,* **or upon the uncircumcised** (the Gentiles); **also? For we say**[30] that is, Paul and his missionary companions have constantly been announcing; **that faith was accounted to Abraham for righteousness. How** or in what way, an interrogative particle; **then** or therefore; **was it accounted** (to him)? **While he was circumcised** (while a Jew); **or uncircumcised?**

Paul answers and says:

Not while circumcised, but[31] **while uncircumcised. And he received the sign of circumcision**, or the distinguishing outward mark or token by which something is known (which sign of circumcision was the sign of the Abrahamic covenant between Abraham and God as we are told in Genesis 17:11);[32] **a seal**[33] or the signet, stamp and sanction; **of the righteousness of faith which Abraham had while still uncircumcised** **that** the conjunction stating the purpose uniquely for Abraham; **he might be**[34] and continue to be; **the father** that is to say, the spiritual father; **of all** each and every one; **who believe, though they are uncircumcised** (Gentile believers); **that** the conjunction stating a second purpose for this; **righteousness might be imputed to them also, and the father** (once more, the spiritual father); **of circumcision** (Jewish believers), **to those** or the specific ones; **who not only** *are* **of the circumcision** that is, those who are of Abraham's natural seed; **but** or rather; who **also:** or indeed;[35]

---

29 Moo, NIGNT, p. 267.

30 Grk. present, active, verb.

31 The use of *ouk alla* is a very emphatic negation in the Greek text setting forth a strong contrast, "stating unequivocally that God declared Abraham righteous before he was circumcised." Harvey, p. 110.

32 Ibid.

33 Circumcision did not *confer* righteousness to Abraham; it simply *confirmed* it. In a similar way, baptism *does not confer* anything to us, rather it *confirms* that we have faith in Christ, which, according to the New Testament, is the prerequisite to one being baptized. See for example Acts 2:41; 8:37; 10:43-48; 16:31-34; 18:8.

34 Grk. present, active, verb.

35 Lloyd-Jones helpfully says here in his commentary on Romans, p. 186: "We have to be careful as we face this verse because it is one that can be, and often has been, misunderstood and misrepresented. It is taken by some to mean 'both those who are

walk[36] (Abraham's spiritual seed); or are walking;[37] **in the steps of** or in line with and in conformity to; **the faith** that is, the belief in God and His Messiah who was to come;[38] **which our father Abraham** *had while still* **uncircumcised.**[39]

These questions and answers from Paul would have been especially important for his Gentile Roman readers to understand, since in the previous verses he just spoke of two Jewish believers who had been saved.

The question is: What about the Gentiles? Are they included in Abraham's spiritual fatherhood of faith? Are they part of his true posterity? The answer is clear: they are, for just as God accepted Abraham by faith while uncircumcised, God accepted them in the same manner.[40] Thus, he is the great spiritual ancestor of all true believers, both Jews and Gentiles alike. This was Abraham's unique position given to him in redemptive history. He is the spiritual father of both the circumcised and the uncircumcised who trust in Jesus the Messiah. These are his spiritual descendants. They are part of his family, which makes them part of the true people of God. As Spurgeon said:

> The historical argument is a forcible one. The blessing was not given to Abraham as a circumcised man, but as a believing man; and hence it comes also to all of us who believe. What a mercy it is that there is, in this sense, no distinction between Jew and Gentile now! I hate that plan

circumcised together with those who believe'. It cannot possibly mean that, for if so, it would be tautology and simply a partial repetition of what had already been said. No! What the apostle is saying here is that Abraham is also the father in the faith of those who belong to the circumcision if they have also believed. Notice the way in which he puts it. He does not say simply that Abraham is the father of the circumcision and leave it at that, for the good reason that a person can be circumcised and yet be lost. He therefore adds the qualification that the circumcised person to whom he is referring is one who has also believed, one who walks in the same faith as Abraham. In other words, Abraham is not only the father of all the uncircumcised who believe, but also the father of all the circumcised who walk in the same faith as Abraham. It is very important to remember the negative that Paul has put into this verse in this way."

36 Grk. present, active, participle.

37 A well-known military term meaning "to march in file." Rogers and Rogers, p. 323.

38 These verses raise an important question: who are Abraham's true seed? The answer of the Bible is plain. It is all who have believed on Jesus the Messiah and have been saved by Him, for as Paul says in Galatians 3:29: "If you are Christ's, then you are Abraham's seed and heirs according to the promise." This is why of course Jesus said to the unbelieving Jews in his day in John 8:37: "I know that you are Abraham's descendants" (his physical offspring). But then he went on to say, "if you were Abraham's children (his spiritual seed, those who like him had faith in Christ, John 8:56), you would do the works of Abraham." And so simply stated, according to the Bible, Abraham has two seeds, one physical (Hebrew Israel), one spiritual (all believers in Christ made up of both Jews and Gentiles). Consequently, in speaking specifically about the nation of Israel as a whole, Paul says in Romans 9:6: "for they are not all Israel who are of Israel."

39 In commenting on this verse McClain says in his commentary on Romans, p. 116, "Verse 12 makes it clear that circumcision alone will not suffice for the Jew. He must also walk in the steps of his Father Abraham. Paul takes the Jew away from external rites and sends him back to that faith which Abraham exercised. Abraham had righteousness; he got it by faith, apart from works and apart from human ordinances."

40 Cf. Gal. 3:29.

of reading the Scriptures in which we are told, when we lay hold of a gracious promise, "Oh, that is for the Jews." "Then I also am a Jew, for it is given to me." Every promise of God's word belongeth to all of those who have the faith to grasp it. We who have faith, are all in the covenant, and are thus the children of faithful Abraham; so be not afraid, ye who are the true seed, to take every blessing that belongs to your father Abraham and to all the seed.[41]

Suggested applications from the text for the church:

1- We must never forget that there is a big difference between regeneration by the Holy Spirit and participation in a ritual.

2- We must never forget that while rituals (or sacraments, or ordinances of the church, i.e., baptism and the Lord's Supper), cannot save, for they are powerless to do so, we must be careful not to undervalue them because they are true means of grace for New Covenant believers, just as circumcision was for the Old Covenant community of faith.

3- We must never forget that since Abraham is the spiritual father of all true believers, Jews and Gentiles alike, then all true believers are brethren, members of the same spiritual household, purchased by the same blood of Christ, filled with the same Holy Spirit (whoever they are, wherever they are from, regardless of their age, race, education, income, etc.). Thus, we are to treat them accordingly. Do we? Do you?

Suggested application from the text for the non-Christian:

1- Would you become a spiritual child of Abraham? Or, more importantly, would you become a spiritual child of Jesus? Then trust in Jesus alone for your soul's salvation, for there is no other way to be saved (Acts 4:12).

Text: Romans 4:13-25

General theme: The Case of Abraham (III). The expansion of justification by faith alone apart from works.

Homiletical outline of the verses:

A. The promise: [13] For the promise that he would be the heir of the world *was* not to Abraham or to his seed through the law, but through the righteousness of faith. [14] For if those who are of the law *are* heirs, faith is made void and the promise made of no effect, [15] because the law brings about wrath; for where there is no law *there is* no transgression. [16] Therefore *it is* of faith that *it might be* according to grace, so that the promise might be sure to all the seed, not only to those who are of the law, but also to those who are of the faith of Abraham, who is the father of us all [17] (as it is written, "I have made you a father of many nations") in the presence of Him whom he believed—God, who gives life to the dead and calls those things which do not exist as though they did;

---

41 Spurgeon, pp. 35, 36.

B. The person: [18] who, contrary to hope, in hope believed, so that he became the father of many nations, according to what was spoken, "So shall your descendants be." [19] And not being weak in faith, he did not consider his own body, already dead (since he was about a hundred years old), and the deadness of Sarah's womb.

C. The perseverance: [20] He did not waver at the promise of God through unbelief, but was strengthened in faith, giving glory to God, [21] and being fully convinced that what He had promised He was also able to perform. [22] And therefore "it was accounted to him for righteousness."

D. The participation: [23] Now it was not written for his sake alone that it was imputed to him, [24] but also for us. It shall be imputed to us who believe in Him who raised up Jesus our Lord from the dead, [25] who was delivered up because of our offenses, and was raised because of our justification.

Summary of section: In the opening words of this third section of this chapter, Paul shows us that the grand promise that Abraham would inherit "the world" (that is, the renewed, renovated and restored world in the age to come with all who, like him, have faith in Christ, and will reign with Christ forevermore), was not obtained because he observed the law, but because he believed God to the saving of his soul.[42] As the apostle continues to develop his instruction concerning *the case of Abraham* with reference to justification by faith alone apart from works, he tells us what Abraham, along with his heirs, will receive on the last day through Jesus, who Himself was promised "the nations for an inheritance and the ends of the earth for His possession" (Ps. 2:8). Further, in verses 18-22, the apostle portrays the great faith of Abraham toward God and His Word. Finally, in verses 23-25, Paul takes us back to his main theme in this chapter, showing us that just as Abraham received the gospel promise of salvation, having Christ's righteousness imputed to him (v. 3, 22), so also "it shall be imputed to us who believe in Him who raised up Jesus our Lord from the dead" (vv. 23-24).

Exegetical & Practical Insights:

Obs. 1- (vv. 13-17) That as Paul opens another implication of the spiritual fatherhood of Abraham for all believers, he writes:

For the conjunction connecting us to and confirming what Paul just wrote of Abraham in the previous verse and shows that just as circumcision was not the means of Abraham being made right with God,

---

42 This is a great gospel promise that is spoken of in many places in the Bible though not specifically in the book of Genesis. One day all true believers will inherit the earth as Jesus said in Matthew 5:5 (see also Eccles. 1:4). One day, this sin-laden, Satan-inhabited planet where we now dwell, shall be regenerated and renovated, when Christ returns it back to its original state before the fall. At that time, the ungodly will be cast out and only God's true people will populate this planet enjoying life with Him, and in it righteousness will dwell. What a glorious future prospect this is for us. Even so, come, Lord Jesus! (cf. 2 Pet. 3:10-13; Rev. 21). For further discussion on this topic, I point the reader to *The End Times Made Simple* by Sam Waldron, *The Bible and the Future* by Anthony Hoekema, and *The Promise of the Future* by Cornelis Venema.

neither was his law-keeping,[43] **the promise** that is, the promise of the world to come for Abraham and his spiritual children: **that he would be the heir**[44] or the inheritor; **of the world**[45] this planet; *was* **not to Abraham or to his seed** or natural offspring; **through** or by means of; **the law** that is, the condition of keeping its requirements; **but** or on the contrary; **through** or by means of; **the righteousness of faith.**

For the conjunction is explanatory, giving the reason why the promise must be through faith rather than through the law;[46] **if those who are of the law** (those who are trying to be justified before God by their obedience to it, cf. Rom. 10:3); *are* **heirs** (unbelieving Jews); **faith is made void**[47] or stands empty and invalid; **and the promise made of no effect**[48] or continually nullified, since to try to receive from God through law-keeping stands in opposition to believing God; **because** the conjunction is causal, giving the confirmation for the previous verses; **the law brings about**[49] or constantly produces; **wrath** not salvation, not justification, not gospel blessings, but wrath (cf. Rom. 1:18), that is to say, punishment and condemnation from God because people do not and cannot keep it fully as they are required to do; **for** the word explaining why the law brings wrath;[50] **where there is no law,** i.e., no moral code (Paul speaks here about a general principle); *there is* **no transgression** or a going beyond a specified boundary so as to "cross the line." And so while of course, wrongdoing is still wrongdoing, with the presence of

---

43 Of course this could not be the case anyway since Abraham lived hundreds of years before the Mosaic Law was ever given, some 430 years as Paul says in Galatians 3:17.

44 I realize that some commentators take the words that Abraham would be the "heir of the world" simply as Paul saying that Abraham would have many spiritual descendants both from the Jews and Gentiles and that he would be a channel of blessing to all the nations of the world. However, I think the apostle's language here includes much more. Abraham always had his sights higher than such earthly matters, for as the writer of Hebrews says in Hebrews 11:9-10: "By faith he dwelt in the land of promise as in a foreign country, dwelling in tents with Isaac and Jacob, the heirs with him of the same promise; for he waited for the city which has foundations, whose builder and maker is God."

45 We might wonder where this promise was made to Abraham in the Old Testament. While we know that God would make him a great nation and that all of the families of the earth would be blessed through him (Gen. 12), and that his descendants would be as the stars of the heaven and as the sand which is on the seashore (Gen. 22), and that he would inherit the land of Canaan which ultimately pointed to heaven (Heb. 11:10), in Genesis chapters 12 and 22, however, nothing is said about him being the "heir of the world." So how then should we understand Paul? We should understand him as taking all of this data about Abraham and his spiritual posterity as speaking in an eschatological sense with reference to the worldwide implications of the gospel for believers in the final day. The point is, Abraham (and all his spiritual seed, who, like him, have believed on Christ alone for salvation), will inherit the world, not just Canaan, because this is what Christ promised to His people who will reign with Him forever in the new heavens and the new earth (cf. Rev. 21).

46 Harvey, p. 115.

47 Grk. perfect, passive, verb.

48 Grk. perfect, passive, verb.

49 Grk. present, middle, verb.

50 Moo, NICNT, p. 276.

a stated law, violations of it become a transgression.[51] **Therefore** or on account of this; *it* (the promise to Abraham and us of the eternal world, the promise of salvation and everything in between); *is* **of faith** (not of works, but by believing as Paul has been stating); **that** or for the purpose that; *it might be* **according to** or in line with; **grace,**[52] that is, God's free, and unmerited favor shown to us who do not deserve it;[53] **so that** stating a second purpose; **the promise** (that is the promise of verse 13); **might be sure** or strong, and certain;[54] **to all the seed** (both believing Jews and Gentiles); **not only to those who are of the law** (believing Jews); **but** or rather; **also to those who are of the faith of Abraham** (believing Gentiles); **who is**[55] and continues to be in the spiritual sense; **the father of us all** (converted Jews and Gentiles); (**as** or just as; **it is written**[56] or stands written, indicating its abiding results;[57] **"I have made**[58] or forever appointed and constituted, a present state of actuality;[59] **you a father of many nations"**)[60] **in the presence** or in the sight; **of Him** (God); **whom he** (Abraham); **believed—God, who gives life** or quickens; **the dead and calls**[61] **those things which do not exist as though they did**[62] or more literally, the things not existing, as existing;[63]

---

51 An example of this would be if someone did not want you to park on his driveway. To park there would already be wrong because it is not your property. However, if the owner of the driveway put up signs saying, "No Parking" or "Private Driveway," and you were to continue doing it anyway, these violations against it would bring the wrongdoing to a heightened level of offense. Moo therefore says that Paul is not claiming that there is no "sin" where there is no law, but, in almost a "truism" that there is no deliberate disobedience of positive commands where there is no positive command to disobey. Or as Calvin puts it: "He who is not instructed by the written law, when he sins, is not guilty of so great a transgression as he is who knowingly breaks and transgresses the law of God" (cf. Rom. 5:13).

52 Cf. 3:24.

53 Lloyd-Jones says, "We can sum it up like this. It has to be of faith, otherwise it cannot be by grace," pp. 196-97.

54 A legally-guaranteed security. Rogers and Rogers, p. 323.

55 Grk. present, active, verb.

56 Grk. perfect, passive, verb.

57 Paul, as the good biblical scholar, reinforces the fact that Abraham is our spiritual father by quoting from the Bible at Genesis 17:5.

58 Grk. perfect, active, verb.

59 Interesting to note that back in the original text in Genesis chapter 17, God did not say to Abraham, I *will* make you the father of many nations. No, he said I *have* (past tense) made you this, even though at the present time this was not so for Abraham. So in God's mind, this was a done deal, and Abraham believed exactly what God had told him. There is a lesson here for all of us to learn from Father Abraham: that the just shall live by faith. We walk by faith and not by sight, trusting and believing what God has said to and about us in His Word, even though things may not seem to be that way. "Faith is the substance of things hoped for, the evidence of things not seen" (Heb. 11:1).

60 Not just the Jews.

61 Grk. present, active, participle.

62 Grk. present, active, participle.

63 While certainly this phrase is true with reference to salvation, for only He could give life to the spiritually dead (cf. Eph. 2:1-6), in this context, it seems best to interpret these words as speaking about God giving life to Abraham's dead body, that is to say, making his and Sarah's reproductive systems alive as Paul proceeds to say in verse 19 of this chapter.

Obs. 2- (vv. 18-19) That as Paul in these verses gives us something of a biographical sketch of the patriarch Abraham, he does so by saying with reference to him:

who, contrary to or beyond all; **hope** that is to say, above all reasonable expectation that one would have in a particular situation;[64] **in** or more literally upon; **hope** "hoping against hope"[65] **believed**[66] or was fully convinced concerning the divine promise told him; **so that** or the result being; **he became the father of many nations** Jews and Gentiles alike; **according to** or in line with; **what was spoken, "So shall your descendants be."**[67]

And not being weak or feeble; **in faith** (cf. 21), that is, in the exercise of faith in the promise that God had made to him; **he did not consider** or regard (literally, he did not put down in his mind); **his own body already dead** or completely ineffective **(since he was about a hundred years old), and the deadness** or barrenness; **of Sarah's womb**.[68]

What is the apostle doing here? He is developing his portrait of Abraham's character, describing his active faith in God. He is highlighting the fact that Abraham believed God's promise that he would be the "father of many nations" even though there were no observational grounds of this due to his advanced age. He continued to believe this even though he had no children at the time when the promise was given back in Genesis 15:5, and even though the promise would not actually come to pass for another fourteen years or so. The point is, despite how things looked or felt or were (considering the infertility of his and Sarah's bodies), Abraham held fast to God's promise, trusting that his descendants would be as numerous as the stars of heaven. As Calvin says: "When Abraham had no ground for hoping, he yet in hope relied on the promise of God; and he thought it a sufficient reason for hoping, that the Lord had promised, however incredible the thing was in itself."[69] Or as Matthew Henry says,

> All the arguments of sense, and reason, and experience, which in such cases usually beget and support hope, were against him; no second causes

---

64 Or we could say: Who without reason for hope, in faith went on hoping. Thiselton says, "Abraham believed God, when it was hardly a human possibility to hope," Thiselton, p. 120. Chrysostom said, "Past hope according to nature, but in hope of the promise of God" (as quoted in Gifford, p. 106).

65 Rogers and Rogers, p. 324.

66 Grk. aorist, active, verb.

67 Abraham heard God's Word to him and he rested in it completely. May we do the same!

68 In commenting on these verses, McClain writes in his commentary on Romans, pp. 118, 119: "Here is a man a hundred years old, with his wife almost as old, and yet God comes to him and says, 'Abraham your seed shall be as the stars of heaven'! Now this man believed God in spite of circumstances, and that is the kind of faith God wants us to exercise. The devil can always raise up circumstances and say, 'Now, look here and look there. God can't fulfill His promise.' But never mind the circumstances. Believe God, 'who quickeneth the dead and calls the things that are not as though they were.'"

69 Calvin, pp. 176, 177.

smiled upon him, nor in the least favored his hope. But, against all those inducements to the contrary, he believed.[70]

Obs. 3- (vv. 20-22) That as Paul continues his sketch of Abraham's great faith, he goes on to write:

He did not[71] **waver at** or vacillate, being a "double-minded man,"[72] literally the word means to be divided or at odds with; **the promise of God through unbelief** or want of faith or doubt;[73] **but** or rather, or in contrast to this; **was strengthened**[74] or made strong, and empowered, (by God); **in faith**[75] that is to say, with respect to his faith;[76] **giving glory,** i.e., honor and praise as an outcome; **to God;**[77] **and being fully convinced** not barely believing that God would do this for him, but being thoroughly assured; **that** or the thing which; **He** (the Lord); **had promised; He was**[78] **also able** or mighty; **to perform** since nothing is impossible for Him.[79] **And therefore** or because of this or for this reason, a conjunction of summary; *"it was accounted to him for righteousness"* or a right standing with the Lord."[80]

---

70 Henry, p. 316.

71 Harvey points out that the negative *ou* here establishes a strong contrast with *alla* in the next clause, p. 120.

72 Cf. James 1:8

73 We might wonder how it is that Paul could say in truth that Abraham did not waver at the promise of God concerning his promised son to him because when we look back in the Old Testament we see that at times it looked like Abraham had lapses in faith regarding this issue (in Genesis chapter 16, he became impatient for God to fulfill His promise concerning Isaac and so he listens to his wife's suggestion to have a son through Hagar. And then in Genesis 17:17, we are told that Abraham fell on his face and laughed when God told him that he would have a son through Sarah). What do we do with these seeming contradictions? Was Paul mistaken in our text? Are there contradictions in the Bible? The answer is no to both questions. When Paul speaks in our passage about Abraham's great faith not wavering at the promises, he is, as Douglas Moo rightly says in *Encountering the Book of Romans*, p. 80, "... generalizing. He is not claiming that Abraham's faith was perfect or that he never had any doubts whatsoever. Rather, his point is that Abraham, despite some very human doubts, always came back in the end to faith in the promise of God. He, therefore, is an outstanding biblical example of a person who walked by faith rather than 'by sight.'" Or as Leon Morris says in his commentary on Romans, p. 213, "Paul is referring to the settled attitude that endured all this, not to Abraham's initial reaction. The unbelief was momentary, the faith was consistent. Abraham was assured that God could and would do what he had promised."

74 Grk. aorist, passive, verb.

75 The phrase shows us that indeed he always had true faith, although at times, it fluctuated as with all of us.

76 Moo, NICNT, p. 285.

77 MacArthur says, "Godly faith glorifies God; the One who gives faith receives all the credit." MacArthur, p. 265.

78 Grk. present, active, verb.

79 I believe Abraham could have such strong faith in God ultimately because he knew something about His *character* (unfailing and consistent), and His *capability* as the great I am (all-powerful and able to do all His holy will).

80 Note how the apostle brings us back once again with this quotation from Genesis 15:6 to his main point regarding Abraham in this chapter, namely, that he was justified by faith alone and not by works, as something of a bookend to the opening words of cf. 4:3.

Obs. 4- (vv. 23-25) That in these final verses, Paul now applies all that was true for Abraham to the lives of believers living in every generation, showing us its timely relevance. This is one of his main points in this chapter for all that he has been saying.

Heinrich Bullinger remarks,[81]

> The Holy Spirit in the Scriptures did not wish merely to demonstrate how Abraham alone was justified, but rather how every race of mortal men and women can be justified. For Abraham is the father and model of all believers. What do those who contend with Paul in speaking of their works, who are under the law and not under grace, have to say to this? For we hear that both the old way of being justified and that of our own is one and the same. Therefore, even if Abraham was faithful and already under grace, it was still by none of his merits but only by faith that he was justified. Therefore, it must be that all Christians are justified by nothing else but faith or by grace.[82]

Here Paul answers the personal "so what" question for all believers, both Jews and Gentiles, when he writes:

Now it was not written for or on account of; **his sake alone** or only; **that it was imputed to him, but** or quite to the contrary; **also for** or on account of **us** that is, all of us who are Christians, Abraham's spiritual offspring, Paul included. **It shall be imputed to us who believe**[83] or are believing;[84] **in** or better translated *upon*, that is, upon God for salvation in His Son, not merely *in* Him as the Creator (cf. Rom. 1:19-21) or one who exists; but upon; **Him** for redemption; **who raised up;**[85] **Jesus our Lord from:** or out of; **the dead, who was delivered up**[86] or handed over,[87] once for all time, never to be repeated again; **because** or on account of; **our**

---

81 Bullinger was a second-generation Swiss Reformer after Zwingli (1491-1551).

82 *Reformation Commentary on Scripture, Romans,* p. 260.

83 Grk. present, active, participle.

84 MacArthur is right when he says in his commentary on Romans, p. 267, "faith is the necessary condition for salvation."

85 Grk. aorist, active, participle.

86 Grk. aorist, passive, verb.

87 We should ask the question, who was it that delivered up our Lord? Was it Jewish leadership? Judas? The Romans? Or Pontius Pilate? Well, in part, yes. But much more vital than this in connection to the gospel is that ultimately it was God the Father himself who delivered Christ up to the cross, so that there He could take our sins upon Himself and be punished in our place, so that we could go free. For as Paul says in Romans 8:32, God "did not spare His own Son, but delivered Him up for us all." This was God's predetermined plan even from before the foundation of the world (cf. Acts 2:23; 4:27-28). Note finally, then, that God, being the ultimate author of the death of Christ, does not at all mean that He can be charged with murder since He is not the author or the approver of sin. Rather, God sinlessly used the murderous sin that was already in the hearts of our Lord's enemies to bring about His great plan of redemption. For a helpful discussion of this matter, I direct the reader to chapter three in the 1689 London Baptist Confession of Faith concerning God's decree, especially paragraph one.

offenses[88] not His offenses, because he had none,[89] but for our offenses, that is, our sins, and our heinous crimes against God and His law; **and was raised,** i.e., raised up by God the Father;[90] **because** or on account of; **our justification** that is, because we were in fact justified through Jesus' work on the cross for us (cf. Rom. 3:24). And so while Jesus' resurrection does not grant our justification, it does clearly attest to it.[91]

As this chapter winds down, it is important to note that these last three verses are a wonderful summation of the gospel. It makes sense that Paul would write about the gospel at this point in this epistle, especially in view of all that he has previously written. Here is a beautiful synopsis of the good news, clearly showing how sinners can be made right with God through the substitutionary death and resurrection of Jesus Christ our Lord. The apostle says that as it was for Abraham, so also it shall be for us who believe. Perfect righteousness will be given to us by imputation—not by our works, but through faith in the God, who delivered up Jesus for our offenses and raised Him up for our justification. In summarizing the heart of this chapter, McClain says:

> Now then, what is the conclusion of the matter? Did Abraham get anything by works? Not a thing! He got his righteousness by faith; his inheritance by faith; his posterity by faith. Abraham did not get a single thing by human works, and yet the Jews look back to Abraham and said, "We are walking in his steps," while trying to keep the law. At this point Paul not only answers the argument, but he also turns it against them. This is the great faith chapter of the Bible. The word *faith* or believe occurs no less than 16 times in this chapter. Everything that Abraham had was by faith.[92]

Suggested applications from the text for the church:

1- Rejoice because God in Christ by grace has made you the true spiritual seed of Abraham, and thus all of his spiritual blessings in Jesus are your blessings as well.

---

88 Here Paul could be thinking of the clearest Old Testament passage in this regard which speaks of the death of the Lord Jesus Christ, namely, Isaiah chapter 53.

89 Cf. 2 Cor. 5:21; 1 Pet. 2:22; 1 John 3:5.

90 As the aorist, passive, verb signifies.

91 As Lloyd-Jones rightly says, "The resurrection is the proclamation of the fact that God is fully and completely satisfied with the work that His Son did up on the cross," *Romans*, p. 244. Or as J. V. Fesko says in his commentary on Romans published by Reformation Heritage Books regarding this matter on p. 111: "What is the connection between Christ's resurrection and our justification? His resurrection means that God the Father accepted His sacrifice and that Christ conquered death. If Christ were still in the grave, then His sacrifice would have been null and void. The wages of sin is death; hence, Christ's continued state in death would have signaled that His sacrifice was ineffective and that at some point in His life He transgressed the law of God. But blessedly, the opposite is true: Christ fulfilled every jot and tittle of the law, He suffered the penalty of the law, and therefore the Father and the Spirit raised Him from the dead. Christ's resurrection was the Father's reversal of the false verdict that had been passed over His Son. And therefore, Christ's resurrection is intimately tied to our justification. Without the public declaration of His righteousness in His resurrection confirming His perfect obedience to the law, we would have no legal ground for our own justification" (cf. Rom. 1:4; 1Tim. 3:16).

92 McClain pp. 119, 120.

2- Recall that while the spiritual blessings of Abraham are yours in Jesus, the patriarch's committed faith in God is to mark your life as well (cf. Rom 1:17). Like him, you must have an ever-abiding trust in the Lord who never fails his people, regardless of what the situation might be.

3- Remember that like Abraham, trusting in the Word of God without wavering is pleasing to the Lord and brings His blessings.

4- Recollect that when your faith is strengthened by God as you go through trials, you, like Abraham, are to give all the glory to God.

Suggested application from the text for the non-Christian:

1- Know that the God of the Bible is still the God who "gives life to the dead." Consequently, He in Christ, can, this very day, quicken and save your never dying soul, as you go to Him for this. Flee therefore to Him, who is the God of sovereign, life-changing grace.

ROMANS
CHAPTER FIVE

Text: Romans 5:1-11

General theme: The Seven Blessed Benefits of Justification

Homiletical outline of the verses:

    A. The Christian has peace with God: [1] Therefore, having been justified by faith, we have peace with God through our Lord Jesus Christ

    B. The Christian has access to God: [2a] through whom also we have access by faith into this grace in which we stand.

    C. The Christian has hope in God: [2b] and rejoice in hope of the glory of God.

    D. The Christian has growth from God: [3] And not only *that,* but we also glory in tribulations, knowing that tribulation produces perseverance; [4] and perseverance, character; and character, hope.

    E. The Christian is loved by God: [5] Now hope does not disappoint, because the love of God has been poured out in our hearts by the Holy Spirit who was given to us. [6] For when we were still without strength, in due time Christ died for the ungodly. [7] For scarcely for a righteous man will one die; yet perhaps for a good man someone would even dare to die. [8] But God demonstrates His own love toward us, in that while we were still sinners, Christ died for us.

    F. The Christian is preserved through God: [9] Much more then, having now been justified by His blood, we shall be saved from wrath through Him.

    G. The Christian is reconciled with God: [10] For if when we were enemies we were reconciled to God through the death of His Son, much more, having been reconciled, we shall be saved by His life. [11] And not only *that,* but we also rejoice in God through our Lord Jesus Christ, through whom we have now received the reconciliation.

Summary of section: In verses 1 to 11 of this chapter, the apostle now moves from the specific need (Rom. 1, 2), way (Rom. 3), and illustration (Rom. 4) of justification by faith alone to its striking benefits for us who believe.[1] In this splendid section, he enumerates the blessings that come to those who have a right standing with God because of Jesus. Concerning these opening verses, John Murray triumphantly comments, "We cannot escape the notes of assurance and exultation—'we exult in the hope of the glory of God' (vs. 2), 'we glory in the tribulations' (vs. 3), 'hope does not make ashamed, because the love of God is shed abroad in our hearts' (vs. 5), 'much more then, having been justified now in his blood, we shall be saved through him from the wrath' (vs. 9), "we glory in God through our Lord Jesus Christ'" (vs. 11)." Murray asks, "What are the consequences flowing from justification which invoke such unrestrained rejoicing and assurance? Examination of the text will show."[2]

Exegetical & Practical Insights:

Obs. 1- (vv. 1-5) That as Paul begins to describe the gospel privileges we possess as justified sinners, at the very top of the list, he says first:

Therefore[3] or consequently, a word of conclusion, summing up all that he has been saying concerning the topic of justification in the previous words; **having been justified**[4] or acquitted once for all time,[5] instantaneously, not in stages;[6] **by** or upon the exercise of;[7] **faith**[8] not our own sin-tainted, unfinished works, but by a complete reliance on Jesus' finished work in our place as the only ground of our acceptance with

---

1 Martin Luther said concerning this entire chapter, "In the whole Bible there is hardly another chapter which can equal this triumphant text." Luther, Romans, p. 88.

2 Murray, p. 158.

3 This verse can be outlined in this way: The channel of the believer's peace (1a); The character of the believer's peace (1b); The conduit of the believer's peace (1c).

4 Grk. aorist, passive, participle.

5 The topic of justification is still very much on Paul's mind. He just concluded the last chapter by mentioning this word. In verse one of Romans chapter 5, Paul is looking back concerning this matter. Then he moves forward in his thinking into chapter 8 to highlight more benefits that come from it. Moo has a helpful discussion about this "backward and forward" look in his commentary on Romans, NICNT, pp. 290-95. He concludes on page 295 by saying, "In chaps. 5-8, then, Paul invites the Christian to join with him in joyful thanksgiving for what the gospel provides — a new life given to God's service in this life and a certain, glorious hope for the life to come. At the same time Paul is continuing his defense of the gospel. His opponents (probably Jewish, mainly) attacked his message as proclaiming no more than a legal fiction—a 'declaration' of a relationship that cannot be proved and which effects no change!— and requires no change!—in this life and which offers no security for the day of judgment. Quite the contrary, Paul affirms, the person who has experienced the gospel as the justifying activity of God (cf. 1:17) is assured of finding that gospel to be truly "God's power for salvation" (cf. 1:16)—power for dedicated Christian service in this life and for deliverance from all the forces of evil and of judgment in the next."

6 The aorist tense highlights the past completed action and the passive voice highlights that it is God who justifies us and not we ourselves.

7 Paul makes it clear that justification before a holy God happens at the time of faith and not before. And certainly not from all eternity as some have falsely taught (cf. Eph. 2:1-9).

8 Note that we are not justified before God by our "faithfulness" to Him which would equate to works salvation. Rather, we are justified/declared not guilty before Him "by faith" alone in what His Son has done for us.

God; **we**[9] **have,**[10] that is, we have now and will have and as a continual possession;[11] **peace**[12] or harmony,[13] i.e., no more hostility (similar to the Hebrew word *shalom*);[14] **with God** or more literally, facing God, the preposition "with" emphasizing the warm fellowship that we have with Him since we are now blameless in His sight; **through** or by means of, the word expressing the agency or the avenue through whom peace with God is realized; **our Lord Jesus Christ.**[15]

Obs. 2- That as Paul speaks about the next blessed benefits that come to believers, he writes:

through whom also, that is, through Jesus our only mediator; **we have**[16] or we have now and will continue to have forevermore;[17] **access**[18]

---

9 Notice how Paul includes himself, which means that even though at one time he was a religious Jew, he did not have true peace with God until he was justified by faith in Christ. This is the only way a person, religious or not, could ever truly find rest in his soul with reference to his relationship with his Maker.

10 Grk. present, active, verb.

11 Although some important Greek manuscripts state this verse as saying, "let us have peace with God" (the different readings being the difference of one Greek letter, the omicron or omega), I agree with most scholars that Paul is not giving an exhortation, but rather stating a proposition. This fits better with the overall context of these words, telling us in short that, having been justified by faith, we have (as a present-day reality) peace with God.

12 The word carries the idea of binding together that which was separated.

13 This, of course, assumes that before the believer was converted there was hostility between him and God (cf. 1:18, 8:7 and Isa. 48:22). Also, note, that in the Greek text, the word peace is placed first in its clause for the sake of emphasis. Lastly, it should be noted that while first and foremost, the peace which is spoken of here is a reference to the *objective peace of God* that we have with Him as a settled fact, because Jesus reconciled us to God through His sacrifice and bloodletting on the cross on our behalf (cf. 11 and Col. 1:20), this does not negate the *subjective peace of God* which we experience in our hearts when we are saved (cf. Phil. 4:7). Frank Thielman helpfully ties these two thoughts together when he writes, "This peace is foremost a cessation of hostility between God and believers, as the emphasis on salvation from God's wrath and on reconciliation with God in 5:9-10 demonstrates (cf. 8:6-7), but Paul probably also intended to express a subjective understanding of peace with God. This is a peace stemming both from the happiness that comes to those whose lawless deeds God has forgiven (4:7-8; cf. Ps 32:1-2) and from the love that, as Paul will say shortly, God has poured into the hearts of believers (5:5; cf. 5:8). Calvin, then, was not incorrect to say that peace here means 'serenity of conscience, which originates from the awareness of having God reconciled to oneself.' Paul means more than this, but not less." Thielman, pp. 263, 264.

14 The Puritan John Trapp said that this peace is, "A blessed calm lodged in our consciences like as when Jonah was cast overboard there followed a tranquility." John Trapp, p. 498. Spurgeon said concerning this peace, "We have peace, we know that we have, we enjoy it, it is not a thing of the future, we have peace, a deep calm like that which came to the disciples when Christ hushed the winds and the waves to sleep." Spurgeon, p. 54.

15 Notice how Paul begins this chapter not only by saying that all we have as Christians comes through "our Lord Jesus Christ." But he also speaks about this in verses 2, 9, 10, 17, 19, and then, like a reinforcement to this entire chapter, he ends by mentioning it one last time in verse 21.

16 Grk. perfect, active, verb.

17 Note the two perfect tense verbs in this verse denoting past accomplishment, with present, ongoing, permanent results.

18 This word appears only two other times in the Pauline corpus: Ephesians 2:18; 3:12. Several commentators note that the word was used in secular Greek to describe one who was introduced into the presence of a higher authority such as a king. Concerning this

(not only peace v.1), but the right, or freedom to joyfully enter God's holy presence as His children; **by faith into,** i.e., into the experience and realm of; **this grace,** that is, this free, saving, merciful and justifying grace and favor of God which has caused us to know peace with Him; **in which we stand,**[19] that is, stand in a present and perpetually state because of our past justification in Christ (v.1); **and rejoice**[20] or habitually boast[21] in the proper sense of the word,[22] not merely in our hearts, but also with "the grateful and confident utterance of the lips"[23] and this "on the highest level";[24] **in** or upon; **hope**[25] or in the complete confidence[26] or "happy certainty;"[27] **of the glory of God,**[28] which is to say, the future glory of God in the age to come,[29] which, as McDonald says means,[30] "that we joyfully

---

matter, Lloyd-Jones says, "It is generally agreed, and I am certainly in full agreement, that a better word here would be the word 'introduction'. It is roughly the same idea as we have in the word which we use about people being 'presented' at Court. That helps to explain the access. You have no access to the Queen as you are. Certain formalities and procedures are essential before that becomes possible. There is a way whereby you can have access — you can be 'presented at Court', you have an introduction. The apostle is still working on the same idea. There was a time when we were in sin, when we had no right of entry, no entrée into the presence of God, no access. We had no introduction, we had not been presented, and we could not come into His presence. But now, he says, as the result of this justification by faith, and through the Lord Jesus Christ, we have our introduction, we are introduced into 'this grace wherein we stand.'" Lloyd-Jones says further, "What our Lord Jesus does is to introduce us to God. We cannot go to Him as we are. We are sinful and vile and polluted. Our righteousness is but as 'filthy rags', says the Scripture. We have nothing to commend us, our clothing is unworthy and unsuitable, and we have no right in our own name to ask to be allowed to enter in. But here comes One who has a right of access and entry Himself, who having dealt with our sins can take us and present us to God the Father. He introduces us. It is the Lord Jesus Christ who does it all — 'By whom also....'" Lloyd-Jones on Romans, pp. 31-22.

19 Grk. perfect, active, verb.

20 Grk. present, middle, verb.

21 The same verb is also used in v. 3 and v. 11, although in v. 3 it is translated "glory."

22 Contrary to the arrogant, false boasting that we are told of in 2:17, 23, etc. Speaking of proper Christian boasting Haldane says, "The Christian should speak nothing boastingly, so far as concerns himself; but he has no reason to conceal his sense of his high destination as a son of God, and an heir of glory. In this he ought to exult, in this he ought to glory, — and, in obedience to His Lord's commandment, to rejoice, because his name is written in heaven. The hope of eternal salvation through the grace of our Lord Jesus Christ cannot but produce joy; for as there can be no true joy without such a hope, so it carries with it the very essence of joy." Haldane, p. 187.

23 E. F. Gifford, p. 110.

24 Murray, p. 161.

25 Paul will speak more about hope in verses 4 and 5 and pick it up once again in 8:20; 12:12; 15:4; 15:13.

26 The word "hope" in the Bible is not a "hope so" wishful thinking kind of attitude. The word does not express doubt or uncertainty as the word can in English. Simply stated, the word "hope" in the Scripture carries the idea of a confident expectation.

27 Phillips translation.

28 The glory of God which we fell short of as non-Christians (Rom. 3:23).

29 Cf. 1 Pet. 5:1.

30 McDonald, p. 1696.

look forward to the time when we will not only gaze on the splendor of God, but will ourselves be manifested in glory."[31]

In commenting on the last part of this verse, Spurgeon summarizes,

> Our joy is in the past and the present in some measure, but it is still more in the future: "We rejoice in the hope of the glory of God." We have three windows — the one out of which we look back with gratitude upon the past, the one out of which we look with joy in the present, and the one out of which we look with expectation upon the future.[32]

And not only *that*,[33] which is to say, that as Christians, we not only have this third blessed benefit of the confident expectation of the glory of God; **but** the strong contrast emphasizing that Paul's rejoicing is not "limited to that which is glorious, but that it also includes that which is inglorious;"[34] **we also glory** or constantly rejoice (same word as found in verse two); **in** the preposition denoting sphere; **tribulations**[35] or extremely difficult afflictions[36] (note the plural use of the word), which Morris observes, "does not refer to minor inconveniences, but to real hardships;"[37] **knowing**[38] not necessarily feeling or seeing, but being fully persuaded; **that** the conjunction identifying "the content of that knowledge"[39] and giving the rationale for the foregoing statement; **tribulation produces**[40]

---

31 Both matters are spoken of in Scripture (8:17, 18; Jude 24 cf. John 17:5; 22).

32 Spurgeon, p. 59.

33 Note that the exact Greek construction appears in verse 11a.

34 Earnest R. Campbell, *A Commentary of Romans* (Silverton, OR: Canyonview Press, 1987), 153.

35 It is important that the apostle dealt with the matter of tribulations and the Christian response to it, especially for those living in Rome in the first century which was a very anti-Christian context (cf. Rom. 12:12). Derek Thomas informs us that within a decade of this letter being written "many of the Roman Christians to whom the letter was addressed were brutally slaughtered in the Roman amphitheaters. The original readers of Romans faced a terrible dilemma: they could deny Jesus or profess Him knowing that, if they did, they face certain death. Tacitus' account, written half a century later, and with unmeasured contempt for Nero, is often cited: 'Mockery of every sort was added to their deaths. Covered in the skins of beasts, they were torn by dogs and perished, or were nailed to crosses, or doomed to the flames.'" Derek Thomas, *How The Gospel Brings Us All The Way Home*, p. 141.

36 Several commentators note that the Greek word here for "tribulations" basically means to squeeze or to crush or to apply pressure. They also say that in Paul's day the word referred to crushing associated with the extraction of oil from olives or getting juice from grapes.

37 Morris, p. 220.

38 Grk. perfect, active, participle.

39 Harvey, p. 129.

40 Grk. present, middle, verb.

or generates and grows in us;[41] **perseverance**[42] a word which is derived from a preposition prefixed to a verb and literally means to remain under or steadfastness.

The apostle tells us here that by the power of the Spirit, his trials fashioned in him a gospel fortitude giving him the ability to press on in life despite problems. His hardships produced a deep persevering grace and thus, although he was "hard pressed on every side," he was "not crushed." Although he was "perplexed" he was "not in despair" (2 Cor. 4:8).[43] He continues:

and perseverance, **character**[44] or we could say "proven character,"[45] the word referring to approval that comes from testing[46] or that which "has been proven by trial;"[47] **hope.**

By restating the word "hope" here, Paul now comes full circle from where he started back in verse two. He tells us that instead of trials and tribulations weakening the Christian's hope, by God's grace toward us, they actually are the soil out of which hope grows. Like Abraham of old, "in hope," we believe God.[48]

Moo aptly remarks,

---

41 Paul was rejoicing *not* because he enjoyed tribulations, but *because* he knew that in God's goodness to him, his trials would not break him, but make him a better believer. He rejoiced in his hardships, which were many (cf. 2 Cor. 11:22-33), because he realized that all of these things were, as one has said, "the shaking of the torch that it might blaze brighter." Paul rejoiced in his difficult circumstances because he knew that God, in His mysterious providence, would work all things together for his good (Rom. 8:28). As Christians we should know the same and take comfort.

42 Cf. James 1:2-3; Job 23:10.

43 McClain challengingly remarks: "Here is a principle by which you can discover the difference between a true child of God and one who is just a professed child of God. It is by the effect that tribulation has on him. In the life of a true child of God, tribulation brings him close to God, makes him steadfast, makes him more patient. There is another sort of person. Troubles come into the life and instead of bringing him close to God, tribulation makes him hard. If tribulation comes into your life and does not make you more tender, if it does not make you love Him more, then it would be wise to examine your life in order to discover what the trouble is. In justified people, tribulation works steadfastness and patience" (McClain, pp. 127, 128). Lloyd-Jones says, "Tribulations also work in this way, that they not only bring out God's love to me, but at the same time test my love to God, and prove it. If I only love God when everything is going well, I am not truly Christian. It is the man who can say with Job, 'Even though he slay me, yet will I trust him', who is truly Christian" (Lloyd-Jones, p. 70).

44 Scholars tell us that in Paul's day this term was used of testing precious metals such as silver or gold in order to demonstrate their purity and "character." In speaking along these lines, Peterson says, "As when precious metals are passed through fire to remove baser metals, so a greater Christ-likeness may emerge from the refinement of suffering." Peterson, p. 234.

45 Compare Paul's commending comment concerning Timothy in Philippians 2:22.

46 One has said that "Fiery trials make golden Christians" and that "The hotter the fire, the purer the gold!"

47 Mounce, p. 135. Mounce also says on the same page (footnote 103) concerning this term that "No occurrence of this word has been found before Paul, and in the NT it is only used by him."

48 Cf. James 1:12.

Sufferings, rather than threatening or weakening our hope, as we might expect to be the case, will, instead, increase our certainty in that hope. Hope, like a muscle, will not be strong if it goes unused. It is in suffering that we must exercise with deliberation and fortitude our hope, and the constant reaffirmation of hope in the midst of apparently "hopeless" circumstances will bring ever deeper conviction of the reality and certainty of that for which we hope.[49]

Again, Spurgeon summarizes,

You cannot make an experienced Christian without trouble. You cannot make an old sailor on shore, nor make a good soldier without fighting. Here is that window of hope again, standing at the back of our experience, we look out of the window, and what God has done for us is a token of what God will do for us.[50]

Now a conjunction summarizing what Paul began to speak of in verse two; **hope** (the hope of partaking of and seeing the glory of God); **does not disappoint**[51] or will never deceive,[52] disgrace,[53] embarrass or put to shame;[54] **because** the causal conjunction giving the reason and rationale for this; **the love**[55] or goodwill[56] and gospel generosity; **of God**[57] toward us

---

49 Moo, NICNT pp. 303, 304.

50 Spurgeon, p. 55.

51 Grk. present, active, verb.

52 The Greek preposition prefix to the verb literally means "to bring shame down on."

53 Moo remarks, "Paul wrote Romans in a culture often focused on honor and shame. To be shamed was one of the worst things that could happen to you" (Moo, *Encountering the Book of Romans*, p. 87).

54 Perhaps Paul, being the Jewish scholar that he was, had Psalm 22:5 or Isaiah 54:4 in his mind at this point.

55 Leon Morris astutely notes that, "Paul's emphasis on love is strangely overlooked; the apostle is often seen as somewhat pugnacious and argumentative, while John, by contrast, is 'the apostle of love.' But the word love occurs 75 times in Paul out of a New Testament total of 116 (nine in Romans). For this apostle love is supremely important, and he comes back to it again and again." Morris, p. 221. Also, note that Paul brings up this topic again in 8:39 as something of a bookend to this theme. This is the first time that the word *love* appears in Romans. It will show up next in verse 8 of this chapter.

56 This phrase "the love of God" is to be understood as an objective genitive, i.e., *His* love for us, *not* our love for Him.

57 The "love of God" is that which a person receives through the agency of the Holy Spirit in their innermost beings when they trust in Christ alone for salvation. This experience of God's love assures them that they know God, are known by Him, and have entered into a special, redemptive, fatherly love relationship with the triune God which will last throughout eternity. Further, this love of God is objectively based on Jesus' work for us and, subjectively, on the application of the work of the Holy Spirit in us. When it is experienced in truth, it produces at least three things: 1- a love back to God (1 John 4:19), 2- a desire to keep God's Word (1 John 2:5), and, 3- a love for the brethren (1 John 3:17). Greg Nichols defines this love for Christians as God's "Special affection for them, his unique attachment to them, and His irrevocable commitment to benefit them in accordance with His unconditional covenant with them. Thus, His redemptive affection under the new covenant consists in His disposition and sworn commitment to bless His people in Christ with every spiritual benefit. This redemptive affection in Christ embraces every individual Christian and the entire Christian Church, the society of the saved" (*Lectures in Systematic Theology, Volume 1, Doctrine of God*, by Greg Nichols, p. 442).

His people in Christ, being not "a vague, mystical feeling that 'somebody up there' cares about humanity, but the deep-seated conviction that a personal God really loves you as an individual;"[58] **has been poured out,**[59] i.e., poured out at conversion,[60] and continues to stand poured out as a permanent state all of our days,[61] the word denoting "both abundance and diffusion";[62] **in** the preposition denoting the realm where the love of God has been poured; **our hearts:** that is, our innermost beings, the core of who we are; **by** or through, the preposition denoting the means or agent by which this is done;[63] **the Holy Spirit**[64] **who was given to us,**[65] that is, given to us as a gift from God[66] at conversion, in the fullness of His person, once for all time.

What is Paul saying here? It is this: The great future hope that we have as believers in partaking of and seeing the glory of God is not an empty hope or a vain promise because the love of God has *already* been poured out into our innermost beings by the Holy Spirit.

This eschatological reality is based upon the internal reality that we have been regenerated. It is rooted in the present fact that we have become partakers of the Holy Spirit, who was given to us in salvation. In other words, the proof of the former is based on the latter. Since we have experienced one now, we will most surely experience the other one later. What extraordinary news this is then for us who are true Christians! If we have been made new creations in Christ Jesus by God's sovereign work through the power of the gospel, we can have complete certainty that our futures are bright.

In capturing the essence of these opening verses, Haldane helpfully remarks:

---

58 McDonald, p. 1696.

59 Grk. perfect, passive, verb.

60 Cf. Joel 2:28; Acts 2:17-18, 33; Titus 3:6.

61 William Hendriksen comments: "Moreover, God's love is not rationed out drop by drop. On the contrary, by the Holy Spirit it is 'poured out' into the hearts of the redeemed; in other words, it is supplied freely, abundantly, copiously, lavishly, as is true with respect to God's gifts in general" (Hendriksen, p. 171). Hodge concurs and says "the love of God does not descend upon us as dew in drops, but as a stream which spreads itself abroad through the whole soul, filling it with the consciousness of his presence and favor. And this inward persuasion that we are the objects of the love of God, is not the mere result of the examination of evidence, nor is it a vain delusion, but it is produced by the Holy Ghost" (Hodge, p. 135). Spurgeon says, "When Mary, the sister of Lazarus, anointed the feet of Jesus with the very costly ointment of spikenard, 'the house was filled with the odour' of it, and in a similar fashion the love of God perfumes every part of our nature." Spurgeon, p. 52.

62 Rogers and Rogers, p. 325.

63 Observe how the preposition highlights the personality of the Holy Spirit, for He is a person who works, not merely a force which operates. He is the one who enables us to know the love of God in our hearts (Cf. Rom. 15:13 with reference to the topic of hope).

64 The Holy Spirit has also been mentioned in 1:4 and 2:29.

65 Grk. aorist, passive, participle.

66 As the passive participle suggests.

What fullness and variety of instruction and consolation are contained in the first five verses of this chapter! The work of the Father, of the Son, and of the Holy Ghost is exhibited, all severally acting, as God alone can act, in the various parts of man's salvation. The righteousness of God is imputed to the believer, who is therefore justified, and pronounced by the Judge of all the earth righteous. As righteous, he has peace with God, and free access to him through Jesus Christ; and being thus introduced into the favor of God, he stands in the justified state, rejoicing in hope of future glory. Being justified, he is also sanctified, and enabled to glory even in present afflictions. He enjoys the indwelling of the Holy Ghost, through whose Divine influence the love of God is infused into his soul. Here, then, are the peace, the joy, the triumph of the Christian. Here are faith, hope, and love, the three regulators of the Christian life.[67]

Obs. 3 – (vv. 6-8) That as Paul expands on the wonder of God's love for us in Jesus, "which secures for believers every benefit previously mentioned,"[68] he writes:

For the explanatory conjunction giving the reason why God's divine love has been poured out in our hearts in salvation as spoken of in the last verse;[69] **when we were**[70] the present tense participle highlighting a continual state; **still without strength,** that is, completely powerless and helpless to save ourselves or do ourselves any good, morally or spiritually speaking, since we were dead in trespasses and sins (Eph. 2:1);[71] **in due time,** that is, at "the right time" or in the "fullness of time" (Gal. 4:4-5), when in God's divine program He ordained for this to come to pass; **Christ,**[72] that is, Jesus the Messiah; **died,**[73] that is, He actually gave up His life, willingly substituting Himself;[74] **for**[75] the preposition denoting

---

67 Haldane, p. 191. Cf. 1 Cor. 13:13.

68 Peterson, p. 236.

69 Osborne says, "Paul here builds on the emphasis in verse 5 regarding God's love poured out into our lives by plumbing the depth of this love and explaining that its true meaning is exemplified in the sacrificial death of Christ for us" (Osborne, p. 139).

70 Grk. present, active, participle.

71 The London Baptist Confession of Faith of 1689 (updated version for the twenty-first century by Founders Press) makes this point plain when it says, concerning the topic of *free will* in chapter 9, paragraph 3: "Humanity, by falling into a state of sin, has completely lost all ability to choose any spiritual good that accompanies salvation. Thus, in their natural state are absolutely opposed to spiritual good and dead in sin, so that they cannot convert themselves *by their own strength* or prepare themselves for conversion."

72 In the Greek text the word Christ is emphatic, highlighting the significance of this monumental event.

73 Grk. aorist, active, verb. The aorist tense verb pointing to this once-for-all, historical fact. The active voice pointing to Christ's willingness to do this.

74 Concerning what Paul says here, that Christ died, Lloyd-Jones says, "This is most important. Do you notice what he picks out? It is not the life, it is not the teaching, it is not the miracles; but 'Christ died'. This is what he emphasizes in order to show and to prove God's love toward us. This is how God commends His love toward us, in that Christ not only came but that He died," (Romans, p. 108).

75 Paul will use this same preposition three more times in the next two verses. For a discussion on the meaning of the preposition, see Leon Morris on *Romans*, p. 222, footnote 20.

"for the sake of" or "on behalf of;" **the ungodly**[76] not for good people, or the morally upright, because in God's eyes there are none (Rom. 3:12). Quite literally, He died for the God-*less*. He died for the *un*-holy. In love, sinless Jesus died for sinners.[77] He died "the just for the unjust, that He might bring us to God" (1 Pet. 3:18). He died "for our sins, that He might deliver us from this present evil age, according to the will of God the Father" (Gal. 1:4). What wonderful news this is! What marvelous mercy! Geoffrey B. Wilson summarized this thought nicely when he wrote:

> The amazing character of God's love thus lies in the fact that it was exercised towards those whose natural condition was absolutely repugnant to his holiness. And it is only as we are taught by grace to acknowledge this unpalatable truth that the boundless nature of God's love begins to dawn upon us.[78]

Kruse further elaborates:

> What distinguishes the love of God for humanity more than anything else is that 'Christ died for the ungodly', those who actually violate God's expectations of humanity, those whom Paul will shortly describe as God's 'enemies' (5:10). It was not unknown in the ancient world that someone might lay down his/her life for a friend, but to do so for one's enemy was unheard of. Within the Jewish context it was well known that one might die out of loyalty to the law (2 Macc 7:9; 8:21) or on behalf of the nation (John 18:14), but to die for the ungodly, those whose wickedness attracts the wrath of God (1:18), was unthinkable.[79]

For the conjunction explaining how truly extraordinary and otherworldly[80] God's love for us in Christ is and this by comparing it with "two examples from human experience;"[81] **scarcely** or hardly, literally with great difficulty, since people typically love their own lives so much, over and against the lives of others "and the yearning to live is strong;"[82] **for** or on behalf of, or in the place of; **a righteous man,** that is, one who, although he was a sinner before God, nonetheless, he had a strong regard for justice and was law-abiding in character, being marked by integrity of conduct; **will one die; yet perhaps** or possibly, but not likely; **for a good man,** which is to say, someone who was known for being kind, and generous[83] "governed by love; he goes the second mile; asked for his cloak

---

76 That Christ died for the ungodly shows us that there is hope for all who seek Him in truth (cf. 4:5).

77 There are three simple gospel truths found in this passage that must always be remembered by us: 1- Christ died for the ungodly; 2- Christ died when we were still without strength; 3- Christ died at the appointed time.

78 Wilson, pp. 82, 83.

79 Kruse, p. 234.

80 Hendriksen calls it, "Both unprecedented and unparalleled." Hendriksen, p. 173.

81 Harvey, p. 131.

82 Mounce, p. 136.

83 Perhaps a philanthropist.

he gives his coat also;"[84] **someone would even dare,** that is, muster up enough courage and confidence; **to die** (although the chances are slim).

But God, that is, in contrast to human love which is "very reticent to lay down its life even for good causes and law-abiding people,"[85] with divine love, the Father;[86] **demonstrates**[87] or is constantly showing and displaying as an endless proof of the matter, as a portrait of the greatest love in all the world;[88] **His own love,**[89] that is, love which comes directly from Himself, "springing from the depths of the Divine nature; not called into existence by any goodness in its object;"[90] **toward us** (believing sinners); **in that** or because; **while we were still**[91] or at that time, referring to our ongoing, former state of being; **sinners,** i.e., not good people, but those who were missing God's standard of righteousness, morally depraved, corrupt and ungodly enemies (v. 10); **Christ** (the centerpiece of heaven, the Redeemer whom God sent into the world, sinners to save, cf. 1 Tim. 1:15); **died,**[92] i.e., suffered the death penalty and God's judgment, being cut off from the land of the living (cf. Dan. 9:26); **for,** that is, in the place of, or for the sake of; **us.**

Hendriksen remarks:

> The unique character of this love becomes apparent when we consider the fact that while for a righteous person a man will scarcely die — though, by rare exception, it might after all happen for such a good person someone would dare to die, God, on the other hand, demonstrates his own love in this remarkable way, namely, that while we were still in our helpless and sinful state Christ died for us.[93]

Spurgeon concurs:

> And that is the glory of his love. While we were rebels against his government, he redeemed us. While we were far off from him by wicked works he sent his Son to die and bring us nearer. Free grace, indeed, was this—not caused by anything in us, but springing freely from the great heart of God.[94]

---

84 Lloyd-Jones on Romans, pp. 120, 121.

85 D. Stuart Briscoe, *The Preacher's Commentary Romans Vol. 29*, p. 113

86 What man hardly does for the best of men, God did for the worst of men.

87 Grk. present, active, verb.

88 The death of Jesus in the place of believing sinners is God's clearest and constant way of saying "I love you!" It is as Leon Morris rightly says, "The cross is an event of the past but it keeps showing the love of God." Morris, p. 224, footnote 27.

89 The reflexive pronoun "His" stated for the sake of emphasis (cf. 8:39; John 3:16; 1 John 4:10).

90 Gifford, p. 113.

91 Grk. present, tense, participle.

92 Grk. aorist, active, verb.

93 Hendriksen, p. 172.

94 Spurgeon, p. 50.

Obs. 4 - (vv. 9-11)[95] That as Paul sets forth the sixth blessed benefit of our justification which is, that we are preserved by God in Christ from His own coming wrath,[96] he writes:

Much more then[97] or better translated "much more therefore"[98] or "to a far greater extent" the words comparing the "greater to the lesser"[99] which is to say, that "since God has already removed the greatest obstacle to future glory, the guilt and enmity of believers, then he will surely see to it that believers will be spared from his eschatological wrath;"[100] **having now been justified,**[101] that is, declared not guilty and accounted positively righteous in God's sight the moment we believed on Christ[102] (and this, as an act of His free grace toward us as the Greek passive voice highlights); **by** or in connection with, or perhaps more broadly, "at the cost of," the preposition denoting means or instrumentality; **His blood,**[103] that is, Jesus' sacrificial blood, upon which God bases our justification; **we shall be saved,**[104] i.e., preserved and delivered in the

---

95 Everett F. Harrison remarks in *The Expositor's Bible Commentary,* p. 60, concerning verses 9-11 of this chapter that, "Whereas the preceding paragraph dealt with the depth of the love of God as seen in the cross, the present section moves on to declare the height of that love, its refusal to stop short of effecting final and everlasting salvation in which the enmity created by sin has been completely overcome.' In these words, Paul lets us know that all Jesus did for us at Calvary is completely effective in getting us to heaven. As one has said, "If He didn't give up on us when we were at war with Him, what could we do to make Him give up on us now that we are at peace with Him?"

96 According to Scripture, God saves us *from* Himself, *for* Himself and *by* Himself through Jesus.

97 This is the first time that this comparative construction "much more then" is used in Romans. It is used four times and they are all found in this chapter (vv. 10, 15, 17, 20). These statements have been called the five "much mores" and they all highlight the glories of the gospel of God's Grace.

98 This type of arguing was popular among the rabbis in Paul's day.

99 Spurgeon says, "This is a fine piece of argument, and strictly logical. If, when we were sinners, Christ died for us, will he let us be condemned now that he has washed us in his precious blood? Is it possible that, after dying for us, he will let us fall from grace, and perish after all? That will never be" (Spurgeon, p. 53).

100 Schreiner, p. 262.

101 Grk. aorist, passive, participle.

102 Cf. 5:1.

103 Paul spoke of Jesus' blood back in 3:25. Jesus' blood signifies that Christ's death was sacrificial in nature and it was the ransom price paid to God in order to satisfy His divine justice against us so that our sins could be righteously pardoned before Him (cf. Lev. 17:11; Matt. 26:28; Eph. 1:7; 2:13; Col. 1:20; 1 Pet. 18, 19; Heb. 9:23; Rev. 1:5; 5:9).

104 Grk. future, passive, verb.

final Day of Judgment;[105] **from wrath**[106] or God's judicial anger against our sin; **through** or by; **Him:**[107] again, Jesus, who is "the mediator who turns aside the ultimate expression of God's wrath."[108]

For the conjunction giving further exposition of verse 9; **if** or since "the construction implies the truth of the supposition;"[109] **when we were enemies**[110] not friends, but haters of and hostile toward the God of the Bible through wicked works in our pre-Christian days (cf. Col. 1:21); **we were reconciled,**[111] that is, we were once for all time rejoined; **to God,**[112] (from whom we were once separated because of our sins against Him, cf. Isa. 59:1, 2), and rendered no longer opposed, the moment we put our faith in Jesus;[113] **through** the preposition stating the means of our reconciliation with God; **the death of His Son**, (i.e., Jesus' substitutionary

---

105 Clearly in these words and many others we see the eternal security of the believer. Donald Grey Barnhouse expounds it like this: "The principle is that God never does anything by halves. He did not set out to save us and then leave us to our own devices. Here is the security of the believer, and no honest student of the Scriptures can make anything else out of it. If God moved toward us when we were helpless, ungodly sinners, His enemies, will He be deterred by that helplessness, that ungodliness, that enmity? Let us reiterate that God has never been astonished by anything in us. He did not find anything good in us. He did not love us because we were lovely or lovable, but because His nature is love. This being the case, we know that He will carry the whole plan of redemption through to its logical conclusion" (Barnhouse, Romans, p. 188). For a detailed exposition of this doctrine, see *The London Baptist Confession of Faith* chapter 17 on *The Perseverance of the Saints*.

106 Cf. Rom. 2:5, 8.

107 Cf. John 3:36; 1 Thess. 1:10; 1Thess. 5:9; Rev. 6:16, 17.

108 Peterson, p. 239.

109 Morris, p. 225.

110 First we were called *ungodly* (v. 6), and then *sinners* (v. 8), but now *enemies* in (v. 10). An enemy is not merely one who falls short of being someone's friend, but an enemy is an opponent who is actively hostile to someone or something. He is a combatant at war; he is a foe on the field.

111 Grk. aorist, passive, verb. The work of reconciliation with God through the cross of Christ is a completed action as the aorist tense highlights. Also, the passive voice verb highlights that God is the specific author of our reconciliation with Himself.

112 This is the first time the word reconciled/reconciliation appears in this book, and to be sure, reconciliation between God and man is at the heart of the gospel. This Greek word literally means "to change or to exchange" or "to make otherwise" and thus, in the sense that it is being used here, it refers to a change from enmity to friendship; from hostility to harmony. Longenecker insightfully notes: "Somewhat surprisingly, the language of reconciliation is not found in any of the other writings of the N.T. Nor does it appear in any of the extant Christian literature of the second century. It has often, therefore, been considered not only distinctive to Paul among the earliest extant Christian writers but also to have been 'coined by him'" (Longenecker, p. 568).

For a detailed exposition of this subject, see Leon Morris' classic book: *The Apostolic Preaching of the Cross*, pp. 214-50.

113 Reconciliation is a relational term. On our part, it happens with God when we repent of our sins against Him and by faith look to Christ for salvation. On God's part, He reconciles us to Himself by providing an atonement for our sins against Him, and this through the sacrifice of His Son which cancels out all our sins, as Paul says in the previous words. Douglas Moo concurs when he says, "Reconciliation in Paul has two aspects, or 'moments': the accomplishment of reconciliation through Christ on the cross (cf. 2 Cor. 5:19: 'in Christ God was reconciling the world to himself') and the acceptance of the completed work by the believer" (cf. 2 Cor. 5:20b: 'We beseech you on behalf of Christ, be reconciled to God'). Moo, NICNT, p. 311.

work in our place, cf. Col. 1:19, 22); **much more,** that is, "all the more" or "much more easily," in contrast to the removal of sin by our Lord's death; **having been reconciled**[114] or having been put in a right relationship with God since the sin opposition has been obliterated and a new relationship established; **we shall be saved,**[115] that is, we shall be saved or kept unto the last aspect of our salvation, which is glorification in the final day (cf. 8:30); **by**[116] **His life:**[117] that is, Jesus' life which we share in Him, because of our union with Him,[118] which, as Matthew Henry states, "is not to be understood of his life in the flesh, but his life in heaven, that life which ensued after his death"[119] (namely, His resurrection life in glory, cf. John 14:19b; Rom. 8:34; Heb. 7:25; Rev. 1:18).

Charles Hodge puts it like this:

> There is, therefore, most abundant ground for confidence for the final blessedness of believers, not only in the amazing love of God, by which, though sinners and enemies, they have been justified and reconciled by the death of his Son, but also in the consideration that this same Saviour that died for them still lives, and ever lives to sanctify, protect, and save them.[120]

And not only *that*,[121] that is, not only do we glory in the aforementioned gospel blessings in the prior verse; **but**[122] the conjunction emphasizing a sharp contrast; **we also rejoice**[123] or are constantly rejoicing and giving shouts of triumph (cf. vv. 2, 3); **in God:**[124] i.e., in God the Father Himself, not just for the good gifts He gives as previously stated; **through** or by the agency and mediation of; **our Lord Jesus Christ;**[125] **through whom**

---

114 Grk. aorist, passive, participle.

115 Grk. future, passive, verb.

116 The preposition denoting agency.

117 There are three aspects to Jesus' resurrected life which pertain to our getting to glory. They are, 1- He intercedes for us as our High Priest (Heb. 7:24-28); 2- He is our heavenly advocate (1 John 2:1); 3- He is our Helper in time of need (Matt. 28:20b; Heb. 2:17, 18; 4:14-16).

118 Paul expounds union with Christ some more in the following chapters. In chapter five, he speaks of union with Christ concerning our *salvation*. In chapter six, he speaks about union with Christ concerning our *sanctification*. In chapter six verses 1 to 6, he speaks about our union with Christ concerning our *standing* with the law.

119 Henry, Romans, p. 321.

120 Hodge, p. 140.

121 Same Greek construction as found in 3a.

122 The strong Greek adversative.

123 Grk. present, middle, participle.

124 What an amazing thought it is that we, who were once rebel sinners and found no pleasure in the Lord, now, by sovereign grace in salvation, rejoice "in God!"

125 MacArthur warmly remarks, "Every blessing a Christian has comes from Christ. Through him we have peace with God (Rom. 5:1), grace and the hope of glory (v. 2), perseverance, proven character, and hope (vv. 3-4), God's love poured into our hearts by His Spirit, who is Himself the Savior's gift to us (v. 5), deliverance from sin by His atoning death (vv. 6-8), deliverance from God's wrath (v. 9), reconciliation with God the Father (v. 10a), and perseverance during this present life (v. 10b)." MacArthur, p. 287.

Spurgeon says concerning this phrase, "Every blessing comes to us through him.

once again, Jesus; **we have now** not just later, but as a present-day reality; **received**[126] not earned, or worked for, but received completely as a gift of grace through Jesus' death on our behalf; **the reconciliation**[127] or the, "establishment of harmony between God and man through the sacrificial work of the Savior."[128]

In summarizing these words, John Gill, the noted Baptist pastor and scholar of the eighteenth century wrote:

> Something seems here to be understood, and which is to be supplied thus; not only we are saved by his life, and from wrath through him, not only are we reconciled to God by his Son and Spirit; not only Christ has died for us while sinners and ungodly; not only do we glory in tribulations, and rejoice in the hope of the glory of God: "but we also joy in God"; himself, as our covenant God and Father in Christ, as the God of all grace, peace, and salvation; in his perfections, as engaged on our side, and as glorified in our salvation; in the purposes of God, and his covenant transactions with his Son, as they are made known in the everlasting gospel; in all his providential dispensations, which are mercy and truth; and in our being of him in Christ, and Christ being made unto us wisdom, righteousness, sanctification, and redemption; in all the blessings of grace we received from him, the glory of which is due him; and in his sight and presence, and in the enjoyment of him.[129]

We see in this last verse that Paul concludes this section of this epistle the same way he began it, namely, with glorying in God. As he has set forth the seven blessed benefits that come to believers, he is absolutely ecstatic, not stoic. He is enthusiastically praising God. May this be our disposition as well in view of all that God in Christ has done for us! In finishing this crucial unit in his commentary on Romans, author Kent Hughes quotes John Stott when he rightly says of Christians:

> We should be the most positive people in the world. We cannot mooch round the place with a dropping, hang-dog expression. We cannot drag our way through life, moaning and groaning. We cannot always be looking on the dark side of everything, as negative prophets of doom. No, "we exult in God." Then every part of our life becomes suffused with glory. Christian worship becomes a joyful celebration of God and Christian living a joyful service of God. So come, let us exult in God together![130]

How Paul delights to harp upon that string! He says continually, 'through our Lord Jesus Christ.'" Spurgeon, p. 58.

126   Grk. aorist, active, verb.

127   The King James Version has the word *atonement* here, which has the root sense of creating unity, hence, reconciling.

128   McDonald, p. 1697.

129   Online commentary: www.biblestudytools.com/gills-exposition-of-the-bible/romans-5-11.html.

130   R. Kent Hughes, Romans, p. 111.

Suggested applications from the text for the church:

1- Our peace with God should cause great gratitude to well up in our hearts.

2- Our access to God should motivate us to come to Him regularly in prayer.

3- Our hope in God should encourage us, knowing that our future is bright.

4- Our growth from God should teach us that in all of our afflictions, God will bring spiritual good from it for us as He promised.

5- Our love from God should cause us to praise His Name, knowing that in truth, we deserve nothing but His wrath.

6- Our preservation through God should strengthen us for all of our trials in life.

7- Our reconciliation with God should inspire our worship to Him for who He is and what He has done for us through Christ.

Suggested applications from the text for the non-Christian:

1- Since you will never know the joyful peace *of* God until you first know peace *with* God, today is the day for you to be reconciled to Him through Jesus.

Text: Romans 5:12-21

General theme: Two Men, Two Acts, Two Outcomes

Homiletical outline of the verses:

A. The condemnation in Adam: [12]Therefore, just as through one man sin entered the world, and death through sin, and thus death spread to all men, because all sinned— [13](For until the law sin was in the world, but sin is not imputed when there is no law. [14]Nevertheless death reigned from Adam to Moses, even over those who had not sinned according to the likeness of the transgression of Adam, who is a type of Him who was to come.

B. The commendation in Christ: [15]But the free gift *is* not like the offense. For if by the one man's offense many died, much more the grace of God and the gift by the grace of the one Man, Jesus Christ, abounded to many. [16]And the gift *is* not like *that which came* through the one who sinned. For the judgment *which came* from one *offense resulted* in condemnation, but the free gift *which came* from many offenses *resulted* in justification. [17]For if by the one man's offense death reigned through the one, much more those who receive abundance of grace and of the gift of righteousness will reign in life through the One, Jesus Christ.)

C. The contradistinction in both: [18]Therefore, as through one man's offense *judgment came* to all men, resulting in condemnation, even so through one Man's righteous act *the free gift came* to all men, resulting in justification of life. [19]For as by one man's disobedience many were made sinners, so also by one Man's obedience many will be made righteous.

[20]Moreover the law entered that the offense might abound. But where sin abounded, grace abounded much more, [21]so that as sin reigned in death, even so grace might reign through righteousness to eternal life through Jesus Christ our Lord.

Summary of section: Having just mentioned in the last word of the prior verse, the topic of "reconciliation," in these last ten verses of this chapter the apostle goes back to the first man ever in human history who needed reconciliation with God because of what he did, and explains what that means for all who are spiritually connected to him. Further, he brings the Lord Jesus Christ into the portrait, showing how all who are spiritually connected to Him receive justification and the free gift of perfect righteousness through what He has done. This magnificent portion in this epistle, "begins in the abyss with man's ruin and ascends through his rescue to the pinnacle of his reign."[131] This text is theologically rich and vital for us to understand.[132] Herman Hoeksema is correct when he writes:

> The rest of this fifth chapter of this epistle to the Romans, from verse 12 to the end, is a parallel between Adam and Christ, between the first and the second Adam. This parallel is drawn by the apostle for the sake of confirming, establishing, and making plain the truth that he has been developing, the truth, namely, that our righteousness is in Christ by faith, without the works of the law. This is the theme of all that precedes.
>
> Strictly speaking, the development of this theme the apostle finishes in verse 11. But he adds this parallel between Adam and Christ to forestall a possible objection that might arise in the minds of some. The objection is that it is an unheard of thing that we should be righteous because of the righteousness of another, without any works on our own part. By drawing this parallel, the apostle shows that there is nothing strange in this, because all our life is constituted just this way. As all are in Adam, so all are in Christ. As Adam is the head and all are represented in him as a legal body, so the elect are in Christ because they are a legal body, represented by him.[133]

---

131 R. Kent Hughes, on Romans p. 113.

132 While I think the point of this text is plain, it is commonly agreed among scholars that it is one of the most difficult passages in the book of Romans to interpret. Even Luther called it "an entertaining outbreak and excursion."

133 Herman Hoeksema on Romans, p. 217. David Steele and Curtis Thomas say a similar thing in their commentary on Romans, pp. 41, 42 when they write: "In Romans 5:12-21 Paul compares the saving work of Christ to the condemning work of Adam. By means of this comparison he illustrates that the methods of justification and condemnation are the same in principle. Sinners are justified through the imputation of Christ's righteousness just as they were condemned through the imputation of Adam's sin. The point of the passage is that just as the race was lost through the representative act of the 'first' Adam even so believers are saved through the representative act of the 'last' Adam." Thomas Goodwin, the great Puritan, famously said, "In God's sight, there are two men— Adam and Jesus Christ— and these two men have all other men hanging at their girdle strings."

Exegetical & Practical Insights:

Obs. 1- (vv. 12-14)[134] That as Paul traces out the specific root of human sin which has affected all of us and how our alienation from our Creator first occurred, he writes: **Therefore** that is, on account of what he just wrote in the previous verse concerning why it is that we all need reconciliation with God and putting forth "a new stage in the argument;"[135] **just as**[136] the conjunction introducing a comparison; **through** or by means of; **one man**[137] (Adam with his transgression, cf. v.14);[138] **sin** "sin" singular, "not the many other sinful acts that Adam eventually committed, but the indwelling sin *nature* that he came to possess because of his first disobedience that he passed on to all his posterity;"[139] **entered** the sense

---

134 I received some helpful insights on this passage from Guy Prentiss Waters' video series entitled *The Life and Theology of Paul* by Ligonier Ministries.

135 Peterson, p. 245.

136 Many commentators say that Paul completes his thought in this verse, in verse 18 of this chapter. Grammatically speaking, this is what is known as *anacoluthon* from the Greek language which means, "not following," which is to say, that Paul here purposefully left the sequence to this sentence out until later. Personally, I am not convinced this is the case. To me, it seems much more likely that he completed his thought in the sentence in the second half of the verse by saying "and thus." Further, the apostle reversed the order of these words "and thus" *kai houto* in the Greek text for the sake of emphasis, in contrast to what he says, for example, in verses 15, 18, 21 *houto kai*.

137 Although, technically speaking, it was Eve who first disobeyed God's command and ate of the tree which was in the midst of the garden, nonetheless, because she was not the federal head of all mankind, the blame is not placed at her feet. It is also interesting to note that Paul says in 1 Tim. 2:14 that Eve was "deceived" and "fell into transgression." However, Adam apparently committed his treason against God with both eyes wide open, fully knowing what God had commanded him not to do (Gen. 2:17). It is important to note that Paul speaks about Adam in this portion of Scripture as a real historical person, just as Jesus did (cf. Matt. 19:4-6).

Lloyd-Jones comments on this matter when he writes, "Our study has sustained our contention that it is not a matter of indifference as to what view you hold of Genesis 1, 2 and 3. If you do not believe that there was a literal Adam, and that what Paul says about him in this Epistle is true, why is there any need of forgiveness? Why is there any need of Atonement? Why did Christ have to take human nature upon Him? Reject a literal Adam and the whole of the Christian case and the Christian message, it seems to me, collapses. You cannot play fast and loose with the Bible. It is a consistent whole. Each part is intertwined with all the others, and they all depend upon one another in this amazing unity. The one great theme of the Bible from beginning to end is man and his world in relationship to God. It tells us how he went wrong and the consequences of that; but thank God it also tells us how he can be put right. Adam! Christ! 'As in Adam, so in Christ.'" Lloyd-Jones, p. 197.

For further information about this topic, I point the reader to *The Quest for the Historical Adam* by William VanDoodewaard, Reformation Heritage Books.

138 I found it interesting that in his helpful commentary on Romans, Paul Barnett shows that before the coming of Christ some Jewish writers believed that Adam's sin was the sin of us all. In speaking about this a devout Jew wrote: "O Adam, what have you done? When you sinned, your fall occurred not only for you, but for us your descendants." Another Jewish writer said: "For when Adam first sinned [he] brought an untimely death over all." Barnett, p. 116.

139 MacArthur p. 293. He also correctly notes on the same page, "Mankind is a single entity, constituting a divinely ordered solidarity. Adam represents the entire human race that is descended from him, no matter how many subgroups there may be. Therefore when Adam sinned, all mankind sinned, and because his first sin transformed his inner nature, that now depraved nature was also transmitted to his posterity. Because he became spiritually polluted, all his descendants would be polluted in the same way. That pollution has, in fact,

is, came in and gained access as a violent intruder to do great harm; **the world,**[140] i.e., the realm of human existence; humanity, all people,[141] so that Adam's sin was not only *imputed* to us, but his fallen nature was *imparted* to us giving us polluted hearts;[142] or an "inherent propensity to unrighteousness;"[143] **and death,** i.e., physical[144] and spiritual death[145] (and then ultimately eternal death or hell, for those who remain unsaved);[146] **through sin and thus** or in the very same way that it did with Adam; **death** again, physical and spiritual death; **spread**[147] or more literally, went through, or extended and forever permeated;[148] **to all men**[149] all individuals universally, none excluded;[150] **because**[151] or "upon the fact" or "the basis;" **that all sinned,**[152] that is, all sinned in that one man—[153]

The logical question to ask and answer is this: When was it that we all sinned *in* and *with* Adam, in what theologians typically call "representative sin"?[154] When did all humanity sin collectively? Our

---

accumulated and intensified throughout the ages of human history. Instead of evolving, as humanists insist, man has devolved, degenerating into greater and greater sinfulness."

140 For an outstanding exposition of man's fall into sin, I refer the reader to *Lectures in Systematic Theology, Volume 2, Doctrine of Man,* by Greg Nichols, pp. 443-575.

141 It is also true that Adam's sin plunged the whole of creation under a curse and thus it groans even until this day, waiting for its final redemption (cf. Rom. 8:19-22).

142 This is what theologians typically call Original Sin which sinners inherited from fallen Adam. Many passages of Scripture speak about this (cf. Gen. 6:5; Prov. 20:9; Psa. 51:5).

143 MacArthur, p. 293

144 Verse 14a highlights this in part. Further, in view of the statement, it seems that from the Genesis 2 narrative, man was originally created to live forever.

145 Clearly, spiritual death is also in view, because concerning this narrative as found in Genesis 2:17 (cf. Gen 3:6, 7), God said to Adam that the very "day" that he ate he would "surely" die. Literally the Hebrew text reads, "dying you shall die." And so since Scripture tells us that Adam lived to a ripe 930 years (Gen. 5:5), it is clear that his death on the "day" when he rebelled against God in eating of the forbidden fruit of the tree of the knowledge of good and evil, was spiritual to begin with.

146 Cf. Matt. 25:46a; Rom. 6:23a; Rev. 21:8.

147 Grk. aorist, active, verb.

148 The verb containing "the force of distribution," Rogers and Rogers, p. 325.

149 Even though Augustine's translation of these words from the Latin Vulgate as *"in whom* all sinned" may not be the best translation, he was certainly correct theologically.

150 Except Christ of course, who was born without sin. Jesus was not conceived through the normal relations of a father and mother therefore, he inherited no sin nature (cf. Matt. 1:18; Luke 1:35; 2 Cor. 5:21; 1 Pet. 2:22).

151 For a helpful discussion at this point concerning the clause in view, see Bird. 178, 180.

152 Grk. aorist, active, verb.

153 A proper understanding of this verse is critical because it answers key questions in life, one of which is this: Why are sin and death so universal in the world? One has said concerning this matter that original sin is "the only Christian doctrine that is empirically verifiable." Further, Paul's language of death spreading to "all men because all sinned" in Adam proves his earlier point found in Rom. 3:9, namely, that both Jews and Greeks are "all under sin."

154 Many people find this doctrine difficult to accept, claiming that it is "not fair" that the sin of the one, should become the sin of all. Fair or not, facts are facts. And the fact is, we were in Adam when he fell and thus his sin is our sin. Further, before we criticize this matter, we ought to remember that positively speaking, the same thing is true concerning Christ. Just as Adam's sin was imputed to us, so also, the sins of the elect were imputed to

verse is plain: we all sinned in Adam the very moment he ate from the tree and disobeyed God.

According to the Bible, Adam represented all of us in the garden, for there he was not acting as a private individual, but as a public one.[155] The fact is, "in Adam all die," as Paul says in 1 Corinthians 15:22a, and this is because he acted both *for* us and *as* us. Consequently, "when a man is born, he is already born with death, because he contracts sin from Adam."[156]

In Eden, Adam acted as the federal head and legal representative of all humanity and hence again, when he fell, we fell in him and with him. This is because spiritually speaking, we all came from him.[157] Spiritually speaking, there is a relationship of representative solidarity between Adam and his natural posterity, for "Adam *was* the race."[158] And so when he reached out his hands, we reached out our hands. When he ate, we ate, and when he died, we died.[159] Accordingly, the Westminster Shorter Catechism is correct when it says in question 16 that, 'all mankind, descending from him by ordinary generation, sinned in him, and fell with him, in his first transgression.'[160]

And as if this were not bad enough, Scripture also teaches that we are not only sinners by nature, but we are sinners by practice (as we have already seen in chapters 1 to 3 of this book). As a people, we all sinned in Adam collectively, and yet, we have also all sinned in our lives personally "for there is none righteous, no not one" (3:10). Consequently, our own personal need for reconciliation with God through Christ is clear and crucial.

Jesus and His righteousness is imputed to them. Biblically speaking, if we reject the one, we have to reject the other, and who would want to do that, seeing that these things stand or fall together?

155 John Murray's small book entitled *The Imputation of Adam's Sin* is outstanding regarding this whole topic.

156 Augustine as quoted in the *Ancient Christian Commentary on Scripture, Romans* p. 95

157 The New England Primer of the Puritans is right when it says, "In Adam's fall, we sinned all."

158 *The Expositor's Bible Commentary* p. 62.

159 The aorist tense of the verb "sinned" makes this point plain. The aorist tense is the tense which points to a single, decisive, non-repeatable past action in time highlighting the exact time when "all humanity sinned" which, as has been stated, was the time when Adam first sinned. Strikingly enough, Paul uses this tense three times in this verse in order to strengthen the force of his point. Moreover, if the apostle was only saying that "we all sinned" when we just sin "by ourselves," he would have used the imperfect or present tense verb to stress this. It is also clear that because when Adam sinned, all sinned (because all were in him), that the teaching of Pelagius from the fourth-century is patently wrong. Pelagius taught that every person born into the world is born innocent and that they are only guilty when they follow after Adam's poor example. This is not so, for clearly Paul is saying much more than this (see particularly vv. 18-19).

160 Several commentators note that this matter of "the sin of the one," being "the sin of the rest," is seen in the Old Testament in several places with the classic example being that of Achan, whose sin of keeping for himself some of the plunder from the battle of Jericho is also said, to be the sin of Israel as a whole (cf. Josh. 7:1).

As Paul continues to pursue and even defend[161] the thought that "as through one man sin entered the world, and death through sin, and thus death spread to all men, because all sinned," he parenthetically writes:[162]

For the conjunction explaining and confirming the previous words concerning the universality of human sin and death; **until** or before; **the law** that is, the Ten Commandments as revealed through Moses; **sin was in the world,** i.e., it was in and among men, and they were accountable for it (a statement of fact, stressing that people were not only born in sin through Adam, but actively pursued sin themselves),[163] for men were "sinners, and were so regarded and treated;"[164] **but sin is not imputed** or was not being reckoned, charged, or invoiced to one's account in a point by point way, the term is "a commercial metaphor indicating that sin would be registered in God's official law book as transgression;"[165] **when there is no law** (which is to say, while men were still guilty for sin, there was no standard of legal assessment officially existing in codified form to set it forth as such).[166] **Nevertheless** or but, the strong adversative stressing that even though Paul's last assertion in verse 13b was true, yet "as a second argument for the presence of sin between Adam and Moses,"[167] Paul says; **death reigned**[168] that is, it reigned and ruled definitively and universally over all humanity both spiritually and physically "so that none can stop it or escape its power,"[169] **from Adam to Moses**[170] (a period of roughly 2,500 years); **even over** or better translated, upon; **those who had not sinned according to** or on the same basis of; **the likeness of the transgression of Adam**[171] (who violated a direct commandment to

---

161 No doubt there were some in Paul's day, as in ours, who denied this doctrine.

162 Osborne sums up vv. 13-14 nicely when he writes: "When did sin come into this world? Many would say that it arrived with the law and not earlier, so Paul breaks his thought and addresses the presence of sin before the law. He has stated in verse 12 that 'all have sinned' and that therefore death came 'through sin.' Many Jews would believe that this should mean that people did not sin or die before Moses, because 'where there is no law is no transgression' (4:15). Paul responds that this takes place through corporate identity with Adam— we have all sinned in Adam— and so this connection meant there was still sin among those who had lived between Adam and Moses and thus that sin existed from Adam's transgression on." Osborne, p. 149.

163 Cf. Gen. 4:8; Gen. 12:10-20; Gen. 18:16-33; 19:1-29. Also, note that before the official giving of the Ten Commandments, the work of the law was written in people's hearts so they knew what sin was (cf. Gen. 39:9; Rom. 2:15).

164 Hodge, p. 157.

165 Osborne, p. 150.

166 MacArthur says, "Though all men were regarded as sinners (Rom. 5:12), because there was no explicit list of commands, there was no strict accounting of their specific points of violation." MacArthur, *One Faithful Life* (2019), p. 284. Cf. 5:20.

167 Osborne, p. 150.

168 Grk. aorist, active, verb.

169 Mahan, p. 41.

170 The two exceptions are Enoch and Elijah in the Old Testament because God took them up without their dying.

171 "The death of every human, even infants who never consciously sinned, proves that God's standard of legal assessment was not personal and conscious transgression of God's revealed will" (Nichols, Doctrine of Man, p. 514). Spurgeon says, "Children died who had not actually sinned themselves, but died because of Adam's sin" (Spurgeon, p. 70).

him from God); **who is a type,**[172] i.e., a foreshadow, and figure;[173] **of Him** (Jesus);[174] **who was to come.**[175]

Obs. 2- (vv. 15-17) That as Paul begins to lay out three clear contrasts between Adam and Christ in each one of these verses, he thoroughly exalts Christ over Adam,[176] "who is a type of Him who was to come," he says:[177]

---

172 The origin of our English word typology. The word means to make an impression by molding, or a figure formed by a strike or a blow as many scholars note.

173 Albeit a flawed foreshadow, figure and form.

174 Adam is a type of Christ who was to come in one main way, namely, that just as Adam was the head of one group of people and what he did affected them, so also Christ is the head of another people and what He did affected them. Haldane states it well when he writes, "The resemblance, on account of which Adam is regarded as the type of Christ, consists in this, that Adam communicated to those whom he represented what belonged to him, and that Christ also communicated to those whom He represents what belonged to Him." Haldane, p. 212.

Chrysostom concurs and says, "Adam is a type of Christ in that just as those who descended from him inherited death, even though they had not eaten of the fruit of the tree. So also those who are descended from Christ inherit his righteousness, even though they did not produce it themselves." *Ancient Christian Commentary on Scripture, Romans* p. 137.

It should also be noted that after this one singular point of resemblance, the differences between Adam and Christ are vast. The following verses in this chapter make this abundantly plain. Paul wants there to be no mistake about this matter. He sets it forth quite strongly in the following words. If we were to line up Adam and Christ next to each other, we could list, for example, under Adam: a living being, but under Christ: a life-giving spirit. Under Adam: of the earth, but under Christ: Lord from heaven. Under Adam the words: tasted death from a tree, but under Christ the words: tasted death on a tree. Under Adam: blamed his bride, under Christ: died for his bride. Under Adam: transgression, but under Christ: righteousness. Under Adam: curse, but under Christ: blessed. Under Adam: in him all die, but under Christ: in Him all shall live. Under Adam: condemnation, but under Christ: justification. Under Adam: death reigned to all, but under Christ: free gift of grace reigning to many.

175 Moo helpfully notes that this language here concerning Jesus "who was to come" may "reflect the contemporary Jewish designation of the Messiah as 'the coming one,' and the future tense is probably used because Paul is viewing Christ's work from the perspective of Adam." Moo, NICNT, p. 334.

176 Osborne comments, "Here we have the two groups that comprise humanity, the only two groups that matter. It is irrelevant to think of Jew and Gentile or the racial and ethnic divides that are so crucial to the earthly scene. The fact is that these differences no longer matter. We who are black or yellow or red or white are all united in one of these two groups for eternity, and that alone is what counts. The most important questions we will ever face in this life are, 'Which group do you belong to?' And, 'Is your destiny death or life?'" Osborne, p. 152.

177 It is vital that we understand in these verses, especially through Paul's repeated use of the words, "much more" (vv.15, 17, & v.20) and "grace" and the "free gift" (vv. 15-17) concerning Christ's work over Adam's work, that it is not merely that Jesus has undone and cleaned up the damage brought about through Adam, but rather, He abundantly restores us and sets us on a much higher spiritual plane, bringing us to the place where we "reign in life." Thus, Christ's victory is much greater than Adam's defeat! Paul wants us to feel and know this to be so that we can truly, "rejoice in God through our Lord Jesus Christ" (5:11).

Frank Thielman says it like this "The atoning death of Christ has reversed Adam's introduction of sin and death into the world. This reversal, moreover, does not merely correct Adam's missteps and its consequences but overwhelms them with the lavish grace of God. God has decisively defeated the power of sin and death and brought the era of their reign to an end. Now the era of the eternal reign of God's grace has begun." Thielman, p. 278.

John Murray says this "Adam before he fell was righteous in the sight of God, but he

But the strong adversative conjunction setting forth the first contrast in the parallelism between these two figureheads and focal points of history, clarifying how they are different; **the free gift**[178] that is, the extremely gracious, unmerited, and unearned gift which comes from God, to sinners, through their representative union with Christ,[179] which is "the gift of righteousness conferred upon those who have put their faith in Christ"[180] (cf. 17); *is* **not like** or absolutely nothing at all as;[181] **the offense** or Adam's deviation from the path of truth i.e., "from the one command, from the single norm for obedience, that God had given."[182] **For** the conjunction stating the reason why the gift of God is far greater; **if by the one man's offense** (Adam's sin in the garden); **many**[183] (the many who came from him; i.e., all people); **died,**[184] i.e., died spiritually and eventually would die physically; **much more** or all the more lavishly since "much more efficacious is the grace of God to the benefit of many; inasmuch as it is admitted that Christ is much more powerful to save, than Adam was to destroy;"[185] **the grace** or goodwill and favor; **of God and the gift by the grace of the one Man** "the last Adam,"[186] **Jesus Christ, abounded** or overflowed and became supremely and savingly beneficial; **to many** (those represented by Jesus).[187] **And** the conjunction continuing Paul's thought and expanding it in order to make his second contrast; **the gift** *is* **not like** *that which came* **through the one who sinned. For** again the explanatory conjunction; **the judgment,** i.e., the punishment or verdict which was handed down and; *which came* **from one** *offense resulted* **in condemnation** that is, the sentence of eternal damnation for all of Adam's unsaved posterity; **but** in contrast to this; **the free gift** *which came* **from** (or in the context of);[188] **many offenses** *resulted* **in justification**[189] or a right standing with God, acquittal and pardon before Him. **For** another explanation setting forth the third and final

---

was still under the possibility of becoming unrighteous. Those who have been saved by the Lord Jesus Christ not only are righteous in the sight of God but they are beyond the possibility of becoming unrighteous. In their case, the probation is over... because Christ has stood in for them." John Murray, "The Active obedience of Christ," *The Presbyterian Guardian*, November 10th, 1940, pp. 131-32.

178 MacArthur says that the word could be rendered "grace gift." MacArthur, p. 302.

179 Genitive of possession.

180 Osborne, p. 142. Broadly speaking, this covers everything pertaining to salvation and eternal life (cf. Rom. 6:23).

181 The comparison is emphasized by the strong negation.

182 MacArthur p. 302.

183 That is, "the many" who were connected to him by natural descent also identified as "all men" in verses 12 and 18 (Jews and Gentiles).

184 Grk. aorist, active, verb.

185 Calvin, p. 206.

186 Cf. 2 Cor. 15:49.

187 Cf. Isa. 53: 10-12; Matt. 20:28; 26:28; John 10:27, 29.

188 Thielman, p. 288.

189 For a discussion on Paul's different use of the Greek word for *righteousness* here I point the reader to Kruse, p. 248, footnote 70.

great contrast between Adam and Christ; **if** or since or because; **by the one man's offense death reigned**[190] that is to say, reigned definitively as a malicious tyrant;[191] **through the one** (Adam); **much more** or to a much greater degree so that mercy abounds over misery; **those who receive**[192] or are receiving, not working for or obtaining based on any preconditions met in or by them; **abundance** or superabundance; **of grace,** i.e., kindness and goodness; **and of the gift of righteousness** or the status of being righteous before God through the imputation of Christ's righteousness; **will reign**[193] "not only be saved as sinners but reign as kings;"[194] **in life** that is, in the eschatological life to come in glory with God;[195] **through** the preposition denoting agency, highlighting that all the aforementioned blessings that we receive, come solely through the mediation and merits of; **the One, Jesus Christ.**[196]

In commenting on this last matter concerning Christ, James Boice helpfully summarizes:

> The apostle never leaves the idea out because, as we have been seeing, it is the one glorious and absolute essential truth in this passage. We were in Adam once, and we fell in him. His sin brought death on the human race. What then? Good news! We can escape the effects of Adam's fall, Paul tells us. More than that, we can rise above the position in which Adam first stood. We can stand in a divine righteousness, which is perfect and which can never be taken away from us. It enables us to reign in life, triumphing over sin, as Adam and his own human (though once perfect) righteousness, could not. Therefore we can sing:

> On Christ the solid rock I stand;
> All other ground is sinking sand.[197]

Obs. 3- (vv. 18-19) that as Paul winds down his contrasting parallelism between Adam and Christ and compares the operation and impact of the representative solidarity between the two, he writes:

---

190 Grk. aorist, active, verb.

191 Cf. v. 14.

192 Grk. present, active, participle.

193 Grk. future, active, verb.

194 Robinson, Book 1, p. 310.

195 This of course is not to negate that believers are reigning right now through Jesus Christ for surely we are "more than conquerors through Him who loved us" (cf. Rom. 8:37). We do reign in life as believers by God's grace in true holiness and happiness through Jesus and thus we have victory over sin, self, Satan, and our situations, praise be to God! Mounce remarks, "The future tense of the verb probably points to a time yet to come when believers will join with Jesus Christ in his reign (cf. 2 Tim 2:12; Rev 22:5). It is possible, however, to understand the reign as the present experience of believers who have already passed from death unto life (cf. John 5:24). If the sin of the one man caused death to reign, the obedience of the one man brings triumph over death to all who believe." Mounce, p. 144.

196 Peterson comments, "This verse forms a triumphant climax to vv. 15 – 17, offering hope to all who are captive to the rule of sin and death but trust in Jesus and his saving work." Peterson, p. 253.

197 Boice, pp. 591, 592.

Therefore or consequently, the emphatic inferential particle with the conjunction stressing the decisive conclusion or sum of the whole passage (vv. 12-17);[198] **as through** or by means of; **one man's offense** (Adam's trespass in crossing over the line which was set before him); *judgment came* **to all men,** i.e., all people, all humanity connected to him by natural descent; **resulting in condemnation, even so** or in the same manner or likewise, these words "introducing the second part of the comparison;"[199] **through** or by means of; **one Man's righteous act,**[200] that act being, our Lord's obedience to His Father in offering Himself up as a sacrifice for our sin which was "the single action by which Jesus overturned the disastrous effects of Adam's single action;"[201] *the free gift came* **to all men**[202] to be precise, all people who are spiritually connected to Christ; **resulting in justification of life,** "a justification by which we are recalled from the death of sin unto the life of grace and glory."[203] **For as** the words explaining the mechanism behind verse eighteen;[204] **by one man's disobedience many were made,**[205] i.e., definitively and legally constituted or rendered as a judicial verdict by the imputation of Adam's sin; **sinners**[206] or "miss-the-markers;" **so also by one Man's obedience**[207] (in opposition to the disobedience of Adam); **many will be made,**[208] i.e., legally constituted or rendered as a judicial verdict on the last day by the imputation of Christ's perfection;[209] **righteous,** that is, fully accepted

---

198 The Greek conjunction *oun* would have been sufficient to summarize the account but Paul goes further than that.

199 Harvey, p. 143.

200 I realize that there are several commentators who view this language as both the totality of Jesus' life in His representative law keeping and His death on our behalf at the cross, i.e., His active and passive obedience. At one time I believed this was the case also. However, now I think that the main focus here really is the cross, as the one righteous "act" of our Lord's death for us (although of course, both aspects of His life and death are connected).

201 Peterson, p. 244. cf. Phil. 2:8.

202 This obviously cannot be teaching "universal salvation" as some have erroneously taught. To say this would be to flatly contradict all that Paul has already written in this letter, namely, that God is "the justifier of the one who has faith in Jesus" (3:26). Also, verse 17 speaks of those "who receive" the abundance of grace and of the gift of righteousness. McDonald helpfully remarks: "It is futile for universalists to use these verses to try to prove that all men will eventually be saved. The passage deals with two federal headships, and it is clear that just as Adam's sin affects those who are 'in him,' so also Christ's righteous act benefits only those who are 'in Him.'" McDonald, p. 1699.

203 E. H. Gifford, p. 120.

204 Harvey calls it the "mechanics", p. 143.

205 Grk. aorist, passive, verb.

206 "Adam's sin did not put us on trial and make us only susceptible to sin nor lead us into sin, but by his fall we were actually *made sinners*. Even so Christ's obedience did not render us saveable nor enable us to be righteous before God by our own works, but we were *made righteous*." Mahan, pp. 40-41.

207 This language is strikingly and wonderfully similar to what we read in Isaiah 53:11.

208 Grk. future, passive, verb.

209 This verse is a nice bookend to the truth set forth in verse 1 of this chapter which tells us that we have already been justified and rendered righteous in this life and that this pronouncement will be the same in the life to come.

and acquitted and free from all condemnation before God with a title to heaven, and this is all because of Jesus' representative and redemptive work on our behalf.[210]

Obs. 4- (vv. 20-21) That as Paul highlights for one last time, the glories of what Jesus did for His people over and against that which Adam did for his, he writes:

Moreover the law, that is to say, the Mosaic Law, the Ten Commandments which Paul spoke of in verse 13;[211] **entered** or came in or alongside the sin which was already in the world (cf. 13a); **that** the conjunction denoting purpose; **the offense** that is, our transgressions against God; **might abound,**[212] i.e., abound by causing it to be clearly seen as sin, by defining it,[213] and intensifying the consequences for breaking it.[214] **But where sin abounded** or was set forth as "exceedingly sinful," (Rom. 7:13); **grace,** i.e., God's goodwill and unmerited favor and kindness toward us in Jesus;

---

210 Cf. 1 Cor. 1:30; 2 Cor. 5:21. In commenting on this verse, Thomas Brooks, the great Puritan, writes: "The imputed righteousness of Christ is the only true basis for a believer to build his happiness, joy, comfort, peace, and quiet of his conscience upon. If a judge acquits the prisoner at the bar, he cares not if the jailer or fellow prisoners condemn him. There are no accusers that a believer needs to fear since it is God, the supreme Judge, that absolves him. The consideration of this should arm us, comfort us, and strengthen us against all the terrors of conscience, guilt, accusation of the law, or cruelty of Satan. If God justifies, none can reverse it. If any come against you, true or false, they shall never hurt you. He from whom there is no appeal has fully acquitted you, and none can take your peace." As cited in Richard Rushing, *Voices from the Past*, vol. 2, Banner of Truth, p. 161.

John Bunyan, another great Puritan, put it like this in his book entitled *Grace Abounding:* "One day as I was passing into the field, this sentence fell upon my soul: 'Thy righteousness is in heaven.' And with the eyes of my soul I saw Jesus at the Father's right hand. 'There,' I said, 'is my righteousness!' So that wherever I was or whatever I was doing, God could not say to me, 'Where is your righteousness?' For it is always right before him. I saw that it is not my good frame of heart that made my righteousness better, nor yet my bad frame that made my righteousness worse, for my righteousness is Christ. Now my chains fell off indeed. My temptations fled away, and I lived sweetly at peace with God. Now I could look from myself to him and could reckon that all my character was like the coins a rich man carries in his pocket when all his gold is safe in a trunk at home. Oh I saw that my gold was indeed in a trunk at home, in Christ my Lord. Now Christ was all: my righteousness, sanctification, redemption."

Martin Luther the great reformer famously said something similar "Lord Jesus, You are my righteousness, I am your sin. You took on you what was mine; yet set on me what was yours. You became what you were not, that I might become what I was not."

211 We might wonder why Paul thought it necessary to bring up this matter of the law once again at this point in this chapter. Some commentators say that these words are very much out of place or an afterthought. But I believe that especially after speaking of salvation through another, namely, the representative and redeeming work of Christ, Paul knew that there still might be some (maybe some self-righteous Jews) who thought they could get right with God on their own apart from the Savior. By bringing up the matter of the law again, Paul once again seeks to shut every mouth that all the world may become guilty before God and understand that no one will, by partial obedience to the commandments of God be justified in His sight (cf. Rom. 3:19-20; James 2:10). Moreover, Paul might be mentioning the law here so as to teach us what he writes in Galatians 3:24, namely, that "the law was our tutor to bring us to Christ that we might be justified by faith."

212 Some commentators take these words to mean that because the law incites men to do more sin, since they hate the things of God, and live in rebellion to him, that this is what Paul is speaking of at this point (cf. Rom 7:7-9). I am not convinced this is the case.

213 "Sin is transgression of the law," 1 John 3:4 (KJV). Cf. Rom. 7:7.

214 Cf. Rom. 4:15a.

abounded[215] **much more**[216] or "superabounded," or, "hyperabounded," since sin could never exceed the lavished free grace of God provided for us in Christ; **so that** the conjunction denoting result;[217] **as sin reigned** or ruled; **in** the preposition denoting the realm or sphere of; **death,** i.e., physical and spiritual death over us; **even so** or in a similar way; **grace might reign** or rule; **through righteousness,** that is, "the law-fulfilling righteousness of Christ"[218] on our behalf; **to eternal life** or never ending blessedness in glory; **through** or by means of the mediation of; **Jesus Christ our Lord.**[219]

In verse 20a, Paul teaches a very important point regarding the law of God: the law was never given to show sinners how they could be made right with God (cf. Rom: 3:19, 20). Rather, it was given to show them how much they are not right with God and thus how desperately they need Jesus the Savior. "The law came not to make a man a sinner, but to show him how great a sinner he is."[220] Here Paul does not say that the law entered so that by keeping it perfectly (which of course we could never do), we might have everlasting life. No, he says that contrary to the expectation of some (the Jews especially), the law shows that we are completely helpless before God — helpless to be right with Him, in and of ourselves.

In 20b, and 21, Paul teaches that "as deep as sin goes, God's grace goes deeper. As wide as sin is, God's grace is wider."[221] As Spurgeon said, "Sin may be a river, but grace is an ocean. Sin may be a mountain, but grace is like Noah's flood, which prevailed over the tops of the mountains fifteen cubits upward."[222]

Paul teaches that our sin and failure to keep the law is absolutely no match for the grace of God because where our sin abounded, God's grace toward us in Christ did much more abound, so that "as sin reigned in death, even so grace might reign through righteousness to eternal life through Jesus Christ our Lord."

In commenting on these last few words, Vaughan and Corley warmly remark,

> This statement, which is a fitting summation of both the similarities and the dissimilarities set forth in the preceding verses, is solemnly triumphant. Denney describes it as having 'almost the value of a doxology.'

---

215 Grk. aorist, active, verb.

216 This Greek word only appears one other time in the New Testament in 2 Cor. 7:4.

217 Or perhaps purpose.

218 Robinson, Book 1, p. 318.

219 It is glorious to see Paul ending this chapter on this note with the emphasis on Christ. He began it this way (5:1), now he ends it this way, letting us know that all that we have, our justification, our righteousness, our forgiveness and acceptance with God, etc., is all bound up in the doing and dying of Jesus Christ our Lord.

220 The *King James Bible Commentary* p. 1416.

221 Ibid.

222 Spurgeon, p. 69.

Adam, whose name loomed large in the opening verses of the paragraph, now drops out of sight, and in his place stands 'Christ Jesus our Lord.[223]

McDonald thoughtfully concludes his comments on this section of Scripture by saying:

> Perhaps we have in these verses a partial answer to the familiar question, "Why did God allow sin to enter the world?" The answer is that God has received more glory and man has received more blessings through Christ's sacrifice than if sin had never entered. We are better off in Christ than we ever could have been in an unfallen Adam. If Adam had never sinned, he would have enjoyed continued life on earth in the Garden of Eden. But he had no prospect of becoming a redeemed child of God, an heir of God, or a joint-heir with Jesus Christ. He had no promise of a home in heaven or of being with Christ and like Him forever. These blessings come only through the redemptive work of Jesus Christ our Lord.[224]

Suggested applications from the text for the church:
1- Learn the importance of believing every single word of the Bible, including the fact that there was a real, historical Adam as Paul has assumed throughout this chapter. This point is vital for us to get, for if there was no real, historical Adam, why believe that there was a real, historical Christ? And if there was no real, historical Christ, then there is no real, historical gospel through which we can be saved.

2- Learn the importance of growing in genuine humility, since, according to our passage, we are not only rebel sinners in ourselves, but we are also ruined sinners in our first father Adam.

3- Learn the importance of rejoicing in God through Christ the Savior who has delivered us from our fallen condition in our first federal head and has freely granted to us justification, righteousness, and eternal life.

Suggested application from the text for the non-Christian:
1- Learn the importance of being justified by Jesus Christ. This is because in your current state, you bear the condemnation of Adam, and it is only through Jesus that you can have any hope for an eternal future with God.

---

223 Vaughan and Corley, p. 71.

224 McDonald, p. 1700. Further, it should be noted that although in pre-fallen Adam, we had the *righteousness of a creature*. In Jesus, however, we have the *righteousness of God*. Sinclair Ferguson said something similar when he wrote, "Perhaps the most wonderful thing of all is this: God lifts us not only from what we are by nature to what Adam was in the Garden of Eden, but to what Adam was to become in the presence of God, and would have been had he persevered in obedience. The gospel does not make us like Adam in his innocence – it makes us like Christ, in all the perfection of His reflection of God." Sinclair Ferguson, *The Christian Life*, Banner of Truth, 2013, p. 14.

ROMANS
CHAPTER SIX

Text: Romans 6:1-10[1]

General theme: Sanctification and the Saved (I)[2]

Homiletical outline of the verses:

A. The knowledge we must have for success over sin: [1]What shall we say then? Shall we continue in sin that grace may abound? [2]Certainly not! How shall we who died to sin live any longer in it? [3]Or do you not know that as many of us as were baptized into Christ Jesus were baptized into His death? [4]Therefore we were buried with Him through baptism into death, that just as Christ was raised from the dead by the glory of the Father, even so we also should walk in newness of life. [5]For if we have been united together in the likeness of His death, certainly we also shall be *in the likeness* of *His* resurrection, [6]knowing this, that our old man was crucified with *Him,* that the body of sin might be done away with, that we should no longer be slaves of sin. [7]For he who has died has been freed from sin. [8]Now if we died with Christ, we believe that we shall also live with Him, [9]knowing that Christ, having been raised from the dead, dies no more. Death no longer has dominion over Him. [10]For *the death* that He died, He died to sin once for all; but *the life* that He lives, He lives to God.

Summary of section: In this chapter, the apostle begins to take up the vital subject of sanctification or the justified believer being set apart from sin and set apart unto the Savior.[3] Sanctification is a moral renewal

---

1 I received some help in my understanding of Romans 6–8 from Guy Prentiss Waters' excellent video series entitled *The Life and Theology of Paul* by Ligonier Ministries.

2 We could also call this chapter *Strategies for Success over Sin*. As I will set forth in the following words, in verses 3-14, the apostle gives *five keys* concerning the sanctification process. They are: 1- *Remembering* our spiritual union with Christ (v. 3). 2- *Recalling* that our baptism portrayed our death to sin and rising to a new life (vv. 4-5). 3- *Realizing* that our old man was crucified with Christ (vv. 6-10). 4- *Reckoning* these things to be so (v. 11). 5- Responding accordingly (vv. 12-14). Further, note that Paul uses the word "know" four times in these verses (vv. 3, 6, 9, 16), helping us to see that a true comprehension of what God has done in our lives through Jesus is a key factor for us having success over sin.

3 For a detailed exposition of the topic of sanctification, I invite the reader to listen to

throughout our whole person which progressively produces consecration of life to the will of God as revealed in the Word of God and conformity to Christ by the working of His grace in our hearts.[4] Simply stated, it is the process by which we who are Christians are freed more and more from the practice of sin.[5] Paul seems to take up this subject in order to defend his statement in the second half of Romans 5:20 when he said,

---

my sermon online regarding the subject on sermonaudio.com. In that message, I give the meaning, mechanisms, means, mediators, movements, and motivations for sanctification. I also speak about how sanctification and justification are always vitally linked together, which is to say, that all whom God justifies He sanctifies. However, whereas justification speaks about what God has done *for us*, sanctification speaks about what He does *in us*. In justification, God deals with the *penalty for* our sin, in sanctification He deals with the *power of* sin. The former (justification) is external and legal, once for all time, entirely a work of God, perfect in this life, and the same in all Christians (as Wayne Grudem mentions in his *Systematic Theology*, p. 746). The latter (sanctification) is internal and personal, first definitive and then progressive, worked out by us with God's help, not perfect in this life, and varying in degrees in all Christians.

The *Westminster Shorter Catechism* provides a good general definition of sanctification in its answer to question 35: "What is Sanctification?" The authors say: "Sanctification is the work of God's free grace, whereby we are renewed in the whole man after the image of God, and are enabled more and more to die unto sin and live unto righteousness."

Further, it is important to note that the word "sanctification" appears for the very first time in this letter first, in verse 19 and then second, in verse 22 although it is translated in most versions as *holiness*. Lastly, the reader should note that the topic of sanctification which begins in Romans 6 goes all the way into Romans 8, so that Romans 6 deals with the subject of sanctification concerning the believer and his relationship to sin. Romans 7 deals with the subject of the believer and his relationship to the law. And then Romans 8 deals with the subject of the believer and his relationship to the Holy Spirit.

In a video published by the *Banner of Truth* entitled *Romans in 40 Minutes*, Sinclair Ferguson gives a helpful overview of Romans 6, 7, and 8, highlighting some "already, not yet" aspects to them concerning sanctification. He said that in Romans 6, Paul says that the believer has died to the dominion of sin, but sin has not yet been fully banished in their life. However, one day this will be so. In chapter 7, Paul says that the believer has died to the condemnation of the law, but he has not yet been fully perfected according to the standard of the law. However, one day this will be so. And then in chapter 8, the believer is no longer in the flesh, that is to say, dominated by the flesh, our sinful nature, because they are now in the Spirit, but their life lived in this world does not perfectly conform to the life of the Spirit. However, one day this will be so.

4 The London Baptist Confession of faith of 1689 updated version for the 21st century by Founders Press, describes sanctification this way in chapter 13: "Those who are united to Christ and effectually called and regenerated have a new heart and a new spirit created in them through the power of Christ's death and resurrection. They are also further sanctified, really and personally, through the same power, by his Word and Spirit dwelling in them. The dominion of the whole body of sin is destroyed, and the various evil desires that arise from it are more and more weakened and put to death. At the same time, those called and regenerated are more and more enlivened and strengthened in all saving graces so that they practice true holiness, without which no one will see the Lord. This sanctification extends throughout the whole person, though it is never completed in this life. Some corruption remains in every part. From this arises a continual and irreconcilable war, with the desires of the flesh against the Spirit and the Spirit against the flesh. In this war, the remaining corruption may greatly prevail for a time. Yet through the continual supply of strength from the sanctifying Spirit of Christ, the regenerate part overcomes. So the saints grow in grace, perfecting holiness in the fear of God. They pursue a heavenly life, in gospel obedience to all the commands that Christ as Head and King has given them in his Word."

5 Some passages which point to the progress nature of sanctification are: 2 Cor. 3:18, 7:1; Phil. 3:13, 14; Col. 3:9, 10; Heb. 10:14, 12:14; 1 Pt. 1:15.

"But where sin abounded, grace abounded much more."[6] In this verse, the apostle explains that even though we are sinners both by nature and practice, nevertheless, God's conquering grace toward us in Christ was greater than all our sin. Though we were rebels and lawbreakers against God, He was rich in mercy toward us in Jesus, so that while we were still sinners Christ died for us.

Even though this is a glorious gospel truth which should bring great joy to our hearts, Paul anticipates that some will twist his words or perhaps that was already happening in his day, for "some men are bad enough for anything; they will curdle the sweet milk of love into the sourest argument for sin"[7] (cf. 3:8b). As he looks ahead, he expects that some would distort what he has said to make it seem as if he taught, "Since there is an abundance of grace to exceed all of our sins, why not sin as much as we like?"[8]

In this chapter, he lists several reasons why the true Christian would not want to go on living in sin. The most fundamental reason for this is because the Holy Spirit produces gospel holiness in everyone who is united to Christ.[9] But what is more, the thought that sinning would produce more grace, is absurd and completely contradicts the essence of the gospel. Thus, in these verses, the apostle defends the doctrine of justification by faith alone from all such slander. Charles Hodge put it this way,

> The most common, the most plausible, and yet the most unfounded objection to the doctrine of justification by faith, is, that it allows men to live in sin that grace may abound. This objection arises from ignorance of the doctrine in question, and of the nature and means of sanctification. It is so preposterous in the eyes of an enlightened believer, that Paul deals with it rather by exclamations at its absurdity, than with logical arguments. The main idea of this section is, that such is the nature of the believer's union with Christ, that his living in sin is not merely an inconsistency, but a contradiction in terms, as much so as to speak of a live dead man, or a good bad one.[10]

---

6 Many commentators make this point.

7 Spurgeon, p. 79.

8 This erroneous thinking is similar to what Paul has already dealt with back in 3:8a and also 6:15. However, in saying this, we must not miss how important it is that he deals with this topic once again because the doctrine of justification of faith alone is constantly being criticized by the enemies of the gospel who say that it leads to a licentious life. However, as we shall see, Paul powerfully shuts down such foolish argumentation.

9 Many commentators point out that the subject of sanctification really begins back in chapter 5:12 to 21 in connection with the whole topic of union with Christ. I agree with them.

10 Hodge, p. 191.

Exegetical & Practical Insights:

Obs. 1- (vv. 1-10) That as Paul begins his defense of the ethical implications of the teaching of justification by faith alone, he writes first in verse one:[11]

What shall we say then[12] or what conclusion should be drawn regarding all that has been written in the previous chapter concerning the free grace of God toward us in Christ? **Shall we continue,**[13] that is, shall we habitually persist as a pattern of life; **in sin that** or for the purpose that; **grace,** or God's unmerited, and undeserved goodness to us in Christ; **may abound** or increase?

Paul answers this rhetorical question in verse two by saying:

Certainly not[14] or may this never be![15] Or, "what a ghastly thought"[16] since "Christ came to free us from our vices, not feed them."[17] **How** or with what right or warrant; **shall we** or, such ones as have become true believers and are no longer under Adam's federal headship (cf. Rom. 5:12-21); **who died**[18] **to sin**[19] (a statement of fact),[20] that is, died definitely to sin as a ruling and reigning principle in our lives the very day we were converted, so that we do not consistently obey it

---

11 These two verses frame Paul's entire discussion of sanctification as set forth in this chapter. Further, some commentators have noted that as Paul was in Corinth writing this letter (see my background overview comments in this commentary), he could be thinking about some of the problems that were going on in that very church among the professed membership.

12 Paul uses the same phraseology in 3:5, and 4:1, and he will use it in 7:7; 8:31; and 9:14. He does this to prevent a potentially false conclusion to any of his particular arguments. This could have been a rabbinical way of reasoning with people as an apologetic technique.

13 Grk. present, active, verb. The preposition attached to the verb in the original intensifies the force of it cf. Acts 12:16; Gal. 1:18.

14 Paul has used this language several times already in this epistle as I have noted. MacArthur calls it, "the strongest idiom of repudiation in the Greek New Testament." MacArthur, p. 316.

15 Plainly, Paul rejects the invalid inference as stated in verse one of this chapter, as the language shows how appalled he is at the suggestion that any should sin that grace may abound.

16 Phillips translation.

17 Edwards, p. 158.

18 Grk. aorist, active, verb.

19 As unbelievers, we were dead *in* sin (Eph. 2:1); now as believers, we are dead *to* sin.

20 Technically speaking we could say that we "died to sin" in a fivefold sense: *Legally,* because we were cleared of all its charges through Christ. *Representatively,* because Jesus dealt with our sin at the cross and severed us from our connection to Adam. *Personally,* because it is at conversion when we actually experienced this in our lives. *Pictorially,* because this is what our baptism symbolized. And then later, as Paul speaks of it in this chapter, *progressively,* because this is what happens through the process of sanctification.

anymore;[21] **live,**[22] i.e., continue to live in the realm of it; **any longer?**[23] Robert Rogland helpfully summarizes these words,

> What does Paul mean by the phrase "dead to sin"? What aspect of death reflects our relationship to sin now that we have been justified by faith in Christ? Paul certainly cannot mean that we are insensitive to temptation and unable to sin (as a corpse cannot sense or respond to stimuli). We know from personal experience that Christians feel temptation and are frequently overcome by it. Indeed, Paul devotes most of chapter 7 to the Christian struggle against sin. The aspect of death that now corresponds to our relationship to sin is *severance*, the termination of all ties, affections, and obligations. When one dies, he or she *leaves this world* and *enters a new world*. Old debts, old relationships, old bonds are completely severed and done away with. An irreversible, total breach is made between the dead and this life. In Christ, we died to sin in this radical sense. The real me, the new me, has no citizenship in this world anymore. I am alive to God now. My loyalty, allegiance, obligations, affections, relationships, and interests are all in the new world. Paul's point is that we already have passed over to the other side in spirit. Despite the reality of indwelling sin, we have no business letting the old, unregenerate nature prevail when it seeks to dominate our thoughts and actions. *It* was nailed to the cross in the person of Christ; *it* is not the new me created in Christ Jesus, the me with whom God now has to do (7:17; 2 Cor. 5:17; Gal. 2:19-20).[24]

John Murray further remarks:

> What the apostle has in view is the once-for-all definitive breach with sin which constitutes the new identity of the believer. A believer cannot therefore live in sin; if a man lives in sin he is not a believer. If we view

---

21 Whereas some take the words that "we died to sin" to mean that we died to the allurement of sin, or that our sin nature has been eradicated, or that the Christian is not responsive to sin anymore, or that the Christian has died to sin's guilt, etc., (some of these matters are helpfully considered in James Boice's commentary on Romans, pp. 651-653), biblically speaking, these ideas should be rejected (cf. 7:15-24). Rather, the idea presented above is the most likely understanding of Paul's words. Simply stated, definitive sanctification is the basis of our progressive sanctification. This view is supported by Lloyd-Jones in his treatment of this passage, pp. 19-20.

Also, note that while Paul says that we "died to sin" that does not mean that sin is dead to us. Death does not mean extinction. Rather, it means separation. When Paul says we "died to sin" he does not mean that sin ceases to exist in our lives or that the ability to sin is no longer with us. Rather, we are "dead to sin" in that through our union with Christ, we are separated from its dominion and dominant influence over us. The strength of sin has been broken in our lives once for all time and has been replaced with the "reign of grace" as Paul speaks of in 5:21.

22 Lloyd-Jones comments, "The word live is obviously important. It means 'continue and abide'. The Apostle is asserting that in view of our position – the fact that we are under the rule and reign of grace – it is impossible that we should continue and abide in sin, or that a life of sin should be our life." Lloyd-Jones, on Romans, p. 22.

23 As we think about the subject of the free, justifying grace of God toward us in Christ, there are two extremes that we must always avoid. On the one hand, there is the matter of licentiousness or loose living, antinomianism. On the other hand, there is legalism or creating our own standards of righteousness apart from God's as found in His Word, either as a way to be made right with God, or as a way to be made holy before Him. Both of these matters are inconsistent with New Testament morality.

24 Rogland, pp. 58, 59.

sin as a realm or sphere then the believer no longer lives in that realm or sphere. And just as it is true with reference to life in the sphere of this world that the person who has died "passed away, and, lo, he is not: yea, I sought him, but he could not be found" (Psalm 37:36; *cf.* 103:16), so it is with the sphere of sin; the believer is no longer there because he has died to sin. Failure to appreciate this premise upon which the subsequent argument rests and of which it is an expansion will distort our understanding of this chapter.[25]

How then can the Christian who is dead to sin because of salvation in Christ have victory over it? Paul gives *five keys* in this regard. The first three are dealt with in these verses and are:

First, *remembering* our spiritual union with Christ (v. 3).[26] Second, by *recalling* that our water baptism symbolized our death to sin and rising to a new life (vv. 4, 5). And third by *realizing* that our old man was crucified with Christ (vv. 6-10).[27]

(vv. 3-5) Or do you not know[28] or are you continually unaware; **that** the conjunction setting forth the content of what they were to know;[29]

---

25 Murray, p. 213.

26 Sinclair Ferguson helpfully says, "Failure to deal with the presence of sin can often be traced back to spiritual amnesia, forgetfulness of our new, true, real identity. As a believer I am someone who has been delivered from the dominion of sin and who therefore is free and motivated to fight against the remnants of sin's army in my heart." www.ligonier.org/blog/how-mortify-sin/.

27 Usually, at this point, commentators deal with the issue of the old man/new man relationship to the Christian. In other words, is the believer both an "old self" and a "new self?" Although many good writers differ on this point, even good reformed writers, my current understanding of Scripture is that the believer is not both an old self/new self (in some type of Jekyll and Hyde scenario), since our old self, i.e., our old man in Adam who was ruled and dominated by sin, was crucified with Christ (Rom. 6:6, 2 Cor. 5:17). Having said this, of course, this is not to deny the fact that the believer who is a new man in Christ, still has remaining sin within himself. But he is no longer the old self in his first Federal head, Adam. He is a new man, but not yet a perfect man.

John Murray put it this way in his book *Principles of Conduct,* p. 218: "The old man is the unregenerate man; the new man is the regenerate man created in Christ Jesus unto good works. It is no more feasible to call the believer a new man and an old man than it is to call him a regenerate man and an unregenerate. And neither is it warranted to speak of the believer as having in him the old man and the new man. This kind of terminology is without warrant and it is but another method of doing prejudice to the doctrine which Paul was so jealous to establish when he said, 'our old man has been crucified'."

For a further discussion of this matter, see Anthony A. Hoekema's book *Saved by Grace,* Eerdmans, 1994, pp. 209-14. On page 214 in his book, Hoekema makes this practical observation regarding this discussion: "One important implication of this teaching is that believers should have positive images of themselves. The basis for such a self-image is not sinful pride in our own achievements or virtues but seeing ourselves in light of God's redemptive work in our lives. Christianity not only means believing something about Christ; it also means believing something about ourselves, namely, that we are indeed new creatures in Christ."

28 Grk. present, active, verb. Paul uses this phraseology throughout Romans: 6:16; 7:1; 11:2, etc.

29 Paul seems to believe that these Roman Christians should have had this information. Additionally, he continues to remind these believers, and us as well, about what we should *know* (6:6; 6:9; 6:16). Hence, it is clear from his language, that a lack of knowledge in the Christian life is a key factor for spiritual failure.

as many of us, i.e., professing believers; **as were baptized,**[30] that is, definitively and spiritually immersed; **into Christ Jesus** once for all time at salvation, which means, "baptized into union with Christ;" [31] **were baptized into His death** or with reference to the particular design of His death, which was to free us from the penalty and power of our sin. **Therefore** or consequently; **we were buried with Him** (Christ); **through** or by means of; **baptism**[32] (i.e., the symbolic ordinance of water baptism);[33] **into death, that** or so that, the conjunction highlighting the purpose of us partaking of the ordinance; **just as Christ was raised from** or out of; **the dead by the glory of the Father** or "by that illustrious power by which he exhibited himself as really glorious;"[34] **even so** or in like manner; **we also should walk** that is to say, morally conduct our lives; **in newness of life** "which refers to newness of quality and character"[35] as opposed to our old former ways of living. **For** the conjunction explaining and confirming what Paul meant by bringing up water baptism in verse four; **if** or since; **we have been united** or planted together; **in the likeness** or form; **of His death** (pictorially portrayed through water baptism); **certainly** or indeed; **we also shall be** *in the likeness* **of His resurrection**[36] which is to say, that as Jesus died and rose from the grave and lived, so also we,

---

30 Grk. aorist, passive, verb.

31 Murray, p. 214. Union with Christ is a real, spiritual joining with Him, which all true Christians experience in regeneration. It is the essence of all true, saving religion, whereby we are in Christ and He is in us by the Holy Spirit. Without this saving union, we are still in union with Adam our first federal head, and thus we are still dead in trespasses and sins and separated from the life of God.

32 Baptism portrays our death to our old selves and our new life with Christ. Symbolically it is like dying and rising again. It is a picture ordinance that reminds us of what God in sovereign grace has accomplished for us in salvation. MacArthur says, "It is a public symbol of faith in God... a mark of salvation because it gives outward evidence of an inward faith in Christ." MacArthur, p. 321.
Bobby Jamieson has perhaps the best full-fledged definition of baptism I have ever heard when he writes that "baptism is a church's act of affirming and portraying a believer's union with Christ by immersing him or her in water, and a believers act of publicly committing him or herself to Christ and his people, thereby uniting a believer to the church and marking off him or her from the world." https://www.9marks.org/article/baptism-is-a-churchs-act.

33 Obviously, the apostle is not teaching salvation by water baptism in this verse as the so-called "Churches of Christ" falsely teach. Paul has just spent several chapters teaching that a man is justified by faith alone, in Christ alone apart from anything that he does. See his words also in 1 Corinthians 1:17.

34 Calvin, p. 222.

35 MacArthur, p. 322.

36 The words here may be speaking about the future at Christ's return. Hodge says that, "the resurrection here spoken of is a spiritual rising from the dead, seems plain, both from what precedes and from what follows. The whole discussion relates to sanctification, to sin, and the holiness of his people. Those who are cleansed from the guilt of sin, are cleansed also from its pollution. Although this is obvious, yet all reference to the future resurrection of the body is not to be excluded. In chapter 8:11, the apostle represents the quickening of our mortal bodies as a necessary consequence of our union with Christ, and the indwelling of his Spirit. If, therefore, we are baptized unto the death of Christ, united and conformed to him in his death, the sure result will be, that we shall be conformed to him in a holy life here, and in a life of glorious immortality of the soul and body hereafter. All this is included in the life which flows to us from Christ." Hodge, p. 196.

in the ordinance of baptism, symbolically rise from an old course of sinning and live a new life in Him as we partake of His resurrected life and rising power. This life and power give us the strength to overcome sin and its suggestions.[37]

In these verses, Paul sets forth the significance and symbolism of two baptisms that we are always to be mindful of if we are to grow in our sanctification. The first is our *spiritual* baptism *into* Christ when we were first saved. Now that this has happened, we are no longer spiritually dead men and women in Adam and have the power to live uprightly through our union with Jesus. We have been spiritually incorporated into the Savior and thus in Him, "we live and move, and have our being."

The second is our *symbolic* baptism as believers *into* water showing that we have been saved.[38] These are two magnificent events that the apostle wants us to constantly look back on and so remember key truths about ourselves in order to drive us away from sin. The point is, we have forever been joined to Christ through regeneration and thus we should live accordingly. Further, we made a public declaration of this when we obeyed the Lord and were baptized as His disciples. Consequently, we should follow hard after Him all of our days (Matt. 28:19).

Spurgeon remarks:

> The operations, therefore, of the Spirit of God forbid that a saved man should live in sin. He is dead; he is raised into newness of life: at the very entrance into the church, in the very act of baptism, he declares that he cannot live as he once did, for he is dead: he declares that he must live after another fashion, for has not he been raised again in the type and raised again in very deed from the dead?[39]

McDonald also helpfully comments:

> There is a sense in which a believer attends the funeral of his old self when he is baptized. As he goes under the water he is saying, "All that I was as a sinful son of Adam was put to death at the cross." As he comes up out of the water he is saying, "It is no longer I who live, but Christ lives in me."[40]

The apostle continues and says thirdly in verses six to ten:

(Vv. 6-10) knowing this,[41] or already having this knowledge based on what they had been previously taught; **that** the conjunction putting forth the knowledge they were to have; **our old man,** which is to say, our old unregenerated sinful selves, the people we were in Adam before we were

---

37 Cf. Eph. 1:19-20; Col. 1:28-29.

38 Note the order here as Paul presents it. One cannot live *for* Christ until one first has been spiritually joined to Christ. Or, to put it another way, one is not fit to be baptized in water *by another,* until one has first been baptized into Christ by God.

39 Spurgeon, p. 75.

40 McDonald, p. 1701.

41 Grk. perfect, active, participle.

saved;[42] **was crucified**[43] or *representatively* put to death, once for all time, never to be repeated again; **with Him**, (i.e., with Jesus at the cross, for we were chosen "in Him" before the foundation of the world, cf. Eph. 1:4; cf. Gal. 2:20);[44] **that** or in order that, the conjunction denoting purpose; **the body of sin**[45] not the physical body, but the old self, completely ruled and dominated by the power of sin; **might be done away with,**[46] i.e., *actually* done away in us at conversion, not annihilated, but rendered ineffectual, or powerless in its relation to sin "as a controlling power;"[47] **that** or so that; **we** that is, we who are Christians who have experienced the grace of God in salvation, through sanctification;[48] **should no longer be slaves of sin**[49] (which of course is what our former condition was as non-Christians).[50]

For the conjunction explaining and expanding the previous verse; **he who has died,** i.e., died to sin's power when he was saved and became a new creation at conversion; **has been freed** literally "has been justified";[51] **from sin** that is, *legally* he stands acquitted from sin's punishment and *practically* he stands delivered from sin's rule over him. **Now if** or since; **we died with Christ,** that is, died with Christ spiritually speaking when we were saved; **we believe**[52] or are believing as a firm conviction; **that** the conjunction setting forth the essence of our belief; **we shall also live**[53] or coexist; **with Him,** that is live with Jesus both now and into eternity; **knowing**[54] or standing fully persuaded of the fact just stated in verse eight based on what Paul is now about to say; **that Christ, having been raised from the dead, dies no more. Death no longer has dominion** or rule and mastery; **over Him,** since He "was raised to an endless life."[55] **For** an explanatory conjunction confirming the previous words;[56] *the death* **that He died, He died to sin** or with respect to our sin when, as the

---

42 Or as John Murray puts it, "Our old man is the old self or ego, the unregenerate man in his entirety in contrast with the new man as the regenerate man in his entirety." Murray, p. 218.

43 Grk. aorist, passive, verb.

44 Hodge says, "We are united to Christ as our head and representative, so as to be partakers of his death and resurrection as a matter of law or right." Hodge, p. 197.

45 The language of "the body of sin" depicts our old, unsaved, sinful selves as an entity that had evil coursing throughout its entire being.

46 Literally, the word translated "be done away" in Greek means "to work down, or exhaust." McBeth, p. 168.

47 McDonald, p. 1702.

48 So Harvey, p. 152.

49 The language of slaves here would have been familiar to the Romans, since the first century was full of slave/master relations.

50 Cf. 6:17a

51 Same Greek verb is used in 3:20, 24.

52 Grk. present, active, verb.

53 Grk. future, active, verb.

54 Grk. perfect, active, participle.

55 Vaughan and Corley, p. 77.

56 Ibid.

sinless One, He bore sin's consequence for us; **once for all** or decisively;[57] but *the life* that He lives, i.e., a Godward, heavenly life; **He lives to God**, as the resurrected, exulted and reigning Son of God.

Suggested applications from the text for the church:

1- Since continuing in unrepentant sin as a pattern of life is inconsistent with being in a state of grace, if we are doing this, we need to ask ourselves, are we genuinely converted?

2- Since we have died to sin and have been joined to Christ, we are to live as though this really has happened to us. Do we?

Suggested application from the text for the non-Christian:

1- Since Christ alone is the one who can break the power of sin over you, do you see your great need for Him?

Text: Romans 6:11-14

General theme: Sanctification and the Saved (II)

Homiletical outline of the verses:

B. The duties we must perform to have success over sin: [11] Likewise you also, reckon yourselves to be dead indeed to sin, but alive to God in Christ Jesus our Lord. [12] Therefore do not let sin reign in your mortal body, that you should obey it in its lusts. [13] And do not present your members *as* instruments of unrighteousness to sin, but present yourselves to God as being alive from the dead, and your members *as* instruments of righteousness to God. [14] For sin shall not have dominion over you, for you are not under law but under grace.

Exegetical & Practical Insights:

The fourth key to overcoming sin is by our *reckoning* that all of the above facts are so.[58]

Obs. 1- (v. 11) That as Paul has just laid out all that is true of us who have been saved, that in the very first command in this entire chapter, and yes, in this entire epistle[59] he sums up and applies all that he has been saying and writes:

---

57 MacArthur says about Jesus, "He achieved a victory that will never need repeating, a profound truth that the writer of Hebrews stresses again and again (7:26-27; 9:12, 28, 10:10; cf. 1 Pet. 3:18)." MacArthur, p. 328.

58 We see from verse eleven and what follows, that although the *power* of sin has been broken over our lives through Christ's work on our behalf, nevertheless, its *presence* is still with us. In other words, although sin no longer *reigns*, it still *remains*. Although we are dead to it, it is not dead to us! And so, what are we to do? Are we to let remaining sin conquer us? Or, are we to be passive when it comes to our sanctification? Absolutely not! And thus, as I said earlier, sanctification is the believer working with God by the enablement of the Holy Spirit so that we regularly say, "no to sin" and "yes to the Savior." We by the Spirit's help, are to put to death the deeds of the flesh, and thus, Paul says in Romans 8:13b, "if by the Spirit you put to death the deeds of the body, you will live."

59 The commands in Scripture (imperatives), are built on what is true of us by grace (indicatives). In other words, because such and such has happened to us in salvation, we are to live therefore in such a manner as commanded us. Further, it should be noted that

Likewise you also, or in view of what was just mentioned in verses six to ten, so in this way; **reckon**[60] (not merely imagine)[61] but continuously regard, believe and acknowledge yourselves; **to be** (as a present reality throughout the entirety of your Christian life); **dead indeed to sin**[62] (or dead with respect to sin's sway over you as the case really is through Christ); **but** (now positively speaking); **alive**[63] **to God** or as being constantly in fellowship with Him; **in** or through our union with; **Christ Jesus our Lord.**[64]

Vaughan and Corley succinctly remark,

> The meaning is that just as Jesus died once for all to sin, the believer is to regard himself, by virtue of his union with Christ, as forever dead to the dominion of sin; and just as Christ lives endlessly unto God, the believer, who shares Christ's life, is to regard himself as forever alive to God.[65]

Grant Osborne comments regarding the word "reckon" in the verse saying that it is,

> ...a present-tense command, and it means that even though we are dead to sin, we must continually reckon ourselves dead to the power of sin in our lives. While it has been "done away with" (v. 6), it is still an invading army trying to regain control and enslave us, so we must as an act of will consider ourselves in every instance of temptation to be dead to it.[66]

The fifth key to overcoming sin is by our *responding* to God positively in His gracious commands to us.[67]

---

although we have been "crucified with Christ" (6:6), nevertheless, since sin still remains in us until the consummation, we must continue to reckon ourselves to be "dead indeed to sin" (6:11) all of our days. This is popularly known as the "already/not yet" tension of the Bible. We are already dead to sin, but we are not yet fully dead to sin.

60 Grk. present, middle, verb.

61 This Greek word is an accounting term that means to calculate. It highlights to us the fact that if we are going to live holy/sanctified lives as believers, then every day we are to compute in our own minds what is true about us spiritually speaking according to Scripture because of our union with Christ.

62 An incident from Augustine's life illustrates what it means to "consider ourselves dead to sin and alive to God in Christ Jesus (v.11) One day after his conversion, as he was walking through a marketplace, a woman who had been his lover cried out to him saying, "Augustine, it's me! It's me!" To this Augustine replied, "I know, but it's no longer me!" This is the essence of what it means to reckon yourselves dead to sin and alive to God through Christ Jesus our Lord.

63 Grk. present, active, participle.

64 Wilson says that this is the "first time in the epistle that Paul uses this pregnant phrase, 'in Christ Jesus our Lord.'" Wilson, p. 101.
MacArthur remarks concerning this prepositional phrase and says: "No religion in the world can or does make such a claim. Even the most ardent Muslim does not claim to be *in* Mohammed or *in* Allah. Buddhists do not claim to be *in* Buddha or Hindus to be *in* any of their multitude of gods. As Christians, however, we know that God 'has blessed us with every spiritual blessing in the heavenly places in Christ'" (Eph. 1:3). MacArthur, 336.

65 Vaughan and Corley, p. 77.

66 Osborne, p. 172.

67 Clearly, by this heading, the popular notion which says that when it comes to growing in sanctification and Christ-likeness we are to "let go and let God" is wrong.

Obs. 2- (vv. 12-14) That as Paul gives another imperative based on what it means to "reckon ourselves to be dead indeed to sin, but alive to God in Christ Jesus our Lord" (v.11), he writes negatively speaking and says:

Therefore or in light of the previous words and as "a call to action;"[68] **do not let sin reign,**[69] that is, regularly resist its rule as an evil oppressor; **in** the preposition denoting the sphere of the reign; **your mortal body,** i.e., the whole person; **that** or with the result that; **you should obey it in its lusts** or sinful desires.[70]

In commenting on this verse Augustine says:

> We must engage in a constant, daily struggle not to obey those desires which are forbidden or improper. For from this sort of fault it comes about that the eye is turned to where it ought not to look, and if this fault grows strong and prevails, even bodily adultery is carried out, which is committed in the heart as much more quickly as thought is quicker than action and has nothing to hinder or delay it.[71]

As Paul explains specifically how we can have mastery over sin in our mortal bodies,[72] he writes again by way of a command and says now positively:

And[73] **do not present**[74] or offer and yield; **your members** (whatever members they are, whether our hearts, our hands, our feet, our tongues etc.); *as instruments*[75] literally, as tools or weapons;[76] **of unrighteousness** or wrongdoing and injustices; **to sin, but**[77] or on the contrary; **present**[78] or positively and definitively as a daily choice give;[79] **yourselves,** i.e., all that you are; **to God as being alive from the dead,** (the very thing which

---

68 Harvey, p. 154.

69 Grk. present, active, imperative, verb.

70 Commentators discuss the significance of the present imperative verb preceded by the negative particle in the Greek text, as to whether Paul is calling them to stop an action that was already taking place or warning them to not start engaging in one (cf. Rom. 12: 1-2). If the former, then the sense in the language would be, "Therefore *stop* letting sin reign in your mortal body, that you should obey its lust." Over the years I have taught it this way to my Greek students, as that which *potentially* might be the case. For further discussion of the matter I point the reader to Moo, in the NICNT pp. 381-82.

71 *Ancient Christian Commentary on Scripture, Romans* p. 158. John Owen the English Puritan famously said, "Be killing sin or it will be killing you!"

72 Evidently, all that Paul is teaching in these verses shows us that sinless perfection is not possible in this life.

73 Or more literally, "neither."

74 Grk. present, active, imperative, verb.

75 The word is a military term (as several commentators note), depicting our bodies as weapons either for good or for evil.

76 "Sin fights for the mastery; it calls out an army of the lust of the body, and seeks to use the members, hand, eye or tongue, as weapons wherewith the lust may re-establish the rule of unrighteousness." Gifford, p. 130.

77 The strong Greek adversative.

78 Grk. aorist, active, imperative verb.

79 This is to be "a daily choice" as opposed to a once for all action being that Paul uses both the present tense and aorist tense verbs in the verse.

is true of us spiritually speaking); **and your members *as* instruments** (again, tools or weapons); **of righteousness** that is, what is right or upright according; **to God** (and His Word).[80]

In verse fourteen Paul now summarizes his teaching concerning sanctification, but he "changes from admonition to declaration,"[81] offering words of encouragement and promise and writes: **For** the conjunction explaining why we are to do what he said in verse thirteen: not, "*Do not let* sin have dominion over you," (a command by Paul, no) but (as a statement of fact); ***sin shall not* have dominion** or mastery, rule control and governance; **over you** (since in fact you are dead to it through Jesus vv. 3-6); **for** or because, the conjunction joyfully explaining why 14a is so; **you are not under** (the power of); **law but**[82] or on the contrary; **under** (the power of); **grace.**

What is Paul saying in these words? Simply this: first, because of our true union with Christ, sin shall not and cannot dominate us any longer. This is a tremendous truth that should cause us to rejoice. When we were unconverted, sin ruled over us and in us. When it said jump we replied, saying, "How high?" But no longer! Now we have been freed from sin's dominion through Christ. Now we have been spiritually raised from the dead by the glory of the Father to walk in newness of life (6:4).

And why is this so? This is the second thing that Paul tells us when he says, "We are not under law but under grace." What does this mean? The phrase "under law" has been variously understood by the commentators.[83] However, in this context, and especially in connection to Romans chapter 7, where Paul once again speaks about his "body," (7:24), and his "members," (7:23a), as he has done in this chapter, it seems that the phrase "under law" refers to being under "the law of sin"

---

80 So the choice before us every day is to whom or to what will we give ourselves? To the service of sin or God? Or we could ask, "What spiritual army will we enlist to use our weapons, sin's or God's?"

81 MacArthur, p. 338.

82 The strong Greek adversative.

83 For example, some take these words to mean that we are no longer "under the curse of the law," which of course is true because of Jesus' work in our place. But in this context, this does not seem to make much sense. Others take the words to mean that we are not "under the requirements or obedience of the law" as a standard or covenant of works through which we could be made righteous with God or a means of justification with Him, which also is true. But again, in this context, this does not make much sense. Lastly, there are some who take these words to mean that we are no longer "under the Mosaic law" that is, the Ten Commandments even as a guiding principle in our lives, in order to direct us in our sanctification, which is to be rejected since 1- Paul has already told us in (3:31), that we do not make void the law through faith but rather we establish it (cf. Matt. 5:17-19). 2- Paul says in 7:12 that the law is "holy and just and good" (cf. 13:8-10). 3- There is no definite article in the Greek text so that the passage says "the law" which typically refers to the Mosaic Law. And then 4- Paul points the believer to the law to show him what love does not do towards others in 13:8-10, showing us that is still of use for us today. And thus, to say that the law has no relevance for the believer in his/her growth in Christ-likeness, cannot be right. And so while the law of God in and of itself does not have the ability to sanctify us, because of the weakness of the flesh (cf. 7:7-11; 8:3) — besides, only the Savior by the Spirit can do this (cf. 1 Thess. 5:23)—it is still a helpful tool in the hand of God to help us to know how we could live righteously before our God and others. For further comments see my notes on Rom. 3:31.

(see Romans 7:23c he uses this exact language). Sin shall not have dominion and authority over us because as believers, we are no longer under the law, i.e., under the rule or regime of sin. Rather, we are under the law, i.e., the rule, and regime of grace. We are now under the power of grace and what a power it is! Grace, grace, amazing grace, is that which now dominates and drives our lives as believers, "so that as sin reigned in death, even so grace might reign through righteousness to eternal life through Jesus Christ our Lord" (5:21).[84]

Plainly then, based on what we have seen in the first fourteen verses of this chapter, according to Paul, the doctrine of justification by faith alone, in Christ alone, is not at all incompatible with sanctification. In reality, it is the very foundation of and impetus for it. As the apostle has instructed us in it so far, he has given us *five keys* to help us in this regard: *remember, recall, realize, reckon, and respond.*

Suggested applications from the text for the church:

1- Remember that in your sanctification there are moral duties that God lays upon you to fulfill by the help and strength of Christ. Therefore, daily seek Him for help.

2- Remember that in your sanctification passivity is not an option if you want to have greater measures of success. Therefore, daily "reckon yourself to be dead indeed to sin, but alive to God in Christ Jesus our Lord."

Suggested application from the text for the non-Christian:

1- Remember that because you are not saved, you are under the law of sin and not under grace. Therefore, go to Christ at once so that He can change this horrible spiritual condition for you.

Text: Romans 6:15-23

General theme: Sanctification and the Saved (III)

Homiletical outline of the verses:

C. The metaphor we must think on to have success over sin:
[15] What then? Shall we sin because we are not under law but under grace? Certainly not! [16] Do you not know that to whom you present yourselves slaves to obey, you are that one's slaves whom you obey, whether of sin *leading* to death, or of obedience *leading* to righteousness? [17] But God be thanked that *though* you were slaves of sin, yet you obeyed from the heart that form of doctrine to which you were delivered. [18] And having been set free from sin, you became slaves of righteousness. [19] I speak in human *terms* because of the weakness of your flesh. For just as you presented your members *as* slaves of uncleanness, and of lawlessness *leading* to *more* lawlessness, so now present your members *as* slaves *of* righteousness for

---

84 John Piper says, "Grace is not simply leniency when we have sinned. Grace is the enabling gift of God not to sin. Grace is power, not just pardon." www.gracequotes.org.

holiness. [20] For when you were slaves of sin, you were free in regard to righteousness. [21] What fruit did you have then in the things of which you are now ashamed? For the end of those things *is* death. [22] But now having been set free from sin, and having become slaves of God, you have your fruit to holiness, and the end, everlasting life. [23] For the wages of sin *is* death, but the gift of God *is* eternal life in Christ Jesus our Lord.

Exegetical & Practical Insights:

Obs. 1- (v. 15) That as the apostle reinforces and restates aspects of his teaching so that one should not miss his point concerning the relationship between justification and sanctification, he writes in similar language to verses one and two of this chapter saying:

What then? That is, what shall we conclude since we are under grace; **Shall we** as believers in Christ, like Paul was; **sin**[85] (not merely "continue in sin" as was stated in verse one, but the idea is sin *even* a little bit);[86] **because** or since; **we are not under law,** i.e., not under the law of sin as a governing rule in our lives; **but**[87] or on the contrary; **under grace,** i.e., the governing rule of grace? **Certainly not** or "No, no, a thousand times no!"[88]

Once again, Paul is "up in arms" at the thought that a truly converted individual would ever turn the grace of God into a license or an evil occasion for sin, even if it is a little bit.[89] We have been freed from such a lifestyle therefore, to do this, is to turn *grace* into *dis*grace, since a life under the reign of grace is to issue forth in a life of evangelical obedience to the Word of God (1 John 2:4). Simply stated, grace works in the hearts of those who are saved to want what God wants, and to do what God wants them to do (cf. v. 17; Phil. 2:12-13).[90]

Schreiner notes,

> If one claims to be "under grace" and yet lives as a slave to sin, then the claim is nullified by one's conduct. Those who live under grace show that they are under grace because they have a new master (God) and are liberated from their old master (sin). Paul refuses to accept any abstract understanding of grace separated from concrete daily living. Grace does not merely involve the forgiveness of sins. It also involves power in which the mastery and dominion of sin are broken.[91]

Obs. 2- (vv. 16-18) That as Paul answers his own question, as stated in verse 15, he replies rhetorically and says unequivocally:

---

85 Spurgeon exclaims, "Oh! This old question keeps coming up." Spurgeon, p. 77.

86 McDonald, p. 1703.

87 The strong Greek adversative.

88 MacArthur, p. 342.

89 This is what false professors of faith do (cf. Jude 4).

90 This is not to say that believers obey the Word of God perfectly, but they do obey it purposefully.

91 Schreiner, p. 332.

Do you not know[92] or are you not knowing as a simple fact of life; **that** the conjunction giving the content of what they should have known; **to whom** or to that which; **you present**[93] or are offering and yielding; **yourselves** under subjection; **slaves to obey, you are**[94] and will continue to be; **that one's slaves whom you obey**[95] **whether** or either; **of sin** *leading to death,* i.e., eternal death in the final analysis (cf. v. 23); **or of obedience** (to God and His Word); *leading* **to** or connected with; **righteousness,** i.e., right living before God?[96] **But God be thanked**[97] not man (or their so-called "free will"), but God, the sole Author of their salvation; **that** the conjunction setting forth the reason and ground for the thanks; *though* **you were slaves of sin,**[98] that is to say, before conversion they were habitually in bondage to a sinful lifestyle; **yet** or in opposition to that now that you are saved; **you obeyed,**[99] or at once, willingly put yourself in subjection; **from the heart**[100] or out of the heart, or "wholeheartedly" not merely outwardly, but from the new heart given in regeneration (cf. Ezek. 36:26, 27); **that form** or pattern; **of doctrine,** or apostolic teaching, i.e., the Christian gospel that was preached to them which was to be molding their lives with all of its moral implications; **to**[101] **which you were delivered**[102] or once for all time entrusted.[103] **And** the apostle recapping all that he has been saying in the previous verses; **having been set free**[104] **from** or away from; **sin** (a statement of fact, again, not from the presence of sin, but the rule and reign and power of sin because we died to it when we were saved); **you became**[105] **slaves of righteousness** (a statement of fact) or right living according to God's Word.[106]

---

92 Grk. perfect, active, verb.

93 Grk. present, active, verb.

94 Grk. present, active, verb.

95 Clint Arnold says, "Making the analogy even more exact is the fact that people in the ancient world could sell themselves into slavery" (e.g., to avoid a ruinous debt). Arnold, p. 38.

96 Paul very much sounds like Jesus here when he said, "No one can serve two masters; for either he will hate the one and love the other or else he will be loyal to the one and despise the other" (Matt. 6:24).

97 Or more literally "grace to God" reminding us that "God's grace makes the change of masters possible." Harvey, p. 161.

98 Grk. imperfect, active, verb.

99 Grk. aorist, active, verb.

100 Kruse, p. 281, notes that this is an expression which is only found here in the New Testament.

101 Or more literally from the Greek text: *into* which you were delivered.

102 Grk. aorist, passive, verb. Schreiner helpfully notes, "The verb form emphasizes that God is the one who delivered believers from the slavery of sin to the imprint of teaching that they now embrace" Schreiner, p. 336.

103 Cf. Jude v. 3.

104 Grk. aorist, passive, participle.

105 Grk. aorist, passive, participle. The two passive verbs in this verse are striking, showing us that salvation is completely of the Lord! (Jonah 2:9).

106 Kruse, p. 282, notes, "This is a paradoxical statement – set free to become slaves!"

What is Paul saying? Simply this: Christians are, in reality, new people! By God's working in their hearts through the Holy Spirit, they have experienced a glorious change in their lives so that they have been delivered from the service of sin and have become the joyful servants of Christ (cf. Rom. 1:1). They have been emancipated from their old ways of living in order to become lovingly enslaved to Him who is the Savior of their souls. What an amazing thing it is then, to be a true Christian! Indeed it is the greatest miracle in all the world.

Obs. 3- (v. 19) That as Paul continues his slave/master analogy in order to set forth the essence of what he is teaching, he writes first in verse nineteen:

I speak[107] **in human** *terms,* that is, I am speaking in a familiar way so that you do not miss what I am saying; **because of** or on account of; **the weakness of your flesh,** i.e., because of any limitation that you might have in understanding me; **For just as you presented**[108] or decisively offered and yielded; **your members** *as* **slaves of uncleanness** or moral impurity in many ways in their pre-Christian days; **and of lawlessness** or rebellion against God and His commandments;[109] *leading* to *more* **lawlessness,** which is the regular progression of such living; **so now**[110] or in the same manner "in consideration of the past;"[111] **present**[112] or decisively offer and yield; **your members,** i.e., all that you are; *as* **slaves** *of* **righteousness** that is, as slaves with a new master who now live uprightly according to God and His Word; **for holiness** or toward sanctification or a life which is increasingly separated from sin unto the Savior.[113]

Spurgeon notes concerning these words that,

> It wants no explanation. In the days of our sin, we sinned with all our power. There was not one part of us but what became the willing servant of sin: and we went from iniquity into iniquity, and now the Cross has made us entirely new, and we have been melted down, poured out into a fresh mold. Now, let us yield every member of our body, soul, and spirit to righteousness, even unto holiness, till the whole of us, in the wholeness and consequently the holiness of our nature, shall be given unto God.[114]

---

107 Grk. present, active, verb (cf. Rom 3:5).

108 Grk. aorist, active, verb.

109 Note the double description of sin in the verse: uncleanness and lawlessness.

110 Paul speaks here as something of a challenge to the Roman Christians and us as well.

111 Robinson, Book 1, p. 357.

112 Grk. aorist, active, imperative, verb (cf. Rom. 6:19).

113 Paul's comparison here in this verse is striking especially if we get what he is saying, namely, that if we give the amount of energy that we once spent in living in sin as non-Christians now to living holy before the Lord, we will grow in sanctification. May it be then, that by God's grace, we will now employ all of our former energies spent on sin and Satan, for the things of God and His glory! Chrysostom speaks similarly and says, "In the past you did not split your service between righteousness and sin but were wholly given over to sin. So now that you have come over to the side of righteousness, you should do the same thing and give yourselves over entirely to righteousness, doing nothing at all that is wicked." *Ancient Christian Commentary on Scripture, Romans,* p. 165.

114 Spurgeon, p. 83.

(Vs. 20) For the conjunction giving the reason why we are to obey Paul's words in verse 19; **when** or at the time; **you were slaves of sin,** while in an unconverted state; **you were free,**[115] i.e., completely void; **in regard** or with respect to the practice of; **righteousness,**[116] that is to say, you were absolutely *un*holy, *un*godly and totally depraved.[117]

(Vv. 21-22) What fruit[118] the sense is, what advantage or benefit; **did you have**[119] or did you habitually experience; **then,**[120] i.e., in the past, at that time when you were not saved and spiritually and morally fruit*less*; **in the things of which you are now** in the present, as a Christian; **ashamed**[121] or continually embarrassed both "inwardly, before God and conscience and outwardly, before men?"[122] **For** the conjunction confirming what Paul just said; **the end** or the outcome; **of those things is death,** i.e., eternal destruction in hell (cf. v. 23). **But now**[123] that is, in stark contrast to your former way of life with its evils; **having been set free**[124] **from sin,** that is, once for all time being gloriously liberated from its bondage as master over you; **and having become**[125] definitively; **slaves** or willing and joyful servants; **of God,** through the transforming power

---

115 They were free concerning righteousness being completely void of it, but still slaves of sin, hence they had no true freedom at all (cf. John 8:36).

116 MacBeth may be right when he says that since the Greek text has the definite article before the word *righteousness* it denotes, "The righteousness of God and not of man; imputed and not personal." McBeth, p. 175.

117 McClain says concerning this verse, "There was a time in your life when you were a servant of sin, and righteousness had nothing to do with you. Now turn around. Once you are free from sin, just the opposite is true. When you are the servant of righteousness, you have nothing to do with sin. You are free from it!" McClain, pp. 147-48.

118 In these opening words Thiselton notes that Paul's probing "invites self-reflection." Thiselton, p. 151.

119 Grk. imperfect, active, verb.

120 Of course, the question is rhetorical and the answer is, none. Paul's question raises another question which is, "Do Christians or should Christians who have been forgiven of all of their past sins feel shame for their old sinful lifestyles?" In a sense, the answer is yes, as Paul articulates it here. However, it should not be a crushing or crippling shame, for if that is the case, we in effect deny the work of Christ on our behalf who died on account of our sins. However, it should be a *motivating* shame that drives us far from the vile things which we used to do while in an unconverted state.

Calvin further adds, "Indeed the godly, as soon as they begin to be illuminated by the Spirit of Christ and the preaching of the gospel, do freely acknowledge their past life, which they have lived without Christ, to have been worthy of condemnation; and so far are they from endeavoring to excuse it, that, on the contrary, they feel ashamed of themselves. Yea, further, they call to mind the remembrance of their own disgrace, that being thus ashamed, they may more truly and more readily be humbled before God." John Calvin, p. 241, Baker Books edition.

121 The preposition attached to the verb in the Greek text intensifying the force of what is being said.

122 Robinson, Book 1, p. 360.

123 Same two words found in Rom. 3:21.

124 Grk. aorist, passive, participle. The passive verb highlights to us that it was God's work completely and not ours, in freeing us from our horrible past spiritual condition.

125 Grk. aorist, passive, participle. The passive verb highlights to us that it was God's work completely in enslaving us to Christ as His servants. Both participles in this verse highlight God's sovereignty in these matters.

of the gospel; **you have**[126] as a present reality; **your fruit,** that is, your spiritual development; **to holiness,** or more literally into sanctification or growth in Christ-likeness; **and the end,** or the outcome which comes from a real relationship with God through Jesus is the free gift of; **everlasting life** or life without end with Him in glory.[127]

Obs. 4- (v. 23) That as Paul summarizes all that he has been saying about sanctification and sets forth a principal motivation for us to live as he has called us to live in presenting our members as slaves of righteousness, (as opposed to our old way of life), he puts before us a crucial end-time reality that we must always keep in mind to help us in this regard, when he writes:[128]

For the conjunction condensing and reconfirming all that has been said in the two previous verses; **the wages**[129] or the payout and compensation in the final analysis from God; **of sin**[130] or from a life lived in habitual rebellion to God and His law; *is* **death** or eternal hell;[131] **but** in contrast to this, now positively speaking; **the gift,**[132] that is, the extremely gracious, unmerited, unearned and undeserved gift to believers or we could say the "grace-gift;" **of God** *is* **eternal life** or that of knowing God fully and forevermore in glory; **in** the preposition denoting the specific agent through whom eternal life comes to those who believe; **Christ Jesus our Lord,**[133] i.e., through His person and substitutionary work in our place.

Here then the apostle concludes this masterful treatment concerning what the life of a truly justified and increasingly sanctified believer will be like with the help and grace of God. According to him, in opposition to those who say that those who have been truly saved will live lawlessly afterward, Paul says, not a chance (6:1)! He says this is completely not the case for, "How shall we who died to sin live in it any longer" (6:2).

---

126 Grk. present, active, verb.

127 Michael Bird could be right when he says that in this verse we have "traveled full circle from Romans 5:21." Bird, p. 214.

128 Contextually, it is important that we first understand this verse in this way as referring to Christians and their sanctification, before we use it evangelistically for non-Christians and their salvation. It works both ways, but this point is important to note.

129 The Greek word is a military technical term for what soldiers received from their service in the army as pay in Paul's day, so that they could buy such things as food or clothing etc. as many commentators note.

130 Sin is being portrayed in this verse as an evil captain who pays out his followers a most dreadful wage.

131 Obviously, this is not merely speaking about physical death, because that will happen to all apart from the Lord's return. Cf. Matt. 25.46a; 2 Thess. 1:9. McBeth says, "Sin pays faithfully, promptly, and eagerly. But in the final analysis, the dying sinners do the paying." McBeth, p. 177.

132 Cf. Eph. 2:8. Note that Paul does not say, "but the wages or payout or compensation of a 'good life' from God is eternal life" so as to say, that eternal life is something we earn or gain perhaps even through the process of sanctification. No, eternal life is never something we merit because we cannot. Rather it is freely given to us by God because of Christ. As McBeth says, "Sin pays according to justice; God gives according to grace." McBeth, p. 178.

133 It is glorious to see that Paul ends this chapter by mentioning Jesus Christ our Lord once again just as he did in chapter five. Christ is at the heart of all that the apostle has to say concerning not only the believer's justification but also his sanctification.

Suggested applications from the text for the church:

1- Reflect on your past spiritual state as a non-Christian and be ashamed of your former sins so as to never go back to them again.

2- Remember your present spiritual state and your one-day future spiritual state in glory and greatly rejoice.

Suggested application from the text for the non-Christian:

1- Right away, face the fact that the wages of sin is death, but the gift of God is eternal life in Christ Jesus our Lord and go to Him for salvation.

ROMANS
CHAPTER SEVEN

Text: Romans 7:1-6[1]

General theme: The Believers' Release from the Penalty of the Law of God

Homiletical outline of the verses:

    A. Paul's general assumption: [1] Or do you not know, brethren (for I speak to those who know the law), that the law has dominion over a man as long as he lives?

    B. Paul's graphic analogy: [2] For the woman who has a husband is bound by the law to *her* husband as long as he lives. But if the husband dies, she is released from the law of *her* husband. [3] So then if, while *her* husband lives, she marries another man, she will be called an adulteress; but if her husband dies, she is free from that law, so that she is no adulteress, though she has married another man.

    C. Paul's glorious application: [4] Therefore, my brethren, you also have become dead to the law through the body of Christ, that you may be married to another—to Him who was raised from the dead, that we should bear fruit to God. [5] For when we were in the flesh, the sinful passions which were aroused by the law were at work in our members to bear fruit to death. [6] But now we have been delivered from the law, having died to what we were held by, so that we should serve in the newness of the Spirit and not *in* the oldness of the letter.

Summary of section: In verses 1 to 6, the apostle continues his discussion of the saints and their sanctification. However, instead of dealing with

---

1 Historically speaking, chapter 7 is notorious for doctrinal controversy. I will discuss this matter more when we come to verse fourteen. However, in preaching verse by verse through this chapter, I found it to be one of the richest chapters in Romans because of how practical it is for the Christian life. In a way that exceeds others, this chapter helps us to discover the nature of the Christian life when it comes to dealing with remaining sin. Lastly, I acknowledge that I received some help in my understanding of this chapter from sermons preached by the late Dr. Robert P. Martin, one of my former seminary professors. Those sermons can be found on sermonaudio.com.

this topic specifically in terms of the believers' relationship to sin (chapter 6), he now deals with it in terms of their relationship to the law of God.[2] In fact, the word "law" appears over twenty times in this chapter, being used in at least three different ways: first, with reference to the moral law of God, the Decalogue (vv. 1, 22); second, with reference to civil law (vv. 2, 3); and third, with reference to law as a governing principle, power, or propensity (vv. 21, 23).

This chapter begins by showing that through Christ's work on their behalf, Christians are completely free from the *condemning power* of the law of God over them. Even though the *commanding power* of the law is still binding upon them (as it is for all others, 3:31; 6:1; 8:4a), believers are entirely delivered from all of its sentencing against them. This is because Christ the Savior has taken that sentencing for them at the cross. At Calvary, Jesus suffered the righteous judgment of God in their place, so that they would not have to experience it. Calvin states all of this well when he said that the release being spoken of here is "not from the righteousness which is taught in the law, but from the rigid demands of the law and from the curse which follows from its demands."[3]

It is significant that Paul begins this new section on sanctification concerning Christ's work on our behalf. I say this because one of the chief ways in which we grow in Christ-likeness is to continually reflect on Jesus' offering that He made for us. The great love which He demonstrated toward us at Calvary is to be a key motivator for us to habitually give ourselves completely to Him, in true gospel holiness.

Exegetical & Practical Insights:
Obs. 1- (v. 1) That as Paul would have us to keep this matter in mind, he says first:

Or do you not know,[4] **brethren**[5] or are you continually unaware brothers and sisters at Rome; Paul speaks parenthetically and says; **(for I speak to those who know the law)**, that is, the Ten Commandments

---

2 This matter would have been particularly relevant to the believers at Rome in case they misunderstood Paul's words in the previous chapter when he said that believers are "not under law" (6:14).

3 As found in Morris, p. 272.

4 Grk. present, active, verb. By using this language, Paul assumes that his readers anticipated his subject and that they would agree with his analogy (cf. 6:3). His Jewish audience would have understood the relationship of the law of God to an individual, since they had been instructed out of the Word of God about it. The God-fearing Gentiles, who often worshiped in synagogues before they were saved, would have known this as well, as commentators note.

5 Note the warm term of affection. Hendriksen writes with insight saying that the word "brethren" should not be passed by unnoticed. He says, "As here used, it is an affectionate term of address. Previously Paul has used it only in 1:13. Careful examination of all the instances of its occurrence in this epistle shows that whenever the apostle employs this term in addressing his readers, he is deeply moved. He is writing about a subject which emotionally affects him. He, as it were, embraces those whom he addresses with his arms of love. In this light examine also the use of the same word in 1:13; 8:12; 10:1; 11:25; 12:1; 15:30; 16:17. In each case the subject discussed is one filled with emotion." Hendriksen, p. 214.

(although what he says here is true concerning any law or rule over us); **that the law has dominion;** literally lordship, from the Greek word *kurios*; **over a man,**[6] i.e., any person, whoever they are for; **as long as he lives?**

What is his point? It is that while we were non-Christians, the law of God had mastery over us, in the sense that we were held liable to it just as a criminal is subject to the law for breaking it. We were legally answerable to its claims, which say in essence, "do this flawlessly and live." Sadly, however, none of us has done this, and so we must die. We must be punished eternally.[7] This is what the strictness of the law of God requires for everyone who has not kept it perfectly, perpetually, and personally all his or her days in thought, word, and deed. For as Paul says in Galatians 3:10, "Cursed is everyone who does not continue in all things which are written in the book of the law to do them."

This, of course, is bad news. But he gives the good news in Galatians 3:13 and says that "Christ has redeemed us from the curse of the law, having become a curse for us (for it is written, 'cursed is everyone who hangs on a tree')".

Obs. 2- (vv. 2-3) That having set forth his general assumption in verse 1, Paul now makes clear what he means by using a graphic or life-like analogy:

For an explanatory conjunction; **the woman** that is, the wife; **who has a husband is bound,**[8] or fastened "till death do us part;" **by the law,** i.e., the civil law of marriage; **to** *her* **husband as long as he lives.**[9] **But if the husband dies, she is released**[10] or stands discharged; **from the law of** or concerning; *her* husband. **So then** or consequently; **if, while** *her* **husband lives, she marries another man, she will be called**[11] or labeled and known as one operating as; **an adulteress;** a violator of the Seventh Commandment, one who is unfaithful and has committed that which is unlawful; **but if her husband dies, she is free** in the civil, matrimonial sense, not bound, but emancipated; **from that law,** again, the law of marriage; **so that** as a result; **she is no adulteress, though she has married another man.**

Paul's analogy is plain.[12] Death dissolves all legal marital obligations. Once a spouse dies, the other is free to marry without transgression. As

---

6 The Greek word here for man is a general reference to all mankind.

7 Cf. Rom. 2:12b.

8 Grk. perfect, passive, verb.

9 Cf. 1 Cor. 7:39.

10 Grk. perfect, passive, verb.

11 This Greek word has the idea of doing business.

12 It is vital that we see that Paul's language here is an analogy because, sadly, some have taken his words out of context so as to mean that under no circumstances whatsoever can a person remarry while his or her spouse is still alive. This is not Paul's point here at all as the matter of being married to another person is not in view. But rather being married to the law is as the context shows. The Bible teaches, and the historic Confessions of faith confirm, that there are two reasons which make divorce and remarriage permissible, adultery and abandonment (cf. Matt. 5:19; 1 Cor. 7:10-15).

John MacArthur says, "Marriage laws are binding only as long as both partners are alive."[13]

Obs. 3- (vv. 4-6) That as Paul makes his spiritual application from all that he has been saying in connection to the believer's relationship to the condemning power of the law of God, (since we are no longer "married to the law," in that we are no longer subject to its curse and condemnation), he writes:

Therefore, or consequently; **my brethren, you also have become dead**[14] or have been made dead definitively at the point of salvation, once for all time; **to the law** in that you are no longer legally answerable to its judgments again; **through** or by the instrumentality of; **the body of Christ,** that is, the crucified body of Christ who met the punishment of God's law for us, in our place;[15] **that** or for the purpose that; **you may be married to another—to Him,** i.e., Jesus; **who was raised from the dead,**[16] **that** or for the purpose that; **we should bear fruit to God** which is to say spiritual fruit to Him.[17]

In connecting this verse to the previous one, Paul says that just as civil law has no jurisdiction over a person after he or she dies, in a similar way, since believers are in union with Christ and have been crucified with Him the moment they believed, they are dead to the penalty of the law, since that penalty has been met in their Savior.

Further, since all of this is so (that we have been married to another, even Jesus, who was raised from the dead), we are to bear fruit unto His Name through sanctification, because of our union with Him. We are to bear the fruit of godliness since we have been forever joined to Christ in a holy spiritual matrimony.

Charles Hodge comments:

> As far as we are concerned, redemption is in order to [produce] holiness. We are delivered from the law, that we may be united to Christ; and we are united to Christ, that we may bring forth fruit unto God.... As deliverance from the penalty of the law is in order to [produce] holiness, it is vain to expect that deliverance, except with a view to the end for which it is granted.[18]

---

13 MacArthur, p. 360.

14 Grk. aorist, passive, verb. The passive verb highlights my translation of it above. Further, it highlights God as the one who by grace, through Christ, has made us dead to the law's penalty when we believed.

15 Cf. Col. 2:14.

16 Moo makes a good point concerning the phrase "who was raised from the dead" when he says, "This new relationship, Paul implies, will be a never-ending one. For the 'other' to which the Christian is joined is 'the one who has been raised from the dead' – never to die again." Moo, p. 418.

17 This is what should come forth from all who are truly joined to Christ (cf. John 15:4-5; Gal. 5:22, 23).

18 As quoted in MacArthur, p. 361.

Having spoken of what is to be true of our present condition as believers, Paul in verse 5, digresses for a moment to contrast this with our former unconverted days when he writes:

For or because; **when we were in the flesh,**[19] that is, in an unconverted state; **the sinful passions** or "the overwhelming impulses to think and do evil, which characterize those who are 'in the flesh;'"[20] **which were aroused** not created by, but stirred up; **by the law** specifically the means of the Ten Commandments;[21] **were at work**[22] or were working and operating; **in our members,** i.e., our bodies,[23] **to bear fruit to death** that is eternal death, under the wrath of God in hell (cf. 6:23).

Here Paul is saying that before our regeneration, our spiritual condition was so bad that along with God's holy law exposing our sin, it also stimulated it negatively speaking, so that when the law told us not to do something, we defiantly said we will do it anyway. It is like when we encounter a sign which reads "wet paint, do not touch." What is typically our natural impulse? To touch the paint!

In like manner, concerning God's law, this is how it goes for the unbeliever.[24] The law says, "Thou shalt not." They say, "Yes, I shall!" It says, "Thou shalt." They say, "I shall not!" This highlights how great the rebellion is toward God. It shows us what Paul means in Romans 8:7: "the carnal mind is enmity against God; for it is not subject to the law of God nor indeed can it be."

The question which should be asked and answered now is, Is the problem of sinning, then, with the law of God or with our fallen sinful hearts?[25] Clearly, the answer is our fallen sinful hearts. For just as a sign is not to be blamed when our fingers are covered with paint, neither are God's commandments to be blamed when we break them. The problem is not the law of God, but us. MacArthur notes, "When a person is justly convicted and sentenced for murder, there is no fault in the law or with those responsible for upholding it. The fault is in the one who broke the law."[26]

In contrast then with our former unregenerate condition, Paul reverts to speaking about us as Christians and says in verse 6:

But now, that is, at the present time, in opposition to our past; **we,** i.e., Christians, Paul included; **have been delivered**[27] or completely cleared and set free, once for all time, by God's doing; **from the law,** i.e., from its

---

19 Geoffrey Wilson astutely notes, "Here for the first time in the epistle Paul uses the expression 'in the flesh' to describe the old unregenerate life of sin in contrast to the new life 'in the spirit' (v.6). Wilson p. 111.

20 John MacArthur, *One Faithful Life,* Thomas Nelson, 2019, p. 290.

21 Cf. Rom. 7:7-11.

22 Grk. imperfect, middle, verb.

23 Cf. Gal. 5:19-21.

24 Cf. Rom. 1:32.

25 Paul will deal with this question further in verses 7 to 12 of this chapter.

26 MacArthur, p. 374.

27 Grk. aorist, passive, verb.

curse and condemnation through Christ; **having died to what we were held by** or what detained us under its sentencing; **so that** as a result;[28] **we should serve,** that is, serve God as willing bondservants;[29] **in the newness of the Spirit**[30] or with the new life and help that the Holy Spirit gives; **and not *in* the oldness of the letter** or in a way that marked out our old relationship to the law in our pre-converted state, which was a relationship of external, formal service.

Here is where Paul ends his opening discussion with reference to the believer's release from the penalty of the law of God. As Christians, we are free from the curse and condemnation which comes by breaking God's law, for we are dead to it (for the law has no claim over the dead). This is our position through Christ, for through His death on our behalf and our union with Him, we have been discharged from the debt-claims that God's law had upon us. Because we are spiritually joined to Him, we can now positively love God and His law and seek to obey it, since we have been graciously saved from its dreadful judgment.

William Hendriksen summarizes:

> Just as a woman, by means of a death (that of her husband) is released from her marriage bond and allowed to marry another man, so also by a death (the believers' death with Christ) God's children are released from indebtedness to the law, the latter's "bill" having been fully paid by Christ's voluntary and vicarious sacrifice. Believers have, accordingly, obtained *liberty*. This liberty is freedom *from* and a freedom *for*. It is a freedom *from* the obligation to keep the law in order to be saved, and is therefore also a freedom *from* the curse which the law pronounces upon the disobedient. But it is at the same time a freedom *for* or *with a view to*, a freedom *in order* to render service to God "in newness of the Spirit, not in oldness of the letter."[31]

Suggested applications from the text for the church:

1- Rejoice because Jesus, your wedded spiritual spouse, has freed you from the curse and condemnation of the law forevermore, having taken that curse and condemnation for you, in your place.

2- Remember that being freed from the curse and condemnation of the law is not an encouragement to live lawlessly but rather to bear spiritual fruit unto God.

3- Recall that while the Ten Commandments are helpful in our lives as a rule of life for our sanctification, it is not our union to the law or our self-righteous strivings after the law which will ever make us truly holy. Rather, it is only as we look to Christ for help in holiness, that we will see growth in our lives to this blessed end (cf. John 15:4-5; Rom 7:25).

---

28 Note the paradox: freed so that we can serve.

29 Cf. Rom. 1:1; 6:20-22.

30 Paul will speak more about the Spirit's role in our sanctification in the following chapter.

31 Hendriksen, pp. 239, 240.

Suggested application from the text for the non-Christian:

1- Renounce all other spiritual lovers (such as self-righteousness and the like) as a means to be made right with God, and be married to Jesus, who alone can forgive you of all of your sins and make you right with Him.

Text: Romans 7:7-13

General theme: The Believer's Respect for the Purpose of the Law of God

Homiletical outline of the verses:

A. Paul's question: [7] What shall we say then? *Is* the law sin? Certainly not! On the contrary, I would not have known sin except through the law. For I would not have known covetousness unless the law had said, "You shall not covet."

B. Paul's explanation: [8] But sin, taking opportunity by the commandment, produced in me all *manner of evil* desire. For apart from the law sin *was* dead. [9] I was alive once without the law, but when the commandment came, sin revived and I died. [10] And the commandment, which *was* to *bring* life, I found to *bring* death. [11] For sin, taking occasion by the commandment, deceived me, and by it killed *me*. [12] Therefore the law *is* holy, and the commandment holy and just and good.

C. Paul's question and explanation: [13] Has then what is good become death to me? Certainly not! But sin, that it might appear sin, was producing death in me through what is good, so that sin through the commandment might become exceedingly sinful.

Summary of section: In these verses, the apostle gives testimony concerning how the law of God was used in his life as a tutor or "schoolmaster"[32] to bring him to Christ when he was an unsaved man (Gal. 3:24). He shows that although as a Jew he had sought to keep the Ten Commandments externally, nevertheless, he had not realized that God's commandments judged not only his outward actions but his inward motives as well. This is because the law of God is spiritual, searching us deep within (vs.14a, cf. Matt. 5:21-28) and when the commandments did their heart-work on the proud Pharisee, he had come to see himself in truth, as a hell-deserving sinner, in desperate need of Christ for life and salvation.[33]

This is a primary function of the law of God toward the unbeliever. Thus, Spurgeon is correct when he says, "If men do not understand the law, they will not feel that they are sinners. And if they are not consciously sinners, they will never value the sin offering. There is no

---

32 As translated by the King James Version.

33 In this we see that the law of God and the gospel are not at odds. Rather, they work hand-in-hand. They are allies, not enemies, for as Stephen Charnock wrote, "The law is a hammer to break us, the gospel God's oil to cure us."

healing a man till the law has wounded him, no making him alive till the law has slain him."[34]

The Puritan John Flavel summarizes these words before us succinctly when he writes,

> The scope of the apostle ... is to state the due use and excellence of the Law which he does accordingly. First, by denying to it a power to justify us which is the peculiar honor of Christ. Second, by ascribing to it a power to convince us, and so prepare us for Christ. Neither attributing to it more honor than belongs to it, nor yet detracting from it that honor and usefulness which God has given it. It cannot make us righteous, but it can convince us that we are unrighteous; it cannot heal, but it can open and discover the wounds that sin has given us; which he proves in this place by an argument drawn from his own experience.[35]

Exegetical & Practical Insights:

Obs. 1- (v. 7) That as Paul begins to speak about his esteem for the law of God, especially concerning its evangelistic effect in his life, he writes:

What shall we say then?[36] *Is the law sin* or evil since it arouses sin (v. 5)? **Certainly not!** Or God forbid, an absolute negation; **On the contrary,**[37] or in complete contrast to this; **I would not have known sin,** i.e., the deep depravity of it; **except through** or by means of; **the law.**[38] **For**[39] **I would not have known,** that is, known experientially; **covetousness** a violation of the Tenth Commandment;[40] **unless** or except; **the law had said, "You shall not covet"** or "You shall not be greedy."

In this verse, Paul clears the law of God from critiques which people might make against it when it reveals their sin. Paul in no way says the law itself is sin. Rather, it is the instrument in God's hand to reveal sin. This is because sin is "transgression of the law of God."[41] It is law-*less-ness* (1 John 3:4). Or, as the *Westminster Shorter Catechism* says, "Sin is any want of conformity unto, or transgression of, the law of God."

And so while, before his conversion, Paul knew what sin was *intellectually*, he did not know it *personally* until he was saved. Before he was converted, he had the law in his head, but did not have its spiritual meaning in his heart. Before he was saved, he "looked at the law as most people do, in the coldness of the letter, as an outside thing. He did not see the sin of thoughts, attitude, desire, nature and will."[42]

---

34 As found on gracequotes.org/topic/law-general.

35 John Flavel, *Works*, II: 287, 288. I have taken the liberty to update the language.

36 Paul uses the same language in 6:1 and 9:14, so as to be sure that no one misunderstands him.

37 The strong Greek adversative.

38 Cf. Rom. 3:21.

39 The Greek explanatory conjunction confirms the preceding words.

40 Cf. Ex. 20:17; Deut. 5:21.

41 As translated by the King James Version.

42 Mahan, 51.

This is why, in reflecting on his pre-conversion days, he could say of himself as a man full of self-righteousness that "concerning the righteousness which is in the law, blameless" (Phil. 3:6).[43] Now, however, in Romans chapter 7, Paul is singing a different song. Now he sees himself in truth, and it was the law of God that helped him in this regard. Apparently, then, this is what was going on in his heart right before he met Christ on the Damascus Road.[44] At that time, he not only met Jesus *outwardly*, but *inwardly* he met the law of God which had been "goading" him on his way to Damascus.[45] The law had been exposing him as a man full of greed and lust and in desperate need of God's forgiveness.

By highlighting covetousness as the specific sin which the law pointed out in his heart, Paul again shows the internal work which the law often does in the sinner whom God is drawing to the Savior. Covetousness is a sin of the heart, not necessarily of the hands. It takes place in the mind. It means to crave inordinately, and it includes "every kind of illicit desire."[46] It means to want something so badly that you will do anything for it. Thus, by coveting, one will break many commandments of God (e.g., the first, third, sixth, and the seventh commandment, etc.). Is it any wonder, then, that Jesus said in Luke 12:15, "take heed and beware of covetousness"? And is it any wonder that Thomas Watson the Puritan once said that covetousness is "a moral vice which infects and pollutes the whole soul."[47]

In commenting on all of this in Paul's life McDonald insightfully says:

> Although Paul may not have committed any of the grosser, more revolting sins, he now realized that his thought life was corrupt. He understood that evil thoughts are sinful as well as evil deeds. He had a polluted thought life. His outward life may have been relatively blameless, but his inward life was a chamber of horrors.[48]

Obs. 2- (v. 8) That as the apostle identifies the real culprit of the wrongdoings in his life, he says:

But sin, i.e., his own personal transgression against God's law; **taking** or seizing; **opportunity by** or through means of; **the commandment, produced**[49] or definitively brought out and effected; **in me all** or every; *manner of evil* **desire** or covetous longings. **For apart from the law** i.e., apart from a true knowledge of its full-fledged requirements both

---

43 The sense in the Greek text on this verse is that Paul viewed himself as one who had attained sinless perfection before God.

44 Cf. Acts 9:1-9.

45 Cf. Acts 9:5. Pastor Nichols very helpfully tied these two texts together and made this point in a sermon preached on them on sermonaudio.com.

46 Rogers and Rogers, p. 329.

47 Thomas Watson, *The Select Works of the Rev. Thomas Watson,* Comprising His Celebrated Body of Divinity, in a Series of Lectures on the Shorter Catechism, and Various Sermons and Treatises (New York: Robert Carter & Brothers, 1855), 334.

48 McDonald, p. 1705.

49 Grk. aorist, middle, verb.

internally and externally; **sin *was* dead** not that it was nonexistent, but that it did not bother him. It was operative in him,[50] but it did not present a conscious problem until it was prohibited.

In speaking from this verse as if he were Paul himself, Spurgeon writes:

> I did not know how sinful I was until God's commandments came to me. Sin seemed to be dead within me and I thought myself a righteous man; but when the law of God came home to my heart and conscience, and I understood that even a sinful thought would ruin me, that a hasty word had the essence of murder in it, and that the utmost uncleanness might lurk under the cover of what seemed a mere custom of my fellow-men,—when I found out all this, sin did indeed live, but I died so far as righteousness was concerned.[51]

Obs. 3- (vv. 9-12) That as Paul continues to talk on this topic, he uses some figurative language to say:

I was alive not spiritually alive, but alive in the sense that he thought everything was fine with him; **once without the law,** i.e., before the law came home to his conscience with conviction; **but when the commandment came** that is, came by the power of the Spirit and exposed him as a self-righteous, deluded individual; **sin revived** or reenergized; **and I died,** i.e., he died to his self-inflated notions about himself and his ability to be right with God on his own.

And the commandment, which *was* to *bring* life, (Paul is probably thinking here of Leviticus 18:5 where God said, "You shall therefore keep My statutes and My judgments, which if a man does, he shall live by them,"[52] which ideally promised life to all who obeyed God's commandments perfectly); **I found** or discovered; **to *bring* death. For** the conjunction explaining what Paul means; **sin,** not the law, but again sin; **taking occasion** or an opportunity; **by** or through; **the commandment, deceived me,** or misled and cheated me into believing that I was better than I truly was before God;[53] **and by it killed *me*.**[54] **Therefore** or consequently, Paul draws the logical conclusion from all that he has been writing about in verses 7 to 11; **the law *is* holy,** again Paul defends the

---

50 Cf. Rom. 5:13.

51 Spurgeon, p. 87 (self-print).

52 Several commentators point this out.

53 Spurgeon says, "There was sin in his nature, but he did not know it. But when the commandment came, then that evil nature said, 'I won't keep that commandment,' and it took occasion at once to show itself by breaking that commandment." Spurgeon, p. 93.

54 It is interesting to see here reflections of Paul's language from the original fall of man in the Garden of Eden in Genesis chapter 3. There God gave the command: Do not eat. But the woman was "deceived" by the serpent and her sin and ate (1 Tim. 2:14). Further, it could be argued that the sin in the garden was one of "covetousness" that is, a desiring to be "like God" but in a wrong way Gen. 3:5.

law from any negative critiques (cf. v.7); **and the commandment holy and just and good**[55] (just as the God who wrote it). John Murray remarks,

> As "holy" the commandment reflects the transcendence and purity of God and demands of us the correspondent consecration and purity; as "righteous" [or just] it reflects the equity of God and exacts of us in its demand and sanction nothing but that which is equitable; as "good" it promotes man's highest well-being and thus expresses the goodness of God.[56]

Obs. 4- (v. 13) That as Paul further establishes all that he has been saying in this section, he asks one last question:

Has then what is good again, the law of God (cf. v. 11) **become death to me** in other words, is it the law's fault that he is being condemned for his sins against it? **Certainly not!** Again, the strong Greek negation. **But**[57] or to the contrary, **sin,** (there is the villain!); **that** or for the purpose that; **it might appear** or be revealed and shown in its true colors as; **sin, was producing**[58] or achieving; **death in me through what is good** (again the law); **so that** as a result; **sin through** or by the agency and instrumentality of; **the commandment might become exceedingly sinful** or excessively wicked, as it always is.

Vos helpfully recaps this second section of Romans 7:

> Here Paul tells us a bit about his own personal experience. The law of God, he tells us, finally convicted him that he was a sinner. "I had not known sin, but by the law: for I had not known lust, except the law said, 'Thou shall not covet' (7:7). Think of Saul the Pharisee, the strict, conscientious, scrupulous observer of all the details of the law of God, both the moral law and the ceremonial law. If we had asked Saul the Pharisee, "Are you a poor, lost guilty sinner?" what would he have replied? Beyond question, he would have said, "No; I am a righteous Pharisee, for I have observed the law blamelessly." Yes, he thought he had. He tells us, "I was alive without the law once" (7:9). That represents Paul's former opinion of himself. We might paraphrase it this way: "There was a time when I thought I was all right; there was a time when I thought I had lived a perfect life in my own strength."

But something happened. But when the commandment came, sin revived, and I died (7:9b). There came a time when light—spiritual light from God—dawned in his soul. He came to understand the true meaning of God's law, the Ten Commandments. When he came to understand the true meaning of God's law, then he came to see himself as he really was. His bubble burst. His illusions about himself faded out. "When the commandment came, sin revived, and I died." That is to say: "When I

---

55 All of the true people of God concur with this thought, see Psalms 19:7-11; 119:86a, 127, 137, 138.

56 Murray, p. 253.

57 The strong Greek adversative.

58 Grk. present, middle, participle.

came to a real understanding of God's law, I realized myself a helpless victim and slave of sin—guilty before God and spiritually helpless."

The result was that Saul the Pharisee became Paul the Christian. It was the tenth and last commandment—"Thou shalt not covet"—that brought him to conviction of sin, to the end of his own resources, at last. Paul tells us that this commandment "slew" him, or rather that "sin taking occasion by the commandment, deceived me, and by it slew me" (7:11).

The law, Paul tells us, is holy, just and good (7:12), but it cannot make a sinful human being holy, just, and good. Far from it. It works on that sinful human being and shows his sin in its true colors, "that sin... might become exceedingly sinful" (7:13). The law cannot make us holy. On the contrary, it makes us realize that we are exceedingly sinful. For the law of God is spiritual, but we sinners are not spiritual."[59]

Suggested applications from the text for the church:

1- Remember to use the law of God when evangelizing the lost since Paul said, "I would not have known sin except through the law" (Rom. 7:7; cf. 5:20a; 3:20b).

2- Remember that while the law cannot sanctify you, it is of use in your sanctification for showing you what holiness is in God's sight.

3- Remember never to speak disparagingly against the law of God as many do in our day, since the law of God is "holy and just and good."

Suggested application from the text for the non-Christian:

1- Remember that one day you have to stand before God in order to give an account for all of the violations which you have committed against His holy law. Are you prepared for that day?

Text: Romans 7:14-25

General theme: The Believer's Relationship to the Precisions of the Law of God

Homiletical outline of the verses:

A. Paul's realization: [14] For we know that the law is spiritual, but I am carnal, sold under sin.

B. Paul's confirmation: [15] For what I am doing, I do not understand. For what I will to do, that I do not practice; but what I hate, that I do. [16] If, then, I do what I will not to do, I agree with the law that it is good. [17] But now, it is no longer I who do it, but sin that dwells in me. [18] For I know that in me (that is, in my flesh) nothing good dwells; for to will is present with me, but how to perform what is good I do not find. [19] For the good that I will to do, I do not do; but the evil I will not to do, that I practice. [20] Now if I do what I will not to do, it is no longer I who do it, but sin that dwells in me. [21] I find then a law, that evil is present with me, the one who wills to do good. [22] For I delight in the law of God according to the

---

59 Vos, pp. 93, 94.

inward man. [23] But I see another law in my members, warring against the law of my mind, and bringing me into captivity to the law of sin which is in my members. [24] O wretched man that I am! Who will deliver me from this body of death?

C. Paul's jubilation: [25] I thank God—through Jesus Christ our Lord! So then, with the mind I myself serve the law of God, but with the flesh the law of sin.

Summary of section: As Paul continues his discussion of the saints and their sanctification in this concluding section of this chapter, he sets forth the internal battles he faced even as a mature believer in Christ.[60] While he had been judicially freed from the curse and condemnation of the Law of God through Christ's sacrifice in his place (as previously mentioned in verses one to six), this did not mean that he was perfectly sanctified thus, he still sinned. Sadly, this was so for Paul and this is what honest believers also acknowledge to be true of them, for although sin no longer reigns in them, it still remains. Although it is no longer president, it still is resident.[61] Paul began to speak about this inner conflict back in chapter 6 when he said in verses twelve and thirteen, "Therefore do not let sin reign in your mortal body, that you should obey its lust. And do not present your members as instruments of unrighteousness to sin, but present yourselves to God as being alive from the dead, and your members as instruments of righteousness to God."

The fact that the apostle allows us to see this side of his sanctification is enormously important. Without this portrait of the warfare within, or this "spiritual realism" as J. I. Packer called it,[62] we might be discouraged to think that we are the worst Christians who ever lived, or that we are

---

60 When I preached through these verses, I entitled the messages: The Christian in Conflict. Although there are commentators who understand these verses as Paul writing about his *pre*-converted days, I reject this idea for the following reasons: 1- Because there is no getting around Paul's repeated use of the present tense verb beginning at verse 14 down to verse 25. Unless he was trying to trick us by switching from the past tense verb in verses 7 to 12 to the present tense verb, I think it is clear that he is speaking about his life presently as a believer. Here he is using language similar to 1 Tim. 1:15, when he wrote, "This is a faithful saying and worthy of all acceptance that Christ Jesus came into the world to save sinners of whom I *am* chief." 2- Because Paul's purpose in writing this chapter was to instruct us about our sanctification as believers, why would he then take twelve verses to write about his non-Christian experience? 3- Because nowhere in any other portion of Scripture do we see Paul lamenting his sinfulness as an unconverted Pharisee. As a matter of fact, as an unsaved Pharisee he did not say "For I know that in me (that is, in my flesh) nothing good dwells (v. 18a) ... rather he said, "if anyone else thinks he may have confidence in the flesh, I more so" (Phil. 3:4). 4- Because unbelievers do not "delight in the law of God according to the inward man" (v. 22). This is the language of the regenerated soul since the unregenerate mind is "enmity against God; for it is not subject to the law of God, nor indeed can it be" (8:7). 5- Because unbelievers do not desire to obey God's law and do not feel great grief when they sin against God as Paul expresses throughout these verses. 6- Because unbelievers do not thank God "through Jesus Christ our Lord" for the deliverances that they receive over sin in life, as Paul himself did (v. 25a).

61 Matthew Henry, in his animated way, describes this matter "The struggle here is like that between Jacob and Esau in the womb, between the Canaanites and the Israelites in the land, between the house of Saul and the house of David." Henry, p. 332.

62 See Boice, Romans, Vol. 2, p. 766.

not even saved because at times our battles with remaining sin are so severe. We might be discouraged by the amount of internal turmoil we experience, forgetting that although our old man has been crucified with Christ, practically speaking, at times he is "slowly dying."

Here then, through Paul's experience, we see our own. We see that his struggles are our struggles. Although at times these are tough realities to face, nonetheless, the promise of victory through Christ is set before us, as well as the help of the Holy Spirit, as Paul goes on to speak of at the end of this chapter into chapter 8.

The nineteenth-century Presbyterian preacher William M'Clure helpfully encapsulates the verses before us:

> Having exhibited the operation of the law in producing conviction of sin, the apostle in this section comes to show its effects on the mind of the believer. Knowing that the law is spiritual, he feels how much he falls short of its requirements. Though renewed in the spirit of his mind, he laments that his sanctification is far from being complete. Though ardently aspiring to conform with the divine will, he feels that the power of sin is not yet subdued. He finds a law in his members opposing his better judgment; and he describes, in earnest and vivid language, the contest between the power of sin and his desire after holiness....
>
> Struck with a sense of danger lest he might fall again into bondage of sin.... his feelings burst out in the bitter exclamation, "O wretched man that I am, who shall deliver me from the body of this death?" But calling to mind the finished work of the Redeemer, his bosom glows with gratitude. His struggling spirit hears the cheering voice, "Sin shall not have dominion over you;" "if you know the truth, the truth will make you free." And in view of certain and glorious victory, he exclaims, "I thank God through Jesus Christ our Lord."[63]

Exegetical & Practical Insights:

Obs. 1- (v. 14) That as Paul speaks about the believer's sanctification and the battle with remaining, indwelling sin, he writes:[64]

For or because, the conjunction explaining why sin through the commandment became "exceedingly sinful" (v.13b); **we know**[65] not just Paul, but all true Christians, freely admit and stand convinced; **that** the conjunction setting forth the content of what we know; **the law is**[66] and continues to be; **spiritual,** which is to say, not only that is it of the Holy Spirit and of divine origin,[67] but that it also has the ability to search the inner man; **but** or in opposition to this; **I am carnal**[68] a metaphoric

---

63 As found in *Family Worship Bible Commentary, Walking Through the Scriptures with our Forefathers,* edited by Andrew Camp, p. 286, 287.

64 I would strongly encourage the reader to study A. W. Pink's excellent treatise called *The Christian in Romans 7,* published by *Chapel Library.*

65 Grk. perfect, active, verb.

66 Grk. present, active, verb.

67 Most commentators highlight these facts.

68 Clearly, when Paul uses this same term when calling the Corinthians "carnal" he was not saying that they were not saved, for he describes in 1 Cor. 1:2 as those who

reference which means, of the flesh, human, weak, and subject to the "gravitational pull of the old sinful nature;"[69] **sold under sin.**[70]

When Paul speaks about the law being "spiritual" in the opening part of this verse, he highlights the fact that the Ten Commandments have a "spiritual purpose,"[71] which again, is to set forth sin as "exceedingly sinful." The law of God exposes us since its requirements reach to "the understanding, will, affections, and all other powers of the soul; as well as words, works, and gestures."[72]

In contrast to this good use of the commandments, Paul again says, "but I am carnal sold under sin." What does he mean in this word picture? Simply this: even though the dominion of sin in his life had been completely broken at conversion, and he was thus no longer a slave to it (Rom. 6), nevertheless, as a Christian he could never be completely freed from his remaining sin until he arrived in glory. Being "sold under sin" was his state in his "already/not yet condition"[73] since he could not reach sinless perfection in this life, although he desperately desired it. This was his spiritual condition and that of every believer after him. Thus, they are all in a cycle of being "sold under sin" *which means* they still commit sin, they still repent of sin, and they still believe on Christ for fresh forgiveness of sin.

And so we ask: is the fact that Paul is liberated from his sin (Rom. 6) a contradiction to him being "sold under sin" (Rom. 7)? The answer is: certainly not! This is because although the power of sin had unquestionably and wonderfully been broken in his life once for all time at the point of his conversion, lingering sin was not and could not be entirely eradicated from him in this life.

Obs. 2- (vv. 15-21) that as Paul continues to show what he means by being "carnal and sold under sin" he writes:

For a validation of the preceding statement; **what I am doing,**[74] or more literally, what I am producing that is, producing under the influence of remaining sin; **I do not understand** or fully know. **For** the conjunction explaining what Paul means; **what I will** or desire; **to do, that I do not**

---

are "sanctified in Christ Jesus, called to be saints." Moreover, he was not saying that there are three classes of people in the world: saved, lost, and carnal. This is a perversion of his teaching and is utterly foreign to the teaching of Scripture. For the Bible only recognizes two classes of people: saved or lost, believer or nonbeliever.

69 James Edwards says something similar to this in his commentary on Romans p. 190.

70 The perfect tense participle highlights a continual state of struggling with remaining sin until the believer gets to heaven. The passive voice highlights that Paul did not, with his new nature, actively seek to sin. Or as David Garland helpfully notes, "The verb *sold* in the Greek a perfect passive participle that refers here to his human condition as fallen and corrupt that continues after becoming a believer. Paul has not sold himself into this slavery (contrast Lev. 25:39; 1 Kgs 21:20, 25; 2 Kgs 17:17); he was born into it." Garland, p. 246.

71 Peterson, p. 295.

72 *Westminster Larger Catechism,* Question 99.

73 That is, he is already saved and justified but not yet glorified.

74 Grk. present, middle, verb.

practice or perform; **but**[75] or in sharp contrast to this; **what I hate,** or detest and despise; **that I do**[76] or am doing.

Paul here is not saying that he is not responsible when he sins. Rather, he is saying that when he sins, he is a contradiction in terms. He is a puzzle to himself since he has two opposite principles at work in his being "the flesh lusts against the Spirit, and the Spirit against the flesh; and these are contrary to one another so that you do not do the things that you wish."[77] Thus, he is bewildered by his behavior. He does the very thing that his renewed nature in Christ does not want to do.

Spurgeon explains,

> This is the believer's riddle. To say that this is not a believer's experience is to prove that the man who says it does not know much about how believers feel. We hate sin, and yet, alas! alas! we fall into it! We would live perfect lives if we could, we that are renewed. We make no justification for our sin: it is evil and abominable; yet do we find these two things warring and fighting within.[78]

Sproul further remarks,

> When we have been born again and the Spirit has been shed abroad in our hearts, we have new natures, new desires, new inclinations, new attitudes, new love for the things of God. But that love is not perfect, it is not pure, it is not yet completely realized in our lives. There is a constant daily struggle and warfare with the old self whose desires are battling the desires of the new self. It is precisely this battle, with which every Christian has struggled, that Paul is setting forth here.[79]

Paul continues:

If, then, I do what I will not to do, I agree[80] or I consent and am confirming; **with the law**[81] **that** *it is* **good,** i.e., noble and right[82] for "the tragic irony of our contrary behavior does not negate the law, but actually confirms it."[83] **But now,** *it is* **no longer I**[84] specifically, the new man in Christ; **who do it, but**[85] or on the contrary; **sin,** that is, the sinfulness; **that dwells**[86] or is living and residing; **in me.**

---

75 The strong Greek adversative.

76 Grk. present, active, verb.

77 Cf. Gal. 5:17.

78 Spurgeon, p. 94.

79 Sproul, pp. 155, 156.

80 Grk. present, active, verb.

81 MacArthur says, "Paul's new nature defends the divine standard—the perfectly righteous law is not responsible for his sin. His new self longs to honor the law and to keep it perfectly." John MacArthur, *One Faithful Life* (2019), p. 292.

82 Cf. v. 12.

83 Edwards, pp. 191, 192.

84 The "I" is emphatic in the Greek text.

85 The strong Greek adversative.

86 Grk. present, active, participle. See the same phraseology in verse 20b.

As Paul expands on the previous verse by explaining what he means by sin "dwelling in him" he writes:

For I know, that is, I perceive by personal experience; **that in me (that is, in my flesh,** not his literal, physical flesh, but in his "old humanness, which has not yet been completely transformed");[87] **nothing good dwells; for to will,** i.e., to desire what is right according to God's law; **is present with me, but**[88] or in contrast to this; **how to perform**[89] or continually accomplish; **what is good I do not find. For the good that I will** *to do,* **I do not do; but**[90] or in opposition to this; **the evil I will not** *to do,* **that I practice**[91] or am practicing. **Now if I**[92] (with my remaining sin); **do** or am doing; **what I will not** *to do,* (as a believer) **it is no longer I who do it, but**[93] or to the contrary; **sin that dwells**[94] or is habitually housed; **in me. I find**[95] **then** or I am continuously discovering; **a law,** i.e., an influence or an operative power, principle, or propensity;[96] **that** the conjunction giving the content of the inner law; **evil is present with me,** or is always ready at hand to stir up trouble; **the one who wills** or purposes; **to do good.**

In these verses, the apostle repeats some of what he has already said in verses fifteen and sixteen of this chapter. He identifies once again the true culprit behind why he does what he wills not to do; *namely,* his lingering sin. Here again, he is not excusing himself when he sins, but he is saying that when he does, this is not an accurate reflection of who he really is in Christ.[97] It is not the real Paul as a redeemed man for although he is purchased and paid for by Christ, his restoration process had not yet been fully completed.

Obs. 3- (v. 22) That as he continues to write about his Christian experience, he says:

For the conjunction confirming that he was the one who wills to do good as he said in the previous verse; **I delight**[98] or more literally, I constantly rejoice together with or; **in the law of God** or, the law that

---

87 MacArthur, p. 387.

88 The strong Greek adversative.

89 Grk. present, middle, verb.

90 The strong Greek adversative.

91 Grk. present, active, verb.

92 Grk. present, active, verb.

93 The strong Greek adversative.

94 Grk. present, active, participle.

95 Grk. present, active, verb. This Greek verb is where we derive our English word "eureka."

96 The Puritan John Owen has an excellent treatment of this matter in his *Works,* VI: 157-163.

97 Of course, this is not to say that "the body" is evil. No, the body is good and is to be "nourished and cherished" by us (cf. Eph. 5:29). But the sinful nature contained within this carcass is evil.

98 Grk. present, middle, verb. Interestingly, this is the only place in the New Testament where this particular form of this verb appears. Further, in the Greek text, this verb is emphatically placed in the front of the sentence for the sake of emphasis.

has its origin and source from God; **according to** or concerning, **the inward man**; or as a regenerated person.

This verse is significant, showing us that even though at times Paul was a wearied warrior from inward battles with sin, nevertheless, because he was saved, he was also able to delight in the things of God. He tells us that unlike his pharisaical days where he merely gave mental assent to the law of God, now, because he was a true child of God, a justified believer, who was freed from the condemning power of the law, he was habitually happy with it in the deepest recesses of his being. Why?

Many answers could be given. Foundationally though, it is because, as he contemplated the commandments of God (commandments which by virtue of the new birth were inscribed upon his new heart),[99] he found the law to reveal to him the very nature and person of God Himself. The law of God reflects the lawgiver. And so, as Paul thought about the perfections, principles, purity, and purposes of God's law, he thought about God and was glad.

Here the apostle says essentially the same thing as the psalmist: "I will delight myself in your statutes; I will not forget your word" (Ps. 119:16), and, "Oh, how I love your law! It is my meditation all the day" (Ps. 119:97).

Obs. 4- (vv. 23-25) That as Paul winds down his discussion of the Christian in conflict, he writes:

But I see[100] or I am seeing (within himself);[101] **another law,** that is, another competing spiritual power or principle of a different kind;[102] **in my members,** i.e., the parts of his body still influenced by sin residing in his nature; **warring**[103] or going to battle; **against the law of my mind,** or his renewed understanding as a Christian; **and bringing me into captivity** (like an evil foe); **to the law** or strength; **of sin which is in my members.**[104]

Paul exclaims:

O wretched or miserable; **man that I am** or continue to be as a believer whenever I sin![105] **Who** (*not what*, for Paul was looking to his Savior since

---

99 Cf. Jer. 31:31-34; Ezek. 36:26, 27; Heb. 8:7-11.

100 Grk. present, active, verb.

101 Cf. v. 21.

102 Same Greek verb is found in Gal. 1:6.

103 Cf. 1 Pet. 2:11. The military language lets us know how strenuous this battle is with remaining corruptions at times.

104 In speaking about Paul's words here MacArthur rightly says, "It is not that Paul's salvation was imperfect or in any way deficient. From the moment he receives Jesus Christ as Lord and Savior, the believer is completely acceptable by God and ready to meet Him. But as long as he remains in his mortal body, in his old unredeemed humanness, he remains subject to temptation and sin." MacArthur, p. 391.

105 Cf. Job. 40:4; Isa. 6:5. It is interesting to note that Paul does not say, speaking as a mature believer, "Oh how good I am!" or, "Look how sanctified I am." No, the mature believer has nothing to boast about except Christ (v. 25). The sanctified saint has learned that even in his best days before God, in and of himself, he is still an unprofitable servant. Thus it is true that the holier a man gets, the more he cries out in this way. This is the testimony found not only in Scripture but throughout church history.

his strength was so small in his sanctification); **will deliver**[106] **me,** i.e., save and rescue in the ultimate sense; **from this body of death,**[107] that is, this body which is so full of persistent, remaining sin. **I thank**[108] **God**—or I am continually grateful to God; **through** or by the mediation and agency of; **Jesus Christ our Lord!**[109] **So then,** or consequently, Paul's summary statement concerning all that he has been writing in this last section; **with the mind,** that is, with the renewed mind, understanding, and will; **I myself**[110] Paul speaks emphatically about what is true for him in the main as a Christian; **serve**[111] or he habitually gives himself to; **the law of God,** showing us that he "does not serve sin so much as he serves

---

Pink points out a few. "Mr. Bradford (1510-1555)... who was martyred in the reign of bloody Queen Mary, in a letter to a fellow prisoner in another penitentiary, subscribed himself thus:

'The sinful John Bradford: a very painted hypocrite: the most miserable, hardhearted, and unthankful sinner, John Bradford' (1555 A.D.).

Godly Rutherford (1600-1661) wrote: 'This body of sin and corruption embitters and poisons our enjoyment. Oh that I were where I shall sin no more' (A.D. 1650).

Bishop Berkeley wrote: 'I cannot pray, but I sin; I cannot preach, but I sin; I cannot administer, nor receive the holy sacrament, but I sin. My very repentance needs to be repented of: and the tears I shed need washing in the blood of Christ' (A.D. 1670).

Jonathan Edwards (1703-1758): 'When I look into my heart and take a view of its wickedness, it looks like an abyss infinitely deeper than hell. And it appears to me, that, were it not for free grace, exalted and raised up to the infinite height of all the fullness and glory of the great Jehovah, I should appear sunk down in my sins below hell itself; far below the side of everything, but the eye of sovereign grace, that alone can pierce down to such a depth. And it is affecting to think how ignorant I was, when a young Christian, of bottomless depths of wickedness, pride, hypocrisy and deceit left in my heart' (A.D. 1743).

C. H. Spurgeon (1834-1892): 'There are some professing Christians who can speak of themselves in terms of admiration; but, from my inmost heart, I loathe such speeches more and more every day that I live. Those who talk in such a boastful fashion must be constituted very differently from me. While they are congratulating themselves, I have to lie humbly at the foot of Christ's cross, and marvel that I am saved at all, for I know that I am saved. I have to wonder that I do not believe Christ more, and equally wonder that I am privileged to believe in Him at all—to wonder that I do not love Him more, and equally to wonder that I love Him at all—to wonder that I am not holier, and equally to wonder that I have any desire to be holy at all considering a polluted, debased, depraved nature I find still within my soul, notwithstanding all that divine grace has done in me.'" *Chapel Library* booklet pp. 9-13.

106 Grk. future, middle, verb. Paul's use of the future tense verb seems to be pointing primarily to the final removal of all sin from his body at death or at Christ's return. However, what Jesus will do then completely, He, by the Spirit helps us to do now daily as we look to Him for help in this regard (cf. Rom 8:2).

107 A. W. Pink rightly notes: "This is not the language of despair, but of earnest desire for help from without and above himself" (Chapel Library booklet p. 13). Further, what an encouragement it is that one day this "body of death" will be a glorified body, completely unable to sin anymore! (Rom. 8:30).

108 Grk. present, active, verb. Note also, how without hesitation Paul immediately and triumphantly answers his own question.

109 Cf. 5:1, 5:9, 5:21, 6:23, 7:4.

110 The words "I myself" are doubly emphatic in the Greek text, Harvey, p. 186. Additionally, it is vitally important to note the significance of these words being connected to the words "serve the law of God" verses the words "serve the law of sin." If this were not the case, we might question how effective salvation is in a person's life.

111 Grk. present, active, verb.

holiness;"[112] **but** or although at times; **with the flesh,** that is, the old sinful tendency; **the law of sin.**

This is Paul's summary about the matter. Even though he struggles with remaining sin, and even though at times it gets the best of him, the general thrust of his life is that by God's unfailing grace, his thoughts and actions, are obedient to the good law of God. However, though much less predominantly, at times with his flesh, he serves the law of sin.

This was his true condition as a believer while still in the process of sanctification. This is the condition of all believers, while in the same process.[113] James Edwards helpfully recaps the apostle's teaching in verses fourteen to twenty-five:

> The chapter closes with a reminder that the Christian life is one of tension and struggle.... To be righteous with God is not to be fully free from the effects of sin. Believers must run the race with perseverance, and though there is progress, sin and sorrow and death do not in this life fade away. These remain enemies, death the greatest of them. Through all this the Christian learns to walk 'by faith, and not by sight' (2 Cor. 5:7). Our one anchor is the promise and presence of the resurrected Lord who gives grace for the present struggle and eternal life in the world to come.[114]

Suggested applications from the text for the church:

1- Reject any form of Christianity which says you can have "your best life now" or that you can reach some "higher-life" type of Christian experience that frees you from all remaining sin in this life, since such teaching does not square with Scripture or with Christian experience.

2- Rejoice if you find that your greatest burden is your remaining sin in this life. This is good proof that you truly are in a state of grace, for this is not the case with the non-Christian.

---

112 William G. T. Shedd as quoted in Wilson, p. 125.

113 This of course does not mean that the believer has a divided life—quite the opposite. Whereas at one time they served *only* the law of sin with the flesh, now they do it *only* to a limited degree. Indeed there has been, by the grace of God, a radical spiritual and ethical paradigm shift in their lives. They are indeed new people in Jesus! This is all because of the transforming power of the gospel (Rom. 1:16).

114 Edwards, pp. 194-95. Vos also helpfully concludes when he writes "There is one practical application that we should consider in this connection. The conflict in our souls is nothing to be discouraged about. Some people have a wrong idea of the Christian life. They expect everything to be peace and joy—"a bed of roses." When they find a battle going on day after day in their soul, they think that maybe they are not really saved after all. They become terribly discouraged. But we should not be discouraged. The battle in our souls is a good sign. It is a sign of life. If we were not saved Christians, there would be no battle. If we did not have a new nature from God, there would be no battle. Because we are spiritually alive, there is a continual battle in our souls. God has put enmity there between the old nature and the new nature. This conflict is the experience of all of God's true children. It is not something exceptional that you and I have to face alone. All of us have this same ordeal to pass through. It is a battle that is sure to end in victory. Our Lord Jesus Christ is going to give us the victory in the end. All armies expect to lose some battles at times, but what counts is to win the war. So if we lose sometimes in the battle with sin, we must not let the devil throw us into a fit of discouragement and despair. He will if he can, but we must not let him do it. Remember, victory is sure." Vos, p. 97.

3- Reflect often on the fact that although at times your present lot in this life is one of internal conflict, nevertheless, a day is coming when Christ will return or you will go to be with Him through the portal of death, and then all the remaining vestiges of sin will be completely eradicated from your life forevermore. Even so, come Lord Jesus!

Suggested application from the text for the non-Christian:

1- Remember that while it is true that sin remains in the believer, nevertheless, sin perpetually reigns in you all the time. Therefore, your only hope is to turn to the mighty Christ who alone can deliver you from such a pitiful spiritual state, for "if the Son makes you free, you shall be free indeed" (John 8:36).

ROMANS
CHAPTER EIGHT

Text: Romans 8:1[1]

General theme: No condemnation for those who are in Christ Jesus (I)

Homiletical outline of the verse:

A. The present position of those who are in Christ Jesus: [1a] *There is therefore now no condemnation to those who are in Christ Jesus,*

B. The present description of those who are in Christ Jesus: [1b] *who do not walk according to the flesh, but according to the Spirit.*

Summary of section: "What's so great about Romans chapter 8?" I asked my congregation this when I preached this chapter to them. I answered with one word: "Everything!" Romans chapter 8 (which is the longest chapter in this epistle) is exceptional indeed. This chapter both begins and ends with the phrase "in Christ Jesus." What is more, it begins with the marvelous words *no condemnation* and ends with the glorious words *no separation*.[2] Then, sandwiched between these two high points, we are told that there is to be *no consternation* for us who are Christians, since we know that "all things work together for good to those who love God, to those who are called according to His purpose" (v. 28).

Many have commented on the majesty and magnificence of this chapter. Luther called it "the masterpiece of the New Testament." Moo called it "the inner sanctuary within the Cathedral of the Christian faith; the tree of life in the midst of the Garden of Eden; the highest peak in the range of mountains."[3] And still, another has said that "if the Holy Scripture was a ring, and the Epistle to the Romans its precious stone, chapter 8 would be the sparkling point of the jewel."[4]

Along these same lines, commentator Robert Mounce writes:

---

1 A book that I found helpful for this chapter is *How the Gospel Brings Us All the way Home* by Derek Thomas.

2 Many commentators highlight this matter.

3 Moo, on Romans, NICNT, p. 467.

4 A quote from the commentator Spencer, as cited in Vaughan and Corley, p. 90.

With chap. 8 we arrive at what may be called the inspirational highlight of the Book of Romans. Here the apostle is swept along in a wave of spiritual exultation that begins with God's provision of the Spirit for victory over the old nature, breaks through the sufferings that mark our present existence, and crests with a doxology of praise to the unfathomable love of God revealed in Christ Jesus . . . we are not dealing here with mere theology. As Paul wrote, his pen gave evidence that he was caught up in an experience of profound worship and spiritual adoration.[5]

But how do we outline this breathtaking chapter? Many writers have struggled with this since Paul's subjects are so tightly stitched together. After laboring with this matter for some time, this is the outline I have come up with: the Christian's salvation (vv. 1-4), the Christian's sanctification (vv. 5-14), the Christian's sonship (vv. 15-17a), the Christian's sufferings (vv. 17b-30), and the Christian's security (vv. 31-39).

Exegetical & Practical Insights:
Obs. 1- (v. 1) That as Paul gathers his various strands of thought that he has been speaking of up to this point in this epistle, such as the blessings of being justified by faith (Rom. 5), freedom from the bondage of sin (Rom. 6) and battles with remaining corruption (Rom. 7), he says first:

There is **therefore** an inferential particle which looks backward and draws a conclusion from the previous chapter, (but perhaps most especially in 7:25a concerning what he just said about our great deliverance through Christ); **now,** i.e., right at the present time; **no**[6] quite literally from the Greek text, not even one; **condemnation**[7] a forensic term meaning eternal judgment or a guilty verdict coming down from God which includes "both the sentence and the execution of the sentence;"[8] **to those** and only those; **who are in** or spiritually joined by means of an "incorporative union"[9] by faith to;[10] **Christ Jesus,** and Christ Jesus alone versus being in Adam as a federal head;[11] **who** that is, true believers in Christ; **do not walk**[12] or act and behave as a habitual pattern of life; **according to** or in conformity with, or after, in the sense of living "under the control of and according to the values of;"[13] **the flesh,** that is the old, corrupt, Adamic, sinful, depraved "fleshly" nature which has as

---

5 Mounce, p. 173.

6 This one Greek word is derived from three other Greek words. It stands first in the Greek text for the sake of emphasis.

7 Cf. Rom. 8:33-34. Paul uses this exact Greek word only two other times in all of his epistles and they are both in this letter, 5:6, 5:18.

8 Morris, p. 300.

9 Harvey, p. 189.

10 Luther famously said that "Faith unites the soul with Christ as a spouse with her husband."

11 Not only is there no condemnation for us who are in Christ Jesus because He took our condemnation for us at the cross, but because we are in Him, God does not see us in our sins. We are completely "accepted in the Beloved" (Eph. 1:6b).

12 Grk. present, active, participle.

13 Moo, NICNT, p. 485.

its object carnal, worldly things;[14] **but**[15] or in strong opposition to this code of conduct; **according to** or in conformity with, or after, in the sense of living "under the control of and according to the values of;"[16] **the Spirit,** that is, being governed by His guidance, influence and will as found in Scripture.[17]

These are wonderful words, but what makes them so wonderful? It is this: not only will there be no condemnation for believers in the *future* because Christ died for their sins and they have been legally justified before God's judgment bar through Him, but there is no condemnation *right now*, even in our present situation amid all of the inward struggles against remaining sin.

This matter is crucial for the apostle to state here as he continues to speak about the subject of sanctification and the saved.[18] Simply stated, even though what he willed to do as a Christian he did not always practice (Rom. 7:15), and that with the flesh he still at times served the law of sin (7:25b), nevertheless, this matter of no condemnation or doom during such difficulties would have been incredibly encouraging to him.

To know that whenever he fell short of the glory of God (as we all do, cf. Rom. 3:23) there was still no reversing of God's judicial clearing of him would have brought him great joy, and no doubt would have been useful in alleviating any *self*-condemnation that he might have.[19] Again, Christ would ultimately deliver him in the final analysis from his "body of death" (7:24), but in his present condition, his current status because of Jesus' justifying righteousness was "no condemnation" whatsoever; thus, he could take great comfort.

Leon Morris comments concerning these words:

> His *now* is surely temporal, now in contrast to times gone by before we had entered into the justification Christ brought. It is possible also in contrast to the time to come. He has a strong eschatological thrust in many places, and he may be hinting that, though we do not as yet experience all the fullness of what salvation in Christ means, we do enjoy all that

---

14 Cf. Gal. 5:19-21; 1 Pet. 4:2.

15 The strong Greek adversative.

16 Moo, NICNT, p. 485.

17 Cf. Gal. 5:22, 23. I realize that there is a textual variant here whereby half of this verse is omitted in some Greek texts. However, I agree with the great Bible commentator Haldane when he said that these words "connect perfectly well with the preceding clause of the verse, as characterizing those who are in Christ Jesus." Haldane also goes on wisely to say "In no respect, however, do they assign the cause of exemption from condemnation to them who are in Christ. The apostle does not say, *because* they do not walk, but *who* walk, not after the flesh but after the Spirit. There is an essential difference between asserting the character of those who are freed from condemnation, and declaring that cause of their being delivered from it." Haldane, p. 314.

18 Paul began to speak about this subject back in Romans 6.

19 This of course does not negate the fact that when Paul sinned against God he needed to repent. He did this, not in order to stay in union with Him, but to stay in fresh communion with Him.

no condemnation means. Now believers have a wonderful gift of salvation from God in Christ.[20]

MacArthur further elaborates, "No sin a believer can commit—past, present, or future—can be held against him, since the penalty was paid by Christ and righteousness was imputed to the believer. And no sin will ever reverse this divine legal decision."[21]

Suggested applications from the text for the church:
1- From this verse there is a call for us to praise Christ for all that He has done in our lives, but especially for completely removing at the cross all the condemnation we deserve from God both now and forevermore.

2- From this verse there is a call to pause and examine ourselves to be sure that we, by the grace of God, have been transformed in our lives, so that now we are characterized as those who do not walk "according to the flesh, but according to the Spirit."

3- From this verse there is a call to pursue a life of gospel holiness, always asking God the Holy Spirit to empower us to this righteous end.

Suggested application from the text for the non-Christian:
1- From this verse there is a call to ponder that there is great condemnation for you from God both now and forevermore because you have not come to Christ for the salvation of your soul. May this fact cause you to own your unrighteousness before Him and to flee to Jesus by faith for mercy and the forgiveness of your sins.

Text: Romans 8:2-4

General theme: No Condemnation for those who are in Christ Jesus (II).

Homiletical outline of the verses:
A. Freedom from sin and death by the Spirit: [2] For the law of the Spirit of life in Christ Jesus has made me free from the law of sin and death.

B. Freedom from curse and condemnation through the Son: [3] For what the law could not do in that it was weak through the flesh, God *did* by sending His own Son in the likeness of sinful flesh, on account of sin: He condemned sin in the flesh,

C. Freedom from lawless and fleshly living by the Spirit: [4] that the righteous requirement of the law might be fulfilled in us who do not walk according to the flesh but according to the Spirit.

Summary of section: In these verses, Paul continues to tie together two crucial aspects of the Christian life: justification and sanctification. He did this in 8:1b, showing that all who have been truly saved will live like it.[22]

---

20 Morris, p. 300.

21 John MacArthur, *One Faithful Life* (2019), p. 294.

22 It is sad to see so many professors of faith separating these two doctrines which

In doing this, he also puts forth in verse three, one of the most splendid statements about the gospel found anywhere in Scripture. Additionally, he introduces us to the person and work of the Holy Spirit which, up until this point in this epistle, he has hardly mentioned. In fact, from verse 2 to verse 27, the Holy Spirit is mentioned no less than fifteen times, showing that He indeed is a principal operator in our sanctification and that a "new and wonderful life opens out before those who put their trust in Christ and that this depends heavily on the work of the Spirit of God."[23]

Exegetical & Practical Insights:

Obs. 1- (v. 2) That as Paul gives the reason why those who are not condemned by God walk according to the Spirit and not according to the flesh, as he spoke of in the previous verse, he says, practically speaking:

For or because; **the law** or the operation, influence and power; **of the Spirit of life** which is another way of saying the Holy Spirit who gives life;[24] **in** that is, in conjunction with; **Christ Jesus has made me free**[25] or liberated him as a pattern of life, once for all time, at the point of salvation; **from the law of sin** i.e., the operation, influence and power of reigning sin and its ultimate consequences; **and death** i.e., spiritual death and its ultimate consequences, which used to have mastery over him when he was unconverted.

Now that Paul says here that the Holy Spirit in concert with Christ made him free from the prevailing operation of "sin and death" when he was saved is "good news" to be sure. This demonstrates the power and practical import of the gospel in freeing men and women from their former lost spiritual condition. It shows that the Almighty Spirit of God radically delivers believers when He regenerates them, releasing them from such horrible states as "sin and death," which He continues to do all their days.

Mounce puts the point this way:

> The apostle was contrasting two different laws (or principles). The old law is the power of sin that inevitably results in death. The new law, which sets the believer free from the power of the old, is the law of the Spirit . . . It is the Spirit of God who provides victory, and that Spirit is the possession of every true child of God.[26]

Obs. 2- (v. 3) That as the apostle speaks about how this freedom over sin and death was procured for us who are Christians, he speaks

---

God has joined together. May it never be so for us.

23 Morris, p. 299. For example, in this chapter Paul tells us: 1- That the Holy Spirit helps us to keep God's law (8:4). 2-That the Holy Spirit indwells us (8:9). 3- That the Holy Spirit will give life to our mortal bodies at the resurrection (8:11). 4- That the Holy Spirit helps us to put to death the deeds of the body (8:13, 14). 5- That the Holy Spirit bears witness with our spirit that we are the children of God (8:16); and 6- That the Holy Spirit helps us to pray (8:26).

24 Cf. John 3:5-8.

25 Grk. aorist, active, verb. See 2 Cor. 3:17 for similar language.

26 Mounce, pp. 174, 175.

now concerning the Ten Commandments and the work of Christ on our behalf, providing yet another reason why there is no condemnation for us. He says:

For what the law, that is, the Decalogue; **could not do** or more literally, was completely powerless to do, which is to say, save or sanctify us, so as to deliver us from the penalty and power of sin; **in that** or because; **it was weak,**[27] i.e., without strength, not in and of itself, but; **through** or by means of; **the flesh,** that is, our fallen, frail, sinful nature which is unable to keep the law as it requires;[28] **God,** i.e., God the Father; ***did*** or remedied our problem; **by sending**[29] or dispatching on a rescue mission;[30] **His own Son** (the words are placed in the front of the sentence in the Greek text for the sake of emphasis); **in the likeness of sinful flesh** or the form of sinful flesh, not in sinful flesh, since Jesus knew no sin,[31] but in flesh nonetheless; **on account of** or concerning both our actual and indwelling; **sin: He** (the Father); **condemned**[32] **sin** or punished our rebellious sin against Him, once for all time, "in the sense of consigning to destruction as well as of pronouncing the sentence of condemnation"[33] upon it when Jesus sacrificed Himself as a sin offering for our sins,[34] when He died; **in the flesh,**[35] that is, in His real human body, the prepositional phrase "in the flesh" indicating "the sphere where God's judgment was carried out."[36]

---

27 Grk. imperfect, active, verb.

28 Cf. Rom. 3:20.

29 Several commentators point out that this matter of God "sending" His Son presupposes His preexistence.

30 Cf. John 3:16; Gal. 4:4; 1 Tim. 1:15.

31 2 Cor. 5:21; 1 Pet. 2:22; 1 Jn. 3:5.

32 Grk. aorist, active, verb.

33 Murray, p. 278.

34 This language points back to the Old Testament sacrificial system by which God temporarily instructed the Old Covenant people to offer animal sacrifices for their sins. These sacrifices could never remove their sins, only cover them (cf. Heb. 10:4). Thus, they pointed forward to the time when Christ, the Lamb of God would shed His innocent blood on behalf of sinners and cancel out their sins altogether (cf. Lev. 17:11; John 1:29).

35 This proves yet again that Jesus came into the world as a real human being with real human flesh and not as some mere phantom or ghost as the Docetists falsely taught (cf. Rom. 1:3b; 1 Jn. 4:2). John Murray put it well when he wrote "In that same nature which in all others was sinful, in that very nature which in all others was dominated and directed by sin, in that nature assumed by the Son of God, but free from sin, God condemned sin and overthrew its power. Jesus not only blotted out sin's guilt and brought us nigh to God. He also vanquished sin as power and set us free from its enslaving dominion. And this could not have been done except in the 'flesh'. The battle was joined and the triumph secured in that same flesh which in us is the seat and agent of sin." Murray, p. 282.

Chrysostom further remarks "For Christ did not have sinful flesh but flesh which, though it was like ours by nature, was sinless. From this, it is plain that flesh is not sinful by nature. It was not by taking on a different kind of flesh nor by changing ours into something different that Christ caused it to gain the victory over sin and death. Rather, he allowed the flesh to keep its own nature, giving it the crown of victory and after its resurrection life immortality." *Ancient Christian Commentary on Scripture, Romans* p. 196.

36 Harvey, p. 191.

Again, as I stated above, this verse is one of the most glorious gospel statements found anywhere in Scripture.[37] Here we see that what the law of God could not do, the Son of God could! The law, which is "holy, just, and good" (Rom. 7:12) could point out sin, however, it was powerless to purge us from sin. The law could call us to holiness, but it could not make us holy. It could terrify, but it does not have the power to justify or sanctify. It could condemn, but could not cleanse or cause us to stop sinning.

This is why we needed a Savior! And this is why God sent His Son into the world, so that through Him taking on flesh by means of the incarnation, He could take our sins upon Himself and be punished for them as our substitute, so that through His sacrifice on our behalf, our sins could be condemned in His flesh. This is what happened 2000 years ago at the cross when Jesus died for us.

This is what the Bible predicted Jesus would do and this is what He actually did. And thus, at the cross (as the Old Testament prophet Isaiah predicted), our Lord was "wounded for our transgressions, He was bruised for our iniquities; the chastisement of our peace was upon Him; and by His stripes we are healed" (Isa. 53:5).

This is the heart and glory of the gospel which Paul nicely summarizes when he says in Second Corinthians 5:21 that God the Father "made Him (Jesus) who knew no sin to be sin for us, that we might become the righteousness of God in Him." This is the core of the message we believe and preach. And this entire salvific arrangement and accomplishment was done by the entire Godhead: the Father (v. 3), the Son (v. 3) and the Holy Spirit (v. 4).

The English Reformer Thomas Cranmer caught something of the wonder of these words when he wrote:

> Although this justification is free for us, it was not free without any ransom being paid at all. Here we may be astonished, reasoning after this fashion: If a ransom was paid for our redemption, then it was not given to us freely. For prisoners who pay their ransom are not let go freely; for if they go freely, then they go without ransom. For what does it mean to go freely, other than to be set at liberty without the payment of ransom? This reason is satisfied by the great wisdom of God in the mystery of our redemption, who so tempered his justice and mercy together that he would neither by his justice condemn us to the perpetual captivity of the devil and his prison of hell remediless for ever, without mercy; nor by his mercy deliver us without justice or payment of a just ransom. Rather, he joined his most upright and equal justice to his endless mercy. He showed his great mercy to us in delivering us from our former captivity without requiring any ransom to be paid or amends to be made on our part, which would have been impossible for us to do. And since it did not lie within us to do that, he provided a ransom for us; that was the most precious body and blood of his dearest and most beloved Son Jesus Christ, who,

---

37 Strikingly, MacArthur calls it "perhaps the most definitive and succinct statement of the substitutionary atonement to be found in Scripture." MacArthur, p. 405.

besides his being a ransom, fulfilled the law for us perfectly. And so the justice of God and his mercy embraced together and fulfilled the mystery of our redemption.[38]

Obs. 3- (v. 4) That as Paul puts forth the ethical purpose for why God saved us, in tying our justification and sanctification together once again he writes,

that or in order that; **the righteous requirement** or regulations; **of the law,** i.e., the Ten Commandments; **might be fulfilled in us**[39] the preposition "in" denoting sphere, that is to say, might be daily kept by us; **who do not walk according to the flesh but according to the Spirit** (cf. 8:1b).

In these words, the apostle shows us that God's gracious act of pardoning us from the judgment of His law through the sacrifice of His Son does not free us from the moral obligation to keep the commandments as an expression of our love to Him for such great deliverance. While of course the terrors of the law no longer hang over our heads, the point is, the directives of the law are to be under our feet as a rule and guide for our lives.[40] Not so that by keeping them we might be saved, but because we are saved, we seek to keep them.

This is not something we do *perfectly* but *purposefully* and *actually* by the power of the Holy Spirit. God did not save us so that we would become law-*breakers*. Rather, He saved us so that we might be law-*abiding* Christians who with hearts made new, gratefully uphold His commandments with gratitude for being freed from their judgments. This has historically been called an evangelical keeping of the commandments of God.[41] James Edwards explains this well:

---

38 *Reformation Commentary on Scripture, Romans* p. 478.

39 I have trouble with the thinking of some commentators who connect these words to Christ's active and passive obedience on our behalf as that by which the righteous requirements of the law might be fulfilled in us. While of course this is true legally speaking regarding our justification, this is not what Paul is saying here. Here he is speaking practically about gospel sanctification and how that connects to our keeping of God's commandments as Christians.

Some argue that the passive form of the verb "fulfilled" confirms that we are not involved in this matter at all. This is an exegetical mistake, for the passive verb is highlighting to us that the Holy Spirit is the primary worker in our fulfilling the commandments. However, what He works in, we work out (cf. Phil. 2:12, 13). Thus, I agree with Schreiner when he says "it would be a serious mistake to conclude from this that the actual obedience of believers is excluded. The obedience of believers has its basis in the work of Christ on the cross, and this provides the platform on which believers receive ability to keep the law. The keeping of the law is God's work, yet this does not exclude human activity and obedience. The two are not mutually exclusive. The word fulfilled in the passive does not rule out human activity, even when God's work is envisioned." Schreiner, p. 405.

Additionally, the preposition "in" in the verse can carry the meaning of agency so that it could read: "That the righteous requirement of the law might be fulfilled 'by' us who 'do not walk according to the flesh but according to the Spirit.'" To me, this second part of the verse makes it abundantly plain that Paul is putting a gospel obligation upon us and is not primarily speaking about what Christ has done for us. All of this is what God said He would do when He would put His Spirit within us cf. Ezek. 36:27.

40 Cf. Rom. 13:8-10.

41 Cf. Rom. 3:31.

Those who live in the Spirit are for the first time enabled to acknowledge the true intent of the law, and they are empowered to begin to fulfill it.... The Spirit is the supernatural reinforcement of God's grace who empowers Christians to fulfill the intent and requirements of the law. Paul does not say that one must keep the law in order to be saved but that one must be saved in order to keep the law! Augustine understood Paul correctly, 'The law is given that grace might be sought; grace is given that the law might be fulfilled.[42]

Suggested applications from the text for the church:

1- From these verses there is an encouragement to praise our God for sending His own Son in the likeness of sinful flesh on account of sin that He might condemn sin in the flesh. This was His great plan of salvation and for it we should forever bless His Name.

2- From these verses there is an exhortation to seek Christ daily so that by the power of the Holy Spirit we could live as He would have us to live.

Suggested application from the text for the non-Christian:

1- From these verses there is an entreaty to call on the living Christ by faith, for He alone can give you freedom from "sin and death" both in this life and in the life to come.

Text: Romans 8:5-8

General theme: The Christian in contrast to the non-Christian

Homiletical outline of the verses:

A. Two spiritual conditions: [5]For those who live according to the flesh set their minds on the things of the flesh, but those *who live* according to the Spirit, the things of the Spirit.

B. Two spiritual certainties: [6]For to be carnally minded *is* death, but to be spiritually minded *is* life and peace. [7]Because the carnal mind *is* enmity against God; for it is not subject to the law of God, nor indeed can be. [8]So then, those who are in the flesh cannot please God.

Summary of section: Having just ended verse four by speaking broadly about those who "walk according to the flesh" in contrast to those who walk "according to the Spirit," Paul now speaks about both categories of people in specific terms. He describes the lifestyle of the saved in contrast to the unsaved, showing how utterly opposed they are to one another. As he does this, he begins by saying:[43]

---

42 Edwards, p. 203.

43 Unfortunately, some commentators see these words as referring to two different ways that believers live as opposed to defining two vastly different categories of people, namely, believers and unbelievers. This is not correct, especially since Paul literally writes that those who "are" of the flesh or "exist" according to the flesh set their minds on the things of the flesh, but those who "are" of the Spirit or "exist" according to the Spirit, the things of the Spirit. These are references to two spiritual states of being, i.e., saved or lost, each with their corresponding behavior patterns, not two different approaches to the Christian life.

Exegetical & Practical Insights:

Obs. 1- (v. 5) For or because; **those,** i.e., unbelievers; **who live**[44] or more literally, "are" continually living; **according to** or in conformity with, or after; **the flesh,** i.e., their fallen, corrupt, Adamic natures;[45] **set**[46] or are setting; **their minds** that is to say, their thinking; **on the things of the flesh, but,** that is, in contrast to such ones; **those** *who live* **according to** or in conformity with, or after; **the Spirit, the things of** or which pertain to; **the Spirit** which means to have the things of the Holy Spirit as "the absorbing objects of thought, interest, affection, and purpose."[47]

Here once more, Paul is putting forth the radical differences between the unbeliever and the believer. Unbelievers are continually setting their minds on the things of the flesh. This means that their worldviews, opinions, pursuits, and desires are all influenced by and regulated according to their corrupt natures. It means that their approach to and outlook on life are all shaped by their fallen hearts, which are focused on and occupied with their sinful selves and the base things of this world, which are not of God.

By contrast, those who live or "are" of the Spirit (by virtue of being regenerated by Him), are setting their minds on the things of the Spirit. But what does this mean?[48] It means to be occupied with the things that the Spirit of God is occupied with; it means to be taken up with the things that the Spirit of God is taken up with. Such things include, but are not limited to: the Word of God, which the Spirit inspired (cf. 2 Pet. 1:20-21); the Son of God, whom the Spirit came to glorify (cf. John 16:14); and the gospel of God, which the Spirit makes real to every heart whom He regenerates (cf. John 3:6).

To be spiritually minded is to *mind* "spiritual things." It is to have one's heart on the things of God—not so as to have one's head in the clouds, but to have his feet on the earth with his heart on heavenly matters. It is to be one who is being shaped by the things of the Spirit and to have "holy affections," and deep longings after God and sanctification as Jonathan Edwards liked to say.[49]

Obs. 2- (v. 6) That as Paul speaks about two spiritual certainties which are connected with the lifestyle of the Christian versus the non-Christian, he begins first by explaining the essence of the mind which is set on the flesh versus the mind which is set on the Spirit, and says:

For to be carnally minded or to have a mind which is focused on the flesh because it belongs to the one who is unsaved; *is* **death, but** in opposition to this; **to be spiritually minded** or to have a mind which

---

44 Grk. present, active, participle.

45 Galatians 5:19-21 shows what this looks like.

46 Grk. present, active, verb.

47 Murray, p. 285.

48 I highly recommend John Owen's classic treatment on *Spiritual-Mindedness*.

49 MacArthur, p. 416.

thinks on the things of the Spirit because it belongs to one who is saved; *is* **life and peace.**

It is important to note that the apostle here is not describing the *consequences* of the carnal mind as opposed to the saved mind. He is not saying that the carnal mind *leads to* death and the spiritual mind *leads to* life and peace, though in some sense that is true. Rather, he is stating a spiritual equation; he is letting us know what is true about both.[50] He is saying that the carnal mind which occupies the unbeliever is in fact *death,* and that the spiritual mind which occupies the believer is in fact *life and peace.*

The terms "death," and "life and peace" are being contrasted. The carnal mind is death, because it is dead to God in its thinking and affections toward Him. It is spiritually dead because the unbeliever is spiritually dead and thus, he does not "receive the things of the Spirit of God, for they are foolishness to him; nor can he know them, because they are spiritually discerned" (1 Cor. 2:14).

In distinction to this, Paul says concerning the Christian that to be spiritually minded is "life and peace." Again, these terms stand in opposition to "death." They mean, firstly, that for the one who is saved and has eternal life through Christ, they have true "spiritual life," i.e., communion and fellowship with God. They know Him in truth and are known by Him in truth,[51] and they receive all true meaning and purpose from Him. Secondly, they have peace with God, which is that *subjective peace,* or tranquility with Him in their hearts. This inner peace is based on the *objective peace* which Christ accomplished on their behalf when He died in their place on the cross and reconciled them to God, from whom they were once estranged.[52]

Concerning these two joyful matters of "life and peace" for the Christian, Charles Simeon, that great expository preacher of the nineteenth century, fittingly comments, "Happy they who are of this description! Let such adore the grace that has caused them to differ from others. Let them endeavor to improve in spirituality of mind; let them guard against relapses, which will destroy their peace; and let their eyes be fixed upon the eternal state, where their present bliss shall be consummated in glory."[53]

Obs. 3- (v. 7) That as Paul gives the reason why the mindset on the flesh is death, he says firstly,

Because the carnal mind *is* **enmity** or actively antagonistic; **against** or directly towards; **God; for** the conjunction explaining the previous words; **it is not subject**[54] or continually not submissive to and unwilling

---

50 Both John Murray and John MacArthur highlight this in their commentaries: Murray, p. 285; MacArthur, p. 417.

51 Cf. Gal. 4:9.

52 Cf. Rom. 5:1.

53 Simeon, pp. 201, 202.

54 Grk. present, passive, verb.

to line up under; **the law of God,** that is, the Ten Commandments; **nor indeed can be**[55] or ever has the inherent power to do this.

These words are eye-opening in what they tell us about the condition of unbelievers. They tell us three specific things:

1- That even though non-Christians may not externally express enmity against God and may even think themselves on good terms with Him, this is not the case. For whether they are actively shaking their fists at Him or passively neglecting Him by not fleeing to Jesus by faith for salvation (cf. John 6:29), their disposition of heart toward Him is one of "downright hostility."[56]

2- Paul says that such people with such mindsets are not subject to God's commandments. The word "subject" here is a military term. It is used concerning one being in subjection to the orders of a commanding general.[57] The point is, the non-Christian is not in subjection to God, the great commanding general of mankind, who gave His laws for our good. Man by nature and by practice is a great rebel against God the commander in charge. Thus, with a lawless life and heart, he wants what he wants, but not what God wants. As a result, he is continually insubordinate to his Maker.

3- As if this were not bad enough, Paul takes it one step further: The non-Christian's unwillingness to subject himself to God is rooted in his powerlessness to do this. His condition is that he is absolutely spiritually dead and cannot even submit to God. Here Paul teaches that the lost are not only morally *depraved* before God, but they are also morally *incapable* of doing what God requires of them. This is sad to be sure. Consequently, they desperately need the Lord Jesus Christ to save them and make them able to do His will by His great power!

Spurgeon stated it correctly when he said:

> That mind with which we are all born is enmity against God, and however much refined or polished a man may be, however amiable [friendly] or polite, however he may shine amongst his fellow-creatures, if he has not had a new heart and a right spirit, he is at "enmity against God," and he cannot enter heaven until there has been a divine change wrought in him. Some of you suppose because you have never been guilty of any vice, because you have not indulged in any great transgression, that therefore you do not require the work of regeneration in your hearts. You will be mightily mistaken if you continue under that delusion until the last great day. "For to be carnally minded," even though that carnal mind is in a body that is dressed in silks and satins, "To be carnally minded is death," even though it be whitewashed till it looks like a spiritual one. "To be carnally minded," even though you sow the carnal mind with a few good garden seeds of the flower of morality, will still be nothing but damnation to you at the last. "To be carnally minded is death;" only,

---

55 Grk. present, middle, verb.

56 Morris, p. 306.

57 Several commentators note this.

"to be spiritually minded is life and peace. Because the carnal mind is enmity against God."[58]

Obs. 4- (v. 8) That as Paul rounds off and reinforces all that he has just said in the previous verse, he gives his summary statement concerning the lost and writes:

So then, those who are[59] or are existing; **in the flesh,** i.e., in fallen Adam; **cannot**[60] or can never under any circumstances, not even on their best days though they may try; **please** or earn favor with; **God** (it is simply impossible).

This is the state of the fallen, unsaved man, with his carnal, disobedient and rebellious mind. Although he might think that his good deeds, religious works, fasting, and tithing, etc., might win him favor with God — Paul says no! He says this is entirely an impossibility, for apart from Christ and His merits imputed to one's account, and the indwelling Holy Spirit, all stand lost and wholly unacceptable before God.

Suggested applications from the text for the church:

1- In these verses we have a call to plead with God daily to help you to walk "according to the Spirit and not the flesh," so that you may regularly choose His way throughout the day.

2- In these verses we have a call to praise God daily for the great, supernatural transaction which has taken place in your life in that you have been delivered from the prevailing condition of "the flesh" to "the Spirit," since all of this is God's doing, and not your own.

Suggested application from the text for the non-Christian:

1- In these verses you have a call to pursue God daily until you know that He has made you a new person in Christ, with the evidence that you begin to live for Him in joyful subjection to His will and ways.

Text: Romans 8:9-11

General theme: The Christian's habitation by the Triune God

Homiletical outline of the verses:

A. The indwelling presence of God the Holy Spirit: [9] But you are not in the flesh but in the Spirit, if indeed the Spirit of God dwells in you. Now if anyone does not have the Spirit of Christ, he is not His.

B. The indwelling presence of God the Son: [10] And if Christ *is* in you, the body *is* dead because of sin, but the Spirit *is* life because of righteousness.

C. The indwelling presence of God the Father: [11] But if the Spirit of Him who raised Jesus from the dead dwells in you, He who raised Christ

---

58 Spurgeon, pp. 102, 103.

59 Grk. present, active, participle.

60 Grk. present, middle, verb.

from the dead will also give life to your mortal bodies through His Spirit who dwells in you.

Summary of section: In these verses, Paul continues his instruction concerning the Christian's sanctification. However, now he takes up matters that have a more direct bearing on the personal and inner experience of the true child of God.[61] He lets us know that through salvation, each distinct person of the Holy Trinity actually lives in us, which is proof positive that we know the Lord and He knows us. He lets us know what God said concerning His true people, namely, "I will dwell in them."[62] This fact is emphasized by Paul's repeated use of the prepositional phrase "in you" which appears four times in these three verses.[63] All of this is enormously significant and should have a direct bearing on how we live as believers.

In fact, so significant is this matter that Octavius Winslow, the prominent 19th-century preacher and author, comments concerning this topic from these verses and says that although it is,

> Scoffed at by the proud boaster of human reason, rejected by the cold formalists, and hated by the avowed enemy of practical godliness, as this doctrine is, it is yet a vital truth, and of marvelous interest of the child of God. It is, in fact, his life. We admit its profoundness, mysteriousness, and inexplicability; yet, apart from its individual, heartfelt experience, all religion, so-called, is a counterfeit and a delusion.[64]

How then does this teaching practically impact our Christian life? Simply, in that since God who is thrice holy lives in us, we who are believers should live in a way that reflects this deep reality. Through the process of sanctification, we are to live cognizant of the fact that God dwells personally and permanently within us. Because this is so, living in a way that is contrary to Him will be a most miserable condition for us. It will be to live in opposition to the God who inhabits His people, which will rob us of our joy, comfort and communion with Him. This is something we must never let happen.

Exegetical & Practical Insights:
Obs. 1- (v. 9) But that is in sharp contrast to the non-Christians spoken of in verse 8 who cannot please God; **you**[65] specifically, you believers and no one else; **are not in the flesh** or in the realm and sphere of being ruled by the flesh, i.e., the old, unregenerate, sinful, Adamic, corrupt

---

61 I was helped in my understanding of these verses from the excellent book entitled, *No Condemnation in Christ Jesus* by Octavius Winslow, pp. 111-45. Additionally, John Owen's book on *Communion with God* was useful.

62 1 Cor. 6:16a.

63 Longenecker notes the same, p. 700.

64 Winslow, p. 114.

65 The pronoun is emphatically placed in the Greek text.

nature which belongs to "the old age of sin and death";[66] **but**[67] or in strong opposition to this; **in the Spirit,** which is to say, because they had been "born of the Spirit" they were now in the realm and sphere of being ruled by the Spirit and belonging "to the new age of righteousness and life;"[68] **if indeed**[69] or better translated from the original, "if as the case is," or "since in fact this is so"; **the Spirit of God** (the Holy Spirit); **dwells**[70] or habitually and everlastingly resides or lives;[71] **in you. Now if anyone** whoever they are, and whatever they profess to be; **does not have**[72] or is destitute of as an ongoing reality in their lives; **the Spirit of Christ,**[73] (again, the Holy Spirit); **he is not His** which is to say, they never, at any point savingly belonged to Jesus.

In this verse, Paul puts forth two drastically different spiritual states of being. The first is one to which every person in the world is born into by nature as children of fallen Adam. It is the spiritual state of "the flesh." It is the spiritual state of deadness before God which demonstrates itself by a life of disobedience to Him. It is "fleshly," and "worldly." It is "earthly, sensual, demonic" (James 3:15).

The other spiritual state, however, is entered into by virtue of the new birth. It happens when one experiences salvation. And when this occurs, the Holy Spirit of God inhabits that individual permanently with His person and presence making that individual His property.[74] This is a

---

66 Moo, p. 489.

67 The strong Greek adversative.

68 Moo, p. 489.

69 The Greek conjunction assumes a condition fulfilled. There is no reason at all to think that Paul doubted whether or not the Holy Spirit of God indwelt the Roman believers. If this were not the case, he would not have opened this letter by addressing them as "beloved of God" and "called to be saints." His words here are not a negation but rather a confirmation. They are a validation of all that he has been expressing throughout this epistle.

70 Grk. present, active, verb.

71 Leon Morris is correct when he says that, "The Spirit is not an occasional visitor." Morris, p. 308.

72 Grk. present, active, verb.

73 This is a phrase which shows up three times in Scripture. Here in Rom. 8:9 and also in Phil. 1:19; and 1 Pet. 1:11. And again, each usage refers to the Holy Spirit. He is the "Spirit of Christ," because He is "none other than the 'Spirit of God' of the preceding clause and indicates that the Holy Spirit sustains to Christ a relationship similar to that which he sustains to the Father." John Murray, p. 288.

Lloyd-Jones asks: "What is the significance of the variation?" He answers, "There is only one conclusion to draw, namely, that these terms are interchangeable; they all convey exactly the same meaning. In each instance the Apostle is referring to the Holy Spirit, the third Person in the blessed Holy Trinity." Lloyd-Jones, *Romans*, p. 55.

Note also that the Holy Spirit is also referred to in Scripture as "the Spirit of Holiness" or the Spirit who helps in our holiness (Rom. 1:4), "the Spirit of life" or the Spirit who gives life (Rom. 8:2), and "the Spirit of adoption" or the Spirit who bears witness to our adoption (Rom. 8:15). Lastly, Chrysostom correctly notes that "Paul is not saying here that the Spirit is Christ but is showing rather that anyone who has the Spirit has Christ as well. For where the Spirit is, there Christ is also. Wherever one person of the Trinity is present, the whole Trinity is present too. For the Trinity is undivided and has a perfect unity in itself." *Ancient Christian Commentary on Scripture, Romans*, p. 204.

74 John 7:38, 29, 14:17; 1 Cor. 3:16; 1 Cor. 6:19; 2 Cor. 1:22; 2 Tim. 1:14; James 4:5.

promise which is spoken of in many places in Scripture for all who trust Christ alone for salvation (cf. Eph. 1:13). The Holy Spirit living in us is a chief hallmark of the Christian religion and when this occurs it greatly affects one's life so that the individual begins to "walk in" or by the help of "the Spirit" (Gal. 5:16), to bear "the fruit of the Spirit" (cf. Gal. 5:22, 23), and to mortify the deeds of the flesh "by the Spirit" (cf. Rom. 8:13).

He or she becomes a "spiritual individual" who experiences "joy in the Holy Spirit" (Rom. 14:17), approaches God "by one Spirit" (Eph. 2:18), and now worships God "in the Spirit" (Phil. 3:3). These salvific certainties bring Christians to commune[75] or fellowship[76] with the Spirit, who lives in them. The Spirit is their great comforter. Hence, the Puritan John Owen said, "The foundation of all our communion with the Holy Ghost [consists] in his mission, or sending to be our comforter, by Jesus Christ."[77]

Further, Paul says in the second part of the verse that whatever else someone might have in life, if he does not have the Holy Spirit of God residing in him, then he does not truly belong to Jesus.[78] This is the litmus test for all true saving religion. Thus, I agree with MacArthur when he writes that,

> The person who gives no evidence of the presence, power, and fruit of God's Spirit in his life has no legitimate claim to Christ as Savior and Lord. The person who demonstrates no desire for the things of God and has no inclination to avoid sin or passion to please God is not indwelt by the Holy Spirit and thus does not belong to Christ.[79]

In other words, no indwelling Holy Spirit, no new birth; no indwelling Holy Spirit, no true Christian; no indwelling Holy Spirit, no part in the people of God; and no indwelling Holy Spirit, no heaven, but an eternity in hell at the final judgment.

Obs. 2- (v. 10) And if or since in fact; **Christ,** i.e., God's Son, the Messiah; *is* **in you, the body** that is, the human, physical body; *is* **dead** or dying; **because of sin,** that is, because of Adam's sin imputed to us;[80] **but** or in contrast to this; **the Spirit** to be precise, the Holy Spirit; *is* **life** or will give life to our bodies; **because of righteousness,** that is to say, because of the impeccable righteousness of Christ imputed to us.

---

75 Cf. 2 Cor. 13:14.

76 The Puritan Matthew Barker gave the best definition of "communion with God" that I know. He wrote that it "consisteth in the divine operations of our souls toward God, when the faculties of the soul are tending toward him, and terminated upon him; when the mind is exercised in the contemplation of him, the will in choosing and embracing him; when the affections are fixed upon him, and centre in him; when by our desires we pursue him, by our love we cleave to him, and by delight we acquiesce and solace ourselves in him." *Puritan Sermons, vol. 4, p. 41.*

77 *A Puritan Theology* by Beeke and Jones p. 111.

78 Cf. Jude 17-19.

79 MacArthur, p. 420.

80 Cf. Rom. 5:21.

The first part of this verse is particularly striking for the fact that whereas the Old Testament promises Messiah would come *to us*, it never actually tells us that He would come and live *in us*. This is a profound "mystery" as Paul calls it in Col. 1:27, but it is a true mystery nonetheless. In salvation Christ comes and inhabits us. He makes His abode in His people as their living Lord, giving us spiritual life as He said he would do in John 14:23, and John 15:4, 5. Jesus dines with us, and we with Him, as He said would happen in Revelation 3:20.[81] So magnificent is this matter that once more John Owen said, "If this is not fellowship, then I do not know what fellowship is."[82] He wrote: "Christ will dine with believers. Christ refreshes himself with his own graces in his people, by his Spirit which he has given them."[83]

The second part of this verse is a bit more challenging to comprehend.[84] However, given what Paul says in the following verse, we can paraphrase his words like this: 'Seeing that Christ dwells in you, even though your body will be subject to decay and death, which are consequences of sin, in the final analysis, the Holy Spirit who also dwells in you, will give life to it and resurrect it because of Christ's righteousness credited to you.'

Here the apostle highlights the fact that although our corruptible bodies will end up in the grave (if we die before Jesus returns), they will not always remain in the grave! He draws attention to the reality that because Christ lives in us, our total persons will one day be redeemed including our bodies, for "Death is swallowed up in victory." Therefore, may we always say: "O Death, where *is* your sting? O Hades, where *is* your victory?"[85]

Obs. 3- (v. 11) But if or since in fact; **the Spirit of Him**[86] that is, the Holy Spirit, who is a distinct person yet related to and associated with the Father;[87] **who raised Jesus** which was a confirmation that our Lord paid our sin debt in full at Calvary; **dwells**[88] or is habitually housed; **in**

---

81 Cf. John 6:56, 14:20, 15:4-5, 17:23; 2 Cor. 13:5; Gal. 2:20, 4:19; Eph. 3:17; Col. 3:11; 1 John 3:24.

82 John Owen, *Communion with God*, p. 38.

83 Ibid.

84 I realize that some scholars understand the term "body" to refer figuratively to the old man, the term "dead" a reference to being "dead to sin" (Rom. 6), and the term "Spirit" a reference to the "human spirit" receiving "spiritual life" through Christ because of His righteousness imputed to us. While all of this is certainly true, I think what I have written above fits better in the overall context of these words, especially with what Paul will go on to say in the next verse.

85 1 Cor. 15: 54, 55.

86 Grk. genitive of relationship.

87 That this is a reference to God the Father seems clear from the context of these words and several commentators take this position. Scripturally speaking, we know that the Father raised Jesus from the dead (cf. Acts 2:24, 32; Rom. 6:4; Gal. 1:1; Eph. 1:20). Thus, we see that along with Jesus being involved with raising Himself from the dead (John 2:19-21, 10:17, 18), and the Holy Spirit (Rom. 1:4), this was also a supernatural act of the Father making the entire event a work of the whole Trinity. Additionally, it should be noted the entire Godhead is set forth here in a single sentence.

88 Grk. present, active, verb.

you, He who raised Christ from the dead (the Father); **will also give**[89] **life to** or quicken; **your mortal** or subject to death; **bodies,** i.e., at the resurrection; **through** or by means of; **His Spirit** (the Holy Spirit); **who dwells in you.**

Here Paul tells us lastly that along with Christ, and the Holy Spirit, God the Father dwells in us, for where the One is, the others are always present. This fact is also spoken of in Scripture and Jesus confirms it in John fourteen, verse twenty-three when he said:[90]

"If anyone loves Me, he will keep My word; and My Father will love him, and We will come to him and make Our home with him."

Once again this is a weighty reality. In many senses it is beyond full comprehension. But Paul's focus here is eschatological. The point is, this present-day reality of God living in us and we having union with Him has a future promise and pledge, and that future promise and pledge is rooted in the reality that what He did for Christ He is going to do for us! For "God both raised up the Lord and will also raise us up by His power" (1 Cor. 6:14).[91]

Here then is great comfort for the Christian! Here is an anchor for our souls which should give us great encouragement, knowing that as we continue to work through the daily process of sanctification, there will be a definitive day of glorification.

Octavius Winslow warmly concludes concerning all that Paul has written,

> In this marvelous work of resuscitation each Person of the ever blessed Trinity will be engaged. The Father will welcome home, as from a long exile, his adopted family; the Son will openly espouse his ransomed bride; and the Spirit will rebuild and re-occupy his sacred temple. Then will the Prophet's prediction receive its fullest and sweetest accomplishment— "The Lord God in the midst of thee is mighty; he will save, he will rejoice over thee with joy; he will rest in his love, he will joy over thee with singing."[92]

Suggested applications from the text for the church:

1- Because the entire Trinity lives in us, let us remember to live holy lives as God Himself is holy.

2- Because the entire Trinity lives in us, let us remember to thank God because this is all of His doing.

3- Because the entire Trinity lives in us, let us be encouraged knowing that although we still groan within because of remaining sin, there is coming a time when we will experience "the redemption of our body" (Rom. 8:23).

---

89 Grk. future, active, verb.

90 2 Cor. 6:16; Eph. 4:6; 1 John 4:4, 12, 13.

91 Cf. 1 Cor. 15:20; 2 Cor. 4:14.

92 *No Condemnation in Christ Jesus* by Octavius Winslow, p. 145.

Suggested application from the text for the non-Christian:

1- Because you are not saved, God does not dwell in you. Unless this changes, your present, sad, spiritual situation will remain and your future situation will be ruinous. Therefore, turn from your sins and put your trust in the wonderful person and finished work of Jesus Christ, who 2000 years ago, died as a sacrifice for sinners and made a complete, once-for-all satisfaction to the Father for them and then was raised from the dead as a validation of this. This is the good news of the Bible (1 Cor. 15:1-4). This is the gospel which is "the power of God to salvation for everyone who believes" (Rom. 1:16).

Text: Romans 8:12-14

General theme: Gospel-driven Mortification

Homiletical outline of the verses:

A. Paul's exhortation: [12] Therefore, brethren, we are debtors—not to the flesh, to live according to the flesh.

B. Paul's explanation: [13] For if you live according to the flesh you will die; but if by the Spirit you put to death the deeds of the body, you will live. [14] For as many as are led by the Spirit of God, these are sons of God.

Summary of section: In these verses, Paul shows that the adage is true, "With great privilege comes great responsibility." Having put forth in the previous verses the glorious reality of the Triune God dwelling in His people (vv. 9-11), he tells us now that there are real Christian duties which flow from this reality. By the help and grace of the Spirit of God, we are to fulfill these duties as we abound more and more in sanctification. Lloyd-Jones pointedly explains:

> ...We have here an exhortation and an appeal on the basis of what has gone before. This statement is important for two main reasons. Firstly, for our understanding of the actual teaching of the Apostle. It enables us to follow his argument as he works it out in this whole section. It is not enough to note his doctrine; the Apostle always applies it. It is because many fail to follow him when he comes to the application that they become guilty of what is called antinomianism, that is, the failure to put into practice what you claim to believe; indeed, still worse, the danger of imagining that if you believe the doctrines nothing else matters. This is a complete denial of the Apostle's teaching, for he always applies the truth. There is nothing more dangerous than to have a merely intellectual or theoretical interest in Christian truth. This 'therefore' comes to us as a warning of that terrible danger. We must pay careful heed always to every 'therefore' used by this Apostle.
>
> But secondly, the statement in these two verses is of crucial importance from the standpoint of the New Testament doctrine of sanctification, and especially in light of the various theories that are current with respect to that doctrine. I maintain that in many ways these two verses are perhaps

the most important statement with regard to the practical aspect of the New Testament doctrine of sanctification in the whole of Scripture.[93]

Exegetical & Practical Insights:

Obs. 1- (v. 12) That as Paul speaks very practically and pastorally now, he writes,

Therefore, or consequently, the emphatic inferential particle with the conjunction stressing the decisive conclusion of the former words;[94] **brethren**,[95] a "term of affectionate pastoral appeal"[96] to all the believers at Rome; **we,** that is, each and every one of us who have been saved by the free grace of God in Christ Jesus (Paul and all other gospel ministers after him included); **are debtors**[97] or are "under obligation in a moral or social sense;"[98] **—not to the flesh,** that is, not to our old, corrupt, propensities which we inherited from Adam, which are still prompted in our hearts by remaining sin; **to live** or for the purpose of continually being "governed and directed;"[99] **according to** or by the demands of; **the flesh**.

Paul argues here that because we are redeemed, we are now debtors to God in Christ. We owe Him everything and the flesh absolutely nothing, since we have been set free from sin and have become the slaves of God (Rom. 6:22). Consequently, when the flesh seeks to entice us we are to respond by saying: "I am not your debtor!" Frank Thielman's comments are helpful,

> If God has condemned sin in the flesh through the death of Christ (8:3) and believers do not walk according to the flesh (8:4), do not have the mindset of the flesh (8:5-7), and in some sense are not in the flesh (8:9), then they owe the flesh nothing.[100]

Again, Lloyd-Jones makes the point plain,

> 'The flesh' is the cause of all our troubles. What has our flesh done for us? It makes us sin, brings us into misery, and into the realm of death. That has been the result of Adam's original fall. That is why we are all born 'in the flesh'. But the Apostle urges upon us that we are under no obligation to it any longer. Realize, he says, what the flesh did for you; but now you do not owe it anything, you are not a debtor to it in any sense. Do not pay it any allegiance, he says; do not show any subservience to it; have nothing

---

93 Lloyd-Jones, *Romans* pp. 91, 92.

94 Cf. 5:18; 7:3, 25; 8:1. I agree with John Murray when he says that these words have "hortatory implications, though not expressly in the language of exhortation" Murray, p. 293.

95 It is worth noting that Paul did not begin by putting them on a guilt trip to do what he is about to say to them, but rather he appealed to their status as beloved brothers in Christ.

96 Yarbrough, p. 130.

97 Cf. Rom. 15:27.

98 BDAG, p. 742 2a.

99 Murray, p. 293.

100 Thielman, p. 388.

to do with it at all. It is entirely against you; and you do not belong to it now. Our obligation is to Someone else.[101]

Obs. 2- (vv. 13-14) That as Paul gives the reason for why we are not to "live according to the flesh" (v.12), he puts forth two "if" clauses with two options connected to them and writes:

For if[102] **you live,**[103] i.e., continually conduct your life; **according to** or in line with; **the flesh you will**[104] without question; **die;**[105] or be eternally condemned by God; **but if by** or through the agency and help of; **the Spirit,**[106] i.e., the Holy Spirit of God;[107] **you put to death**[108] not "let go and let God" but continually mortify, kill, and "cut the nerve of;"[109] **the deeds of the body**, not the body itself, but the ill-behaved activities "of" or which come forth through "the body;"[110] **you will live,** that is, live *happily now* as a true believer (because you did not stop mortifying your remaining sin), and then live *happily ever after* (because Jesus died for you, which was evidenced by how you lived for Him in a life of gospel holiness). **For** the conjunction confirming the previous words; **as many as** or "only such"[111] who; **are led**[112] or are continuously guided; **by the Spirit of God,** that is to say, led (not *mystically* but rather, *ethically*) by the Holy Spirit to mortify remaining sin (v. 13b); **these** and these only; **are**[113] and will always continue to be; **sons**[114] not merely servants; but "sons;" **of** or who actually belong to; **God.**

The apostle's words are straightforward. They teach us that those whose lives are characterized by a habitual living after the sins of the flesh will undoubtedly experience God's condemnation in the life to

---

101 Lloyd-Jones, *Romans* p. 100.

102 Concerning the word "if" James R. Edwards notes that it may "function as a gentle prod to Paul's readers to encourage them to consider whether or not they belong to the Spirit. For the solid church members in Rome it would have been an inducement to humble self-examination, and for inquirers about the faith, an invitation to its grateful acceptance." Edwards, pp. 205, 206.

103 Grk. present, active, verb.

104 Grk. present, active, verb. The verb in the Greek text stresses this point.

105 Cf. Gal. 6:8.

106 Schreiner helpfully states: "Victory is by means of the Spirit, which means that believers conquer sinful passions by relying on and trusting in the Spirit to provide the strength to resist the passions that wage war within us." Schreiner, p. 422.

107 Paul has already mentioned various ministries of the Holy Spirit to us in this chapter in vv. 2, 5-9.

108 Grk. present, active, verb. Cf. Col. 3:5-7. I can recommend no greater resource on this subject than John Owen's classic treatment in Volume 6 of His works. Owen has famously said, "Be killing sin or it will be killing you."

109 Phillips translation.

110 Cf. Gal. 5:19-21.

111 Robinson, Book 1, p. 448.

112 Grk. present, passive, verb. It is interesting to note how in verse 13 that the call to "put to death" our sins is in the active voice. But here the words "are led" are in the passive voice. This shows us that in sanctification, it is both God and us working together.

113 Grk. present, tense verb.

114 I will speak about the subject of sonship more in the next section.

come. If, as a pattern of life, one "professes Christ" but is not living as one "in Christ" (demonstrated by a life of evangelical godliness) then he has deceived himself and will be damned forever at last.[115]

Now, of course, since the believer has been made new by Christ (2 Cor. 5:17), he will not habitually engage in the sins of the flesh and perish in the end. These individuals have, in fact, been changed by the power of the gospel (1:16). Even though at times they will fall short of the glory of God (3:23), nonetheless, they will not allow sin to progress in their lives unchecked, unmortified, and unrepented of. Thus, this is why Paul can describe these individuals in this chapter as those who as a pattern of life "do not walk according to the flesh but according to the Spirit" (8:4). Consequently, he says that there is "no condemnation" for them (8:1).

However, having said this, the sense of Paul's words should not be blunted towards us who are the true people of God. As the apostle moves from the "we" of verse 12 to the personal "you" of verse 13, he gives a call for all who name the name of Christ to examine their lives in order to be sure that they genuinely belong to the Lord (for surely Paul realized that in every church there could be false believers cf. Gal. 2:4; 2 Cor. 11:13, 26). Simply stated, if one names the name of Christ and is not living in obedience to the Word of God by the help of the Holy Spirit, so that one is denying the flesh and regularly saying "no" to it, then he needs to seek Christ in true repentance and faith so that He might make him a true believer who lives like this.

MacArthur states the matter well:

> The apostle is not warning genuine believers that they may lose their salvation and be condemned to death if they fall back into some of the ways of the flesh. He has already given the absolute assurance that there is therefore now no condemnation for those who are in Christ Jesus (8:1). He is rather saying that a person whose life is characterized by the things of the flesh is not a true Christian and is spiritually dead, no matter what his religious affiliations or activities may be. If he does not come to Christ in true faith, he must die the second death under God's final judgment.[116]

Suggested applications from the text for the church:

1- Never despise a pulpit ministry that directly applies the Word of God to your life. Never despise preaching that challenges you to be more and more conformed to Christ. Instead, greatly desire it, for this is how Paul ministered to the churches through his epistles (cf. v.13).

2- Never be content to live comfortably with your sins. Instead, through the lifelong process of sanctification and with the aid of the Holy Spirit, seek daily to put them to death.

---

115 Cf. 1 John 2:4.
116 MacArthur, p. 422.

Suggested application from the text for the non-Christian:

1- Never rest comfortably until you know that by the grace of Christ, you have been converted and that you are no longer a debtor "to the flesh" but only to Him.

Text: Romans 8:15-17a

General theme: The Christian's Sonship

Homiletical outline of the verses:

A. The sure evidences of being a child of God: [15] For you did not receive the spirit of bondage again to fear, but you received the Spirit of adoption by whom we cry out, "Abba, Father." [16] The Spirit Himself bears witness with our spirit that we are children of God,

B. The splendid effects of being a child of God: [17] and if children, then heirs—heirs of God and joint heirs with Christ,

Summary of section: In these verses, Paul opens up what it means that believers are the "sons of God," as mentioned in the previous verse. In doing this, he raises the glorious topic of adoption,[117] and that we have God as our Father. Then, he lays out the cosmic spiritual riches which are ours in Christ.

Concerning this subject, the late, Reformed luminary J. I. Packer famously wrote,

> You sum up the whole of the New Testament teaching in a single phrase, if you speak of it as a revelation of the fatherhood of the holy creator. In the same way, you sum up the whole New Testament religion if you describe it as the knowledge of God as one's holy Father. If you want to judge how well a person understands Christianity, find out how much he makes of the thought of being God's child, and having God as his Father. If this is not the thought that prompts and controls his worship and prayers and his whole outlook on life, it means that he does not understand Christianity very well at all. For everything that Christ taught, everything that makes the New Testament new, and better than the Old, everything that is distinctly Christian as opposed to merely Jewish, is summed up in the knowledge of the fatherhood of God. "Father" is the Christian name for God.[118]

Exegetical & Practical Insights:

Obs. 1- (v. 15) That as Paul speaks about what is true concerning every genuine Christian he writes saying:

For[119] a conjunction explaining what it means that we who are Christians have become the sons and daughters of God; **you did not**

---

117 I have written a piece on this topic which the reader might find helpful. It appears in *Growing in Grace*, Reformation Heritage Books, a Chapel Library booklet, and in *A New Exposition of the London Baptist Confession of Faith*.

118 J. I. Packer, *Knowing God* (Downers Grove, Ill.: InterVarsity Press, 1973), 182.

119 This is Paul's third time that he has begun his words with the word "for" (vv. 12, 13).

receive,[120] i.e., receive at the point of salvation from God; **the spirit of bondage again to fear,** that is to say, a disposition or "frame of mind"[121] of dread concerning our relationship to God and His impending judgment (as the case was when we were not saved);[122] **but**[123] or in sharp contrast to the previous negative statement; **you received,**[124] i.e., received at the point of salvation; **the Spirit of adoption**[125] or the Holy Spirit who testifies *to* our adoption[126] or has been given to us *as* the gift[127] of our adoption;[128] **by whom,** that is, the Holy Spirit; **we** (all who are real Christians, Paul included); **cry out,**[129] that is, we cry out with a regenerated heart to God persistently in prayer saying; "Abba, an Aramaic term for Father which expresses warmth, closeness and security as when we call someone we love "dear;" **Father.**"[130]

In commenting on the term Abba, Luther tenderly writes,

> This is but a little word, and yet notwithstanding it comprehendeth all things. The mouth speaketh not, but the affection of the heart speaketh after this manner. Although I be oppressed with anguish and terror on every side, and seemed to be forsaken and utterly cast away from thy presence, yet I am thy child, and thou art my Father for Christ's sake: I am beloved because of the Beloved.[131]

---

120 Grk. aorist, active, verb.

121 Mahan, 57.

122 Cf. Heb. 2:14, 15. I realize that there is scholarly discussion regarding how best to understand the two instances of the word "spirit/Spirit" in the passage. Most commonly, commentators understand both instances as referring either to the human spirit or to the Holy Spirit. However, I think that the way I present it here seems most natural to the passage, firstly, because Paul will speak about the Holy Spirit and then our own spirits in the following verse once again. But secondly, because in 15a he says "you did not receive the spirit of bondage *again* to fear." In commenting on these words, Haldane says "Paul uses the word *again* to indicate a double opposition,—the one of the state of man before and after his regeneration, the other of the New Testament and the Old. Before regeneration, a man, sensible that he is a sinner, must be apprehensive of punishment, not having embraced the only remedy provided for the remission of his sins by Jesus Christ." Haldane, p. 354.

123 The strong Greek adversative.

124 Grk. aorist, active, verb.

125 The Greek word for "adoption" here is made up of two individual Greek words and it literally means to "place as sons" or to "put in the position of a son," hence, to adopt as a son. The word describes the supernatural change of relationship that happens to Christians in salvation from being slaves of sin, to the legal and loved sons and daughters of the living God, which takes place at the moment of conversion by faith (cf. John 1:12; Gal. 3:26; 4:3–7). Scholars are almost unanimously agreed that Paul's use of the term is rooted in a Roman custom in his day. In the context of the Roman Empire, a person could become a son to a father by the father adopting the son into his family, who was not his son by natural procreation. When this happened, it secured for the adopted child all of the rights, status, privileges, and property of the one who had adopted him.

126 Cf. 8:16.

127 The second "gift" or "token" of our adoption is the glorifying of our bodies at Christ's return as Paul speaks of in 8:23.

128 Gal. 4:6.

129 Grk. present, active, verb. Note also that the same Greek verb is used in 9:27.

130 These words come from our Lord's lips in Mark 14:35.

131 Cited in Moo NICNT, p. 503.

Moo further comments,

> In crying out "Abba, Father," the believer not only gives voice to his or her consciousness of belonging to God as his child but also as to having a status comparable to that of Jesus Christ himself. The Aramaic *abba* was the term Jesus himself used in addressing his Father, and its preservation in the Greek gospel of Mark (14:36) and in the Greek-speaking Pauline churches attest to the fact that it was remembered and treasured as distinctive and meaningful. In ascribing to Christians indwelt by the Spirit the use of this same term in addressing God, Paul shows that Christians have a relationship to God that is like (though, of course, not exactly like) Christ's own relationship to the Father. In "adopting" us, God has taken no half measures; we have been made full members of the family and partakers of all the privileges belonging to members of that family.[132]

In this passage Paul describes the practical implications of our spiritual status as sons and daughters of the Most High. He tells us that through the power of the gospel, there has been a radical transformation that has taken place in our lives so that when we were saved, we became part of God's family. In our lost estate, we were "the children of the devil"[133] and the "sons of disobedience." Now, however, by grace, we have become "members of the household of God."[134] This is fantastic news to be sure! And it is all connected to the fact that as Paul says in this verse God has spiritually adopted us.[135] Thus, Packer is right again when he said that, "The revelation to the believer that God is his father is in a sense the climax of the Bible."[136]

Obs. 2- (v. 16) That as Paul speaks about how the Christian can know of his sonship[137] he writes that:

---

132 Ibid.

133 Cf. John 8:44.

134 Cf. Eph. 2.2, 19.

135 It should be noted that the foundation of our adoption is rooted in God's eternal plan to save us (cf. Eph. 1:5). Additionally, our spiritual adoption differs from the adoption of the nation of Israel as mentioned in 9:4. Their adoption was theocratic but *not* salvific for all individuals. Their adoption set them apart to God as a people. However, this does not mean that they all savingly knew God, for this only happens by receiving Jesus by faith alone (John 1:12, cf. 9:6).

136 Packer, *Knowing God*, 182.

137 Christian assurance can be defined as the joyous certainty that we, in fact, have been saved through Jesus Christ the Lord. It is, as Sinclair Ferguson says, "The conscious confidence that we are in the right relationship with God through Christ. It is the confidence that we have been justified and accepted by God in Christ, regenerated by his Spirit, and adopted into his family and that through faith in him we will be kept for the day when our justification and adoption are consummated in the regeneration of all things" [The Reformation and Assurance, *The Banner of Truth*, cf. p. 30 fn. 1, no. 643 (Apr. 2017): 20]. I would also recommend the excellent treatment of this subject by Dr. Joel Beeke in his book entitled *Knowing and Growing in Assurance of Faith*.

The Spirit Himself[138] (again the Holy Spirit of God, the third person in the blessed Trinity); **bears witness**[139] or continually testifies;[140] **with** or together with; **our spirit,** i.e., our own human spirits, our inner selves; **that** the conjunction stating what the witness is; **we are children** (i.e., the beloved children); **of God.**

These words help us to understand the divine work of the Holy Spirit in our lives in confirming our sonship, for they show that "The Holy Spirit is not only instrumental in *making* us God's children; he also makes us *aware* that we are God's children."[141] In fact, Paul puts forth two witnesses in our verse, the Holy Spirit and our own spirit. Here the apostle applies the Old Testament principle found in Deuteronomy 19:15, which says, "By the mouth of two or three witnesses the matter shall be established."

But how does the Holy Spirit do this? In summary, He does not do it *mystically* by some inner whisper, saying, "You are a child of God." Rather, He does it *scripturally* and then *experientially*. Scripturally, He does this by describing for us in the Word (the Bible which He inspired) what a true Christian is. Experientially, He does this in our own hearts by helping us know that we really are what a true Christian is according to Scripture.

Simply stated, the Holy Spirit takes the *objective, external* Word of God and confirms it to us *subjectively and internally* so that when, for example, we read in 2 Corinthians 5:17, "Therefore, if anyone *is* in Christ, *he is* a new creation; old things have passed away; behold, all things have become new," we cry out in our hearts saying, "Yes, that's true of me by God's grace!" Moreover, when we read a promise of God which says that He is our God and we are His people (2 Cor. 6:16), we say, "It's so for me Lord, glory be to Your Name!"

Haldane's thoughts are helpful here:

> The Holy Spirit, in the heart of a believer, joins His testimony with his spirit, in confirmation of this truth, that he is a son of God. It is not merely the fruits of the Holy Spirit in the lives of believers which afford this testimony, but the Spirit Himself, by imparting filial confidence, inspires it in the heart. This is a testimony which is designed for the satisfaction of believers themselves, and cannot be submitted to the scrutiny of others. The witnesses here spoken of are two,—our spirit, and the Holy Spirit of God together with our spirit.[142]

---

138 The word "Himself" in the Greek text is placed first in the sentence for the sake of emphasis. Further, it should be noted that the King James Version use of the word "itself" concerning the Holy Spirit is not at all a theological denial of the personhood and deity of the Holy Spirit. Instead this is a grammatical issue. In Greek, words have gender according to their word form, and so, because the word "Spirit" in the text is a neuter form, it calls for a neuter pronoun, which is the word "itself."

139 Grk. present, active, verb.

140 It should be noted that this assurance will not always be experienced in the same measure for all of God's children, and that things like sin in our lives will cause these testimonies to fluctuate.

141 Moo, NICNT, p. 503.

142 Haldane, p. 362.

Obs. 3- (v. 17a) That as Paul highlights some further splendid effects of Christian sonship, he writes:

and if children (again, the adopted children of God); **then** (we are); **heirs**[143] or those who will receive a royal inheritance—**heirs of God** (or those upon whom God will bequeath His inheritance and receive God Himself as their great inheritance);[144] **and joint** or fellow; **heirs with Christ,** which means that "all that Christ inherits will belong to all of us as well!"[145]

What an incredible promise this is for us who are God's adopted children! Regardless of who we are, each of us will have an unspeakable inheritance from God the Father. We will inherit glory and innumerable spiritual blessings from Him which will last throughout eternity. And with Christ, as His co-heirs, we will share in His inheritance of receiving the renewed earth on which we will reign at His return. As MacArthur correctly notes, "Everything that Christ receives by divine right, we will receive by divine grace"[146] (Ps. 2:8; Matt. 25:34; Rom. 4:13-16; Col. 1:12, 3:24; 2 Tim. 2:12; 1 Pet. 1:3, 4; Rev. 5:10).

Suggested applications from the text for the church:

1- Our Christian sonship should cause us regularly to reflect on this stunning teaching of Scripture and all that it means for us personally.

2- Our Christian sonship should cause us regularly to recall what our new identity is as the adopted sons and daughters of God and live in light of it.

3- Our Christian sonship should cause us regularly to reject the ways of the world, which belong to the children of the devil.

4- Our Christian sonship should cause us regularly to reach out to God in prayer, knowing that His ears are always open to our petitions.

5- Our Christian sonship should cause us regularly to rejoice, knowing that what awaits us in the eternal state is truly wonderful.

Suggested application from the text for the non-Christian:

1- The subject of Christian sonship should regularly remind you of all that could be yours in Christ!

Text: Romans 8:17b-18

General theme: The Christian's Sufferings (I)

Homiletical outline of the verses:

A. A biblical condition concerning our sufferings: [17b] if indeed we suffer with *Him,* that we may also be glorified together.

---

143 Cf. Gal. 3:29; 4:7; Eph. 3:6; Titus 3:7; Heb. 6:17.

144 Cf. Ps. 16:5; 73:25.

145 Phillips translation.

146 MacArthur, p. 455.

B. A biblical comparison during our sufferings: [18] For I consider that the sufferings of this present time are not worthy *to be compared* with the glory which shall be revealed in us.

Summary of section: In these verses, the apostle turns our minds to the unavoidable and unpleasant subject of the sufferings of the saints. Suffering is one of the most terrible words in the English language. It is the state of being in great anguish or distress, whether internally or externally, brought about by a variety of circumstances. Suffering has been called "the chief burden of history." Every person on the face of the planet will experience it to one degree or another. Christians will experience sufferings of various sorts. They will experience the pains of disappointment in others and in themselves; they will experience the sadness of sin, sickness, loss and trials with Satan. As Job said in Job 5:7, "Man is born to trouble as the sparks fly upward." Jesus said in John 14:33, "In the world you will have tribulation."

What is more, a true believer will also experience persecution for his faith as he seeks to live uprightly in the world as a witness for Jesus and the gospel. He can be certain that Paul's words in 2 Timothy 3:12 will be true for him, "All who desire to live godly in Christ will suffer persecution."[147]

Where then is the believer's hope? Paul wrote this letter to Christians living in first-century Rome, people who were experiencing hardships for their monotheistic beliefs among a polytheistic society. As a man with a great pastor's heart for the people of God, what encouragements did he give them? This is his topic in the next part of Romans 8, as he sets forth three particular ways for us to have hope amidst all that we will experience in life.[148]

First, *we are to remember the great glory which will be revealed in us, which will absolutely outweigh all of our present hardships* (vs. 18).

Second, *we are to remember the great groanings that the Holy Spirit makes for us which helps us to endure in the midst of our trials* (vv. 26, 27).

And third, *we are to remember the great guarantee that our God will work all things together for good to those who love Him, to those who are the called according to His purpose* (v. 28).

Here then is how Paul cheers us on through all that we will face in life. These are three bedrock truths which we must come back to repeatedly, especially in our times of discouragements and disappointments.

Exegetical & Practical Insights:
Obs. 1- (v. 17b) That as Paul begins the subject, in speaking about those who prove their co-heirship with Christ (v.17a), he writes:

if indeed we that is to say, we Christians are willing to; **suffer with** *Him* (Jesus); that or as a result; **we may also be glorified** or made perfect

---

147 Cf. Acts 14:22.

148 Other commentators have also picked up on this three-fold line of encouragement from Paul.

both in body and soul; **together** that is together as God's people at Christ's return.

What is Paul saying? *Negatively*, it is not that our suffering for Jesus and the gospel is that which will merit or be the basis of our future glorification (which is the final act of our salvation [8:30]). For if the apostle were to say that, then he would be completely overturning all that he has already written throughout this epistle; it would undermine his doctrine that salvation and a right standing with God are received by means of faith alone, on the ground of Christ alone, because of grace alone (1:16; 3:22-26, 28; 5:1). *Positively*, he is saying that although our sufferings in this life do not save us, they do, prove the genuineness of our salvation.

Our willingness to suffer with Christ is a strong indicator that we, in fact, belong to Him and He belongs to us. It is a genuine badge that we are His followers, and therefore we will experience final glorification (and then glory itself) because we have been saved by Jesus' free grace.[149] In this verse, Paul teaches us that there is a definite link between suffering and glory, even like Jesus experienced in His own life. John Murray aptly remarks,

> There is no sharing in Christ's glory unless there is sharing in his sufferings. Sufferings and then glory was the order appointed for Christ himself. It could not be otherwise in terms of his messianic undertaking and design (cf. Luke 24:26; Phil. 2:6-11; 1 Pet. 1:11). The same order applies to those who are heirs with him.[150]

Here, then, Paul once again separates false professors of faith from the faithful followers of Christ (cf. v.13). False professors of faith do not have the root of Christian salvation in them, and thus, they only identify with Jesus for a little while. For "when tribulation or persecution arises because of the word, immediately he stumbles" (Matt. 13:21). True professors of faith, however, are willing by the grace of God to stand for Jesus in the face of suffering for His sake and for the gospel. They know that, like their Savior, this is what they were called to do (1 Pet. 2:21).

Obs. 2- (v. 18) That as Paul puts forth a biblical perspective to remember during all of our sufferings, he views them all in a "larger, world-transcending context,"[151] and writes:

For the word "introducing this verse and, indeed, the entire paragraph that follows, as an elaboration of the sequence of suffering and glory attributed to believers in 17b;"[152] **I consider**[153] not merely "I think," but I continually reckon and calculate with great certainty "by careful

---

149 Cf. 2 Tim. 2:11. When I preached on this passage at my church I put forth this little rhyme: "If there is no cross to bear, then there will be no crown to wear. And if there is no suffering to endure, then there will be no glory for sure!"

150 Murray, p. 299.

151 Moo, NICNT, p. 511.

152 Moo, NICNT p. 511.

153 Grk. present, middle, verb. Paul has used this verb already in this epistle: 2:3; 3:28; 6:11.

study and reasoning;"[154] **that** the conjunction putting forth the content of Paul's consideration; **the sufferings,**[155] i.e., all the sufferings which a Christian can experience in all the various forms;[156] **of this present time** literally "the now time;" **are not worthy** or we might say, are relatively insignificant or "less than nothing"[157] so as; **to be compared** with the glory or, the glorifying of us; **which shall be revealed in us** not merely all around us but, more literally from the Greek text, *into* us at Jesus' return.[158]

Here Paul puts two matters on a scale. On the one side, he puts all of the sufferings and difficulties of this life that we could ever endure. On the other side, he puts all the glory which shall be revealed in us. Then he says that what awaits us in the eternal state (being free of all suffering, sin and sadness) is going to be so magnificently wonderful that our present trials should be viewed as very little in comparison.[159]

This of course does not mean that we make light of the crosses that we bear as Christians. But neither are we to make too much of them. It means that as we put the two matters side-by-side and consider the duration and the degree of both, we are to agree with Paul that the two are not worthy of being compared. Ultimately, this is because earth will have no sorrows which heaven will not heal. In heaven, we will have glorified hearts, minds, bodies and souls, and every single hardship that we ever experienced in this life will be gone forevermore—glory be to God!

Suggested applications from the text for the church:

1- Our passage provides us with a biblical realism for all of life, teaching us that the pathway to glory is the pathway of suffering. As it was for Christ, so also it will be for His true followers for "a servant is not greater than his master" (John 13:16).

2- Our passage provides us with a biblical resilience for all the opposition we will face in life, knowing that although present-day difficulties are hard, they will not last forever.

3- Our passage provides us with a biblical recognition that all of our sufferings are with Christ, as Paul says in 17b. They are never apart from our union with Him. Consequently, He will always be for us, "a very present help in trouble" (Ps. 46:1).

Suggested application from the text for the non-Christian:

1- Our passage provides you with a biblical rationale to seek the Lord Jesus Christ for the forgiveness of your sins now, knowing that unlike

---

154 MacArthur, p. 449.

155 Recall that the Apostle Paul himself was no stranger to sufferings. He lists many of them in 2 Cor. 11:23-31.

156 Paul lists some of these things out in verses 35 and 36 of this chapter.

157 Phillips translation.

158 Cf. 2 Cor. 4:17.

159 Cf. Rev. 21:3-4.

true Christians whose sufferings are limited to this life, your greatest sufferings will only begin in the life to come.

Text: Romans 8:19-22

General theme: The Christian's Sufferings *and the Sighs of Creation* (II)

Homiletical outline of the verses:
   A. The expecting, waiting, and revealing: [19] For the earnest expectation of the creation eagerly waits for the revealing of the sons of God.
   B. The subjecting, delivering, and groaning: [20] For the creation was subjected to futility, not willingly, but because of Him who subjected *it* in hope; [21] because the creation itself also will be delivered from the bondage of corruption into the glorious liberty of the children of God. [22] For we know that the whole creation groans and labors with birth pangs together until now.

Summary of section: In these verses, the apostle continues his discussion on the sufferings that we will experience in life. However, now he adds a new dimension to his dialogue when he speaks about the world at large which also suffers from the dreadful effects of Adam's fall (Gen. 3:17-19). When Adam fell not only did his posterity fall in and with him, but the cosmos also was cursed and thus (figuratively speaking) it is also longing to be liberated from such a matter.
   We may wonder, "Why does Paul now connect our sufferings as Christians with the sufferings of the created world? What is his point in all this?" It is this: in his mind (and yes, in "the mind of God"), there is a very close connection between *our destiny* at the return of Christ and *the destiny of the creation*. "... and the one follows the other."[160] Simply stated, there is a solidarity between redeemed sinners and this world, so that just as when our Savior returns and we experience total freedom from all of our sufferings, so also at this time the creation itself will be freed from all of its suffering.
   When Jesus returns, closes out this age, and ushers in the age to come, everything in God's created order that experienced the ravages of the fall will be emancipated. What a day this is going to be! Yes, at this time Psalm 98:8 will be fulfilled: "The rivers will clap their hands and the hills will be joyful together before the Lord," and in fulfillment of Isaiah 11:6: "The wolf also shall dwell with the lamb, the leopard shall lie down with the young goat, the calf and the young lion and the fatling together; And the little child shall lead them."

Exegetical & Practical Insights:
   Obs. 1- (v. 19) That as Paul highlights and supports how majestic the glory will be, which shall be revealed in us who are Christians, when

---

160 Lloyd-Jones, *Romans* p. 50. Concerning this whole matter Lloyd-Jones says, "This is most remarkable teaching. It is found only in the Bible" p. 50.

Jesus returns (as he spoke of in the previous verse), he writes now of the creation:

For the conjunction confirming the greatness of the previous comparison in 18b; **the earnest expectation** or confident anticipation; **of the creation,** that is, the material, *non*-human, *non*-angelic creation, "both animate and inanimate;"[161] **eagerly waits for**[162] or is expecting; **the revealing,** i.e., the manifestation and unveiling; **of the sons of God** (in their true dignity, as the redeemed of the Lord).

This is a sweeping statement! In speaking about the creation, Paul says that the whole natural world (the hills, the rocks, the plants, the trees, and the animals etc.)[163] is intensely looking forward to the time when believers shall be publicly revealed and perfected in glory in front of the entire universe. "The whole creation is on tiptoe to see the wonderful sight of the sons of God coming into their own."[164] Thus, it must be, that this will be a spectacular event when, for example, believers will be changed "in a moment, in the twinkling of an eye" (1 Cor. 15:52). This will be the great day when that which is "corruptible has put on incorruption, and this mortal has put on immortality" (1 Cor. 15:54). And so although now we are the children of God, "it has not yet been revealed what we shall be, but we know that when He is revealed, we shall be like Him, for we shall see Him as He is" (1 John 3:2).[165]

Obs. 2- (vv. 20-21) That as Paul gives the reason why the creation is eagerly waiting for the revealing of the sons of God, he writes:

For the creation was subjected to[166] or definitively placed under at the fall; **futility** or "uselessness," in that it was unable to "accomplish the purpose for which it was created;"[167] **not willingly** or of its own accord; **but**[168] or in sharp contrast to this; **because of**[169] or on account of; **Him** not Adam or Satan, but God who is the Lord of creation; **who subjected** *it* (because this was part of Adam's punishment who was the head of creation, for when he fell "all that was under him fell"[170]); **in hope**[171] "not wistful optimism but certain expectation;"[172] **because the creation**

---

161 Harvey, p. 203.

162 Grk. present, middle, verb. It is interesting to note that this verb appears seven other times in the New Testament and every time it is connected to the return of Christ (8:23, 8:25; 1 Cor. 1:7; Gal. 5:5; Phil. 3:20; Heb. 9:28).

163 MacArthur rightly notes, "The term obviously does not include Satan and his host of fallen Angels, the demons. They have no desire for a godly, sinless state and know they are divinely sentenced to eternal torments." MacArthur, p. 453.

164 Phillips translation.

165 Cf. Col. 3:4; 1 Pet. 4:12-13.

166 Grk. aorist, passive, verb. The aorist tense verb points to a single event.

167 Thielman, p. 403.

168 The strong Greek adversative.

169 The Greek preposition *dia* with the accusative case denotes cause.

170 Lloyd-Jones, *Romans*, p. 54.

171 The word "hope" picks up a theme which Paul mentioned last time back in 5:5. Paul will mention this word again in this chapter in verses 24 and 25.

172 Yarbrough, p. 127.

itself also[173] or along with the children of God; **will be delivered**[174] i.e., set free at Jesus' second coming; **from** or away from; **the bondage** or we might say, the curse that was placed upon it; **of corruption** (such as the corruption which it experiences daily: decay, disease, distress, and death itself);[175] **into** or in a manner corresponding with; **the glorious liberty** or the complete freeing; **of the children of God** (from all of the negative things that they were subjected to in this life such as, sin, sadness and Satan etc.).

MacArthur remarks, "In other words, just as man's sin brought corruption to the universe, so man's restoration to righteousness will be accompanied by the restoration of the earth and its universe to their divinely-intended perfection and glory."[176]

Obs. 3- (v. 22) That as Paul further asserts that the subhuman creation is in great bondage and in need of deliverance, he concludes his comments concerning the creation by saying:

For we know that is to say, Christians, know with great certainty that the world is in fact subjected to bondage and corruption whether from the teaching of Scripture (cf. Isa. 24.4) or from what we see happening all around us; **that** the conjunction putting forth the content of what we know; **the whole creation** "not just some limited portion of it;"[177] **groans**[178] not sings with joy, for "nature's music is in the minor key,"[179] but habitually laments; **and labors** or travails; **with birth pangs together** or in its entirety; **until now,** that is, till the present time.

Paul's imagery is plain. It teaches that just as a mother greatly labors toward her delivery when giving birth (which, recall, was a judgment placed on her at the fall as well, Gen. 3:16), Paul says that this is what is true of the creation. All the effects of the fall that this world experiences (such as thorns and thistles, floods, fires, famines, and even "earthquakes in various places"), are as Jesus says in Matthew 24:8, "the beginning of the birth pains" (ESV).

Lloyd-Jones nicely summarizes,

> We see then the unity between man and his surroundings, the creation. What happens to man happens to it. The negative has already happened; but what the Apostle is about to say is that the positive is also in the plan of God. That is why the whole creation is 'earnestly expecting,' craning

---

173 Frank Thielman is correct when he says that "The term 'also' (kai), although translations often leave it out (RSV, NAB, NIV, NRSV, ESV, CEB), is important because it illustrates the immensely glorious nature of 'the revelation of the sons of God' (8:18-19). The time in which God's family experiences the glory of full union with Christ (cf. 8:17) will be so glorious that not only his children but all creation will be caught up in the transformation." Thielman, p. 404.

174 Grk. future, passive, verb.

175 Cf. Isa. 65:17, 66:22, 23; 2 Pet. 3: 10-13; Rev. 21:1-5.

176 MacArthur, p. 455.

177 Yarbrough, p. 127.

178 Grk. present active, verb. Note further that this is the first of the three "groanings" which are mentioned in this chapter: vv. 23, 26.

179 McDonald, 1712.

its neck, waiting with eager expectation for the manifestation of the sons of God.[180]

Suggested applications from the text for the church:
1- These verses should produce in us a Christian environmentalism, which is to say, a healthy regard for the world we live in, which God made, seeing that He cares for it so much that one day He will entirely redeem it.

2- These verses should produce in us Christian holiness, because the final redemption of the creation is inextricably connected to Jesus' sure return. Thus, Apostle John says that "everyone who has this hope in Him purifies himself, just as He is pure" (1 John 3:3).

3- These verses should produce in us Christian optimism, because although everything in this world is failing and falling (ourselves included!), one day God is going to fix the whole thing, for He "will wipe away every tear from their eyes; there shall be no more death, nor sorrow, nor crying. There shall be no more pain, for the former things have passed away" (Rev. 21:4).

Suggested application from the text for the non-Christian:
1- These verses should produce in you a compelling urgency to get right with God through Christ immediately, since nobody knows the day or the hour when the Lord will return to restore the earth and judge the world in righteousness (Acts 17:31; 2 Pet. 3:10).

Text: Romans 8:23-27

General theme: The Christian's Sufferings (III)

Homiletical outline of the verses:
A. The groanings of the saints: [23] Not only *that*, but we also who have the firstfruits of the Spirit, even we ourselves groan within ourselves, eagerly waiting for the adoption, the redemption of our body. [24] For we were saved in this hope, but hope that is seen is not hope; for why does one still hope for what he sees? [25] But if we hope for what we do not see, we eagerly wait for *it* with perseverance.

B. The groanings of the Spirit: [26] Likewise the Spirit also helps in our weaknesses. For we do not know what we should pray for as we ought, but the Spirit Himself makes intercession for us with groanings which cannot be uttered. [27] Now He who searches the hearts knows what the mind of the Spirit *is*, because He makes intercession for the saints according to *the will of* God.

Summary of section: In these verses, Paul continues to put forth some of the "hurts and hallelujahs"[181] of the Christian life. He tells us that while in fact our lives will be filled with distresses of various sorts as

---

180 Lloyd-Jones, *Romans* p. 54.

181 Boice, p. 845.

we continue to make our way to the glory, nonetheless, we will know God's enabling grace to make it through the difficult days. Consequently, his words in 2 Corinthians 6:10 capture the heart of our verses in view, when he writes that as believers, we are "sorrowful, *yet always rejoicing*."

Exegetical & Practical Insights:

Obs. 1- (vv. 23-25) That as Paul writes these verses, he does so by connecting his thought to the previous words which spoke about the created world groaning and laboring with birth pangs. He says:

Not only *that,* which is to say, not only does the creation suffer and sigh because the fall of Adam; **but we also,** i.e., we who are Christians in like manner do the same; **who have,**[182] i.e., have as a present-day reality and will continue to have all of our days; **the firstfruits**[183] **of the Spirit,** or better understood: the firstfruit *who is* the Holy Spirit, whom we received at conversion as the first token or "first installment/down-payment"[184] of our spiritual adoption into God's family (cf. v.15, the term "firstfruits," refers to a foretaste of more to come, much like the firstfruits or early sampling of a farmer's crop pointed forward to further fruits); **even we ourselves**[185] **groan**[186] or habitually sigh (cf. 7:24; Ps. 13); **within ourselves,** or inwardly; **eagerly waiting for the adoption,** or we might say, the second part of our adoption (v. 15); **the redemption of our body** which is, the perfecting and complete deliverance of our bodies from all sin and decay at the return of Christ (either by resurrection or instant glorification, which is the second fruit or token given to us because of our adoption by God). **For** the conjunction explaining why we are eagerly waiting for the adoption, the redemption of our body; **we were saved** or perhaps better understood with the idea that we are kept and sustained; **in this hope,**[187] that is to say, we who are already saved by faith alone (cf. 1:16, 17; 3:22-31; 5:1) are saved "with this hope" before us of the final redemption and renewing of our bodies; **but hope that is seen** or fully realized; **is not hope; for why does one still hope for what he sees** (the point is, nobody does this since seeing the thing hoped for takes away hoping for it). But if we hope for what we do not see, i.e., the glorifying of our bodies; **we eagerly wait for** *it* with perseverance or endurance.[188]

Obs. 2- (vv. 26-27) That as the apostle gives yet another encouragement in connection to the hope that was just put forth concerning the future redemption of our bodies, he writes:

Likewise or in a similar way; **the Spirit** that is to say, the Holy Spirit of God who is in us (v. 9), leads us (v. 14), bears witness to our sonship that we are the children of God (v. 15, 16), and is the firstfruits of our

---

182 Grk. present, active, participle.

183 Cf. 1 Cor. 15:20, 23.

184 Cf. Eph. 1:14.

185 Note the repetition of the pronoun for the sake of emphasis.

186 Grk. present, active, verb.

187 See similar language to this concerning Abraham in Rom. 4:18.

188 Cf. 5:3, 4.

adoption (v. 23); **also helps**[189] or continually cooperates and comes to our aid; **in** (the midst of); **our weaknesses** (whatever weaknesses they might be: physical, emotional, spiritual, etc.). **For** the explanatory conjunction telling us why the Spirit helps us; **we do not know what** (not merely "how," but "what"); **we should** or is appropriate to; **pray for as we ought** (sometimes our situations are so dire that we are at a loss for words); **but**[190] or in sharp contrast to this; **the Spirit Himself** (comes to our rescue and fills us so that we are not left in such a pitiful state); **and makes intercession**[191] or constant entreaties to God; **for** or concerning; **us** (not instead of us, but alongside of us to help us in our praying); **with groanings** or sighs which "carry profound appeals for the welfare of every believer;"[192] **which cannot be uttered**[193] or are too deep for words. **Now** or perhaps better translated "and;" **He,** that is, God the Father; **who searches**[194] or continually examines; **the hearts,** i.e., our hearts, our inner beings; **knows** or understands; **what the mind of the Spirit** *is,* ("because of their essential and perfect unity")[195] or we might say, what the Holy Spirit's thoughts are; **because He** (the Holy Spirit); **makes intercession for** or on behalf of; **the saints according to** or in harmony with; *the will of* God[196] (which means that although we may not know God's will in any particular situation, the Holy Spirit knows it perfectly, and thus all of our prayers—though weak and feeble in themselves—are always wonderfully heard and answered by God the Father because of Him).

Paul speaks profoundly in this passage. In it he teaches us that along with there being *one in heaven* who is at God's right hand praying for us as believers (even the Lord Jesus Christ, as he mentions in verse 34 of this chapter), there is also *one on earth* in our hearts, who has been given to us to help us in our deepest trials. According to the apostle, there are two divine persons who help believers amid every life experience: Christ who intercedes *for us*; and the Holy Spirit who intercedes *in us*. What great news this is for the wearied soul! This gives us a double assurance that as we continue to bear the hardships of life, God the Father will always hear our prayers and respond in the fullness of time.[197]

Calvin comments are useful:

---

189 Grk. present, middle, verb.

190 The strong Greek adversative.

191 Grk. present, active, verb.

192 *MacArthur Study Bible,* p. 1708.

193 It is unfortunate that some in the Pentecostal church say that these words are referring to tongues-speaking. This is incorrect, especially since according to the Bible tongues were known languages that individuals *spoke* to God (Acts 2:8), not *groanings* that "cannot be uttered." For further discussion on this topic, I point the reader to Schreiner on Romans, pp. 444-47.

194 Grk. present, active, participle. Cf. 1 Sam 16:7; Heb. 4:12, 13.

195 Yarbrough, p. 130.

196 Cf. 1 John 5:14, 15.

197 Clearly then, in the ultimate sense, the Holy Spirit is the best "prayer partner" that any Christian could have.

That the faithful may not make this objection—that they are so weak as not to be able to bear so many and so heavy burdens, he (Paul) brings before them the aid of the Spirit, which is abundantly sufficient to overcome all difficulties. There is then no reason for anyone to complain, that the bearing of the cross is beyond their own strength, since we are sustained by a celestial power. And there is great force in the word συναντιλαμβάνεται (helps) which means that the Spirit takes on himself a part of the burden, by which our weakness is opposed; so that he not only helps and succors us, but lifts us up; as though he went under the burden with us.[198]

The noted Greek scholar, A. T. Robertson, further says concerning the word "helps" that "The Holy Spirit lays hold of our weaknesses along with us and carries His part of the burden facing us as if two men were carrying a log, one at each end. The word is found elsewhere in the New Testament only in Martha's plea to Jesus to tell Mary to get into the kitchen and help her (Lk 10:40)."[199]

In summary, Paul teaches here that when we are weak the Holy Spirit is strong. He teaches us that when we can barely utter a word to the Father because our hearts are breaking, the Holy Spirit of God is interceding about the burdens of our hearts, for "when we cannot find words in which to express our prayer and can do no better than make inarticulate sounds, the Spirit takes those sounds and makes them into effective intercession."[200]

Suggested applications from the text for the church:

1- The teaching of this passage should cause us to be immensely encouraged, knowing that in all of our sufferings, we have a divine helper in our hearts to aid in carrying the burdens of the day to our Father in heaven as we pray to Him.

2- The teaching of this passage should cause us to be immensely thankful that all of this is so!

Suggested application from the text for the non-Christian:

1- The teaching of this passage should cause you to go to Christ at once for deliverance from the penalty of your sins. God "searches the hearts." Since this is so, He knows the truth about who you really are, deep within.

Text: Romans 8:28[201]

General theme: A glorious gospel promise for the children of God (I).

---

198 John Calvin, p. 311 Baker Books edition.

199 A. T. Robertson, *A Grammar of the Greek New Testament in Light of Historical Research* (Nashville: Broadman, 1947), p. 593.

200 Morris, p. 328.

201 I was helped in my understanding of these words by Lloyd-Jones' treatment of this section of Scripture in his multivolume set. I also found help in Thomas Watson's book entitled *All Things For Good*.

Homiletical outline of the verse:

   A. The confidence in the promise: [28a] And we know,

   B. The content of the promise: [28b] that all things work together for good to those who love God, to those who are the called according to *His* purpose.

Summary of section: In these words, Paul is still thinking about the various sufferings that we will face in life either because we live in a fallen world or because ungodly individuals will oppose us for the sake of Christ and the gospel. His mind is still very much on the difficulties of the evil days in which we live. In giving us a third set of encouragement for such times, he puts forth words which have been beloved by believers throughout the ages. These are words which make the heart sing and the soul soar. They give great comfort to Christians.

Exegetical & Practical Insights:

   Obs. 1- (v. 28) That as Paul puts forth this glorious gospel promise which is "breathtaking in its magnitude, encompassing absolutely *everything* that pertains to a believer's life"[202] he writes:

   And we know[203] not "and we feel" or "and it always immediately appears to be," but we continually are confident as a standing conviction because God has pledged it and we have seen it to be the case time and again in our lives and in the lives of God's people; **that** the conjunction stating the content of what we know; **all things** whatever they are, the good things, the bad things, and the ugly things; **work together,**[204] or harmonize and continually cooperate; **for good**[205] or "for our own ultimate blessing"[206] (spiritually, naturally, temporarily or eternally); **to those**[207] and only those; **who love God,**[208] that is, those who have a strong regard for and habitual commitment to Him because they been saved by

---

   202 MacArthur, p. 471.

   203 Grk. perfect, active, verb. Paul uses this language throughout this epistle: 2:2; 3:19; 7:14; 8:22. In verse 26 he uses it negatively when he writes, "For we *do not know* what we should pray for as we ought..."

   204 Grk. present, active, verb. This one Greek word forms our English word *synergism* or the working of various matters together to produce an effect.

   205 It is important to note that Paul does not say here that "all things *in and of themselves* are good." This is not the case. Death is not good. Murder is not good. Rape is not good. Abortion is not good. Consequently, in view of such bad things, we should be sensitive not to *unsympathetically* quote this verse to others especially in their times of grief. The verse is true, but so is Romans 12:15b which tells us that we are to "weep with those who weep."

   206 MacArthur, p. 472. While I think MacArthur is right here (for surely God will work whatever comes into our lives for our ultimate blessing), it is important to note that God will do this mostly *Christocentrically* in that He will use whatever comes our way to make us more like Christ, as Paul goes on to say in the following verse.

   207 This language makes it plain that this is not a universal promise for all humanity.

   208 Grk. present, active, participle. It is worth noting that the words, "to those who love God," are placed in the front of the sentence in the Greek text for emphasis. It is also interesting to note that although Paul often speaks of God's love for us in this epistle (1:7; 5:5, 8; 8:35, 37, 39), Frank Thielman points out that this is "his only reference in this letter to their love for God." Thielman, p. 409.

Him; **to those** and only those; **who are the called**[209] **according to** or in line with; *His* purpose, that is God's intentional plan to save His people.

This is a comprehensive, comforting expression—one which should act as a soft pillow for our heads concerning all of the sorrows of life. Amid all our difficulties, we must be absolutely persuaded that our God is at work, producing glorious good for us. He is synchronizing all of our trials in such a way that at the end of them, we will be able to say with the psalmist in Psalm 119:71, "It was *good* for me that I have been afflicted." He is orchestrating all the events that we experience (even from the hands of those who trouble us) in such a way that we will be able to say with Joseph of old, "But as for you, you meant evil against me; but God meant it for *good*..." (Gen. 50:20).[210]

Haldane's comments are useful:

> Nothing is more necessary for Christians than to be well persuaded of the happiness and privileges of their condition, that they may be able to serve God with cheerfulness and freedom of spirit, and to pass through the troubles and difficulties of the world. Here, then, is further consolation: Christians are often in sorrows, sufferings, and trials. This is not in itself joyous, but grievous; but in another point of view it is a matter of joy. Though afflictions in themselves are evil, yet in their effects as overruled and directed by God, they are useful. Yea, all things, of every kind, that happen to the Christian, are overruled by God for his good![211]

Suggested applications from the text for the church:

1- This verse calls us to praise God for the grand truth it contains.

2- This verse calls us to be patient in all of our trials (not grumbling or complaining) knowing that God always has our best in view.

3- This verse calls us to persevere through all of our hardships in life, knowing that this is what glorifies the Lord (cf. James 5:11).

Suggested application from the text for the non-Christian:

1- This verse calls you to be persuaded that until you become a true Christian who loves God for all that He is, this promise cannot be yours. In fact, if you are not a true Christian, the very opposite is true for you, for even the good things that happen in your life will work out for your eternal ruin because of your sin and God's righteous judgment.

Text: Romans 8:29-30

General theme: A glorious gospel promise for the children of God (II).

Homiletical outline of the verses:

C. The confirmation from the promise: [29] For whom He foreknew, He also predestined *to be* conformed to the image of His Son, that He might be

---

209 See verse 30 explanation.

210 Cf. Acts 14:17.

211 Haldane, Romans p. 390.

the firstborn among many brethren. [30] Moreover whom He predestined, these He also called; whom He called, these He also justified; and whom He justified, these He also glorified.

Summary of section: In these words Paul begins to unpack what it means to be one who is "called according to God's purpose" (v. 28b) in what is commonly known as the *ordo salutis* (a Latin term which speaks about the order of the causes and effects in our salvation). The *ordo salutis* does not list every theological point concerning our salvation. For example, Paul here does not mention regeneration, repentance, faith, or sanctification. Still, the ones he does mention are some of the central doctrines in the matter. Concerning these doctrines, two of them are eternal (foreknowledge and predestination), and three of them happen in time (calling, justification, and glorification).

Exegetical & Practical Insights:

Obs. 1- (v. 29) That as Paul puts forth the first two causes or reasons for our becoming Christians, in this "series of five verbs outlining what God has done in fulfillment of his saving purpose"[212] he writes:

For whom[213] that is, the specific individuals ordained by God for salvation (again, the called according to His purpose); **He** (God the Father); **foreknew,**[214] not merely *fore-saw* that such ones would put their faith in Christ and then, in response to this, God decided to choose them,[215] "for it is certainly true that God foresees faith; he foresees all that comes to pass."[216] But rather Paul says "whom the Father *fore-knew*," or more literally "knew in advance,"[217] "knew from eternity," or fore-chose" and "fore-loved,"[218] so that this knowledge "characterizes an intimate personal relationship;"[219] **He also predestined**[220] or "decided

---

212 Morris, p. 332.

213 It is important to note that Paul does not speak here about "what" God foreknew (which of course is everything) but rather of "whom" He foreknew. The point is: he is speaking about specific individuals and not some general matter. He is talking about "God's elect" as he defines them in verse 33 of this chapter.

214 The Old Testament background to this word (the Hebrew word *yada*) shows that this knowledge is not some bare knowledge that God has of His people but rather it is that which is warm and tender. It is a love which "refers to his covenantal love in which he sets his affection on those whom he has chosen," as Schreiner notes, p. 452. Many passages bring out the sense of the word: Gen. 18:19; Ex. 33:17; Jer. 1:5; Hos. 13:5; Amos. 3:2. It should also be noted that this word stands in sharp contrast to Jesus' words which He will speak to unbelievers when he will say to them, "I never knew you; depart from Me, you who practice lawlessness!" (Matt. 7:23).

215 Cf. Rom. 9:11. MacArthur notes, "Scripture is clear that repentant faith is essential to salvation and is the first step that *we* take in response to God, but repentant faith does not initiate salvation." MacArthur, p. 494.

216 Murray, p. 316.

217 This word in the Greek text is the basis for our English word "prognosis."

218 Murray, p. 317.

219 MacArthur's Systematic Theology, p. 499.

220 Cf. Eph. 1:4-6. It should be noted that while predestination and election are interrelated and are inseparable dimensions of God's eternal decree, the doctrine of predestination speaks about God's divine will, intention, and ultimate plan which includes

upon beforehand"[221] (and this ultimately for salvation which is rooted in the fact that God fore-loved them);[222] *to be* conformed or for the purpose of being progressively molded morally (in our thoughts, words, and deeds) through the daily process of sanctification[223] and then ultimately at glorification, when we will have sinless souls, inhabiting deathless bodies like our Lord's (v. 30);[224] **to the image,** i.e., the likeness and character; **of His Son,**[225] (Jesus); **that He** (Jesus) **might be the firstborn** *not the first created*[226] since "all things were made through Him, and without Him nothing was made that was made" (John 1:3). But the firstborn, which is Old Testament language for the most honored son who had the priority and preeminence in a family; **among many brethren,** i.e., all who have become the children of God through faith in Christ.

Paul's words here are significant. They show us that along with a major goal in our lives being that we would be made more Christ-like in our daily lives (and not merely that we would have heads full of Bible knowledge or "enter heaven at last"),[227] that in addition to having saved a people for Himself, Jesus would not merely be "One among equals, but the One who has supreme place of honor among His brothers and sisters."[228] Simply put, in saving His spiritual family "which no one could number, of all nations, tribes, peoples, and tongues"[229] who, through grace, bear His family likeness, Jesus will be the One who will have the supremacy in their midst. He and He alone will be the main focus of our attention in glory—and praise be to God for that!

Lloyd-Jones correctly notes,

> It is most important that we should look at our salvation from this standpoint. We must not only think of it in terms of ourselves, but we must realize that God's ultimate object in ever planning and introducing

---

determining our destinies for our conformity to the image of Christ (Rom. 8:29) and our adoption as sons (Eph. 1:5). The doctrine of election however (which is the positive part of predestination and a subset of it), speaks about the method by which God initiates His predestining plan of salvation. He does this by selecting or choosing those individuals whom He is determined to save in Christ for Himself before the foundation of the world (Eph. 1:4).

221 BDAG, 873.

222 *Predestination* stands in opposition to *postdestination* which says that God determined our destinies *after* He foresaw how we would respond to the gospel.

223 Cf. 2 Cor. 3:18.

224 Cf. Phil. 3:20-21; 1 Cor. 15:49.

225 As opposed to us being conformed to this world (Rom. 12:1-2). Chrysostom helpfully comments on the words about our being "conformed to the image of His Son" and writes, "What a superb honor! For what the only begotten Son was by nature, we have become by grace. Christ in his human nature has become the firstborn of many brethren, even though in his divine nature he remains the only begotten." *Ancient Christian Commentary on Scripture, Romans* p. 227.

226 This is a deadly error which is taught by the cult group known as the Jehovah Witnesses.

227 Hendriksen, p. 283.

228 McDonald, 1713.

229 Rev. 7:9.

the scheme of salvation is to glorify His Son.... It is as the result of what He has done that He is thus exalted. In other words, the ultimate object of salvation is that the Son might be set in the position in which at His Name 'every knee should bow, of things in heaven, and things in the earth, and things under the earth: and every tongue should confess that Jesus Christ is Lord.'[230]

Obs. 2- (v. 30) That as Paul now moves down the golden chain of events in our salvation to the last three items which all happen *in time*, he writes:

Moreover whom He (God the Father); **predestined,**[231] **these** (the sense in the original language is, these and these only); **He also called;**[232] that is, called not merely *outwardly* through the preaching of the gospel,[233] but *inwardly, irresistibly*, sovereignly, and savingly by the regenerating work of the Holy Spirit as a divine summons from the King of Heaven to come to Christ;[234] **whom He called, these He also justified,** i.e., declared them not guilty and imputed to them the impeccable righteousness of Christ when they believed on Him alone for salvation, so that they are not just "declared not guilty," but also "declared righteous" before God (this righteousness alone commends them to God cf. Rom. 1:17; 3:21, 22; 5:19; 10:3, 4); **and whom He justified, these He also glorified** or will surely bring about the final act of their salvation at which time they will receive glorified souls and bodies at Christ's return.

With these words, Paul closes the circle of the *ordo salutis* and shows that what God purposes eternally, He accomplishes in time. The point is, all whom God foreknows, He, in fact, glorifies! Paul is so convinced about this matter that all of the five verbs in his chain of salvation are listed as past tense events, as if they were already done. This is the case because it is absolutely sure they will be! Here then is comfort amid all that we will face in life despite our hardships, inward or otherwise. Despite persecutions and the like, the glorious promise of the gospel is: God will never let His people go.[235] As Jesus says in John 6:39, "This is the will of the Father who sent Me, that of all He has given Me I should lose nothing, but should raise it up at the last day."

Spurgeon condenses the matter nicely when he says that in our verses there are,

No breaks between the links of this chain. Foreknowledge is welded to the predestination: the predestination is infallibly linked with the calling, the

---

230 Lloyd-Jones, *Romans* pp. 229, 231.

231 See explanation in verse 29.

232 Cf. Rom. 1:6; 8:30; 9:24; 2 Thess. 2:14; 2 Tim. 1:9; 2 Pet. 1:3; Jude 1:1; Rev. 17:14. For a helpful statement concerning effectual calling, see the London Baptist Confession of Faith of 1689, chapter 10.

233 Cf. Mark 16:15.

234 Cf. Matt. 22:14; 1 Cor. 1:9. Lewis Berkhof reminds us in his Systematic Theology that according to the Westminster Confession of Faith effectual calling includes regeneration. He does distinguish between the two but rightly sees them as intimately connected, pp. 470, 471.

235 Cf. John 3:16; 10:28-30; Rom. 8:31-29; Eph. 1:13, 14, 4:30; Phil. 1:6; 1 Pet. 1:5; Jude 25.

calling with the justification, and the justification with the glorification. There is no hint given that there may be a flaw or break in the series. Get a hold of any one, and you possess the whole. The called man is the predestined man. Let him be sure of that. And the justified man shall be a glorified man. Let him have no doubt whatever about that.[236]

Suggested applications from the text for the church:

1- Although such terms as "foreknowledge" and "predestination" are not always liked by some professing Christians, we are to believe them and rejoice over them since they are true and part of the infallible Word of God.

2- Although many claim to be Christians, the real test is not what people say about themselves, but rather, if their lives are truly being progressively molded morally into Christ's image.

Suggested application from the text for the non-Christian:

1- Although you may wonder whether you are one of God's foreknown, predestinated ones, this is not a concern that the Bible lays upon you. Rather, the concern that the Bible lays upon you is that you see yourself in truth as a great sinner before God and in need of Jesus as your great Savior! Having done this, you turn from your sins and go to Him by faith for mercy, forgiveness, and pardon. You go knowing that, according to Him, "the one who comes to Me I will by no means cast out" (John 6:37).

Text: Romans 8:31-39

General theme: The Christian's security (six vital questions).

Homiletical outline of the verses:

A. **First question:** [31] What then shall we say to these things?

B. **Second question:** [31b] If God *is* for us, who *can be* against us?

C. **Third question:** [32] He who did not spare His own Son, but delivered Him up for us all, how shall He not with Him also freely give us all things?

D. **Fourth question:** [33] Who shall bring a charge against God's elect? *It is* God who justifies.

E. **Fifth question:** [34] Who *is* he who condemns? *It is* Christ who died, and furthermore is also risen, who is even at the right hand of God, who also makes intercession for us.

G. **Sixth question:** [35] Who shall separate us from the love of Christ? *Shall* tribulation, or distress, or persecution, or famine, or nakedness, or peril, or sword?

[36] As it is written: "For Your sake we are killed all day long; We are accounted as sheep for the slaughter."

[37] Yet in all these things we are more than conquerors through Him who loved us. [38] For I am persuaded that neither death nor life, nor angels nor principalities nor powers, nor things present nor things to come, [39] nor

---

236 Spurgeon, p. 183.

height nor depth, nor any other created thing, shall be able to separate us from the love of God which is in Christ Jesus our Lord.

Summary of section: Paul concludes this chapter on a crescendo. Having just expounded the enormous comfort that is ours in Christ amidst all that we will experience in life, he now celebrates these grand realties. Here he even challenges the whole moral universe with six crucial questions. He asks in light of what God has done for us in Christ, who could possibly do anything to overturn or thwart His great work on our behalf? He answers by telling us: no one! Thus, I agree with the Puritan Richard Sibbes when he writes concerning our passage that, "The words are a glorious conclusion and triumph of faith: the conclusion upon all the former particulars in the chapter, and the foundation of all the comforts that follow after, to the end of the chapter. They are as the centre of the chapter. All the beams of heavenly comfort in this divine chapter, they meet, as it were in one, in this short clause, 'What shall we say then to these things?'"[237]

Exegetical & Practical Insights:
Obs. 1- (v. 31) That as Paul is thinking about all that he just wrote (in the immediate context in verses 28 to 30) about the goodness of God in orchestrating all things together for our good and for saving and keeping us saved to the end, he writes:

What then or therefore, the conjunction drawing a conclusion from the previous words; **shall we say to** or "in response to" or, "in view of;"[238] **these things?** ("In the face of all of this, what is there left to say?).[239] **If** or better translated, since in fact; **God *is* for us,**[240] the idea being "because He is on our side"[241] in every sense of the word because of Jesus our Savior; **who *can be*** (not necessarily "who *is* against us" because that could be the case with many people or spiritual beings because of our commitment to Christ, cf. Eph. 6:10-20; 2 Tim. 3:12; 2 Tim. 4:14; 1 Pet. 5:8, 9), but who *can be*; **against us** in the sense of prevailing against us or "being successful in standing against us"[242] in the ultimate sense of the word, to which the answer is no one.[243]

Obs. 2- (v. 32) That as Paul puts forth the ultimate demonstration for how God is for us, he writes:

---

237 Richard Sibbes, Works, vol. 7 p. 386.

238 Harvey, p. 215. Paul asks this same question in several places in this epistle to make other points: 3:5; 4:1; 6:1; 7:7; 9:14; 30.

239 Phillips translation. No doubt the answer to the question is "Praise the Lord!"

240 Paul might be reflecting on words found in Psalm 46:7, which read: "The Lord of hosts is with us; the God of Jacob is our refuge."

241 Rogers and Rogers, p. 332.

242 Ibid., p. 332.

243 Thielman says that "Paul's rhetorical question comes out of the same understanding of God's saving power that prompted David's rhetorical question about Goliath: 'For who is this uncircumcised Philistine, that he should defy the armies of the living God?'" (1 Sam 17:26; cf. Ps. 27:1; 118:6-7; Isa 50:9; 54:17). Thielman, p. 421.

He (God the Father); **who did not spare**[244] or keep back and withhold judgment from; **His own Son,** that is, His very own Son Jesus, His unique Son (the second person of the Holy Trinity), His "beloved,"[245] His "co-equal"[246] the One who is "the brightness of His glory and expressed image of His person,"[247] who was in His "bosom;"[248] **but**[249] or in sharp contrast to this, in love He (again, God the Father); **delivered Him up** or orchestrated that Jesus would die as a sin-sacrifice on the cross;[250] **for** or on behalf of; **us all,** i.e., all of His people (vv. 29, 30); **how shall He** (God the Father); **not with Him** (Jesus); **also freely** or graciously bestow and most definitely; **give us all things,** that is, all things pertaining to life and godliness as we continue to live for Him on our way to glory.

Here we have irrefutable proof that the Father is for us in that He gave His very best for the very worst. He gave the altogether lovely One for us who were not at all lovely in ourselves and deserved nothing but His wrath.

Lewis Johnson rightly remarks:

> The evidence that God is for us is found in the cross of Christ. That is the sign of love fulfilling justice. It is a magnificent display of the nature of man and the nature of God. It is a display of the justice of God in that in order to find a way for man to be forgiven, the Son of God must be sacrificed. The same God who three times is said by Paul in Romans 1 to have given up men and women (cf. 1:24, 26, 28) is now said by Paul to have given up his only Son for us. Why? So that he might justly forgive sinners through the Son's suffering of their penalty by his sacrifice of blood. Thus, the cross shows that God is just and righteous in his dealings, and he does not deviate from his law even when he wishes to save people out of love for them.[251]

Additionally, Paul says that since God the Father gave Christ to be a sacrifice for our sins to save us, then surely with Him, He will also give us all things in this life spiritually speaking so that we will experience the fullness of that salvation in heaven. Since God has done the greater, He will surely do the lesser for "if he gave the best, then he will give the rest."[252]

Obs. 3- (v. 33) That as the apostle brings our minds back once again to the courtroom scene (as he did in earlier chapters), he asks his fourth question and writes:

---

244 The Father did not spare Jesus from the judgment which fell upon Him, in order that He could spare us of that judgment.

245 Matt. 3:17.

246 John 1:1.

247 Heb. 1:3.

248 John 1:18.

249 The strong Greek adversative.

250 Matt. 20:17-19; Acts 3:22, 23; 4:27, 28.

251 Johnson, pp. 142-43.

252 Ibid., p. 145.

Who shall bring a charge,[253] that is, a legal accusation or indictment on the final Day of Judgment;[254] **against** or towards; **God's elect** or His chosen ones? *It is* God who justifies or declares us not guilty.

Since God, the great judge of heaven and earth, has already legally acquitted us of all of our debts to His law (because Jesus at the cross made a full and final atonement to Him for our lawlessness, "having wiped out the hand writing of requirements that was against us, which was contrary to us... having nailed it to the cross, Col. 2:14), no one can justly condemn us. Since we have already been completely acquitted once for all time by Him, there can be no higher court of appeal beyond Him. Geoffrey Wilson is right when he says, "Those who press charges against believers are doomed to disappointment, for they fight against God's decree. It is impossible to curse, still less to condemn, those whom God has determined to bless."[255]

Obs. 4- (v. 34) That as Paul hypothetically raises the stakes even higher against the Christian from him being *charged* to now being *condemned*, he asks fifthly:

Who *is* he who condemns? Answer? No one! Then, in putting forth four clear reasons why this is so (in what we might call the "Golden Chain of Eternal Security") he writes:

1- **It is** Christ who died, because Jesus paid the penalty for our sins at the cross and satisfied all of God's just punishment against us as our substitute, we could never be condemned, for "by his death, as an atonement for our sins, all ground of condemnation is removed"[256] (John 19:30).

2- **and furthermore is also risen,** which means that because Jesus was raised from the dead, His sacrifice for us at Calvary has been completely accepted by the Father, for "the efficacy of the death resides in the reality of the resurrection"[257] (cf. Rom. 4:25; 1 Cor. 15:12-20; Gal. 1:1).

3- **who is even at the right hand of God,** which means that because Jesus occupies the highest place of honor at God's right hand, by God's appointment (Acts 2:33-35; 5:31) and all authority in heaven and earth has been given to Him, granting Him universal dominion over all things (Matt. 28:18), then clearly His work for us at Calvary is approved by the Father (Heb. 10:12).

4- **who also makes intercession for us,** which means that although Jesus' atonement on our behalf is finished, the fact that Christ continues to plead the merits of His blood to the Father for the sins that we commit at the present time, we have further assurance, for Jesus "acts as our advocate, pleads our cause before God, presents those considerations

---

253 Grk. future, active, verb.

254 Satan even attempts to do this now but he is unsuccessful (Rev. 12:10).

255 Wilson, p. 151.

256 Hodge, p. 289.

257 Wilson, p. 153.

which secure us pardon and the continued supplies of the divine grace"[258] (Heb. 7:25; 9:12).

Here then is why we can never be condemned as Christians. As Paul builds his argument point by point, he firmly sets four rock-solid pillars upon which we can stake our eternal destiny.

MacArthur nicely summarizes:

> If we understand what Christ did on the cross to save us from sin, we understand what it means to be secure in His salvation. If we believe that God loved us so much when we were wretched and ungodly that He sent His Son to die on the cross to bring us to Himself, how could we believe that, after we are saved, His love is not strong enough to keep us saved? If Christ had power to redeem us out of bondage to sin, how could He lack the power to keep us redeemed?
>
> Christ, the perfect Priest, offered a perfect sacrifice to make us perfect. To deny the security of the believer is therefore to deny the sufficiency of the work of Christ. To deny the security of the believer is to misunderstand the heart of God, to misunderstand the gift of Christ, to misunderstand the meaning of the cross, to misunderstand the biblical meaning of salvation.
>
> Even when we sin after we are saved, "if we confess our sins, He is faithful and righteous to forgive us our sins and to cleanse us from all unrighteousness," because in Him "we have an Advocate with the Father, Jesus Christ the righteous" (1 John 1:9; 2:1). When we sin, our Lord intercedes on our behalf and comes to our defense against Satan and any others who might bring charges against us.... Through our remaining days on earth and throughout all eternity, our gracious Lord will hold us safe in His everlasting love by His everlasting power.[259]

Obs. 5- (v. 35-37) That as Paul puts forth his final challenge in the last step of his argument concerning the great security that we have in Christ, he asks sixthly:

Who or what individual, the "who" pictures a "human agent who might stand behind one or more of the seven threats Paul cites;"[260] **shall separate** or divide and sever; **us from** or away from; **the love** or the unending, goodwill and affection; **of Christ** or that which comes to us from Him both now and forevermore.

Shall tribulation affliction or extreme pressure; **or distress** perplexing circumstances or hardships; **or persecution** harassment or maltreatment; **or famine** hunger or lack of food; **or nakedness** being without clothing, poverty; **or peril** danger or looming threat on one's life; **or sword**[261] a large knife or dagger which could take our life. As it is written, i.e., written in Psalm 44:22 as a confirmation of the suffering of the people of God in all generations:

---

258 Hodge, p. 290.

259 MacArthur, p. 509.

260 Yarbrough, p. 133.

261 Church history tells us that Paul was most likely killed by the sword by beheading.

"**For Your sake** that is, God's sake, in His cause; **we** (because of our faith attachment to Him); **are killed all day long; We are accounted** or considered; **as sheep for the slaughter.**"

Yet[262] which is to say, instead of our sufferings separating us from the love of Christ, in strong opposition to this; **in,** i.e., right in the midst of; **all these things** which is to say, in each and every hardships listed above (we are not failures, or left without the love of Christ no, rather); **we are more than conquerors,**[263] literally, we are hyper-conquerors or super-abounding victors (the words "more than conquerors" in the original language describe "winning in the face of every obstacle")[264] not because of ourselves, but; **through Him,** that is, through Jesus, the supreme Agent of our success; **who loved us,** which is to say, *loved* us unquestionably as demonstrated by Him specifically giving Himself for us at the cross.

These words are full of encouragement for us who live in the twenty-first century, just as they were for those Christians to whom Paul originally wrote, especially in light of everything they would suffer in the days ahead under the persecution of Nero.[265] Christians throughout the centuries have often been ill-treated. In fact, even in today's world, some "90,000 Christians die of persecution annually (nearly 250 per day worldwide)."[266] This is tragic! Nevertheless, the truth of our passage stands. Regardless of what we experience in life, Christ's eternal love will continue to be with us and He will continue to give us success over our situations. He who daily intercedes for us (vs. 34) will continue to be merciful toward us and will make our roadblocks into stepping stones whereby we advance in life, seeing that nothing can ever sever His commitment to do us good all of our days (Jer. 32:40). Through His grace, He will bring triumph out of our tragedies. By His never-ending kindnesses, He will give us "beauty for ashes, the oil of joy for mourning, the garment of praise for the spirit of heaviness" (Isa. 61:3).

Obs. 6- (v. 38-39) That as the apostle gives the reason for the Christian's conquest amidst suffering, he writes:

For I am persuaded[267] not merely "I think" or "I hope," but rather, I stand convinced (his words indicating a "rock-solid conviction");[268] **that** the conjunction putting forth the contents of what Paul is convinced of; **neither death** which is what we will all experience at the end of our journeys here; **nor life** with all of its current trials and temptations; **nor angels nor principalities nor power,** i.e., spiritual, demonic powers, Satan and his associates, cf. Eph. 6:12; **nor things present nor things**

---

262 The strong Greek adversative.

263 Grk. present, active, verb. Paul speaks about what some of this victory looked like in his life practically speaking in 2 Cor. 4:7-12.

264 Harvey, p. 218. Some scholars say that Paul might have coined this Greek term himself.

265 See my comments on 5:3.

266 Yarbrough, p. 134.

267 Grk. perfect, passive, verb. See also 14:14; 15:14, for the same type of language.

268 Yarbrough, p. 134.

to come which represents everything we are experiencing now or will experience in the days ahead; **nor height nor depth** nothing overhead or underneath, big or small; **nor any other created thing** with these words, Paul includes anything that he did not specify already; **shall be able** or have the strength or power; **to separate** or divide and sever; **us from the love of God** now the all-embracing love of the Father is in view, cf. 5:5, 8; **which is in** or inextricably connected to and secured for us by; **Christ Jesus our Lord.**[269]

Here Paul lists ten specific terms which move from "physical danger through the hierarchy of superhuman powers, those that now exist or ever will, powers from on high or from below"[270] covering "all dimensions of time and space."[271] He shows that there is absolutely no circumstance, no situation, and no spiritual being whatsoever, either in the present or in the future, which will be able to divorce us from the covenantal love of God which is in Christ Jesus our Lord. Paul says this is simply impossible. What great joy this should bring to our hearts!

As the apostle ends his main doctrinal portion of this epistle, he does so on an extremely high note showing us how wonderfully secure we are in the Savior through the promises of the gospel. He shows that God, having loved us, will love us all of our days. Consequently, we are safe now and forevermore. Here is our great confidence! Here our hearts can be settled and our faith strengthened as we continue to make our way toward the celestial city. Hodge fittingly comments:

> How wonderful, how glorious, how secure is the gospel! Those who are in Christ Jesus are as secure as the love of God, the merit, power, and intercession of Christ can make them. They are hedged around with mercy. They are enclosed in the arms of everlasting love. "Now unto Him that is able to keep us from falling, and to present us faultless before the presence of his glory with exceeding joy; to the only wise God our Savior, be glory and majesty, dominion and power, both now and for ever. Amen!"[272]

Suggested applications from the text for the church:

1- This passage calls us to trust God concerning our present and future standing with Him, knowing that Christ has secured everything that we need to be right with God both for time and for eternity.

2- This passage calls us to resist the devil with the truths of our text, seeing that he seeks to rob us of our Christian joy and security.

3- This passage calls us to love Christ and the Father in return, seeing that they have such a great love for us.

---

269 It is worth pointing out again that Paul ends this glorious chapter where he began, namely by speaking about "Christ Jesus" our Lord (cf. 8:1).

270 Mounce, p. 192.

271 *Reformation Heritage Study Bible,* p. 1630.

272 Hodge, p. 293.

Suggested application from the text for the non-Christian:

1- This passage calls you to understand that you will never find real, lasting, inner love in your life, until you find that love in God through Christ. God offers His love to you through His Son and He promises to give that love to you as you seek it from Him in truth.

ROMANS
CHAPTER NINE

Text: Romans 9:1-5[1]

General theme: Paul's Passionate Heart for His People

Homiletical outline of the verses:
   A. The pain Paul endured: [1] I tell the truth in Christ, I am not lying, my conscience also bearing me witness in the Holy Spirit, [2] that I have great sorrow and continual grief in my heart. [3] For I could wish that I myself were accursed from Christ for my brethren, my countrymen according to the flesh,

   B. The privileges Israel enjoyed: [4] who are Israelites, to whom *pertain* the adoption, the glory, the covenants, the giving of the law, the service *of God*, and the promises; [5] of whom *are* the fathers and from whom, according to the flesh, Christ *came,* who is over all, *the* eternally blessed God. Amen.

Summary of section: Beginning in this chapter, all the way to Chapter 11,[2] Paul opens up the major subject of the salvation of the Jewish people and God's faithfulness concerning His redemptive promises towards them. Having told us in 1:16 that the gospel is for "the Jew first," and having just spoken of "the love of God which is in Christ Jesus our Lord" in the previous chapter (8:39), Paul's heart and mind now move very naturally to his "countrymen according to the flesh" (9:3).

   In fact, it is important to see that chapters 9 to 11 of this letter form one major unit which addresses the topic of Abraham and his descendants. As the apostle thought about many of the Jews in his day who rejected

---

1 The reader should note that I write this next portion of this commentary with great love and care for Jewish people. In fact, half of my family is Jewish and not saved, therefore my "heart's desire and prayer to God for them" is that they might be saved through faith in Jesus the Messiah (10:1). Further, it should be noted that I found some useful instruction on these chapters from the book entitled *Three Views on Israel and the Church: Perspectives on Romans 9–11*. Mainly, the chapters written by Benjamin L. Merkle were most helpful.

2 We could outline these chapters as: *ethnic Israel and their salvation in the past* (chapters 9 and 10), and *ethnic Israel and their salvation in the present* (Chapter 11).

Jesus, the promised Messiah, the question is: "Has the word of God failed concerning its promise to bless Abraham and his posterity" (9:6)? Thankfully, Paul answers this question with a resounding no (11:1). He teaches that among the Jewish nation even "at this present time there is a remnant according to the election of grace" (11:5). This is good news to be sure, and it shows that just as with the Gentiles (whom Paul also addresses in these chapters, cf. Rom 11:13), God will continue to call a Jewish remnant to Himself for salvation through the gospel.[3]

John Murray captures the heart of the matter:

> But what of chapters 9 to 11? It might seem that there is discontinuity in this portion of the epistle and its length appears to aggravate the question raised. It is only as we fail to discern or overlook the relation that these chapters sustain to the thesis of this epistle that any thought of irrelevance or discontinuity is entertained. On closer inspection this part of the epistle is seen to bring to climactic vindication the thesis stated in 1:16, 17 and correlative [corresponding] doctrines unfolded later in chapters 1 to 8. If this section of the epistle were absent, there would be a hiatus leaving us with unanswered questions and the corresponding perplexity. It is not that we may demand or expect answers to all questions. But in this instance we may be profoundly grateful that the supreme author of Scripture inspired the apostle to deal with questions so germane to the grand theme of this epistle and urgently pressing upon the minds of intelligent readers.[4]

Exegetical & Practical Insights:

Obs. 1- (vv. 1-3) That as Paul puts forth a triple declaration concerning his passionate heart for his own native people, he says:

I tell the truth in Christ, that is to say, he is speaking as a redeemed man, a Christian, who is in saving union with Jesus the Messiah; **I am not lying** or being dishonest; **my conscience,** i.e., his inner God-given sense of right and wrong; **also bearing me witness**[5] or constantly testifying to him the truthfulness of the matter; **in** or by the agency of; **the Holy Spirit; that** the conjunction putting forth the content of the truth which he speaks; **I have**[6] or am continually experiencing; **great** not small, but huge; **sorrow** or pain; **and continual** or unceasing; **grief** or anguish; **in my heart,** which is to say, deep within. **For** the conjunction explaining why this is so; **I could wish**[7] or I was desiring if it were proper[8] or permissible in the will of God; **that I myself** (the personal pronoun "myself" is being used for the sake of emphasis and could be translated as: "I could wish that I, even I myself"); **were accursed** or cut off by God and anathematized

---

3 Cf. Jer. 31:7.

4 Murray, pp. xii, xiv.

5 Grk. present, active, participle.

6 Grk. present, active, verb.

7 Grk. imperfect, middle, verb.

8 Hodge, p. 298.

or "abandoned to perdition;"[9] **from Christ** "the only source of life and light and joy;"[10] **for** or on behalf of; **my brethren** (note the term of warm affection); **my countrymen,** i.e., his natural family members and relatives; **according to the flesh** or those from his own ethnicity.

Paul's words here are moving. In them, we see that he was willing to do whatever it took if it meant that his unsaved fellow Jews would escape the judgment of God due them for their sins against Him. We see that he was willing to "lose anything and everything if they but be saved" as Spurgeon said.[11] Of course, he knew that he could never be severed from Christ and so lose his salvation, as he said in the previous chapter (8:35). Further, he knew that as a sinner, he could never actually atone for others' sins (7:24, 25). However, here he is showing his heart. He is expressing his "deep concern for his fellow-Jews"[12] out of his all-consuming love for them. Or, as Murray says again, "The intensity of the apostle's love for his own people is hereby disclosed."[13]

Paul's words remind us of Moses' words in Exodus 32 verses 31 and 32. There as God's wrath was burning hot against His old covenant people because of their idolatry against Him regarding the golden calf incident, Moses cried out to the Lord saying, "Oh, these people have committed a great sin, and have made for themselves a god of gold! Yet now, if You will forgive their sin—but if not, I pray, blot me out of Your book which You have written."

Paul's heart is also similar to the prophet Jeremiah, when he said concerning his apostate countrymen in Jeremiah 8:18 to 9:1:

> I would comfort myself in sorrow; my heart *is* faint in me. Listen! The voice, the cry of the daughter of my people from a far country: "*Is* not the LORD in Zion? *Is* not her King in her?" "Why have they provoked Me to anger With their carved images—With foreign idols?" "The harvest is past, the summer is ended, and we are not saved!" For the hurt of the daughter of my people I am hurt. I am mourning; Astonishment has taken hold of me. *Is there* no balm in Gilead, *Is there* no physician there? Why then is there no recovery for the health of the daughter of my people?

And most significantly, Paul's heart is like the Lord Jesus Christ, who, in thinking about Israel's stubborn impenitence in not receiving Him as Savior, cried out, in Matthew 23:37, 38:

> O Jerusalem, Jerusalem, the one who kills the prophets and stones those who are sent to her! How often I wanted to gather your children together, as a hen gathers her chicks under *her* wings, but you were not willing! See! Your house is left to you desolate.

Calvin summarizes this matter nicely:

---

9   Murray, Vol. 2, p. 3.
10 Robinson, Book II, p. 5.
11 Spurgeon, p. 188.
12 Morris, p. 347.
13 Murray, pp. 2, 4.

Paul could not have expressed a greater ardor [passion] of love than what he testifies here. That is surely perfect love that does not refuse to die for the salvation of a friend. But there is another word added, *anathema*, which proves that he speaks not only of temporal but also of eternal death; but he explains its meaning when he says "from Christ," for it signifies a separation, and what is it to be separated from Christ, but to be excluded from the hope of salvation? It was then proof of the most ardent love that Paul hesitated not to wish for himself that condemnation which he saw impending over the Jews, in order to deliver them.... Many indeed doubt whether this was a lawful desire; but this doubt may be thus removed: the settled boundary of love is that it proceeds as far as the conscience permits; if then we love in God and not without God's authority our love can never be too much. And such was the love of Paul; for seeing his own nation endued with so many of God's benefits, he loved God's gifts in them, and them on account of God's gifts, and he deemed it a great evil that those gifts should perish, hence that his mind being overwhelmed he burst forth into this extreme wish.[14]

Obs. 2- (vv. 4-5) That as Paul speaks next, specifically about his countrymen according to the flesh, he puts forth eight things about them **"who are Israelites,"** which is to say, they are the "descendants of Abraham through Jacob, whose name God changed to Israel (Gen. 32:28)."[15] He writes:

1- **to whom *pertain*** the adoption, that is, not the spiritual, saving, individual adoption that believers received when they trusted in Christ alone for salvation, as Paul mentions in 8:15. But here the language speaks of a theocratic or national adoption which set the nation apart from all other people groups in the world (Ex. 4:22).

2- **the glory**, i.e., the Shekinah (or dwelling) glory of God which He revealed to them in the tent and the temple (1 Kgs. 8:10, 11). Or perhaps, this refers to the glory cloud which guided the Israelites during the day during their exodus from Egypt, which cloud represented God's presence with them (Ex. 13:21).

3- **the covenants**, that is all of God's divine covenants to them, including the Abrahamic covenant (Gen. 15), the Mosaic covenant (Ex. 19), and the Davidic covenant (Ps. 89).

4- **the giving of the law**, which speaks about God giving them the Ten Commandments on Mount Sinai (Ex. 20).

5- **the service *of God***, or the ordinance of His worship, which He ordained and appointed by Himself, in connection with the tent and the temple and the Aaronic priesthood (Ex. 29).

6- **and the promises**, i.e., all the promises that God gave to them from Genesis to Malachi, the chief one being the coming of Messiah-Jesus.[16]

---

14 *Reformation Commentary on Scripture, Romans* p. 11 Book II (9-16).

15 *MacArthur Study Bible*, p. 1710.

16 For these references, see my footnote comments on Rom. 1:3.

7- **of whom** *are* the fathers, that is to say, the patriarchs, Abraham, Isaac and Jacob (Ex. 3:6).

8- **and from whom** or out from; **according to the flesh** (a clear statement of Jesus' humanity and Jewish ancestry);[17] **Christ** (the long-expected, promised Messiah);[18] *came,* **who is**[19] (or more literally, "who being"); **over all** (as the Supreme One);[20] *the* **eternally blessed God**[21] (a clear statement of Jesus' deity).[22] **Amen.**[23]

These are all outstanding privileges which were given to the nation from God's kindness toward them. It shows that He highly favored the Hebrew people. Perhaps this is why Paul was so sad. With all that they had received from God's hand, they did not receive the crowning

---

17 Cf. John 1:14.

18 Cf. John 4:25, 26.

19 Grk. present, active, participle.

20 Cf. Rom. 10:12.

21 Grant Osborne helpfully comments: "Paul concludes with a note of worship that celebrates this wonderful gift of the Messiah. The question is whether this doxology affirms the deity of Christ. The key to finding an answer is the punctuation. If we place a period after Christ, the ascription centers on God rather than Christ, as in the RSV (also REB, TEV), 'of their race, according to the flesh, is the Christ. God who is over all be blessed forever. Amen.' If we place a comma there, it affirms the deity of Christ, as in the NIV (also KJV, NASV, ESV, NLT, LEB, NET), 'the human ancestry of the Messiah, who is God overall, forever praised! Amen.' Doxologies tend to be connected to their preceding context, and if God the Father was the object of worship here, one would expect that to be indicated in the context. It is Christ who is foremost in 9:1-5, so he is the object of worship in this doxology. Most of those who opt for the first reading also say that Paul does not call Jesus God in his writings, yet he does so clearly in Titus 2:13; Philippians 2:6; and Colossians 1:15. Here, too, he is praising Jesus as God. The greatest gift of all is that God himself should become incarnate in Jesus and become the suffering servant who gives his life for the salvation of sinners (Phil 2:6-8). He is supreme 'overall,' meaning cosmic Lordship over all creation (Col 1:15-18). As God, he is sovereign Lord over the universe, the history of this world, and all beings, good and evil, that inhabit his creation. This is the one Paul's kindred, the Jews, are rejecting. He is not only Messiah but also God himself, and so the Jewish people refuse to believe in their God, their creator. The 'Amen' is a formal closing affirmation to the validity of such worship (as in 1:25; 11:36; 15:33, 16:27)." Osborne, p. 278.

Leon Morris also helpfully comments: "The view that the passage refers to Christ is supported by a number of considerations. (1) The word order favors it: 'of whom is the Christ as far as flesh is concerned, who is over all, God blessed forever.' To understand it as 'God, who is over all...' is to do violence to the word order; the relative pronoun does not precede the noun to which it refers (CF. 2 Cor. 11: 31, a passage similar to this and where there can be no doubt that 'who is' refers to a proceeding noun). (2) A doxology begins 'Blessed be...' whereas here 'God' precedes 'blessed'. (3) A joyful doxology is out of place. Why should Paul bless God that Christ was born a Jew in a passage where he is expressing his grief over the Jewish rejection of Jesus? To take the words to refer to Christ is understandable; Paul speaks of him as being of the Jewish nation according to the flesh and goes on to bring out his greatness. (4) The reference to Christ 'according to the flesh' looks for an antithesis. It would be very unexpected to have this as all that is said of him. (5) To have the doxology applied to God requires a very abrupt change of subject. (6) The early church Fathers, including many whose native language was Greek, usually take the words to refer to Christ." Morris, p. 350.

22 Cf. Rom. 1:3, 4.

23 As Paul lists this final, grand privilege, he could not help but say: so be it!

privilege of the Christ, who, as Paul says, came "according to the flesh,"[24] who is "over all, the eternally blessed God."[25]

This fact is heartbreaking, but it is true nonetheless. Consequently, the apostle John says that our Lord "came to His own, and His own did not receive Him" (John 1:11). Thank God, though, that this is not the whole story for all Jewish people. The Apostle John himself was a Jew who received Jesus as Lord and Savior as did many other Jews before and after him.[26] However, in general, the nation as a whole has not received our Lord whom God sent to be their Redeemer from sin (Matt. 1:21). Even though Christ presented Himself to them in this way (John 3:16-18; 4:13, 14; 5:24, 39, 40; 8:24; 10:9-11; 14:6) and Paul preached Him from the Scriptures, in their synagogues, as their Savior (Acts 17:1-3), their response to Christ was not warm. It was not welcoming, just as the Old Testament predicted (Isa. 53:1; Ps. 118:22; Rom. 9:33).

So, the question to be answered is: was all of this because God's Word to them failed? Was it because somehow the gospel was not "the power of God to salvation for everyone who believes" (1:16)? This is the topic that Paul will take up in verse 6 of this chapter, which we will consider subsequently.

Suggested applications from the text for the church:

1- There is to be absolutely no anti-Semitism in us, but rather a sincere love for Jewish people as Paul had.

2- There is not to be a cold heart concerning the lost, but rather a passionate heart and plan of action to see them saved through the work of evangelism.

3- There is not to be any ingratitude in us toward God for all the glorious gospel privileges which He has given to us, but rather a sincere thankfulness and praise.

Suggested application from the text for the non-Christian:

1- There is to be in you a deep appreciation for, and an obedient listening to, every gospel minister and Christian who, like Paul, desperately desires your salvation.

Text: Romans 9:6-13

General theme: Two Israels with Two Scriptural Examples

Homiletical outline of the verses:

A. Paul's enlightening statement and his first scriptural example:
[6] But it is not that the word of God has taken no effect. For they *are* not all Israel who *are* of Israel, [7] nor *are they* all children because they are

---

24 This is why we are told in the Gospels that Jesus ate (Luke 24:43), slept (Mark 4:38), and wept (John 11:35). See also: Luke 24:39; 1 John 4:3. Further, there is a helpful statement in this regard in the London Baptist Confession of Faith of 1689, in chapter 8, paragraphs 2-5.

25 Cf. John 1:1.

26 Cf. Acts 2:41; 4:1-4; 21:20.

the seed of Abraham; but, "In Isaac your seed shall be called." [8] That is, those who *are* the children of the flesh, these *are* not the children of God; but the children of the promise are counted as the seed. [9] For this *is* the word of promise: "At this time I will come and Sarah shall have a son."

B. Paul's expanding statement and his second scriptural example: [10] And not only *this*, but when Rebecca also had conceived by one man, *even* by our father Isaac [11] (for *the children* not yet being born, nor having done any good or evil, that the purpose of God according to election might stand, not of works but of Him who calls), [12] it was said to her, "The older shall serve the younger." [13] As it is written, "Jacob I have loved, but Esau I have hated."

Summary of section: In these verses, Paul still has the topic of salvation on his mind, given what he just said at the beginning of this chapter. Here he is thinking about what this topic has to do with the overall rejection of Jesus by the Jews. In other words, could it be that God's gospel toward Israel has been unsuccessful? Paul answers negatively. He says this is emphatically not the case, for as Douglas Moo rightly says, "God's word never promised salvation to all the biological descendants of Abraham (9:6b-13)." He writes, "Salvation is never a birthright, even for Jews, but always a gift of God's electing love (vv. 14-23), a gift he is free to bestow on Gentiles as well as Jews (vv. 24-29)."[27]

Exegetical & Practical Insights:

Obs. 1- (vv. 6-9) That as Paul begins to unpack and reinforce the aforementioned matter, he writes:

But it is not that the word of God, i.e., God's redemptive promises to bless Israel through Christ or more specifically, the gospel itself;[28] **has taken no effect**[29] or has ever fallen away from its intended saving purposes towards the Jews. **For** the explanatory conjunction telling us why this is so; **they** *are* not all Israel (i.e., spiritual/elect Israel); **who** *are* of Israel (i.e., Hebrew/ethnic Israel);[30] nor *are they* all children, that is to say, children of God, redeemed, saved, born-again individuals as Paul says in the next verse; **because** or on account of the fact that; **they are the seed of Abraham** or his offspring, for "if Abraham's faith be not in your hearts, it will be no advantage that Abraham's blood runs through

---

27 Moo, NICNT, p. 554.

28 Ibid., p. 572.

29 Grk. perfect, active, verb.

30 Paul's words here make it abundantly plain that, according to Scripture, there is not *one* Israel, but *two*. Additionally, it should be noted that there are not *two peoples of God*, but rather there is *one*. These individuals come from both Jewish and Gentile backgrounds. They are only those who have put their faith in Jesus Christ our Lord as Savior. Consequently, they are His followers, are part of the church, and are of Abraham's true, spiritual, believing seed (Acts 3:23; Gal. 3:26-29). It should also be noted that with the distinction which Paul makes here between the "two Israels," he (as the first end of a bookend) puts forth who in fact "all Israel" are who "will be saved" (11:26).

your veins;"[31] **but,**[32] or in sharp contrast to this; **"In Isaac your seed shall be called"** a quote from Genesis 21:12, where God says to Abraham that he intended to call his offspring not through Ishmael (whom he had with Hagar the Egyptian), but rather, through Isaac only (whom he had with Sarah).

This fact shows not only God's sovereignty in choosing Isaac (who represented all of spiritual/elect Israel) over Ishmael (who represented Hebrew/Ethnic Israel), but it establishes the fact that God draws distinctions between individuals right from the early pages of Scripture. In this Genesis 21 quote, God emphasizes divine election as a foundational principle of His dealings with people on the earth, even among His Jewish people.[33]

Thielman states the matter well:

> After tension arose between Hagar and Sarah over their sons by Abraham, God told Abraham he intended to "call" Abraham's offspring through Isaac rather than Ishmael. Paul probably saw significance in the use of the word to refer to God's choice of one child over another: God "calls" his people into existence elsewhere in Romans (8:30; cf. 1:6; 4:17; 8:28; 9:24), and he called a special people into existence from among Abraham's offspring. God's free decision, then, defines the identity of his people, not merely their physical relationship to the right patriarch.[34]

This matter of Abraham's natural descendants not *automatically* being the children of God is asserted in many places in the Bible. For example, John the Baptist spoke of it concerning the Jewish religious leaders of his day. Matthew 3:4-9 tells us:

> Now John himself was clothed in camel's hair, with a leather belt around his waist; and his food was locusts and wild honey. Then Jerusalem, all Judea, and all the region around the Jordan went out to him and were baptized by him in the Jordan, confessing their sins. But when he saw many of the Pharisees and Sadducees coming to his baptism, he said to them, "Brood of vipers! Who warned you to flee from the wrath to come? Therefore bear fruits worthy of repentance, and do not think to say to yourselves, 'We have Abraham as *our* father.' For I say to you that God is able to raise up children to Abraham from these stones.

In this interaction with the Jewish leadership, John went after the very thing that they would do: lean on their ancestry with Abraham as their acceptance with God, especially since many of them viewed Abraham as the gatekeeper to heaven. John said to them that this would not cut it! This is why, along with calling his people to repentance, he said that they should "believe on Him who would come after him, that is, on

---

31 The Puritan John Flavel, as quoted by Wilson, p. 160.

32 The strong Greek adversative.

33 Paul has already made this distinction between a true Jew and who is not in Romans 2:28-29.

34 Thielman, p. 450.

Christ Jesus" (Acts 19:4). Because John understood that salvation was not by *physical procreation*, but rather *spiritual regeneration*, he spoke to his brethren after the flesh in this way.

Our Lord Himself spoke similarly to the Jews in John 8:37-47:

> "I know that you are Abraham's descendants, but you seek to kill Me, because My word has no place in you. I speak what I have seen with My Father, and you do what you have seen with your father." They answered and said to Him, "Abraham is our father." Jesus said to them, "If you were Abraham's children, you would do the works of Abraham. But now you seek to kill Me, a Man who has told you the truth which I heard from God. Abraham did not do this. You do the deeds of your father." Then they said to Him, "We were not born of fornication; we have one Father—God." Jesus said to them, "If God were your Father, you would love Me, for I proceeded forth and came from God; nor have I come of Myself, but He sent Me. Why do you not understand My speech? Because you are not able to listen to My word. You are of *your* father the devil, and the desires of your father you want to do. He was a murderer from the beginning, and does not stand in the truth, because there is no truth in him. When he speaks a lie, he speaks from his own *resources,* for he is a liar and the father of it. But because I tell the truth, you do not believe Me. Which of you convicts Me of sin? And if I tell the truth, why do you not believe Me? He who is of God hears God's words; therefore you do not hear, because you are not of God."

As the apostle continues to open up all that he has just been speaking about, he writes next saying:

That is, those who *are* the children of the flesh, i.e., Abraham's natural, earthly descendants;[35] **these** *are* not the children of God, i.e., saved individuals who are on their way to heaven; **but**[36] or on the contrary; **the children of the promise,**[37] that is, the children to whom the salvific promises of God belong through Jesus; **are counted** or reckoned; **as the seed,** that is, God's true, messiah-believing children as Isaac was (thus, Paul says to the church in Galatians 4:28 "Now we, brethren, as Isaac *was,* are children of promise"). **For** the conjunction explaining what the heart of the promise was to Abraham concerning Isaac as stated in Genesis 18:10, 14; **this** *is* the word of promise: **"At this time** (when you and your wife are both past childbearing years); **I** (God) **will come** (by a supernatural, sovereign miracle); **and Sarah shall have a son"** (which was what the promise was all about).

Henry Mahan helpfully notes:

> The birth of Isaac was by promise; without a miracle, it would never have taken place. The birth of Ishmael was not by promise but in the ordinary course of nature. Ishmael is a type of those who are born after the flesh

---

35 Cf. 1 Cor. 10:18.

36 The strong Greek adversative.

37 Cf. Rom. 4:16, Gal. 3:14, 29.

and are carnal men. Isaac is a type of those who are born of the Spirit and are the children of God (John 3:5-7; Gal. 4:28; Phil. 3:3).[38]

Hendriksen adds further:

> God's people are here called "the children of promise," a strikingly beautiful designation! Their spiritual birth was due not to anything residing in them but entirely to God's covenant promise. It was the promise that gave them birth! They "were born not of blood nor of the will of the flesh nor of the will of man, but of God" (John 1:13), a fact exemplified clearly in the story of the birth of Isaac, to which reference is made in verse 9."[39]

Obs. 2- (vv. 10-13) That as the apostle gives yet another proof that the Word of God has not failed concerning Israel (and makes the point of sovereign election even plainer), he now moves down one generation to develop his distinction further between *spiritual Israel* and *natural Israel* and writes:

And not only *this,* i.e., as the case was with Sarah; **but when Rebecca also had conceived by one man,** *even* by our father Isaac Paul now writes parenthetically and says: **(for *the children,*** i.e., Jacob and Esau; **not yet being born,**[40] a matter which is mentioned "to show God's free election;"[41] **nor having done any good or evil** (and so God's choice was not based on one child being "better" than the other); **that** or in order that; **the purpose** or the eternal plan and intention; **of God** (concerning the two brothers); **according to election,**[42] that is, according to God's divine prerogative to choose or select a remnant of fallen humanity (both of Jews and Greeks), whom He in history actually saves, according to "the good pleasure of His will, to the praise of the glory of His grace;"[43] **might stand,**[44] or continue to remain as "an abiding condition;"[45] **not of works**[46] or of human effort which we do "actual or foreseen"[47] or anything that we could ever attempt to merit God's favor;[48] **but**[49] or in sharp contrast to this; **of Him** that is, God; **who calls,**[50] i.e., sovereignly and savingly calls to Himself; **it was said to her** (Rebecca); **"The older** (Esau, "who first came

---

38 Mahan, p. 68.

39 Hendriksen, p. 318.

40 Cf. 2 Thess. 2:13.

41 Robinson, Book II, p. 20.

42 This is the first time Paul uses this term in this letter.

43 Cf. Eph. 1:5, 6.

44 Grk. present, active, verb.

45 Vaughan and Corley, p. 105.

46 Cf. Eph. 2:9; Titus 3:5.

47 Robinson, Book II, p. 21.

48 Cf. Rom. 3:20.

49 The strong Greek adversative.

50 This language of "not of works but of God who calls" shows us, in fact, that the topic of salvation is at hand as Paul has used these terms all throughout this epistle in the same way: 1:6; 3:20, 27, 28; 4:2-6; 8:28, 29.

out of the womb");[51] **shall serve** or be in subjection to, which involved the "transfer of the birthright and of the parental blessing;"[52] **the younger** (Jacob, "who thus had no claim to superiority")."[53] **As it is written**[54] or just as it stands written in Malachi 1:1-3 proving the aforementioned point (the use of the Greek perfect tense verb "emphasizing the lasting and binding authority of that which was written");[55] **Jacob I have loved,** i.e., loved with saving and special favor; **but Esau I have hated,**[56] not hated as unsaved people do in the world, with an emotional, vindictive, out-of-control kind of hatred which is condemned in Scripture, for "it would be blasphemy to predicate [or assert] the same of God."[57] But, it is a hatred which caused Esau to be "rejected" by God as Calvin says.[58]

Paul establishes here once again the point that although the nation of Israel on the whole had rejected Jesus, God nonetheless still had an elect remnant among them whom He had chosen to be saved. He had a people who would come to faith in Christ in due time. These people were marked out for such an end, even from "before the foundation of the world,"[59] so that "the purpose of God according to election might stand not of works but of Him who calls."

In speaking about this second scriptural example of God's sovereignty in salvation, from Genesis, Johnson remarks:

> There is no problem of complex parentage now [as the case was in the previous example with Abraham, Sarah, and Hagar], for Rebecca was the mother of twins by one man (in the Greek text the emphasis rests on the fact that the two sons came from one man). Yet the destiny of the two was to be infinitely different, for Jacob was loved but Esau was hated. The story on which the apostle builds his teaching is found in Genesis 25:19-26, where the birth of these twins is recorded. God had

---

51 Robinson, Book II, p. 22.

52 Ibid.

53 Ibid., p. 23.

54 Grk. perfect, passive verb.

55 Rogers and Rogers, p. 333.

56 Some people ask, "Why would God hate anyone?" However, in view of all that Paul has already taught in this epistle, I ask, "Why would He love anyone seeing that we are all fallen in Adam by nature and rebels against Him by practice?

57 Murray, p. 22.

58 Calvin, p. 352. Schreiner asks about our passage, "Does the text suggest double predestination?" He answers, "Apparently it does" (Schreiner, p. 501). I agree with him. Double predestination refers to the twin doctrines of election and reprobation, and considers them both to be aspects of God's eternal decree. Reprobation, as the London Baptist Confession of Faith of 1689 says, is the teaching that by God's decree, some of His fallen in Adam, hell-deserving, rebellious creatures are "left to live in their sin, leading to their just condemnation, to the praise of His glorious justice." This is a difficult doctrine for some to swallow, but it is true nonetheless. Paul anticipates opposition to this doctrine in the following verse when he writes, "What shall we say then? Is there unrighteousness with God (that Jacob should receive blessing and Esau judgment, cf. verse 19 also)?" The apostle answers: Certainly not! Other passages which speak about the doctrine of reprobation are Prov. 16:4; John 13:18, 19; 17:12; Matt. 11:20-27; Rom. 9:17, 18, 21, 22; 1 Thess. 5:9; 1 Peter 2:6-8; Jude 4.

59 Cf. Eph. 1:3-4.

promised Isaac that he should have a seed, but Rebecca was barren (cf. v. 21). So the patriarch entreated the Lord for his wife, which illustrates aptly that divine predestination is not contrary to earnest supplication, that the patriarch was being taught patience, and that God accomplishes the fulfillment of his promises in his own way, not in ours.

The Lord answered the prayer, and Rebecca was pregnant with twins. As they struggled within her womb, she, troubled by the meaning of it all, went to ask the Lord about it. She received this prophetic word: "Two nations are in your womb, and two peoples from within you will be separated; one people will be stronger than the other, and the older will serve the younger" (Gen. 25:23). History makes it plain that the prophecy is one that covers the history of the descendants of Jacob and Esau, but as the final clause makes clear, it also refers specifically to the destiny of two individuals, Jacob and Esau. Contrary to ancient Eastern customs, the elder son will serve the younger.

The important words for Paul in Romans 9 are the last ones of the prophecy, "The older will serve the younger" (v.12). It is from them that Paul reasons to his conclusion. The blessing of the unborn Jacob and the preferring of him to Esau, before they had an opportunity to do anything good or evil, teaches the doctrine of sovereign distinguishing grace and election. He points out that the children were not yet born when the choice was made. Further, they had not done any works. Thus, the election of Jacob was according to the divine purpose, and it was not based on works but on the will of the one calling, that is God. Furthermore, the choice involved individuals, not simply nations.[60]

Wilson further elaborates:

> It cannot be denied that in this quotation from Malachi 1:2-3 the prophet has in view the nations of Israel and Edom, but it must not be assumed that their respective destinies can be considered in isolation from the difference which God first made between their respective heads. As the election of Jacob is the proof of God's love, so the rejection of Esau is the evidence of God's hatred. The two aorists [the tense of the verbs "hated" and "loved" which point to past, one time actions] look back to the acts which caused these twins to differ. Both were hateful on account of Adam's sin, so that it is in fact easier to explain God's hatred of Esau than his love for Jacob. For as Warfield well says, 'When all deserve death it is a marvel of pure grace that any receive life; and who shall gainsay the right of him who shows his marvelous mercy, to have mercy on whom he will, and whom he will to harden?' Certainly Jacob deserved this mercy no more than Esau. But God sovereignly chose Jacob in Christ, whereas he just as sovereignly passed by Esau. Hence God hated Esau for no other reason but his sin—for God hates nothing but sin—and his holy hatred of sin may not be defined in terms of a loving less, as some commentators try to do. 'Nothing, then, is said of Esau here that might not be said of every man who shall finally perish' (Haldane).[61]

---

60 Johnson, pp. 153, 154.

61 Wilson, pp. 162, 163.

It is unfortunate that some Christians balk at the biblical doctrine of election. Perhaps this is the case because our Western culture has such a high view of democracy where *we elect* our governing officials, both in the government and often those in the church. We have much freedom in this regard in choosing whom we want, for what we want. Thus, the notion that *God alone decides* whom He wants to choose for salvation (apart from our initial choosing of Him) is loathsome to some.

To think that by His sovereign decree, for the demonstration of His glory, God predestined some human beings to eternal life through Jesus Christ, "to the praise of His glorious grace," and that others are "left to live in their sin, leading to their just condemnation to the praise of His glorious justice,"[62] is just cutting things too close for some. It grates against their democratic sensibilities.

Perhaps the late Dr. James Kennedy got it right when he wrote in his book entitled *Truths that Transform*:

> The reason people today are opposed to it is because they will have God to be anything but God. He can be a cosmic psychiatrist, a helpful Shepherd, a leader, a teacher, anything at all ... only not God.[63]

These words are arresting, and they get to the heart of the issue, which should cause us to ask ourselves "Are we willing to let God be God?" This is what Paul is highlighting in our passage when he illustrates "God's absolute freedom in salvation by pointing to his discriminating choice between Jacob and Esau."[64] Paul here speaks about God's *un*-conditional election of individuals before they are born and apart from anything they will ever do.[65]

Johnson states the matter correctly:

> We may sum it up by saying that, first, the sovereignty of the divine choice is taught in the choice of Jacob (v.11). Second, the particularity of the choice is taught in the preferring of Jacob to Esau (vv.12-13). This prenatal love of God for Jacob raises, of course, the doctrine of election and the basis on which God makes his selection. There are no other alternatives, since God does not choose on the basis of moral qualities. The ultimate choice is that of God, who freely chooses. God is not simply a ratifier of man's fundamental choice.
>
> In addition, if God looked down through the years of time and saw who would believe, he would have gained in knowledge. Thus, before that time, he would not have been omniscient. Instead, God elects those whom he has purposed to save through faith in Jesus Christ. Is the reason

---

62 London Baptist Confession of Faith of 1689, in chapter 3, paragraph 3.

63 As quoted in Michael Horton's book, *Putting Amazing Back into Grace: An Introduction to Reformed Theology*, p. 43.

64 John MacArthur and Richard Mayhue, *Biblical Doctrine: A Systematic Summary of Bible Truth*, p. 493.

65 Spurgeon said it well: "I believe the doctrine of election, because I am quite sure that if God had not chosen me I would never have chosen him; and I am sure he chose me before I was born, or else he never would have chosen me afterward." John Blanchard, *The Complete Gathered Gold* (Darlington, England: Evangelical Press, 2006), 165.

in man or in God? The Bible teaches that election is not grounded in man's will (cf. Rom. 9:16), nor in human works (cf. 2 Tim. 1:9), nor in human choice (Eph. 1:4). It is grounded in the divine good pleasure of his will (Eph. 1:5, 11; 2 Tim. 1:9). Faith is the effect, not the ground or basis of election (John 6:44; Rom. 8:7-8).[66]

So, does all this mean that the ungodly do not need to believe on Christ to be saved, or that we do not need to evangelize the lost because God has already ordained who will be saved and who will not be saved? Does it mean there are people who really want to be saved but God refuses them? The answer to these three questions is an emphatic *no*. Consequently, Paul says in Romans 10:13-15:

> ... whoever calls on the name of the LORD shall be saved. How then shall they call on Him in whom they have not believed? And how shall they believe in Him of whom they have not heard? And how shall they hear without a preacher? And how shall they preach unless they are sent? As it is written:
>> "How beautiful are the feet of those who preach the gospel of peace,
>> Who bring glad tidings of good things."

It is clear then, that biblically speaking, the doctrine of sovereign election is no hindrance to unbelievers coming to Christ for life and salvation, nor is it a hindrance to the preaching of the gospel. The concern of unbelievers is not to be whether they are elect or not, but rather that God in grace and love has provided a glorious Savior for sinners, even Jesus Christ the Lord. If they break with their sins and self-righteousness and seek Him by faith, they will be saved (Rom. 9:30-32).

Concerning evangelism, election does not kill this desire either. Rather, rightly understood, it fuels it.[67] If we truly believe that God has a people whom He has marked out from all eternity to be saved and that these people will hear Jesus' voice and follow Him through the preaching of the gospel (John 10:27), it should cause us to go to the lost with great zeal. It should cause us to say with Paul in 2 Timothy 2:10, "Therefore I endure all things for the sake of the elect that they also may obtain the salvation which is in Christ Jesus."

Suggested applications from the text for the church:

1- The doctrine of God's sovereign choice of us is to produce in us great humility, knowing that there was nothing in us, or accomplished by us, that caused Him to select us to be His own in Christ.

2- The doctrine of God's sovereign choice of us is to produce in us a growing holiness (a hatred for all known sin and a desire to be morally

---

66 Johnson, p. 154.

67 This is clearly seen historically speaking. Consequently, the biblical evangelists throughout church history were Calvinistic. This list would include Luther, Calvin, the Puritans, George Whitefield, Jonathan Edwards, Spurgeon, Lloyd-Jones etc. Also, the doctrine of sovereign election helps to banish the fear of engaging in evangelism. This is because we do not need to be concerned about eloquence or our presentation in presenting the gospel as that which wins souls, since salvation is of the Lord.

pure in His sight according to His Word), even as He Himself is holy, knowing that this is a great end of our election (Eph. 1:4).

3- The doctrine of God's sovereign choice of us is to produce in us great praise to His Name for His unfathomable grace in not leaving us to perish in our sins but rather, to know Him savingly, through His Son, by the power of the gospel.

Suggested application from the text for the non-Christian:

1- The doctrine of God's sovereign choice of sinners should remind you that while salvation ultimately rests in His hands, you are nonetheless a responsible moral agent who is accountable to go to Christ for the forgiveness of your sins. If you do this, He will save and forgive you (John 6:37). If you do not, in the final analysis, your damnation will be your own election (cf. Rom. 9:30-32).

Text: Romans 9:14-29

General theme: The Potter's Freedom[68]

Homiletical outline of the verses:[69]

A. Paul's ending statement and his third scriptural example [14] What shall we say then? *Is there* unrighteousness with God? Certainly not! [15] For He says to Moses, "I will have mercy on whomever I will have mercy, and I will have compassion on whomever I will have compassion." [16] So then *it is* not of him who wills, nor of him who runs, but of God who shows mercy. [17] For the Scripture says to the Pharaoh, "For this very purpose I have raised you up, that I may show My power in you, and that My name may be declared in all the earth." [18] Therefore He has mercy on whom He wills, and whom He wills He hardens.

[19] You will say to me then, "Why does He still find fault? For who has resisted His will?" [20] But indeed, O man, who are you to reply against God? Will the thing formed say to him who formed *it*, "Why have you made me like this?" [21] Does not the potter have power over the clay, from the same lump to make one vessel for honor and another for dishonor?

[22] *What* if God, wanting to show *His* wrath and to make His power known, endured with much longsuffering the vessels of wrath prepared for destruction, [23] and that He might make known the riches of His glory on the vessels of mercy, which He had prepared beforehand for glory, [24] even us whom He called, not of the Jews only, but also of the Gentiles?

[25] As He says also in Hosea:
"I will call them My people, who were not My people,
And her beloved, who was not beloved."
[26] "And it shall come to pass in the place where it was said to them,
'You *are* not My people,'

---

68 James White's book with this title is helpful.

69 When I preached on these verses, I outlined them like this: the protest v. 14; the pronouncements vv. 15, 16; the Pharaoh vv. 17, 18; the pushback vv. 19, 20; the Potter vv. 21-24; the passages vv. 25-29.

There they shall be called sons of the living God."
[27] Isaiah also cries out concerning Israel:
"Though the number of the children of Israel be as the sand of the sea,
The remnant will be saved.
[28] For He will finish the work and cut *it* short in righteousness,
Because the LORD will make a short work upon the earth."
[29] And as Isaiah said before:
"Unless the LORD of Sabaoth had left us a seed,
We would have become like Sodom,
And we would have been made like Gomorrah."

Summary of section: In these verses, the apostle deals with the accusation that God's choice to elect some to salvation and not others is unfair. Given all that he has written in the previous verses, he now anticipates this opposition and addresses it. His response essentially boils down to the question: "Is it not lawful for God to do what He wants with His own?" (cf. Matt. 20:15). Since He is the supreme King over all, what could be wrong with Him allowing some sinners who deserve nothing but His judgment, to experience His mercy, and yet others who do not deserve His mercy to experience His justice? The answer is nothing at all. As Dan Doriani says, "Is election unjust? No, for humans stand before God in sin, not in neutrality."[70]

Since none deserve God's mercy, surely, if He decides to pity a number of those hell-deserving sinners, then this is nothing but pure grace, amazing grace. How sweet the sound!

MacArthur summarizes nicely:

> The question behind this paragraph is a question of God's fairness. If He only chose some to be the heirs of promise, and not others, people will say He is unfair. Paul had just reminded his Jewish readers that God sovereignly chose Isaac above Ishmael and Jacob above his twin brother Esau before they were born (Rom. 9:16-13). They were not chosen or rejected because of who they were or would be or because of what they had done or would do, "but of Him who calls" (v. 11), that is, wholly on the basis of God's sovereign will. Isaac and Jacob were "the children of the promise" (v. 8); Ishmael and Esau were not. So, in the sense of spiritual salvation, God has chosen some to believe.
>
> The natural human response is to assert that God was unjustly arbitrary in choosing one over the other long before they would have opportunity to trust or reject Him or to be obedient or disobedient. That natural response, however, is tantamount to saying that there is injustice with God. So Paul asks rhetorically if we have a right to accuse God of being unjust.
>
> That accusation has been raised throughout the history of the church and is still heard today when God's election and predestination are proclaimed. How can God elect one person and reject another before they are even born? In light of human wisdom and standards especially in democratic societies, where all people are considered equal before the law,

---

70 Doriani, p. 11.

the ideas of election and predestination are repulsive and unacceptable. Those doctrines, it is claimed, could not possibly characterize a God who is truly just and righteous. To the saved but ignorant and immature mind, God simply could not do such a thing, and to the unsaved mind, a god like that would not be worthy of recognition, much less worship.

... Because all men are sinful and deserve God's condemnation, no person is wronged or treated unjustly if God chooses to condemn him. That is justice. His mercy toward any person is purely by His grace.[71]

Exegetical & Practical Insights:

Obs. 1- (v. 14) That as Paul begins to answer a popular protest concerning God's sovereignty in salvation, he writes:

What shall we say then?[72] *Is there* unrighteousness or unfairness and wrongdoing; **with God** (in Him choosing Isaac over Ishmael and Jacob over Esau)? **Certainly not** or perish the thought! Again, how could there be? There cannot, since when God made His choice of certain ones for salvation (and not others), He viewed them all with His omniscient mind as already god*less* and *guilty* in His sight. Since He owes none of us anything but to damn us for all eternity because of our wayward lives, if some, who were already considered fallen in Adam and lost in themselves are judged for this, there is no unrighteousness with God. He is free to do whatever He decides to do with His unruly creation.[73] As McDonald notes:

> All people are condemned by their own sin and unbelief. If left to themselves, they would *all* perish. In addition to extending the general gospel invitation to all people, God chooses some of those condemned people to be special objects of His grace. But this does not mean that He arbitrarily chooses the others to be condemned. They are already condemned because they are lifelong sinners and have rejected the gospel. Those who are chosen can thank God for His grace. Those who are lost have no one to blame but themselves.[74]

Obs. 2- (vv. 15-16) That as Paul explains why God, the Ruler of all, is not unrighteous in His dealing concerning His sovereignty over humanity, he quotes God Himself saying, **For He** (God) **says to Moses,**

---

71 MacArthur, pp. 30, 32.

72 Paul asks this question typically when he summaries his instruction, cf. 3:9; 4:1; 6:1; 8:31. 9:30.

73 These statements about God choosing some (and not others) for salvation whom He viewed as already created and fallen in Adam is historically known as *Infralapsarianism.* This is the position that is held by all of the historic Reformed Confessions and Creeds. This perspective seems to me to make the best sense especially in this context, for how else would God exercise "mercy and compassion on whomever He wills" (v. 15) if people did not need such things? If such individuals were not already considered fallen and condemned in Adam, what need would there be for any grace to be expressed towards them? A different position is known as *Supralapsarianism.* This perspective teaches that God's choice of some to salvation logically preceded His decree to create mankind and to permit the fall. In other words, that God viewed mankind as *un*fallen in His decree of election.

74 McDonald, 1718.

(in Exodus 33:19); **"I will have mercy** or pity; **on whomever I will have mercy, and I will have compassion** or sympathy; **on whomever I will have compassion."**

It is crucial to understand the context in which this quote from Exodus 33 appears because it follows on the heels of the golden calf incident in the previous chapter. In Exodus 32, the Old Covenant Community had grievously sinned against the Lord through their idolatry.

They broke the First and Second commandments given back in Exodus 20. Because of this, God's just wrath was burning hot against them and He was ready to consume them (Ex. 32:10). All the people justly deserved this, as they all partook of this sin (Ex. 32:3). However, in grace and mercy we are told that only "three thousand men of the people fell that day" (Ex. 32:28). Only a small fraction of the entire nation, generally estimated to be around one million individuals, died for their corporate rebellion against the Lord.

Then in Exodus 33, as God was revealing something about Himself and His sovereign dealings with men to Moses while they fellowshipped together "as a man speaks to his friend" (Ex. 33:11), God said, "I will be gracious to whom I will be gracious, and I will have compassion on whom I will have compassion."

This is the passage that Paul quotes in Romans 9 as he affirms from Scripture the matter of God's distinguishing grace among disobedient individuals. Even though all people in the world rightly deserve His just judgment (as the case was with the rebellious Israelites in Moses' day), God did not cause all of them to experience this. Instead, in grace, He decided to have mercy on some who did not deserve this at all. This was God's sovereign prerogative, and no one could justly fault Him for it.

As Paul speaks to this matter summarily, he writes saying next in verse 16,

So then[75] a double conjunction in the Greek text emphasizing a clear conclusion and summary to what has just been said; *it is* not of him who wills[76] or is willing; **nor of him who runs**[77] or is running; **but**[78] or in sharp contrast to this; **of God who shows mercy.**

Paul is teaching in these words that our election by God is not that which is determined or conditioned by our choice or effort. Rather, it is determined by God's unconditional, sovereign good pleasure to show mercy and compassion on whom He wills.[79]

Obs. 3- **(vv. 17-18)** That as Paul continues to unpack the doctrine of God's sovereignty among men, he shows next that not only is His sovereignty seen in Him showing mercy to some, but it is also seen in Him hardening others, as the case was with Pharaoh. He writes:

---

75 The Greek words *ara ouv*.

76 Grk. present, active, participle.

77 Grk. present, active, participle.

78 The strong Greek adversative.

79 The Puritan Bible commentator Matthew Poole said that "This text wounds Pelagianism under the fifth rib," as quoted in Wilson, p. 164.

For the Scripture says to the Pharaoh, that is, it says to him in Exodus 9:16;[80] **For this very purpose** or reason; **I** (God); **have raised you up** i.e., raised you up to your office as king; **that** or for the purpose that; **I may show** or demonstrate and make known; **My power** that is, "His divine power;"[81] **in** or perhaps better translated "through" **you;"[82] and that** or for the purpose that; **My name may be declared** or proclaimed; **in all the earth. Therefore**[83] Paul summarizes his teaching again (cf. v.16); **He** (God) **has mercy on whom He wills** or chooses; **and whom He wills** or chooses; **He hardens** (or removes His restraining influences upon them, leaving them in their native hardness towards Himself so that they continue to remain "resistant to his warnings and reject his gracious overtures").[84]

These words have troubled some readers of Romans. They wonder, "Why would God harden anyone?" This is an honest question, but we must remember that it is one that must be answered in light of God being able to do what He wants to do with His own disobedient creatures.[85] If He chooses to save some of them then, as was stated earlier, that is His sovereign choice. And if He chooses in His judicial sentence to further harden others (much like Paul tells us that God did regarding certain sinners in "giving them up" to their sins in chapter one of this book), in order to accomplish His own purposes in the earth, then that is His sovereign prerogative as well.

In this passage, Paul shows us God's twofold purpose in hardening the godless Pharaoh. First, he says that it was done so that God may demonstrate His great power in him. This was seen, for example, in God exercising His divine strength over the earthly king and his false gods through the plagues that He sent, which forced Pharaoh to let the Israelites go. The second purpose for God's hardening disobedient Pharaoh was so that God's great name would be proclaimed throughout all the earth. This was seen because many of the surrounding peoples "heard of God's fame and all that He did in Egypt" (Josh. 9:9).

Sproul has a lengthy but helpful comment about these verses. He writes:

> Paul is saying that the purpose of God in elevating Pharaoh to his position of power was not to reward Pharaoh's righteousness, or because he merited his prestigious position. Rather, God put him in that position for God's purposes. Here we have an insight into God's providential rule as the Lord of all of history. He raises kingdoms up, he brings kingdoms

---

80 Kruse is insightful when he says, "It is noteworthy that Paul here equates what Scripture says with what God said." Kruse, p. 382.

81 Herman Hoeksema on Romans, p. 412.

82 Moo, p. 595.

83 The Greek words *ara oun.*

84 Peterson, p. 359. This hardening effect of God on some is another form of His reprobation, cf. v. 13, 22.

85 The London Baptist Confession of Faith, chapter 5, paragraph 6, speaks about God sometimes hardening wicked and ungodly people.

down. Pharaoh could not have become the most powerful man in the world, apart from the providential rule of God. And the purpose of God in establishing Pharaoh was to show God's power. Pharaoh was the most powerful man in the world at that time, but when his power was brought to bear against the power of God, Pharaoh appeared impotent, and God's manifestation of his own authority reigned supreme.

God was using an evil man to bring about his good purposes and redemptive activity. This is a common theme of the Bible ... A classic example of this is the story of Joseph. His brothers, filled with jealousy and envy, sold him into slavery. Joseph was taken down to Egypt and remarkable events transpired by which he was elevated to the level of prime minister and was set in a strategic position to bring relief and redemption to his own family at a time of crisis and famine in the promised land.

Finally, Joseph had a meeting with his brothers when they recognized him and repented of their evil deed. Joseph responded to their confession by saying, 'You meant it for evil, but God meant it for good' (Gen. 50:20). God's holy, powerful providence can make use of the wicked intentions of men to bring about the good purposes of his own plan...

Of course, the supreme example of God's control of evil is in the betrayal of Jesus by the hands of Judas. Judas was not forced, he did exactly what he wanted to do. He manifested his own treachery, his own lust for power and his own selfish motives in taking 30 pieces of silver for handing Jesus over to his enemies. But in so doing, there is a sense in which Judas did the world the greatest favor it has ever known. By means of this betrayal, Jesus was crucified, an act which, considered in terms of the intentions of Judah and the intentions of those who crucified Jesus, was an act of diabolical wickedness, yet from God's perspective was the supreme salvific event in world history. Without the cross we have no salvation. Does that mean, then, that we should go up to Judas and say, 'Congratulations Judas, thank you so much for your benevolent act on behalf of mankind; if it weren't for you we wouldn't be redeemed.' No, we should still regard Judas' actions for what they were: self-centered and wicked. Rather than showing any evil in God, this shows the overwhelming power of God to bring about his good purposes by means of wicked men.[86]

Obs. 4- (v. 19) That as Paul expects some more potential pushback concerning God hardening some so that they remain "resistant to his warnings and reject his gracious overtures" he writes, saying:

You will say to me then, Why does He (God) **still find fault** or a cause for blaming people when they continue to sin?; **For who has resisted**[87] or ever withstood; **His will** or His purpose in people's lives (even when that purpose is to leave them in their sins so that as sinners they continue to sin)?[88]

It seems clear in this question that the hypothetical objector is seeking to avoid any sense of personal guilt or responsibility before the Almighty. It is almost as if he views himself as wholly innocent and God worthy

---

86 Sproul, pp. 211-12.

87 Grk. perfect, active, verb.

88 A similar question is asked in 3:7.

of all the blame for arbitrarily hardening him against Himself. But this is not the case, for God does not randomly harden innocent people, since according to the Bible there are no innocent people (Eccles. 7:20; Rom. 3:23). No, all are guilty before Him (in Adam, cf. Romans chapter 5 and verse 12, and in themselves, as the case was with Pharaoh, cf. Romans chapters 1-3). Thus, God is just in finding fault with such people. They resisted Him from birth, they resisted Him and His truth all of their days, even "suppressing the truth in unrighteousness" (Rom. 1:18; cf. Acts 7:51).

Obs. 5- (vv. 20-21) That as Paul thinks about this objection and sees the foolishness behind the creature calling the Creator to account, and as he "rebukes the insolence [audacity] of any creature who dares to find fault with his Creator"[89] he says:

But indeed, or on the contrary; **O man,**[90] "The address, 'O man' is more than dramatic flair; it is surely a reminder of the wide chasm that separates humanity from God;"[91] **who are you**[92] **to reply against** or to criticize and answer back to; **God** (the supreme king)?[93] **Will the thing formed** (man) **say to him who formed** *it* (God), **"Why have you made me like this?"**[94] Paul is beside himself as he thinks, "How dare the creature (molded-man) call God (man's-Maker) on the carpet?" Then in vindicating God's sovereignty in all that He does among His creation, Paul illustrates the matter and says,[95] **Does not the potter** (God) **have power** or absolute right; **over the clay** (fallen humanity) **from the same lump** (that is, the same created, fallen lump in Adam)[96] **to make one vessel for honor and another for dishonor?**

What is the answer to the question that Paul poses? The answer is, of course, God does! Of course He has the authority to exercise His sovereignty over the lost in any way that He pleases. For even if He decided to damn the entire fallen lump of sinful humanity, there would be no wrongdoing in Him.

McDonald helpfully captures the essence of verse 21:

---

89 McDonald, 1718.

90 Cf. 2:1.

91 James Edwards, 240.

92 Note that in the Greek text the personal pronoun "you" is placed in the front of the sentence for the sake of emphasis.

93 Peterson is right when he says, "Paul is not condemning people who honestly seek to understand God's ways but rather those who arrogantly challenge his justice and how he orders human affairs." Peterson, p. 361.

94 A quotation from Isaiah 29:16.

95 His illustration comes most likely from Jeremiah 18:1-10.

96 Whereas in verse 11 of this chapter, Paul spoke about our election happening before we were born, this verse shows us that God's choosing of us was in view of our fallenness in Adam. B. B. Warfield says, "The body out of which believers are chosen by God's unsearchable grace is the mass of justly condemned sinners, so the destruction to which those that are passed by are left is the righteous recompense of their guilt," as quoted in Wilson, p. 167.

The potter comes into his shop one day and sees a pile of formless clay on the floor. He picks up a handful of clay, puts it on his wheel, and fashions a beautiful vessel. Does he have a right to do that? The potter, of course, is God. The clay is sinful, lost humanity. If the potter left it alone, it would all be sent to hell. He would be absolutely just and fair if He left it alone. But instead He sovereignly selects a handful of sinners, saves them by His grace, and conforms them to the image of His Son. Does He have a right to do that? Remember, He is not arbitrarily dooming others to hell. They are already doomed by their own willfulness and unbelief.[97]

Obs. 6- (vv. 22-24) That as Paul continues his pottery image, he now applies it to the two different groups that he just spoke of in verse 21. He says:

What if God, "a statement of fact in the form of a rhetorical question;"[98] **wanting** or choosing; **to show** or to demonstrate; *His* wrath[99] **and to make His power** or ability; **known, endured** or bore; **with much longsuffering** or patience; **the vessels of wrath prepared**[100] **for** or more literally, fitted into; **destruction** or ruin, and that He might make known the riches or spiritual abundance and wealth; **of His glory on the vessels of mercy,** i.e., His elect; **which He had prepared beforehand for glory,** which speaks about God predestinating some people to salvation and then heaven at last (Rom. 8:29, 30); **even us,** i.e., we whom He saves by grace; **whom He called,** that is, called effectively through the gospel; not of the Jews only, but also of the Gentiles?

The apostle addresses two matters here. The first is with reference to God's dealings with those who will experience His wrath (v. 22). Such ones are described as "vessels of wrath prepared for destruction." The question is often asked, "Who is it that prepared these individuals for destruction?"

It could be said, that in one sense, such individuals *prepared themselves* for this through their sinful lives (Rom. 1:18 cf. John 3:36); however, since the Greek passive voice is used for the word "prepared," this indicates that they were prepared for this by someone else, but who? The answer is, God (the potter who prepares the clay, cf. 9:18). The perfect tense is also used for the word "prepared," and it points to a present result of a past action. The point is: those who are vessels of God's wrath are in a state of preparedness from God as sinners to receive His wrath, from the moment they were conceived.

Even though this is the case, Paul tells us that God has patiently endured with sinners in their sinfulness with "much long-suffering" (as the case was with Pharaoh and the rest of lost humanity). God could have cut off rebellious sinners the first moment they ever sinned against Him. But, thanks be to God that He has not done that, though one day

---

97 McDonald, 1719.

98 MacArthur, *One Faithful Life* (2019), p. 303.

99 Cf. 1:18; 2:5; 2:8; 3:5; 4:15; 5:9; 12:19.

100 Grk. perfect, passive, participle.

He will![101] One day, the judge of all the earth will bring complete justice in the strictest sense, and on that day, all those who were *born in sin* and continued to *live in sin* and *died in sin* will be "turned into hell" (Ps. 9:17). Because of their hardness and impenitent heart, they have treasured up for themselves "wrath in the day of wrath and the revelation of the righteous judgment of God" (Rom. 2:5).

Secondly, and to the contrary, in choosing some for salvation who were "no better or wiser than the others or because they deserve it,"[102] He has also made known "the riches of His glory on the vessels of mercy which He had prepared beforehand for glory" (v. 23). These are tremendous words and they show us the truth of what Paul says in 1 Thessalonians 5:9 when he writes concerning Christians: "For God did not appoint us to wrath, but to obtain salvation through our Lord Jesus Christ."

This is a glorious truth which shows us who are believers, God's great, undeserved kindness toward us who were once lost sinners, but are now, magnificent trophies of His grace, and this "not of the Jews only, but also of the Gentiles" (v. 24).

In commenting on the last two verses, Luther wisely notes:

> It is not wise for the novice to meddle too much with divine purposes and mysteries. Nothing has greater tendency to confound the understanding and to harden the heart then to take strong meat too early. Let us not talk of these matters too lightly. Hidden things belong to God; things that are revealed belong to us. Touching the Almighty we cannot find him out, but he is excellent in power, judgment and grace. He will not afflict without cause. Let us rejoice that the great truth of divine grace is written in the Word and revealed in Christ.[103]

Obs. 7- (vv. 25-29) That as Paul proves from Scripture the aforementioned point (that God will have an elect people for Himself from among the Jews and the Gentiles), he quotes now from two Old Testament passages, first, from Hosea (Hos. 2:23; 1:10) applying them to the Gentiles, and then two passages from Isaiah (Isa. 10:22, 23; Isa. 1:9), applying them to the Jews. He writes,

²⁵ **As He says also in Hosea:**
"I will call them My people, who were not My people,
And her beloved, who was not beloved."
²⁶ **"And it shall come to pass in the place where it was said to them,**
'You *are* not My people,'
There they shall be called sons of the living God."
²⁷ **Isaiah also cries out**; i.e., cries out with a loud voice concerning Israel:
"Though the number of the children of Israel be as the sand of the sea,
The remnant will be saved.

---

101 Of course, this is not to negate that God does, in fact, deal with sinful men in this life and does cut them off and send them to hell.

102 Mahan, p. 72.

103 As quoted in Mahan, p. 72.

[28] **For He will finish the work and cut** *it* **short in righteousness,**
Because the Lord **will make a short work upon the earth."**
[29] **And as Isaiah said before:**
"Unless the Lord **of Sabaoth had left us a seed,**
We would have become like Sodom,
And we would have been made like Gomorrah."

Concerning these passages, Vaughn and Corley aptly summarize:

There can be no sentiment against the calling of the Gentiles and the
rejection of the majority of Israel because the matter is confirmed by
Scripture. The redemptive goal, seen in the dual operation of wrath and
mercy in Israel, complemented two results, as shown in the Old Testament
prophets: (1) divine mercy has been extended to the Gentiles, a people
"not beloved" (vv. 25, 26; Hos. 2:23; 1:10) and (2) because Divine Mercy
preserved a "seed" (v. 29; cf. 9:8), a remnant of Israel has been saved
(vv. 27-29; cf. Isa. 10:22, 23; 1:9).

Paul cites Hosea to prove that God promised to call the Gentiles;
however, the passage originally applies to the restoration of Israel. He
probably understood the promise of Israel's restoration, "either by parity
[sameness] of reason or as a typical prophecy" (Gifford, p. 175), to include
the calling of the Gentiles....

The proof from Isaiah shows that only a "remnant" (v. 27) of the Jews
continues to inherit God's promise and carries out the divine purpose.
The remnant doctrine (cf. "seed," v. 29; 9:8) forms a link between what
God did among the patriarchs (9:6-13) and what happened to Israel in
Paul's time. Additionally, it shows a progressive narrowing in the scope
of election from the nation, to a remnant, and finally to Christ, the Elect
One (9:30-33). Furthermore, the remnant is an evidence of God's mercy at
work and a pledge that Israel as a whole has not been rejected (cf. 11:1, 5).[104]

Suggested applications from the text for the church:

1- The teaching of this section should cause us to always side with
God concerning His dealings with men since there is no unrighteousness
in Him.

2- The teaching of this section should cause us to always marvel at
God's great grace in our lives in making us "vessels of mercy prepared
beforehand for glory."

3- The teaching of this section should cause us to always know our
Bibles well, so that we, like Paul, can demonstrate from the Bible all that
we believe.

Suggested application from the text for the non-Christian:

1- The teaching of this section should cause you to always remember
that God is a God of "mercy" and "compassion." He is the God who
promises you in His Word that all who seek Him in truth and with all
of their hearts will find Him (Jer. 29:13).

---

104 Vaughan and Corley, pp. 111, 112.

Text: Romans 9:30-33

General theme: Faith-righteousness versus Works-righteousness

Homiletical outline of the verses:
    A. What the Gentiles did not pursue but found: [30] What shall we say then? That Gentiles, who did not pursue righteousness, have attained to righteousness, even the righteousness of faith;
    B. What the Jews did pursue but did not find: [31] but Israel, pursuing the law of righteousness, has not attained to the law of righteousness. [32] Why? Because *they did* not *seek it* by faith, but as it were, by the works of the law. For they stumbled at that stumbling stone. [33] As it is written:
    "Behold, I lay in Zion a stumbling stone and rock of offense,
    And whoever believes on Him will not be put to shame."

Summary of section: Paul concludes this chapter by bringing our minds back to the main gospel teaching of this letter: we are saved by grace alone, through faith alone, in the finished work of Christ alone. We are not saved by what we do or by how we live. We are not saved by personal performance or by trying to make ourselves savable in God's sight by attempting to keep His commandments as a way of gaining a right standing with Him. No, Paul has already demolished this idea throughout this epistle, saying definitively, for example, in 3:28: Therefore we conclude, that a man *is justified by faith apart from the deeds of the law.*

    Paul teaches here that the righteousness of God (which is the righteousness of Christ, the only righteousness which commends us to God) is a righteousness which is received by faith and not by works (cf. 1:16, 17, 3:21, 26). He illustrates this fact from the lives of the *believing-Gentiles* versus the lives of the *working-Jews*. As he does, he puts forth the difference between true and false religion—the difference between God's way of salvation and man's way of damnation.
    Moo helpfully summarizes:

> In this paragraph Paul uses a critical feature of the gospel — the indispensability of faith in attaining a right relationship with God (cf. 3:27 – 4:25 especially) — to explain the current state of affairs in salvation history. It is by their faith that Gentiles have attained a righteous status with God (v. 30); and it is because of their lack of faith that Israel has failed to attain the righteousness that the law demanded (vv. 31-32a). By means of a composite quotation from Isa. 8:14 and 28:16, Paul shows that Israel's failure is ultimately Christological; by failing to believe in him, he has become for Israel the cause of her downfall (vv. 32b-33).[105]

Exegetical & Practical Insights:
    Obs. 1- (v. 30) That as the apostle touches on the above-mentioned topic, he writes:

---

105 Moo, NICNT, p. 620.

What shall we say then?[106] That is, what should we conclude?; **That,** the conjunction giving the answer to the question; **Gentiles**[107] (pagan, idolaters); **who did not pursue**[108] or zealously go after as their chief attainment in life; **righteousness,** i.e., a right standing with the one true living God of heaven and earth; **have attained**[109] or definitively grasped and apprehended once for all time; **to righteousness,** i.e., have become justified; **even the righteousness of** or which is received by and credited through; **faith** (alone).

What is the apostle saying in these words? Firstly, *he is not saying* that the Gentiles were not religious or "spiritual people."[110] In fact, elsewhere he says that they were. This is why when he was preaching to a crowd of them (the Epicurean and Stoic philosophers, in Athens, on Mars Hill), he said to them in Acts 17:22, "I perceive that in all things you are very religious."

Even though the Gentiles were all born dead in trespasses and sins (just like the rest of us), because they knew that God existed, "for His invisible attributes are clearly seen, being understood by the things that are made" (Rom. 1:20), they knew that He was to be worshiped. All people know this. Sadly, however, the Gentiles did not worship God in spirit and in truth (John 4:23, 24). Instead, as Paul tells us earlier in Romans 1, they "changed the glory of the incorruptible God into an image made like corruptible man—and birds and four-footed animals and creeping things" (Rom. 1:23). This was tragic. It was disastrous, and indeed, it led them into many gross depravities which continue till this day.

Secondly, *he is saying* that in their pagan idolatry, being made acceptable with their Creator was not high on their list of spiritual priorities. Simply stated, for the Gentiles, asking the simple question, "'How can a man be right and just with God?' had never occurred to them, they were not interested in it,'" as Lloyd-Jones correctly remarks.[111] Thus, although Gentiles were very religious, they were spiritually very lost. They were those who *lived in their sins, loved their sins, and were led by their sins,* being those whom Paul describes in Ephesians 4:18, 19, as, "having their understanding darkened, being alienated from the life of God, because of the ignorance that is in them, because of the blindness

---

106 Paul often asks this question whenever he concludes a teaching on a particular topic cf. 3:5, 9; 4:1; 6:1; 7:7; 8:31; 9:14.

107 Paul is speaking broadly here of the Gentiles as a class of individuals, in contrast to the Jews as a class of individuals. Obviously, he is not speaking about *every single* Gentile or *every single* Jew, but only of those Gentiles who believed and Jews who did not believe.

108 Grk. present, active, participle.

109 Grk. aorist, active, verb.

110 Nor is the apostle saying that none of the Gentiles were moral individuals as far as people in the world consider this matter. Some of them may have been, since the work of God's law was written on their hearts, helping them to know the difference between right and wrong (Rom. 2:14, 15). However, having said this, none of this made them right with God, who requires perfect righteousness from people in order to be accepted by Him (Gal. 3:10).

111 Lloyd-Jones, *Romans* p. 275.

of their heart; who, being past feeling, have given themselves over to lewdness, to work all uncleanness with greediness."

Just like all non-Christians throughout the world, the Gentiles as a people had "no hope and [were] without God in the world" (Eph. 2:12). Thanks be to God then, that by His immeasurable grace, for many of them, this was dramatically changed! By God's doing, these *non*-seekers became *seekers* of the Savior. By His drawing of them through the gospel, these *non*-pursuers became *pursuers* of Christ, and attained righteousness before God, *even* the righteousness which comes through faith in Jesus.[112]

Historically speaking this was amazing because of the sad spiritual condition of the Gentiles before they were saved. Paul gives an eye-witness perspective that as he went about preaching the good news of Jesus on his various missionary journeys, he saw repeatedly that the Gentiles who were "far off have been brought near by the blood of Christ" (Eph. 2:13). He saw that they were turning "to God from idols to serve the living and true God, and to wait for His Son from heaven, whom He raised from the dead, even Jesus who delivers us from the wrath to come" (1 Thess. 1:9, 10).[113]

Spurgeon joyfully speaks about this matter in a sermon on this verse:

> The wonder grows when we consider that these persons who had attained to righteousness had come to it under great disadvantages; for they were Gentiles. The Gentiles were considered by the Jews to be off casts and outcasts, aliens from the commonwealth of grace. They were given up to idolatry or to atheism—and the most degrading lusts were rife among them. They had gone very far from original righteousness. A true picture of the Gentile world in the days of Paul would have terribly dark colours in it: it would be injurious [harmful] to morals to describe in public the details of the lives of the best of the heathen....
>
> The strange thing is that such, originally, were those men who attained unto righteousness. The gospel came into their streets, and at first they heard it with opposition, saying, "What will this babbler say?" Their attention was attracted, and they were willing to hear the preacher again concerning this matter. Conscience was aroused, and soon they began to enquire, "What must we do to be saved?" Having no righteousness of their own, and being convinced that they needed one, they fled at once to the righteousness which God has prepared in his dear Son for all who believe in him; and multitudes believed and turned to God. Thus those who knew not the Lord became his obedient worshippers, and those who were far off were made nigh by faith.[114]

What a wonderful testimony this is! It demonstrates that, indeed, the God of the Bible shows "no partiality" (Acts 10:34). It demonstrates that He will call a people to Himself who were once not a people, and that

---

112 Cf. John 6:44.

113 Cf. Acts 13:46-49.

114 www.spurgeon.org/resource-library/sermons/s-s-or-the-sinner-saved /#flipbook/, Charles Haddon Spurgeon May 1, 1887, From: Metropolitan Tabernacle Pulpit Volume 33.

He will call a people who were once not beloved, beloved (Rom. 9:25). Praise be to His Name![115]

Obs. 2- (vv. 31-32) That as Paul now contrasts his countrymen according to the flesh with the Gentiles, he writes somewhat paradoxically and says,

but Israel, i.e., Hebrew, ethnic Israel; **pursuing**[116] or zealously going after as their chief attainment in life (the same word as found in verse 30); **the law of righteousness** or a legal-righteousness which seeks to be made right with God by one's efforts to keep His commandments; **has not attained to** or arrived at; **the law of righteousness,** which is to say, the kind of perfect righteousness which the law requires.[117] **Why?** Or for what reason? (Simple!); **Because** *they did* not *seek it* by faith, but[118] or in sharp opposition to this; **as it were, by** or on the basis of; **the works of** or the strivings after; **the law. For they** (the Jews); **stumbled** or struck hard;[119] **at that stumbling stone** (the stone being the Lord Jesus Christ, for surely He was not like they expected).[120] As it is written[121] that is written in Isaiah 8:14 and 28:16:

"Behold, or look and see; **I** (God speaking); **lay in Zion** that is Jerusalem the city of the Jews; **a stumbling stone and rock of offense,** as Christ was to the self-righteous Jews, who did not recognize Him for who He was in truth, their Redeemer (Isa. 53:1);[122] **And whoever** (each and every one who); **believes on** or sincerely puts their trust in **Him** (Jesus alone); **will not be put to shame**[123] or be disappointed and made sorry when they stand before God in the final day."

The apostle's words here are straightforward and twofold. First, he shows that, according to Romans 3:20, the Jews (just like all other

---

115 This is seen in Scripture for example in the salvation of Cornelius and his household, Lydia and her household, the Philippian jailer and his household, and all others like them throughout Corinth, Galatia, Ephesus, Philippi, Colossae, and Thessalonica who believed. Through faith, God gave them all perfect righteousness in His Son.

116 Grk. present, active, participle.

117 MacArthur says, "What a tragic commentary on a wasted effort. God's righteousness cannot be achieved by man's works, because they are always sin-tainted and fall short of God's perfect and holy standard." MacArthur, p. 50.

118 The strong Greek adversative.

119 Of course they did not all stumble beyond being able to be saved (cf. Rom. 11:1, 11).

120 Cf. Zech. 4:7; Acts 4:11; 1 Cor. 3:11, 10:4; Eph. 2:20; 1 Pet. 2:6. Haldane is correct when he says, "A free salvation becomes an offense to men on account of their pride. They cannot bear the idea of being indebted for it to sovereign grace, which implies that in themselves they are guilty and ruined by sin. They desire to do something, were it ever so little, to merit salvation, at least in part. Salvation by a crucified Saviour was in one way opposed to the pride of the Jews.... The Jews expected a mighty conqueror, who should deliver them from a foreign yoke, and render them so powerful as to triumph over all the other nations of the earth; and in order to reconcile with these ideas what the Scriptures said of His humiliation, some among them supposed that there would be two messiahs" (Haldane, p. 496). In summary, we can say that for the Jews, putting their faith in a carpenter's son from Nazareth, turned Rabbi, who then hung and died on a cursed tree, was scandalous. For them, it was a stumbling block (1 Cor. 1:23)! However, this was God's way of reconciling them to Himself. This is what God had long before foretold in Holy Scripture (see Isaiah 53).

121 Note how Paul grounds all that he believes in Scripture just as we should do.

122 Cf. 1 Cor. 1:23.

123 Grk. future, passive, verb.

unsaved religious people in the world), did not understand a very basic principle of Scripture, namely "by the deeds of the law no flesh will be justified in His sight, for by the law is the knowledge of sin." He also shows the truthfulness of what he says in Romans 10:3 when he writes concerning the Jews that "they being ignorant of God's righteousness, and seeking to establish their own righteousness, have not submitted to the righteousness of God."[124] Hodge summarizes the matter well concerning Israel on the whole when he succinctly says, "In other words, they would not submit to the method of justification proposed by God, which was alone suitable for sinners, and persisted in trusting to their own imperfect works."[125]

Second, in these words, Paul shows us positively that all who put their faith in Jesus' person and work alone for salvation will never be put to shame. While they will certainly experience various hardships in this life (Rom. 8:17, 18), they will nonetheless have an abundant entrance into glory (Rom. 5:2). They will hear those most spectacular words from the Savior when He says to them, "Come you blessed by My Father, inherit the kingdom prepared for you from the foundation of the world" (Matt. 25:34).

Suggested applications from the text for the church:

1- Our passage shows us that God's sovereignty in election (vv. 6-29) and human responsibility to believe (vv. 30-32) are both taught in Scripture; therefore they both are to be believed.

2- Our passage teaches us that there is a biblical way to get to heaven, which is by faith alone, in Christ alone, versus the wrong way which cannot save, which is by trusting in ourselves and our efforts. Consequently, this is the only message that we are to proclaim.

3- Our passage teaches us that the Jesus of the Bible will see to it that at the last day His saved people will not be "put to shame," therefore, we must reject any other teaching which speaks in opposition to this.[126]

Suggested application from the text for the non-Christian:

1- Our passage teaches you that if you put all of your hope in Jesus, who died for sinners, was buried and rose again on the third day, you will be saved (1 Cor. 15:1-4).

---

124 Despite what some scholars tell us in our day, this verse makes it abundantly plain that the Jews of the first-century sought acceptance with God by their works. They sought it through human effort. Cf. Luke 18:9-14.

125 Hodge, p. 330.

126 Cf. John 3:16, 6:39, 10:27-30, 14:1-3.

ROMANS
CHAPTER TEN

Text: Romans 10:1-13

General theme: Israel's Need for Salvation (I)

Homiletical outline of the verses:

    A. The prayer concerning Israel's salvation: [1] Brethren, my heart's desire and prayer to God for Israel is that they may be saved. [2] For I bear them witness that they have a zeal for God, but not according to knowledge. [3] For they being ignorant of God's righteousness, and seeking to establish their own righteousness, have not submitted to the righteousness of God.

    B. The person given for Israel's salvation: [4] For Christ *is* the end of the law for righteousness to everyone who believes. [5] For Moses writes about the righteousness which is of the law, "The man who does those things shall live by them." [6] But the righteousness of faith speaks in this way, "Do not say in your heart, 'Who will ascend into heaven?'" (that is, to bring Christ down *from above*) [7] or, "'Who will descend into the abyss?'" (that is, to bring Christ up from the dead). [8] But what does it say? "The word is near you, in your mouth and in your heart" (that is, the word of faith which we preach): [9] that if you confess with your mouth the Lord Jesus and believe in your heart that God has raised Him from the dead, you will be saved. [10] For with the heart one believes unto righteousness, and with the mouth confession is made unto salvation. [11] For the Scripture says, "Whoever believes on Him will not be put to shame." [12] For there is no distinction between Jew and Greek, for the same Lord over all is rich to all who call upon Him. [13] For "whoever calls on the name of the Lord shall be saved."

Summary of section: In this unit, Paul continues his discussion from the previous words at the end of chapter 9 concerning the topic of "the way of salvation and how to be right before God."[1] Having laid the groundwork for this subject, he puts forth this matter once again as he seeks to correct

---

1 Lloyd-Jones, *Romans*, p. 2.

the ignorance of the Jews and all others in the world who think that, by their strivings, they will be made right with their Maker. John Murray puts it like this:

> In this chapter the apostle is concerned with the same subject as that dealt with in the latter part of the preceding chapter. In 9:32, 33 the stumbling of Israel consisted in seeking righteousness by works and not by faith. This is but another way of saying that they sought to establish their own righteousness and did not subject themselves to the righteousness of God, the way it is stated in 10:3. Thus there is no break in the thought at 10:1.[2]

Why repeat this theme after having stated it so plainly? The answer is simple: we can never hear too much about the doctrine of justification before a holy God by faith alone in Christ alone. This is a vital point which we must hear repeatedly so that we never move away from this central truth of the gospel, by which we are made acceptable in God's sight. If we lose this truth, we lose everything! If we lose it, we lose our souls![3]

Exegetical & Practical Insights:

Obs. 1- (v. 1) That as Paul begins this chapter in a similar way to chapter 9 verses 2 and 3, where he wrote "I have great sorrow and continual grief in my heart, for I could wish that I myself were accursed from Christ for my brethren, my countrymen according to the flesh," he now writes:

Brethren, i.e., the beloved Christian brothers and sisters at Rome (not a reference to his Jewish brethren according to the flesh); **my heart's desire** or more literally, the good pleasure of my inner being; **and prayer** or specific supplication; **to God for** or on behalf of; **Israel,** i.e., unsaved, ethnic Israel; **is**[4] or will always be; **that** or for the purpose that; **they may be saved** or delivered from the wrath of God due them because of their sins against Him.

These opening words are particularly striking, especially in light of how the Jews had treated Paul. Ever since the day he was converted and started preaching Christ to them that He is the "Son of God" (Acts 9:20), we are told that they "plotted to kill him" (Acts 9:23). They followed him and dogged his steps wherever he went, seeking to turn the crowds away from the message of life that he preached. On one occasion they even stoned him, with the result being that they "dragged him out of the city supposing him to be dead" (Acts 14:19).

Even though this was the case, Paul still loved them deeply. Since he knew that Jesus was the One whom God "raised up for Israel [as] Savior" (Acts 13:23), he obeyed Him when He said to "pray for those who spitefully use you and persecute you" (Matt. 5:44). Since he knew that

---

2 Murray, 2:46.

3 Cf. Gal. 1:6-9.

4 Grk. present, active, verb.

Jesus was their long-awaited promised Messiah, he passionately longed for them to put their faith in Him so that they might be saved.

Obs. 2- (vv. 2-3) That as the apostle explains why his heart's desire and prayer to God for Israel was that they might be saved, he writes:

For I bear them witness[5] or continually testify about or concerning them; **that** the conjunction putting forth the content of his witness; **they** (the Jews); **have**[6] (and that constantly); **a zeal** or fervor "marked by a sense of dedication;"[7] **for God but**[8] or in sharp contrast to this; **not according to** or in line with; **knowledge** which is to say, a full knowledge of God's completed revelation in Jesus as outlined in the gospel; **For** the conjunction giving the reason for Paul's previous words; **they** (the Jews); **being ignorant**[9] or constantly ill-informed; **of** or with respect to; **God's righteousness,** not the righteousness which God is in Himself, but the perfect righteousness He provides, freely out of His grace in His Son, by faith;[10] **and seeking** or eagerly going about; **to establish** or set up; **their own righteousness** (this was the heart of the problem) which righteousness was a self-produced righteousness, which God calls filthy rags;[11] **have not submitted to** or placed themselves under; **the righteousness of God,** again, His righteousness in Christ given to believing sinners.[12]

Paul's testimony here regarding those of his own flesh and blood shows again why he was so heartbroken about them. Simply put, he sympathized with them because, before he was converted, he also had this type of "zeal for God." He even said of himself, "And I advanced in Judaism beyond many of my contemporaries in my own nation, being more *exceedingly zealous* for the traditions of my fathers" (Gal. 1:14).

Unfortunately, that zeal was misplaced and misinformed because it was not for the Messiah Jesus. In fact, it was deadly and destructive, for as he says in Philippians chapter 3 and verse 6 *"concerning zeal,* [I was] persecuting the church." Paul was so blinded at that time that no doubt he thought that he was offering service to God by persecuting Christians, even as Jesus had predicted (John 16:2). Nevertheless, God laid hold of him, showed him the error of his ways, and forgave him his sin. However, he never forgot how he acted. Consequently, years later, he could say of himself, "for I am the least of the apostles, who am not worthy to be called an apostle, because I persecuted the church of God" (1 Cor. 15:9).

Regarding this matter about the Jews, Spurgeon aptly comments:

---

5 Grk. present, active verb.

6 Grk. present, active verb.

7 BDAG, p. 427.

8 The strong Greek adversative.

9 Grk. present, active, participle.

10 Cf. Rom 1:16, 17, 3:21-26, 5:17-19.

11 Cf. Isa. 64:6.

12 The Jews said of Jesus in John 19:15, "Away with Him, away with Him!" And, "We have no king but Caesar!"

They were very zealous; but it was blind zeal. They were very energetic; but they used their energy in going the wrong way. God has a righteousness, and our wisest course is to submit to it. Our righteousness, if we set it up in opposition to God's way of salvation, will only increase our sin. You can be ruined by your righteousness, as surely as by your unrighteousness, if you set it in the place of salvation by grace through faith in Jesus Christ.[13]

Obs. 3- (v. 4) That as Paul now puts forth where all of our righteousness before God and His holy law is to be found, he writes:

For Christ, i.e., Jesus the Messiah; *is* **the end** or the fulfillment;[14] **of the law for righteousness** or for one's attaining a right standing and acceptance with God; **to everyone who believes** or is completely trusting in Jesus' person and work alone for life and salvation.[15]

These words are thrilling. They tell us that Jesus has done everything in His life and death to fulfill all righteousness for us. Through His active life of obedience to all the commandments of God, and then His passive obedience in His death on the cross in our place to satisfy the wrath of God for our transgressions, we who have put our trust in Him have received His perfect righteousness credited to our account. We have been made "accepted in the Beloved" (Eph. 1:6). Thus, the law of God no longer has any judicial claims over us to condemn us. This is glorious news! It is fantastic truth, which is well expressed by the hymn writer when he wrote:

Jesus, thy blood and righteousness
My beauty are, my glorious dress;
Midst flaming worlds, in these arrayed,
With joy shall I lift up my head.

Bold shall I stand in thy great day;
For who aught to my charge shall lay?
Fully absolved through these I am
From sin and fear, from guilt and shame.

Again, Spurgeon's comments are helpful:

He that believes in Christ is as righteous as the law could have made him, if he had kept it perfectly. The end of the law is righteousness; that is, the fulfilling of it; and he that hath Christ will see the law fulfilled in Christ, and the righteousness of Christ apply to himself.[16]

---

13 Spurgeon, p. 215.

14 Cf. Matt. 5:17; Acts 13:38, 39. It should be noted that the word "end" in the Greek text is placed in the front of the sentence for the sake of emphasis.

15 Phillips translates the verse like this: For Christ means the end of the struggle for righteousness-by-the-Law for everyone who believes in him.

16 Spurgeon, p. 209.

Matthew Henry further expounds:

> Christ is thus the end of the law for righteousness, that is, for justification; but it is only to *everyone that believeth*. Upon our believing, that is, our humble consent to the terms of the gospel, we become interested in Christ's satisfaction, and so are justified through the redemption that is in Christ Jesus.[17]

Obs. 4- (v. 5) That as Paul continues to contrast the difference between faith-righteousness versus law-keeping-righteousness (which will always fail us because we are full of sin), he turns now to the Old Testament to prove his point. Since all that he is teaching concerning how a person is justified before God is not original to him, but rather firmly rooted in Scripture, he turns first to Moses in Leviticus 18:5, and says:

For the word providing the grounds for what Paul just said;[18] **Moses writes about the righteousness which is of** or out from or by; **the law,** i.e., a legal righteousness; **"The man who does those things shall live** or conduct himself entirely; **by them,** 'for a righteousness based on obedience to the law requires perfect conformity in every detail.'"[19]

What is Paul's point in quoting this passage? It is that for the one who seeks to be made righteous, (i.e., justified in God's sight by his performance or obedience to the law of God), he needs to live by that standard all of his days personally, perpetually, and perfectly. As he says in Galatians 3:10 (in quoting Moses, from Deuteronomy 27:26), "Cursed is everyone who does not continue *in all things* which are written in the book of the law, to do them." This attempting to be made right with God by our own strivings is a tyranny of the highest order and tragic for the one who does not comply. Nevertheless, if (hypothetically speaking) one could comply with all of the demands of the commandments in thought, word, and deed, then God would grant the individual perfect righteousness and justification in His sight. However, since the law of God was given to individuals who were *already rebel sinners*, keeping the law perfectly as it requires was never in their ability; thus, "any hopes that men may have for obtaining righteousness by law are doomed to failure from the outset."[20]

That is why we need a Savior to keep the law of God for us as our representative, and die as our substitute in order to pay our penalty for breaking it. This is why God sent Jesus into the world, for as Paul says in Galatians 3:13, "Christ has redeemed us from the curse of the law, having become a curse for us (for it is written, 'Cursed is everyone who hangs on a tree')."

---

17 Henry, p. 354.

18 Morris, p. 381.

19 MacArthur, *One Faithful Life* (2019), p. 306. Cf. James 2:10.

20 McDonald, 1720.

Obs. 5- (vv. 6-8) That as Paul illustrates the above point in verse 5, he quotes now from Moses in Deuteronomy 30:11-14, which in that context speaks about obeying God and His law. The original quote went like this:

"For this commandment which I command you today [again, to follow God's laws] *is* not *too* mysterious for you, nor *is* it far off. It *is* not in heaven, that you should say, 'Who will ascend into heaven for us and bring it to us, that we may hear it and do it?' Nor *is* it beyond the sea, that you should say, 'Who will go over the sea for us and bring it to us, that we may hear it and do it?' But the word *is* very near you, in your mouth and in your heart, that you may do it."

What is the essence of what Moses is teaching in these words? It is that because the law of God was accessible to the people and not hidden, they could know and do it (albeit imperfectly). Getting the gist of what God required of them was in no way "mysterious." It did not require them to search it out or to travel far to find it. Rather, everything they needed had been set right before them through the instruction which they regularly received, and in the Decalogue.

Here as Paul quotes this passage, it is interesting to note that the Holy Spirit directed him to add three parenthetical ("that is") remarks which explain the relationship that this quote has to Jesus Christ.

Here is what he writes:

But the righteousness of or out from or by; **faith** (in opposition to the righteousness which is of the law, v.5) **speaks in this way** or "after this manner;"[21] **"Do not say in your heart, 'Who will ascend into heaven?'" (that is, to bring Christ down** *from above)* [7] **or, "'Who will descend into the abyss?' " (that is, to bring Christ up from the dead). But**[22] or in sharp contrast to this; **what does it say? "The word is near you, in your mouth and in your heart" (that is, the word of faith** or the word about the faith, i.e., the proclamation of the gospel; **which we preach):**

What has Paul done in these words? He has taken the general sense of Moses' words and applied them to Jesus, showing that *just as* the Old Testament law was not hidden, or distant, or unreachable to the people of God such that they could not get to it, *the same is true* for Christ whenever the saving message of the gospel is preached.

Paul is telling us that the way to be saved from the curse of the law—that curse which we all deserve, having broken it thousands of times in our flawed attempts at righteousness—is not difficult to attain. Jesus Christ, who is the Savior from the sentencing which that curse brings about, is brought within reach of all who hear the preaching of the Word, and who respond to it in faith (as the Jews had multiple opportunities to do when Paul traveled to and preached in their synagogues, cf. Acts 17:1-4).

As Spurgeon says about the matter, "How very simple! No climbing, no diving, no imagining, no long reckoning of the understanding, no

---

21 Robinson, Book II. p. 71.

22 The strong Greek adversative.

strangling of the mental faculties. It is just believe God's testimony concerning his Son, and thou shalt be saved."[23]

Kruse remarks similarly:

> Paul's main point in 10:6-8 is clear enough. He uses Deuteronomy 30:12-14 to emphasize that, just as the law was not something hidden and distant from the Israelites, so likewise the gospel of faith-righteousness is not something hidden or distant from Paul's contemporaries — it is freely available to both Jews and Gentiles through the gospel he proclaims.[24]

Obs. 6- (vv. 9-10) That as the apostle explains how one partakes of the accessible "word of faith" (the gospel) which is "near," and gives its essential contents, he writes:

that if you confess[25] not do religious works, but openly proclaim or say the same thing that Scripture says (which is what the essence of the Greek word *confess* means);[26] **with** or by means of; **your mouth the Lord** (*kurios*, a term which evidently speaks about Christ's deity,[27] and is used in the Septuagint, the Greek version of the Old Testament, over "6000 times for the name of God"[28]);[29] **Jesus** or Jehovah incarnate, God made flesh;[30] **and believe** or sincerely trusts; **in your heart** not just the head, but with the deepest inner recesses of one's being;[31] **that God has raised Him from the dead,** that is, raised Jesus from the dead as a validation of His completed work on the cross on our behalf;[32] **you will be saved. For,** the conjunction explaining why this is so; **with the heart one believes unto** (or with the immediate result being);[33] **righteousness,** i.e., a perfect standing with God through Christ; **and with the mouth confession is made unto** or with the immediate result being); **salvation,** i.e., deliverance from the wrath of God due us because of our sins against Him.

---

23 Spurgeon, p. 206.

24 Kruse, p. 408.

25 Here the idea is clearly not that of making some bare, empty *acknowledgment* that the Lord Jesus lived and died and rose again. Rather, it is a verbal, public affirmation of one's allegiance to this Lord who is their God. These words are not some formulaic "sinner's prayer" that we have people pray and then afterward assure them that they are now saved. No, for as MacArthur rightly says, "This is the deep personal conviction, without reservation, that Jesus is that person's own master or sovereign. This phrase includes repenting from sin, trusting in Jesus for salvation, and submitting to Him as Lord. This is the volitional element of faith." *MacArthur Study Bible,* p. 1712.

26 This often takes place at one's baptism.

27 Cf. John 20:28.

28 Morris, p. 385.

29 These words make it plain that for the true Christian, they cannot merely have Jesus *as Savior* and *not* Lord. This is because the Jesus who saves, is the Lord, verse 9, cf. Acts 16:31.

30 John 1:1, 14.

31 Obviously, these words are not just some intellectual agreement with the facts of the gospel, sometimes called easy believism.

32 Cf. Rom. 4:25; 1 Cor. 15:1-4, 17-20.

33 The preposition plus accusative denoting result.

Here Paul gives us the touchstone of the Christian faith. This is its sum and substance, and every true Christian has unreservedly embraced these truths for themselves. They have embraced Jesus' person and work wholeheartedly and are resting alone in His person and work as their only ground of acceptance with God. This is the core of the issue for them, and they by the grace of God will not be moved from it.

Boice remarks:

> The first truth is that "Jesus is Lord." What a tremendous statement! It is impossible to overestimate the significance of these three words (only two in Greek), for this was not only the first essential element of the gospel proclamation as well as of the first Christian confession. It was also a confession of their faith for which believers of the first Christian centuries were willing to die.
>
> How can those three words be that important? The answer, as we know, is that they are literally crammed with meaning. They testify to: (1) the person of Christ, (2) the unique work of Christ, and (3) the ongoing all-embracing rule of Christ over his people and the church.[34]

Johnson further comments:

> In confessing "Jesus is Lord," a person confesses the divine nature and attributes in him. This acknowledgment can be made only by the Holy Spirit (cf. 1 Cor. 12:3), which indicates, in an incidental way, that faith is the gift of God.[35]

The second article of the faith, that "God raised [Jesus] from the dead," is an important corrective for those who use the term "Lord" too broadly (cf. 1 Cor. 8:5). There is only "one Lord, Jesus Christ, through whom all things came and through whom we live" (1 Cor. 8:6). All other "lords" are not lords at all. The Christian faith is not one among many, as Peter puts it so plainly in Acts 4:12. Salvation is only through Christ, "for there is no other name under heaven given to men by which we must be saved." Christianity is an exclusive truth.

The fact that Jesus is Lord and has been raised from the dead is an affirmation that he stands both within history and outside history, and not as a teacher, but as the conqueror of death. As he said in his encounter with Martha, "I am the resurrection and the life. He who believes in me will live, even though he dies; and whoever lives and believes in me will never die. Do you believe this?" (John 11:25-26).

Paul concludes with that statement that righteousness and salvation come from believing in confessing (cf. v.10).

Obs. 7- (vv. 11-13) That as Paul brings an end to this section concerning *faith*-righteousness versus *works*-righteousness, he does so by means of three Greek conjunctions ("for")[36] at the beginning of each sentence. They,

---

34 Boice, p. 1191.

35 Johnson, p. 167.

36 The Greek word *gar.*

in turn, prove, explain and support from Scripture what he taught in verses 9 and 10.[37] In telling us why these things are so, Paul writes:

For the Scripture says, i.e., says in Isaiah 28:16; **"Whoever believes on Him will not be put to shame"**[38] or humiliated and disgraced before God on the final day.

And then, explaining why this is so, he says in verse 12,

For there is no distinction or difference; **between Jew and Greek,**[39] **for the same Lord over all** (that is, over all the world and those in it); **is rich** or generous; **to all** (each and every one, regardless of who they are or what they have done); **who call upon Him,** that is, call upon Him in humble, repentant faith, out of a true sense of need for deliverance from God's judgment having seen His gracious provision of mercy toward them in Jesus.

And then, in explaining why this is so, Paul quotes from Joel 2:32, when finally he says in verse 13,

For "whoever calls on the name (Jesus' name, which represents all that He is in His person, specifically the Savior who is kind, compassionate, and ready to forgive all who call upon Him by faith); **of the LORD** (Jehovah Jesus); **shall be saved"** that is to say, instantaneously justified, reconciled to God, covered with the righteousness of Christ and adopted into God's family both for time and for eternity.

These words are tremendously reassuring, being both profound and simple at the same time. They offer all people everywhere great hope and the scriptural way to be saved from their sins and the judgment to come. Therefore, may we be found believing on Christ to the saving of the soul!

Suggested applications from the text for the church:

1- We learn from these verses that prayer does not stand in contradiction to God's sovereign choice of only some to be saved because Paul prayed for the salvation of the entire nation of Israel.

2- We learn from these verses that religious sincerity is not a basis for truth because people can be sincerely wrong.

3- We learn from these verses that Jesus is to be everything for the believer. He alone has done everything for us to make us right with God through His representative life, and substitutionary death, and resurrection on our behalf.

Suggested application from the text for the non-Christian:

1- You learn from these verses that Jesus is rich to all who call upon Him for salvation. Therefore, call upon Him even now for this!

---

37 These three verses could be outlined as: the promise of the gospel v. 11, the scope of the gospel v. 12, and, the certainty of the gospel v. 13.

38 Grk. future, passive, verb.

39 Cf. Rom. 3:22.

Text: Romans 10:14-21

General theme: Israel's Need for Salvation (II)[40]

Homiletical outline of the verses:
   A. The preachers "assisting" in Israel's salvation: [14] How then shall they call on Him in whom they have not believed? And how shall they believe in Him of whom they have not heard? And how shall they hear without a preacher? [15] And how shall they preach unless they are sent? As it is written:
   "How beautiful are the feet of those who preach the gospel of peace,
   Who bring glad tidings of good things!"
   B. The passages about Israel's salvation: [16] But they have not all obeyed the gospel. For Isaiah says, "LORD, who has believed our report?" [17] So then faith *comes* by hearing, and hearing by the word of God.
      [18] But I say, have they not heard? Yes indeed:
      "Their sound has gone out to all the earth,
      And their words to the ends of the world."
      [19] But I say, did Israel not know? First Moses says:
      "I will provoke you to jealousy by *those who are* not a nation,
      I will move you to anger by a foolish nation."
      [20] But Isaiah is very bold and says:
      "I was found by those who did not seek Me;
      I was made manifest to those who did not ask for Me."
      [21] But to Israel he says:
      "All day long I have stretched out My hands
      To a disobedient and contrary people."

Summary of section: In the last unit of this chapter, Paul (having just spoken in the previous verses of both the prayer concerning Israel's salvation, and the person by whom it was given), now speaks about the means by which salvation would come to them: through human instrumentality.[41] Having told us in verse thirteen that "whoever calls on the name of the Lord shall be saved," the question he tackles now is, "How will this come to pass in people's lives?" How will people hear about "the word of faith," i.e., the glorious gospel of God, which is "the power of God to salvation for everyone who believes, for the Jew first and also for the Greek" (1:16)? Murray states the matter succinctly: "The main point is that the saving relationship to Christ involved in calling upon his name is not something that can occur in a vacuum; it occurs only in a context created by proclamation of the gospel on the part of those commissioned to proclaim it."[42]

---

40 While the words of this passage are directly applied to Israel, it is apparent that they could apply broadly to all who are lost, either Jew or Gentile.

41 Cf. 1 Cor. 3:5.

42 Murray, 5:58.

Exegetical & Practical Insights:

Obs. 1- (vv. 14-15) That as Paul addresses the aforementioned question, he sets forth four interconnected "how" questions which are meant to stir up our thinking about this matter and then move us into action. He writes:

How then shall or better understood, "how could;"[43] **they call on Him** (Jesus); **in whom they have not believed? And how shall** or could; **they believe in Him of whom they have not heard? And how shall** or could; **they hear without** or apart from; **a preacher? And how shall** or could; **they preach,** that is, herald and announce the Word; **unless they are sent?** (The answer to these questions is: they cannot). **As it is written,** that is, written in Isaiah 52:7:

"How beautiful or lovely; **are the feet**[44] **of those who preach the gospel of peace,** or bring good news about peace with God through faith in Jesus Christ; **Who bring glad tidings of good things!"**[45]

Paul's words here are plain. They show us that he understood the vital necessity of preaching the gospel to the lost. Even though he clearly understood God's sovereignty in saving specific sinners (whom He had foreordained to be saved even from before the foundation of the world, cf., Rom. 9:6-13; Eph. 1:3-5), he also knew that those sinners would come to faith through God's ordained means of the preaching of the Word of God. Consequently, he says in 1 Corinthians 1:21, "it pleased God through the foolishness of the message preached to save those who believe."[46]

Here he is telling us about what Spurgeon calls, "the whole machinery of salvation."[47] Spurgeon goes on to say, "God provides salvation in Christ Jesus, he sends the preacher to tell of it, men hear, they believe, and salvation is theirs."[48] The apostle is telling us that there is a responsibility

---

43 I translate the four verbs this way because they are in the subjunctive mood in the Greek text. In Greek, the subjunctive mood is the mood of potentiality—of whether or not something will or could happen. In our passage, the answers are all assumed to be negative so that people could not do what is being asked in the questions. Paul here is not speaking absolutely but relatively, hence for example this does not negate the fact that many people are saved just by simply reading the Word of God and not by hearing a preacher. But in either case (the hearing or the reading of the Word) are necessary (cf. James 1:18; 1 Pet. 1:22-25).

44 Leon Morris says, "It is interesting to have the feet selected as the beautiful parts of the body. But, of course, the messengers normally traveled on foot and the feet were the significant members. They might be dirty and smelly after a long, hot journey, but to those who eagerly awaited good news they were beautiful." Morris, p. 390.

Spurgeon further said about the reference to the feet, "And they are so beautiful because, you see, God has put them at the root of everything. God makes the preacher whom he sends to be the source of so much good, or the channel of so much good, for by his preaching comes the hearing, and by the hearing comes the believing, and out of the believing, the calling upon the name and the salvation." Spurgeon, p. 212.

45 Leon Morris notes that the word "good" following the words "glad tidings" emphasizes the "goodness of the good news." He says, "Paul is not thinking of some run-of-the-mill good tidings, but of something really outstanding, the gospel." Morris, p. 391

46 Clearly, Paul was no hyper-Calvinist who did not stress the importance of evangelism.

47 Spurgeon, p. 218.

48 Ibid.

which is laid upon all of us to do all that we can to be like the early church in Jerusalem, who "went everywhere preaching the word" (Acts 8:4).[49] He is telling us that we have a responsibility to open our mouths on behalf of our Great King toward the lost, to tell them about God's glorious message of reconciliation with Himself through Christ, as we have opportunity.

Spurgeon challenged his church in this regard. He writes:

> If sinners will be damned, at least let them leap to hell over our bodies. And if they will perish, let them perish with our arms about their knees, imploring them to stay. If hell must be filled, at least let it be filled in the teeth of our exertions, and let not one go there unwarned and unprayed for.[50]

He said:

> The fact is, brethren, we must have conversion work here. We cannot go on as some churches do without converts. We cannot, we will not, we must not, we dare not. Souls must be converted here and if there be not many born to Christ, may the Lord grant to me that I may sleep in the tomb and be heard of no more. Better indeed for us to die than to live if souls be not saved.[51]

More specifically though, in this setting, Paul seems to highlight his own "official sending" as a missionary.[52] He is writing to the church at Rome while he was on the mission field as a commissioned man, who himself was "sent" to do this work through the local church in Antioch (Acts 13:1-3).[53] This of course also helps us then to see the important job that local churches have in sending out gospel ministers, missionaries and evangelists to preach the Word throughout the world. This is a task which we must seek to fulfill so that the lost will hear about Jesus and be saved.

Henry comments:

> They cannot preach except they be sent, except they be both commissioned and in some measure qualified for their preaching work. How shall a man act as an ambassador, unless he have both his credentials and his instruction from the Prince that sends him? This proves to the regular ministry that there must be a regular mission and ordination. It is God's

---

49 In this regard, some helpful books to instruct us in this matter are: Paul Washer's trilogy on the gospel. Jeremy Walker's book, *The Brokenhearted Evangelist*. Denton's *Even If None*, Denton and Smith's, *A Certain Sound*, and the classic Puritan work by Joseph Alleine, *A Sure Guide to Heaven*.

50 As quoted in *2200 Quotations from the Writings of Charles H Spurgeon*, p. 67.

51 Ibid., p. 67.

52 It should be noted that the word "sent" is a similar verb to the noun "apostle." Thus, it seems to be pointing to the idea of an "official sending."

53 It is striking to consider that although Paul had seen the risen Lord Jesus Christ with his own eyes and had direct communication from Him, that he still felt it necessary to submit himself to be sent out by a local congregation. Many commentators miss this point of what this sending in our passage is about. I believe that this reveals a poor understanding of the local church in God's great plan for the spreading of the gospel throughout the world.

prerogative to send ministers; he is the Lord of the harvest, and therefore to him we must pray that he would send forth labourers, Matt. 9:38.

He only can qualify men for, and incline them to, the work of the ministry. But the competency [skill] of that qualification, and the sincerity of that inclination, must not be left to the judgment of every man for himself: the nature of the thing will by no means admit this, but, for the preservation of due order in the church, this must needs be referred and submitted to the judgment of a competent number of those who are themselves in that office and of approved wisdom and experience in it, who, as in all other callings, are presumed the most able judges, and who are empowered to set apart such as they find so qualified and inclined to do this work of the ministry, that by this preservation of the succession the name of Christ may endure forever and his throne as the days of heaven. And those that are thus set apart, not only may, but must preach as those that are sent.[54]

When the apostle quotes from Isaiah 52:7, in v. 15b, he is referencing a passage which in its original context spoke about the Old Testament footmen who, in the sixth-century B.C., announced the good news of freedom from Babylonian captivity. These individuals joyfully announced that the Babylonian exile had ended and the people were now free to return to Jerusalem. This was good news to be sure! Thus, as Paul thinks about how the gospel emancipates people from spiritual captivity to sin, Satan and self, and ultimately God's punishment for their sins, he applies this text to the situation with far more significant implications to be sure. He uses the text to show the glorious work of believers whenever they bring the gospel to those who are in spiritual bondage.

Obs. 2- (vv. 16-17) That as the apostle thinks now about the negative reaction to the gospel from many of the Jews in his day, he remarks about it and says in verse 16:

But[55] that is to say in sharp contrast to those who receive and obey the preached Word when it came to them; **they** (specifically the unsaved Jews, and then all other gospel-rejecters like them); **have not all obeyed**[56] **the gospel** or definitively placed themselves under it, in submission to the good news about Christ which is what it requires since it is not only "a gracious offer but a command to believe and repent."[57] **For** or because; **Isaiah says,** i.e., says in Isaiah: 53:1 (which is a superb Old Testament gospel passage); "Lord, **who has believed our report?**"

Here Paul shows us that the Jews' refusal to bow the knee to Christ as Lord and Savior was hardly something new or unexpected; it had been prophesied long ago. In the Hebrew Scriptures, God had foretold that many of His people would be stiff-necked[58] and reject the Savior. As Chrysostom observes, "Paul is saying that by disbelieving, the Jews

---

54 Henry, p. 356.

55 The strong Greek adversative.

56 Grk. aorist, active, verb.

57 MacArthur, *One Faithful Life* (2019), p. 307.

58 Cf. Ex. 32:9; Acts 7:51.

are not disbelieving the apostles only but also the prophet Isaiah, who foretold many years before that they would be sent to preach the gospel."[59]

Even though this was the case, because Paul also saw that Isaiah had said in 53:1, that belief in the "report" concerning Christ was the vital matter for salvation (as he has been teaching), he summarizes in verse 17 and says next:

So then or therefore; **faith** or belief; *comes* by or out from; **hearing,** "not with the outward ear only, but with the heart:"[60] **and hearing by** or through the instrumentality of; **the word of God.**[61]

We must grasp these words because they show us that along with faith being a gift of God to sinners (Eph. 2:8; Phil.1:29), in a real sense, faith to believe on Christ alone for salvation comes as people listen to the gospel. Paul says that as people sit under the Word of God, faith to believe in Jesus to the saving of the soul is produced. Therefore, we must always preach the Word of God! It must be proclaimed week by week, "precept upon precept, and line upon line" (Isa. 28:10).

Again, Henry wisely comments:

> The beginning, progress, and strength of faith, are by hearing. The word of God is therefore called *the word of faith:* it begets and nourishes faith. God gives faith, but it is by the word as the instrument. *Hearing* (that hearing which works faith) is *by the word of God.* It is not hearing the enticing words of man's wisdom, but hearing the word of God, that will befriend faith, and hearing it as the word of God, cf. 1 Thess. 2:13.[62]

Obs. 3- (v. 18) That as Paul raises an objection against the unbelieving Jews who might argue and say that they had not been given ample opportunity to hear the Word preached and appropriately respond to its message so that they might be saved, he says:

But I say, have they (again the Jews); **not heard?**[63] To which he immediately replies saying; **Yes indeed** or certainly: and then in quoting from Psalm 19:4 he writes:

> "Their sound has gone out to all the earth,
> And their words to the ends of the world."

What is Paul's point in quoting this verse from this psalm? It is that just as God's general revelation about Himself (which is what this verse in this psalm is speaking about),[64] has gone out through the world, so

---

59 *Ancient Christian Commentary on Scripture, Romans* p. 270.

60 Mahan, p. 78.

61 I realize that there is a textual variant here which speaks about faith coming by hearing and hearing "by the word of Christ." If this is the better option, it teaches us that as we preach the gospel to the lost, Jesus Himself is actively involved in calling His sheep to Himself, through us (cf. 2 Cor. 5:20).

62 Henry, p. 357.

63 Paul's words in the Greek text are very emphatic as he uses a double negation to stress his point. The words could be translated as: But I say have they not heard? Haven't they?

64 Cf. Rom. 1:19-21.

also has the gospel spread widely through commissioned preachers.[65] Paul takes this verse in Psalm 19 and applies it similarly to sent ministers of the Word, thus, *"Their sound* has gone out to all the earth, And their words to the ends of the world."

Obviously, the gospel had not gone to every single place in the world in the same way as God's general revelation of Himself has (thus the great commission still needed to be fulfilled and Paul still had plans to travel to Spain for this very reason, cf. Rom. 15:24). But the point is, Paul and others had made the gospel broadly known in their day; consequently the Jews were without excuse. As he said earlier in this chapter concerning the Jews in verse 8, God's word was "near" them. And as he says in Colossians 1:23 he had preached the gospel "to every creature under heaven."[66]

Obs. 4- (vv. 19-21) That as the apostle winds down his words in this section of Scripture, he does so by quoting a few passages from the Old Testament (one from Deuteronomy and two from Isaiah), to show once again (as he did in Romans 9:24-26), that along with God intending to save many of the Jews, He also intended to save many of the Gentiles. This was something that the Jews should have fully known, for it was predicted in their scriptures. Paul writes:

But I say, did Israel not know,[67] i.e., know about God's plan to save the pagans, those who are not Abraham's physical descendants? **First Moses says** (Deut. 32:21);

"I (God speaking); **will provoke** or incite; **you to jealousy** or envy;[68] **by** or through; **those who are not a nation** (the Gentiles, who would provoke Israel to jealousy because Israel thought that God's mercies belonged only to them); **I** (God speaking); **will move you to anger by a foolish nation** (foolish because of their senseless idolatry, and blatant immorality)."

Paul says next in verse 20 about the Gentiles:

But Isaiah is very bold or forthright; **and says** (Isa. 65:1);

"I (God); **was found by those who did not seek Me** (the Gentiles);

I (God); **was made manifest to those who did not ask for Me** (the Gentiles)."

Finally, he says in verse 21:

But to Israel he says (Isa. 65:2);

"All day long I (God); **have stretched out My hands** "calling for repentance and faith;"[69]

To a disobedient and contrary people."

---

65 Col. 1:5, 6.

66 Incidentally, we should note that the connection Paul makes between gospel preachers and his reference to Psalm 19 confirms that general revelation is not enough to bring people to a saving knowledge of Christ. Hence, preachers must preach the gospel "in all the world to every creature" (Mark 16:15).

67 The double negative is being used again, cf. v. 18.

68 Note that Paul takes up this theme of *jealousy* again in 11:11.

69 Robinson, Book II. p. 96.

In commenting on these last words, Sproul rightly says:

> Paul uses the imagery of God with his palms open, beseeching people, exhorting them, inviting them, telling them, to come to him. And he stands there not just for a second, not just for a moment, not for a five-minute altar call, but all day long.
>
> The reason why people don't come to God is not because God fails to invite them, nor is it a logical conclusion from the doctrine of predestination, but it is rooted in disobedience and obstinacy. It is precisely because man is in a state of rebellion that he will never respond to the gospel, unless God sovereignly conquers that rebelliousness in his heart. To state the matter another way: anyone can be saved if he wants to be saved, but therein lies the problem. No one wants to be saved, unless God sovereignly plants a desire in the rebellious heart to come to him. If we were left to ourselves, if there were no election, if there were no predestinating grace, none of us would ever come to Christ, simply because we would never want to come, because we are by nature disobedient and rebellious.[70]

These closing words in our chapter are significant and sad at the same time, for "against this picture of the Gentiles flocking to Jehovah, Isaiah portrays the Lord standing all day long with outstretched, beckoning hands to the nation of Israel, and being met with disobedience and stubborn refusal."[71]

And so, what will God do with His people who continue to spurn His free grace in Christ through the gospel? Will He utterly cast them all off? Will He totally reject them all at last? This is what Paul will take up in the next chapter.

Suggested applications from the text for the church:

1- We learn from our verses that just as with prayer (10:1), preaching the gospel does not stand in contradiction to God's sovereign choice of only saving some. In fact, it is the primary means by which they will be saved.

2- We learn from our verses that churches have a duty to be involved in training up ministers and missionaries for the gospel as God gives them opportunity to do so.

3- We learn from our verses that as believers, we have ample cause to give God praise, because, by His doing, we have not only heard the good news report concerning Jesus, but we have also believed it to the saving of the soul — glory be to God!

Suggested application from the text for the non-Christian:

1- You learn from our verses that your refusal to come to Jesus for salvation is blameworthy, for indeed, through the gospel, He stretches His hands out toward you in love that you may be saved. Humble yourself, then, before Him, and receive Him as Lord and Savior before it is too late. Believe on Him with all your heart, and then confess Him with your mouth all the days of your life.

---

70 Sproul, pp. 228, 229.

71 McDonald, 1723.

ROMANS
CHAPTER ELEVEN

Text: Rom. 11:1-10[1]

General theme: Israel – A Castaway People?

Homiletical outline of the verses:

A. The probing:[1a] I say then, has God cast away His people? Certainly not!

B. The proofs: [1b] For I also am an Israelite, of the seed of Abraham, *of* the tribe of Benjamin. [2] God has not cast away His people whom He foreknew. Or do you not know what the Scripture says of Elijah, how he pleads with God against Israel, saying, [3] "LORD, they have killed Your prophets and torn down Your altars, and I alone am left, and they seek my life"? [4] But what does the divine response say to him? "I have reserved for Myself seven thousand men who have not bowed the knee to Baal."

C. The practical point: [5] Even so then, at this present time there is a remnant according to the election of grace. [6] And if by grace, then *it is* no

---

1 I realize that there are good and godly commentators and pastors who will differ with some of my perspectives on this chapter. None of this should cause animosity between us. Rather we should have Christian love for each other (John 13:35) and open dialogue as we seek to sharpen one another (Prov. 27:17). Lloyd-Jones speaks to this matter when after he says that Romans chapter 11 is "one of the great and noble chapters in the whole of the Bible" and that it is "much more difficult than either chapter 9 or 10." He writes, "Certainly, there has been disagreement about some of its content and it is therefore essential that as we come to consider it we should begin with a kind of general introduction. But before we do that there is something which is even more important. It relates to the spirit in which we approach this chapter. We must come with reverence and humility. Of course, the Scriptures are always to be approached in that way but it is necessary at times and for particular reasons to enforce that requirement and one of those relates to the fact there are matters in this chapter which are the subject of great dispute. Let us therefore resolve at the outset that our object in examining this chapter is not going to be to prove that we are right while others are wrong. We must avoid a spirit of controversy. There are several differing points of view here and they are all conscientiously held." Lloyd-Jones, *Romans,* p. 1. Finally, I remind the reader again that I write on this section of Scripture as one whose family is half Jewish. I love Jewish people as with all people. I trust that what I have written in this chapter in no way detracts from that position at all but rather accurately and honestly reflects God's teaching regarding the nation of Israel as a whole.

longer of works; otherwise grace is no longer grace. But if *it is* of works, it is no longer grace; otherwise work is no longer work.

D. The pronouncement: [7] What then? Israel has not obtained what it seeks; but the elect have obtained it, and the rest were blinded. [8] Just as it is written:

"God has given them a spirit of stupor,
Eyes that they should not see
And ears that they should not hear,
To this very day."
[9] And David says:
"Let their table become a snare and a trap,
A stumbling block and a recompense to them.
[10] Let their eyes be darkened, so that they do not see,
And bow down their back always."

Summary of section: In these verses, Paul speaks about God's plan of salvation for the nation of Israel. Having just described them in the last verse of the previous chapter as a "disobedient and contrary people," he speaks now about their relationship to God. He asks, "Has God *completely* washed His hands of all the Jews or in their present state of rejecting Christ as a whole, has He *entirely* cast them all off?" Thankfully, Paul will tell us that this is not the case. Rather, he shows here that within *ethnic Israel* God has an *elect Israel* who will come to faith in Christ and be saved. Hendriksen helpfully comments:

> The description (in 10:21) of Israel as "disobedient and obstinate" naturally introduces the question of whether God has perhaps rejected his people (11:1). This theme, divine rejection, is not new. The apostle has already shown that divine rejection, though in a sense real, is *not complete* (chapter 9) and *not arbitrary* (chapter 10). Here in chapter 11 he will point out that it is also *not absolute or unqualified*. It is not the whole story. Running side-by-side with rejection there is also election. Divine saving activity parallels divine hardening. See 11:7, 25, 26. In a sense some of the ideas of chapter 9—see especially verses 6-13; 23-27—recur in Chapter 11. But Chapter 11 goes farther. It shows that between hardening and saving, between breaking off and grafting in, there is a kind of cause and effect relationship: the disobedience of the Jews brings about the obedience of the Gentiles (verses 11, 12, 15, 30); the mercy shown to the Gentiles is a blessing for the Jews (verse 31b); so that, in the end, not only *the fullness of the Gentiles* but also the salvation of *"all Israel"* is secured.[2]

Exegetical & Practical Insights:
Obs. 1- (v. 1a) That as Paul addresses his topic at hand concerning the nation of Israel, he writes:

---

2 Hendriksen, pp. 359, 360.

I say then,[3] or "This leads me to the question;"[4] **has God cast away** or utterly rejected, thrust off and abandoned; **His people** (Hebrew Israel) [which of course He could have done because of their rejection of Christ]? **Certainly not** or banish the thought forever![5]

Obs. 2- (v. 1b) That as Paul goes on to give support for his last statement, he speaks about himself as a full-blooded "Hebrew of Hebrews" in order to establish his point.[6] He writes:[7]

For the conjunction explaining why God has not cast off His people completely; **I** literally, "I, even I myself;" **also am an Israelite,** i.e., a descendent of Jacob (Israel); **of the seed of Abraham** or one of his physical offspring; *of* the tribe of Benjamin[8] (which was one of the most regarded tribes in the nation which descended from Benjamin himself, who was Jacob's youngest son).[9]

Sproul comments: "There is, within the nation of Israel, some whom God determines in advance to save, to overcome their rebelliousness; and exhibit A for that is Paul. Who was more rebellious than Paul? Who set out to destroy the Messiah and his people more than did Paul? And yet, when God intervened in his life on the Damascus Road, giving him the vision of the risen Christ, his life was changed."[10]

Obs. 3- (vv. 2-4) That as Paul goes on to explain the fact that God has not fully and finally cast away "His people" (v.1) he begins this verse by establishing exactly who "His people" truly are by giving an important qualifier. He says:

God has not cast away His people whom He *foreknew* (italics mine). The word "foreknew" should be given the full weight and emphasis here that it was given back in chapter 8:29, the only other place where Paul uses it in this epistle. There we saw that the term spoke of those whom

---

3 Paul uses similar words in 10:18, 19; 11:11. His question in this verse sounds similar to that of Samuel and the psalmist in the Old Testament (see 1 Samuel 12:22 and Psalm 94:14).

4 Phillips Translation.

5 Paul uses these words throughout this epistle: cf. 3:4, 3:31, 6:2, 9:14, 11:11.

6 Paul speaks of himself in this way in other places: cf. Acts 22:3, 26:4-5; Rom. 9:3; Phil. 3:4-5; 2 Cor. 11:22.

7 Haldane says, "Had his doctrine involved the total rejection of the Jews, he would have pronounced his own condemnation." Haldane, p. 523.

8 Benjamin Merkle says, "It is instructive that Paul does not answer, 'May it never be!' For you know that in the Millennium God will restore Israel to its former glory.'" *Three Views on Israel and the Church: Perspectives on Romans 9–11* p. 179.

9 Merkle notes again (*Ibid.* 178-79): "This question is not dealing with the future but with the past and the present. Paul is asking whether the ethnic people of Israel, although they receive special blessings (3:1-2; 9:4-5), are cut off from God's promises because they have rejected the Messiah. Thus the question is whether God has *completely* or *utterly* rejected them because of the hardness of their hearts. Again, the question is not, 'Has God cast off ethnic Israel with respect to his special plan for their future?' It seems, however, that people often subconsciously read the question that way, but that misses Paul's real question and prejudices one toward interpreting the rest of the chapter as advocating a special future for Israel. The nature of the question does not anticipate a future mass-conversion. The question Paul asked is, 'Has God cut off ethnic Israel altogether?' or, 'Is there any hope that God will continue to save Israelites?'"

10 Sproul, p. 229.

God "knew in advance," or "knew from eternity," or "fore-chose," and "fore-loved" so that this knowledge "characterizes an intimate personal relationship."[11] It spoke about a *saving knowledge* of specific individuals who were predestined to be saved and conformed to the moral image of God's Son.

And so, what is Paul's point? It is that although the nation as a whole should be completely cast off from God for rejecting Jesus the Messiah, nonetheless, those whom God foreknew from the foundation of the world among the nation would be spared this. Although many of the Christ-rejecting Israelites will be cast-off in the final analysis, nevertheless, those upon whom God set His love from all eternity will not experience such a thing. Consequently, God has not cast off His people whom He *foreknew*.

But we ask, "Who are these people whom God foreknew among the Jews?" They are the Israel within Israel whom Paul spoke of back in chapter 9:6. They are the "remnant according to the election of grace" as Paul will speak of in verse 5 of this chapter.[12]

Hodge's comments are helpful:

> This verse admits of two interpretations. The words *his people* may be understood, as in the preceding verse, as meaning *the Jewish nation*, and the clause *which he foreknew*, as, by implication, assigning the reason for the declaration that God had not cast them off. The clause, according to this view, is little more than a repetition of the sentiment of the preceding verse...
>
> The second interpretation requires more stress to be laid upon the words *which he foreknew*, as qualifying and distinguishing the preceding phrase, *his people*. 'God has indeed rejected his external people, the Jewish nation as such, but he has not cast away his people whom he foreknew.' According to this view, *his people* means the elect, his spiritual people, or the true Israel. This interpretation seems decidedly preferable, **1.** Because it is precisely the distinction which Paul had made, and made for the same purpose in chapter ix 6-8, 'The rejection of the external Israel does not invalidate the promises of God, because those promises did not contemplate the natural seed as such, but the spiritual Israel. So, now, when I say that the external Israel is rejected, it does not imply that the true chosen Israel, to whom the promises pertain, is cast away.' **2.** Because this is apparently Paul's own explanation in the sequence. The mass of the nation were cast away, but "a remnant, according to the election of grace," were reserved, ver. 5. Israel as such, Paul says in ver. 7, failed of admission to Messiah's kingdom, "but the election hath obtained it." It is, therefore, evident that the *people which God foreknew*, and which were not cast off,

---

11 MacArthur, *New Systematic Theology*, p. 499.

12 It is unfortunate that some good commentators take the word *foreknew* here *merely* to mean that God "foreknew" the nation of Israel *corporately* or *nationally*. While of course this is true (cf. Deut. 7:1-11; Amos 3:2), this does not seem to be Paul's particular point here, especially since he goes on to speak in just a few verses about a "remnant" among the corporate, national Jewish people who are saved "according to the election of grace." Paul's main point in mentioning the word "foreknew" in this context is to prepare us for what he will say in the following verses, based on what he has already said in the previous chapter, 9:6-8, 27.

is "the remnant" spoken of in ver. 5, and "the election," mentioned in ver. 7. **3.** Because the illustration borrowed from the Old Testament best suits this interpretation. In the days of Elias [Elijah], God rejected the great body of the people; but reserved to himself a remnant, chosen in sovereign grace. The distinction, therefore, in both cases, is between the external and the chosen people.[13]

Haldane concurs:

The term people, in the preceding verse, refers to the whole of Israel as the typical people of God, but is here restricted to the elect among them who were His true people, and are distinguished as 'His people which He foreknew.' God had cast off the nation, but even then He had a people among them whom from eternity He foreknew as His people. The word foreknow, as formerly observed, signifies to know before, or it denotes a knowledge accompanied by a decree, or it imports a preconceived love, favour, and regard.[14]

Paul writes next in verses 2b-4:

Or do you not know or recall and understand; **what the Scripture says of Elijah** (that is, says of the well-known Old Testament prophet in 1 Kings 19); **how he pleads**[15] or continually makes intercession; **with God against Israel,** (not for, but against Israel because of the nation's apostasy from God); **saying, "Lord, they have killed Your prophets and torn down Your altars, and I alone am left, and they seek my life"? But**[16] or in stark contrast to this; **what does the divine response** or communication; **say to him? "I have reserved** or kept; **for Myself**; "as His own children, people, and property"[17] (amid the spiritual wickedness of the society); **seven thousand** "seven a symbolic number denoting sufficiency and completeness;"[18] **men who have not bowed the knee** "the outward sign of idolatrous worship;"[19] **to Baal** (the false, "weather-god" and Canaanite deity).

In these words, Paul gives his second proof for why God had not entirely cast away all of ethnic Israel. As he thought about how most (not all, but most) in his day had rejected Jesus whom God had sent to them, he reflects on the nation's dark history. He brings to our minds the account of Elijah. After the prophet's glorious defeat of the false prophets of Baal at Mount Carmel (1 Kings 18), we are told that Jezebel—the mad queen who herself was a worshiper of Baal—threatened Elijah, which prompted him to run for his life into the wilderness.

---

13 Hodge, pp. 353, 354.

14 Haldane, pp. 523, 524.

15 Grk. present, active, verb.

16 The strong Greek adversative.

17 Robinson, Book II. p. 103.

18 Ibid.

19 Ibid., p. 104.

After escaping her clutches, we are told that Elijah received some food, drink, and then some sleep, and that God came to him and said, "What are you doing here, Elijah?" In other words, God said to His servant, "Why are you hiding out as if there was no God in Israel to protect you?"

In response to God, Elijah spoke the words which Paul records in verse 3 of our chapter. As he thought about how most of his kinsman according to the flesh had rejected the Lord (and no doubt Paul was feeling the same in his day), Elijah cried out against Israel saying, "LORD, they have killed Your prophets and torn down Your altars, and I alone am left, and they seek my life."

After this time of self-pity, we are told that God came to the prophet with a divine response through a still small voice, saying to him the words of verse 4 in our chapter (as found in 1 Kings 19:18), "I have reserved for Myself seven thousand men who have not bowed the knee to Baal."

Paul's point in citing this Old Testament narrative is plain: regardless of the unfaithfulness of the nation of Israel on the whole to God, He will always have a true, believing people among them. He will always have a believing seed "reserved for Himself" for His own glory and honor, despite how things may seem.

Obs. 4- (v. 5) That as Paul now applies this fact practically to his current situation and "draws a conclusion from Elijah's encounter with God"[20] he says:

Even so then, or accordingly "the language making it clear that Elijah's experience is a typical example of how God works;"[21] **at this present time** or more literally "at the now time;"[22] that is, right while Israel continues to reject Jesus the Messiah in Paul's day; **there is**[23] or has come to be at the current time as a result of a past action which is now part of all who have ever been saved; **a remnant** or a godly, believing seed or group which is left from the larger number of apostate Jews; **according to** or because of; **the election of grace**[24] which means that this selecting of them was "*gracious*, not merely in the sense of *kind*, but

---

20 Harvey, p. 268.

21 Ibid.

22 As Paul puts forth his "remnant theology," it is essential to note that he highlights what God has done *in his day in the apostolic generation* (see also verses 30, and 31, where Paul emphasizes what God is doing presently in his time [note the double use of the word "now"] and throughout the ages, as opposed to primarily in the future). As Merkle says, "Paul's point is *not* that God has rejected his people temporarily but in the future he will once again show mercy to them. Rather, his point is that just as God did not reject Israel in the past (but preserved the faithful remnant as in the days of Elijah) so too God has not rejected his people during Paul's day." Merkle, p. 182.
Furthermore, I agree with William Hendriksen when he writes, "The view of some—and among them those whose writings we regard highly—that a day is coming when this rule [of a remnant from the larger group of Jews being saved] will no longer apply, in fact that the very principle of the remnant implies that one day the nation of Israel as a whole will be saved, seems rather strange." Hendriksen, p. 363.

23 Grk. perfect, active, verb.

24 Once again, we see Paul highlighting the matter of *grace* when it comes to salvation. This is something which is always on his mind.

gratuitous, sovereign, not founded on the merits of the persons chosen, but the good pleasure of God."[25]

Once again, Paul here identifies the *true Israel within apostate Israel* whom God foreknew calling them now in verse 5 "a remnant." This remnant (whom God has saved in Old Covenant times and in New Covenant times even till this day) proves that God has not completely rejected all of His people. These are those whom, although they deserve to go to hell just like everybody else, God has marked them out from among the Jewish nation for salvation (just as He does with other individuals from other nations as well). Thus again Paul says in Romans 9:27:

> Isaiah also cries out concerning Israel:
> "Though the number of the children of Israel be as the sand of the sea,
> *The remnant will be saved*" (italics mine).

Jeremiah the prophet said something similar when he writes in Jeremiah 31:7:

> [7] For thus says the LORD:
> "Sing with gladness for Jacob,
> And shout among the chief of the nations;
> Proclaim, give praise, and say,
> 'O LORD, save Your people,
> *The remnant of Israel!*'" (italics mine).

William Hendriksen makes this important observation:

> The doctrine of *the salvation of the remnant* is taught throughout Scripture: At the time of *Noah* the many perished, the few were saved (Gen. 6:1-8; Luke 17:26, 27; 1 Peter 3:20). The same thing happened in the days of *Lot* (Gen. 19:29; Luke 17:28, 29). *Elijah* too, as we have just now been told, was acquainted with the idea of the saved remnant, though he did not realize that it amounted to no less than seven thousand. Previously (Rom. 9:27; cf. Isa. 10:22 f.) the apostle has reminded us of the remnant in the days of *Isaiah.* It does not surprise us therefore that also "at the present time," that is, in the apostle's own day, there was a saved remnant, and that *Paul* belonged to it. In Romans the remnant doctrine is either taught or implied also in the following passages: 9:6 f.; 9:18a; 10:4, 11, 16; 11:14, 24, 25. Further substantiation of the doctrine that salvation is for the elect remnant can be found in such Old Testament passages as Isa. 1:9 (=Rom. 9:29); 11:11, 16; 46:13; 53:1; Jer. 23:3; 31:7; Joel 2:32; Amos 5:15; Mic. 2:12; 4:5-7; 7:18; Zeph. 3:13, to mention but a few.
> As to the New Testament, it may or may not be significant that in the parable of The Sower (or The Four Kinds of Soil)—see Matt. 13:1-9, 18-23; Mark 4:1-9, 13-20; Luke 8:4-15— it is *only the final kind of soil* that yields a good crop. But even if no conclusion can be drawn from this parable as to the portion of saved to unsaved among those who hear the gospel, we hear the Master's clear statement, "For many are called, but few chosen" (Matt. 22:14) Cf. Luke 22:32.[26]

---

25 Hodge, p. 356.
26 Hendriksen, p. 363.

Obs. 5- (v. 6) That having just mentioned at the end of the previous verse the word "grace" concerning God's merciful choosing of some in Israel, Paul writes now saying,

And if by grace, i.e., by God's unmerited, unearned, and uncaused favor in Christ; **then it is no longer of works** or our own human attempts to get right with God; **otherwise** the word supplying the reason election cannot be by works;[27] **grace is no longer grace. But if it is of** or on the grounds of; **works, it is no longer grace; otherwise work is no longer work.**

What is Paul saying? It is simply what he has been saying throughout this entire epistle; namely, that God's plan of salvation which is entirely based on grace is wholly antithetical to any salvation plan of works.[28] Why is this? It is because the two completely cancel each other out, since they are thoroughly "distinct and opposite, [so] that salvation cannot be of any combination or mixture of both."[29] Consequently Paul says in Romans 4:4, 5, "Now to him who works, the wages are not counted as grace but as debt. But to him who does not work but believes on Him who justifies the ungodly, his faith is accounted for righteousness."

McDonald comments: "God doesn't choose this remnant on the basis of their works, but by His sovereign, electing grace. These two principles—grace and works—are mutually exclusive. A gift cannot be earned. What is free cannot be bought. What is unmerited cannot be deserved. Fortunately, God's choice was based on grace, not on works; otherwise no one could ever have been chosen."[30]

Haldane further obverses: "The opponents of the doctrine of election maintain that men are chosen on account of their good works *foreseen*. But here it is expressly declared by the Apostle that it is not on account of works at all, whether past, present, or future. What, then, is the source of election? Grace."[31]

Obs. 6- (vv. 7-10) That as Paul raises and answers a question so as to summarize all that he has been saying in the previous words he writes,

What then? Israel, i.e., Hebrew/ethnic-Israel; **has not** (because they sought it by works); **obtained** or arrived at; **what it seeks**[32] or diligently goes after, which is to say, righteousness and acceptance with God;[33] **but the elect,** i.e., the foreknown/remnant who were chosen "according to the election of grace" v. 5; **have obtained it,** that is, obtained it by God's merciful predestining of them to salvation and them ultimately coming to faith in Christ; **and the rest** or the others in national Israel who

---

27 Harvey, p. 268.

28 Cf. Rom. 1:7; 3:23-28; 4:1-8; 5:20; 9:11; 9:30-10:13; 16:24. See also: Deut. 7:7, 8; Gal. 2:16, 21; Eph. 2:8, 9; 2 Tim. 1:9; Titus 3:5.

29 Wilson, p. 186.

30 McDonald, 1724.

31 Haldane, p. 526.

32 Grk. present, active, verb.

33 Cf. 9:31-32, 10:2.

continue in unbelief; **were blinded** so as to be left spiritually calloused to Christ and the gospel.

Just as it is written[34] or stands written in Scripture in Deuteronomy 29:3, 4; and Isaiah 29:10,[35] **"God has given them,** i.e., Christ-rejecting Israel; **a spirit of stupor** or a disposition of spiritual slumber or numbness; **Eyes that they should not see** (spiritually speaking); **And ears that they should not hear, To this very day"** (Paul's current time). **And David says** that is, says in Psalm 69:22, 23: **"Let their table** which represents the spiritual privileges which God in grace gave them; **become a snare and a trap, A stumbling block and a recompense** or righteous retribution; **to them. Let their eyes be darkened, so that** or for the purpose that; **they do not see, And bow down their back always"** which is to say, let them be like blind people who sometimes are hunched over as they grope about in the dark.[36]

These are sobering words which show that to whom much is given much shall be required (Luke 12:48). They teach us that because Jesus came to His own "and His own did not receive Him" (John 1:11), as a judgment upon them for this, God brought a judicial blindness to them. This is the case with the majority of ethnic Israel "to this very day" v. 8, so that "even to this day, when Moses is read, a veil lies on their heart" (2 Cor. 3:15).[37] But we ask, "Will this horrible spiritual condition continue with *all the Jews forever*? Have they all completely stumbled so as to never rise again?" This is the matter that Paul takes up in the following verses.

Suggested applications from the text for the church:

1- We learn from our passage (specifically in verse 1b) about the power of our testimonies in showing that our God is mighty to save sinners from all different backgrounds including those from a Jewish background.

2- We learn from our passage about the promise that God will always have a remnant for Himself by grace. This should cause us who are Christians to rejoice, seeing that we are part of this remnant.

3- We learn from our passage about the particular results which should come from us who are part of the elect remnant: deep humility, great gratitude, and earnest praise.

Suggested application from the text for the non-Christian:

1- You learn from our passage about a present-day sentencing that God gives to those who reject Christ—a spirit of stupor. May it be then that this knowledge of such horrific consequence will cause you to break with your sins and to go to Christ by faith to be saved.

---

34 Grk. perfect, passive, verb.

35 In verses 8 to 10, R. C. Sproul insightfully says in his *Reformation Study Bible*, p. 2000, that all of Paul's Old Testament citations from Deut. 29:4; Is. 29:10; Ps. 69:22, 23 (the law, the Prophets and Psalms) "represent each major section of the canon of OT Scripture [and] describe a biblical pattern of divine activity in the judicial hardening of hearts, a pattern Paul sees repeated in his own day."

36 MacArthur, p. 104.

37 Cf. Mark 4:10-12; Luke 8:10; Acts 28:23-29.

Text: Romans 11:11-24[38]

General theme: Israel – Provoked to Jealousy!

Homiletical outline of the verses:

A. Paul's examination: [11] I say then, have they stumbled that they should fall? Certainly not! But through their fall, to provoke them to jealousy, salvation *has come* to the Gentiles. [12] Now if their fall *is* riches for the world, and their failure riches for the Gentiles, how much more their fullness!

[13] For I speak to you Gentiles; inasmuch as I am an apostle to the Gentiles, I magnify my ministry, [14] if by any means I may provoke to jealousy *those who are* my flesh and save some of them. [15] For if their being cast away *is* the reconciling of the world, what *will* their acceptance *be* but life from the dead?

B. Paul's exemplification: [16] For if the firstfruit *is* holy, the lump *is* also *holy;* and if the root *is* holy, so *are* the branches. [17] And if some of the branches were broken off, and you, being a wild olive tree, were grafted in among them, and with them became a partaker of the root and fatness of the olive tree, [18] do not boast against the branches. But if you do boast, *remember that* you do not support the root, but the root *supports* you.

[19] You will say then, "Branches were broken off that I might be grafted in." [20] Well *said.* Because of unbelief they were broken off, and you stand by faith. Do not be haughty, but fear. [21] For if God did not spare the natural branches, He may not spare you either. [22] Therefore consider the goodness and severity of God: on those who fell, severity; but toward you, goodness, if you continue in *His* goodness. Otherwise you also will be cut off. [23] And they also, if they do not continue in unbelief, will be grafted in, for God is able to graft them in again. [24] For if you were cut out of the olive tree which is wild by nature, and were grafted contrary to nature into a cultivated olive tree, how much more will these, who *are* natural *branches,* be grafted into their own olive tree?

Summary of section: In these verses, Paul begins to speak about what has been called God's jealousy-provoking strategy. In His sovereignty, God ordained that the salvation of elect Gentiles would be used by Him to provoke the Jews to jealousy so that through their jealousy of seeing Gentiles being converted, some of the Jews themselves would ultimately seek the Savior and be saved. In fact, Paul tells us in verse fourteen of this chapter that this jealousy-provoking strategy toward the Jews concerning the Gentiles was part of his ministry so that the Jews would be saved; thus, he says, "If by any means I may provoke to jealousy those who are my flesh and save some of them." All of this might sound a bit mysterious to us, however it shows us that God's thoughts are not our thoughts and His ways are not our ways (Isa. 55:8). In His infinite wisdom, God has His

---

38 I received help in my understanding of these verses all to the end of the chapter by a written sermon online by Charles Alexander entitled: *Romans Eleven and the Two Israels.*

own ways of getting things done. This is no less true than when it comes to bringing about the spiritual recovery of many in Israel.

Exegetical & Practical Insights:

Obs. 1- (v. 11) That as Paul continues to reflect on unsaved, ethnic Israel he writes,

I say then or therefore; **have they,** that is, Israel as a whole who had not yet been saved; **stumbled** or tripped so badly in their rejection of Christ (who became to them a stumbling stone cf. 9:32); **that** or so that; **they** (like a runner in a race); **should fall** or utterly be left in ruin with absolutely no hope of ever recovering? Paul is asking, "Has God absolutely washed His hands of every single unbelieving Jew so that their blindness would be irreversible" (cf. v. 7b)? **Certainly not!** Or perish the thought! **But**[39] or on the contrary; **through their fall** or better understood from the Greek text, through *the sin* of the Jews not receiving Christ by faith alone; **to** or in order to; **provoke** or stir;[40] **them** (again, unsaved, ethnic Israel); **to jealousy** or envy,[41] (by God's design); **salvation,** i.e., deliverance from the wrath of God due them because of their sins against Him (along with peace and forgiveness of sin); *has come* to the Gentiles (non-Jews).[42]

As the apostle here recaps much of what he has already written in the earlier verses, he assures us that although Israel stumbled in rejecting Jesus the Messiah and was judged for it, their fall was not designed by God to bring about their *complete and collective* ruin. This is clear by what Paul says again in verse 5, "Even so then *at this present time there is a remnant according to the election of grace.*" The point is plain: God is still saving elect Jews (as well as elect Gentiles) whom He foreknew (cf. v. 2). As He did in Old Covenant times and in Paul's day, He will continue to do throughout the generations (not just in the future)[43] until the end of time, when Jesus returns, as Paul will continue to explain.[44]

Further, we see here that God used Israel's sin for good. He used it sinlessly so that a door of grace might be opened on a broader scale toward other people groups besides the Jews and that the Jews themselves, who witness this happening, might realize what they are missing and seek the Savior. As Hodge says, "The stumbling of the Jews was not attended with

---

39 The strong Greek adversative.

40 Since ethnic Israel provoked God in rejecting Christ, God, in turn, provoked them back by saving Gentiles whom they despised.

41 Cf. 10:19.

42 Of course, it was always God's plan to save Gentiles (cf. Isa. 42:6, 49:6) but this became much more pronounced when the Jews as a whole rejected our Lord (cf. Acts 13:46-48).

43 Merkle is correct when he writes, "Again, this question does not presuppose the reversal of Israel's fortune in the future. Paul is merely asking if God has *utterly* rejected his covenant people. To read this question as if Israel is now fallen but will later be redeemed is to misread the question." Merkle, p. 174.

44 This is what I call the *non-future-steady-stream conversion of the Jews*. This perspective stands in opposition to a *future-mass conversion of the Jews*.

the result of their utter and final ruin, but was the occasion of facilitating the progress of the gospel among the Gentiles."[45]

Obs. 2- (v. 12) That as Paul speaks about the above-stated matter, he writes:

Now if their fall again, ethnic Israel's initial sin in stumbling over Christ which led to God's spiritual blinding upon them; *is* riches or great gospel blessings; **for the world,** i.e., the non-Jewish world (because again, now, by God's grace, the gospel door of salvation is wide open to them); **and their failure,** that is, the Jews' failure in rejecting the gospel and in not receiving Christ by faith alone as their Savior; **riches** (i.e., spiritual wealth: regeneration, justification, adoption, sanctification, etc.,); **for the Gentiles, how much more their** (Israel's); **fullness**[46] not their *full inclusion,* which is to say, the salvation of all Jews or most of them at the return of Christ as some teach. But rather, their *full number* as God continues to save a steady-stream of elect-remnant Jews throughout history (even as He was doing in Paul's day and will continue to do until Christ returns). Paul's argument is, "If the national rejection of Israel [on a whole] has meant great blessing to the world at large, how much more blessing will it be when out of the wreck of Israel there comes a steady stream of Jewish converts, an election of grace to join the main stream of divine election flowing from the Gentile world? Is this not indeed, life from the dead?"[47]

Obs. 3- (vv. 13-14) That as Paul confirms this present day, side-by-side work that God is doing between the elect Jews and elect Gentiles (again, even in his own day, not exclusively in the future cf. v. 5, 14, 30, 31), in speaking to the Gentiles directly for the first time in this letter about the Jews he writes:[48]

For I speak to you Gentiles i.e., the Gentile believers at Rome; **inasmuch as I am an apostle to the Gentiles,**[49] **I magnify**[50] or continually exalt and take glory in; **my ministry,** that is, his service to God in preaching the gospel since as he was doing this the blessings of the gospel were coming to the Gentiles; **if by any means I may provoke** or awaken; **to jealousy** or envy; *those who are* my flesh (his own, ethnic family members from among the Jewish nation); **and save some of them**[51] (again, not the entire nation or most in it at Christ's return), but some, i.e., the chosen Jewish remnant, and this once more, as they throughout

---

45 Hodge, p. 361.

46 Merkle is also correct when he says that there is "no clear evidence in this passage that 'fullness' refers to a future event when Israel returns to their God. One clue to the meaning of 'fullness' is in v. 25 where Paul speaks of the 'fullness' of the Gentiles. Since virtually every scholar interprets 'the fullness of the Gentiles' as the full number of elect Gentiles throughout history, is it not also likely that the 'fullness' of Israel refers to the full number of elect Jews throughout history?'" Merkle, p. 190.

47 Charles Alexander from the sermon entitled: *Romans Eleven and the Two Israels.*

48 The words "to you" are placed first in the sentence in the Greek text for the sake of emphasis.

49 Cf. Acts 9:15

50 Grk. present, active, verb.

51 Cf. Rom. 9: 1-4, 10:1.

time see all that they are missing spiritually speaking taking place in the lives of the pagans who are embracing Jesus. In short, converted Gentiles become God's instruments for turning elect Jews to Christ.

Obs. 4- (v. 15) That as Paul explains his previous thought he writes:

For if their (the ethnic Jews); **being cast away,** i.e., the unbelieving, Christ-rejecting Israelites being cast away by God for rejecting His Son; *is* the reconciling of the world, that is, the ongoing salvation of elect Gentiles to God through faith in Christ; **what *will* their acceptance *be*,** i.e., the acceptance of all the believing Jewish remnant to God, through Christ; **but life from the dead** which is exactly what happens spiritually to elect Jews at conversion, for indeed, this is "life from the dead" (cf. Rom. 6:13; Eph. 2:1-5). "We must be careful to observe that Paul has not yet mentioned the future even once. His whole discussion has been about a hardened nation and an election of grace within it. The hardening of the nation has meant the opening of the door of salvation to the Gentiles. In this sense both blessing and reconciliation have come to the world. But the elect remnant of the Jews is a source of even *more* blessing, as his single example shows. The 'casting away' and 'receiving' was something which was going on then, and is still going on now, side by side. There is no mention whatever of its being two consecutive stages of history."[52]

Obs. 5- (v. 16-24) That as Paul illustrates all that he has written in verses 1 to 15 concerning God's saving only some individuals from among the Jewish nation, he now puts forth a metaphor in order to reinforce all he has been saying. He paints a picture from nature in order to drive home a practical application and exhortation to Gentiles. Simply stated, he does not want them to conclude that the unbelief of most of the Jews meant that there was little or no hope of seeing more of them saved. God, in fact, has a remnant among them (Rom. 9:5). There is an election of grace, thus he writes:[53]

For if the firstfruit *is* holy or separated unto God, the term "firstfruit" is an Old Testament reference to the first piece of dough from the annual harvest of grain which was to be offered by the Israelites to the Lord as mentioned in Numbers 15:17-21. The "firstfruit" or "first-portion,"

---

52 Olyott, p. 100.

53 Merkle wisely notes, "Those who affirm a special future for Israel claim that Paul teaches that a great majority of ethnic Israelites will be grafted into the tree of salvation. There are at least three difficulties with such an interpretation. First, Paul's primary purpose for using this metaphor is to warn the Gentiles of pride; they are not the natural branches. In other words, this metaphor does not demonstrate that in the future Israel will be grafted back into the olive tree; it cautions the Gentiles not to become arrogant. Second, nowhere does Paul state or imply that God is going to graft *all* unbelieving Jews back into the tree. Rather, he states that those who believe will be grafted into the olive tree. In fact, Paul prefaces his statement with the conditional clause ('if [ἐάν, *ean*] they do not continue in their unbelief, will be grafted in' (11:23). Third, the focus is not only on the future but also on the present. Robertson notes, 'This participation by being 'grafted in' cannot be postponed to some future time, while Gentile believers immediately experience the blessing of the covenant. Just like every present Gentile believer, every present Jewish believer will be grafted in.' Paul is not predicting or prophesying that Israel *as a nation* will be grafted back into the tree of salvation. Rather his point is that when individual Jews believe in Christ, they will be grafted back in.'" Merkle, pp. 192, 193.

"sample" or "piece" is a reference most likely to the remnant of Jews who were first converted under Paul's ministry (cf. Rom. 16:5; 1 Cor. 16:15 see also Acts 18:8); **the lump,** that is to say, all believing Jews who would come after them, for this is what the firstfruit was a pledge of; *is also holy;* and if the root a reference most likely to the believing Jewish patriarchs or the fathers: Abraham, Isaac, and Jacob who are spoken of in verse 28; *is* holy, so *are* the branches, i.e., all believing Jews after them in all generations collectively. "The apostle's point is that we can expect to see a remnant of grace continuing, by virtue of the Jewish origins of the plant. The old plant is not completely devoid of life. But the life that is there consists of those Jews who were coming to believe the gospel."[54]

And if some, not all, but some; **of the branches** that is, individual unbelieving Israelites like many of the Pharisees; **were broken off,** or cut off from the people of God for rejecting Jesus (cf. Acts 3:23); **and you** (you Gentiles); **being a wild olive tree, were grafted in among them** which is to say supernaturally incorporated into the people of God; **and with them became a partaker of the root and fatness** or spiritual richness; **of the olive tree, do not boast** or become haughty and prideful (a present tense command in the original language which stresses the point);[55] **against the branches** or the Jews who were broken off because of unbelief. **But if you do boast,** *remember that* you do not support the root, but[56] or in sharp contrast to this; **the root** *supports* **you** (in other words, Paul says to his Gentile readers at Rome [cf. v.13], "Be humble, because you are what you are, only by the grace of God. You stand by faith alone and this, upon the shoulders of the believing remnant who have gone before you in history").

Paul writes:

You will say then (Paul anticipates a Gentile saying), **Branches were broken off** (Jesus-rejecting Jews); **that** or for the purpose that; **I might be grafted in. Well** *said* or true enough (Paul agrees). **Because of unbelief they were broken off, and you stand,**[57] that is, stand presently and will continue to stand; **by faith,** that is, the personal faith that they expressed in Christ as individuals when they first heard the gospel. **Do not be haughty, but**[58] or in contrast to this; **fear** (two more present tense commands in the original language). For the conjunction explaining the previous words; **if God did not spare the natural branches,** i.e., the unbelieving Jews; **He may not spare you either,**[59] that is, spare you if you become unbelieving [clearly a warning to false professors of faith cf. Matt. 7:21-23]. **Therefore** the word drawing Paul's concluding results

---

54 Olyott, p. 100.

55 The present tense verb with the negative particle may indicate that this was something that was already happening with the Gentiles. If so, Paul's words could be translated as: Stop boasting!

56 The strong Greek adversative.

57 Grk. perfect, active, verb.

58 The strong Greek adversative.

59 The double negation in the Greek text emphasizing the point.

from the previous verses; **consider** or note carefully; **the goodness and severity of God: on those who fell** (unbelieving Israelites); **severity** or sternness for their unbelief (in that He gave them a spirit of stupor, "to this very day" v. 8, and then He will finally cast them into hell if they continued in that state); **but toward you** (believing Gentiles); **goodness** or kindness, i.e., gospel goodness and kindness: the forgiveness of sins, reconciliation with God, peace with Him; if you continue in *His* goodness (which of course is what all true Christians do, cf. Phil. 3:13, 14; Heb. 10:39; 1 John 2:19). **Otherwise you also will be cut off** (as the case was with apostate Israel). **And they also** (current unbelieving Israel); if they do not continue in unbelief (as the case was with Paul himself by God's electing grace); **will** (surely); **be grafted in** which is something that God continues to do throughout the centuries; **for** the conjunction explaining why this is so; **God is able** or has the divine strength; **to graft them in again.**[60] For the conjunction confirming why everything that Paul has just said is so; **if you** (Gentiles); **were cut out of the olive tree which is wild by nature, and were grafted contrary to nature into a cultivated olive tree** or the group of God's believing Jews throughout the ages thus, they were now no longer "aliens from the commonwealth of Israel and strangers from the covenants of promise;"[61] **how much more will these, who** *are* natural *branches* (unbelieving Israelites); be grafted into their own olive tree, i.e., be grafted in when they receive Jesus as Lord and Savior?

In summarizing Paul's words, Fesko writes:

> The likely scenario at Rome was that Gentile Christians were boasting about their salvation. They knew of the large-scale Jewish rejection of Christ and the gospel and bragged about the fact that they were included in God's covenant despite the fact that they were once aliens and strangers. Like the humble country boy who skyrockets to fame, the fast-moving cancer of pride swelled in Gentile hearts. But Paul wanted both Jews and Gentiles to understand the wave pattern of God's grace. The Jews needed to recognize how God's grace works so that they would know that God had not forgotten them—He was still faithful to His promises to Abraham, Isaac, and Jacob. The Gentiles however needed to grasp the nature of the movement of God's grace so that they would not become prideful and arrogant. They needed to know that they were originally wild branches, pagans, those with whom no God-fearing Jew would even deign [agree] to share a meal. But God nevertheless grafted them into the holy people of God. Moreover, they were grafted in by God's grace through faith, not by their own inherent superiority or worthiness. A Jewish root also supported these Gentiles — the promises God gave to Abraham, Isaac, and Jacob. So, contrary to Gentile misperceptions, they had not taken over the house of Abraham. Rather they were guests in

---

60 O. Palmer Robertson remarks: "This participation of being 'grafted in' cannot be postponed to some future time, while Gentile believers immediately experience the blessing of the covenant. Just like every present Gentile believer, every present Jewish believer will be grafted in. Like the previous sections of Romans 11, this paragraph emphasizes the present significance of the Jews in fulfilling God's purposes of salvation." Robertson, p. 170.

61 Eph. 2:12.

Abraham's house, and Paul wanted them to remember this. Therefore, he warns his Gentile recipients at Rome about the dangers of pride.

Remember the old saying: "Pride goes before the fall." In this case, Paul wanted the Roman Gentile Christians to recognize that they were saved by grace, not by works. As such, salvation by God's grace precluded all grounds for boasting and pride. If they boasted in their own self-worth, works, or supposed superiority, they would reveal that they were not truly united to Christ and would be broken off the tree. Recall Christ's words to his disciples: 'if anyone does not abide in Me, he is cast out as a branch and is withered; and they gather them and throw them into the fire, and they are burned' (John 15:6). Rather than sink into a pit of pride, the Gentile Christians at Rome are encouraged to meditate on the mercy and grace of God. Not only this, he implicitly gives the Gentile Christians something for which to pray— that the Jews would be regrafted onto the tree."[62]

Suggested applications from the text for the church:

1- We are to marvel at God's amazing plan of salvation, for who but He could formulate such a strategy!

2- We are to be humble, avoiding all spiritual pride and elitism since our entire salvation rests solely on God's wonderful grace toward us in Christ.

3- We are to ponder the great goodness of God which He has richly lavished upon us in Jesus, knowing that in truth, we deserve nothing but His severity.

Suggested application from the text for the non-Christian:

1- You are to remember that not receiving Christ as your Lord and Savior is keeping you from the goodness of God. Repent therefore and put your faith in Him who died in the place of guilty sinners and took the penalty due them for their sins against God and was raised on the third day as a validation of His completed work on their behalf.

Text: Romans 11:25-36

General theme: Israel – All Saved?

Homiletical outline of the verses:

A. Paul's explanation: [25] For I do not desire, brethren, that you should be ignorant of this mystery, lest you should be wise in your own opinion, that blindness in part has happened to Israel until the fullness of the Gentiles has come in. [26] And so all Israel will be saved, as it is written:

"The Deliverer will come out of Zion,

And He will turn away ungodliness from Jacob;

[27] For this *is* My covenant with them,

When I take away their sins."

[28] Concerning the gospel *they are* enemies for your sake, but concerning the election *they are* beloved for the sake of the fathers. [29] For the gifts and

---

62 Fesko, pp. 317-19.

the calling of God *are* irrevocable. [30] For as you were once disobedient to God, yet have now obtained mercy through their disobedience, [31] even so these also have now been disobedient, that through the mercy shown you they also may obtain mercy. [32] For God has committed them all to disobedience, that He might have mercy on all.

D. Paul's exultation: [33] Oh, the depth of the riches both of the wisdom and knowledge of God! How unsearchable *are* His judgments and His ways past finding out!

[34] "For who has known the mind of the LORD?

Or who has become His counselor?"

[35] "Or who has first given to Him

And it shall be repaid to him?"

[36] For of Him and through Him and to Him *are* all things, to whom *be* glory forever. Amen.

Summary of section: In these verses, Paul continues to speak specifically to his Gentile readers as he continues to lay out to them God's redemptive dealings with the Jews (cf. v. 13a). This is something that he did not want them to be unaware of, and this "so to prevent them from becoming conceited and thinking that God has chosen them instead of Israel."[63] In commenting on the remaining words in this chapter, Lloyd-Jones wisely remarks:

> We must be careful that our proper interest in the content of this chapter does not become carnal excitement. There is more than one way of being excited. We can be excited intellectually as well as emotionally. I warn those who are keen to find out what is going to be said on this matter or that and particularly on 'So all Israel shall be saved'. This attitude is quite inappropriate when one comes to study the Scriptures.
>
> Let us remind ourselves at the outset of two things which we find in this chapter. The first is that the Apostle refers in it to a mystery. If therefore we think that we have this chapter all sorted out and tabulated and that there can be no other view worth considering, we are already wrong. But the second is the way in which the Apostle concludes this chapter. Having written it he finds himself in a state of mind and heart in which he can think of and do nothing else but praise and worship God—'O the depth of the riches both of the wisdom and knowledge of God.' The consideration of this truth had that effect on him. So it should on us and on all who consider it and that is what we now begin to do.[64]

Exegetical & Practical Insights:

Obs. 1- (vv. 25-27) That as Paul has just been informing his Gentile readers that Jewish believers will continue to be grafted into the household of faith, he says to them:

For, the conjunction introducing a further explanation of Paul's claim that if Israel does not continue to reject the gospel, then God will graft

---

them back into the olive tree of His people (11:23-24);[65] **I do not desire or wish; brethren, that you** again, primarily his Gentile readers; **should be ignorant** or unaware; **of this mystery** or a particular truth which had been previously concealed but is now formally and fully revealed, which mystery Paul is about to identify explicitly; **lest** or for fear that; **you should be wise** or conceited; **in your own opinion,** "evidently some Gentile believers were tempted to think that there was no future for Israel. She had rejected the gospel and it had now passed to the Gentiles; Israel was finished, rejected, cast off. God had chosen them instead. It is this kind of pride that Paul is opposing;"[66] **that,** the conjunction putting forth the substance of *the mystery* (or secret) which Paul did not want the Gentiles to be ignorant of; **blindness** or spiritual callousness (God's judicial sentencing upon the Christ-rejecting, unbelieving Jews cf. v. 7); **in part,** not temporarily so that sometime in the future this blindness will be lifted, but rather, *only on some,* not all of the Jews (but part of Israel);[67] **has happened** or "befallen" or "has come" (the perfect tense verb denoting a continual state);[68] **to Israel** (ethnic/Hebrew Israel); **until** the word should not be understood *sequentially* so that blindness in part has happened to Israel *until* their hardening status changes, when God will then turn from saving the Gentiles to now saving Israel corporately just before Jesus returns or at the very moment of His return.[69] Instead the word is to be understood as a word of *termination*[70] so that Paul is saying

---

65 Thielman, p. 546.

66 Morris, p. 419. This quote indirectly raises the question of whether or not the church now replaces God's dealings with the nation of Israel. While I do not care for the so-called "replacement theology," I do believe that a "fulfillment theology" fits the biblical testimony better, which is to say, that God's Old Testament salvific promises to the Jews are fulfilled in the elect remnant who believe in Jesus Christ the Messiah. These saved individuals ultimately become part of the Christian church (thus, there is one true people of God on the earth not two) which is made up of both Jews and Gentiles alike. This is the clear teaching of the New Testament (Acts 2:36-47; 15:14-17; Gal. 6:16; Eph. 2:11-22; Phil 3:3; 1 Pet. 2:9, 10).

67 O. Palmer Robertson says: "The phrase 'in part' *(apo merous)* is often interpreted as having a temporal meaning. The passage is thus read, 'For a while hardening has happened to Israel.' But this interpretation has little to support it. It is doubtful that the phrase has a temporal meaning anywhere in the New Testament. The phrase declares either that 'partial hardening' has happened to Israel or that 'part of Israel' has been hardened. Either of these understandings would fit with Paul's earlier discussion of a remnant from Israel that will be saved. Probably the apostle is saying that a part of Israel has been hardened. But in either case, 'in part' does not have temporal meaning. This phrase does not provide an exegetical basis for the idea that God intends to initiate special saving activity in Israel at some time in the future." Robertson, pp. 176, 177.
    Merkle further notes that this "hardening will occur throughout the whole of the present age until the return of Christ. As such, Paul is not suggesting a time when the hardening will be reversed but a time when the hardening will be eschatologically fulfilled." Merkle, p. 94.

68 Morris, p. 420, footnote 111.

69 This view is typically held by those who hold to dispensational, pre-millenarian theology. After this supposedly happens, our dispensational brethren tell us that "Christ will rule over the converted Jewish nation, now regathered in its ancient homeland, from a throne in Jerusalem for a period of a thousand years." Anthony A. Hoekema, *The Bible and the Future,* Eerdmans, 1979, 1994, p. 140.

70 Merkle, p. 185.

that blindness has happened to part of Israel while God's saving work keeps happening through the generations, concerning;[71] **the fullness** or the full-number, **of the Gentiles** (elect Gentiles); **has come in** or has been brought to faith in Christ and into the blessings of the gospel, *until* Christ returns.[72] **And so** (here Paul now confirms all that he has been saying in the previous words concerning the salvation of elect Gentiles being that which will run side-by-side with the salvation of elect Jews until Jesus returns); "And so" not "and then after that" (so as to make the salvation of Jews a next step in God's plan of redemption); but literally: *in the very same manner* (that is, in the very same *remnant manner* that elect Gentiles keep getting saved throughout the ages, through the gospel as Paul just spoke of in the preceding verse); "And so" **all Israel**[73] or the foreknown

---

71 O. Palmer Robertson says: "Too often 'until' has been understood as marking the beginning of a new stage of things with regard to Israel. It has hardly been considered that 'until' more naturally should be interpreted as reaching an eschatological termination point. The phrase implies not a new beginning after a termination, but the continuation of a circumstance until the end of time." Robertson, p. 180.

Merkle concurs: "This phrase is essentially terminative in its significance, implying the end of something. Yet only the context can determine where the emphasis lies after the termination. Often the phrase occurs in an eschatological context where the termination envisioned contains a finalization aspect that makes questions concerning the reversal of the circumstance irrelevant. In other words, what is important is not what will take place *after* the event is completed, but *that* the event is eschatologically fulfilled. For example, in 1 Corinthians 11:26 Paul states that the church is to partake of the Lord's supper and thus proclaim the Lord's death "until" *(achris hou)* he comes. Paul's purpose is not to stress that one day the church will not celebrate the Lord's Supper. Instead, his point is that this celebration will continue "until" the end of time. Also, 1 Corinthians 15:25 states that Christ must reign "until" *(achris hou)* he has put all enemies under his feet. The intended stress is not that a time will come when Christ will no longer reign, but that he must continue to reign until the last enemy is conquered at the final judgment. Likewise, the hardening of Israel that will occur "until" the fullness of the Gentiles comes in refers to an eschatological termination. A hardening will occur throughout the whole of this present age until the return of Christ. Paul is not suggesting a time when the hardening will be reversed but a time when the hardening will be eschatologically fulfilled (i.e., it will have served its full, God-ordained purpose). Merkle, pp. 185, 186.

72 There will be no opportunity for Jews or Gentiles to be saved when Christ returns. In that day, He will "gather together His elect from the four winds, from the farthest part of the earth to the farthest part of heaven" (Mark 13:24, 27). He will "judge the world in righteousness" (Matt: 25:31-46; Acts 17:30, 31). He will close out this age and usher in "the new heavens and the new earth" (2 Pet. 3:10-13).

73 Not "All the Jews" as some read the words, but "All Israel." Typically there are three major views concerning these words:
1- That "all Israel" refers to the elect both Jews and Gentiles (i.e., the church). This was Calvin's view. And while there is much to commend it, I do not think it fits best in this context as it would be completely obvious that this is going to happen. Of course, all the church will be saved. There is no "mystery" here. This would be however my second interpretative choice. As Hendriksen says: "To be sure, at the close of verse 25 the apostle makes mention of the Gentiles, but only in order to indicate that the partial hardening of the Jews will not cease until every elect Gentile will have been brought into the kingdom. Accordingly, Paul is still talking about the Jews. He does so also in verse 26b. Even verse 28 contains a clear reference to the Jews. Not until verses 30-32 are reached does the apostle cause the entire body of the elect, both Jews and Gentiles, to pass in review together. Therefore, while appreciating the good elements in Calvin's explanation, we cannot agree with him in interpreting the term 'all Israel' in 11:26 as referring to all the elect, both Jews and Gentiles. A passage should be interpreted in light of its context. In the present case the context points to Jews, not to Gentiles, nor in verses 26-29 to a combination of Jews and Gentiles." Hendriksen, pp. 380, 381.

(v. 2), remnant (vv. 5, 7), full number of elect Jews (cf. v. 12); **will be saved,** i.e., redeemed and reconciled to God through Christ; **as it is written,**[74] or as it stands written in Isaiah 59:20, 21. Here Paul grounds the reason why it is that elect Jews [and of course elect Gentiles also] will keep being saved "at this present time" (v. 5), and all times after that until the arrival of our Lord:

2- That "all Israel" refers to the ethnic nation of Israel as a whole or most of them in the last generation before Christ's return. Again, this is the view which is typically held by those who hold to dispensational, pre-millenarian theology. My exposition above shows that this understanding of the passage does not square with Scripture. Further, we must always keep in mind that nowhere are we ever told in Holy Scripture that God promised to save every or most of the Israelites in the end times.

Louis Berkhof addresses this matter: "Both the Old and the New Testament speak of a future conversion of Israel, Zech. 12:10; 13:1; 2 Cor. 3:15, 16 and Rom. 11:25-29 seems to connect this with the end of time. Premillennialist have exploited this Scriptural teaching for their particular purpose. They maintain that there will be a *national* restoration and conversion of Israel, that the Jewish nation will be re-established in the Holy Land, and that this will take place immediately preceding or during the millennial reign of Jesus Christ. It is very doubtful, however, whether Scripture warrants the expectation that Israel will finally be re-established as a nation, and will as a nation turn to the Lord. Some Old Testament prophecies seem to predict this, but these should be read in the light of the New Testament. Does the New Testament justify the expectation of a future restoration and conversion of Israel as a nation? It is not taught nor even necessarily implied in such passages as Matt. 19:28, and Luke 21:24, which are often quoted in its favor. The Lord spoke very plainly of the opposition of the Jews to the spirit of His kingdom, and of the certainty that they, who could in a sense be called children of the Kingdom, would lose their place in it, Matt. 8:11, 12; 21:28- 46; 22:1-14; Luke 13:6-9. He informs the wicked Jews that the Kingdom will be taken from them and given to a nation bringing forth the fruits thereof, Matt. 21:43. And even when He speaks of the corruptions which in course of time will creep into the Church, of the troubles it will encounter, and of the apostasy which will finally ensue, He does not hint at any prospective restoration and conversion of the Jewish people. This silence of Jesus is very significant. Now it may be thought that Rom. 11:11-32 certainly teaches the future conversion of the nation of Israel. Many commentators adopt this view, but even its correctness is subject to considerable doubt. In chapters 9-11 the apostle discusses the question, how the promises of God to Israel can be reconciled with the rejection of the greater part of Israel. He points out first of all in the chapters 9 and 10 that the promise applies, not to Israel according to the flesh, but to the spiritual Israel; and in the second place that God still has His elect among Israel, that there is among them still a remnant according to the election of grace, 11:1-10. And even the hardening of the greater part of Israel is not God's final end, but rather a means in His hand to bring salvation to the Gentiles, in order that these, in turn, by enjoying the blessings of salvation, may provoke Israel to jealousy. The hardening of Israel will always be only partial, for through all succeeding centuries there will always be some who accept the Lord. God will continue to gather His elect remnant out of the Jews during the entire new dispensation until the fullness (pleroma, that is, the number of the elect) of the Gentiles be come in, and so (in this manner) all Israel (its pleroma, that is, the full number of true Israelites) shall be saved. "All Israel" is to be understood as a designation, not of the whole nation, but of the whole number of the elect out of the ancient covenant people. Premillenarians take the 26th verse to mean that, after God has completed His purpose with the Gentiles, the nation of Israel will be saved. But the apostle said at the beginning of his discussion that the promises were for the spiritual Israel; there is no evidence of a change of thought in the intervening section, so that this would come as a surprise in 11:26; and the adverb houtos cannot mean 'after that,' but only 'in this manner.' With the fullness of the Gentiles the fullness of Israel will also come in." Berkhof, Systematic Theology, pp. 698-700.

3- That "all Israel" refers to all the elect (the remnant) among the Jewish nation who believe in Christ throughout the centuries. This last view makes the most sense. It is clearly in line with all that Paul has been teaching contextually in this chapter.

74 Grk. perfect, passive, verb.

"**The Deliverer** or the rescuer from God's wrath[75] (Jesus); **will come**[76] **out of Zion** (not out of heaven at His second coming when He will judge the world as He says in Matt. 25:31-46, but out from among the Jews in Jerusalem at His first coming);[77]

And He (Jesus) **will turn away ungodliness from Jacob** (which is what He does when Jews turn to Him by faith);

For this *is* My (Jesus') **covenant,** that is, the new covenant which He ratified and executed when He shed his blood for the forgiveness of sins at Calvary, cf. Jer. 31:31-34; Matt. 26:28; **with them, When I take away their sins** (which is the very thing He did at the cross, once for all time, for everyone who believes cf. John 19:30; Acts 13:38, 39; Heb. 8:6-13, 10:1-16)."

These words are packed. They are also pretty plain. The key to understanding them, again, is by remembering *why* Paul wrote them. Here, as always, context is king. And in this context Paul has told us that he did not want the Gentiles to be ignorant of the fact that along with them being saved, God would keep saving elect Jews. Recall again that earlier Paul lamented the fact that many of his countrymen according to the flesh had rejected the gospel, thus he desperately desired and prayed to God that they might be saved (Rom. 9:1-3, 10:1). Of course, God had always saved Jews both in Old and New Testament times, even thousands of them (cf. Rom. 4:1-8; Acts 2:36-47, 4:4, 21:20). But nonetheless, when considered as an entire nation, the numbers of those saved among them seemed quite small. In view of this, Paul wrote these verses. All of this information was given specifically to the Gentiles so that they should not be wise or conceited in their own opinion (v. 25b).

In these words, Paul puts forth a powerful point to keep the Gentiles in check. As they thought about how mightily God was working among them, it seems their hearts were swelling with pride and thus, again, Paul says in verse 18 of this chapter, by way of a command, "Do not boast against the branches." He says in verse 20, "Do not be haughty but fear." In helping the Gentiles with all of this, he lets them know that which was not revealed in days gone by, namely, that although it might look like God had utterly cast away the Jews (v. 1) this was not the case (and praise God for this)!

God, in grace, will keep saving elect Jews right alongside elect Gentiles until the Lord Jesus Christ returns. Thus, His word toward them has not

---

75 Cf. Rom. 1:18.

76 Concerning the use of the future tense verb, Merkle says, "Although it is true that Paul uses the future tense, the question is whether or not Paul understood it as future from his point in history. It was future from the perspective of Isaiah, but when Paul quotes the passage, he is quoting it because he sees it as past." Merkle, p. 95.

77 Hendriksen concurs, "Paul is not thinking of what Jesus will do at his second coming, when he will come not 'out of Zion,' but 'from heaven' (1 Thess. 4:16), and when forgiveness of sin will no longer be possible. Paul is thinking of Christ's first coming when, by means of his vicarious death, he established the basis for the forgiveness of sins, and therefore also for the salvation of 'the fullness of the Gentiles' and of 'all Israel.'" Hendriksen, p. 383.

failed (Rom. 9:6). Therefore, there ought not to be any conceit or carnal, racial pride in the hearts of Gentiles (or any people group) that would look arrogantly down on others who do not seem to be receiving the same type of divine favor from God. Paul instructs that God is not done with the Jews and that as He keeps saving non-Jews, He is going to keep saving Jews until our Lord returns. This news should keep Gentiles humble and also thankful for God's marvelous redemptive mercies to Israel. Consequently, it seems to me that Paul's main focus in these verses is not *primarily* on *eschatology* (the end times) but rather *ecclesiology* (the church), the very topic which he will take up in the following chapters of this epistle.

So we ask, "Will *all Israel* be saved?" The answer is absolutely! However, the question is "Which Israel?" for Paul has spoken of two (ethnic Israel and elect Israel, Rom. 9:6-8). The answer is simple: each individual Jew whom God has elected to eternal life will be converted to Christ in the same way that each elect Gentile is. Both are saved through hearing the gospel and trusting in Jesus the Messiah for salvation, who died as a sacrifice for their sins. This is the teaching that Paul would have us all know in order that we would not gloat over what appears to be God's rejection of His Old Covenant people.[78]

The Reformed theologian Herman Bavinck nicely summarizes these thoughts:

> If in 11:26 Paul is seeking to convey a new fact, the manner in which he does it is very odd indeed. For he does not say *and then*, or *thereupon*, that is, after the fullness of the Gentiles has come in, all Israel will, but "and in *that way* all Israel will be saved" (*kai outos pas Israel sothesetai*). That can only mean: in the way prescribed in the preceding verses. Just prior to this, in verse 25, Paul stated that a hardening has come over only a part (*apo merous*) of Israel. Believers among the Gentiles might perhaps begin to think—as Israel used to think—that they alone were the elect people of God and that Israel was totally rejected. But Paul says that this is not so. No: Israel as such has not been rejected. Among them there has always been a remnant chosen by grace. True enough, some branches have been broken off, and in their place a wild olive shoot has been grafted in, but the stem of the tame olive tree has been preserved. When the *pleroma* (fullness) of the Gentiles comes in, also the *pleroma* (fullness) of Israel is brought in and in that way all Israel is saved.
>
> This fact, that a hardening has come *upon a part* of Israel Paul calls a mystery (*mysterion*, 11:25). Elsewhere he frequently calls by that name the fact that now the Gentiles are fellow heirs and fellow citizens with the saints, fellow members of the household of God, and here he describes with the same word the fact that the Jews have only in part become

---

78 I realize that there are good Reformed men (such as John Murray and many of the Puritans who were postmillenarian) who hold to much of what I have put forth regarding Israel in these words. However, they anticipated that there will be a large-scale conversion of elect Jews right before Jesus returns. Nothing that I have written here negates this from happening. In fact, I hope it is true. However, my present understanding of Paul's teaching has not led me to affirm this conclusion. For a further discussion of this topic, I point the reader to Robert L. Reymond, *Paul, Missionary Theologian*, pp. 539-48.

hardened and that God continually brings numerous elect from among them into his church. For that *partial* hardening will last until the *pleroma* (fullness) of the Gentiles will have come in. Never, up until the end of the ages, will God totally reject his ancient people; he will always bring to faith in Christ, alongside a part from the Gentile world, a part from Israel as well. The Gentiles, but also the Jews, had deserved a very different fate. But this is the great mystery: that God is rich in mercy; that he gathers his elect from every nation, also that of the Jews who rejected him; that he imprisoned all in disobedience that he might be merciful to all. That mystery sends the apostle into ecstasy and causes him to marvel at and adore the depth of God's wisdom and knowledge (11:33-36).

All Israel (*pas Israel*) in 11:26 is not, therefore, the people of Israel that at the end of time will be converted in mass. Nor is it the church of the Jews and the Gentiles together. But it is the *pleroma* (fullness) that in the course of centuries will be brought in from Israel. Israel will continue to exist as a people alongside the Gentiles predicts Paul. It will not expire or disappear from the earth.[79]

Obs. 2- (v. 28) That as Paul continues to speak about "the present and continuing pattern of things,"[80] concerning both the Jews and the Gentiles in the last half of this chapter, he has some summarizing thoughts concerning God's redemptive workings among them which leads him finally to praise and bless the name of the Lord our God. He begins by speaking first to the Gentiles about the Jews and says:

Concerning the gospel or we might say, "with respect to" or "regarding" the good news of salvation in Jesus the Messiah; *they are,* that is, the blind, unbelieving, Christ-rejecting Jews whom Paul just mentioned in verse 25; **enemies,** i.e., enemies of God; **for your sake** or on account of your spiritual advantage (this is because as Paul said in verse 12 and 15 of this chapter, their rejection of Christ has meant gospel riches for pagans throughout the world); **but concerning the election,** that is, the saved group of Messiah-believing Jews from among the apostate nation identified in verses 5 and 7 as the "remnant according to the election of grace" and "the elect;" *they are* beloved that is, highly regarded of God in Christ (as Paul says they are along with elect Gentiles in Romans 1:7); **for the sake of the fathers** or the patriarchs. This love of God toward them on account of the fathers, is not of course, because of any merit or worth in them. Rather, it is because God has not forgotten the promises that He made to the patriarchs, which was to bless their descendants. This is what God keeps doing as He keeps saving a chosen, believing number among them throughout the generations. Simply stated, from the children of

---

79 *The Last Things,* Herman Bavinck, p. 105, 106. It should be noted that there are other noted reformed theologians who hold to the same view: Louis Berkhof, Herman Ridderbos, William Hendriksen and Anthony A. Hoekema.

80 Stuart Olyott notes: "Paul is not talking about the future, but about the present and continuing pattern of things. This is proved by what he says next, in verse 28. He does not fly off to reveal what will happen at some distant time, but soberly tells his readers what the present situation is, summing up his previous teachings." Olyott, p. 108.

Abraham, Isaac, and Jacob (the root, v. 16) there will always be a saved people who believe on the Lord Jesus Christ alone for life and salvation.

Obs. 3- (v. 29) That as Paul goes on to explain and establish why it is that God will keep saving a people from among the Jews who come from the lineage of the patriarchs, he writes:

For the gifts that is, God's gracious, special salvific blessings to undeserving Israelites (such as election, regeneration, repentance, faith, justification, adoption); **and the calling of God,** i.e., His effectual calling through the gospel to elect Jews;[81] *are* **irrevocable,**[82] thus, they are unchangeable. This is so because what God has purposed to fulfill concerning the "Israel within Israel," He will never stop doing until the return of Christ.[83]

Regarding these words, Olyott writes:

> The believers reading Paul's letter are themselves a fulfillment of the promises made to the patriarchs. God promised them descendants as numerous as the stars of heaven and the sand of the seashore. Paul has taught us that the true descendants of Abraham are not an earthly people, but a people united to Christ by faith. This explains how Paul can go immediately from the question of 'all Israel' being saved, to the truth that God's gifts and calling cannot be cancelled, and then straight to a personal address to his Gentile readers.[84]

Obs. 4- (vv. 30-32) That as Paul speaks to the Gentiles at Rome and explains how it is that God will fulfill His irrevocable, covenantal promises to the patriarchs, and their elect seed, in speaking in a similar way that he did throughout this chapter, he writes summarily saying:

For as, or just as; **you** (Gentiles); **were once disobedient to God, yet have now** (not in the future at Christ's second coming, but right now at the present time); **obtained mercy,** i.e., gospel, salvific mercy; **through their disobedience** (the Jews cf. vv. 11, 12); even so or in a similar way; **these also** (the Jews); **have now** (not in the future at Christ's second coming, but right now at the present time); **been disobedient that,** the conjunction stating the divine purpose for this; **through the mercy,** i.e., gospel, salvific mercy; **shown you** (Gentiles); **they also may obtain** or receive; **mercy** (v. 14). For the conjunction explaining and summarizing the entire "discussion of Chapter 11 and 9-11 as a whole"[85] [and really the whole Bible, for the next statement is "the closest that the Bible ever comes

---

81 Cf. Rom. 1:6, 7, 8:28, 30.

82 The word irrevocable is placed at the front of the sentence in the Greek text for the sake of emphasis, showing us that God will never be negligent to save some of the offspring of the patriarchs through Jesus Christ our Lord.

83 Hendriksen says, "There are those who interpret this entire passage (verses 28-31) as a description of God's love for the people of Israel in general. The present clause shows that this interpretation is incorrect, for it refers to *God's irrevocable calling, a calling that is not subject to change and is never withdrawn.* This is certainly the inner or effectual call, one that pertains only to the elect." Hendriksen, p. 384.

84 Olyott, p. 108. See also Louis Berkhof, *Systematic Theology,* p. 469.

85 Schreiner, p. 629.

to relating the sin of man to the mercy of God"[86]]; **God has committed** or consigned or spiritually bound;[87] **them all** (all unsaved humanity, Jews and Gentiles alike); **to disobedience** (which He does when He gives people over to their sins which they pursue for themselves cf. 1:24, 26, 28, 3:9, 22, 23); **that** or for the purpose that; **He** (God); **might have mercy on all,**[88] that is, immeasurable mercy on all who call on the name of the Lord Jesus Christ for salvation (Rom. 10:13), repent of their sins and trust in His finished cross-work alone for their deliverance from the wrath of God.[89]

Obs. 5- (vv. 33-36) That as Paul is completely astonished by the amazing design of God's sovereign plan concerning the salvation of sinners (both Jews and Gentiles alike), in view of all that he has written, he now bursts into a song of praise and says:

Oh, "the interjection suggests strong emotion"[90] (of awe and wonder); **the depth** or the greatness and "deep inexhaustible fullness;"[91] **of the riches**[92] or the spiritual treasures, wealth and gospel blessings; **both of the wisdom and knowledge of God!** (His ability to carry out His divine plan of salvation and the insight that He has into all things). **How unsearchable** or unfathomable; *are* His judgments or eternal decrees and counsels; **and His ways,** i.e., His plans, and providences in all that He does in the world in accomplishing His strategy concerning the salvation of His people (and no doubt everything else He does); **past finding** or tracing; **out!**[93]

"**For** the conjunction giving the reason for the previous words; **who has known the mind of the Lord?** (Paul quotes Isaiah 40:13); **Or who has become His counselor** or advisor?" In other words, who could ever say in truth that he completely comprehends all that the infinite God does among people in the world? Who could possibly ever give Him better instruction in this regard? Could we who are finite honestly instruct He who is infinite? As McDonald rightly says, "No created being can know the mind of the Lord, except to the extent that He chooses to reveal it. And even then we see in a mirror, dimly (1 Cor. 13:12). No one is qualified

---

86 McClain, p. 203.

87 Gal. 3:22.

88 Obviously, Paul is not teaching the heretical doctrine known as Universalism which teaches that in the final analysis, all people will be saved whether they trust in Christ alone for salvation or not. Rather, Paul is teaching that God will have mercy on *all without distinction, not all without exception.* This is His great, global gospel plan for the nations, seeing that He shows no partiality (Acts 10:34).

89 MacArthur rightly notes: "Though not the author of sin (Ps. 5:4; Hab. 1:13; James 1:13), God allowed man to pursue his sinful inclinations so that He could receive glory by demonstrating His grace and mercy to disobedient sinners (cf. Eph. 2:2; 5:6)." MacArthur, *One Faithful Life* (2019), p. 312.

90 Harvey, p. 291.

91 Robinson, Book II. p. 147.

92 Cf. Rom. 2:4.

93 The Phillips translation captures the heart of these words: "I stand amazed at the fathomless wealth of God's wisdom and God's knowledge. How could man ever understand his reasons for action, or explain his methods of working?"

to advise God. He doesn't need our counsel, and wouldn't profit by it anyway (see Isa. 40:13)."[94]

"Or who has first given to Him (again God, Paul quotes Job 40:11); **And it shall be repaid to him?"** In other words, no one has ever made God indebted to himself, for as David says to the Lord, "all things come from You, and of Your own we have given You" (1 Chron. 29:14). Consequently, God could never be put in a position where he had to repay someone or something back. Again McDonald says, "What gift of ours would ever put the Eternal in a position where He had to repay?"[95]

For or more literally from the Greek text "because" the word putting forth the causal reason for the previous verse; **of Him** (God); **and through Him** (God); **and to Him** (God); *are* all things, to whom (God); *be* glory or honor; **forever** or more literally "to all eternity." **Amen** or indeed, the word giving the "solemn affirmation and approval"[96] for what was just said.

What is Paul's point in these final words? It is this: since God is *the Author* of all things, "for of Him,"—and *the Agent* of all things, "and through Him,"—and the *Aim* of all things, "and to Him"—He alone is to be the sole focus of our worship and praise for all things. This is to be especially true for us who are saved since He has had so much gospel mercy on us in redeeming our souls through Christ. Consequently, may it be that with Paul, our theology will always lead to doxology all of our days.

Suggested applications from the text for the church:

1- We are to remember never to write off any unsaved people (Jew or Gentile) because of their initial rejection of Christ. This is because we do not know whether or not God has foreordained that they might be saved or not.

2- We are to remember that we are not to forget to evangelize our Jewish friends with the gospel since God, in fact, will keep saving an elect number of them until Jesus returns.

3- We are to remember constantly to give glory to our great God for all that he has done for us in Christ. For of Him and through Him and to Him *are* all things, to whom *be* glory forever. Amen.

Suggested application from the text for the non-Christian:

1- You are to remember that God has shut you up to your sins for the very purpose that you might seek Him for forgiveness in His Son. May you be found doing that very thing this very day!

---

94 McDonald, 1728.

95 Ibid.

96 Hendriksen, p. 393.

ROMANS
CHAPTER TWELVE

Text: Romans 12:1-2[1]

General theme: A Call to Complete Consecration to God

Homiletical outline of the verses:

A. The motive for our consecration to God: [1a] I beseech you therefore, brethren, by the mercies of God.

B. The character of our consecration to God: [1b] that you present your bodies a living sacrifice, holy, acceptable to God, *which is* your reasonable service.

C. The means for our consecration to God: [2a] and do not be conformed to this world, but be transformed by the renewing of your mind.

D. The purpose of our consecration to God: [2b] that you may prove what *is* that good and acceptable and perfect will of God.

Summary of section: In these verses, all the way to chapter 15:13, Paul begins the last major section in this magnificent epistle. Having dealt with deep doctrinal matters in the previous chapters such as sin, salvation, sanctification, and sovereignty, he now shows what service to the living Lord looks like for us who have been saved by God's free, unmerited grace.[2] Simply stated, Paul now puts forth the ethical implications and practical applications of the gospel for daily living for those who have been redeemed. As he moves from *belief to behavior* and from *doctrine to duty*, he shows that the transforming power of the gospel is to affect every single area of our lives. Broadly speaking, he says that it is to impact:[3]

---

1 A good title for a sermon on these two verses could be: Not conformed, but transformed!

2 It should be observed that this is Paul's typical pattern in his epistles. The first part of them typically deals with *doctrine*. The second part typically deals with *duty* (cf. Gal. 1-4, 5-6; Eph. 1-3, 4-6; Col. 1-2, 3-4).

3 Schreiner summarizes this matter nicely when he says, "Romans 12:1–2 serve as the paradigm for the entire exhortation section (12:1–15:13). If all the exhortations contained here could be boiled down to their essence, they would be reduced to the words: Give yourselves wholly to God; do not be shaped by the old world order, but let new thought

- our relationship to God, 12:1-2
- our relationship to our brethren and others, 12:3-21
- our relationship to the government, 13:1-7
- our relationship to our neighbors and to our remaining sins in view of Jesus' return 13:8-14, and
- our relationship to our differing brethren in the church, 14:1–15:13

Michael Bird helpfully summarizes these matters:

> Romans 12:1–15:13 can be likened to "Christ College" where Paul attempts to engender certain attitudes and behaviors appropriate for those whom Romans 1–11 is true. In essence, Paul begins to expound the "imperative" that follows from the "indicative" of the gospel. Or, because of what God has done for us in Christ, this is how we ought to live before God. Paul wants those who are declared righteous and united to the Messiah to exhibit a set of distinctive behaviors that show that they live under Jesus' Lordship and are led by the Spirit. Call it ethics, applied theology, or Christian living, label it whatever you like, but remember that Paul's goal is to bring Gentiles[4] to the obedience of faith (1:15; 15:18; 16:26), and he shows us now what this obedience looks like in real life. Paul is outlining how the gospel is lived out in faithful obedience among the tenements [apartments], markets, and hustle and bustle of ancient Rome.[5]

Exegetical & Practical Insights:

Obs. 1- (v. 1) That as Paul puts forth the foundation for everything that he will say in the following chapters, he writes:

I beseech[6] or I continually urge and lovingly appeal to; **you brethren,** that is, all of the cherished Christians at Rome collectively (both believing Jews and Gentiles alike); **therefore,** or in light of all that he has just written in the previous chapters and is about to write in the following chapters;[7] **by** or "through" or "in view of" the preposition highlighting the great gospel motive of our consecration to God; **the mercies of God,**[8] which is to say, all of the divine, salvific, multiple merc*ies* and compassions which come to us from God through Christ, which Paul has already described in the previous chapters (e.g., predestination, justification, union with Christ, the receiving of the Holy Spirit, sanctification, eternal security to name a few[9]); **that you present**[10] or offer daily to God

---

patterns transform your life. The subsequent context (12:3–15:13) fleshes out the nature of this dedication in concrete ways." Schreiner, p. 640.

4   Of course, the same thing is true for believing Jews.

5   Bird, p. 411.

6   Grk. present, active, verb.

7   I believe that the conjunction "therefore" looks both backward in this letter and forward from this point onward.

8   Phillips translation: With eyes wide open to the mercies of God, I beg you my brothers.

9   It should be noted that Paul just mentioned the word "mercy" several times in the previous chapter in verses 30-32.

10 Although the verb "present" in the original language is in the aorist tense, signifying a once for all offering, I agree with Osborne when he says that "this verb draws

(the word "present" is a term which should bring to our minds the imagery of an Old Testament priest presenting an animal sacrifice to the Lord); **your bodies,** that is, the whole of your physical bodies, the totality of your redeemed faculties to Him as; **a living sacrifice,**[11] not dead, like the Old Testament sacrifices, but metaphorically as an active and energetic sacrifice,[12] the term "living" recalling Paul's earlier description of "the believer's transformation from the realm of death because of sin to the realm of life through union with the risen Christ (Rom 5:10, 17-18, 21);"[13] **holy,** or separated from sin; **acceptable to God**, or well-pleasing to Him,[14] which is what it is through Christ, "the three modifiers ["living," "holy," and "acceptable"] are best understood as parallel and define the character of the sacrifice;"[15] *which is* **your reasonable**[16] or "rational;"[17] **service** or that which accords with sound logic in consideration of all that God has done for us in Christ. Simply put, it makes complete sense.

As mentioned above, verse 1 of this chapter is the foundation from which the fulfilling of all our gospel obligations is to flow. Before Paul even begins to speak about our various relationships in the church and in the world, there is a matter which is absolutely crucial in our lives: our complete consecration to God. It is that of our total devotion to Him in the light of all that He has done for us by grace. As we think about this, we will be able to say with the psalmist, "What shall I render to the LORD for all of His benefits towards me?" (Ps. 116:12). We will be able to say with the hymn writer:

> Love so amazing, so divine,
> demands my soul, my life, my all.

And,

> Take my life, and let it be
> Consecrated, Lord, to Thee.

Obs. 2- (v. 2) That as Paul tells us exactly how to live as consecrated Christians for the Lord, as those who have been bought with a price so that we are no longer our own (1 Cor. 6:19, 20), he writes firstly by way of negative command:

---

its force from the main verb, the present-tense 'I exhort,' and it is followed by two present-tense imperatives in verse 2. This means there is no one-time action in it." Osborne, p. 379.

11 Chrysostom famously said, "And how is the body, it may be said, to become a sacrifice? Let the eye look on no evil thing, and it hath become a sacrifice; let thy tongue speak nothing filthy, and it hath become an offering; let thine hand do no lawless deed, and it hath become a whole burnt offering," as quoted in Moo, NICNT, p. 754.

12 Cf. Rom. 6:13.

13 Thielman, p. 567.

14 Cf. Rom. 14:18.

15 Harvey, p. 295.

16 Our English word "logic" is derived from this original Greek word.

17 Murray, 2:112.

And the conjunction continuing the apostle's previous thought from verse 1; **do not be conformed**[18] or constantly formed and fashioned;[19] **to this world**[20] or more literally, to this age which is fallen and dominated by sin and Satan;[21] the sense is: "Don't let the world around you squeeze you into its own mold"[22] so that you "allow yourselves to become like your surroundings;"[23] **but,**[24] which is to say, in sharp contrast to this (Paul now speaks positively by way of another present tense command and says); **be transformed**[25] or habitually changed from the inside out;[26] **by** the preposition highlighting the means by which this is to be done; **the renewing** or we might say reprogramming and renovating;[27] **of your mind,** or our thought life (which previously as non-Christians was debased and carnal, Rom. 1:28; 8:7);[28] **that** or for the purpose that; **you may prove** or better understood "know," and "put in practice;" **what** *is*

---

18 Grk. present, active, verb.

19 Cf. 1 Pet. 1:14.

20 Mahan writes, "The word 'world' means the nature, character, opinions, goals, and attitudes of unregenerate men." Mahan, p. 86. Further note that since one of God's major goals in our sanctification is that we become "conformed to the image of His Son" (Rom. 8:29), how antithetical is it for us then to be "conformed to this wicked world."

21 Cf. John 15:18-19; James 4:4; 1 John 2:15-17; 5:19. Of course, this is not to say that as believers, we may not enjoy the many wonderful things which God has made in this world, such as its vast landscapes, oceans and nature. But those things which stand in opposition to God, the gospel, and Christ (such as pagan practices, perspectives, and philosophies which abound all around us) are not to be accepted or adopted by us at all. Further, it is interesting to note that God commanded His Old Covenant people in Deuteronomy 18:9, about a similar thing that Paul says to us here. Sadly, many in the Old Covenant did not heed God's Word to them and they greatly suffered for it.

22 Phillips translation.

23 Bird, p. 415.

24 The strong Greek adversative.

25 Cf. 2 Cor. 3:12. Our English word "metamorphosis" is derived from this original Greek word.

26 This happens in many ways in our lives as Christians, but perhaps most especially, it occurs as we *privately* read, memorize and meditate upon the Scriptures daily (Ps. 1) and pray. And then *corporately* as we sit under the Word of God weekly in biblical churches, and listen to Scripture expounded "line upon line and precept upon precept" (Isa. 28:10).

27 Hendricksen helpfully discusses the use of the passive voice in the verb "be transformed" and says, "It is important to pay close attention to the exact manner in which the apostle expresses himself in this exhortation. Note the following details. A. He uses *the present tense:* 'Continue to let yourselves be transformed.' Accordingly, this transformation must not be a matter of impulse: on-again, off-again. It must be continuous. B. The verb used is in *the passive voice.* Paul does not say, 'Transform yourselves,' but 'Let yourselves be transformed.' Transformation is basically the work of the Holy Spirit. It amounts to progressive sanctification. 'And we all, with unveiled faces, reflecting the glory of the Lord, are being changed into his likeness from one degree of glory to another, which comes from the Lord, who is the Spirit' (II Cor. 3:18). C. Nevertheless, the verb is in *the imperative mood.* Believers are not completely passive. Their responsibility is not canceled. They must allow the Spirit to do his work within their hearts and lives. Their duty is to co-operate to the full. See Phil. 2:12, 13; II Thess. 2:13.'" Hendriksen, p. 406.

28 Schreiner rightly says, "Human beings are transformed as their thinking is altered." Schreiner, p. 648. Additionally, it should be noted that if as Christians we are going to be spiritually minded, which is "life and peace" (8:6), then this transformation of our mind must be a matter of priority.

that good (morally and spiritually speaking); **and acceptable** or well-pleasing; **and perfect** or without flaw; **will of God.**

As Christians living in the twenty-first century, these words are vital for us to understand and to live out practically by the grace of God. This is because we are constantly being attacked with so much moral filth through multiple outlets like music, the media, and many anti-God mouthpieces all around us. Through the influences of secularism, humanism, hedonism, postmodernism, relativism and materialism, etc., we are continually being bombarded with the lies of the enemy. Therefore, if we would live as God's holy people in the world, we must seek regularly to implement the opening words of this chapter in Romans.

We must earnestly heed them so that our lives of *dedication to the Lord* will lead us to clear *discernment of His will* in every area of life through His Word, whether we are, for example, employees in the workplace, mothers at home, students at school, retired folks, or people on the missionary field. In a true sense, then, we are to be Christian *non*-conformists.[29] We should live distinguished lives, in how we think, act, dress, talk, and all the rest as the people of God, being salt and light "in the midst of a crooked and perverse generation" (Phil. 2:15).

This matter would have been exactly the same for Paul's original readers living in the first century. As it is in our day, so it was in Paul's day. Unsaved people were and still are "filled with all unrighteousness, sexual immorality, wickedness, covetousness, maliciousness, full of envy, murder, strife, deceit, [and] evil mindedness..." (Rom. 1:29). They were and still are "backbiters, haters of God, violent, proud, boasters, inventors of evil things, disobedient to parents" (Rom. 1:30). And they were and still are full of "revelry and drunkenness, lewdness and lust, strife and envy" (Rom. 13:13).

Michael Bird speaks to this matter:

> Despite the historical grandeur, cultural wealth, and promotion of virtues like justice in the Roman Empire, truth be told, the Romans were often little more than Latin-speaking savages dressed in a toga. The Roman Empire was cruel, repressive, and merciless, especially to non-elites and those on its margins....
>
> In this context, Paul says Christians are consciously to resist and to reject the attempt to bring them into concord with their surrounding culture. On the contrary, they are to be 'transformed.' As far as I am aware, no moral philosopher in the ancient world ever touted the virtues of a moral reconstruction of the self. You can find teachers advocating conformity to nature, advocating the necessity of self-mastery, or disengaging from the desires of the world. But the idea of "transformation" as a moral do-over was not a category anyone seems to have been seriously entertaining. Yet Paul is urging a fundamental renovation of a person at the deepest level of his or her desires, intellect, and will.... Paul calls for a transformation conceived as a 'renewing of the mind'....

---

29 Of course, this does not negate that we are to be excellent citizens in the world, who serve others and submit to the "governing authorities" (Rom. 13:1-7).

The purpose of a transformed self and a renewed mind is then spelled out: 'Then you will be able to test and approve what God's will is — his good, pleasing and perfect will' (v. 2b). A renewed mind is able to recognize and appreciate that which belongs to God proper.... The mind renewed by the Spirit is able to discern the good, the pleasing, and the perfect purposes of God with a view to aligning their own attitudes and values with it.[30]

May God help all of us then to be such consecrated Christians. May He help us to understand that it is this fundamental matter which will help us in all areas of our lives to be His shining representatives and sterling ambassadors in the world.

Suggested applications from the text for the church:

1- If we are going to obey this call to a consecrated life we must constantly reflect on all the mercies of God toward us in Christ which are new every morning (Lam. 3:23).

2- If we are going to obey this call to a consecrated life we must daily choose not to crawl off the altar of God as a living sacrifice and then to pursue our own ways. Rather, we must say daily to God with Christ, "not as I will, but as You will" (Matt. 26:39).

3- If we are going to obey this call to a consecrated life we must habitually remember that to live according to this world's unholy principles and practices is to be disloyal to Christ who "gave Himself for our sins, that He might deliver us from this present evil age, according to the will of our God and Father, to whom be glory forever and ever. Amen" (Gal. 1:4-5).

Suggested application from the text for the non-Christian:

1- If you are going to obey this call to a consecrated life then you also must immediately offer yourself to God. But before doing this, you first need to come to Him through Christ as a hell-deserving sinner who desperately needs to be forgiven and cleansed by Him.

Text: Romans 12:3-8

General theme: Spiritual Gifts and the Saints

Homiletical outline of the verses:

A. The injunction[31] regarding spiritual gifts: [3] For I say, through the grace given to me, to everyone who is among you, not to think *of himself* more highly than he ought to think, but to think soberly, as God has dealt to each one a measure of faith.

B. The illustration of spiritual gifts: [4] For as we have many members in one body, but all the members do not have the same function, [5] so

---

30 Bird, pp. 415, 416.

31 The word means "warning."

we, *being* many, are one body in Christ, and individually members of one another.

C. The identification for spiritual gifts: [6] Having then gifts differing according to the grace that is given to us, *let us use them:* if prophecy, *let us prophesy* in proportion to our faith; [7] or ministry, *let us use it* in *our* ministering; he who teaches, in teaching; [8] he who exhorts, in exhortation; he who gives, with liberality; he who leads, with diligence; he who shows mercy, with cheerfulness.

Summary of section: In these verses, Paul speaks about the subject of serving God in the church with spiritual gifts.[32] Having just told us in the previous verses that we are to live consecrated lives to the Lord (and this by not being conformed to this world), interestingly, the very first place where the apostle tells us that this consecrated life is to manifest itself is in the context of the local church. This idea might be foreign to some. However, this is what the context and connection of this verse to the previous one clearly shows. The opening, explanatory word "for" in verse 3 makes this point plain.

Olyott astutely comments:

> We need to put away vague views of consecration. The first place where it is seen is in the way in which a believer lives and behaves in the Body of Christ. If you want to display your gratitude to God for His mercies, you must start here. You must submit to what He has revealed concerning church life. People who appear to be keen Christians, but are not obeying the Lord in this area, are not keen Christians at all. They have not put themselves at His disposal in the area where He expects obedience first. If first things are not put first, how can anything else be right?[33]

---

32 The best definition for spiritual gifts that I found is in the *International Standard Bible Encyclopedia* vol. 4, p. 602, by R. P. Spittler. It says that spiritual gifts are "Varied endowments graciously bestowed by the triune God upon individual Christians, but particularly intended to enhance the community, worship, and service of locally gathered Christians and thereby to enrich the whole church."

John MacArthur also helpfully says that a spiritual gift is "a God-given capacity through which the Holy Spirit ministers. It is not a natural human ability such as playing piano, singing, or writing. Such talents may be used to express your gift, but they are not spiritual gifts in themselves. For example, if you have the gift of teaching, you might express that gift through writing. Or if you have the gift of exhortation, you might write letters that exhort." John MacArthur, *Spiritual Boot Camp*, p. 62. It should also be noted that Paul discusses the topic of spiritual gifts in 1 Corinthians chapters 12 to 14. Peter discusses them in 1 Peter. 4:10, 11.

For further study on this topic, I would recommend the books: *Spiritual Gifts: What They Are and Why They Matter* by Tom Schreiner and *Dynamics of Spiritual Gifts* by William McRae. Both of these authors take the classic cessationist view of the gifts, as I do, which says that miraculous spiritual gifts such as prophecy and speaking in tongues have ceased. However, we do believe that God still does work in the world in supernatural ways. He does this often when we call upon Him in prayer to do so.

33 Olyott, pp. 114, 115.

Exegetical & Practical Insights:

Obs. 1- (v. 3) That as Paul begins his discussion concerning the use of spiritual gifts in the church, he begins by speaking against the matter of pride:

For I say through the grace given to me, that is, he speaks with the authority of a duly authorized apostle of the Lord Jesus Christ (Rom. 1:1, 5; 15:5), and yet, he humbly acknowledges that he does this only "through" or "by virtue of"[34] the grace given to him, that is to say, the *effectual grace* which first saved him, followed by the *equipping grace* which made him an apostle; **to everyone who is among you,** no one is excluded from Paul's words here (be that the pastor in the pulpit or people in the pew); **not to think**[35] or ever to think;[36] *of himself* more highly or "over" and "beyond;"[37] **than he ought to** or should; **think,**[38] in other words, "Don't cherish exaggerated ideas of yourself or your importance;"[39] **but**[40] or in sharp contrast to this; **to think soberly,**[41] not like a man who is intoxicated with his own self-worth, but sanely and soundly (which does not mean to think poorly of ourselves), but rather sensibly, "He is not to overvalue his abilities, his gifts, or his worth but make an accurate estimate of himself;"[42] **as God has dealt** or distributed; **to each one** again, no one is excluded; **a measure** or amount; **of faith** that is, a measure of faith to humbly trust Him to enable us to arrive at an accurate evaluation of our spiritual gifts and then to use them in the assembly in complete dependence on Him.

We might wonder why Paul began the subject of spiritual gifts by speaking against the matter of conceit. While, of course, it seems obvious that he did this because pride is present in all of us from birth and is the "oldest sin in the universe,"[43] could there be another reason? I think there is. It has to do with the context in which Paul was writing this letter. Remember, he wrote Romans while he was in Corinth, nearing the end of his third missionary journey (see my opening comments in the *Brief Overview*).

---

34 Harvey, p. 299.

35 Grk. Present, active, verb.

36 The progressively renewed mind mentioned in verse 2, should help us in this regard.

37 The idea is: do not be high-minded. Do not be a constant braggart, showman, and a know-it-all.

38 R. Kent Hughes insightfully notes that, "Our Adamic nature loves to over-think about itself. This can take two classic forms. Primarily it is that of the self-elevating braggart — the person who tells you how smart he is, how much he has done, how strong he is, how rich he will be when he gets his big break — legends in their own mind... The other form of overestimation is more subtle... those who self-consciously talk about themselves as if they were nobodies." R. Kent Hughes, *Romans, Righteousness from Heaven*, p. 220.

39 Phillips translation.

40 The strong Greek adversative.

41 Cf. Titus 2:11, 12.

42 MacArthur, p. 158.

43 John Blanchard in *The Complete Gathered Gold* (Darlington, England: Evangelical Press, 2006), 503.

Consider then, what was happening at Corinth while Paul was there. There was a misuse and abuse of spiritual gifts. In fact, Paul essentially takes three chapters (1 Corinthians 12, 13, and 14) to correct much of the carnal pride and lack of love in that church. He said to the Corinthians, "And though I have *the gift of* prophecy, and understand all mysteries and all knowledge, and though I have all faith, so that I could remove mountains, but have not love, I am nothing" (1 Cor. 13:2).

So it may be that as the apostle was writing to the Romans and was still entrenched in fixing the spiritual mess at Corinth, that he felt it necessary to speak to them first and foremost about the matter of humility. He had already corrected them earlier in Romans chapter 11, verses 18 and 20, concerning being boastful and haughty. Now it seems that he wants to lay this foundation afresh as he takes up this new topic so that the Romans would not "parade themselves" and become "puffed up" (1 Cor. 13:4). A superiority complex among anyone who names the name of Christ will be devastating to the church. Pride will go before their destruction (Prov. 16:18). So all of us must take special heed to Paul's words.

Obs. 2- (vv. 4-5) That as Paul explains why each of us should not to think of ourselves more highly than we ought to think, he writes using an illustration and says:

For as or just as; **we have many members** or parts and limbs; **in one body,** i.e., our physical body, **but all the members** or parts and limbs; **do not have the same function** or activity; so in a similar manner, the adverb completing the point of Paul's comparison in the illustration; **we,** that is, we who are Christians both locally and universally in the church, in the same way; *being* many, which is to say, being many different people from many diverse backgrounds and ethnicities, etc.; **are one body** or one spiritual organization and organism; **in** or in union with; **Christ, and** at the same time are; **individually members of one another.**

Paul's "body language" here is language that he uses elsewhere in his epistles (see especially 1 Cor. 12:12-27; Eph. 1:22, 23; 4:23; 5:23). This language conveys two chief things: first, that there is both diversity and unity within the Christian community,[44] and second, that the church is made up of "many interrelated and mutually dependent parts."[45] Simply stated, as it is with our physical bodies, so it also is with Jesus' spiritual body, the church of which He is the Head (Eph. 1:22, 23). Those who are truly born again and filled with the Holy Spirit are part of the body of Christ and spiritual members of each other. Because this is so, it is to have a profound impact on how we treat each member in the body and act among ourselves. Since we are not only in spiritual union with Jesus, but also with each other, we should treat one another extremely well in our assemblies. We should "let nothing be done through selfish ambition or conceit, but in lowliness of mind let each esteem others better than

---

44 Moo, NICNT, p. 762.

45 John MacArthur, *The Body Dynamic,* Study Guide, 2000, p. 8.

himself. Let each of you look out not for his own interest, but also for the interest of others" (Phil. 2:2, 3). As Charles Hodge rightly says:

> In these verses we have the same comparison that occurs more at length in 1 Cor. 12, and for the same purpose. The object of the apostle is in both cases the same. He designs to show that the diversity of offices and gifts among Christians, so far from being inconsistent with their union as one body in Christ, is necessary to the perfection and usefulness of that body. It would be as unreasonable for all Christians to have the same gifts, as for all the members of the human frame to have the same office. This comparison is peculiarly beautiful and appropriate; because it not only clearly illustrates the particular point intended, but at the same time brings into view the important truth that the real union of Christians results from the indwelling of the Holy Spirit, as the union of several members of the body is the result of their being all animated and actuated by one soul. Nothing can present in a clearer light the duty of Christian fellowship, or the sinfulness of divisions and envying among the members of Christ's body, than the apostle's comparison.[46]

This illustration by the apostle sets the stage for what he will say in the following verses. His point is that because we are a body, we need one another; thus, no spiritual gift is unnecessary, and none is self-terminating or for self-promotion.

Obs. 3- (vv. 6-8) That as Paul has put forth his illustration concerning the church, he now identifies seven spiritual gifts that are to be exercised in our midst.[47] He writes:

Having then gifts or we might say, because we have divine, spiritual deposits or endowments; **differing according to the grace that is given to us:**[48] "It is not a matter of the believer making an earnest effort in order to produce some spectacular results in Christian character or achievement, but something God has given;"[49] *let us use* or exercise; **them:**

if prophecy,[50] this spiritual gift which originally referred to one speaking forth divine, inspired truth from the Lord has ceased with the close of the apostolic age,[51] but nevertheless, continues today in the

---

46 Hodge, p. 387

47 Concerning spiritual gifts, I believe that it is important to note that, according to the Bible, every Christian has received at least one (see 1 Cor. 12:6-7; 1 Pet: 4:10). Further, since Paul's language in this passage carries the sense of a command, we are under apostolic obligation to exercise them. Finally, as far as discerning what spiritual gift or gifts we have, perhaps after studying the Scriptures and praying, asking God to show us the answer to this question, we can discover our gifts by satisfying at least three criteria: 1- do we have *an ability* to perform the gift, 2- is there *an affinity* [desire] for us to exercise the gift; and 3- is there is *an affirmation* of the gift by the church that we, in fact, have it.

48 The aorist tense participle highlights to us that our spiritual gift or gifts were given to us once for all time at conversion. The passive voice shows that we did not generate it ourselves. Rather, it was freely bestowed upon us by God.

49 Morris, p. 440.

50 Murray says that in the apostolic generation, "Prophecy refers to the function of communicating revelations of truth from God. The prophet was an organ of revelation; he was God's spokesman." Murray, 2:122.

51 MacArthur highlights this point when he says, "The spiritual gifts mentioned

form of preaching or the proclaiming of God's inspired truth from the Bible;[52] "There can be no inspired, prophetic additions to the body of Christian doctrine today since the faith has been once for all delivered to the saints (see Jude 3);"[53] *let us prophesy* **in proportion to** or in accord and agreement with the analogy of; **our faith** or better understood "the faith" (since the definite article is in the original language, the idea being that prophecy must correspond with the objective rule of faith which has already been proclaimed by the apostles and believed by the churches);

or ministry, which is a broad term that stands for any service in the church which could be done by any member in the congregation, or the deacons especially[54] towards those in need. "The person who has the gift of ministry has a servant-heart. He sees opportunities to be of service and seizes them;"[55] *let us use it* **in** *our* **ministering;**

he who teaches, or has the ability to instruct others out of the Word of God faithfully, clearly, helpfully, pointedly and practically; **in teaching;**

he who exhorts, or has the ability to encourage the fainthearted, comfort the distressed, or warn the disobedient; **in exhortation;**

he who gives, or freely shares with others without expecting anything in return whether it be food, finances or clothing. "Giving is the ability to provide for others who can't meet their own needs. It flows from a

---

in the New Testament, primarily in Romans 12 and in 1 Corinthians 12, fall into three categories: sign, speaking, and serving.... The sign gifts authenticated the teaching of the apostles—which was the measure of all other teaching—and therefore ceased after the apostles died probably even earlier. "The signs of a true apostle were performed among you with all perseverance," Paul explained to the Corinthian church, "by signs in wonders and miracles" (2 Cor. 12:12). The writer of Hebrews gives further revelation about the purpose of the spiritual gifts: "After [the gospel] was at the first spoken through the Lord, it was confirmed to us by those who heard, God also bearing witness with them, both by signs and wonders and by various miracles and by gifts of the Holy Spirit according to His own will" (Heb. 2:3-4). Even during Jesus' earthly ministry, the apostles "went out and preached everywhere, while the Lord worked with them and confirmed the word by the signs that followed" (Mark 16:20). First Corinthians was written about A.D. 54 and Romans some four years later. It is important to note that none of the sign gifts mentioned in 1 Corinthians 12:9-10—namely, the gifts of healing, miracles, speaking in tongues, and interpreting tongues—is found in Romans 12. The other two New Testament passages that mention spiritual gifts (Eph. 4:7, 11; 1 Pet. 4:10-11) were written several years after Romans and, like that epistle, make no mention of sign gifts. Peter specifically mentions the category of speaking and serving gifts ("whoever speaks" and "whoever serves," v. 11) but neither the category nor an example of the sign gifts. It seems evident, therefore, that Paul did not mention the sign gifts in Romans because their place in the church was already coming to an end. They belong to a unique era in the church's life and would have no permanent place in its ongoing ministry. It is significant, therefore, that the seven gifts mentioned in Romans 12:6-8 are all within the categories of speaking and serving." MacArthur, p. 168.

52 William Perkins, who lived in the sixteenth-century and believed that prophecy by direct revelation had ceased, wrote a book for pastors on preaching entitled, *The Art of Prophesying*. MacArthur also notes that "In the sixteenth-century Switzerland, pastors in Zürich came together every week for what they called 'prophesying.' They shared exegetical, expositional, and practical insights they had gleaned from Scripture that help them more effectively minister to their people in that day." MacArthur, p. 171.

53 McDonald, 1729.

54 Our English word *deacon* is derived from the Greek word *ministry*.

55 Ibid., p. 1730.

decision to commit all earthly possessions to the Lord and His work;"[56] **with liberality** or more literally, sincerity of heart;

he who leads, or more precisely, "stands before" others and presides over them, such as elders do in local churches; **with diligence** or zeal and;

he who shows mercy, or pity and compassion, which refers to an individual who has a unique sensitivity to the sufferings of the saints in the church who are either sick or in need, "with the ability to notice misery and distress that may go unnoticed by others and with the desire and means to help alleviate such afflictions,"[57] and they do this, not merely out of a sense of duty but; **with cheerfulness** or joy.

Of course, in speaking about all of these various spiritual gifts which God in grace gives to His people, through the Holy Spirit for the edifying of the body (1 Cor. 14:26) and for His glory alone (1 Cor. 10:31), the idea is not that it is *only those* who, for example, have the gift of ministry, exhortation, giving or showing mercy who are to do this; no. Rather, the idea is that those who have these specific gifts must exercise them with great zeal. All of us are to minister to one another. All of us are to exhort one another. And all of us are to give and to show mercy as we are able. However, the point is, those who have these specific, spiritual endowments are to excel in them. Therefore, may we all be found doing these very things!

Suggested applications from the text for the church:

1- Be sure that you seek to discover, develop, and deploy your spiritual gifts in the church, so that your local congregation will be all that God calls her to be.

2- Be sure that as you exercise your spiritual gifts, you remember that like anything else in your walk with God, they will take time to grow and mature. Although your spiritual gifts were given to you at salvation, the benefit of them will become greater and more effective over time, with the blessing of God.

Suggested application from the text for the non-Christian:

1- Be sure that in your life, you seek not the gifts of God but rather God, the gift-giver. Therefore, receive from Him the greatest gift of all which is "eternal life in Christ Jesus our Lord" (Rom. 6:23).

Text: Romans 12:9-21

General theme: Authentic Christianity

Homiletical outline of the verses:

A. Paul's practical directives [9] *Let* love *be* without hypocrisy. Abhor what is evil. Cling to what is good. [10] *Be* kindly affectionate to one another

---

56 MacArthur, *Spiritual Boot Camp,* 2021, p. 64.

57 MacArthur, p. 177.

with brotherly love, in honor giving preference to one another; [11] not lagging in diligence, fervent in spirit, serving the Lord; [12] rejoicing in hope, patient in tribulation, continuing steadfastly in prayer; [13] distributing to the needs of the saints, given to hospitality. [14] Bless those who persecute you; bless and do not curse. [15] Rejoice with those who rejoice, and weep with those who weep. [16] Be of the same mind toward one another. Do not set your mind on high things, but associate with the humble. Do not be wise in your own opinion. [17] Repay no one evil for evil. Have regard for good things in the sight of all men. [18] If it is possible, as much as depends on you, live peaceably with all men. [19] Beloved, do not avenge yourselves, but *rather* give place to wrath; for it is written, "Vengeance *is* Mine, I will repay," says the Lord. [20] Therefore

"If your enemy is hungry, feed him;
If he is thirsty, give him a drink;
For in so doing you will heap coals of fire on his head."

[21] Do not be overcome by evil, but overcome evil with good.

Summary of section: In these verses, Paul shows what true gospel transformation looks like in the lives of God's people.[58] Far from leaving us wondering about this matter, he fleshes out for us in concrete ways how we, who have been redeemed by the blood of Christ should live toward *believers within the household of faith* (vv. 9-13), and then also how we should live toward *unbelievers outside the household of faith* (vv. 14-21). This topic is crucial for us to comprehend if we would honor Christ and the gospel in the world. Thus, this last section in this chapter does not consist of some random list of disconnected directives as some might think. Rather, it shows us very practically and clearly what authentic Christianity looks like in action. These verses show us in a series of "short, sharp, tweet-length statements"[59] what genuine Christianity is all about, ethically speaking. As Paul begins his topic, it is noteworthy that he begins with the subject of love. Love is his starting point, as it should be for us as well. Love is that which is "the cement of the saints, and the bond of perfectness, without which all the gifts that men have, the profession they make, and works they do are of no avail, and they themselves nothing."[60] As Vaughan and Corley note:

> After considering the importance of humility and spiritual gifts, Paul is now ready to show us "a more excellent way" (1 Cor. 12:31). The sequence of ideas is exactly similar to that of 1 Cor. 12, 13, and obviously suggested by it. In the section that follows, love is the ruling thought, but Paul does not entangle it in the sloppy sentimentalism that haunts the word in modern religious talk. It is first of all love "without hypocrisy" (v. 9a),

---

58 It *may be* that Paul was specifically led by the Holy Spirit to address these various topics with the church at Rome because they were falling short of these matters in their midst. Moo discusses this possibility, along with others, on pages 771-74 in his commentary.

59 Bird, p. 430.

60 Online commentary: www.biblestudytools.com/gills-exposition-of-the-bible/romans-5-11.html.

that is, "sincere," "genuine." In the ministry of the church, the Christian's love must be the real thing, not counterfeit.... We can best define the all-embracing character of unfeigned love by briefly commenting on its active features.[61]

Exegetical & Practical Insights:

Obs. 1- (v. 9a) That as Paul begins to speak about authentic Christianity among those within the household of faith, he writes with the force of a command saying:

- *Let* **love**[62] or more literally from the Greek text, let "the love," that is to say, the distinctive Christian love, which is "the greatest virtue of the Christian life;"[63] *be* **without hypocrisy**[64] or without insincerity, so that we are not playacting in our demonstration of it.[65] "In classic Greek drama, the *hypokrites* (actor) wore a facemask. The Christian's loving behavior should not be playing a part or wearing a mask, but an authentic expression of goodwill."[66]

The Bible has much to say about our love for fellow believers.[67] It tells us (among other things) that it: 1- is a genuine mark of true Christianity (John 13:35; 1 John 3:14, 4:20), 2- that it should be natural for us to express toward those who have been born again (1 Thess. 4:9), and 3- that it is to be expressed fervently with a pure heart (1 Pet. 1:22). But what does this type of love really look like among us?

The Puritan John Owen answers this question plainly. In writing on the topic of *Gospel Charity* (or Gospel Love [*agape*]), he says, "It is a fruit of the Spirit of God, an effect of faith, whereby believers, being knit together by the strongest bonds of affection, upon the account of their interest in one head, Jesus Christ, and participating of one Spirit, do delight in,

---

61 Vaughan and Corley, p. 141.

62 The Greek word for love here *agape* speaks about us having a warm, intentional regard for and a strong interest in others (Christians or non-Christians) whether they express this love back to us or not.
It is a love that is sacrificial on our part and is not caused by anything in the one loved. It is a love which cannot be earned; that is, it is unconditional. It is not based on what someone does for us in return. MacArthur says that this love "centers on the needs and welfare of the one loved and will pay whatever personal price necessary to meet those needs and foster that welfare." MacArthur, p. 184.
Although scholars tell us that this type of love was uncommon in the Roman culture because it was seen as a sign of weakness, this is how God would have us, His people, to act toward others. Since God Himself is love (*agape*, 1 John 4:16) and expresses this love towards those who do not deserve it (John 3:16), we must do the same as His followers.

63 Ibid., p. 183.

64 Our Lord often called out the Pharisees for their hypocrisy, Matt. 23:27.

65 In commenting on the deceptiveness of hypocrisy, John Murray says: "No vice [evil trait] is more reprehensible than hypocrisy. No vice is more destructive of integrity because it is the contradiction of the truth. Our Lord exposed its diabolical character when he said to Judas, 'Betrayest thou the Son of man with a kiss?' (Luke 22:48). If love is the sum of virtue and hypocrisy the epitome of vice, what a contradiction to bring these together!'" Murray, 2:128.

66 R. C. Sproul, *The Reformation Study Bible*, p. 2003.

67 Paul will speak more about our love toward believers and unbelievers in the following chapter in Romans (13:8-10).

value, and esteem each other, and are in constant readiness for all those regular duties whereby the temporal, spiritual, and eternal good of one another may be promoted."[68] He said it is, "The principal grace and duty that is required among, and expected from, the saints of God, especially as they are engaged in church-fellowship."[69]

- **(v. 9b) Abhor**[70] or constantly detest, "not only shun but vehemently hate it;"[71] **what is evil,**[72] i.e., morally wicked according to the Word of God or "sin in general"[73] (even the matter of hypocrisy previously mentioned); **Cling** or be cemented and glued; **to what is good**[74] or constantly be fixed and fastened to that which is morally right and excellent according to the Bible (which in this context would especially be authentic love for the brethren);

- **(v. 10)** *Be* **kindly affectionate** or continually devoted; **to one another** as all the loving members of the same spiritual household should be;[75] **with** the preposition expressing the manner by which this affection is to be shown; **brotherly love** or more literally, brotherly *philadelphia*. The Greek word *philadelphia* is a compound which is composed of two other words: "love" and "brother." Although this word for love is similar to the word *agape* [which was mentioned earlier], and is perhaps a subset of it and can be used interchangeably with it, the main difference seems to be that this type of love is a love which all Christians are mutually required to express toward one another. Hence, it is *brotherly love*[76]; in honor giving preference to one another, in other words, be regularly valuing each other so much that you "esteem others better than yourself" (Phil. 2:3);

- **(v. 11) not lagging** or being lazy; **in diligence** or zeal, and this so that we do not "lose steam,"[77] especially as we seek to fulfill the above directives concerning our brethren;[78] **fervent** or more literally from the Greek text, "red hot" and "boiling;" **in spirit** that is our own inner spirit or disposition, and this as we are; **serving the Lord** for as we do it unto Him, we do it unto to His people;[79]

---

68 The Works of John Owen, vol. 9, p. 259.

69 Ibid., p. 258.

70 Grk. present, active, participle. It should be noted that the next several directives by Paul are all present, active, participles and thus they should carry this same ongoing sense.

71 Robinson, Book II. p. 179.

72 Cf. Psalm 97:10.

73 Ibid.

74 Cf. Phil. 4:8; 1 Thess. 5:21.

75 Cf. Acts 2:42-47.

76 In the Greek text, the word for brotherly love is placed first in the sentence for emphasis.

77 Moo, NICNT, p. 778.

78 I imagine that these words could be understood as a standalone idea that we should be very zealous for Christ (cf. Acts 18:25; Col. 3:23). While this is certainly true, I think my above interpretation fits better in this context (cf. Gal. 6:9, 10).

79 Cf. Matt. 25:40.

- **(v. 12) rejoicing** or constantly exulting; **in hope,** which seems to be a reference to that future, blessed hope of glory that we who are Christians have when we appear before the presence of our God forevermore (cf. Rom. 5:2-5); **patient** or enduring continually; **in tribulation** or afflictions (whether those tribulations be our own or those of our brethren[80]); **continuing steadfastly** or persistently; **in prayer** which is one of the most loving things we can do for all the people of God;[81]

- **(v. 13) distributing** or, we might say, constantly contributing; **to the needs of the saints,** i.e., believers in need "when it is in the power of our hand to do so" (Prov. 3:27);[82] given to[83] not just providing but habitually and intentionally going after and pursuing with great effort; **hospitality** or more literally from the Greek text, "the hospitality," that is, the uniquely Christian hospitality. (As we exercise this grace we are to generally think "basic" not "ballroom." "Crockpot" not "caviar." "35 minute meal preparation time" not "3 days").

Haldane speaks aptly to this point. In referring to hospitality, he wrote:

> This does not mean, as it is generally now applied, social intercourse and conviviality [feasting among neighbors], but it means the receiving and entertaining of strangers at a distance from their own habitations. This was a duty of peculiar necessity in the primitive times, when inns and places of entertainment were unusual. But it is a duty still; and the change of times and customs cannot set aside any of the precepts of the Lord Jesus Christ. Christians ought hospitably to receive their brethren coming from a distance, and to assist them in their business. We are here directed not only to practice hospitality, but according to the import of the original, to follow or pursue it. Christians are to seek opportunities of thus manifesting love to their brethren. In another place the Apostle enforces the same duty: 'Be not forgetful to entertain strangers; for thereby some have entertained angels unawares.'[84]

Tony Merida comments further,

> Hospitality was important in Paul's day—Christians lacked accommodations for various reasons. We know that Paul enjoyed the hospitality of many. Throughout Scripture we read of the gracious hospitality of our God, as he who welcomes weak and weary sinners (Isa. 25:6-7; 55:1-3; Matt. 11:28; Luke 14:12-24; Rev 21:3). This should motivate our hospitality (Rom. 15:7), and Peter urges us to do it without grumbling (1 Pet. 4:9). Here in Romans 12 Paul speaks of the intentionality of it: *pursue it.* Be intentional about inviting others into your home and

---

80 Cf. Rom. 5:3; 8:35.

81 Cf. Col. 4:2; 1 Thess. 5:17.

82 Cf. Acts 2:45; Rom. 15:25, 26.

83 Grk. present, active, participle.

84 Haldane, p. 569.

into your life. Use your home to bless others, to bless those in the church, and to bless people in need outside of your church, with wisdom and compassion.[85]

Vv. 14-21 *How We Are to Live Toward Unbelievers outside the Household of Faith.*

- **(v. 14) Bless**[86] or quite literally from the Greek text, continue to "eulogize" or "speak well of;" **those who persecute**[87] or harass; **you,** "The obedient Christian not only must resist hating and retaliating against those who harm him but is commanded to take the additional step of blessing them."[88]

The point is, we are not to act in kind toward unbelievers who often mistreat us. Rather, we are to be like Jesus who, "when He was reviled, did not revile in return; when He suffered, He did not threaten, but committed Himself to Him who judges righteously" (1 Pet. 2:23). We are to obey our Lord when he said that, as his followers, we are to "love our enemies, bless those who curse us, do good to those who hate us, and pray[89] for those who spitefully use us and persecute us" (Matt. 5:44).[90] **Bless** (Paul repeats himself here just in case we thought that he meant something else in his original command in the previous words);[91] **and do not curse** or call down calamity or destruction upon those who persecute us.[92] "When Paul adds, 'bless and curse not', he underlines the fact that our attitude is not to be a mixture of blessing and cursing but one of unadulterated blessing."[93]

- **(v. 15)** "These two verses [vv.15, 16] return to the issue of internal relations in the church, beginning with 'rejoice with those who

---

85 Merida, p. 205.

86 Grk. present, active, verb.

87 Since persecution is part and parcel with the Christian life, we all need to take special heed to these words, cf. 2 Tim. 3:17.

88 MacArthur, p. 195. MacArthur relates this personal story in his commentary: "Some years ago, in the store where he was working, a nephew of mine was murdered by an addict looking for drug money. Although deeply grieved by this tragic loss, my brother-in-law has refused to become bitter or hateful. Instead, his continued desire and prayer has been for the salvation of the man who took his son's life. He even visited him in prison to give him the greatest blessing, the gospel. Such is the kind of distinctive Christian love that seeks to bless those who do us harm." MacArthur, p. 196.

89 We know that both Jesus and his dedicated follower Stephen did this very thing (cf. Luke 23:34; Acts 7:59-60).

90 Cf. 1 Pet. 3:9.

91 We should also note that Paul practiced this very thing in his own life; thus he says in 1 Cor. 4:12, "Being reviled, we bless."

92 While of course, in and of ourselves, obeying the apostle here would be very difficult. Nonetheless, we must continue to go back to the opening words of this chapter where we are told that we are "not conformed to this world, but transformed by the renewing of our mind." R. C. Sproul is right when he says, "If there is any dimension in which Christians are to transcend the normal behavior patterns of fallen man, it is with respect to how they deal with their enemies, with those who have injured them. To say something good about one who has persecuted us, takes as much grace as any virtue ever did, because our natural human tendency is to get even. Sproul, p. 252.

93 Murray, 2:134.

rejoice; mourn and with those who mourn.' Though most agree
this likely includes unbelievers, it is primarily the saints who
have this empathy for one another."[94] **Rejoice** or be glad and
happy; **with those who rejoice,**[95] **and weep**[96] **with those who
weep** or continually come alongside of those who are suffering
and empathize with them. Feel what they feel, for "if one member
suffers, all the members suffer with it; or if one member is honored,
all the members rejoice with it" (1 Cor. 12:26).

Merida helpfully comments on verse 15:

> This often-quoted verse reminds us to come alongside other believers in
> the highs and lows of life. And do not limit that to funerals and weddings!
> Sometimes it is harder for us to rejoice with others than to weep with
> them, if they have obtained that which we want to obtain, envy and
> jealousy and competition make it difficult to rejoice.[97] But this is why we
> need the gospel. A sign of growing in grace is that we are able to rejoice
> in the success of other brothers and sisters. This is a wonderful way to
> love others: rejoice when they rejoice.

What about weeping? How do we do this? Showing up is most of the job,
right? You do not need a great speech. Just be present with the hurting.
This would have been a radical idea in a hierarchical [ranked] Roman
culture: the elite weeping with the poor migrant worker. But that is what
brothers and sisters in Christ do—regardless of background or class.[98]

- **(v. 16) Be of the same mind**[99] or opinion and judgment, which
  does not mean that we must always see eye to eye on secondary,
  nonessential matters. Rather, it means that even when we disagree
  on things like this, we are still earnestly to seek a harmony of
  relationships, and an "endeavoring to keep the unity of the Spirit
  and the bond of peace" (Eph. 4:3);[100] **toward one another.**[101] "To live
  in harmony means working through conflict, misunderstanding,
  miscommunication, and wounds. Through those awkward
  conversations, gracious interactions, and repentance, reconciliation
  and harmony are experienced. Harmony takes hard work, humble
  work, and heart work."[102] **Do not set your mind on high things**

---

94 Osborne, p. 398. I agree with Osborne's perspective here, but of course, we are not
to "rejoice" in those sinful things which might make unbelievers happy.

95 Cf. Phil. 2:17. Of course, this does not require that we rejoice with the ungodly when
they rejoice in that which is evil in God's eyes.

96 Grk. present, active, verb,

97 Chrysostom famously said, "It is easier to weep with those who weep than to
rejoice with those that rejoice, because nature itself prompts the former [weeping], but
envy stands in the way of the latter [rejoicing]," as cited in Johnson, p. 204.

98 Merida, p. 206.

99 Cf. Rom. 15:5, 6.

100 Paul will discuss our treatment of each other when it comes to secondary,
nonessential gospel matters more fully in chapters 14 and 15.

101 Cf. Rom. 15:5.

102 Ibid.

or never be conceited, high-minded, and full of self-importance;[103] **but**[104] or instead of doing this, and no doubt to help neutralize it; **associate** or go along; **with the humble** or those of low degree. "Don't become snobbish but take a real interest in ordinary people."[105] The idea is "not that we should avoid associating with those in high positions of wealth or influence. But as far as our service to them is concerned, we typically have more obligation to associate with the lowly, not because they are more important but because they are more needy."[106] **Do not be wise in your own opinion**[107] or estimation.

In this verse, Paul revisits some of what he said back in verse 3 of this chapter when he wrote that we are "not to think of ourselves more highly than we ought to think." His words are also similar to what he writes in Philippians 2:2: "be like-minded, having the same love, being of one accord, of one mind."[108] Of course, all of this instruction is vital for the ongoing unity of the church. Simply put, things like pride, arrogance, self-will, and egotism among ourselves will be devastating to the church. These are sins that we must seek to mortify in ourselves by the help of the Holy Spirit if we want things to go well in our congregations (Rom. 8:13).[109]

- **(v. 17) Repay** or paying back; **no one**[110] (regardless of who they are, or what they have done, believer or unbeliever, who is Paul's specific focus here again); **evil for evil.** "Private revenge is contrary to our gospel. We are not to repay evil words for evil words or evil deeds for evil deeds."[111]

Here the apostle provides us no loopholes or excuses. His language is similar to what he says in 1 Thessalonians 5:15: "See that no one renders evil for evil to anyone, but always pursuing what is good both for yourselves and for all." And his words are similar to Jesus' words when He said in Luke 6:29: "To him who strikes you on the one cheek,

---

103 Cf. Rom. 11:20.

104 The strong Greek adversative.

105 Phillips translation.

106 MacArthur, p.199.

107 Perhaps in writing this verse, Paul was thinking of the words of Prov. 26:12: "Do you see a man wise in his own eyes? There is more hope for a fool than for him." See also Prov. 3:7.

108 Cf. 1 Pet. 3:8.

109 It should be noted that in putting forth this instruction, Paul might be preparing his original audience for his discussion on Christian unity that he will take up with them more fully in chapters 14 and 15.

110 Paul placed these words at the beginning of the sentence by the direction of the Holy Spirit, for the sake of emphasis.

111 Mahan, p. 90. MacArthur further reminds us that "The Old Testament laws of 'eye for eye, tooth for tooth' (Ex. 21:24; cf. Lev. 24:20; Deut. 19:21) pertain to civil justice, not personal revenge. Not only that, but its major purpose was to prevent the severity of punishment from exceeding the severity of the offense. In other words, someone guilty of destroying other persons' eyes could not be punished with any greater penalty than that of forfeiting one of his own eyes." MacArthur, p. 201.

offer the other also. And from him who takes away your cloak, do not withhold your tunic either."

Thus, while of course our Lord (and Paul) is not saying that we should never protect ourselves against evil people who would seek to hurt us (or those whom we love), He is teaching us that we should not go after them in kind. He is saying that even though this is what the ungodly do, as Christians we are not to do this. Paul will give us the ultimate reason for this in verse 19 of this chapter.

Have regard for good things or better translated from the Greek text, continually giving thought to what is morally and ethically right and noble; **in the sight** or presence; **of all men** which means that genuine Christianity is concerned with rightly presenting Christianity to the world. It is concerned with appropriately adorning "the doctrine of God our Savior in all things" (Titus 2:10), so that our "public behavior is above criticism."[112]

Or, as Leon Morris wisely notes concerning Paul's words to his readers:

> He is calling on them to live out the implications of the gospel. Their lives are to be lived on such a high plane that even the heathen will recognize the fact. They will always be living in the sight of non-Christians, and the way they live should be such as to commend the essential Christian message (cf. Prov. 3:4; Matt. 5:6; Luke 2:52; 2 Cor. 4:2; 8:21; Titus 2:10).[113]

Sproul further elaborates:

> Paul is saying, 'Act with integrity in the sight of all men. Let your honesty be a model to the world.' There is a sense in which even pagans applaud civic virtues of righteousness. Even the pagan will appreciate a man who keeps his word. The pagan will appreciate a man who does his business dealings with integrity. Pagans can appreciate righteousness, at least where they are the beneficiaries of that righteousness.[114]

- **(v. 18) If it is possible** (implying its difficulty);[115] or if it is in our power to do so; **as much as depends on you** (even if the unbeliever will not do it "as far as your responsibility goes"[116]), **live peaceably with all men.**[117] Obviously Paul, in these words, is not calling us to "peace at any price." Nor is he encouraging us ever to compromise our convictions about Christ or the gospel. Rather, he is encouraging us to be sure that there is nothing in our persons or personalities that might cause problems with non-Christians. Simply stated, we are not purposefully to be offensive or odious to them but are to labor to live in harmony with them as much as we can.

---

112 Phillips translation. See also 1 Tim. 3:7.

113 Morris, p. 452.

114 Sproul, p. 255.

115 Robinson, Book II. p. 193.

116 Phillips translation.

117 Cf. Heb. 12:14; James 3:17.

Calvin states the point plainly:

> But here two cautions must be stated: We are not to seek to be in such esteem as to refuse to undergo the hatred of any for Christ, whenever it may be necessary. And indeed we see that there are some who, though they render themselves amicable [friendly] to all by the sweetness of their manners and peaceableness of their minds, are yet hated even by their nearest connections on account of the gospel. The second caution is,—that courteousness should not degenerate into compliance, so as to lead us to flatter the vices of men for the sake of preserving peace. Since then it cannot always be, that we can have peace with all men, he has annexed two particulars by way of exception, *If it be possible, and, as far as you can.* But we are to conclude from what piety and love require that we are not to violate peace except when constrained by either of these two things. For we ought, for the sake of cherishing peace to bear many things, to pardon offenses, and kindly to remit the full rigor of the law; and yet in such a way, that we may be prepared, whenever necessity requires, to fight courageously: for it is impossible that the soldiers of Christ should have perpetual peace with the world, whose prince is Satan.[118]

- **(v. 19) Beloved,** these tender words highlighting "Paul's awareness of the difficulty of this requirement;"[119] **do not avenge** or ever take vengeance for; **yourselves, but** *rather* **give place** or leave room or defer; **to wrath** (which is to say, God's wrath and anger, which Paul has spoken of throughout this letter: 1:18; 2:5, 8; 3:5; 5:9; 9:22); **for** the explanatory conjunction telling us why we should do this; **it is written**[120] (or stands written in Deuteronomy 32:35)[121] **Vengeance *is* Mine** which is to say, it completely belongs to God alone to inflict it; **I** literally, I even I; **will repay, says the Lord.**[122]

In these words, Paul highlights something which is crucial for us to grasp—vengeance is not Christian. Genuine Christianity does not seek to get even. It does not recompense itself because it realizes that vengeance is a usurping of God's sovereign prerogative to deal with our enemies for us in this life or in the life to come. Consequently, biblical Christianity lets God, the sovereign judge of all the earth deal with wrongs done to us in His way, and in His own time. It agrees with Paul when he said, "it is a righteous thing with God to repay with tribulation those who trouble you" (2 Thess. 1:6).

Vos wisely notes:

> Here again we have a solemn admonition not to seek vengeance [cf. v. 17]. The world talks continually about vengeance. As Christians we should not think in such terms. Even a nation at war should not seek

---

118 Calvin, pp. 472, 473.
119 Wilson, p. 207.
120 Grk. perfect, passive, verb.
121 Cf. Ps. 94:1, 2.
122 Cf. Prov. 20:22.

vengeance. Revenge is far from the Christian ideal in spirit. Rather, we are commanded to give place unto wrath, and leave vengeance to the Lord.

God, who is absolutely just as well as merciful, will render retribution to evildoers. He will pay them according to absolute justice. No sin will be overlooked. God will render to all according to their deeds unless they repent and seek His mercy in Christ.[123]

- **(v. 20) Therefore** or perhaps better translated from Greek text "but" or "on the contrary" (Paul quotes from Proverbs 25:21, 22);

"If your enemy is hungry, feed him;
If he is thirsty, give him a drink;
For in so doing you will heap coals of fire on his head."

Here Paul gives a balancing perspective to what he just spoken of in verse 19. He goes "beyond the reactive to the proactive,"[124] showing us that real Christianity does not ignore the needs of others—even if they are our enemies. "Christianity goes beyond non-resistance to active benevolence."[125]

The apostle says here in essence that we are to let our gospel-light shine before men, even toward those who harm us, for "in so doing you will heap coals of fire on his head." Concerning this matter of our good deeds toward our enemies figuratively heaping "coals of fire on their head," MacArthur says that this refers to an ancient Egyptian custom in which a person who wanted to show public contrition carried a pan of burning coals on his head. The coals represented the burning pain of his guilt and shame. When believers lovingly help their enemies, it should bring shame to such people for their hate and animosity.[126]

- **(v. 21) Do not be overcome** or conquered; **by evil, but**[127] or on the contrary; **overcome evil with good.**[128]

The apostle here summarizes all that he has been saying in the previous verses. He says to us by way of another command: do not be overpowered by all the ills that are done to us so that they cause us to be bitter, angry, and depressed. Rather, he says that we are to overpower that evil with good. We are to do good when others treat us badly. We are to treat them well when they deserve nothing but our retribution. And what is the greatest good that we can do for them? It is to give them the gospel. It is to tell them about Christ's person and work! This is what authentic Christianity seeks to do by the grace of God. This is how God would have us to live in the world as we continue to offer ourselves to Him as "living sacrifices" (vs. 1). May He then, by the empowerment of His Holy Spirit, enable us to do this very thing.

---

123 Vos, p. 261.

124 Barnett, p. 284.

125 McDonald, 1731.

126 MacArthur, *One Faithful Life*, p. 317.

127 The strong Greek adversative.

128 Cf. 1 John 5:4.

Lewis Johnson concludes his exposition of this chapter well when he reminds us that,

> As we look over the chapter, it becomes clear that the apostle's emphasis is on the necessity of being something first, and then of doing something. Right conduct can flow only from right being and thinking. Thus, the first step in the fulfillment of 12:3-21 can be accomplished only by the "Christian offering" that Paul refers to in verse 1, and the transformation of the believer by the renewing of the believer's mind through the Word of God (set forth in v. 2).[129]

Suggested applications from the text for the church:

1- Our passage calls us to repent where we have fallen short of these perspectives as God's people.

2- Our passage calls us to a fresh renewal of a commitment to all of these perspectives.

3- Our passage calls us to recall that our Lord Jesus Christ is always willing, able, and ready to help us to do all that He requires us to do.

Suggested application from the text for the non-Christian:

1- Our passage calls you to remember that because you are not an authentic Christian, you need to be born again, just as Jesus said (John 3:7). Since you cannot do this for yourself, you must call out to Him to do this for you, even this day.

---

129 Johnson Jr., p. 206.

ROMANS
CHAPTER THIRTEEN

Text: Romans 13:1-7

General theme: The Christian's Gospel Obligation concerning the Government[1]

Homiletical outline of the verses:

A. The command to obey the governing authorities: [1] Let every soul be subject to the governing authorities. For there is no authority except from God, and the authorities that exist are appointed by God.

B. The caution regarding resisting the governing authorities: [2] Therefore whoever resists the authority resists the ordinance of God, and those who resist will bring judgment on themselves. [3] For rulers are not a terror to good works, but to evil. Do you want to be unafraid of the authority? Do what is good, and you will have praise from the same. [4] For he is God's minister to you for good. But if you do evil, be afraid; for he does not bear the sword in vain; for he is God's minister, an avenger to *execute* wrath on him who practices evil. [5] Therefore *you* must be subject, not only because of wrath but also for conscience' sake.

C. The contribution for the governing authorities: [6] For because of this you also pay taxes, for they are God's ministers attending continually

---

1 When I preached on these verses, I called the sermon: *God, Government, and the Godly*. It should be noted that most scholars agree that God has established three main institutions on the earth: The family (Gen. 2:18-25), the government (Gen. 9:6; Rom. 13:1-7), and the church (Acts 2). Greg Nichols defines civil government in this way, "The organized exercise of civil authority, ordained by God, in which an empowered political regime exercises judicial, legislative, and executive power in its jurisdiction, with incentives and deterrents, taxation and conscription [the ability to draft individuals into public service], to establish justice, tranquility, welfare, defense and stability" *Lectures in Systematic Theology,* vol. 2. Doctrine of man, p. 300. The 1689 London Baptist Confession of Faith makes this helpful statement: "God, the supreme Lord and King of the whole world, has ordained civil authorities to be under Him and over the people, for His own glory and the public good. For this purpose He has armed them with the power of the sword, to defend and encourage those who do good and to punish evildoers." For further instruction about this matter, I point the reader to Wayne Grudem's Christian Ethics, pp. 426-87, and to *A New Exposition of the London Baptist Confession of Faith of 1689*, chapter 24, *Of the Civil Magistrate*, Mentor Books.

to this very thing. [7] Render therefore to all their due: taxes to whom taxes *are due,* customs to whom customs, fear to whom fear, honor to whom honor.

Summary of section: In these verses to the end of the chapter, Paul continues to explain the moral implications and applications of the gospel. He deals with three major topics: The Christian's gospel obligation concerning the government (vv. 1-7), their gospel obligation concerning the godly and all others (vv. 8-10), and their gospel obligation concerning the glorious and sure return of Christ (vv. 11-14). But we ask, "Why spend a whole chapter on these matters, especially when verses 1 to 10 seem to be concerned with a merely civic and social matter?"

The answer is simple: the gospel is to affect the entirety of our lives, both in and out of the church. The gospel, which has radically transformed our lives by grace, is not only a *private thing,* it is also that which is *public and practical.* As Lloyd-Jones says, "The gospel is not only to be believed, it is also to be practiced, and if we fail to carry it out, then there is no point in any amount of intellectual understanding."[2] Paul wants his first century Roman believers to understand this. He would have the same to be true for us who live in the twenty-first century.[3]

Specifically, in verses 1 to 7, he speaks to Christians about their civic responsibility. This can be a controversial subject, but since (as Hodge correctly notes), "The Christian religion is adapted to all states of society and all forms of civil government,"[4] I believe that all people regardless of the form of government under which they find themselves living, are to obey Paul's inspired words here.

Simply stated, Paul was not anti-government, and neither should we be. Christianity is not a call to political revolt or anarchy. Rather, it is a call to "submit to the governing authorities" and to "pray for kings and all who are in authority that we may lead a quiet and peaceable life in all godliness and reverence" (1 Tim. 2:1, 2).[5]

---

2 Lloyd-Jones, *Romans* p. 2.

3 Moo may also be correct when he says, "The specific contextual trigger for Paul's teaching about government and its role in this world may have been 12:19. Forbidding the Christians from taking vengeance and allowing God to exercise this right in the last judgment might lead one to think that God was letting evildoers have their way in this world. Not so, says Paul in 13:1-7: for God, through governing authorities, is even now inflicting wrath on evildoers (vv. 3-4): Moo, NICNT, p. 792. Additionally, he says that Paul might have been motivated to write this section because he is "worried that Christians will take his demand not to 'conform.... To the pattern of this world' (12:2) too far, lumping government into the category of "this world" and therefore refusing to respect its legitimate, divinely ordained position and function." Moo, in *Zondervan Illustrated Bible Backgrounds Commentary,* p. 77.

4 Hodge, p. 414.

5 This is how the transformed Christian mind is to think regardless of what people in the world do or think (Rom. 12:2). Perhaps the two extremes to avoid concerning this topic of government is either that of no *conformity to it or all conformity to it.* Moo makes a helpful comment when he says, "Balance is needed. On the one hand, we must not obscure the teaching of Romans 13:1-7 in a flood of qualifications. Paul makes clear that government is ordained by God — indeed, that every particular governmental authority is ordained by God — and that the Christian must recognize and respond to this fact with

But what about those Christians who live under tyrannical forms of government? Can they then exercise civil disobedience? Well, perhaps. However, this must be done in a non-violent, peaceful way. It is to be done prayerfully, asking God to raise up leaders who will deliver them from such challenging circumstances, just as Moses was used of God to deliver the old covenant people out of the tyrannical rule of Pharaoh.

But what if the government commands us to do what God forbids, like worshiping idols, as was the case in Daniel's day with his three friends?[6] Or, what if the government forbids us to preach the gospel, as the case was with the apostles? In situations like these, the answer is plain: "We ought to obey God rather than men" (Acts 5:29). Consequently, we see that the rule and role of government is not absolute or unlimited.

In our verses, Paul does not answer every question that we might have about government.[7] He does not get into the nitty-gritty matters or issues. In fact, in this chapter, he gives us broad instruction on this subject, which is to be applied generally to any form of government, even such forms of government as faced by the Roman Christians.

In speaking about some of these matters, McDonald wisely notes,

Those who have been justified by faith are obligated to be subject to human government. Actually the obligation applies to everyone, but the apostle here is concerned especially with believers. God established human government after the flood when he declared, "Whoever sheds man's blood, by man his blood shall be shed" (Gen. 9:6). That decree gave authority to men to judge criminal matters and to punish offenders.

In every ordered society there must be authority and submission to that authority. Otherwise you have a state of anarchy,[8] and you cannot survive indefinitely under anarchy. Any government is better than no government. So God has instituted human government, and no government exists apart from His will. This does not mean that He approves of all that human rulers do. He certainly does not approve of

---

an attitude of 'submission.' Government is more than a nuisance to be put up with; it is an institution established by God to accomplish some of his purposes on the earth (cf. vv. 3-4). On the other hand, we must not read Romans 13:1-7 out of its broad NT context and put government in a position relative to the Christian that only God can hold. Christian should give thanks for government as an institution of God; we should pray regularly for our leaders (cf. 1 Tim. 2:1-2); and we should be prepared to follow the orders of our government. But we should also refuse to give the government any absolute rights and should evaluate all its demands in the light of the gospel." Moo, NICNT, pp. 809, 810.

6 See also the example of the midwives in Egypt who refused to murder the newborn Hebrew babies (Ex. 1:15-22).

7 For example, a Christian might wonder if it is okay for a believer to play a role in the government to influence it for good, as the case was with Joseph and Daniel in the Old Testament. I think the answer to this question is absolutely. Again, the London Baptist Confession of Faith of 1689 addresses this matter when it says in chapter 24, paragraph 2, "Christians may lawfully accept and carry out the duties of public office when called to do so. In performing their office they must especially maintain justice and peace, according to the wholesome laws of each kingdom or other political entity. To carry out these duties they are authorized now under the New Testament to wage war in just and necessary situations (2 Sam. 23:3; Psalm 82:3, 4; Luke 3:14)."

8 Think about what we read in the book of Judges, "In those days there was no king in Israel; everyone did what was right in his own eyes" (Judg. 21:25).

corruption, brutality, and tyranny! But the fact remains the authorities that exist are appointed by God.

Believers can live victoriously in a democracy, a constitutional monarchy, or even a totalitarian regime. No earthly government is any better than the men who comprise it. That is why none of our governments are perfect. The only ideal government is a beneficent [merciful and kind] monarchy with the Lord Jesus Christ as King. It is helpful to remember that Paul wrote this section on subjection to human government when the infamous Nero was Emperor. Those were dark days for Christians. Nero blamed them for a fire which destroyed half the city of Rome (and which he himself may have ordered). He caused some believers to be immersed in tar, then ignited as living torches to provide illumination for his orgies. Others were sewn up in animal skins then thrown to ferocious dogs to be torn to pieces.

And yet it still holds that anyone who disobeys or rebels against the government is disobeying and rebelling against what God has ordained. Whoever resists the lawful authority earns and deserves punishment.

There is an exception, of course. A Christian is not required to obey if the government orders him to sin or to compromise his loyalty to Jesus Christ (Acts 5:29). No government has a right to command a person's conscience. So there are times when a believer must, by obeying God, incur the wrath of man.[9] In such cases he must be prepared to pay the penalty without undue complaint. Under no circumstances should he rebel against the government or join in an attempt to overthrow it.[10]

Exegetical & Practical Insights:[11]

Obs. 1- (v. 1) That as Paul begins this new section about our gospel obligation concerning our government, he begins with an apostolic command and writes:

Let every not some, but *every*, which means no one is excluded, not even the Christians at Rome living under Nero's rule; **soul**[12] or everyone, "which is a Hebraic expression meaning the whole person [and] emphasizes individual responsibility;"[13] **be subject**[14] **to** or continually and

---

9 Think of Daniel who refused to obey the decree to not petition any other except King Darius. Daniel knew that his refusal to do this could cost him his life. Yet, he remained faithful to the Lord and only petitioned Him. As a result he was thrown into the den of lions. God, however, was with him and sent His angel so that he was not hurt (Daniel 6).

10 McDonald, 1732.

11 In summarizing the essence of verses 1 to 7, Kevin Deyoung helpfully notes 1- The government's authority is a derived authority, 2- The government's authority is a divine authority, 3- The primary responsibility of government is to restrain and punish evil, 4- The secondary responsibility of government is to approve what is good. https://www.thegospelcoalition.org/blogs/kevin-deyoung/the-nature-and-purpose-of-government/.

12 Luther asked, "Is there some mysterious reason why he does not say 'every person' but rather 'every soul'? Perhaps it is because it must be a sincere submission and from the heart" *Reformation Commentary on Scripture, Romans*, Book 2, p. 153.

13 Edwards, 307.

14 Grk. present, middle, verb. The word is a military term which depicts the kind of submission that a soldier gives his commanding officer. The Greek word is made up of two

willingly place themselves under; **the governing** or higher; **authorities. For** the conjunction explaining the reason for the command; **there is**[15] **no authority,** i.e., none whatsoever; **except from God, and the authorities that exist are appointed**[16] or established and ordered (the use of the perfect tense verb highlighting an ongoing state resulting from past action, meaning that all governments that have ever existed or will exist are all determined); **by God.**

As we read these words, it is essential to remember what was said earlier, namely, that none of this means that God approves of all that human rulers do.[17] God never approves of sin. And He certainly is not the author of it. God hates sin wherever it is found from the lowest form of authority on up. Moreover, He promises to judge all who commit it who have not found forgiveness with Him through Christ (Rom. 2:8, 9).

However, the fact remains, "there is no authority except from God, and the authorities that exist are appointed by God." This is why as Christians, we must be "subject to the governing authorities." We may not like our form of government, or the people in it, or their policies, but this is not the point.[18] Therefore, if we rebel against them, we rebel against God who established them. We rebel against His rule on the earth, and this is sin on our part. As Sproul says, "That means that if I show no respect to a person whom God has set in authority between Himself and me, my disrespect carries beyond that person and ultimately lands on God as the giver of the authority."[19]

Paul's words here are similar to what he says to Titus, in Titus 3:1, "Remind them *to be subject* to rulers and authorities, *to obey,* to be ready for every good work... [emphasis mine]."

And his words are similar to what Peter said, in 1 Peter 2:13-15: "Therefore *submit yourselves* to every ordinance of man for the Lord's sake, whether to the king as supreme, or to governors, as to those who are sent by him for the punishment of evildoers and for the praise of those who do good. For this is the will of God, that by doing good you may put to silence the ignorance of foolish men—[emphasis mine]."

MacArthur nicely summarizes some of these matters:

> Paul says, human government is ordained by God for the benefit of society. In whatever of the many forms that exist, civil authority derives directly from God....
>
> There is no civil authority, Paul says, except from God. No matter what form it takes, no human government at any time in history, at any place

---

words, "under" and "to arrange." The same word is used in verse 5.

15 Grk. present, active, verb.

16 Grk. perfect, passive, verb. Cf. Prov. 8:15, 16; Dan. 2:19-21, 37, 38; 4:17, 25, 32; John 19:11.

17 Think, for example, of the great atrocities of the past two centuries throughout the world.

18 Remember also that in these words, Paul fully realized that the Roman government had ordered the execution of our Lord Jesus (John 19:1-16). Furthermore, as church history tells us, this is the same government that would behead Paul himself.

19 R. C. Sproul, *What is the Relationship Between Church and State*, p. 13.

on the earth, among any people on earth, at any level of society, has ever existed or will exist apart from the sovereign authority of God, because all "power belongs to God" (Ps. 62:11). The entire world, everything in heaven and earth, including Satan and his host, are subject to their Creator. God sovereignly created and absolutely controls the universe, with no exceptions or limitations. Also without exception, the power that any person, group, or society may possess is divinely delegated and circumscribed. How well or how poorly that power is used is another matter. Paul's point here is that this power has only *one source*—God.[20]

Obs. 2- (vv. 2-5) That as Paul gives a warning to us in view of what he just said in the previous words, he writes:

Therefore or consequently; **whoever** (Christian or non-Christian) **resists** or stands against and opposes (by not being subject to v. 1); **the authority resists the ordinance** or order; **of God, and those who resist will bring judgment** or punishment by the authorities for their disobedience and crimes; **on themselves. For** the word explaining why the previous verse is so; **rulers** or governing officials (whether local, state or national leaders); **are not a terror** or a cause for fear; **to good works,** i.e., law-abiding citizens whose conduct is "morally and socially right;"[21] **but**[22] or on the contrary; **to evil. Do you want to be unafraid of the authority? Do what is good,** or lawful; **and you will have praise** or commendation and approval; **from the same,** "peaceful, law-abiding citizens need not fear the authorities. Few governments will harm those who obey their laws. In fact governments usually commend such people."[23] For "the reason for the promise in verse 3;"[24] **he,** i.e., the civil official, governor, mayor, judge, or police; **is God's minister** or servant in the realm of government; **to you for good** or for the good of each one, individually and personally, for the enjoyment of a "quiet and peaceable life" (1 Tim. 2:2). **But if you do evil** which is to say, that which is criminal in nature; **be afraid; for,** the word explaining why this is so; **he does not bear the sword** "this symbolizes the government's right to inflict punishment on wrongdoers—especially capital punishment (Gen. 9:6; Matt. 26:52; Acts 25:11");[25] **in vain** or without purpose; **for he is God's minister, an avenger** or, we might say a revenger; **to** *execute* or carry out; **wrath on him who practices evil. Therefore** or for this reason (Paul draws a conclusion from the above-mentioned verses with a two-fold exhortation); *you* **must,** that is, you must of necessity; **be subject, not only because of wrath,** again, wrath incurred by the government for disobedience to it; **but also for conscience' sake,** which is to say, a good conscience towards God for obeying Him in these matters.

---

20 MacArthur, p. 218.

21 Robinson, *Studies in Romans* Book II. p. 203.

22 The strong Greek adversative.

23 MacArthur, *One Faithful Life* (2019), p. 318.

24 Harvey, p. 317.

25 MacArthur, *One Faithful Life* (2019), p. 318.

These words are clear and concise. Governments are to be obeyed. Therefore, to resist them is to bring their judgment upon us for our disobedience to them. Nevertheless, for us who are believers and good citizens, who seek to do good and not evil, we will receive praise from such ones when we do what is right. And since they execute wrath on evildoers, we must be sure that we are regularly subjecting ourselves to them. Consequently, we not only avoid their anger, but also please the living God who commands us to do these things. By regularly submitting to the authorities we keep a good conscience towards God and men, which is something that Paul highly valued: "I myself always strive to have a conscience without offense toward God and men" (Acts 24:16).

In commenting on these words, John Murray says,

> The meaning here must be that we are to subject ourselves out of a sense of obligation to God. The thought then is that we are not only to be subject because insubjection brings upon us penal judgment but also because there is the obligation intrinsic to God's will irrespective of the liability which evil-doing may entail. God alone is Lord of the conscience and therefore to do anything out of conscience or for conscience' sake is to do it from a sense of obligation to God. This is stated expressly in 1 Peter 2:13: "be subject to every ordinance of man for the Lord's sake". The necessity, therefore, is not that of inevitable outcome (*cf.* Matt. 18:7; Luke 21:23; 1 Cor. 7:26) but that of ethical demand (*cf.* 1 Cor. 9:16).[26]

Obs. 3- (vv. 6-7) That as Paul speaks about our contributions to our various types of governments, he writes:

For because of this, that is, "out of a sense of obligation to God and to keep a clear conscience before Him"[27] **you** (you Romans and every believer by extension) **also pay taxes,** "or public dues of every kind"[28] **for they,** i.e., the ones who collect our taxes; **are God's ministers** or public servants under His charge; **attending** or devoting themselves; **continually to this very thing** or giving of their time to it. Render or give back and pay (the word "render" is not an apostolic suggestion but a command); **therefore to all their due** or we might say what properly belongs to them according to God and by law "taxes are not voluntary or optional offerings given for the support of government, and paying them is the unqualified obligation of every citizen;"[29] **taxes**[30] **to whom taxes *are due*,** customs or fees typically imposed on imported and exported goods and merchandise;[31] **to whom customs, fear** or reverence; **to whom**

---

26 Murray, 2:154.

27 MacArthur, *One Faithful Life* (2019), p. 318.

28 Robinson, Book II, p. 207.

29 MacArthur, p. 239.

30 But someone might argue, saying, "Since my tax dollars are not always used for righteous things, why should I pay taxes?" Obviously, in the first century, the Roman government did not use all of its collected taxes for righteous things. Paul nonetheless still charged the Romans to pay their taxes.

31 Robinson, Book II, p. 208.

fear, honor or respect, value and deference; **to whom honor.** "What Paul probably means is something on this order: 'Simply paying your taxes is not enough.' Telling the officials, 'Here's the money, and now get out,' will never do. You should *respect* these men for the sake of their office, and *honor* them in view of their faithful devotion to their task (see verse 6)."[32]

What is Paul's main point in these two verses? McDonald states it well when he says, that "We owe the government not only obedience but financial support by paying taxes." He writes, "It is to our advantage to live in a society of law and order with police and fire protection, so we must be willing to bear our share of the cost. Government officials are giving their time and talents in carrying out God's will for the maintenance of a stable society, so they are entitled to support."[33]

In summary, if we are to continue to enjoy the many things that we enjoy in our various countries, such as national defense, parks for our children to play in, and generally speaking, nice roads to drive on, these things need to be paid for. They are paid for by our taxes. Taxes are God's provision for the government to be a blessing to us. Thus, instead of encouraging Christians not to pay them, when our Lord was asked if it was lawful to pay taxes to Caesar or not, He promptly replied by saying, "Render (the same verb used in our passage), to Caesar the things that are Caesar's" (Mark 12:17).[34]

Here then, from these opening verses of this chapter, Paul teaches us a few things concerning government:[35]

- Government is God's idea (not man's or Satan's)
- Government is to be submitted to (not rebelled against)
- Government authority is not absolute (only God's is)[36]
- Government officials are God's servants (therefore they are to be respected)
- Government plays a significant role in society in keeping law and order (therefore we should be thankful for it)
- Government is to be supported by our taxes (per God's command)

---

32 Hendriksen, pp. 437, 438. Further, in this regard, as Christians, we are to be careful not to speak abusively about our heads of state, whether it be our President or Prime Minister etc. To do this is to violate God's Word which says, "You shall not speak evil of a ruler of your people" (cf. Ex. 22:28; Acts 23:5).

33 McDonald, p. 1733.

34 Cf. Matt. 17:24-27.

35 Historically speaking, there was a Jewish religious, political group in Paul's day known as the Zealots. These individuals believed that there should be no king over the Jews except God, and they encouraged the people to rebel against the Roman Empire. They also encouraged the people not to pay taxes to the Empire. Paul taught something different, for surely he understood that for the gospel to thrive at that time (and in all other times) God's people needed to work well within their various governmental structures as good citizens and to "render to all their due." Interestingly, the Zealots were ultimately crushed by the Roman Empire. Christianity, however, continued to expand and to influence society with the gospel for decades to come.

36 Cf. Ps. 22:28, 103:19.

Suggested applications from the text for the church:

1- Our passage calls us to pray for our government, firstly, that those who work for it would be converted and follow Christ. But secondly, we are to pray that they would make wise and righteous laws according to God's Word and that Christians would prove to be good citizens so as to stay off their radar (1 Tim. 2:1-2).

2- Our passage calls us to participate in our government. This can be done not only by voting, but also by being involved in a governmental position in any way that we can be, seeking to influence it for good.

3- Our passage calls us to prepare for and long after that great and ultimate government and kingdom which is coming to this world in its full and final form when our Lord Jesus Christ returns. When that happens righteousness will reign, and we shall forever be with the Lord! (2 Pet. 3:13). Even so, come Lord Jesus! (Rev. 22:20).

Suggested application from the text for the non-Christian:

1- Our passage calls you to perpetually remember that your only hope in life and death is not government—but God. It is the Lord Jesus Christ, the only Savior of sinners. Thus seek Him while you can.

Text: Romans 13:8-10

General theme: The Christian's Gospel Obligation concerning the godly and all others—Love!

Homiletical outline of the verses:

A. The responsibility to love: [8] Owe no one anything except to love one another, for he who loves another has fulfilled the law.

B. The regulation for love: [9] For the commandments, "You shall not commit adultery," "You shall not murder," "You shall not steal," "You shall not bear false witness," "You shall not covet," and if *there is* any other commandment, are *all* summed up in this saying, namely, "You shall love your neighbor as yourself." [10] Love does no harm to a neighbor; therefore love is the fulfillment of the law.

Summary of section: In these verses, Paul returns to the vital theme of love (whether it be love for Christians or non-Christians). In fact, love so permeates this short section of Scripture that Paul mentions the word no less than five times. But why repeat this subject when he has already discussed it back in chapter 12:9-21? The answer is simple: we can never hear enough of it. Even though we are Christians, sadly, at times, we can be love-*less*. In being like this, we bring shame to the gospel and to God Himself *who is love* (1 John 4:16).

As those who are loved by God and love God, love toward others is to mark us out as His people. This is how we demonstrate and display the power of the gospel in our lives which at its core is all about love (John 3:16). This is how we obey our Lord when he said that we are to love our neighbors as ourselves (Matt. 22:34-40). Consequently, Leon

Morris is correct when he says, "The Christian should be characterized by love, love to other Christians but also to people in general. In short, the Christian is to be a loving person."[37]

Exegetical & Practical Insights:

Obs. 1- (v. 8) That as Paul takes up our topic at hand, he writes by way of ongoing command and says:

Owe[38] **no one anything except** or we might say "but;" **to love**[39] or to continue to love;[40] **one another,**[41] **for,** the word putting forth the reason for his previous words; **he who loves**[42] or keeps on loving; **another has fulfilled** *not nullified*, but rather, has met the full requirements of; **the law,** which is to say, the second table of the law which speaks specifically about our duties to others.

It is unfortunate that some Bible teachers take the opening words of "owe no one anything" to mean that a Christian can never, under any circumstance, have any debt. To have debt typically means to be in a state of owing money to someone else. However, in most societies, there are all kinds of ways that this could be done legitimately, for "debt is part of every aspect of economic life."[43]

For example, if we buy a house, we would typically owe the bank money for our mortgages. Likewise, we take on debt if we go to college and take a student loan, or if we have a lease on a car so that we can go to work, or if we get a small business loan to start a business and sell merchandise the same would be true. All of these matters are lawful in and of themselves and can be quite helpful for us to establish ourselves in the world and for preparing ourselves for the future.

Paul's opening words here in verse 8 do not forbid such a practice, for if going into debt is always sin, "it's difficult to understand why Scripture gives guidelines about lending and even encourages lending under certain circumstances"[44] as Randy Alcorn says.[45] He also writes, "If debt is always sin, then lending is aiding and abetting sin, and God would never encourage it."[46]

---

37 Morris, p. 467.

38 Grk. present, active, verb.

39 Grk. present, active, verb.

40 The Greek word for love here (as I mentioned in my exposition of 12:9) speaks about us having a warm, intentional regard for and a strong interest in others (Christians or non-Christians) whether they express this love back to us or not. It is a love that is sacrificial on our part and is not caused by anything in the one loved. For more information on this word, see my comments on 12:9.

41 Paul uses this "one another" language to refer to Christians throughout this letter: 12:5; 12:10; 12:16; 14:13; 14:19; 15:5; 15:7; 15:14.

42 Grk. present, active, verb.

43 Jim Newheiser, *Money Debt and Finances, Critical Questions and Answers*, p. 151.

44 Cf. Matt. 5:42.

45 Alcorn, *Money Possessions and Eternity*, p. 307.

46 Ibid., p. 307.

Having said this, nonetheless as Christians, we need to be extremely careful about getting into debt and prudently plan to get out of debt as soon as possible. Going into debt can be dangerous for us and those we love, especially since "the borrower is servant to the lender" (Prov. 22:7). Thus, Alcorn is right when he says that "unless there is an overwhelming need to borrow, it's unwise for God's children to put themselves under the curse of indebtedness."[47]

Perhaps, then, the best way to understand these opening words here is in the way that the NIV does: "Let no debt remain outstanding." This seems to be the essence of Paul's words. As Murray says:

> The force of the imperative is that we are to have no unpaid debts; that we are not to be in debt to any. In accord with the analogy of Scripture this cannot be taken to mean that we may never incur financial obligations, that we may not borrow from others in case of need (*cf.* Exod. 22:25; Psalm 37:26; Matt. 5:42; Luke 6:35). But it does condemn the looseness with which we contract debts and particularly the indifference so often displayed in the discharging of them. "The wicked borroweth, and payeth not again" (Psalm 37:21). Few things bring greater reproach upon the Christian profession than the accumulation of debts and refusal to pay them.[48]

Having made his statement of us to "owe no one anything" (and this probably because he just spoke in the previous verse about us rendering the various ones their "due") Paul now puts forth the main essence of his thought in the rest of the verse when he says that we are to owe "no one anything" *except* to love one another.

What is his point? It is this: there is one debt which is always to remain outstanding among ourselves as believers, namely, that we love each other. Love is a permanent obligation among all the people of God all of our days. Love is a debt that we never pay off and should never be neglected by us. It remains "ever due," as Hodge says.[49] *Agape* love, which is a fruit of the Holy Spirit in our lives,[50] and "signifies a deep, unselfish, superhuman affection which one person has for another"[51] is to be actively expressed and felt in all of our churches.[52] To not express this is to sin. It is to disobey Paul in our passage. It is to disobey the apostle John when he wrote, "My little children, let us not love in word or in tongue, but in deed and in truth" (1 John 3:18).

---

47 Ibid., p. 307.

48 Murray, 2:158, 159.

49 Hodge, p. 409. And this love again, is not only to be expressed toward believers, but also toward our enemies, thus, our Lord says to us, "love [agapao] your enemies, bless those who curse you, do good to those who hate you, and pray for those who spitefully use you and persecute you" (Matt. 5:44).

50 Gal. 5:22, 23.

51 McDonald, 1734.

52 Chrysostom said, "Love is a debt which you owe to your brother because of your spiritual relationship to him.... If love departs from us, the whole body is torn in pieces. *Ancient Christian Commentary on Scripture, Romans* p. 318.

John Gill explains what this type of love looks like:

> This debt should always be paying; Saints should be continually serving one another in love, praying for each other, bearing one another's burdens, forbearing each other, and doing all good offices in things temporal and spiritual that lie in their power, and yet always owing; the obligation to it always remains....
>
> But what the apostles seems chiefly to respect, is love to one another as men, love to one another, to the neighbor, as the following verses show. Love is a debt we owe to every man, as a man, being all made of one blood, and in the image of God; so that not only such as are of the same family, live in the same neighborhood, and belong to the same nation, but even all the individuals of mankind, yea, our very enemies are to share in our love; and as we have an opportunity and ability, are to show it by doing them good.[53]

Finally, in the verse, Paul gives his rationale for owing no one anything except to love one another when he writes, "for he who loves another has fulfilled the law." As was mentioned above, the law which Paul is speaking of here, are those laws specifically contained in the second half of the Ten Commandments, which speak about our responsibilities towards our fellow man. The following verse (v. 9), where Paul quotes these commandments, makes this point plain.

But what is the apostle teaching us by connecting *the law of God with our love toward others*? It is simply this: far from the law of God having no relevance for the life of the Christian, "We need God's law to tell us how to love."[54] God's law describes for us in concrete ways (as opposed to leaving it up to us to figure it out or for our hearts to decide) how we are to love our brethren and our neighbors in truth, and this especially by forbidding unlawful acts against them. The law of God not only describes the negative things we are not to do toward our neighbors (such as Paul will state in the following verse), but all of those commandments have positive corresponding implications. This is the case so that if, for example, we are not going to "commit adultery" then we are required positively to have:

Chastity [purity] in body, mind, affections, words, and behavior; and the preservation of it in ourselves and others, watchfulness over the eyes and all the senses; temperance, keeping of chaste company, modesty in apparel; marriage by those that have not the gift of continency [celibacy]

---

53 Online commentary: www.biblestudytools.com/gills-exposition-of-the-bible/romans-5-11.html. As I read these words by John Gill, I was struck with the fact of how, if more people (even Christian people) embraced his words, there would be so much less racism and hatred in our world. May God help us, then, especially who are Christians, to take his words (and yes, Paul's words!) to heart so that such evils would be progressively eradicated from our societies.

54 *Reformation Heritage Study Bible*, p. 1637. The comments in the Study Bible continue helpfully saying, "There is no conflict between law and love. Love is a command, and the Ten Commandments show us in greater detail what that means. The Old Testament taught love, even to our enemies (Ex. 23:4-5). There is no difference in moral standard between the Testaments, though the same standard is more fully revealed in the New Testament.

conjugal [marital] love, and cohabitation; diligent labor in our callings; shunning all occasions of uncleanness, and resisting temptations thereunto (as the Westminster Larger Catechism says).

Olyott expounds on this point as follows,

> Why refrain from adultery? If I love my neighbor I would not dream of stealing his wife or daughter. If I love my wife, I would not betray her, or give her unnecessary heartache. The same sort of thing can be said about the other laws which Paul quotes. Love is the seeking of the greatest possible good for my neighbor, even at the greatest possible cost to myself. Where such love exists it will inevitably refrain from murder, stealing, and setting my heart on my neighbor's possessions. If my love is genuine, it will be worked out in right action. I will treat others as I would like them to treat me. The observation of God's law is the fullest display of love.[55]

Obs. 2- (vv. 9-10) That as Paul puts forth the regulation for our love toward others, in quoting from Exodus chapter 20:13-15, he writes:[56]

For, the word confirming Paul's previous words; **the commandments,**[57]

"You shall not commit adultery," (the seventh commandment);

"You shall not murder," (the sixth commandment);

"You shall not steal," (the eighth commandment);

"You shall not bear false witness," (the ninth commandment);

"You shall not covet," (the tenth commandment);

and if *there is* any other commandment, that is, any other commandment of God along these same lines; **are** *all* summed up or gathered; **in this saying, namely, "You shall love your neighbor as yourself"** (A quote from Leviticus 19:18);[58]

Love (or more literally from the Greek text *the love*) that is, the distinctive Christian, agape love that Paul has been writing about which believers are to have in their hearts; **does no harm**[59] or never works any evil; **to a neighbor** which of course is anyone in need[60] or more literally, anyone who is "near" us;[61] **therefore,** the word introducing "Paul's conclusion to the paragraph;" **love** *is* **the fulfillment** or again, that which meets the full requirement; **of the law.**

In summarizing these last words Sproul well observes,

> Paul amplifies the statement by saying that love is not just a feeling, it has a behavioral aspect. When the Bible says I am to love my neighbor, it means I am to be considerate to my neighbor. It has to do with action: what

---

55 Olyott, p. 127.

56 Cf. Deut. 5:17-21.

57 It is interesting to observe that Paul rearranged the order of the commandments between the sixth and seventh. Perhaps he did this because adultery was so prevalent at that time in Roman society.

58 Cf. Gal. 5:14; James 2:8.

59 Grk. present, middle, verb.

60 Luke 10:25-37.

61 The Greek word for neighbor is derived from a word that means "near."

I say, what I do with my money, what I do with my body, what I do that may bring harm and injury to another person. I am to care about other people. Christians should be the most caring, considerate and neighborly people in the world. To be a lover of God requires that we show that love through being kind and considerate to people.[62]

Suggested applications from the text for the church:

1- In view of our passage, we are to excel in our love toward one another.

2- In view of our passage, we are to expect this love from one another.

3- In view of our passage, we are to be encouraged in this love, and this especially as this love has been abundantly shown toward us by God through Jesus Christ our Lord (John 3:16; Rom. 5:5).

Suggested application from the text for the non-Christian:

1- In view of our passage, you need to experience the love of God, which is found exclusively in Jesus Christ.

Text: Romans 13:11-14

General theme: The Christian's Gospel Obligation concerning the Glorious and Sure Return of Christ

Homiletical outline of the verses:

A. Wake up: [11] And do this, knowing the time, that now it is high time to awake out of sleep; for now our salvation is nearer than when we *first* believed.

B. Clean up: [12] The night is far spent, the day is at hand. Therefore let us cast off the works of darkness, and let us put on the armor of light. [13] Let us walk properly, as in the day, not in revelry and drunkenness, not in lewdness and lust, not in strife and envy.

C. Suit up: [14] But put on the Lord Jesus Christ, and make no provision for the flesh, to *fulfill* its lusts.

Summary of section: In these verses, the apostle ties together the subject of *ethics* (from the previous verses) to *eschatology* (or the end times) in connection to the second coming of Christ. Jesus often spoke of His second coming in Scripture (Matt. 16:27; 25:31; John 14:1-4). The Bible describes His return as personal (Acts 1:11), physical (Rev. 1:7),

---

62 Sproul, pp. 282, 283.

visible (Col. 3:4), sudden (Mark 13:33-37),[63] glorious and triumphant[64] (1 Thess. 4:16). Hence, when Jesus returns, the "clouds of heaven will be His chariot, the Angels His bodyguard, the archangels His heralds, and the saints of God His glorious retinue [entourage]. He will come as King of kings and Lord of lords, triumphant over all the forces of evil, having put all His enemies under His feet" (1 Cor. 15:25; Rev. 19:11-16).[65]

Our Lord will return one day to judge the wicked and to receive His people to Himself. When that happens, Christians will "inherit the kingdom prepared for them from the foundation of the world" (Matt. 25:34). When Jesus returns, He will close out this age and usher in the age to come. Consequently, Peter says, "We, according to His promise, look for new heavens and a new earth in which righteousness dwells" (2 Pet. 3:13).

All of this should make us as believers extremely encouraged. It should make us regularly say with the apostle John, "Even so, come, Lord Jesus!" (Rev. 22:20). However, this glorious truth should also be a real wake-up call for us to spiritual alertness and moral purity since we do not know when our Lord will return. This is how Paul uses the topic of the return of Christ in this passage. Thus, his eschatology fuels his ethics. Paul uses our Lord's return as a motivation for us to be sure that our lives are in order so that we who have been saved by free grace will be in good spiritual shape when He, Jesus the bridegroom, returns (Matt. 25:1-13). As Morris says, "Paul adds a section drawing attention to the urgency

---

63 In commenting on this matter regarding the sudden return of Christ, Augustine wrote, "Paul said this, yet look at how many years have passed since then! Yet what he said was not untrue. How much more probable it is that the coming of the Lord is near now, when there has been such an increase of time toward the end!'" *Ancient Christian Commentary on Scripture, Romans* p. 322.

Sproul says further, "... If we examine carefully the writings of the apostle Paul, we find that, although Paul may have personally hoped for the return of Jesus in his own lifetime, he certainly didn't teach that concept. The Bible nowhere teaches, emphatically or explicitly, a timetable for the return of Jesus. It does not teach us that Jesus was going to come back in the first century." Sproul, p. 285.

Moo sums up this matter nicely when he says, "Many scholars think that Paul's statement here, along with similar ones in the NT, shows that the early Christians were certain that Christ was going to return within a very short period of time. And, since Paul's imperatives are, to some extent, based on this premise, the failure of Christ to return as soon as Paul expected requires that we critically evaluate the continuing validity of those imperatives. Paul certainly betrays a strong sense of expectation about the return of Christ (e.g., Phil. 4:5) and can even speak at times as if he will be alive at that time (e.g., 1 Thess. 4:15). But nowhere does he predict a near return; and, more importantly, he does not ground his exhortations on the conviction that the Parousia [the return of Jesus] would take place very soon but on the conviction that the parousia was always imminent – it's coming certain, it's timing incalculable. 'On the *certainty of the event*, our faith is grounded: by *the uncertainty of the time*, our hope is stimulated, and our watchfulness aroused. Christ's return is the next event in God's plan; Paul knew it could take place at any time and sought to prepare Christians – both in his generation and in ours – for that "blessed hope." Moo, NICNT, p. 822

64 Berkhof, *Systematic Theology,* p. 704-06.

65 Ibid., p. 706.

of getting on with the business of living as Christians should. In view of the coming of 'the day' they should live wholeheartedly for Christ."[66]

Exegetical & Practical Insights:

Obs. 1- (v. 11) That as Paul takes up our topic at hand, he writes:

And *do* this, that is, continue to walk in gospel love toward all people just as he commanded us to do in verses 8 to 10; **knowing** or understanding and realizing; **the time,** i.e., the appointed time or that decisive moment in history when Jesus will return; **that now,** not tomorrow or next week, but "now;" **it is high time** or already the critical hour; **to awake out of sleep** or our spiritual slumber (figuratively speaking); **for,** the conjunction putting forth the rationale for the previous words; **now,** again, not tomorrow or next week, but "now;" **our salvation** which is to say, the final aspect of our salvation which is our glorification;[67] *is* **nearer** or closer; **than when we** *first* **believed.**[68]

The Bible describes our salvation in three ways:
- that which is past (Rom. 5:1; Eph. 2:8)
- that which is present (1 Cor. 1:18, 2 Cor. 2:15) and
- that which is future (Rom. 5:9, 8:23)

Here as Paul points us to this last aspect of our salvation when Jesus returns, he calls us to moral alertness as was mentioned above. He calls us to be attentive so that our "houses are in order," for as Jesus said in Matthew 24:42, "Watch therefore, for you do not know what hour your Lord is coming."

Paul's language sounds similar to Peter's, when he wrote, "But the end of all things is at hand; therefore be serious and watchful in your prayers." (1 Pet. 4:7). Moreover, he sounds similar to the apostle James, when he wrote, "Do not grumble against one another, brethren, lest you be condemned. Behold, the Judge is standing at the door!" (James 5:9).

Obs. 2- (vv. 12-13) That as Paul puts forth the practical implications of his subject, he writes:[69]

The night is far spent or almost gone (again, he speaks figuratively) but now with reference to this present evil age of sin that has "just about run its course;"[70] **the day is at hand,** i.e., the triumphant day of Christ's glorious, sure return. Therefore or accordingly; **let us cast off**[71] or forsake and immediately lay aside as one does dirty clothing; **the works of darkness** or every single thing in our lives that we know displeases the

---

66 Morris, P. 470.

67 Cf. Rom. 8:30.

68 By mentioning the word belief again in connection to our salvation, Paul highlights a grand truth that he has expressed throughout this epistle, namely, that we are saved by *grace alone, through faith alone, in Christ alone.* It is also important to note that he does not say that our salvation is nearer than when we "first were baptized or joined the church or partook of the Lord's Supper or tried to keep the Ten Commandments" no. He says that our salvation is nearer than when we first *believed* (cf. Rom 1:16, 3:21-31, 5:1, 9:30-32, 10:10).

69 Cf. Eph. 5:11-14; 1 Thess. 5:5-7.

70 McDonald, 1734.

71 Grk. aorist, middle, verb.

Lord; **and let us**[72] **put on** or be covered with immediately; **the armor of light**[73] or we might say, the protective weapon of a godly, holy life which pleases God. "The Christian spiritual armor is the light of God's own holiness and purity, with which He desires His children to be constantly clothed. It is the clothing of spiritual purity and integrity, a reflection of our Lord's holiness that—whether they recognize it or not—all the world can see."[74] **Let us walk properly,** that is, let us conduct our lives as Christians honorably and becomingly according to the rule of Scripture; **as in the day, not in revelry** or wild sinful partying; **and drunkenness** or excessive drinking so that one becomes intoxicated; **not in lewdness** or sexual immorality and self-indulgence; **and lust** or unbridled sensuality; **not in strife** or discord **and envy** or jealousy.[75]

In these words, Paul continues to press the Romans [and us by way of extension] to holy, Christian living based on the reality of Christ's sure return. He does this as Chrysostom says,

> not to frighten his hearers, but to encourage them, so as to detach them from their love of the things of this world. It was not unlikely that at the beginning of their endeavors they would be more dedicated and slacking off as time went on. But Paul wants them to do the opposite—not to slacken as time goes on but to become even more dedicated. For the nearer the King is, the more they ought to be ready to receive him.[76]

In writing this way, Paul speaks like the apostle Peter who said that in view of Jesus' return, the manner of persons we are to be is "holy in conduct and godly" (2 Pet. 3:10, 11). And he speaks like the apostle John, who, when writing about Jesus' return said, "And everyone who has this hope in Him purifies himself, just as He is pure" (1 John 3:1-3).[77]

We might wonder why Paul felt it necessary to use three "not statements" in verse 13 concerning the various sins that we are to avoid. Could it be that these were really sins that the Roman Christians were *habitually committing*? I do not think this was the case. I say this because plainly these individuals had been transformed by the power of the gospel so that "though they were slaves of sin, yet they obeyed from the heart that form of doctrine to which they were delivered. And having become set free from sin they became the slaves of righteousness" (Rom. 6:17, 18).[78]

---

72 Grk. aorist, middle, verb.

73 Haldane says, "The Christian is a soldier, and as such he is furnished with a complete suit of armor, to fit him for the encounter with his enemies. It consists of *faith*, and *love*, and *hope*. 'Let us who are of the day be sober, putting on the breastplate of faith and love; and for a helmet, the hope of salvation'" (1 Thess. 5:8). Haldane, p. 590.

74 MacArthur, p. 265.

75 These last two sins listed by Paul shows us that God is not only concerned with *outward actions*, but also *inward ones* as well.

76 *Ancient Christian Commentary on Scripture, Romans* p. 321.

77 Cf. Titus 2: 11-13; Heb. 10: 24, 25.

78 See also Rom. 1:6, 7. Cf. 1 Pet. 4:3, 4. It should be noted that these sins were very prevalent in the Roman society of the first century thus, it was vital that in order not to fall

However, the fact remains, any one of us as Christians could still regrettably be tempted towards and commit any of these evil deeds. This is a sad reality, therefore Paul's words are vital for us to obey. They are tremendously instructive to help us stay on the narrow path that leads to life so that we avoid any relapses in our lives, which would grieve us and our lovely, returning Lord.

Obs. 3- (v. 14) That as Paul highlights to us how it is that we could have victory over the sins which he just listed, he writes by way of another apostolic command:

But[79] or in strong contrast to living improperly according to the flesh (v. 13); **put on**[80] or be daily and completely clothed with; **the Lord** (not only the "armor of light" v. 12, but with the sovereign Master and Ruler whose "Lordship" we are to be under); **Jesus** (which means, "the Lord is salvation"); **Christ** (or God's promised anointed and appointed Messiah); **and make no provision** or more literally, give no forethought or planning; **for the flesh**[81] or our remaining sinful tendencies within; **to fulfill** or to carry out and indulge; *its* **lusts** or evil desires.

We need to note first from the opening part of these words that when Paul speaks about us "putting on the Lord Jesus Christ," he is not speaking about us doing this legally, with respect to *imputed righteousness and justification*, whereby we receive Jesus' righteousness credited to our account by faith alone. This is because this is a one-time act of God which happened the moment we believed (Rom. 3:21, 22; 4:5-8; 10:3, 4; Gal. 3:27; Phil. 3:9). So, if he is not speaking about this, what is he describing?

He is describing what we are to do daily in the practical sense of *imparted righteousness and sanctification*, whereby we as Christians are consciously sure that we are clothing ourselves with Christlike characteristics such as love (Mark 10:21; John 11:36), truth (John 1:14, 14:6), holiness (Luke 4:34; Heb. 7:26), humility (Matt. 11:29; Phil. 2:5-11), and peace (John 14:27, 16:33).

To "put on the Lord Jesus Christ" is for us to wear Jesus wherever we go, figuratively speaking,[82] so that we are regularly modeling according to Scripture, His Godward life of a holy heart, a holy mind, and a submissive will to God the Father. It is for us to be "Christ's men [and women] from head to foot."[83] In summary, it is to walk "just as He walked," just as we are commanded to do in 1 John 2:6.[84] Or, as Moo says,

---

into them, these believers obeyed Paul when he said in Romans chapter 12:2 "And do not be conformed to this world."

79 The strong Greek adversative.

80 The middle voice in the Greek verb stressing our part in this process. The aorist tense stressing its urgency.

81 Haldane correctly notes, "We are to make provision for the wants of the body, but we are to make no provision for its lust. Whatever then, tends to excite our corrupt propensities ought to be avoided." Haldane, p. 591.

82 I first heard this put this way by Pastor Greg Nichols.

83 Phillips translation.

84 For a helpful exposition of this topic, I point the reader to *The One thing Needful*, by William Mason, p. 27. In this work Mason says, "To put on Christ, may more precisely

it means that we are to "consciously embrace Christ in such a way that his character is manifested in all that we do and say."[85]

How can we do this most effectively in our lives? It is by us growing closer in our communion with Jesus as we spend time daily in His Word and prayer. It is by us sitting weekly under the preaching of Christ and His gospel in the local church, with its holy ordinances as important means of grace. Furthermore, it is by us surrounding ourselves with the godliest people that we know so that we imitate them as they "imitate Christ" (1 Cor. 11:1).

But second, we should also note that when Paul says in the second half of this verse that we are to make "no provision for the flesh, to fulfill its lust" (which is what we are enabled to do when we put on the Lord Jesus Christ), that since God commands this through Paul's pen, we, in fact, can do this by His grace with the help of the Holy Spirit. Paul has already discussed much of this topic in Romans chapters 6 through 8. Yet, it is good that he reminds us of this matter once again *so that we do not forget it.*

Merida sums up this matter well when he says concerning these words:

> This reminds us that we have *power* to say no to sin and yes to God. To make "no provision for the flesh" means to say no to any thought that may lead you to sin; avoid even the desire for it. Do not plan to sin. Do not daydream about sin. Do not seek comfort in sin. Do not flirt with sin. Specifically, in light of this passage, do not entertain the idea that a wild night of drunkenness and partying will cure your loneliness, sadness, or boredom. As a married person, do not entertain the idea that committing adultery will satisfy your unfulfilled romantic desires. As a person frustrated with your current situation, do not entertain the thought of growing jealous of others. As a bitter person, do not begin quarreling with others.
>
> Make no provision for the flesh. Instead, direct your mind to the promises of God in Scripture. Direct your mind to the beauty of Christ! Follow the lifestyle of the Savior in this present age. Direct your mind to the glory that is to come. We have a wonderful Savior who satisfies our human longings and empowers us for this kind of obedience. Jesus is better than sin—the sin of retaliation, the sin of dishonoring the government, the sin of failing to love our neighbors, and the sin of the flesh. One day soon he will come and eradicate the world of sin once and for all, and we will no longer wrestle in these bodies of flesh. Live *this day* in view *of that day*![86]

Lastly, concerning the final half of verse 14, we should remember that it was this very verse (along with the previous one) that God powerfully

---

mean, that we daily, yea constantly clothe our mind, memory, and conscience with Christ, and with the truth as it is in him — which truth holds forth, what he hath done for us, what he is to us, and what he is now doing for us at the right hand of God."

85 Moo, NICNT, pp. 825, 826.

86 Merida, pp. 220, 221.

used to convict and convert the great Christian theologian named Saint Augustine. Before Augustine was converted, he was anything *but* a saint. Actually, he was a great sinner whose life was characterized by many of the sins that Paul listed in this section of Scripture. Still, God got a hold of Augustine and made him a new creation in Christ Jesus! God transformed him through the reading of our passage so that as he himself said, "No further would I read, nor had I any need, instantaneously at the end of the sentence, a clear light flooded my heart and all the darkness of doubt banished away."[87]

May God be pleased then to use this passage in the lives of many in the same way—to the saving of their souls—and to the glorifying of His wonderful name!

Suggested applications from the text for the church:

1- In view of our passage, we are to "look up" to heaven in hope because our Savior will surely return as our final redemption draws nigh.

2- In view of our passage, we are to "get up" and do the work of evangelism since the gospel must be preached to all the nations and then the end will come.[88]

3- In view of our passage, we are to "pray up" to God for all the strength that we need to live as He would have us to live as His people until Jesus returns.

Suggested application from the text for the non-Christian:

1- In view of our passage, you are to "fess up" because you have committed great wickedness before God. Thus, you desperately need Him to save you through Christ. May you call out to Him then even this day, for this very thing (Rom. 10:12, 13).

---

87 Confessions 8.29.

88 Cf. Matt. 24:14.

ROMANS
CHAPTER FOURTEEN

Text: Romans 14:1–15:13

General theme: Christian Liberty with Grace-filled Sensitivity (the Weak and the Strong Must Get Along: Christian Toleration) (I)

Homiletical outline of the verses:

A. Paul's commands: [1] Receive one who is weak in the faith, *but* not to disputes over doubtful things. [2] For one believes he may eat all things, but he who is weak eats *only* vegetables. [3] Let not him who eats despise him who does not eat, and let not him who does not eat judge him who eats; for God has received him. [4] Who are you to judge another's servant? To his own master he stands or falls. Indeed, he will be made to stand, for God is able to make him stand.

B. Paul's counsels: [5] One person esteems *one* day above another; another esteems every day *alike.* Let each be fully convinced in his own mind. [6] He who observes the day, observes *it* to the Lord; and he who does not observe the day, to the Lord he does not observe *it.* He who eats, eats to the Lord, for he gives God thanks; and he who does not eat, to the Lord he does not eat, and gives God thanks.

C. Paul's considerations: [7] For none of us lives to himself, and no one dies to himself. [8] For if we live, we live to the Lord; and if we die, we die to the Lord. Therefore, whether we live or die, we are the Lord's. [9] For to this end Christ died and rose and lived again, that He might be Lord of both the dead and the living. [10] But why do you judge your brother? Or why do you show contempt for your brother? For we shall all stand before the judgment seat of Christ. [11] For it is written:

"*As* I live, says the LORD,
Every knee shall bow to Me,
And every tongue shall confess to God."

[12] So then each of us shall give account of himself to God. [13] Therefore let us not judge one another anymore, but rather resolve this, not to put a stumbling block or a cause to fall in *our* brother's way.

Summary of section: In these verses continuing through to chapter 15 and verse 13, Paul opens up the last major section in this letter concerning the crucial topic of Christian Liberty with Grace-filled sensitivity. He does this by instructing us broadly about the matters of Christian toleration (14:1-13),[1] Christian consideration (14:14-23), Christian imitation (15:1-6), and then Christian integration (15:7-13).[2]

The church in Rome was a culturally diverse congregation. This assembly included believers from both Jewish and Gentile backgrounds, and that presented some unique challenges to them.[3] As a result, the general thrust of these words is about them learning to live and love each other as a saved society despite secondary differences. Having diversities of backgrounds among believers can be problematic for any church. Evidently, this was the situation at Rome.[4] The believers there were expressing their God-given liberties, *but not* with grace-filled sensitivities. This is why Paul wrote this section of Scripture. He wanted to bring healing to the congregation and to set them (and all believers after them) on a path where gospel love would flourish among them.[5]

Paul would not have any racial, social or cultural differences or practices divide brethren in the church, and neither should we. The apostle knew that it was not Jesus' plan to have, for example, Jewish believing congregations and Gentile believing congregations separated from one another doing their "own thing." Rather, He would have them integrated, even with all their various differences, with the goal that they with *"one mind* and *one mouth"* would glorify the God and Father of our Lord Jesus Christ" (Rom. 15:6) [emphasis mine].[6] This is the great end to which he is driving towards in this section which is based on, and really is the pastoral crescendo to all that he has established in the previous chapters concerning their lives together as Christians.

Leon Morris expresses similar thoughts:

> The church was never meant to be a cozy club of like-minded people of one race or social position or intellectual caliber. Christians are not clones, identical in all respects. One of the difficulties the church has always faced is that included in its membership are the rich and the poor, the powerful and the powerless, those from every stratum of society, the old and the young, adults and children, the conservatives and the radicals.

---

1 By using the words "Christian toleration" of course as believers we never "tolerate" sin, error or false teaching in the church. These are not matters with which the apostle is dealing here.

2 Pastor Greg Nichols helped me to see this big picture. Moo also captures this matter in his overview of this section in Romans, Moo, NICNT, p. 833.

3 For more information about this, see my Brief Overview in the front of the book. Further, we see that Paul, throughout his letters, speaks to this matter concerning the Jews and Gentile and their relationship in the church (see Gal. 3:28; Eph. 3:14-16, 3:6; Col. 9-11).

4 Cf. 14:1, 3, 4, 10, 15, 19, 20 etc.

5 It should also be noted that the topic of love among the brethren has been much on Paul's heart in the previous chapters (see Rom. 12:9, 10, 13:8-10).

6 For a fuller treatment on this subject, I point the reader to Greg Nichols' *Doctrine of the Church.*

People from a great number of nations are Christians, and people of every temperament. This is a wonderful thing about the church, and most of us have thrilled at some time at the contemplation of the rich variety in our brothers and sisters in Christ. But this very variety puts strains on us all. How are we to coexist within one church?[7]

In these chapters, Paul answers this key question as he, principally, puts forth a popular motto which has been in the churches over the centuries: In essentials, unity;[8] in non-essentials, liberty; in all things, love.[9] This is a gospel golden rule that he would have us to live by as he teaches us a vital point for our living well together in the church which is: *despite matters of secondary importance where we might disagree, we are never to let non-gospel, non-essential, non-sinful matters become barriers to our fellowship in the Lord.*[10]

This is a crucial point that we must get if we would live as God would have us to live as loving, local, gospel communities. We must remember this especially as we exercise Christian liberty.[11] But what exactly is Christian liberty?[12]

In summary, Christian liberty pertains to believers being able to partake in or practice activities upon which the Scriptures do not speak directly. Christian liberty involves applying biblical wisdom with reference to things which are morally indifferent. It is often associated with social "do's or don'ts."[13] But what kind of social "do's or don'ts" am I speaking of? I am speaking, for example, of whether a Christian could listen to certain types of non-Christian music or watch certain types of non-Christian movies, or if they could dance at weddings, dress fashionably, or drink alcoholic beverages socially (of course without ever getting drunk or losing self-control),[14] or even if they could enjoy

---

7 Morris, p. 476.

8 Of course, it should be noted that *unity* among believers does not mean *uniformity*. Unity is essential in the foundational matters of the Christian life, such as: justification by faith alone, in Christ alone, the deity of Jesus, His resurrection and second coming, and the Trinity. However, uniformity requires something else entirely. Uniformity requires that we are entirely alike in all things disallowing differing opinions about matters of secondary importance. This is something which the Bible does not require.

9 Christian theologians debate the original source.

10 I agree with Doriani when he succinctly says, "Romans 14-15 teaches the church how to retain its unity while its members disagree." Doriani, p. 512.

11 Sinclair Ferguson has a good article on this topic entitled: 4 principles for exercising Christian liberty. It can be accessed here https://www.ligonier.org/learn/articles/4-principles-exercise-christian-liberty.

12 The London Baptist Confession of Faith of 1689 has a useful discussion of this subject in chapter 21 of that treatise. Dan Dodds helpfully notes that this doctrine guards against "the unlawful usurpation or abuse of authority by people or institutions over the consciences of God's people. This doctrine states that if Scripture (or a truth legitimately deduced from it) does not address a particular ethical issue, the Christian is at liberty to decide—his conscience cannot be bound by anyone. Thus, the Christian is protected from the tyranny of human authorities or opinions. His article on this subject can be found here: https://tabletalkmagazine.com/article/2019/06/christian-liberty.

13 The Greek word commonly associated with this by theologians is *adiaphora*.

14 See Eph. 5:18; 1 Cor. 6:10.

certain types of secular holidays, etc. Another area could include if a Christian should use various forms of social media (Facebook, Twitter and Instagram). These subjects are gray areas in the Word of God, which God has neither commanded nor forbidden. Consequently, the Christian is at liberty to partake of them. However, having said this, some words of caution are in order.

- As Christians, we must always remember when exercising any Christian liberty that *we are never at liberty to behave in a way which Scripture flatly condemns* (Rom. 6:1, 2). In other words, Christian liberty is always to be lived out under the Lordship of Christ (Rom. 14:7-9).
- As Christians, we must always remember when exercising any Christian liberty that *we are never at liberty to wound the conscience of or become a stumbling block to another believer who cannot do what we do with a good conscience by flaunting our liberty before them* (Rom. 14:13-21).
- As Christians, we must always remember when exercising any Christian liberty that *we are never to engage in anything which might harm our testimonies as followers of Jesus to the unsaved world* (1 Cor. 10:32).
- As Christians, we must always remember when exercising any Christian liberty that *we are not to hinder our own spiritual growth or communion with the Lord by wounding our consciences; thus, in all that we do, it must be done in faith to the glory of God* (Rom. 14:23; 1 Cor. 10:31).

Summarily, then, all of this teaches us that when it comes to Christian liberty, we must think carefully about what we might do in our lives. On the one hand, we must avoid *an unchecked laxity*, or an antinomian disposition which can lead to an undisciplined life. This violates Paul's words in Galatians 5:13, when he said, "Only do not use liberty as an opportunity for the flesh." On the other hand, we must avoid *a rigid legalism*, which can tend unlawfully to bind our consciences (and at times the consciences of others) with rules, and regulations which are not found in Scripture (cf. Mark 7:1-23), forgetting that there is only one Lord of the conscience, namely, God Himself (Rom. 14:4).

In bringing these thoughts back to Romans chapters 14 and 15, there were essentially two major matters of differences which Paul highlights that were causing divisions in the church between the Jewish and the Gentile believers. These matters were concerning the matters of Old Covenant, ceremonial diets and days.

Simply stated, some in the church had scruples or reservations about eating certain kinds of foods and so they did not partake of them (commentators generally believe that these individuals were Jewish Christians who are identified in the chapters as "the weak").[15]

---

15 Moo, NICNT, p. 829.

Furthermore, they also had personal convictions about keeping certain Old Covenant feast days and so they practiced them.

Then there were others in the church at Rome (generally thought to be by the commentators Gentile believers who are identified in the chapters as "the strong")[16] who, in contrast to the weak, had no issues of conscience at all about eating certain kinds of foods. They also did not keep Old Covenant special days as a matter of conviction because they believed that these matters were not required by God under the New Covenant.

With such diverse opinions on these matters, it is easy to see why such things were becoming a recipe for catastrophe in the church. And so again, what were they to do—divide, and start two separate congregations, *one* Jewish, *one* Gentile? Paul says no! Rather, by the grace of God, they were to live in gospel harmony among themselves. They were to be one in God's Son, graciously tolerating one another despite their differences of opinions and living as a united, diverse, redeemed people. This is how they would reflect Jesus' design for the church in the world. This is how they would display God's salvation blueprint for His people on the earth, who, in heaven are from "every tribe and tongue and people and nation" (Rev. 5:9). Throughout this passage, Paul argues that:

Christ died to save us and accept us, and we should accept one another (14:1-3). Christ then rose to be our Lord, and we are accountable to him (14:6-9). Christ is coming to be our judge (14:10-12). Paul might conclude: Christ has died! Christ is risen! Christ will come again! Accept one another! After all, "the kingdom of God is not a matter of eating and drinking, but of righteousness, peace, and joy in the Holy Spirit (14:17).[17]

Lloyd Jones states this matter succinctly:

> The Apostle is dealing here with our attitude, as Christian believers and as members of the church, to things that are not definitely prohibited in the New Testament. That is why we call them things 'indifferent'. If a thing is prohibited, then there is no need to discuss it, there is no argument. If it is prohibited, it is prohibited; if it is commanded, it is commanded. But there are matters in connection with the Christian life concerning which we do not have a clear commandment, and about which there is no definite prohibition. And, as we have seen, though they are indifferent, they often lead to considerable trouble, as was clearly the case in the church at Rome and also in the church at Corinth.[18] So that is why the Apostle had to deal with these matters, and that is why we also must not ignore them. Though they are not essential to salvation, it is important that we should be right and clear in our thinking with respect to them.[19]

---

16 It is worth noting however that Paul identifies himself as one who was "strong" (15:1). This, of course, is because he understood the liberty that he had in Christ.

17 *The Baker Illustrated Bible Handbook*, p. 768.

18 For a helpful discussion concerning the similarities and dissimilarities between what was happening at the church in Rome versus the church in Corinth, I point the reader to Frank Thielman, ZEC, pp. 627-30; Schreiner, pp. 704-10, and John Murray, 2:172, 174.

19 Lloyd-Jones, *Romans* pp. 19, 20.

Exegetical & Practical Insights:

Obs. 1- (v. 1) That as Paul begins to show how Christians are to behave toward fellow Christians with whom they might disagree concerning non-gospel issues in the Christian life, he begins by addressing "the strong" Gentile believers and writes by way of an ongoing command and says:

Receive[20] *not* reject, or browbeat others until they agree with your particular, secondary perspectives, and keep them at a distance till they do, no. But rather he says, continually and actively embrace from your heart and take to yourself in true friendship and fellowship as "equal in the eyes of the Lord"[21] the; **one** i.e., a Jewish believer; **who is weak in the faith,** not weak in his walk with Christ or trust concerning the gospel (that salvation was by grace alone, through faith alone, in the finished work of Christ alone),[22] but one whose faith was weak to participate in some activates which he was completely free to do biblically speaking; however for whatever reason, his conscience would not allow him to;[23] *but* not that is, do this, but not with other motives so that you then spend the rest of your days given; **to disputes** or criticisms and quarreling; **over doubtful things,** or things which cannot be firmly established by the Word of God as to their rightness or wrongness.

It is noteworthy that as Paul begins this new section in Romans, he does so by commanding these Christians at Rome (and all other Christians after them) to welcome and receive one another warmly. This imperative sets the general tone for everything else that he will say in the following words. Interestingly, Paul not only begins this new section in this way, but he also essentially ends it like this when he says as a bookend to this thought in 15:7: "Therefore *receive one another* just as Christ also *received us* to the glory of God" [emphasis mine].

Concerning the command to welcome one another Garland says:

> The command to accept (welcome) one another is the foundation of Paul's understanding of what God's grand vision for the world intends. It should not be restricted to an attempt to remedy a localized problem in Rome. God's intention is to eradicate the human divisions of Jews and Gentiles, Greeks and barbarians, wise and foolish, the strong and weak, so that all might praise him with one voice. Since Christ's death lays out the welcome mat for all the ungodly, Paul notably shifts the ground for welcoming one another from God who welcomed them (14:3) to Christ who welcomed them. Welcoming persons from different cultures and ethnicities into the church's fellowship, which is most evident when they

---

20 Grk. present, middle, verb.

21 Osborne, p. 429.

22 I realize that the definite article is in the Greek text so that the words read "the faith." However, the following words in this context make it abundantly plain that this is not speaking about one who was weak in his faith concerning how one gets saved through the gospel or about his assurance before God.

23 Or as Garland says, "They are simply not far enough along in their faith to believe that they can safely risk breaking what they regard as taboos without breaking their relationship with God." Garland, p. 425.

celebrate common meals together, testifies to God's righteous impartiality into their justification by faith through Christ's death. The unified church becomes a visible microcosm of God's redemptive intention to unite all humankind in Christ to the glory of God. The ethical injunctions in 12:1–15:7 are about shaping the church's identity for its witness to the world. Only a church bathed in peace can authentically proclaim the message of God's peace to the world that does not know 'the way of peace' (3:7). Welcoming one another also applies to Paul's intent to take the gospel to Spain to win more converts who will need to be welcomed in Christ.[24]

Obs. 2- (v. 2) That as Paul speaks about the first specific instance of difference among the Roman Christians in connection to Christian liberty, he writes:

For one (the Gentile Christian); **believes** or is convinced that; **he may eat all things, but he** (the Jewish Christian); **who is weak eats** *only* vegetables.

Why did the Gentile Christians feel such liberty of conscience to eat whatever was placed before them without any self-condemnation? The answer is simple: they had not been raised in a context where certain Old Testament foods were deemed unclean.[25] They were never required to keep the food restrictions which were placed on the nation of Israel while under the Old Covenant. And so they ate whatever was before them to the glory of God, whether, for example, it was a piece of chicken or a pork chop.

Of course, biblically speaking this was completely fine for them to do since the temporary food laws which were placed on the old covenant people in order to distinguish them from the surrounding pagans (who for example often ate pork and sacrificed pigs to their deities) had been lifted. This is the plain teaching of the New Testament as taught by both Jesus and Paul (Mark 7:14-23; Acts 10:15; Rom. 14:14a; 1 Tim. 4:4).

But what about these Jewish believers? Why did they eat only vegetables or, quite literally, that which came out of the ground?[26] The answer seems to be, as several scholars note,[27] that they did this (not in order to be saved), but in order to avoid eating meats which were consecrated to pagan deities in Rome or because they wanted to keep some of the Old Covenant, Jewish dietary laws because they thought that this would help them in their growth in grace.

As Yarbrough affirms:

In the Roman world some food purchased in the marketplace may have come from a pagan temple, where it had been sacrificed or offered to false deities. Strong believers understood that they could "eat anything" because idols are human figments (1 Cor. 8:4), having no real existence. Weak believers did "not all possess this knowledge. But some, through

---

24 Garland, pp. 444, 445.

25 See, for example, Lev. 11:7, 20:25.

26 *Word Meanings in the New Testament,* Ralph Earle, p. 208. Also Morris, p. 478.

27 See, for example, Vaughan and Corley, p. 121.

former association with idols," if they ate "food... offered to an idol," would end up with a damaged conscience (1 Cor. 8:7). To be safe they would stay away from meat (possibly sacrificed in a temple) and eat "only vegetables."[28]

All of this background information helps us to see that what was stirring in the pot at the church in Rome concerning food preferences was becoming a recipe for disaster. Could you imagine what their fellowship meals looked like? Perhaps some were bringing ham wrapped with bacon to eat, while others were bringing trays full of carrots and broccoli! It is easy to see, then, why there was trouble happening. These believers were beginning to think ill of others because their ideas about what they should or should not eat did not fit with their personal preferences, so Paul addresses it.

Obs. 3- (v. 3) That as the apostle speaks to this matter, he gives two more commands:

Let not him who eats (the Gentile Christian); **despise**[29] or ever disdain and treat with contempt "mock and ridicule ... or poke fun at"[30] or have "an attitude of religious superiority" over;[31] **him who does not eat** (the Jewish Christian); **and let not him who does not eat** (the Jewish Christian); **judge**[32] or ever find fault with and "condemn and censure 'the strong' for participating in activities that 'the weak' deem to be improper;"[33] **him who eats** (the Gentile Christian); **for** the conjunction putting forth the reason for this; **God has received him** or completely welcomed him to Himself [34] once for all time through Christ.

Paul's words here are plain and sadly highlight inner dispositions that all of us tend to have regarding those who do things that we find odd or different. In cases like these, we are often quick to despise others or judge them for their practices. However, the apostle says this is not right. In fact, he forbids such temperaments in us, especially since they are very much not like God. As Olyott says, "Am I more than God? If he has received the person with whom I disagree, who am I to do differently?"[35]

Obs. 4- (v. 4) That as Paul thinks about how wrong it is for a Christian to be critical toward another Christian regarding secondary matters in

---

28 Yarborough, p. 185.

29 Grk. present, active verb. The same Greek word is translated as "contempt" is verse 10b of this chapter.

30 Schreiner, p. 717.

31 Thielman, p. 631.

32 Paul repeats this admonition throughout this chapter in verses 4, 10, and 13. See also Col. 2:16, 17.

33 Schreiner, p. 717.

34 The "him" here seems to be *the strong Gentile believer who the weak Jewish believer might not receive.* Commentators debate this issue, but since Paul already spoke to the strong Gentile believer in this regard concerning the weak Jewish believer in verse 1, this seems most likely to be the case here.

35 Olyott, p. 135.

the Christian life (addressing specifically "the weak," Gentile believers here concerning their Jewish brethren), he asks emphatically:

Who are you to judge[36] or continually condemn; **another's servant,** in other words, he says you are not his Lord or master so cut it out. **To his own master** (and not another) i.e., to Christ; **he stands,** i.e., stands approved in what he does; **or falls,** that is, falls disapproved in what he does. **Indeed, he** (the one whom we might judge negatively) **will be made to stand**[37] that is, stand acceptable before God both now and in the final day for the choices he made before Him with a good conscience regardless of what others think; **for** the conjunction putting forth the reason this is so; **God is able** or has all the supplies of strength and power; **to make him stand.**

What is Paul's point in these words? It is this: in matters of Christian liberty we are answerable to one—God alone. It is not our loving brethren in the church, nor our critical brethren in the church—instead, it is Jesus.

Olyott wisely remarks:

> The one with scruples [or reservations about some matters] must be careful not to judge the person who does not share those scruples. He must remember that God has received the person he is tempted to criticize. God counts him as His servant, and that person is answerable to Him alone, and to nobody else. Who are you to behave as if somebody else's servant was answerable to you? As for questioning his ability to stand, be certain that he *will*, for God is able to make him stand. Stop acting as if you were his master, and be careful that your attitude is not less receiving than God's.[38]

Wilson also wisely remarks:

> This [verse] makes it clear that even the 'strong' do not stand in their own strength. The power to stand is imparted to every believer by Christ himself, apart from whom all would inevitably and irrevocably fall. It is the Lord Christ who grants preserving strength, and who also maintains the present standing of his servants despite the unjust censures of those who are completely unqualified to judge them.[39]

Obs. 5- (vv. 5-6) That as Paul now turns from the subject of Old Covenant ceremonial diets to Old Covenant ceremonial days, he raises the second specific instance of difference among the Roman Christians in connection to Christian liberty and says:

One person (the Jewish Christian); **esteems** or considers; *one* day above another; another (the Gentile Christian); **esteems every day** *alike.*[40]

---

36 Grk. present, active, participle.

37 Grk. future, passive, verb.

38 Olyott, p. 134.

39 Wilson, p. 220.

40 Unlike some Study Bibles which tell its readers that "the day" in view in this passage is the Sabbath, *The Reformation Study Bible,* p. 2005, is correct when it says, "A pattern of holy days characterized the Jewish year, and it is these days that Paul refers, and not the weekly Sabbath. If the Sabbath were in view it would have been more natural to say, "One man

Let each (the Jewish and the Gentile Christian); **be fully convinced** or thoroughly persuaded; **in his own mind** or in his understanding of things.[41] He who observes the day (the Jewish Christian); **observes** *it* to the Lord;[42] and he (the Gentile Christian); **who does not observe the day, to the Lord he does not observe** *it*.

Paul then returns to his previous topic and writes:

He who eats (the Gentile Christian); **eats to** (or with a good conscience towards); **the Lord, for he gives God thanks** this is because his conscience is clear about what he eats; **and he** (the Jewish Christian); **who does not eat, to** (or with a good conscience towards); **the Lord he does not eat, and gives God thanks** this is because his conscience is also clear about what he does not eat.

Concerning these latter words in 6b, Thielman helpfully notes:

> Both those who eat everything and those who do not eat everything at the common meal are on the Lord's side. This is obvious because both groups thank God for their food, whatever it is. Paul's reference to giving thanks to God here reflects the Jewish and early Christian custom of saying grace before meals (Mark 8:6; 14:23; John 6:11, 23; Acts 27:35; 1 Cor 11:24; 1 Tim 4:4).

Concerning vv. 5-6a, there has been much scholarly discussion and debate over the years regarding what *day* Paul refers to. Some say it refers to the Old Covenant Sabbath. Others (like myself) say that it is speaking about Old Covenant feast days such as The Feast of Tabernacles or Booths, or Trumpets, Passover or Pentecost, etc. So which is it?

The key in answering the question is the context, for context is always king.[43] In this context, what has Paul been speaking about? He has been speaking about ceremonial foods, which were optional for Jewish and Gentile believers to partake. In verses 5 and 6, he is dealing with the same category of things.[44] He has not changed his thinking. Thus, it is unthinkable that Paul would now assert that believers are free to choose for themselves whether to keep the Sabbath, when the Sabbath is part of the moral law of God — namely the fourth commandment as contained in the Decalogue. For since when has keeping a commandment of God ever been left up to us whether or not we want to keep it?[45] No, a command of God is a command of God, and it is to be obeyed.

---

considers the Sabbath above the other days."

41 It is important to remember that Paul says that our being "fully convinced in our own mind" is with reference to matters of moral indifference in the Christian life but not the foundational truths of the Word of God. In other words, when it comes to the core truths of Christianity (justification by faith alone, in Christ alone, the deity of Jesus, His resurrection and second coming, and the Trinity etc.) we are not at liberty to reject them. If we do, we do it to our own peril.

42 Paul uses this phrase "to the Lord" four times in this verses. In doing this, he seems to be stressing that what one does or does not do with reference to areas of Christian liberty he does or does not do it *to the Lord's glory*.

43 This is a point that I remind my students of repeatedly in *Rhode Island School of the Bible*.

44 Cf. Gal. 4:10; Col. 2:16, 17.

45 Could it possibly be that, for example, whether or not we want to murder (the sixth commandment), or commit adultery (the seventh commandment), steal (the eighth

Now, while it is true that the Old Covenant, Saturday Sabbath has been abolished with the closing of the Old Covenant itself,[46] this does not negate the fact that there is still a New Covenant day for the New Covenant community to worship God.[47] This day has been transferred by Jesus the Lord of the Sabbath[48] from the last day of the week (Saturday) to the first day of the week (Sunday), and historically, this new Sabbath Day has been called the Lord's Day,[49] the Christian Sabbath.[50]

Regarding this matter, John Murray concurs:

> Ceremonial feast days fall into the category of which the apostle could say: "One man esteemeth one day above another: another esteemeth every day alike." Many Jews would not yet have understood all the implications of the gospel and had still a scrupulous regard for these mosaic ordinances. Of such scruples we know Paul to have been thoroughly tolerant and they fit the precise terms of the text in question. There is no need to posit anything that goes beyond such observances. To place the Lord's Day and the weekly Sabbath in the same category is not only beyond the warrant of exegetical requirements but brings us into conflict with principles that are embedded in the total witness of Scripture. An interpretation that involves such contradiction cannot be adopted. Thus the abiding sanctity of each recurring seventh day as the memorial of God's rest in creation and of Christ's exultation in his resurrection is not to be regarded as in any way impaired by Romans 14:5.[51]

The late Dr. Robert P. Martin also agrees when he says:

> Christ freed his New Covenant people from the Old Covenant ceremonial laws, which were types and shadows imposed "until the time of reformation" (Heb. 9:10). He freed us from any obligation to keep the feast days commanded in the ceremonial law. But that has nothing to do with the weekly Sabbath. God established the Sabbath at creation. He based it on the moral foundation of his own example. The Sabbath existed long before he gave the ceremonial law at Sinai. He made the Sabbath part of the old covenant, but he placed it in the moral law, not in the ceremonial law. Paul here (in Romans 14:5-6), does not refer to the Sabbath day established at creation and commanded in the fourth

---

commandment), or bear false witness (the ninth commandment), is optional and up to us? Well, of course not! In the same way, neither is the fourth commandment concerning our remembering the Sabbath.

46 The Saturday Sabbath was a specific sign given to the nation of Israel under the Old Covenant by God (Ex. 31:12-18). That Sabbath under the Old Covenant continued as long as the Old Covenant remained in force. It remained in force until Jesus ratified the New Covenant by the shedding of His blood at the cross (Matt. 26:28). Thus, when our Lord replaced the Old Covenant with the New, He terminated the Saturday Sabbath sign of the Old Covenant.

47 Acts 20:5-12; 1 Cor. 16:2; Heb. 4:9.

48 Mark 2:27, 28.

49 Rev. 1:10.

50 This topic is expounded in all of the major Reformed Confessions of Faith: Savoy, London Baptist Confession of Faith of 1689, and The Westminster, to name a few.

51 Murray, 2:259, Appendix D.

commandment. In fact, the Sabbath is not mentioned at all. Paul merely speaks of "days." Paul then is not saying that keeping or not keeping the Sabbath is a matter of Christian liberty....

In a word, this text has nothing to do with the Lord's Day Sabbath. There is no basis here to argue that God has set aside the weekly Sabbath, or to think that he has freed us to do as we please with the day. This is a "problem text" only if we remove it from its scriptural context.[52]

In summary then, Paul is saying here that even though Old Covenant ceremonial feast days are done away, if a believer decides to keep one for personal reasons, he does not object, and neither should we. However, he says again, that such a one must be "fully convinced in his own mind." This means that he must believe before God that what he is practicing concerning his liberty in Christ is pleasing to Jesus and good for his soul.

Obs. 6- (vv. 7-9) That as Paul just mentioned the word *Lord* four times in the previous verse concerning Jesus, he now puts forth the practical implications of this and writes:

For the conjunction confirming the previous words; **none of us** (Jewish believer or Gentile believer); **lives** or exist; **to himself** or for his own pleasures and preferences as a Christian; **and no one dies to himself,** which is to say, our deaths, as well as our lives, are not for ourselves.[53] For the conjunction explaining why this is; **if we live, we live to the Lord,** i.e., we live with His glory and honor in view;[54] **and if we die, we die to the Lord,** i.e., we die with His glory and honor in view. **Therefore** (Paul summarizes his thought); **whether we live or die, we are** (and will always be); **the Lord's. For to this end** or with this goal in view; **Christ** (Jesus the Messiah); **died and rose and lived again, that** or for the purpose that; **He might be Lord** or master, king and sovereign; **of both the dead and the living,** that is, the master, king and sovereign of His redeemed people both when they die and when they are alive, i.e., throughout the entirety of their lives.

But we ask, "Why is Paul bringing up our lives in relation to Christ's lordship in his discussion on Christian liberty?" The answer is simple: all of our Christian liberty is to be exercised under Jesus' lordship. Since as Christians we have been bought with a price, (even the precious blood of Jesus),[55] we are no longer our own. We belong to Him. Therefore, what He says goes.

But what is the practical point of all of this for Christian liberty? It is that since the entirety of our existence is to be lived under Jesus' governance, when He says to us, for example, that we should act in certain ways toward our differing brethren in the church (i.e., warmly receiving them and not despising or judging them, vv. 1-4), we are to

---

52 Martin, *The Christian Sabbath*, pp. 228, 229.

53 Robinson, Book II. p. 241.

54 Cf. 2 Cor. 5:15.

55 1 Cor. 6:20.

obey Him. By His grace, we must do His will and not our own. We must follow His desire, not our own.

Merida remarks:

> Paul elaborates on what it means to live under Christ's Lordship in verses 7 to 9. He says that it means you do not live for your own self-interest but for the interest of Christ, the one who died and rose that he may be Lord of all. Whether in life or death, Christ owns us. Therefore the Lord expects our conduct to please him. The Roman Christians were trying to dictate to one another how one should treat the other in debatable matters, but Paul calls for liberty and for both groups to live under the Lordship of Jesus and allow the Lord alone to judge.[56]

Garland also helpfully says:

> The Lordship of Christ is the fundamental premise that grounds Paul's comments.... The gravity of condemning other believers is heightened by the reality that they all are the Lord's slaves. Since only the Lord has the right to pass judgment on them, and his judgment alone carries weight, how much more is it true that our judgment of Christ's servants is of no consequence? Worse, such judgments brazenly infringe on our Lord's authority.

Obs. 7- (vv. 10-11) That as Paul now applies all that he has been saying, he writes:

But why do you[57] **judge your brother,**[58] that is, the weaker Christian judging the stronger Christian who eats whatever he wants? **Or why do you show contempt** or scorn; **for your brother,** that is, the stronger Christian despising his weaker brother?[59] **For,** the conjunction explaining why we are not to do these things towards those who differ with us concerning non-gospel, non-sinful issues; **we shall all** (none of us is excluded); **stand before the judgment seat of Christ. For it is written**[60] (or stands written, that is written in Isaiah 45:23), God speaking says by way of a solemn oath:

"As I live, says the LORD,[61] **Every knee** (both the knees of the weak and strong); **shall bow to Me** (and not another), **And every tongue shall confess** or fully acknowledge; **to God."**

In these words (verses 10b-11), Paul gives the reason why believers must not judge one another when it comes to how we exercise our

---

56 Merida, p. 227.

57 The two uses of the word "you" in the Greek text are emphatic.

58 Paul's double use of the words "your brother" in the passage seems to be intentional so as to heighten how wrong it is for us to judge and show contempt for those who belong to the same spiritual family as we do.

59 Cf. Rom. 14:3, where Paul essentially says the same thing, showing us that his repetition was definitely needed so that the Romans and all other Christians after them would not forget this.

60 Grk. perfect, passive, verb.

61 In connecting this Old Testament passage which speaks about the Lord (Jehovah) as judge to Christ, it is clear that in Paul's mind, Jesus is Jehovah God Himself.

liberties in Christ. Why? The answer is simple: there is only one Judge over us, and it is God Himself! It is Jesus (who is God), for all judgment has been committed to His hands by His Father.[62] Consequently, for us to assume the role of judge over the consciences and choices of others in our churches in connection to the matter of Christian liberty is sin. It is to assume a role to which God has not called us. Hence, "since all believers will eventually have to explain to Christ how they lived out their faith (2 Cor. 5:10), human judgments in the present usurp his authority."[63]

But we ask next, if we are not to spend our time focusing on others in the church when it comes to this topic, what are we to do? Again, the answer is simple: we are to focus on ourselves. We are to be sure that what we have decided to do before the Savior in this regard is that which we can do before Him with a good conscience (as informed by His Word) as we prepare to give a good accounting to Him on the final day.[64]

Obs. 8- (vv. 12-13) That as Paul draws a conclusion from his previous words, he writes:

So then each of us (note the personal responsibility being highlighted here); **shall give account of** or with reference to; **himself** (not someone else); **to God** (not man). Therefore (Paul speaks here by way of a command); **let us** (all of us who are believers, both weak and strong, Paul includes himself); **not judge one another,** i.e., judge one another regarding non-essential, non-gospel, non-salvation issues; anymore (the word "anymore" showing that this in fact was happening in the church at Rome); **but**[65] or in sharp contrast to this; **rather resolve this**[66] or determine immediately; **not to put a stumbling block** or an obstacle; **or a cause to fall** or a snare; **in** *our* **brother's way.**

Paul is saying that when we disobey God by either despising others in the church for what they do not do according to our personal opinions or when we judge them for what they do, we put barriers between them and us that often cause them to stumble or fall into sin in their walk with the Savior. We hurt them with our critical attitudes and conduct. Therefore, instead of being a help to them on their way to heaven, we actually become a hindrance. This is a terrible thing—something which needs to be repented of immediately and forsaken altogether if we have done it.

---

62 Cf. John 5:22, 27.

63 Thielman, p. 634.

64 Concerning the final day of judgment and all of us who are believers standing before the judgment seat of Christ, of course, we must realize that since Jesus paid our sin debt in full at the cross, there is therefore now no condemnation for us who are in Christ Jesus (Rom. 8:1, also compare John 5:24). In view of this, we might wonder what will this final Day of Judgment be about for us. My present understanding of this topic is that it will be a judgment of *rewards* according to our works. It will be a time when all of our works will be on display before God and He, in grace, will graciously recompense each believer to a greater or lesser degree. Consequently, Paul could say in 2 Cor. 3:14, 15, "If anyone's work which he has built on it endures, he will receive a reward. If anyone's work is burned, he will suffer loss; but he himself will be saved, yet so as through fire."

65 The strong Greek adversative.

66 Grk. aorist, active, verb.

Suggested applications from the text for the church:

1- Our passage teaches us that we must always warmly receive each person who names the name of Christ into our hearts and homes despite matters of secondary personal convictions in which we might differ. Do we?

2- Our passage teaches us that it is not our God-given duty to enter into controversy with brethren who differ with us on matters which are not fundamental to the faith.

3- Our passage teaches us that we must be extremely careful to keep the main things the main things in the church and never allow ourselves to pass harsh judgments on others who may differ with us in gray areas.

Suggested application from the text for the non-Christian:

1- Our passage teaches you that just like everyone else in the world, you too will one day stand before the judgment seat of Christ to give an account of the deeds done in the body, whether good or evil.[67] I ask, therefore, are you ready for that day? Are you prepared to meet Jesus the great Judge of the World, because you have been forgiven by Him?

Text: Romans 14:14-23

General theme: Christian Liberty with Grace-filled Sensitivity (the Weak and the Strong Must Get Along: Christian Consideration) (II)

Homiletical outline of the verses:

A. Paul's convictions: [14] I know and am convinced by the Lord Jesus that *there is* nothing unclean of itself; but to him who considers anything to be unclean, to him *it is* unclean.

B. Paul's concerns: [15] Yet if your brother is grieved because of *your* food, you are no longer walking in love. Do not destroy with your food the one for whom Christ died. [16] Therefore do not let your good be spoken of as evil; [17] for the kingdom of God is not eating and drinking, but righteousness and peace and joy in the Holy Spirit. [18] For he who serves Christ in these things *is* acceptable to God and approved by men.

C. Paul's call: [19] Therefore let us pursue the things *which make* for peace and the things by which one may edify another. [20] Do not destroy the work of God for the sake of food. All things indeed *are* pure, but *it is* evil for the man who eats with offense.

D. Paul's conclusion: [21] *It is* good neither to eat meat nor drink wine nor *do anything* by which your brother stumbles or is offended or is made weak. [22] Do you have faith? Have *it* to yourself before God. Happy *is* he who does not condemn himself in what he approves. [23] But he who doubts is condemned if he eats, because *he does* not *eat* from faith; for whatever *is* not from faith is sin.

---

67 Cf. 2 Cor. 5:10.

Summary of section: In these verses, Paul highlights a crucial point concerning the whole matter of Christian liberty which could be summed up in the words of Martin Luther when he said, "A Christian man is a most free lord of all, subject to none. [And] a Christian man is a most dutiful servant of all, subject to all."[68] Luther's point is that when it comes to our consciences in connection to Christian liberty, Jesus Christ is the *only* Lord and judge over them so that no one else can justly bind them (as Paul taught in the previous words). However, we must also note that when it comes to Christian liberty, we are to be mindful of the consciences and choices of our brethren so that in view of them we are willing at any point to place voluntary limits on ourselves when we are with them. Our freedom in Christ should never become an occasion for their stumbling. This is a vital perspective for us to have. Summarily, then, we could say: if there is any liberty in our lives which might cause a brother or sister to be tripped up in their walk with Jesus, we are immediately to deny ourselves that liberty out of love for him or her and the peace of the church, remembering that, according to Scripture, love for others and the peace of the church is much more important than any liberty that we might otherwise legitimately enjoy.[69]

Or, as Geoffrey Wilson succinctly notes, "In practice Christian liberty is limited by the higher claims of Christian love, for love teaches us that this freedom must never be exercised to the spiritual detriment of another."[70]

Concerning the second half of this chapter, Kruse aptly notes:

> In this section Paul makes quite specific his exhortation to his Roman audience regarding food taboos. On the one hand he says that they should stop passing judgment upon others, and on the other that they should avoid putting any stumbling blocks before others. He himself adheres to the fundamental position held by the 'strong', that 'no food is unclean in itself', and urges them not to allow what they consider good to be spoken of as evil, but implying, nevertheless, that if their eating distresses others,

---

68 Martin Luther, *On the Freedom of a Christian Man.*

69 R. Kent Hughes makes another helpful statement concerning this matter. He writes, "Exercising Christian liberty is very much like walking a tightrope. As you walk the rope with a balancing pole in hand, at one end of the pole is *love for others* and at the other is *Christian liberty.* When these things are in balance, your walk is as it should be.... We are immensely free in Christ. Our only bondage is the bond of love to our fellow believers. It is our Christian duty, when exercising our freedom, not only to think about how our actions affect us but others. We must always remember that it is not our display of Christian freedom that commends our faith to the world, but our demonstration of agape love. Jesus said, 'All men will know that you are my disciples if you love one another' (John 13:35). The strong, mature Christian voluntarily limits his freedom out of love for his weaker brothers and sisters." Hughes, p. 269.

MacArthur is also helpful when he says, "Our Christian liberty is vertical, before the Lord. But the exercise of that liberty is horizontal, because it is seen by and affects others. To rightly understand and use our freedom in Christ brings great satisfaction. But that satisfaction is multiplied when we willingly surrender the exercise of a liberty for the sake of other believers. More importantly, it greatly pleases our Lord and promotes harmony in His church." MacArthur, p. 288.

70 Wilson, p. 225.

they should abstain, 'For the kingdom of God is not a matter of eating and drinking, but of righteousness, peace and joy in the Holy Spirit.'[71]

Exegetical & Practical Insights:

Obs. 1- (v. 14) That as Paul returns to the specific subject of Old Covenant, ceremonial food laws (vv. 2, 3, 6), he writes, saying:

I know not merely 'I am of the opinion,' but 'I am completely certain:'[72] **and am convinced**[73] or stand fully persuaded;[74] **by the Lord Jesus,** the prepositional phrase establishing "the authoritative basis for Paul's conviction"[75] (a conviction which he might have received through direct revelation or in a vision as Peter received it in Acts chapter 10); **that** the conjunction putting forth the essence of Paul's persuasion; *there is* nothing unclean itself or ceremonially or morally defiled, unholy or profane on its own; **but to him who considers** or reckons or counts; **anything to be unclean, to him** (personally); *it is* **unclean.**

Paul's words here are emphatic as he speaks concerning Old Testament ritual foods, which were for a time off-limits to the people of God under that economy.[76] These restrictions have now passed under the New Covenant. Therefore, for example, Paul could say, "For every creature of God *is* good, and nothing is to be refused if it is received with thanksgiving; for it is sanctified by the word of God and prayer" (1 Tim. 4:4, 5).[77]

However, having said this, Paul says that for the individual who considers anything to be unclean (for whatever particular reason that might be), to him it is unclean. And so, even though all foods are clean in and of themselves, if for the sake of conscience someone is still not convinced of this, to him it is unclean if he eats. To do this then is to act contrary to one's conscience. Thus, he would defile himself and plague his conscience with guilt. This is something we must never do. As MacArthur says, "If a believer is convinced a certain behavior is sin—even if his assessment is wrong—he should never do it."[78]

Obs. 2- (vv. 15-18) That as Paul gets to the matter at hand he writes:

Yet or but; **if your brother is grieved** or vexed and offended; **because** or through the agency; **of** *your* food, or your "unrestricted diet;"[79] **you are no longer walking** or conducting and carrying yourself toward others; **in** or according to; **love.**[80] Do not destroy or seriously harm and ruin the conscience of your brother (Paul speaks by way of a command); **with**

---

71 Kruse, pp. 519, 520.

72 Lloyd-Jones, p. 151.

73 Grk. perfect, passive, verb.

74 Cf. Rom. 8:38, 15:14 where Paul uses the same Greek verb.

75 Harvey, p. 339.

76 See verse 2 for further explanation of this matter.

77 See also verse 20 in this chapter where Paul essentially says the same thing.

78 MacArthur Study Bible, p. 1720.

79 Phillips translation.

80 Cf. Rom. 12:10; 13:8-10.

your food the one for whom Christ died or voluntarily gave His life on behalf of.[81] **Therefore** (Paul speaks by way of another command); **do not let your good,** that is, the good and lawful things that believers can legitimately do when it comes to the area of Christian liberty; **be spoken of as evil** or slanderously by others (typically weaker believers) because they (the stronger believers) flaunt their freedom before them and cause them to stumble in their lives; **for,** the conjunction putting forth the grand reason why the stronger brethren are not to do this concerning their weaker brethren; **the kingdom of God** (or its present manifestation as seen in the local church); **is not** (and will never be); **eating and drinking** or merely focused on natural, common matters; **but**[82] or in sharp contrast to this; **righteousness** or upright, godly living, **and peace,** that is, harmony with God and others; **and joy**[83] or happiness; **in** or which is produced by; **the Holy Spirit. For** "Paul continues with a further explanation of verse 17;"[84] **he who serves**[85] **Christ in these things,** i.e., continually commits himself to obey Jesus concerning the things Paul just mentioned regarding righteousness and peace and joy in the Holy Spirit being lived out by us in the church; *is* **acceptable** or well-pleasing; **to God and approved** or greatly esteemed; **by men** (for who would not highly value such a person in their midst?).[86]

Obs. 3- (vv. 19-20) That as Paul puts forth some apostolic exhortations in view of all that he has just written, he says:

Therefore a word of summary in light of verses 17, 18; **let us** (he includes himself); **pursue**[87] "not merely wish for it and talk about it"[88] but habitually track down and make every effort to go after; **the things** *which make* for or lead to; **peace** not distractions and divisions among ourselves because of our secondary, side note, inconsequential matters, but rather the things which lead to gospel harmony and accord; **and the things by which one may edify**[89] or build up; **another. Do not destroy** "Satan's aim and work"[90] or ever tear down and slow the progress of (the

---

81 This language highlights the definiteness and greatness of Christ's atonement for His people.

82 The strong Greek adversative.

83 Paul will mention the traits of joy and peace once again in Rom. 15:13.

84 Harvey, p. 341.

85 Grk. present, active, participle.

86 I believe that Hendriksen is correct when in commenting on this last phrase says, "Those who say, 'I don't care at all what people think of me,' may be guilty of an other-worldliness that is not exactly pious." Hendriksen, p. 465.

87 Grk. present, active, verb. Paul uses the same Greek verb in a similar fashion in Rom. 12:13.

88 Robinson, Book II. p. 255.

89 Thielman makes a helpful comment when he writes, "Edification was an important metaphor for Paul. He could summarize his own apostolic vocation as building the community of believers on the foundation of Christ and the gospel (Rom 15:20; 1 Cor 3:9-10; cf. Eph. 2:19-3:13), and he admonished other believers to participate in this work of building up one another and the church generally (1 Cor 3:10 -17; 8:1; 14:3-5, 12, 17, 26; Eph 4:12, 16, 29; 1 Thess 5:11)." Thielman, p. 647.

90 Robinson, Book II. p. 257

opposite of "edifying" or "building up" as mentioned in the previous verse); **the work of God** or the supernatural, saving and sanctifying work of God which He is doing in our churches; **for the sake of** or on account of; **food** (or anything else for that matter) for "surely we shouldn't wish to undo God's work for the sake of a plate of meat!"[91] **All things indeed** *are* **pure,** i.e., all foods are morally, lawfully and ceremonially acceptable in God's sight (cf. v. 14); **but** *it is* **evil** or morally wrong; **for the man** (specifically the strong believer in view); **who eats with offense** which is to say, it is wrong for any of us to eat any specific food (or to do anything else) if in so doing we offend a brother or sister in Christ, and cause them to stumble in their walk with the Savior.

Obs. 4- (vv. 21-23) That as Paul now sums up and concludes all that he has been saying, he writes:

It is **good** or we might say, "right;" **neither to eat meat nor drink wine** (he now adds this additional matter of wine); **nor** *do anything* **by which your brother stumbles or is offended or is made weak,**[92] i.e., made weaker in his faith then he was before.[93] **Do you**[94] **have faith?** That is to say, do you have the conviction and clear conscience that you can eat any food or drink wine? **Have** *it* **to yourself before God** in other words, do not publicly display those liberties, when, for example, you are in the home of or out with a weaker brother. Instead, keep your liberties privately between yourself and God and others who enjoy them. Happy or more literally blessed; *is* he who does not condemn himself in what he approves which is to say, the things that he judges before God based on His Word to be okay to partake of as a believer. **But he who doubts,** that is, doubts what he does is okay in this area of Christian liberty; i.e., he thinks it is wrong; **is condemned if he eats,** *not condemned with eternal condemnation* (Rom. 8:1!), but with a *self-condemnation* in his own conscience; **because** the conjunction providing the causal reason for the previous words; *he does* **not** *eat* **from faith** or with the full persuasion in his own mind that he is right in eating; **for,** the conjunction explaining why this is so; **whatever** *is* **not from faith** or we might say, with a solid conviction that what we are doing is right in God's eyes; **is sin,** which is to say, it is sin to the one who sins against his conscience in what they do. Hence, Spurgeon's counsel is wise when he said something along these lines, "If you are not sure a thing is right, leave it alone, for it will be sin to you."[95]

Hughes nicely summarizes these words:

Paul is saying, what you believe about neutral things is between you and God. Keep it that way. Moreover, you are a happy (blessed) person if in

---

91 Phillips translation.

92 Cf. Matt. 17:27; 1 Cor. 8:13

93 Online commentary: www.biblestudytools.com/gills-exposition-of-the-bible/romans-5-11.html.

94 The word "you" is emphatic in the Greek text.

95 Or we might say, "When in doubt, leave it out!"

exercising your liberty you do not condemn yourself by harming another. You are blessed if your exercise of freedom is free from doubt. You are blessed if no one is being scandalized and led toward sin by you. You are blessed because you feel God's pleasure.

Charles Spurgeon, at the height of his fame, was one day walking down the street and saw a sign which read, "We sell the cigar that Charles Spurgeon smokes," whereupon Spurgeon gave up the habit. He came to see that what was for him a freedom might cause others to stumble. "Blessed is the man who does not condemn himself by what he approves."[96]

Suggested applications from the text for the church:

1- When it comes to Christian liberty, we must never engage in anything with a doubting conscience.

2- When it comes to Christian liberty, we must do nothing which will cause another believer to stumble even if that means restraining our own liberties while we are with them.

3- When it comes to Christian liberty, we must keep our personal practices between us and God and those who share them with us.

Suggested application from the text for the non-Christian:

1- When it comes to Christian liberty, you must understand that just like you, Christians are free to enjoy many things in life. However, before their conversion they, by God's doing, came to the realization that they had done many sinful things in their life that caused a radical breach in their relationship with God. This is why they turned to Him through Christ in repentance and faith in order to be saved. Will you do the same thing now?

---

96 Hughes, pp. 272, 273.

ROMANS
CHAPTER FIFTEEN

Text: Romans 15:1-13

General theme: Christian Liberty with Grace-filled Sensitivity (the Weak and the Strong Must Get Along: Christian Imitation and Integration) (III and IV)

Homiletical outline of the verses:

A. Paul's exhortations: [1] We then who are strong ought to bear with the scruples of the weak, and not to please ourselves. [2] Let each of us please *his* neighbor for *his* good, leading to edification.

B. Paul's example: [3] For even Christ did not please Himself; but as it is written, "The reproaches of those who reproached You fell on Me."

C. Paul's encouragement: [4] For whatever things were written before were written for our learning, that we through the patience and comfort of the Scriptures might have hope.

D. Paul's entreaty: [5] Now may the God of patience and comfort grant you to be like-minded toward one another, according to Christ Jesus, [6] that you may with one mind *and* one mouth glorify the God and Father of our Lord Jesus Christ.

E. Paul's ending: [7] Therefore receive one another, just as Christ also received us, to the glory of God. [8] Now I say that Jesus Christ has become a servant to the circumcision for the truth of God, to confirm the promises *made* to the fathers, [9] and that the Gentiles might glorify God for *His* mercy, as it is written:

"For this reason I will confess to You among the Gentiles,
And sing to Your name."

[10] And again he says:

"Rejoice, O Gentiles, with His people!"

[11] And again:

"Praise the Lord, all you Gentiles!
Laud Him, all you peoples!"

[12] And again, Isaiah says:

"There shall be a root of Jesse;

And He who shall rise to reign over the Gentiles,
In Him the Gentiles shall hope."
[13] Now may the God of hope fill you with all joy and peace in believing,
that you may abound in hope by the power of the Holy Spirit.

Summary of section: In these verses, up to verse 13, Paul continues his
discussion of Christian liberty with grace-filled sensitivity. Tensions
were running high between Jewish and Gentile believers in the church.
Therefore, he continues to speak to them about this crucial subject. In
order to help the situation, the apostle carries his discussion further by
putting forth first, *the example of the Savior* (vv. 3, 5, 7, 8), and, second, *the
explicit teaching of Scripture* (vv. 9-12). These two topics show that believers
are not to selfishly assert their rights over others. Rather, they should be
a united, integrated, and diverse community that worships God together
to the praise of the glory of His grace.[1] This is God's grand design for
His people, for He is not only the God of the Jews but also the God of
the Gentiles (Rom. 3:29).

Merida notes:

> In this section Paul first summarizes how the strong should treat the weak
> (15:1-6). He then roots his teaching in the broader storyline of Scripture,
> showing the global purposes of God in the Messiah (vv. 7-12). The Lord
> Jesus's example of serving others (and not himself) is stressed, and the
> Savior's work of redeeming and welcoming of people from all nations
> is celebrated. Paul has already emphasized the Lordship of Christ in
> his instruction on liberty and love in Romans 14, and here again we are
> drawn to Christ's life, ministry, and saving purposes as motivation for
> Christian unity.[2]

Exegetical & Practical Insights:
Obs. 1- (vv. 1-2) That as Paul continues to teach his topic, he writes:
We then (he includes himself in this group); **who are strong**[3]
(primarily Gentile believers); **ought**[4] or have a biblical obligation before
God and others; **to bear,**[5] not divide over, but to forbear patiently and
graciously; **with the scruples** or weakness; **of the weak** (primarily Jewish
believers); **and not to please ourselves** or "act according to our own
views and inclinations."[6] **Let each of us** (Paul speaks here by way of
a command primarily to the strong believer); **please** or accommodate;
***his* neighbor** or the one who is near to him in the church who holds a

---

1 It is interesting to note that Paul once again calls the church to unity in 16:16a with
the command to "greet one another with a holy kiss." Unless they were going to do this in
pretense, which does not seem to be the case, this command would have been a powerful
means to press them to reconcile with one another if divisions existed.

2 Merida, p. 231.

3 For a further discussion about these two groups of believers, see my introductory
comments in Romans 14.

4 Grk. present, active, verb.

5 Grk. present, active, verb.

6 Robinson, Book II. p. 263.

different perspective than he does in the area of Christian liberty, "Paul's choice of the word *neighbor* rather than 'brother', which he has used in 14:10, 13, 15, 21, recalls his comment that loving one's neighbor 'is the fulfilling of the law' (13:9-10)";[7] **for *his*** good, or "spiritual advantage;"[8] **leading to edification** or with the specific aim of building him up in his walk with Christ (cf. Rom. 14:19).

We might wonder why Paul specifically calls the strong believer to do something regarding the weak, and not vice versa. *The Holman Study Bible* answers the question succinctly when it says, "The strong believer does not forsake his conscience by abstaining from certain of his freedoms, but the weaker believer would have to violate his conscience in order to accommodate the liberties of the strong."[9]

Morris also helpfully notes:

The negative side of carrying the weak is that we are *not to please ourselves*. This does not mean that we never do anything that we want to do, but that we are never to do what pleases us regardless of its effects on others. Consideration for weaker Christians takes precedent over what we ourselves would like to do. Elsewhere Paul can cite his own example; he practices what he preaches (1 Cor. 10:33; cf. Rom. 8:8; Phil. 2:4). Selfishness is always a barrier to effective Christian work, and of course it breaks up Christian unity, which is such an important consideration throughout this discussion.[10]

Obs. 2- (v. 3) That as Paul now motivates the Roman believers to follow the greatest example of One who pleased God and denied Himself for the sake of others, even Jesus, he writes:

For, the conjunction highlighting the causal reason for the previous words; **even Christ**[11] (or God's anointed and appointed Messiah) the word "even" implying that had anyone ever been entitled to please himself, it would have been Jesus;[12] **did not please Himself**[13] or put His personal desires first, so as to please Himself;[14] **but**[15] or in sharp contrast to this; **as it is written**[16] or stands written in Psalm 69:9 (a messianic Psalm); **"The reproaches** or insults; **of those who reproached You** (God the Father); **fell on Me** (Christ the Son)."

---

7 Garland, p. 440.

8 Hendriksen, p. 470.

9 *The Holman Study Bible* 2014, p. 1918.

10 Morris, p. 497.

11 Jesus' example also shows up in verses 5, 7, and 8 of this section of Scripture.

12 Thielman, p. 656.

13 This, of course, does not deny the fact that Jesus came willingly and joyfully to redeem His people who were given to Him by His Father from before the foundation of the world in the covenant of redemption (John 6:39). He did this and it was His great pleasure (Heb. 10:7). However, the point is, in the whole act, He suffered great misery for the sake of others.

14 Recall his famous words in Luke 22:42, "not My will, but Yours be done."

15 The strong Greek adversative.

16 Grk. perfect, passive, verb.

It should be noted first that we have in these words a wonderful gospel verse that speaks of our Lord's substitutionary death for sinners who constantly reproached God through their lives of sin against Him. At the cross, Jesus willingly stood in the place of such ones with their sins (reproaches against God) upon His sinless self and was punished on their behalf so that they could go free. All such guilty individuals deserve God's just wrath to fall on them. Nevertheless, in love Jesus bore the wrath they deserved in order to redeem all who put their faith in Him as their Savior (cf. Isa. 53; Matt. 26:28; Mark 10:45; John 19:30).

But second, and more specific to this context, it should be noted again that Paul here is underscoring all that he just said in the previous verse against pleasing ourselves. In verse 3, he now puts forth the great example of Jesus for our imitation. Simply stated, since our wonderful Lord willingly denied Himself to do the will of God on behalf of others (see for example, Phil. 2:1-11), we also are to do the same as we do God's will in the church. We must give up our liberties and bear with our weaker brethren. Therefore, Jesus' example of self-denial is the pattern that we follow so that we put the needs of others before ourselves.

Obs. 3- (v. 4) That Paul, having just quoted the Bible in verse 3 concerning Christ,[17] now parenthetically has something very encouraging to say about it, when he writes:

For whatever things were written (i.e., written in its precepts, promises or prophecies); **before,** that is, before in the Old Testament (just as in the Psalm he quoted); **were written for our learning** or instruction; **that** or for the purpose that; **we through** or by means of; **the patience and comfort of the Scriptures** or we might say the patience and comfort which the Scriptures give; **might have hope,**[18] that is, continual consolation in the central person of whom the Scriptures speak, namely, Christ[19] (and this especially when trying times are upon us, even as was currently the case in the church at Rome).[20]

Obs. 4- (vv. 5-6) That as Paul now puts forth a prayer-wish for the Romans, pleading that the God who inspired the Scriptures might grant such "patience and comfort" to them he says:

Now may the God of, or we might say, the God who gives; **patience and comfort**[21] **grant** or give; **you to be like-minded** or unified; **toward**

---

17 Paul will quote the Scriptures several more times in verses 9 to 12.

18 Hope is a topic which Paul repeatedly brings up throughout this epistle: 5:2, 5:5, 8:20, 24, 25, 12:12; 15:12, 13, 24.

19 Of course, this is not to say that the accounts of other believers in the Bible who overcame significant obstacles do not give us excellent examples as well to follow, for they surely do.

20 Haldane is certainly correct when he says, "Some persons have blasphemously said that the Old Testament is now out of date. But the writers of the New Testament give no such view of the Old. Instead of this, they refer to it as proof, and treat it as of constant use to the people of God." Haldane, p. 610.

21 It is significant to note that amid all that Paul is discussing in this chapter, he identifies God as the God of patience and comfort (v. 5), the God of hope (v. 13), and the God of peace (v. 33). Cf. 2 Cor. 13:11.

one another, according to Christ Jesus or we might say, in line with His example of not putting Himself and His preferences above others (15:3) which when we do, often causes divisions among us; **that** or for the purpose that; **you,** both the weak and the strong; **may with one mind** (not two); *and* one mouth[22] (again, not two); **glorify** or bring honor as a congregation (not to themselves, but to); **the God and Father of our Lord Jesus Christ.**[23]

As I mentioned in my opening comments on Chapter 14, what Paul has written from that point forward really finds its ultimate goal reached in 15:6. The apostle would not have the Romans divide over secondary matters of opinion (diets and days). He would not have them form separate congregations built around their own preferences and likings. Instead, he would have them pursue "loving, spiritual harmony in regard to matters on which the Bible is silent."[24]

He would have them "with one mind and one mouth glorify the God and Father of our Lord Jesus Christ." And he would have them both *inwardly* (with the heart and mind) and *outwardly* (with the mouth and voice) worship God together and not let any of their petty, non-gospel issues divide them. This is God's will for all of His people in every generation. Since Jesus redeemed us who believe, we are to live as a united, saved society, for as we do, God is greatly honored.

Mounce remarks:

Paul's wish was that God would grant the church at Rome a spirit of unity. His desire that they "mind the same thing among one another" (literal translation) does not mean that they should all come to the same conclusion. That is obvious from his discussion of the weak and the strong—the conscience of each is to guide the conduct of that person. It is unity of perspective that is desired. And that perspective is that of Christ Jesus, our model for Christian conduct. Think as he does. Take on his values and priorities. As each member of the church draws closer to Christ, we will at the same time draw closer to other members of the body. The experience of Christian unity produces a symphony of praise to God in which each voice blends with all the others to the glory of God. It is a

---

22 William McDonald makes an insightful comment when he says, "There are four mentions of the mouth in Romans, forming a biographical outline of a 'well-saved soul.' At the beginning, his mouth was full of cursing and bitterness (3:14). Then his mouth was stopped, and he was brought in guilt before the Judge (3:19). Next he confesses with his mouth Jesus as Lord (10:9). And finally his mouth is actively praising and worshiping the Lord (15:6)." McDonald, 1738.

23 Osborne notes, "The God and Father of our Lord Jesus Christ" is a liturgical title used often in the opening salutations of the New Testament letters (2 Cor 1:3; Eph 1:3; Col 1:3; 1 Pet 1:3) but used elsewhere as well (2 Cor 11:3; Eph 1:17; Rom 15:6). The idea of the Father being 'the God of Jesus' makes sense as a reference to Jesus' incarnate state of being and helps us to understand the offices of the Father and the Son within the Trinity. 'The God of our Lord Jesus' (Eph 1:17) is the God Jesus worshipped and who raised him from the dead. Paul's calling Jesus 'Lord' [15:6] unites him with the God of the Old Testament." Osborne, p. 462.

24 MacArthur, *One Faithful Life* (2019), p. 325.

family affair. We, the adopted sons of God, sing praises to the Father of our Lord Jesus Christ.[25]

Obs. 5- (vv. 7-13) That as Paul now concludes his entire discussion concerning Christian liberty with grace-filled sensitivity which he stated back in 14:1, he "frames the whole unit"[26] and writes with a command saying first in verse 7:

(V. 7) Therefore or on account of all that he has written; **receive,** again, *not* reject or browbeat others until they agree with your particular, secondary perspectives (as I said in my comments in 14:1), no. But, he says, continually and actively embrace from your heart and take to yourself in true friendship and fellowship as "equal in the eyes of the Lord;"[27] **one another, just as** or in a similar way that; **Christ also received us,**[28] that is in the similar way which He warmly welcomed us into His "fellowship, family and fold;"[29] **to** or with the goal being; **the glory of God,** "God's glory was promoted when Christ received us sinners, and it is further advanced when we who are by nature sinners and wrapped up in our own concerns instead receive our brothers and sisters in Christ with warmth and love."[30]

(Vv. 8-12) That as Paul has just mentioned Jesus in the previous verse, he now reminds us that since His earthly ministry included *both Jews and Gentiles alike,* "our hearts should also be big enough to include both,"[31] and so he writes:[32]

Now I say or maintain; **that Jesus Christ has become a servant to the circumcision for the truth of God** which is to say, He first became a minister to the Jews when He preached the gospel of salvation to them as seen throughout the Gospels; **to confirm** or for the purpose of fulfilling; **the promises** *made* to the fathers, that is, all of the Old Testament covenantal promises which were made to the patriarchs concerning His coming to them and then His dying for their sins as their Messiah-Redeemer; **and that the Gentiles** again, not just the Jews; **might glorify God for** *His* **mercy,** or for the great pity and compassion which He has shown towards them also through Jesus' death on their behalf; **as it is written**[33] or stands written in the Pentateuch, Psalms, and in the Prophets (Paul quotes four Old Testament passages here, the first of which is Psalm 18:49, which is attributed to David):

"**For this reason I will confess to You** (God); **among the Gentiles, And sing to Your name.**"

---

25 Mounce, pp. 260, 261.

26 Osborne, p. 463.

27 Ibid., p. 429.

28 Note that Jesus again is central in Paul's argument.

29 Robinson, Book II. p. 270.

30 Morris, p. 503.

31 William, 1738.

32 Cf. Rom. 11:30-32.

33 Grk. perfect, passive, verb.

[10] **And again he says** (that is, says by Moses in Deuteronomy 32:43):
"Rejoice, O Gentiles, with His people!"
[11] **And again** (that is, again by the psalmist in Psalm 117:1):
"Praise the LORD, all you Gentiles!
Laud Him, all you peoples!"
[12] **And again, Isaiah says** (that is, says in Isaiah 11:1, 10):
"There shall be a root of Jesse (Jesus);
And He who shall rise to reign over the Gentiles,
In Him the Gentiles shall hope."

What has Paul done by citing these Old Testament passages? The answer is simple: he has supported his point that God had long predicted through the Scriptures that He would save both Jews and Gentiles and make them into one spiritual family (the very thing which he had been urging this congregation to be). Here, he uses Scripture to prove his point that salvation is for both Jews and Gentiles in Christ (Rom. 1:16).[34] Because it is, both groups were to get along despite any differences that they might have on non-essential matters. This, again, is how they would greatly glorify God. This is how they would honor their Lord who "shows no partiality" (Acts 10:34).

Merida nicely summarizes the matter:

> It is important for believers to see petty squabbles in light of God's glorious plan of salvation. For the believers in Rome, this reminder about God's eternal plan of having a people for himself from among the nations should have made it inconceivable to divide over matters of indifference. The Messiah has come for the Jewish Christians as well as the Gentile Christians, for the weaker brother as well as the stronger brother. The appeal to unity, then, is not based on a thin foundation but on God's saving purposes.[35]

(V. 13) That as Paul puts forth another prayer-wish for the Romans in his last word to them concerning the topic under consideration,[36] he offers supplication to God on their behalf saying:[37]

Now may the God of hope[38] or we might say, the God who is the Ground and Giver of all of their hope; **fill you** or overflow and saturate you; **with all** (not just some, but with all); **joy** or deep happiness; **and peace** or inner serenity of soul; **in,** the preposition stating the means

---

34 Cf. Luke 2:29-32.

35 Merida, p. 233.

36 Cf. Rom. 15:5.

37 Cf. Rom. 14:17 where Paul once again speaks about "joy and peace."

38 Recall that "hope" is a topic that Paul addresses several times in this letter, 5:2, 4, 5; 8:20, 24; 12:12; 15:4, 12. Concerning our God being "the God of hope," Garland warmly writes: "God is the fountainhead of our hope, and those who are without God are also without hope. Those who have been justified by God live in hope for the glory of God for which they have been divinely predestined. This hope is made possible by divine love and secured by divine power. This hope enables believers to bear up under suffering. It enlightens the heart so that it sees the good in others who might otherwise be disregarded as hopeless." Garland, p. 447.

by which all joy and peace comes to us; **believing** not doubting, but by trustingly keeping our eyes on and faith in Christ; **that,** the conjunction stating the purpose for Paul's prayer-wish; **you may abound** or overflow; **in hope** or better understood, in biblical certainty and conviction that what God has promised will surely come to pass; **by** the preposition stating the means for how we abound in hope; **the power of the Holy Spirit** or we might say, by the strength which He supplies.

These are fitting closing words to all that Paul has been saying to the Romans concerning Christian liberty. As he ends his discussion, he directs them heavenward and prays that despite the differences and divisions that were happening among them that God would overrule and give them much "joy and peace" as they believe Him for these things. Paul calls them to cast their faith upward, and as he does he reminds them that although their trials made things look hopeless for a time, nonetheless, their God who is "the God of hope," was able to fix the situation and to work "all things together for their good" (Rom. 8:28).

Haldane helpfully notes:

> The prayer contained in this verse reminds us that there is no blessing which does not come to us from God, Jas. 1:17. He is called the God of love, of peace, of patience, of consolation, of hope, who fills His people with joy and peace. If, then, we desire to be filled with joy and peace, we must look to God. If we desire to *abound* in hope by the power of the Holy Ghost, we must with confidence pray to obtain His sacred influences and Divine teaching.[39]

Suggested applications from the text for the church:

1- When it comes to exercising Christian liberty among our brethren, we must remember to keep our eyes on Jesus and pattern our lives after His life of self-denial and obedience to the will of God the Father.

2- When it comes to exercising Christian liberty among our brethren, we must recall the Scriptures that point us to the fact that God would have the church to be a harmonious house of worshipers who, by His grace, are able to lovingly get along despite matters of secondary opinion.

3- When it comes to exercising Christian liberty among our brethren, we must regularly look to our God in prayer by faith, through Christ, by the power of the Holy Spirit, asking Him to help us to live as He would have us to live.

Suggested application from the text for the non-Christian:

1- When it comes to the salvation of your never-dying soul, you must remember that the same God who gives Christians great hope is the God who can give you this hope as well. But this hope is found only in One, even Jesus Christ the Lord. Therefore, go to Him now by faith, and ask Him to cleanse and forgive you of all your sins so that with Christians, you might also receive "joy and peace in believing."

---

39 Haldane, p. 618.

Text: Romans 15:14-33

General theme: Paul's Personal Comments, Plans, and Prayer

Homiletical outline of the verses:

A. Paul the persuaded: ¹⁴ Now I myself am confident concerning you, my brethren, that you also are full of goodness, filled with all knowledge, able also to admonish one another.

B. Paul the "priest": ¹⁵ Nevertheless, brethren, I have written more boldly to you on *some* points, as reminding you, because of the grace given to me by God, ¹⁶ that I might be a minister of Jesus Christ to the Gentiles, ministering the gospel of God, that the offering of the Gentiles might be acceptable, sanctified by the Holy Spirit.

C. Paul the preacher: ¹⁷ Therefore I have reason to glory in Christ Jesus in the things *which pertain* to God. ¹⁸ For I will not dare to speak of any of those things which Christ has not accomplished through me, in word and deed, to make the Gentiles obedient— ¹⁹ in mighty signs and wonders, by the power of the Spirit of God, so that from Jerusalem and round about to Illyricum I have fully preached the gospel of Christ.

D. Paul the pioneer: ²⁰ And so I have made it my aim to preach the gospel, not where Christ was named, lest I should build on another man's foundation, ²¹ but as it is written:

"To whom He was not announced, they shall see;
And those who have not heard shall understand."

²² For this reason I also have been much hindered from coming to you. ²³ But now no longer having a place in these parts, and having a great desire these many years to come to you, ²⁴ whenever I journey to Spain, I shall come to you. For I hope to see you on my journey, and to be helped on my way there by you, if first I may enjoy your *company* for a while. ²⁵ But now I am going to Jerusalem to minister to the saints. ²⁶ For it pleased those from Macedonia and Achaia to make a certain contribution for the poor among the saints who are in Jerusalem. ²⁷ It pleased them indeed, and they are their debtors. For if the Gentiles have been partakers of their spiritual things, their duty is also to minister to them in material things. ²⁸ Therefore, when I have performed this and have sealed to them this fruit, I shall go by way of you to Spain. ²⁹ But I know that when I come to you, I shall come in the fullness of the blessing of the gospel of Christ.

E. Paul the pleader: ³⁰ Now I beg you, brethren, through the Lord Jesus Christ, and through the love of the Spirit, that you strive together with me in prayers to God for me, ³¹ that I may be delivered from those in Judea who do not believe, and that my service for Jerusalem may be acceptable to the saints, ³² that I may come to you with joy by the will of God, and may be refreshed together with you. ³³ Now the God of peace *be* with you all. Amen.

Summary of section: In these verses, we see a personal side of Paul that we have not seen since the opening portion of this letter. In fact, what we have in these words forms a vital bookend to Romans 1:8-15, which provides valuable information regarding his life and labors. Sadly, this is a section that many could see as miscellaneous or minor. However, since "all Scripture is given by inspiration of God and is profitable" (2 Tim. 3:16), we should not think this. To the contrary, what we have here gives us many useful insights into Paul's pastoral character, commission, and concerns. Because of this, we should take special heed to it.

Exegetical & Practical Insights:

Obs. 1- (v. 14) That as Paul now says several positive things concerning the Roman believers and turns a corner in his subject matter, he writes:

Now I myself, despite all the corrective instruction he just gave them; **am confident**[40] or stand persuaded; **concerning** or with reference to; **you, my brethren,**[41] the words "my brethren" highlighting Paul's deep affection for them; **that** the conjunction putting forth the essence of his confidence; **you also are full of goodness, filled with all knowledge, able** or have the ability; **also to admonish**[42] **one another** or to continually keep one another "on the right road."[43]

In this verse, Paul lets the Romans know that even though he needed to write pointedly to them in the previous words about their need to love brethren who had some different perspectives than they had on non-gospel issues, this did not mean that he did not think highly of them. Indeed, he assures them that none of what he wrote diminishes the fact that he viewed them collectively as true saints who had many spiritual abilities in the congregation.[44]

Of course, all of this is striking because Paul did not know most of these believers in this city. There were some whom he met on the mission field of whom he speaks in the next chapter, but again, he did not know most of them. How then could he make such an assessment of them? He did this most likely on the basis of the testimonies of those whom he knew from the church, like Priscilla and Aquila. Further, he did this because he knew that they had experienced genuine conversion. Consequently he mentions three positive characteristics that were true of them, namely that they were "full of goodness, filled with all knowledge, able also to admonish one another."

- Full of goodness, which does not mean that they had no remaining sin (Rom. 7). Rather it means that because the Holy Spirit had given them new Christian hearts through regeneration and now lived in them, He was producing through them an active, benevolent goodness which sought the welfare of others (Gal. 5:22).[45]
- Filled with all knowledge, which does not mean that at the moment of their conversion they gained all the knowledge that

---

40 Grk. perfect, passive, verb.

41 Cf. Rom. 1:13.

42 Grk. present, active, verb.

43 Phillips translation.

44 Cf. Rom. 1:7, 8; 16:19.

45 BDAG, p. 4.

one could gain. Rather, it means that they intellectually and experientially gained vast spiritual knowledge pertaining to life and salvation which is in Jesus Christ our Lord.[46] Or, as MacArthur says, they gained a "deep knowledge of God's truth in the gospel of Jesus Christ."[47]

- Able to admonish[48] one another,[49] which means that by God's grace they could instruct, encourage, warn, and lovingly confront each other as brethren. Summarily, it means that they could direct each one down a right biblical path when any one of them strayed or just needed some Scriptural guidance for certain decisions in life.

And so whereas at the beginning of this epistle, Paul said that the Romans (just like all others who are in an unsaved state), were "filled with all unrighteousness" (Rom. 1:29), he observes now that they were "filled" with new things by the transforming power of the gospel. They were now filled with gospel graces and Christian goodness, proving the point that if anyone is "in Christ, he is a new creation; old things have passed away; behold, all things have become new" (2 Cor. 5:17).

Obs. 2- (vv. 15-16)[50] That as Paul just spoke encouragingly of the Romans in the previous verse, he now feels it necessary to let them know one of the main reasons why he wrote them in the way that he has, when he says:

Nevertheless, brethren, I have written more boldly or forthrightly; **to you on** *some* **points,** i.e., some points of doctrinal and practical matters in some portions of this epistle; **as reminding you,**[51] because of the grace given to me by God,[52] **that** or for the purpose that; **I might be a minister** or servant; **of Jesus Christ to the Gentiles, ministering** the word "ministering" in the original language carries the idea of ministering as a priest; **the gospel of God** or the good news of Christ which has its source in God (the very gospel which Paul has put forth throughout this letter);

---

46 Cf. 1 Cor. 1:5.

47 MacArthur, p. 327.

48 Cf. Col. 3:16. The word "admonish" is made up of two Greek words, which literally means "to place in the mind." It is so full with meaning that there is no word-for-word translation for it in English, hence Dr. Jay Adams would simply transliterate it into English as nouthetic and use it to summarize his biblical counseling model which he popularized. This type of counseling seeks to use the Word of God to bring God's solutions to problems that people face in life as they, by the power of the Holy Spirit, seek to obey the Bible and align themselves with it. This type of counseling stands in sharp contrast to secular, psychological counseling which is full of the words and ideas of unsaved men and women which are "according to the tradition of men, according to the basic principles of the world, and not according to Christ" (Col. 2:8). For more information about this matter, see "What is nouthetic counseling?" www.gotquestions.org.

49 By highlighting the ability of the church at Rome to "admonish one another," Paul shows that this gospel task is not just for the so-called experts, but it is to be the practice of the rank and file of all God's people when necessary.

50 It is noteworthy that although Paul does not give us a full-blown exposition of the doctrine of the Trinity in these verses, he mentions nonetheless the Father (15c), the Son (16a), and the Holy Spirit (16c).

51 Cf. 2 Pet. 1:12.

52 Cf. Rom. 1:5; 12:3.

that or for the purpose that; **the offering of** or we might say, the offering consisting in; **the Gentiles** (that is, the Gentiles themselves); **might be acceptable** or well-pleasing; **sanctified**[53] or completely consecrated; **by** or through the agency of; **the Holy Spirit.**

As Paul winds down this letter, he first establishes his apostolic credentials once again to the Romans (the very thing that he did in the opening chapter of this book, see 1:5). And as the case was there, so again, he clearly acknowledges that all that he received in his calling as an apostle was because of the "grace of God given to him by God." His office, just as his salvation, was given to him purely out of mercy, *not merit*. It was freely bestowed on him, *not because of who he was* but because of who God was.[54]

Additionally, he reminds his readers of his specific ministry "to the Gentiles."[55] As he does, he describes that ministry figuratively as his priestly ministry whereby he brings an acceptable sacrifice to God that is not *from* the Gentiles but is the believing Gentiles *themselves* who became pleasing to Him through Christ. This is a marvelous truth, one which gives us penetrating insight into how Paul viewed his ministerial service to the Lord. Here he tells the Romans that whenever he preached the gospel, the Gentiles that were saved became a sweet aroma to the Lord. He says that they became a fragrant offering that was pleasing to God. This was because they were now positionally set apart to Him "by the Holy Spirit."

The famous preacher G. Campbell Morgan (1863-1945) gives this pictorial comment on Paul's words in verse 16:

> What a radiant light this sheds on all our evangelistic and pastoral effort! Every soul won by the preaching of the gospel is not only brought into a place of safety and of blessing; he is an offering to God, a gift which gives Him satisfaction, the very offering He is seeking. Every soul carefully and patiently instructed in the things of Christ, and so made conformable to His likeness, is a soul in whom the Father takes pleasure. Thus we labor, not only for the saving of men, but for the satisfying of the heart of God. This is the most powerful motive.[56]

Hodge also makes a useful comment in another regard when he says:

> It is well worthy of remark, that amidst the numerous designations of the minister of the gospel in the New Testament, intended to set forth the nature of their office, they are never officially called priest. This is the only passage in which the term is even figuratively applied to them, and that under circumstances which render its misapprehension

---

53 This establishes the truth once for all that despite what some Jews would have thought, the Gentiles were not unclean because they were not circumcised. No, according to God, they were completely clean in His sight because of Christ.

54 Cf. Eph. 3:6, 7.

55 Cf. Acts 9:15, 16. Of course, this does not mean that Paul's calling was only to the Gentiles, for surely he also was a minister to the Jews, cf. Acts 17:1-4.

56 As quoted in McDonald, 1739.

impossible. They are not mediators between God and man; they do not offer propitiatory sacrifices. Their only priesthood is the preaching of the gospel, and their offerings are redeemed and sanctified men saved by their instrumentality.[57]

Obs. 3- (vv. 17-19) That as Paul just metaphorically described himself as a priest, he now literally describes himself as a preacher and writes:

Therefore he draws a conclusion from his previous words; **I have reason** or cause as a grace-called apostle; **to glory** or boast; **in** the preposition denoting the specific object of Paul's glorying; **Christ Jesus,** *not himself* but Christ Jesus alone; **in the things** *which pertain* **to God** which is to say, God's gospel and Paul's ministry in preaching it.[58] For the conjunction explaining "how Paul's boasting is truly 'in Christ';" [59] **I will not dare** or have the audacity; **to speak of any of those things which Christ has not accomplished through me** which means that he would not take any credit to himself for someone else's gospel work[60] or "claim praise from other persons' labors"[61] (cf. v. 20); **in word** (his speech); **and deed** (his actions); **to make the Gentiles obedient,** i.e., obedient to the faith;[62] — in mighty signs and wonders, two means which were used of God to establish Paul's apostolic work to the Gentiles;[63] **by** or through; **the power of the Spirit of God, so that** or as a result; **from Jerusalem and round about to Illyricum** (or modern-day Albania): "Jerusalem is the birthplace of the church. Illyricum is almost a thousand miles away in a straight line, but nearly two thousand miles by foot."[64]; **I have fully** or comprehensively; **preached the gospel of Christ,** i.e., whenever or wherever Paul preached, he accomplished his mission in a given area by not holding back anything pertaining to the glories of Jesus and the demands of the gospel to repent and believe.[65]

Obs. 4- (vv. 20-21) That as Paul puts forth his grand passion as a pioneer gospel missionary (which is to say, one who labors in fresh fields for Jesus) he writes:

---

57 Hodge, p. 439.

58 Cf. 1 Cor. 1:31; Gal. 6:14.

59 Harvey, p. 359.

60 Cf. 2 Cor. 10:13.

61 Robinson, Book II, p. 440.

62 Cf. Rom. 1:5.

63 Cf. Acts 14:3; 15:12; 2 Cor. 12:12; Heb. 2:3, 4. Concerning "signs and wonders" in the Bible, R.C. Sproul says that this phrase is "rooted in the authentication of Moses' ministry at the time of the Exodus. God periodically gave such miracles at crucial junctures of redemptive history, such as the Exodus, the prophetic ministries of Elijah and Elisha, the preserving of His people in the time of Daniel, and the ministry of Christ and the apostles. These events are unusual rather than normal and point to the successive stages of redemptive history and the new revelation that accompanied them. As signs and wonders expressed God's endorsement of Jesus' ministry and claims (Acts 2:22-24, John 5:36), so Paul can invoke such signs as authenticating his own apostolic authority." R. C. Sproul, Study Bible, p. 2008.

64 Doriani, p. 518.

65 Cf. Acts 20:26, 27.

And so or thus; **I have made it my aim** or chief goal; **to preach** or proclaim; **the gospel,** i.e., the good news of Jesus; **not where Christ** (the Messiah); **was named** or proclaimed and acknowledged; lest or in case; **I should build on another man's foundation** or work for Jesus which someone else had done[66] "that was not because of some peculiar pride that would encourage him to go it on his own but because of his intense desire to reach the known world as quickly as possible"[67] (cf. v. 18); but as it is written[68] or as it stands written in Isaiah 52:15 (the passage providing the reason why Paul ministered in the way that he just mentioned): **"To whom He** (Jesus); **was not announced, they shall see; And those who have not heard shall understand."**[69]

These two verses highlight two primary things about Paul's preaching. First we see in verse 20 that he never shrank back from his pioneer, missionary mode of operation of preaching the gospel "not where Christ was named" even though it would be a more difficult task. This was because that was how he understood his specific commissioning from Christ (although he was not saying that everyone had to follow his exact pattern of ministry. For as McDonald says, "Paul's example in pioneering in new areas does not necessarily bind other servants of the Lord to do this exact activity. Some are called to move in and teach, for example, after new churches have been planted)."[70]

Second, we see in verse 21 that in Paul's use of the Isaiah 52:15 passage (the passage immediately preceding that most notable Old Testament passage which clearly displays the substitutionary work of Christ on behalf of sinners in Isaiah chapter 53) he viewed his gospel preaching as that which prophetically fulfilled these words regarding getting the good news message of Jesus out far and wide. This no doubt was a powerful motive for his missionary preaching since he "knew that God had raised him up for this work — to preach to the heathen"[71] and to tell them about Christ who, in love, came into the world to save sinners.

Moo provides this helpful elaboration on Paul's use of the Isaiah passage:

> As he so often does, Paul clinches his point with an OT quotation. The quotation is from Isa. 52:15b. Paul has probably chosen to quote this text for at least 3 reasons. First, it justifies Paul's decision not "to build on another's foundations (v. 20); for the text speaks of bringing a message to those who have not yet heard. Second, it accords with Paul's sense of calling to Gentiles, since the ones who have not had it announced to them and have not yet heard are "kings" and "nations" (cf. v. 15a). Third, it

---

66 In short, Paul sought to break fresh ground for the gospel, plant churches and then move on and do the same again.

67 Mounce, p. 268.

68 Grk. perfect, passive, verb.

69 Leon Morris notes that this Scripture citation is the "last of 64 quotations from Scripture in Romans in the list given in the UBS Greek New Testament." Morris, p. 515.

70 McDonald, 1739. Cf. 1 Cor. 3:10.

71 Mahan, p. 107.

alludes to the content of Paul's gospel. For Isa. 52:15 is part of the famous fourth "servant" passage, and the "him" concerning whom these Gentiles have not been told is the Servant of the Lord. Paul's pioneering church-planting ministry among the Gentiles is fulfilling the OT prediction about the Gentiles coming to see and understand the message about the Servant of the Lord.[72]

Obs. 5- (vv. 22-24) That as Paul speaks more fully about his plans for new missionary work (plans which commentators say he was making while he was about sixty years old[73] and had been on the mission field for at least twenty years), he writes:

For this reason that is, the reason for not visiting the Romans sooner because he had been caught up in gospel labors in other areas (cf. vv. 19-21); **I also have been much** (not a little, but much); **hindered**[74] or providentially delayed by God for a time until his other work was finished; **from coming to you,** the very thing which he told them in the beginning of this letter that he planned on doing (cf. 1:13). **But now** the words contrasting "the situation in the past, when Paul was prevented by gospel ministry in the East from coming to Rome, with the present situation, in which, having 'completed' that ministry (cf. v. 19b), he is free to move on;"[75] "but now;" **no longer having a place** or opportunity; **in these parts,** i.e., the parts before specified in the previous words which is to say, his work of planting and establishing churches from Jerusalem and round about to Illyricum;[76] **and having a great desire** or longing; **these many years to come to you** (you who are at Rome); **whenever I journey to Spain** (the area in the Far West of the Roman Empire where he had his sights set for new gospel ministry); **I shall come to you** (note his determination). **For** the conjunction explaining why this was so; **I hope to see you on my journey, and to be helped** that is, helped financially and materially; **on my way there by you, if first I may enjoy** or more literally, be filled to the brim and saturated with; **your *company* for a while,** the language anticipating "rich enjoyment and refreshment"[77] (clearly Paul desired not only their *finances* but also their *fellowship* in the Lord).[78]

These verses put forth three vital truths which could be expounded in great detail, but are stated here summarily: 1- That true gospel ministers are extremely busy people: "for this reason I also have been *much hindered*

---

72 Moo, NICNT, pp. 897, 898.

73 Merida, p. 242.

74 Gr. imperfect, passive, verb.

75 Moo, NICNT, p. 899.

76 Morris, p. 517.

77 Robinson, Book II. p. 297.

78 Morris is correct when he says, "Some think that Paul was looking for prayers and good wishes only, and this may indeed be the case. But it seems somewhat more likely that he hoped to have Rome as his base for his work in the Western regions. Until now Antioch had functioned as his base, but this was too far from places like Spain. It would be a very great help to Paul if the Christians at Rome could see their way clear to acting as his home church, so to speak, while he went forward into unknown territory in the regions to the west." Morris, p. 518.

from coming to you" (v. 22). Simply stated, genuine gospel ministers do not work only for a couple of hours on Sunday. 2- That a man's heart plans his way, but the Lord directs his steps (Prov. 16:9).[79] Recall that when Paul first wrote this letter to the Romans, he was a free missionary of the Lord sent out by the church from Antioch.[80] However, by the time he finally arrived in Rome, it was as a prisoner of Rome, after having been arrested in Jerusalem.[81] 3- That local churches are to be involved in supporting gospel missionaries as much as possible as they seek to do global evangelism: "I hope to see you on my journey, and to be *helped on my way there by you*" (v. 24b).

The question commonly asked concerning Paul's trip to Spain (as he mentions in verse 24) is, "Did he ever make it there?" Commentators and others are divided regarding this issue, and it is hard to be definitive.[82] Perhaps he did. Perhaps he did not. But in either case, it is probably more important to ask, "Why did he want to go to Spain anyway? Surely there were other areas to evangelize."

While many reasons could be given, perhaps one of the main ones is that along with what he said in verse 21 of this chapter, of him prophetically fulfilling his gospel labors by preaching to people who had not heard of Jesus in fulfillment of Isaiah 52:15, that he also viewed the words of Isaiah 66:19 as that which also predicted his gospel labors. There, God said through the prophet that the gospel would go to the general area of Spain, where people would hear of the Lord's "fame and see His glory."[83]

Obs. 6- (vv. 25-29) That as Paul speaks about what he first planned on doing before he got to Rome, namely, make a pit stop in Jerusalem to assist struggling saints there, he writes:[84]

But now I am going to Jerusalem to minister to the saints or to take care of and financially assist the impoverished believers there.[85]

---

79 Clearly, Paul understood this point cf. Rom. 1:10, 15:32.

80 Cf. Acts 13:2.

81 Cf. Acts chapters 21-28.

82 Clement, an elder in the church in Rome, seemed to believe that Paul had arrived in Spain. In writing about this around three decades later, he said that the apostle *"reaching the limits of the west* he bore witness before rulers"—(1 Clement 5:7). To those living in Rome, "the west" would have most likely included Spain, as commentators note. And so what happened to Paul after he reached Spain if, in fact, he did? The traditional view is that after this he must have been arrested again and finally executed in Rome, "for tradition is unanimous that he died there sometime during the latter years of Nero's reign (ca. A.D. 64-68)." Edwards, 350.

83 Spain included the city or the region referred to in the Old Testament as Tarshish. Cf. Isa. 11:11, 51:5, 60:9.

84 So his travel plans were first Jerusalem, second Rome, and third Spain.

85 Osborne helpfully notes: "One very important duty remains before Paul can come to Rome — delivering the collection for the poor he had been gathering from the Gentile churches for months. 'In the service of the saints' (NIV 'the Lord's people') probably states the purpose for the trip. He wants to serve the saints with the offering. This was the second such collection. Paul and Barnabas delivered the first in AD 48 after Agabus's prophecy of an empire-wide famine (Acts 11:27-30 = Gal. 2:1-10). This was Paul's second trip to Jerusalem. At that time the "pillars of the church" — James the Lord's brother, Peter, and

For the conjunction explaining why this was; **it pleased** or was good in the eyes of; **those from Macedonia and Achaia,**[86] i.e., the believing Gentile churches in Philippi, Thessalonica, Galatia and Corinth, etc.; **to make a certain contribution** or a voluntary partnership offering; **for the poor among the saints who are in Jerusalem** "poverty was an ongoing problem for Palestinian Christians."[87] **It pleased** or delighted; **them indeed** or for sure; **and they are their debtors,**[88] i.e., their spiritual debtors since the gospel ultimately spread to the Gentiles through the church at Jerusalem. **For if** or since; **the Gentiles have been partakers of their spiritual things,** i.e., the gospel; their duty or moral obligation; **is also to minister to them in material things. Therefore, when I have performed this and have sealed** or secured; **to them this fruit** which is metaphorical language for the financial offering from the Gentile churches, "the fruit of the faith and love of the believers in Macedonia and Achaia and a token of the bond of fellowship existing between these believers and the saints at Jerusalem;"[89] **I shall go by way of you** (you Romans); **to Spain. But I know that when I come to you, I shall come in the fullness of the blessing** "not only blessing, but fullness of blessing;"[90] **of the gospel of Christ,** which is to say, that when he arrived in Rome, God would greatly own his gospel ministry to them as he preached Christ by the power of Holy Spirit.[91]

These words are insightful. Taken at face value, they show us that although the first-century congregations were *independent*, they were also *interdependent*.[92] Since they all made up one spiritual body, when one congregation suffered, they all suffered with it (1 Cor. 12:26). Therefore, the churches sought to help each other in times of need as they were able. This is something they did joyfully, *not reluctantly*, for "it pleased them indeed" (vv. 26, 27) to do this, even while some of them were in financial straits.[93] May God help us then to model such a practice in our lives as local congregations. May it be that as we first give ourselves wholly to

---

John — affirmed Paul as an apostle to the Gentiles and asked only that he "remember the poor" (Gal. 2:10). This must have had quite an effect on him, and he spent a great deal of time collecting another gift from the Gentile churches for the poor in Jerusalem." Osborne, pp. 484, 485. Cf. Acts 12:25 with Acts 19:21.

86 Cf. 1 Cor. 16:1; 2 Cor. 8, 9.

87 Osborne, p. 485.

88 Cf. 1:14.

89 Murray, 2:219.

90 Robinson, Book II. p. 305.

91 Hughes says, "Paul concludes this section on a remarkably positive note: 'I know that when I come to you, I will come in the full measure of the blessing of Christ' (v. 29). Such optimism! Paul was sure that he would come to Rome in blessing. Little did he know his arrival would be in chains, and yet it was indeed in joy. What a way to go — 'in the full measure of the blessing of Christ.'" Hughes, p. 292.

92 Cf. 1 Cor. 16:1; 2 Cor. 8:1; 8:19; 11:8.

93 2 Cor. 8:2.

the Lord that we will then give ourselves wholly to those who belong to Him (cf. 2 Cor. 8:5).[94]

Obs. 7- (vv. 30-33) That as Paul ends this chapter, he does so by making a fervent appeal to the Romans on his behalf and writes:

Now I beg[95] or continually plead with; **you, brethren,** the word "brethren" once again highlighting Paul's deep affection for them (cf. v.14); **through** or we might say, by the authority and mediation of; **the Lord Jesus Christ** "note the solemnity of the expression 'the Lord Jesus Christ,' referring to the Savior in all the fullness of his being and meaning for the church;"[96] **and through the love of the Spirit,** i.e., through or by the love which the Holy Spirit gives us for one another (Gal. 5:22); **that,** the conjunction putting forth Paul's desire in the prayer; **you strive together,**[97] or earnestly engage and wrestle in prayer, which "is not a formal exercise, but a sincere, fervent desire laid before God in the name of Christ;"[98] **with me in prayers to God; for me that,** the conjunction putting forth Paul's first prayer request; **I may be delivered** or rescued; **from** or "not fall into the hands of;"[99] **those in Judea** "the country of the Jews, in a wider or stricter sense;"[100] **who do not believe, and that,** the conjunction putting forth Paul's second prayer request; **my service** or mission; **for Jerusalem may be acceptable** or warmly welcomed; **to the saints, that** or so that, the subordinate conjunction putting forth the goal of all that he just requested; **I may come to you with joy** or a "happy heart;"[101] stemming from the "success of his undertaking;"[102] **by,** the preposition stating the means of Paul getting to them; **the will of God, and may be refreshed** or rested and reinvigorated amid his exhausting ministry; **together with you** (cf. 1:12; 15:24). [And then finally, as Paul gives his benediction to these believers in view of all that he has written to them concerning their being at peace with one another (14:1-15:13), he says:] **Now the God of peace**[103] or the God who is the source and supplier of all our harmony as a church;[104] *be* **with you all.** Amen the word expressing Paul's strong assurance that God will do this very thing.

---

94   Cf. Rom. 12:13.

95   Grk. present active, verb.

96   Hendriksen, p. 496.

97   Cf. Col. 4:12. Our English word agonize is derived from this Greek word. MacArthur says that the word was "originally used from athletic events, especially gymnastics, in which contestants such as wrestlers or boxers, struggled against each other." MacArthur, p. 351.

98   Mahan, p. 108.

99   Phillips translation.

100 Robinson, Book II. p. 308.

101 Phillips translation.

102 Robinson, Book II. p. 309.

103 It is important to see how concerning all that Paul has been writing he calls God in chapter 15 by three outstanding titles, "the God of patience and comfort" (v. 5), "the God of hope" (v. 13), and now "the God of peace" (v. 33).

104 Cf. 2 Cor. 13:11; 1 Thess. 5:23; 2 Thess. 3:16; Rom. 16:20.

If we study Paul's epistles closely, we see that he was never too proud to ask God's people to pray for him.[105] He did not ask this of them because he desired any attention to be brought to himself. Instead, he did it because he clearly understood his weaknesses as a minister and the power of prayer. He understood that God answered the prayers of Christians because of Christ (John 16:23). Because of this, he regularly sought this means of grace for himself.

In verse 31, he makes two specific requests from the Romans, "That I may be delivered from those in Judea who do not believe, and that my service for Jerusalem may be acceptable to the saints." Paul's first request is understandable since the unbelieving Jews regularly persecuted him on the missionary field (as the book of Acts repeatedly shows).[106] They did this because they were "fanatically opposed to the gospel, just as he himself had once been."[107] They viewed the apostle as a traitor to Judaism when in fact nothing could be further from the truth. For when Paul became a believer in Jesus the Messiah, he did not become less Jewish, but, as it were, more Jewish! For Jesus is the Jewish Messiah of whom the prophets foretold would come. This is why we are told that when Paul went to a synagogue of the Jews, "as his custom was," he "reasoned with them from the Scriptures, explaining and demonstrating that the Christ had to suffer and rise again from the dead and saying, this Jesus whom I preached to you is the Christ" (Acts 17:2, 3). And this is why he could say at his trial, "I worship the God of my fathers, believing all things which are written in the law and in the prophets" (Acts 24:14).

Paul's second request seems to anticipate that perhaps some believers in Jerusalem might have been tainted by false reports from the Judaizers against him, namely, that he now was rejecting the moral Law of Moses as a rule of life for Christians.[108] Again, nothing could be further from the truth, for Paul was no antinomian. While he clearly believed that Christians were completely freed from the condemning power of the law and that the ceremonial law had been done away with, he also believed just as strongly that they were obligated to keep the moral law as an expression of their love to God. This they did not for their justification, but for their sanctification. Or, as Paul already said in Romans 3:31, "Do we then make void the law through faith? Certainly not! On the contrary, we establish the law." Thankfully, it seems that God answered the prayers of the Romans on Paul's behalf, for when he finally reached Jerusalem with the contribution for the poor, we are told that the brethren

---

105 Cf. 2 Cor. 1:11; Eph. 6:18-20; Phil. 1:19; Col. 4:2-4; 1 Thess. 5:25; 2 Thess. 3:1, 2; Philem. 22.

106 Cf. Acts 13:45; 14:2; 17:13; 18:5, 6; 19:9; 20:23; 21:27; 23:12.

107 McDonald, 1740.

108 Cf. Acts 21:20-25. Some commentators say that Paul's request here is more connected to the fact that the Jewish believers in Jerusalem might be prejudiced against the Gentile believers who were uncircumcised and, consequently, would not want their money. This seems strange to me because in Galatians 2:9, 10, Paul says that when he was in Jerusalem, he was told by James, Peter and John to remember "the poor" there. The inference is that Paul would do this very thing by the collection which he received from the Gentile churches.

there received him and his traveling companions "gladly" (Acts 21:17 cf. Acts 28:15).

Merida nicely sums up this section,

> Paul spends many chapters in Romans teasing out the gospel and its implications, but in Romans 15:14-33 we find the missionary heartbeat of the letter. Paul's missionary heart is on display. It should not surprise us. When you have a gospel as big as the gospel presented in Romans, you will want to take it to the nations.... If you soak yourself in the good news presented in Romans, I cannot help but believe you too will want to be a Great Commission Christian, pouring your life out for the fame of Christ among the nations. Paul gives us a vision of what that looks like:
>
> * Be part of a healthy, gospel centered church.
> * See life and mission through the lens of worship.
> * Remember that ministry fruitfulness is the result of divine enablement.
> * Have the right kind of ambition: driven by the gospel and a heart for people.
> * Support the work of church planting.
> * Support the work of mercy ministry.
> * Refresh those on the front lines.
> * Pray for those on the front lines.
>
> Jesus Christ has fulfilled his mission, has forgiven us our sins and made us new creations, and has given us the Holy Spirit. Now, compelled by his grace, let's make his final charge our first priority.[109]

Suggested applications from the text for the church:

1- We learn from these verses that although we will all continue to fall short of all that God would have us to be, we should not negate the good things which He in grace has produced both in us and others and freely acknowledge this (cf. v. 14).

2- We learn from these verses that no portion of Scripture is to be overlooked by us regardless of how insignificant it might seem (i.e., Paul's personal comments, plans, and prayer), but rather every portion should be carefully considered, for it is all profitable for our lives as God's people.

3- We learn from these verses that we must never forget, especially in our times of greatest need, that our God is "the God of peace" who is always willing, able, and ready to grant us this through Christ.

Suggested application from the text for the non-Christian:

1- You learn from our passage that the God of the Bible would be "the God of peace" to you. However, for this to happen, you must first cease being at war with Him by turning from your sins and asking Him to forgive you on the basis of Jesus' substitutionary death on behalf of people like you. When you do this, you will be reconciled to your God, and you will know His peace which "surpasses all understanding" (Phil. 4:7).

---

109 Merida, p. 247.

ROMANS
CHAPTER SIXTEEN

Text: Romans 16:1-16, 21-24

General theme: Paul and His Pals

Homiletical outline of the verses:
    A. Paul's commendation of Phoebe: [1] I commend to you Phoebe our sister, who is a servant of the church in Cenchrea,
    B. Paul's concerns for Phoebe: [2] that you may receive her in the Lord in a manner worthy of the saints, and assist her in whatever business she has need of you; for indeed she has been a helper of many and of myself also.
    C. Paul's commendation of other people: [3] Greet Priscilla and Aquila, my fellow workers in Christ Jesus, [4] who risked their own necks for my life, to whom not only I give thanks, but also all the churches of the Gentiles. [5] Likewise *greet* the church that is in their house. Greet my beloved Epaenetus, who is the firstfruits of Achaia to Christ.
    [6] Greet Mary, who labored much for us. [7] Greet Andronicus and Junia, my countrymen and my fellow prisoners, who are of note among the apostles, who also were in Christ before me.
    [8] Greet Amplias, my beloved in the Lord. [9] Greet Urbanus, our fellow worker in Christ, and Stachys, my beloved. [10] Greet Apelles, approved in Christ. Greet those who are of the *household* of Aristobulus. [11] Greet Herodion, my countryman. Greet those who are of the *household* of Narcissus who are in the Lord.
    [12] Greet Tryphena and Tryphosa, who have labored in the Lord. Greet the beloved Persis, who labored much in the Lord. [13] Greet Rufus, chosen in the Lord, and his mother and mine. [14] Greet Asyncritus, Phlegon, Hermas, Patrobas, Hermes, and the brethren who are with them. [15] Greet Philologus and Julia, Nereus and his sister, and Olympas, and all the saints who are with them. [16] Greet one another with a holy kiss. The churches of Christ greet you.
    D. Paul's companions in Corinth at Gaius' place: [21] Timothy, my fellow worker, and Lucius, Jason, and Sosipater, my countrymen, greet

you. [22] I, Tertius, who wrote *this* epistle, greet you in the Lord. [23] Gaius, my host and *the host* of the whole church, greets you. Erastus, the treasurer of the city, greets you, and Quartus, a brother. [24] The grace of our Lord Jesus Christ *be* with you all. Amen.

Summary of section: In these verses, we see that Paul, very much like God Himself, did not forget the work and labor of love which others had shown toward God's name by ministering to the saints (Heb. 6:10). Moreover, Paul plainly understood that in his gospel work, he was part of a team, therefore he joyfully labored with others. Simply put, the apostle was no soloist. He was not a one-man-band. Rather, he was a team player who richly valued others and clearly understood that the kingdom of God advances through the combined efforts of God's diverse people working together for the glory of Jesus and the good of others.[1]

These verses also show us Paul's immense love for fellow Christians. It shows how he felt about them and how much he enjoyed their friendship and fellowship. John MacArthur says that this passage is "by far the most extensive and intimate expression of love and appreciation to come from the tender heart and inspired mind of the apostle Paul. It is a rich and rewarding section that yields many insights into the life of Paul, into the lives of other early Christians, and into the nature and character of the first-century church."[2]

Doriani summarizes these matters:

> Essential points about church life emerge from the greetings of Romans 16:1-23. Above all, we see a church that found unity despite diversity in ethnicity, sex, social status, and native language. The names suggest both high rank and enslavement. Paul mentions people from noble households, people with civil status, and total unknowns. He praises both men and women. As Paul said in Galatians 3:28, "There is neither Jew nor Greek, there is neither slave nor free, there is no male and female, for you are all one in Christ Jesus." Paul's greetings show a diverse yet unified church. The greetings have three noble facets. First, Paul sees the people he greets as a family, as brothers and sisters (Rom. 16:1, 14). Second, he loves his people and often calls them "beloved" (16:2-9). Third, Paul toiled and suffered alongside his friends. By sharing tasks and sorrows, bonds grew strong (16:3-9).[3]

Exegetical & Practical Insights:
Obs. 1- (vv. 1-2) That just before Paul begins greeting his pals, he begins by speaking of Phoebe and says:

---

1 Cf. Col. 4:7-15; Phil. 4:3. Commentators often wonder how Paul knew so many people in Rome since he had never been there. The answer seems to be that he met these individuals while on his various missionary journeys. Doriani notes that when "Emperor Claudius expelled the Jews from Rome in A.D. 49, he scattered Rome's Jewish Christians throughout the region. They often landed in cities that Paul visited in his journeys. When Claudius rescinded his decree in A.D. 54, many returned to Rome, so Paul is greeting people whom he met during his journeys." Doriani, p. 531.

2 MacArthur, p. 358.

3 Doriani, pp. 534, 535.

I commend to you or positively recommend so as to heartily approve of her character and conduct; **Phoebe our sister,** which is to say, our sister in the Lord because she was a true born-again believer; **who is a servant** or helper; **of the church**[4] **in Cenchrea** (a small seaport city of Corinth about seven miles away from it);[5] **that** or for the purpose that; **you may receive** or warmly welcome; **her in the Lord** or as one who is in true spiritual union with Him; **in a manner worthy of the saints,** or as "befitting someone who belongs to Christ;"[6] **and assist** or aid; **her in whatever business** or practical things; **she has need of you** "whether it was of a private or public nature;"[7] **for,** the conjunction giving the reason for Paul's previous words; **indeed she has been a helper** or benefactor;[8] **of many and of myself also** (which probably means that while Paul was in Corinth ministering for months, she ministered to him).[9]

A couple of questions need to be answered concerning this beloved sister named Phoebe, whose name means radiant.[10] First, why did Paul need to commend her to the church in Rome? The answer seems to be that he did this because the Roman Christians had never met her and so they knew little to nothing about her. Therefore, she needed someone to speak on her behalf. Paul was willing to do this. This commendation of Phoebe was something that the early churches often did in order to verify that an individual had a credible profession of faith and was trustworthy.[11]

Paul's warm mention of Phoebe first in his list has caused many throughout the centuries to believe that she was the one who brought this letter from Paul in Corinth to the Romans in Rome. This could be the case. If it was, think about the precious treasure she carried in her purse! In commenting on this matter, Donald Grey Barnhouse warmly notes:

> Never was there a greater burden carried by such tender hands. The theological history of the church through the centuries was in the manuscript which she brought with her. The Reformation was in that luggage. The blessing of multitudes in our day was carried in those parchments.[12]

Second, there is the matter of Phoebe being called "a servant of the church of Cenchrea." The Greek word which is translated "servant" in verse 1 is

---

4 Several commentators note that this is the first time that Paul uses the word church in this letter.

5 Some commentators say that Cenchrea was a church plant of the church at Corinth.

6 Olyott, p. 157.

7 Robinson, Book II. p. 315.

8 Many commentators see from the use of this word that Phoebe was a wealthy individual.

9 Cf. Acts 18.

10 Olyott also says that her name is from a Greek mythological goddess, which indicates that she was from a pagan background, Olyott, p. 152.

11 Cf. Acts 18:24-28; 1 Cor. 16:3, 2 Cor. 3:1. This would be like our modern-day practice of letters of transfer, where one local church testifies to another local church about the saving work of God done in the life of an individual.

12 Donald Grey Barnhouse, Romans, IV. p. 124.

the same word from which we derive the title "deacon." As a result, much ink has been spilled over whether or not she held the office of deacon in the church. I do not believe this was the case for at least three reasons:

1- When we consider the word 'servant' in the passage, it can be rightly understood generically for any person who served, helped, waited on, or took care of others in any capacity. For example, we are told in Romans 13:4 that the governing officials are "God's ministers" or servants (the same Greek word) to us for good. Additionally, this same word is used to describe our Lord Jesus Christ in Romans 15:8, where Paul says, "Now I say that Jesus Christ has become a servant (the same Greek word) to the circumcision for the truth of God to confirm the promises made to the fathers." Paul himself used this very term in 1 Corinthians 3:5 to describe himself and Apollos: "Who then is Paul, and who is Apollos, but ministers (the same Greek word) through whom you believed, as the Lord gave to each one?" And this exact same term is also used of the household servants who drew the water that Jesus turned into wine in John 2:5, and 9. In all these references, we see that none of the people in view held an official office-bearing position of deacon or deaconess in the church. Surely Jesus was not a deacon in that sense, nor Paul. Therefore, are we now to believe that in this one instance where the word is connected to a woman that she occupied an official position in the church? I do not think so.

2- When we see the diaconate in its seed form coming to fruition in Acts 6:2, 3, we are told that "the twelve summoned the multitude of disciples and said, 'It is not desirable that we should leave the word of God and serve tables, therefore brethren seek out from among yourselves *seven men* [not women] of good reputation, full of the Holy Spirit and wisdom, whom we may appoint over this business.'" In light of this directive, it seems safe to deduce that the office of deacon was given specifically to men. That being the case, Phoebe—a woman—would be ineligible.

3- When Paul gives his most straightforward instruction concerning who is to occupy the office of deacon in 1 Timothy chapter 3:12, he says that they must be "the husbands of one wife," not "the wife of one husband."[13] This apostolic statement also appears to confirm that the office of deacon will be occupied by men, and men exclusively.

For these reasons, it seems unlikely that Phoebe was officially a deacon. In fact, these reasons and others make it quite clear that no woman should be permitted to hold the office of deacon in the church. According to the clear teaching of the New Testament, the office of deacon (and, in fact, the office of elder as well) is restricted to men. This is God's design according to His eternal will and infallible Word.

Rogland helpfully comments on this matter:

---

13 I believe that what Paul says in 1 Tim. 3:11 is a specific reference to a deacon's wife, not a broad reference to women in general. This seems to fit the context much better there.

Some writers and some evangelical churches of the present-day contest the proposition that a woman may not occupy the office of deacon. They cite Romans 16:1 as evidence that women occupied the office in the early church. Their argument, however, is without merit. If women were eligible for ordination to the office of deacon, Paul certainly would have made this clear in 1 Timothy 3:8-13. The passage in 1 Timothy is a *didactic* portion of Scripture, i.e., a passage that presents systematic teaching on a subject. On the other hand, Romans 16:1 is an *incidental* passage regarding the diaconate. Paul's intention in 16:1-2 is to commend Phoebe to the care of the church in Rome; only in passing does he refer to her as a *diakonos*. It is a cardinal rule of biblical hermeneutics (the science of interpretation) that didactic passages serve to illuminate the meaning of incidental passages, not vice versa. We must conclude that Phoebe was not a deaconess, but, rather, an unordained servant of the church in Cenchrea.[14]

Having said what Phoebe was not, let us not forget what she was. Phoebe was a great, gifted, godly, gracious, and giving sister and servant of the Lord. She was thoroughly committed to the things of Christ, giving of her time, energy, and finances to the brethren. She was like the other women mentioned in the following words like Mary who "labored much for us" (v. 6), and Tryphena, Tryphosa and Persis (v. 12) who "labored much in the Lord." Indeed, Phoebe was like godly Lydia who, after God opened her heart to Him, opened her home to Paul and his traveling companions and ministered to them (Acts 16:15). Putting all the pieces together concerning Phoebe, William Hendriksen makes a most balanced statement when he says,

> The lesson is clear: Two extremes should be avoided: (a) that of ordaining women to an ecclesiastical office when there is no warrant for doing so in Scripture; and (b) that of ignoring the very important and valuable services devout and alert women are able to render to the church of our Lord and Savior Jesus Christ.[15]

Obs. 2- (vv. 3-4) That as Paul now officially begins his list of greetings (which is his lengthiest list in all of his letters) he says:

Greet or give my warm wishes to; **Priscilla and Aquila,** a Christian wife and husband who were close friends of the apostle, whom he initially met while on the mission field in Corinth, who shared a similar tent trade with him (Acts 18:1-4); **my fellow workers** or helpers and laborers; **in**

---

14 Rogland, p. 156.

15 Hendriksen, p. 501. Perhaps some women reading this commentary might wonder what services they can render to the church. While certainly, older women can teach younger women, especially in matters about domestic piety regarding loving their husbands and children, being discreet, chaste, homemakers, good, obedient to their own husbands that the word of God may not be blasphemed (Titus 2:3-5), they can also visit and pray for sick members in the church, make meals for the needy, greet and invite visitors to their homes for hospitality, encourage the hurting by writing cards to them, show mercy to the poor, hand out gospel tracts when evangelism is done, assist the deacons in practical ways that they might need, and use the many other gifts that God has given them to advance His glory in the earth. In saying these things, we see that while only men can hold official positions in the church, ministry is not only for men. Ministry is for all who want to roll up their sleeves, get their hands dirty, help others and glorify Jesus.

Christ Jesus,[16] which is to say, "in union with Christ and His cause;"[17] **who risked their own necks for my life,** "they put their own lives in jeopardy to protect Paul's;"[18] **to whom not only I give thanks** or am grateful; **but also all the churches of the Gentiles** this, of course, was because Priscilla and Aquila were used by God to preserve Paul's life so that he could bring the gospel to them.

Obs. 3- (v. 5) Likewise *greet* **the church that is in their house.** Scholars say that in the first century, believers did not own church buildings as we do today, so they depended on wealthy Christians with larger homes or apartments to use for their gatherings.[19] **Greet my beloved** or well-loved; **Epaenetus,** whose name means "praiseworthy;" **who is the firstfruits of Achaia to Christ** which apparently means that he was the first convert in that area, which today is the general area of modern Greece.

Obs. 4- (v. 6) Greet Mary, the first of the several women mentioned in this honorable list, of whom we know nothing but that she was one; **who labored** or more literally, from the Greek text, greatly exerted herself; **much for us** (cf. v. 12).

Obs. 5- (v. 7) Greet Andronicus, whose name means "man of victory;" **and Junia** whose name means "youthful." Some commentators say that these two were a husband-and-wife couple. However, since in the Greek text the name Junia is a masculine proper noun, it seems more likely that these two were male believers; **my countrymen** or better translated "kinsman," i.e., they were Jewish believers who were blood relatives of Paul; **and my fellow prisoners,** which means that at one time they were confined with Paul in one of his imprisonments when he was locked up for cause of Christ and the gospel; **who are of note among the apostles,** or well known among them; **who also were in Christ,** "the distinguishing characteristic of a true Christian;"[20] **before** or prior to; **me,** thus, because of this, it seems likely that they prayed for Paul's conversion. As MacArthur says, "the prayers of those relatives for Paul's salvation—and perhaps their witnessing to him—may have been instrumental in his eventual surrender to the Savior."[21]

Obs. 6- (v. 8) Greet Amplias, this name was a common Roman name among household slaves as many commentators note; **my beloved** or

---

16 Paul will use similar language as this throughout these verses (v. 7, 8, 9, 10, 11, 12, 13, 16), highlighting to us the "Christ-centered basis for these diverse relationships" as Merida rightly notes. Merida, p. 259.

17 Robinson, Book II. p. 319.

18 MacArthur, p. 363.

19 This of course, is not a justification for the so-called "house church movement." In the first century, Christianity was an illegal religion. Consequently, they could not rent public spaces. Further, it would have been extremely expensive for the early believers to do this and so they met in their homes not because God commanded it, but because it was convenient.

20 Robinson, Book II. p. 324. Robinson also notes on the same page that the believer has "three positions—1. In Adam by nature; 2. In Christ by faith; 3. In the church by baptism."

21 Ibid., p. 365.

well-loved; **in the Lord** "Beloved—1. For the sake of Christ; 2. With true Christian love; 3. As members of the same body of Christ."[22]

Obs. 7- (v. 9) Greet Urbanus, another common Roman name for a household slave; **our fellow worker in Christ, and Stachys,** whose name means "head of grain;" **my beloved** or well-loved.

Obs. 8- (v. 10) Greet Apelles, approved or "tried and found trustworthy;"[23] **in Christ. Greet those who are of the *household* of Aristobulus** which seems to be a reference to Christian slaves who belonged to Aristobulus. Most scholars say he was Herod the Great's grandson and the brother of Herod Agrippa I.

Obs. 9- (v. 11) Greet Herodion, my countryman, i.e., his "kinsman." This man was another Jewish believer, who might have been a slave of Herod's household and also a blood relative of the apostle (cf. v. 7); **Greet those** i.e., those believers; **who are of the *household* of Narcissus who are in the Lord,** this Narcissus has been identified by many commentators as Tiberius Claudius Narcissus, a wealthy man during the reigns of emperors Tiberius and Claudius. "Even those who are lowest on the social ladder are not excluded from the choicest blessings of Christianity. The inclusion of slaves in this list of names is a lovely reminder that in Christ all social distinctions are obliterated because we are all one in Him."[24]

Obs. 10- (v. 12) Greet Tryphena, which means "delicate;" **and Tryphosa,** which means "dainty," two more dear sisters in Christ;[25] **who have labored** or worked hard, even to the point of exhaustion; **in the Lord. Greet the beloved Persis,** another sister in Christ, who labored much in the Lord (cf. v. 6).

Obs. 11- (v. 13) Greet Rufus who might have been the son of Simon the Cyrene who carried the cross of Jesus (cf. Mark 15:21); **chosen** or elected; **in the Lord,** as all true Christians are from before the foundation of the world (cf. Rom. 8:29, 30; Eph. 1:4). But here, most likely Paul is simply highlighting the fact that he was a choice believer or an "extraordinary Christian, known for his love and work for the Lord and for the Lord's people;"[26] **and his mother and mine,** not that she was Paul's actual mother, but because she had treated him so well, even as a son, she had been *as a mother to him.*

Obs. 12- (vv. 14-15) Greet Asyncritus, Phlegon, Hermas, Patrobas, Hermes, all men's names who perhaps were leaders in one of the local churches in Rome; **and the brethren who are with them. Greet Philologus and Julia,** these two might have been a husband-and-wife couple; **Nereus**

---

22 Robinson, Book II. p. 325.

23 Robinson, Book II. p. 326. The Greek word "approved" carries the idea of being tried and passing that trial having remained faithful.

24 McDonald, 1741.

25 Scholars suggest they were probably sisters, maybe even twins, because of the close connection in their names.

26 MacArthur, p. 368.

and his sister, and Olympas, and all "implying a considerable number,"[27] the saints, i.e., God's redeemed, set apart people; who are with them. It seems that these two groups of Christians who are mentioned in these two verses, made up two different local congregations in Rome. All of these believers are unknown to us—but not to the Lord! In His eyes, they are precious. Before Him, they are those "of whom the world was not worthy" (Heb. 11:38).

Obs. 13- (v. 16) That as Paul concludes this list of the Hall of the Faithful, to continue to encourage lasting love and unity among them (especially given all that he wrote in chapters 14 and 15 concerning Christian liberty with grace-filled sensitivity), he writes:

Greet or give warm wishes to; **one another with** the preposition highlighting the manner in which this was to be done; **a holy** not sensual, but a holy; **kiss. The churches of Christ greet you,** this language is most likely a reference to all the local churches in and around Corinth, where Paul wrote this letter. This greeting would have helped to remind the Romans that they were part of something big, even the universal church, the body of Christ.

What was this holy kiss? It was a symbolic expression of sincere Christian love and warmth which was done men to men and women to women, typically on the cheek or on the forehead. Paul mentions this kind gesture for the churches to express toward one another in several places (1 Cor. 16:20; 2 Cor. 13:12; 1 Thess. 5:26).[28] Even today, where this custom is commonplace in some parts of the world, a holy kiss is still practiced among brethren. In places where it is not commonplace, it seems that a friendly hug or a firm handshake would do.

Obs. 14- (vv. 21-24) That as Paul now gives greetings from his companions at Corinth to those at Rome, he writes:[29]

Timothy, whose name means "one who honors God;" **my fellow worker,** who was Paul's spiritual son in the faith, traveled and labored with Paul on the missionary field, and received two letters from him (Acts 16:1-3; 1 and 2 Timothy); **and Lucius,** some commentators say that this Lucius is Luke, the author of the book of Acts and the third gospel which bears his name, but it seems more likely that he is the believer whose name is in Acts 13:1, who was from the church in Antioch; Jason, whose mentioned in Acts 17:5, 7, and 9 as the one who hosted Paul on the first missionary journey to Thessalonica; **and Sosipater,** this might be the same believer mentioned in Acts 20:4; **my countrymen** or better translated "kinsmen," i.e., they were Jewish believers who were blood relatives of the apostle; **greet you. I, Tertius, who wrote** *this* **epistle greet you in the Lord.** Although Paul authored this letter by the direction of the Holy Spirit, he dictated it to Tertius, who penned it as Paul's secretary or amanuensis; **Gaius,** who was from Corinth and whom Paul personally

---

27 Robinson, Book II. p. 330.

28 Cf. 1 Pet. 5:14.

29 Paul includes greetings from others elsewhere in his letters (Cf. 1 Cor. 16:19, 20; Phil. 4:22; Col. 4:10-14).

baptized (1 Cor. 1:14); **my host,** "Paul lived with Gaius on his second visit to Corinth;"[30] **and** *the host* **of the whole church,** "his large-hearted hospitality further commended;"[31] **greets you. Erastus, the treasurer of the city,** i.e., the city of Corinth from where Paul was writing, thus he was a civil servant showing us that God has His people in all kinds of places; **greets you, and Quartus, a brother,** i.e., a Christian brother. The **grace** or the unmerited, unearned, and uncaused favor and goodwill; **of our Lord Jesus Christ** *be* **with you all. Amen.**[32]

Suggested applications from the text for the church:

1- We learn from these verses that although women are not to hold an office in the church, they are to be held in high esteem by the church.

2- We learn from these verses that we should greatly appreciate and value all our brethren and regularly thank God and them for all that they do for us and Jesus.

3- We learn from these verses that it is not just church leaders who advance the cause of Christ on the earth, but all the varied people of God laboring together for the glory of Jesus and the good of His church.

Suggested application from the text for the non-Christian:

1- You learn from our passage that just as God was merciful to all the saints in our passage, who formerly were lost sinners, the same could be true for you now, if you seek Him by faith, through Jesus.

Text: Romans 16:17-20

General theme: Paul's Words of Warning

Homiletical outline of the verses:

A. His entreaty: [17] Now I urge you, brethren, note those who cause divisions and offenses, contrary to the doctrine which you learned, and avoid them.

B. His explanation: [18] For those who are such do not serve our Lord Jesus Christ, but their own belly, and by smooth words and flattering speech deceive the hearts of the simple.

C. His encouragement: [19] For your obedience has become known to all. Therefore I am glad on your behalf; but I want you to be wise in what is good, and simple concerning evil.

D. His expectation: [20] And the God of peace will crush Satan under your feet shortly. The grace of our Lord Jesus Christ *be* with you. Amen.

---

30 Robinson, Book II. p. 345.

31 Ibid.

32 Paul states these words in verse 20 of this chapter as well, and so why repeat them here in this benediction? The answer is simple. We can never hear them enough. The Christian life means receiving the grace of God in Christ Jesus our Lord for all our daily needs. So significant was this fact for Paul that he began and ended all of his thirteen epistles on this God-giving-grace-note.

Summary of section: In these verses, we see that at his core, Paul was not only a true Christian but a true pastor as well. He was one who truly loved God's people. Consequently, concerning the presence of errorists or troublemakers that were capable of harming them, he played no games. He minced no words. This was because he knew that the stakes were extremely high concerning the eternal welfare of the souls of men and women. Because of this, he now speaks to the church in Rome the way he does. But why did he wait until the end of the letter to warn them?[33] And who were the particular people that he wanted the Romans to note?

Concerning the first question, it seems that Paul wrote this section of Scripture at this point in the epistle, first, because having just sent warm greetings to all of his beloved friends at Rome, he did not want them to be spiritually duped. Because he cared so much for them, he wanted them to be protected. Second, he did this because, having just instructed them in verse 16 to "greet one another with a holy kiss," he would have no one or anything disrupt their unity in Christ. Third, I believe the Holy Spirit led him to write these words at this point in the letter specifically to help them recall it more easily. As one of the last things on their minds, it would have remained prominent in their thinking.

As to the second question regarding the identity of those whom Paul wanted the Romans to note, was he speaking about those who were currently at the church "causing divisions and offenses" or was he speaking prophetically, as it were, about those who would come in the days ahead? Since we know that there were already some at the church who were causing trouble over matters of Christian liberty, so that they were judging and showing contempt towards the brethren (Rom. 14:10), it seems that Paul could be speaking about a current situation among them. Contextually speaking, this makes sense.

However, he could also be thinking about those who might come to the church in the future as wolves in sheep's clothing seeking to devour the flock.[34] Perhaps he was thinking about the Judaizers who troubled some of the churches he had planted with teaching that denied that salvation was by grace alone, through faith alone, in Christ alone. Another possible explanation comes from Hendriksen when he says that, Paul was warning about "antinomians or perhaps ascetics or advocates of a combination of two or more disruptive isms."[35] Regardless of who or what it was, Paul's words were to be heeded. They demanded serious attention both from the original recipients and from us in our own day, so that we will be kept spiritually safe and secure in the Savior.

---

33 Because this passage seems a bit abrupt and out of place here, some commentators regrettably say that Paul did not author it. However, I believe Murray is right when he says, "Severity of mood and expression appears at various points in the epistle (*cf.* 2:1-5; 3:8; 6:1-3; 9:19, 20; 11:20; 14:15, 16). The warning note appears throughout." Murray, p. 234. It should also be noted that Paul ended some of his other letters with similar warnings (Cf. 1 Cor. 16:22; Gal. 6:12-17; Phil. 3:2).

34 Acts 20:28-31. Cf. Matthew 7:15-20.

35 Hendriksen, p. 510.

Exegetical & Practical Insights:

Obs. 1- (v. 17) That as Paul begins his entreaty to the Romans, he writes:

Now I urge[36] or continually exhort and implore; **you, brethren,** the word "brethren" highlighting his tender care and concern for them; **note**[37] or constantly keep a "watchful eye"[38] on (the verb "note" is from the noun form of that word that we get the *scope* in telescope and microscope);[39] **those who cause** (by false teaching, false accusations, gossip, and unholy living, etc.); **divisions** or separations and factions; **and offenses** or stumbling blocks which cause God's people to fall;[40] **contrary** or "different from and opposed;"[41] **to the doctrine** or teaching; **which you learned,** that is, learned directly from Paul in personal interactions with him or from this very epistle; **and avoid** or "steer clear of;"[42] **them.**[43]

Paul's teaching here is plain. While he is not encouraging us to treat false teachers and divisive people badly, he is saying by an ongoing command that we are to keep away from them habitually. Simply stated, we are not to listen to their false teachings or follow them in person, or on the TV, or on YouTube, etc. This is what it means to "avoid them." It means we are not in any way, shape, or form to keep company with those who pose a threat to our spiritual well-being with their errors. It means, as Olyott says, "the true church of Christ is to have *no contact* with them. They are not to be received, or listened to, or permitted to enter into dialogue."[44]

In light of this, someone might wonder if we are not to attempt to reach such individuals with the truth of the gospel or help those being badly influenced by them. I believe that this can be done, but not by every single believer, especially not by those who are new in the faith. Since these errorists are experts in their deceptions, this work should be done primarily by pastors, for as Paul says in Titus 1:9, they are the ones who "by sound doctrine" are to "exhort and convict those who contradict."

Obs. 2- (vv. 18-19) That as Paul gives his explanation for why he wrote the previous words and then encourages the Romans, he says:

For those who are such, that is, such as he just spoke of in verse 17; **do not serve** or give themselves entirely to; **our Lord Jesus Christ but**[45] or in strong contrast to this; **their own belly,** which is to say, these counterfeit believers are slaves to their inner lust, appetites, and ambitions, which,

---

36 Grk. present, active, verb.

37 Grk. present, active, verb.

38 Phillips translation.

39 MacArthur, p. 372.

40 Cf. Rom. 14:13.

41 Robinson, Book II. p. 334.

42 Phillips translation.

43 Cf. 1 Tim. 6:3-5; Titus 3:9-11.

44 Olyott, p. 160.

45 The strong Greek adversative.

are fueled by sin, Satan, and themselves;[46] **and by** or through the means of; **smooth** or kind and plausible;[47] **words and flattering speech**[48] or "false elegance;"[49] **deceive** or seduce; **the hearts,** the word "heart" in Scripture speaks about the inner aspect of who we are, the mind, the emotions, etc.; **of the simple** or unsuspecting. "The Roman Christian should stay away from those who create divisions by their deceptive teaching because such people can use their rhetorical skill to convince others with little theological training to serve the immoral interests of the false teachers themselves."[50] **For,** the conjunction explaining why Paul just said what he said; **your obedience** or wholehearted commitment to Christ and the gospel;[51] **has become known to all,** the point seems to be that because this was so, the Romans were to be on heightened alert because Satan, through his servants, often likes to attack high-profile, well-ordered churches. He knows full well that if he can infiltrate them, it would be a big win for him.[52] Or, as Schreiner says, "perhaps the idea is that the Romans must be on their guard precisely because news of their obedience has reached the entire world. Thus opponents will be anxious to subvert the good that has been accomplished."[53] **Therefore I am glad**[54] or am continually rejoicing; **on your behalf,** i.e., because of the obedience of the Romans; **but I want you to be wise** or have understanding; **in what is good,**[55] which is to say, wise in keeping an eye out for false teachers and troublemakers of whom he just spoke and wise in the truths of the gospel; **and simple** or better understood uncontaminated and pure; **concerning evil,** that is, all the evil doctrines and practices which false teachers promote.

Obs. 3- (v. 20) That as Paul now puts forth his positive expectation in view of all the negative things he just spoke of, his assurance is:

And the God of peace[56] or the God who, because of Jesus' death in our place,[57] is now the source and supplier of our peace (the very thing we especially need when trials and "divisions," as spoken of in verse 17, are upon us); **will crush** or shatter (in Paul's day, the word "crush" was used in a military context and would have been familiar to

---

46 MacArthur says that such people are often identified by their "pretentious, extravagant, and immoral lifestyles (cf. Phil. 3:18, 19; 2 Tim. 3:7, 8; 2 Pet. 1:20–2:3, 10-19; Jude 12, 13). MacArthur Study Bible, p. 1724.

47 Cf. 2 Pet. 2:18.

48 Cf. Jude 16.

49 BDAG, p. 408.

50 Thielman, p. 738.

51 Cf. Rom. 1:5-8.

52 Hodge says the sense of the passage could be this, "Ye ought to be on your guard against these false teachers, for since your character is so high, your faith being everywhere spoken of, it would be a great disgrace and evil to be led astray by them." Hodge, p. 451

53 Schreiner, p. 804.

54 Grk. present, active, verb.

55 Matt. 10:16. Cf. Rom. 12:9.

56 Cf. Rom. 15:33.

57 Cf. Col. 1:19, 20.

the Romans as it "often depicted Roman emperors or armies standing over conquered peoples");[58] **Satan,**[59] i.e., our great spiritual foe; **under your feet** "as your conquered adversary;"[60] **shortly** or swiftly or perhaps unexpectedly.[61] **The grace** or the unmerited, unearned, and uncaused favor and goodwill; **of our Lord Jesus Christ be with you,** the very thing we need for challenging days. **Amen.** "The benediction fittingly concludes this important paragraph."[62]

When Paul says here that in the midst of Satan's crafty attacks against us, the God of peace will be the God of war for us, he seems to be echoing language found in Genesis 3:15. In that first gospel promise (typically called by scholars the *protoevangelium*) we are told that the foretold seed of the woman (who is Jesus the Messiah) would one day bruise or crush the head of the serpent. This blow would be a fatal one against the Devil. But when would this take place?

First, we can say that there is a sense in which this has already taken place because when Jesus died on the cross as our substitute and surety, He freed us from the captivity and power which the devil had over us (Luke 11:18-23; Acts 26:17-18). Indeed, at the cross, our Lord "disarmed principalities and powers, he made a public spectacle of them triumphing over them in it" (Col. 2:15). Second, we can say that there is a sense that God crushes Satan under our feet every time He, by His grace, squashes problems in our midst, problems which Satan is usually behind. This ongoing work might be Paul's particular point in verse 20. Third, along with these things, we can say for sure that the God of the Bible will ultimately crush Satan under our feet, once for all time, and banish him forevermore when our Lord Jesus returns to this earth (Matt. 25:41; Rev. 20:10). Because of this, may we continually say with the apostle John in Revelation 22:20, "even so, come Lord Jesus!"

Suggested applications from the text for the church:

1- If we are to remain vigilant against Satan and those through whom he works, then we must know our Bibles well. We must especially know the gospel well which Paul has been expounding throughout this epistle. Only then will we be able to recognize false teachers in contrast to those who accurately teach the Word of God.

2- If we are to remain vigilant against Satan and those through whom he works so that we can "note them" accordingly (v. 17), then we must be like the Bereans, who "searched the Scriptures daily" to be sure

---

58 Thielman, pp. 739, 740.

59 This is the first time that Paul mentions Satan in this epistle. For a scriptural treatment concerning the devil, his works against us, and our victorious armor against him, I recommend *Spiritual Warfare: A Biblical and Balanced Perspective* by Brian Borgman and Rob Ventura, Reformation Heritage Books.

60 Robinson, Book II. p. 341.

61 MacArthur, p. 377.

62 Wilson, p. 249.

that all that we receive from any Bible teacher is in line with Scripture (Acts 17:11).

Suggested application from the text for the non-Christian:
1- If you are to become a true Christian, then you must stop listening to the lies of Satan and those through whom he works, who, in one way or another, have blinded you up to this point in your life to the truth of who Jesus Christ is, namely, the Son of God, the only Savior of sinners.

Text: Romans 16:25-27

General theme: Paul's Glorious Gospel Doxology

Homiletical outline of the verses:
A. His praise for God's great power through the gospel: [25a] Now to Him who is able to establish you according to my gospel and the preaching of Jesus Christ,
B. His praise for God's great provision in the gospel: [25b] according to the revelation of the mystery kept secret since the world began [26] but now made manifest, and by the prophetic Scriptures made known to all nations, according to the commandment of the everlasting God, for obedience to the faith—
C. His praise for God's great Person because He has given us the gospel: [27] to God, alone wise, *be* glory through Jesus Christ forever. Amen.

Summary of section: In these verses, Paul takes us back to what he wrote in the first chapter of this book.[63] He ends his great epistle the way he began it, with a gospel note. He has come full circle.[64] *To God Alone Be the Glory*[65] is the great chorus of Paul's heart.[66] This is because he understood that "salvation is of the Lord" (Jonah 2:9) and that the gospel is "the power of God to salvation for everyone who believes, for the Jew first and also for the Greek" (Rom. 1:16).
Olyott states the matter well:

> The closing lines are an inscription of glory to God. They underline various truths and, like the close of a great symphony, leave a majestic cord sounding in the ears. The music of the epistle does not weakly fade away. The final cord is glorious, satisfying, and memorable.[67]

Exegetical & Practical Insights:
Obs. 1- (v. 25a) That as Paul glories in God from whom all blessings flow, he writes:

---

63 He also did this in chapter 15 verses 22 and following.

64 In comparing chapter 1:1-5 to what Paul writes here, we see that he speaks in both places, of the gospel (1:1; cf. 16:25); the Scriptures (1:2; cf. 16:26); Jesus Christ (1:3; cf. 16:25); and obedience to the faith among all nations (1:5; cf. 16:26).

65 In Latin, it is *Soli Deo Gloria* or simply S.D.G.

66 Paul praises God in other places in this letter: 1:25; 9:5; 11:36.

67 Olyott, p. 162.

Now to Him[68] (God); **who is able**[69] or has the continual power and strength; **to establish**[70] **you** or to make you stand strong; **according to** or by means of; **my gospel,** i.e., the gospel he received directly from Christ[71] and preached (which was the same gospel preached by the other apostles); **and the preaching** or the heralding; **of Jesus Christ.**

What do these words mean? They mean that as we keep hearing the apostolic gospel faithfully taught and proclaimed, God is going to use it to help us stand steadfastly all of our days. He will use the good news of our Lord Jesus to fortify our souls and to keep us spiritually safe and sanctified on the straight and narrow path that leads to life.

This is a very encouraging word for Paul to put forth at this point in the epistle. As he has just unfolded the gospel throughout this book, he now assures us that as we continue to hear it expounded, God will use it for much good in our lives. This is what will be true of us both individually and corporately as gospel-centered congregations.

Obs. 2- (v. 25b-26) That as Paul now praises God concerning His great provision in the gospel (because it is for all people everywhere, both Jews and Gentiles alike), he says that the gospel is:

according to or in keeping with; **the revelation** or the unveiling; **of the mystery** "in the New Testament [the word 'mystery'] refers to something hidden in former times but now made known;"[72] **kept secret** or "not fully revealed;"[73] **since the world began** or in "the ages before Christ;"[74] **but now,** i.e., since the time of Christ through the apostolic generation onward; **made manifest,** or "brought to light;"[75] **and by the prophetic Scriptures,** which is to say, by that which was concealed in the Old Testament but now fully revealed in the New Testament; **made known to all nations,** i.e., the Jews and the Gentiles; **according to the commandment** or will; **of the everlasting** or eternal; **God, for obedience to the faith**—which is a great purpose or goal of the gospel. This speaks, first, of unsaved people responding to the gospel in repentance and faith, and second of saved people expressing, by the power of the Holy Spirit, evangelical obedience to the objective faith of the Christian religion as expressed in God's Word.

But what is the heart of the "mystery" of which the apostle speaks, which was "kept secret since the world began but now made manifest, and by the prophetic Scriptures made known to all the nations?" The mystery is that through the preaching of the gospel (which is to go to "all the nations" as Jesus commanded in Matthew 28), pagan, outcast Gentiles

---

68 Praise to God is also seen in Ephesians 3:20 and Jude 24.

69 Grk. present, middle, participle.

70 The only other place that Paul uses this same verb to speak about what he hopes to happen to them through his ministry is found in 1:11.

71 Gal. 1:12.

72 MacArthur, p. 386.

73 Robinson, Book II. p. 349.

74 Ibid.

75 Ibid., p. 350.

would be saved and experience God's gospel blessings with elect Jews and made into one spiritual family with them.

In the Old Testament, God spoke about the Gentiles being blessed by Him in many passages. Genesis 12:3; 22:18; Isa. 9:1, 2; and 42:1 are important examples. However, now in New Testament times, we see that this blessing is being fully realized as they are saved, and not only "entering God's kingdom in large numbers but [also becoming] fellow sharers, participants on equal terms, with the elect from among the Jews," as William Hendriksen says.[76] This is fantastic news which shows us God's heart for all the families of the earth. It demonstrates that He indeed "shows no partiality" (Acts 10:34).

Paul speaks more about this in Ephesians 3:1-7 when he writes:

> For this reason I, Paul, the prisoner of Christ Jesus for you Gentiles— if indeed you have heard of the dispensation [or stewardship] of the grace of God which was given to me for you, how that by revelation He made known to me the mystery (as I have briefly written already, by which, when you read, you may understand my knowledge in the mystery of Christ), which in other ages was not made known to the sons of men, as it has now been revealed by the Spirit to His holy apostles and prophets: *that the Gentiles should be fellow heirs, of the same body, and partakers of His promise in Christ through the gospel,* of which I became a minister according to the gift of the grace of God given to me by the effective working of His power.

Obs. 3- (v. 27) That as Paul ends this magnificent epistle, his heart bursts with praise to God concerning His great Person because He has given us the gospel, thus, he says:

to God, alone or we might say "only;" **wise,**[77] i.e., infinitely wise in His plan of salvation concerning the Jews and Gentiles, and infinitely wise in all that He purposes to do; *be* **glory or honor and praise; through** or by the mediation and agency of; **Jesus Christ forever** or to the ages. [And then, as the apostle gives his own strong affirmation to all that he has written, he says,] **Amen,** or so be it.

Suggested applications from the text for the church:

1- This glorious gospel doxology calls us to go forward with the proclamation of the gospel. Will we?

2- This glorious gospel doxology calls us to praise God for the gospel. May it always be!

Suggested application from the text for the non-Christian:

1- This glorious gospel doxology calls you to believe this glorious gospel. It calls you to embrace from the heart the good news concerning God's Son, Jesus Christ the Lord, and all that He has done in love for people like you.

---

76 Hendriksen, p. 517.

77 In verse 25 of this chapter, Paul highlighted God's power. Now he ends by highlighting His wisdom.

Thus ends the examination of this mine of spiritual wealth.
Perused a thousand times, yet ever found still new.
The oftener read the more delightful and valuable.
For the preciousness of its truths and the sublimity of its sentiments;
For the discoveries of divine grace and wisdom which it contains;
And for the influence which it has exercised on the human race;
Unrivaled by any composition in ancient or modern times.
A monument of divine love, and a treasury of blessing to man.[78]

AMEN

---

78 Robinson, Book II. p. 353.

BIBLIOGRAPHY

Clint Arnold, *Romans*, Zondervan Illustrated Backgrounds Commentary, Zondervan, 2002.

Paul Barnett, *Romans*, Focus on the Bible, Christian Focus Publications, 2003.

Donald Gray Barnhouse, *Romans*, multi-volumes, Eerdmans, 1952.

Michael F. Bird, *Romans*, Story of God Commentary Series, Zondervan, 2016.

James M. Boice, *Romans*, 4 vols. Baker Books, 1991-1995.

D. Stuart Briscoe, *Romans*, The Preacher's Commentary, Vol. 29, Thomas Nelson, 1982.

John Calvin, *Romans*, Calvin's Commentaries, Baker Books, 2003.

Earnest R. Campbell, *A Commentary of Romans*, Canyonview Press, 1987.

Daniel Doriani, *Commentary on Romans*, Reformed Expository Commentary, P&R, 2021.

James Edwards, *Romans*, New International Biblical Commentary, Hendrickson, 1992.

John V. Fesko, *Romans*, Reformation Heritage Books, 2018.

David E. Garland, *Romans*, Tyndale New Testament Commentaries, IVP, 2021.

E. H. Gifford, *The Epistle of St. Paul to the Romans*, John Murray, 1886 (also in The Speakers Bible series).

Robert Haldane, *Exposition of the Epistle to the Romans*, Robert Carter, 1849.

Everett F. Harrison, *Romans*, The Expositors Bible Commentary (ed. Frank E. Gaebelein), Zondervan, 1995.

John D. Harvey, *A Commentary on Romans*, Kregel, 2019.

William Hendriksen, *Exposition of Paul's Epistle to the Romans*, New Testament Commentary, Baker Book House, 1981.

Matthew Henry, *Romans*, Commentary on the Bible, Hendriksen, 1991.

Charles Hodge, *Romans*, Grigg and Elliot, 1835.

Herman Hoeksema, *Romans*, Reformed Free Publishing Association, 2002.

R. Kent Hughes, *Romans, Righteousness from Heaven*, Preaching the Word, Crossway Books, 2013.

S. Lewis Johnson Jr. *Discovering Romans*, Zondervan, 2014.

Philip Krey etc., *Romans 9–16: NT Volume 8* (Reformation Commentary on Scripture Series), IVP, 2016.

Colin Kruse, *Romans*, Pillar New Testament Commentary, Eerdmans, 2012.

D. Martyn Lloyd-Jones, *Romans*, multi-volume set, Banner of Truth.

Richard Longenecker, *Romans*, The New International Greek Testament Commentary, 2016.

John MacArthur, *Romans*, 2 Vols., MacArthur New Testament Commentary, Moody Press, 1994.

Henry T. Mahan, *Romans*, Bible Class Commentary, Evangelical Press, 1984.

J. P. McBeth, *Exegetical and Practical Commentary on Romans*, Hennington, 1937.

Alva J. McClain, *Romans, The Gospel of God's Grace*, BMH Books, 1979.

William McDonald, *Believers Bible Commentary*, Thomas Nelson, 1989.

Benjamin L. Merkle, *Three Views on Israel and the Church: Perspectives on Romans 9–11*, Kregel, 2018.

Tony Merida, *Exalting Jesus in Romans*, B&H Publishing Group, 2021.

Douglas Moo, *Encountering the Book of Romans*, Baker Academic, 2012.

Douglas Moo, *Romans*, New International Commentary on the New Testament (NICNT), Eerdmans, 1996, 2018.

Leon Morris, *Romans*, Pillar New Testament Commentary, Eerdmans, 1988.

Robert H. Mounce, *Romans*, The New American Commentary, Broadman and Holman, 1995.

William D. Mounce, *Mounce's Complete Expository Dictionary of Old and New Testament Words*, Zondervan, 2006.

John Murray, *Romans*, New International Commentary on the New Testament (NICNT), Eerdmans, 1968.

Stuart Olyott, *Romans, The Gospel as It Really Is*, Welwyn Commentary Series, Evangelical Press, 2006.

Grant R. Osborne, *Romans: Verse by Verse*, Osborne New Testament Commentaries, Lexham Press, 2017.

David J. Peterson, *Romans*, Evangelical Biblical Theology Commentary, Faithlife, 2021.

Robert L. Reymond, *Paul, Missionary Theologian*, Christian Focus Publications, 2000.

Archibald T. Robertson, *A Grammar of the Greek New Testament in Light of Historical Research*, Broadman, 1947.

Archibald T. Robertson, *Word Pictures in the New Testament*, Vol. 4, Broadman, 1931.

Thomas Robinson, *A Suggestive Commentary on Romans*, 2 Vols., Appleton and Co: New York, 1873.

Cleon L. Rogers Jr. & Cleon L. Rogers III, *The New Linguistic and Exegetical Key to the New Testament,* Zondervan.

Robert Rogland, *Romans,* A Study Manual, P&R Publications, 1988.

Thomas Schreiner, *Romans,* Baker Exegetical Commentary on the New Testament, Baker Publishing Group, 2018.

Charles Simeon, *Romans,* Expository Outlines on the Whole Bible, Zondervan, 1955.

C. H. Spurgeon's Verse Exposition of Romans: *The Expansive Commentary Collection* (self-printed).

R. C. Sproul, *Romans,* St. Andrews Expositional Commentary, Crossway Books, 2009.

David N. Steele and Curtis C. Thomas, *Romans, An Interpretive Outline,* Presbyterian and Reformed, 1963.

Anthony C. Thiselton, *Discovering Romans,* Eerdmans, 2016.

John Trapp, *A Commentary on the New Testament,* Baker Book House, 1981.

Curtis Vaughan and Bruce Corley, Romans, *A Study Guide Commentary,* Zondervan, 1976.

Geoffrey Wilson, *Romans,* Banner of Truth, 1976.

Robert W. Yarbrough, *Romans,* ESV Expository Commentary, Vol. 10, Crossway Books, 2020.

SCRIPTURE INDEX

SUBJECT INDEX

Also Available from Christian Focus Publications...

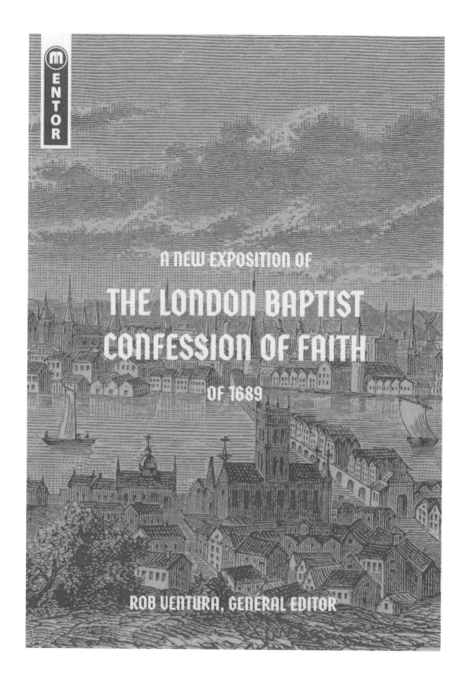

A NEW EXPOSITION OF

THE LONDON BAPTIST CONFESSION OF FAITH

OF 1689

ROB VENTURA, GENERAL EDITOR

ISBN 978-1-5271-0890-5

A New Exposition of
The London Baptist Confession of Faith of 1689

Edited by Rob Ventura

For centuries, Baptists have published confessions of faith as formal statements of their beliefs. Chief among these is the Second London Baptist Confession of Faith of 1689. This doctrinal statement is a spiritual treasure trove worthy of our fresh attention. In this new study, more than twenty contributors unpack its timeless biblical truths, 'things which are most surely believed among us' (Luke 1:1). Our prayer is that the Lord will use this volume to richly edify and sanctify His people worldwide, and to assist the churches in pursuing biblical holiness and doctrinal purity. May these labors send God's people back again and again to the Bible, which is—as the confession states—the 'only sufficient, certain, and infallible rule of all saving knowledge, faith, and obedience' (1.1).

In a most attractive, readable and scholarly way this rich volume presents historic Christianity as Baptists have absorbed it and been confessing it for the last 333 years in this grand statement of our best Confession of Faith. This book is a tremendous achievement.

GEOFF THOMAS
Conference Speaker and author, Aberystwyth, Wales

Christian Focus Publications

Our mission statement –

STAYING FAITHFUL

In dependence upon God we seek to impact the world through literature faithful to His infallible Word, the Bible. Our aim is to ensure that the Lord Jesus Christ is presented as the only hope to obtain forgiveness of sin, live a useful life and look forward to heaven with Him.

Our books are published in four imprints:

CHRISTIAN FOCUS

Popular works including biographies, commentaries, basic doctrine and Christian living.

CHRISTIAN HERITAGE

Books representing some of the best material from the rich heritage of the church.

MENTOR

Books written at a level suitable for Bible College and seminary students, pastors, and other serious readers. The imprint includes commentaries, doctrinal studies, examination of current issues and church history.

CF4•K

Children's books for quality Bible teaching and for all age groups: Sunday school curriculum, puzzle and activity books; personal and family devotional titles, biographies and inspirational stories – because you are never too young to know Jesus!

Christian Focus Publications Ltd,
Geanies House, Fearn, Ross-shire,
IV20 1TW, Scotland, United Kingdom.
www.christianfocus.com